THE DILEMMAS OF CORRECTIONS
Contemporary Readings
Second Edition

THE DILEMMAS OF CORRECTIONS

Contemporary Readings

Second Edition

Kenneth C. Haas
University of Delaware

Geoffrey P. Alpert
University of South Carolina

WAVELAND PRESS, INC.
Prospect Heights, Illinois

For information about this book, write or call:

    Waveland Press, Inc.
    P.O. Box 400
    Prospect Heights, Illinois 60070
    (708) 634-0081

Contents

Part III
The Courts and Corrections

—— **Part IV** ——
The Rehabilitation Debate: What Works?

—— **Part V** ——
Corrections in the Community

——— Part VI ———
Critical Problems and
Issues in Corrections

Preface

Prisons, as they were established in the United States, were to be positive contributions to the new world. They were to be institutions in which the idle, the unmotivated, the hooligans, and the cruel were sent to be transformed into active, energetic, useful, and kind members of our society. Somehow, somewhere, something went wrong. Critics have offered too few constructive solutions for change and too many quick-fixes. One of the more insightful comments was made by George Bernard Shaw in his 1924 book *Imprisonment*:

> Although public vindictiveness and public dread are largely responsible for (the cruelty), some of the most cruel features of the prison system are not understood by the public, and have not been deliberately invented or contrived for the purpose of increasing the prisoner's torment. The worst of these are (a) unsuccessful attempts at reform, (b) successful attempts to make the working of the prison cheaper for the state and easier for the officials, and (c). . .the new state prisons (pp. 80-81).

Shaw directs our attention to problems with prisons that he observed in the early 1900s. Unfortunately, these problems still prevail and they exist for more prisoners in more prisons than Shaw ever imagined. On December 31, 1989, 703,687 men and women were confined to state and federal prisons, over 340,000 were locked up in local and county jails, and approximately three million others were under probation, parole, or some other type of correctional supervision.

Our purpose in bringing together the readings in the second edition of *The Dilemmas of Corrections* (known as *The Dilemmas of Punishment* in its first edition) is to present a timely, issue-oriented perspective on corrections. From the vast number of articles and reports on corrections, we have chosen 37 that demonstrate what Shaw noted so many years ago: there have been recurring attempts to reform shabby prison operations; there have been recurring attempts to find simple answers for complex penal problems; and more and bigger prisons have been constructed. What George Bernard Shaw also told us is that these

ix

attempts are nearly always well-intentioned and nearly always leave a legacy of failure.

A close analysis of the literature on corrections reveals a tendency to criticize each and every aspect. What is written about jails and prisons tends to leave the reader with the impression that practitioners do nothing at all, or actively and maliciously oppress a selected segment of society. While it may be a trend to damn every aspect of corrections, it is in many ways unfair. As we read these articles, we can reflect upon Shaw's comments and keep in mind that most administrators and line staff want to do what is right and what is decent. Unfortunately, the political and budgetary restraints placed upon correctional officials make it extraordinarily difficult to manage prisons and other correctional programs effectively.

Our compilation of materials includes some of the outstanding statements and studies that have been published in books, research reports, and professional journals. In addition, we have brought together new material from several of the best criminologists in the country. These original contributions offer readers the most recent theories and research findings in the field of corrections. Part I provides an overview of the scope and structure of the American correctional system and addresses the all-important question: Who goes to prison? Our second section describes the pains of imprisonment felt by those who are incarcerated. What really happens when the bars slam shut? Part III examines the impact the judiciary has had on the correctional system and the prisoners. No book on corrections would be complete without a chapter on rehabilitation, and our fourth section offers an up-to-date overview of the continuing debate over the effectiveness of correctional treatment programs. The fifth section explores the theory and practice of what has come to be called community-based corrections. Corrections outside the traditional walls and fences may be a sensible alternative to warehousing criminals, but the movement toward community corrections has not succeeded in reducing the nation's reliance upon prisons.

Part VI is an important addition to the second edition of *The Dilemmas of Corrections*. This new section contains readings on six problems and issues that undeniably are among the most pressing and troublesome in the field of corrections today. The first three articles in this section examine the problems involved in meeting the special needs of three distinct types of offenders—the mentally ill inmate, the elderly prisoner, and the incarcerated adolescent female. The final three selections offer insights into three controversial issues in correctional administration—the expansion of prison-employee drug-testing programs, the difficult policy choices concerning how best to prevent the spread of AIDS in

American prisons, and the hotly debated question of whether private corporations can do a better job of running prisons and jails than government agencies have done. We are confident that readers will agree that we have selected essays and articles that are both scholarly and thought-provoking.

Part I

Who Goes to Prison?

Introduction

Many Americans undoubtedly believe that the United States is one of the most lenient nations in the world in punishing offenders. However, the U.S. imprisonment rate is the third highest in the world and it is rising rapidly. As of 1989, only the Soviet Union and South Africa imprisoned their populations at higher rates than the United States. Moreover, the best available data indicate that American prisoners serve longer terms than their counterparts anywhere else in the world. With over 340,000 inmates incarcerated in city and county jails and over 700,000 adults behind bars in state and federal prisons as of December 31, 1989, it is important to find out who is selected to be placed in these facilities and who is not. Our first group of readings addresses these and related issues.

Our first selection is taken from "Prisoners in 1989," a bulletin issued by the Bureau of Justice Statistics in May 1990 that presents population counts for the nation's state and federal prisons on a single day— December 31, 1989. The bulletin shows that prison populations are continuing to rise, with over 73,000 prisoners added in 1989—an increase that equals a demand for more than 1500 new prison beds per week. The total of 703,687 prisoners represents an incarceration rate of 271 prisoners per 100,000 Americans. Among the more interesting findings is that the female prison population has increased at a faster rate than the male population in each year since 1981, raising the female percent of the nation's prison population from 4.2% in 1981 to 5.6% in 1989. The bulletin also indicates that soaring prison populations are

1

at least in part attributable to the steadily worsening drug problem and society's growing willingness to impose imprisonment on serious criminal offenders.

Our second selection, "Census of Local Jails: 1988," has been adapted from a bulletin issued by the Bureau of Justice Statistics in February 1990. The bulletin presents the major findings from the most recent nationwide census of local jails. Whereas state and federal prisons primarily hold convicted offenders serving terms of more than one year, the nation's local (county, city, municipal, etc.) jails primarily house people convicted of misdemeanor offenses who are serving terms of a year or less and people who have been arrested and are awaiting trial or some other disposition of their case. Most of those in the latter group either have been unable to afford bail or have been charged with serious crimes that are not bailable. Readers of the BJS bulletin will note that jail populations, like prison populations, have been increasing rapidly, totaling 343,569 persons on June 30, 1988. Perhaps more startling is that there were nearly ten million jail admissions over the one-year period ending June 30, 1988 and that over that same time period there were 137 jail admissions per 1000 Americans in the 18-34 age group.

The third selection in Part I comes from the *Report to the Nation on Crime and Justice, Second Edition*, issued in March 1988 by the U.S. Department of Justice's Bureau of Justice Statistics. The "Sentencing and Corrections" segment of the Report first examines the objectives and principles of various sentencing alternatives, with the emphasis on how recent sentencing reforms have contributed to striking increases in prison populations. Next, the *Report* describes some of the most noteworthy characteristics of America's jails, prisons, juvenile facilities, and community-based programs. It also examines the impact of tougher sentencing policies on correctional populations, demonstrating that prison populations and death row populations are growing while the use of parole is declining. The *Report* concludes with a disturbing recent research finding: approximately half of all men released from prison will return to prison, most in the first three years after release.

No new research, however, is necessary to document the equally disturbing fact that race and ethnicity are of major importance in determining who goes to prison. It is irrefutable that blacks, who account for an estimated 12% of the total U.S. population, have long been greatly overrepresented in American prisons. The Criminal Justice Institute's *The Corrections Yearbook: 1989* estimates that as of January 1, 1989, blacks and other minorities accounted for 46.8% of prisoners in America (pp.4-5). This statistic, however, only begins to convey the scope and seriousness of the disproportionality problem. In "Our Black Prisons,"

Scott Christianson examines incarceration rates for black males on a state-by-state basis to show that the problem of vastly disproportionate rates of imprisonment for blacks is indeed much worse than generally realized. Christianson discusses the social, political, economic, and legal implications of black overrepresentation in American prisons. He urges scholars, criminal justice officials, and concerned citizens to work together in documenting the causes, extent, and effects of racial disproportionality in criminal sentencing.

In the final article in this section, Jessica Mitford offers some explanations for minority overrepresentation in America's prisons. She invites readers to consider the history of society's efforts to pinpoint a criminal type. This chapter has been reprinted from Mitford's controversial, hard-eyed examination of the inadequacies and hypocrisies of the American prison system, *Kind and Usual Punishment: The Prison Business.* Her thesis in "The Criminal Type" is that although crimes are committed at all levels of society, the criminal justice process sees to it that the prisons are overwhelmingly filled with the young, the poor, the black, the Chicano, and the Puerto Rican.

1

Prisoners in 1989

United States Department of Justice, Bureau of Justice Statistics

The number of prisoners under the jurisdiction of Federal or State correctional authorities at yearend 1989 reached a record 703,687. The States and the District of Columbia added 73,043 prisoners during the year; the Federal system, 3,056. The total increase, about 76,000 inmates, also set a new record, exceeding the 1982 record increase by more than 32,000. The increase for 1989 brings total growth in the prison population since 1980 to 373,866—an increase of about 113% in the 9-year period (table 1).

The 1989 growth rate (12.1%) was greater than the percentage increase recorded during 1988 (7.3%), and the number of new prisoners added during 1989 was more than 33,000 higher than the number added during

Source: Adapted from *Prisoners in 1989* (Washington, D.C: U.S. Department of Justice, Bureau of Justice Statistics), May 1990, pp. 1-9.

Table 1 **Change in the State and Federal prison populations, 1980-89**

Year	Number of inmates	Annual percent change	Total percent change since 1980
1980	329,821		
1981	369,930	12.2%	12.2%
1982	413,806	11.9	25.5
1983	436,855	5.6	32.5
1984	462,002	5.8	40.1
1985	502,507	8.8	52.4
1986	544,972	8.5	65.2
1987	585,084	7.4	77.4
1988	627,588	7.3	90.3
1989	703,687	12.1	113.4

Note: All counts are for December 31 of each year and may reflect revisions of previously reported numbers.

the preceding year (42,504). The 1989 increase translates into a nationwide need for nearly 1,500 new prison bedspaces per week.

Prisoners with sentences of more than 1 year (referred to as ''sentenced prisoners'') accounted for 96% of the total prison population at the end of 1989, growing by 11.9% during the year (table 2). The remaining prisoners had sentences of a year or less or were unsentenced (like those, for example, awaiting trial in States with combined prison-jail systems).

The number of sentenced Federal prisoners grew at a substantially lower rate than sentenced prisoners in the States during the year (1.7% versus 12.7%). Among the 9,535 Federal prisoners with no sentences or sentences of 1 year or less were 1,955 under the jurisdiction of the Immigration and Naturalization Service, an increase of 99 from the number held at the end of 1988 (1,956). The number of Federal prisoners with no sentences or sentences of 1 year or less increased by 2,345 during 1989 (from 7,190 to 9,535), while the number of sentenced prisoners increased by 711.

In Kansas, North Dakota, and Alaska prison populations decreased during 1989. The total decrease for the three States was 234 inmates. Total prison population rose most rapidly during 1989 in Rhode Island

Table 2 **Prisoners under the jurisdiction of State or Federal correctional authorities, by region and State, yearend 1988 and 1989**

	Total			Sentenced to more than 1 year			
	Advance 1989	Final 1988	Percent change, 1988-89	Advance 1989	Final 1988	Percent change, 1988-89	Incarcer-ation rate 1989*
U.S. total	703,687	627,588	12.1%	675,441	603,720	11.9%	271
Federal	52,984	49,928	6.1	43,449	42,738	1.7	17
State	650,703	577,660	12.6	631,992	560,982	12.7	253
Northeast	114,754	99,180	15.7%	110,181	94,522	16.6%	216
Connecticut	9,301	8,005	16.2	6,309	4,723	33.6	194
Maine	1,455	1,277	13.9	1,432	1,214	18.0	116
Massachusetts	7,524	6,757	11.4	7,268	6,455	12.6	123
New Hampshire	1,166	1,019	14.4	1,166	1,019	14.4	104
New Jersey	19,439	16,936	14.8	19,439	16,936	14.8	251
New York	51,227	44,560	15.0	51,227	44,560	15.0	285
Pennsylvania	21,267	17,900	18.8	21,256	17,883	18.9	176
Rhode Island	2,479	1,906	30.1	1,467	1,179	24.4	147
Vermont	896	820	9.3	617	553	11.6	108
Midwest	136,519	120,382	13.4%	136,221	120,077	13.4%	226
Illinois	24,7122	21,081	17.2	24,712	21,081	17.2	211
Indiana	12,341	11,406	8.2	12,220	11,271	8.4	218
Iowa	3,584	3,034	18.1	3,584	3,034	18.1	126
Kansas	5,622	5,817	-3.4	5,622	5,817	-3.4	223
Michigan	31,746	27,612	15.0	31,746	27,612	15.0	342
Minnesota	3,103	2,799	10.9	3,103	2,799	10.9	71
Missouri	13,919	12,176	14.3	13,919	12,176	14.3	269
Nebraska	2,438	2,156	13.1	2,321	2,066	12.3	144
North Dakota	451	466	-3.2	404	414	-2.4	61
Ohio	30,538	28,462	15.4	30,538	26,462	15.4	279
South Dakota	1,277	1,020	25.2	1,277	1,020	25.2	178
Wisconsin	6,788	6,353	6.8	6,775	6,325	7.1	139
South	257,821	233,907	10.2%	249,284	226,735	9.9%	290
Alabama	13,907	12,610	10.3	13,575	12,357	9.9	329
Arkansas	6,409	5,519	16.1	6,306	5,519	14.3	261
Delaware	3,356	3,197	5.3	2,337	2,207	5.9	344
District of Columbia	9,268	8,831	4.9	6,771	6,628	2.2	1,129
Florida	39,999	34,732	15.2	39,966	34,681	15.2	311
Georgia	20,885	18,787	11.2	19,619	18,018	8.9	302
Kentucky	8,289	7,119	16.4	8,289	7,119	16.4	222
Louisiana	17,257	16,242	6.2	17,257	16,242	6.2	395
Maryland	16,514	14,276	15.7	15,378	13,572	13.3	325
Mississippi	7,911	7,384	7.1	7,770	7,251	6.2	294
North Carolina	17,451	17,078	2.2	16,695	16,251	2.7	252
Oklahoma	11,423	10,448	9.3	11,423	10,448	9.3	355
South Carolina	15,720	13,888	13.2	14,808	12,902	14.8	419
Tennessee**	10,621	7,720	—	10,562	7,720	—	213
Texas	40,789	40,437	.9	40,789	40,437	.9	239
Virginia	16,477	14,184	16.2	16,273	13,928	16.8	265
West Virginia	1,536	1,455	5.6	1,536	1,455	5.6	83

West	141,609	124,191	14.0%	136,306	119,648	13.9%	260
Alaska	2,564	2,588	-.9	1,805	1,862	-3.1	342
Arizona	13,251	12,095	9.6	12,726	11,578	9.9	354
California	87,297	76,171	14.6	84,338	73,780	14.3	286
Colorado	7,318	5,765	26.9	7,318	5,765	26.9	220
Hawaii	2,470	2,300	7.4	1,606	1,510	6.4	143
Idaho	1,850	1,581	17.0	1,850	1,581	17.0	181
Montana	1,362	1,272	7.1	1,362	1,272	7.1	169
Nevada	5,387	4,881	10.4	5,387	4,881	10.4	473
New Mexico	3,034	2,825	7.4	2,861	2,723	5.1	186
Oregon	6,744	5,991	12.6	6,744	5,991	12.6	237
Utah	2,378	1,961	21.3	2,355	1,944	21.1	137
Washington	6,928	5,816	19.1	6,928	5,816	19.1	144
Wyoming	1,026	945	8.6	1,026	945	8.6	217

Note: Explanatory notes for each jurisdiction are reported in the appendix. Prisoner counts for 1988 may differ from those reported in previous publications. Counts for 1989 are subject to revision as updated figures become available.
— Not applicable.

*The number of prisoners with sentences of more than 1 year per 100,000 resident population.
**Data for 1989 include prisoners sentenced to State prison but held in local jails; 1989 data are not comparable to counts from prior years.

(30.1%), Colorado (26.9%), South Dakota (25.2%), and Utah (21.3%). Thirty-one States reported total prisoner increases of 10% or more since yearend 1988. California's increase of more than 11,100 prisoners during the year was the largest for any single jurisdiction. At the end of 1989, California institutions confined about 1 in 8 prisoners nationwide. Colorado, for the third year in a row, experienced an annual increase of more than 20% in the number of State prisoners; its yearend 1989 population of 7,318 was 92% higher than the yearend 1986 population of 3,804.

Rates of Incarceration Increase

On December 31, 1989, the number of sentenced prisoners per 100,000 residents was 271, also setting a new record. Ten of the seventeen jurisdictions with rates equal to or greater than the rate for the Nation were located in the South, four were in the West, two were in the Midwest and one was in the Northeast.

Since 1980 the number of sentenced inmates per 100,000 residents has risen nearly 95%, from 139 to 271. During this period, per capita incarceration rates have increased the most in the Northeast (a 148% growth from 87 to 216) and in the West (a 148% growth from 105 to 260).

The per capita number of sentenced prisoners in the Midwest climbed 107% (from 109 to 226), and the rate in the South rose 54% (from 188 to 290). The number of sentenced Federal prisoners per 100,000 U.S. residents has increased 89% (from 9 to 17) over the same period.

Prison populations in Northeastern States grow the fastest

During 1989 the percentage increase in the number of sentenced prisoners was highest in the Northeastern States, with a gain of 16.6%. This marks the first time since 1984 that a region other than the West has had the largest percentage growth in the sentenced prison population. The number of sentenced prisoners grew by 13.9% in the West, 13.4% in the Midwest, and 9.9% in the Southern States. The sentenced Federal prison population grew by 1.7%. Since 1980 sentenced prison populations in Western States have increased nearly 203%, compared to growth of about 155% in the Northeast, 111% in the Midwest, and about 75% in the South. Over the same period the number of sentenced Federal prisoners rose by almost 111%. Overall, the number of sentenced prisoners nationwide has increased by nearly 114% since 1980, from 315,974 to 675,441.

Since 1980, 30 States, the District of Columbia, and the Federal prison system have more than doubled the number of sentenced prisoners. Alaska, California, New Hampshire, and New Jersey have experienced a threefold increase. In 1980 these 4 States housed 29,725 sentenced prisoners or 9.4% of the Nation's sentenced prisoners; in 1989 they housed 106,748 or 15.8% of the sentenced inmates nationwide.

California's increase of 61,074 sentenced prisoners since 1980 accounts for 67% of the increase for the West and 18% of the increase among all States over the period. In 1980, 7.9% of the Nation's sentenced State prisoners were in California; in 1989, 13.3%. (For additional State comparisons, see table 3).

Female prisoner population growth outpaces that of males

Women inmates numbered 39,689, increasing at a faster rate during 1989 (21.8%) than males (11.6%) (table 4). The rate of incarceration for sentenced males (525 per 100,000 males in the resident population), however, was about 18 times higher than for sentenced females (29 per 100,000 females in the resident population).

The female prison population has grown more rapidly than the male

Table 3 **The prison situation among the States, yearend 1989**

10 States with the largest 1989 prison populations	Number of inmates	10 States with the highest incarceration rates, 1989*	Prisoners per 100,000 residents	10 States with the largest percent increases in prison population			
				1988-89	Percent increase	1980-89*	Percent increase
California	87,297	Nevada	473	Rhode Island	30.1%	California	262.5%
New York	51,227	South Carolina	419	Colorado	26.9	New Hampshire	257.7
Texas	40,789	Louisiana	395	South Dakota	25.2	New Jersey	249.4
Florida	39,999	Oklahoma	355	Utah	21.3	Alaska	216.1
Michigan	31,746	Arizona	354	Washington	19.1	Nevada	192.9
Ohio	30,538	Delaware	344	Pennsylvania	18.8	Arizona	191.9
Illinois	24,712	Alaska	342	Iowa	18.1	Ohio	162.0
Pennsylvania	21,267	Michigan	342	Illinois	17.2	Pennsylvania	162.0
Georgia	20,885	Alabama	329	Idaho	17.0	Hawaii	157.4
New Jersey	19,439	Maryland	325	Kentucky	16.4	Utah	153.8

Note: The District of Columbia as a wholly urban jurisdiction is excluded.
*Prisoners with sentences of more than a year.

Table 4 **Prisoners under the jurisdiction of State or Federal correctional authorities, by sex, yearend 1988 and 1989**

	Male	Female
Total		
Advance 1989	663,998	39,689
Final 1988	594,996	32,592
Percent change, 1988-89	11.6%	21.8%
Sentenced to more than 1 year		
Advance 1989	638,807	36,634
Final 1988	573,587	30,133
Percent change, 1988-89	11.4%	21.6%
Incarceration rate, 1989*	525	29

*The number of prisoners sentenced to more than 1 year per 100,000 residents of each sex on December 31, 1989.

population in each year since 1981. The higher growth rates for women over the 1981-89 period have raised the percentage of women in the Nation's prison population from 4.2% in 1981 to 5.6% in 1989.

In 1989, 21 States, the District of Columbia, and the Federal system had more than 500 female inmates. Among these jurisdictions, 20 had increases of at least 10%, led by the District of Columbia's increase of

54.3% (from 372 in 1988 to 574 in 1989). California's increase during 1988, 1,107 inmates, accounted for 15.6% of the nationwide increase of 7,097.

Local jails held more than 18,000 because of State prison crowding

At the end of 1989, 20 jurisdictions reported a total of 18,236 prisoners held in local jails or other facilities because of crowding in their prisons. The number of State prisoners held locally increased by 27.0% over that of yearend 1988. Three States—Louisiana, New Jersey, and Tennessee—accounted for more than half of the prisoners sentenced to prison but incarcerated locally. Because of crowding in State facilities, five States—Kentucky, Louisiana, Mississippi, New Jersey, and Tennessee—held in local jails more than 10% of the prisoners sentenced to State prison. Overall, 2.6% of the State prison population was confined in local jails on December 31, 1989, because of prison crowding.

Prison capacity estimates are difficult to compare

The extent of crowding in the Nation's prisons is difficult to determine precisely because of the absence of uniform measures for defining capacity. A wide variety of capacity measures is in use among the 52 reporting jurisdictions because capacity may reflect both available space to house inmates and the ability to staff and operate an institution. To estimate the capacity of the Nation's prisons, jurisdictions were asked to supply up to three measures for yearend 1989—rated, operational, and design capacities. These measures were defined as follows:

Rated capacity is the number of beds or inmates assigned by a rating official to institutions within the jurisdiction.

Operational capacity is the number of inmates that can be accommodated based on a facility's staff, existing programs, and services.

Design capacity is the number of inmates that planners or architects intended for the facility.

Of the 52 reporting jurisdictions, 39 supplied rated capacities, and 37 submitted design capacities. As a result, estimates of total capacity and measures of the relationship to population are based on the highest and lowest capacity figures provided. (Twenty-two jurisdictions reported one capacity measure or gave the same figure for each capacity measure they reported.)

Most jurisdictions are operating above reported capacity

Prisons generally require reserve capacity to operate efficiently. Prison dormitories and cells need to be maintained and repaired periodically, special housing is needed for protective custody and disciplinary cases, and space may be needed to cope with emergencies. At the end of 1989, 10 States reported that they were operating below 95% of their highest capacity. Forty-four jurisdictions and the Federal Prison System reported operating at 100% or more of their lowest capacity; 38 of these held populations that met or exceeded their highest reported capacities.

Overall, at the end of 1989 State prisons were estimated to be operating at 107% of their highest capacities and 127% of their lowest capacities (table 5). Prisons in Southern States were found to be operating closest to their reported capacity on each measure. The Federal system was estimated to be operating at 63% over capacity.

Table 5 **State prison population and capacity, by region, 1989**

	Prison population	Highest capacity	Lowest capacity	Highest capacity	Lowest capacity
			Population as a percent of:		
Total	631,889	588,650	499,122	107%	127%
Northeast	111,628	96,926	84,491	115	132
Midwest	136,200	112,424	106,787	121	128
South	243,210	246,732	215,120	99	113
West	140,851	132,568	92,724	106	152

Note: Population counts exclude prisoners sentenced to State prison but held in local jails and female offenders in 4 States for which the capacity of women's facilities was not reported.

Between 1988 and 1989, State and Federal prison capacities were estimated to have increased by approximately 40,000-60,000 beds (based on the highest and lowest capacities). At the end of 1989, prisons nation-wide were estimated to be 10%-29% over their capacities based on the following:

	Reported population*	Highest capacity	Lowest capacity
U.S. total	684,873	621,144	531,616
Federal	52,984	32,494	32,494
State	631,889	588,650	499,122

*Reported population excludes prisoners housed in local jails and other facilities where they have been included in the jurisdiction count and female prisoners in four States for which capacity data were not reported.

Prison population growth may reflect increasing certainty of punishment

There is some evidence that during the period from 1980 to 1988 changes in criminal justice policies have increased from earlier levels a criminal's probability of being incarcerated. Murder, nonnegligent manslaughter, rape, robbery, aggravated assault, and burglary are among the most serious crimes and account for approximately half of prison commitments from courts. In 1960 there were 62 prison commitments for every 1,000 of these crimes reported to law enforcement agencies (table 6).

During the rest of the decade this ratio steadily declined, reaching 23 in 1970, and was relatively stable during the 1970s. Between 1980 and 1988 the ratio increased 104% from 25 commitments per 1,000 reported crimes to 51.

Similarly, between 1960 and 1970 the ratio of prison commitments to adult arrests for the selected crimes declined from 299 per 1,000 to 170. This ratio was relatively stable during the rest of the 1970s, but it increased by 48% between 1980 and 1988, from 196 commitments per 1,000 adult arrests to 291.

Besides the increased use of prison relative to reported crime, arrests, and resident population, prison population has also been affected by changes in the extent of the illegal drug problem. An estimated two-thirds of those in State prisons for a drug offense were convicted of trafficking or manufacturing illegal drugs. Since 1980 the number of adult arrests for drug violations has increased by 123%, and the number of arrests for sales or manufacturing of illegal drugs has grown by 180%.

Table 6 **Court commitments to State prisons relative to offenses and arrests, 1960-88**

| Year | Commitments to prison per 1,000: | |
	Selected serious offenses	Adult arrests for same offenses
1960	62	299
1965	45	261
1970	23	170
1975	26	185
1980	25	196
1981	29	214
1982	35	219
1983	39	247
1984	39	246
1985	42	266
1986	43	268
1987	48	301
1988	51	291

Note: Selected offenses include murder, nonnegligent manslaughter, forcible rape, robbery, aggravated assault, and burglary. Date for crimes reported to the police and adult arrests are from Federal Bureau of Investigation, *Crime in the United States*, 1978-88 (Washington, DC: U.S. Government Printing Office). Commitments to prison are inmates admitted from sentencing courts. The data on which this table is based are presented in an appendix table.

2

Census of Local Jails in 1988

U.S. Department of Justice, Bureau of Justice Statistics

Local jails throughout the United States held 343,569 persons on June 30, 1988, 54% more than in 1983, the year of the last National Jail Census. The record level was 117% higher than the number confined in 1978. During the same 10-year period, the number of local jail facilities had decreased 5% from 3,493 to 3,316.

Other major findings from the 1988 census include the following:

- In 1988 there were 144 jail inmates per 100,000 U.S. residents, a rate 47% higher than the 98 per 100,000 in 1983.
- The number of female inmates nearly doubled (93%) between 1983 and 1988, while the male inmate count rose 51%.
- More than 19 million entries and exits (9.7 million admissions and 9.6 million releases) took place in local jails during the annual period ending June 30, 1988.

Source: Adapted from *Census of Local Jails in 1988* (Washington D.C.: U.S. Department of Justice, Bureau of Justice Statistics), February 1990, pp. 1-9.

- Among inmates discharged from jails in the week preceding the census, the median length of stay was 3 days. About 4 in every 10 had stayed a day or less.
- Jail space, as measured by rated capacity—the number of beds or inmates assigned by a State or local rating official—increased by nearly two-fifths between 1978 and 1988.
- For the Nation as a whole, in 1988 the local jail population was 101% of the total rated capacity—up from 85% of capacity in 1983.
- Twenty-nine percent of the jails held prisoners because of crowding in other institutions in 1988, compared with 17% in 1983. One in every twelve inmates—26,513—were in jail because of crowding elsewhere.
- Twelve percent of all jails were under Federal or State court order or consent decree to limit the number of inmates.
- Acquired immune deficiency syndrome (AIDS) accounted for 10% of 667 inmate deaths during the year ending June 30, 1988. Suicide, the leading cause of death, accounted for 43% of deaths in 1988, compared to 53% in 1983.
- The number of jail employees and the number of inmates increased at nearly the same rate during the 1980s. There was an average of 3.5 inmates per employee in 1983 and an average of 3.4 inmates per employee in 1988.
- The number of correctional officers, that is, employees who directly monitor inmates, increased 65% from 1983 to 1988, compared to a 54% increase in the number of inmates. The number of other types of correctional employees increased 31%.
- Jail expenditures totaled $4.5 billion during the annual period ending June 30, 1988. Capital outlays for building, major repairs, and other nonrecurring items were 22% of the total, about the same percentage as in 1983. The average annual operating cost per inmate was $10,639.

The 1988 Census of Local Jails

A record 343,569 persons were held in local jails on June 30, 1988, 54% more than in 1983 when the last jail census was taken and 117% greater than in 1978 (table 1). While the number of jail inmates was rising, the number of jail facilities was declining. A total of 3,316 local jails were operating on June 30, 1988, 1% fewer than in 1983 when they numbered 3,338 and 5% fewer than in 1978 when they numbered 3,493.

In this report a jail is defined as a locally administered confinement facility that holds persons pending adjudication or persons committed after adjudication, usually for sentences of a year or less. Jails incarcerate a wide variety of sentenced and unsentenced persons. Jails —

- receive individuals pending arraignment and hold them awaiting trial, conviction, and sentencing
- readmit probation, parole, and bail-bond violators and absconders
- temporarily detain juveniles pending transfer to juvenile authorities
- hold mentally ill persons pending their movement to appropriate health facilities
- hold individuals for the military, for protective custody, for contempt, and for the courts as witnesses
- release convicted inmates to the community upon completion of sentence
- transfer inmates to State, Federal, or other local authorities
- relinquish custody of temporary detainees to juvenile and medical authorities.

Table 1 **Jails and inmates, by region, February 15, 1978, and June 30, 1983 and 1988**

Region	1978	1983	1988
Number of jails			
U.S. total	3,493	3,338	3,316
Northeast	207	223	223
Midwest	1,042	972	964
South	1,678	1,607	1,599
West	566	536	530
Number of inmates			
U.S. total	158,394	223,551	343,569
Northeast	24,228	36,634	57,613
Midwest	28,452	39,538	50,646
South	67,444	89,479	143,751
West	38,270	57,900	91,559

The South led the Increase in local jail population

Jail populations in Southern States grew 61% between 1983 and 1988, followed closely by increases in the West (58%) and Northeast (57%). The jail population in the Midwest rose 28% during the period.

Nevada led the States with an increase of 149% in the number of jail inmates from 1983 to 1988 (table 2). In Arizona, Florida, and Texas, jail populations doubled or nearly doubled. Only Alaska, with five small local facilities, and the District of Columbia, which reclassified a facility from a jail to a prison, reported population decreases. The slowest population growth occurred in Illinois, Missouri, Alabama, and Oklahoma, where increases ranged from 8% to 17%.

Table 2 **Jails and inmates, by region, State and ratio to general population, June 30, 1983 and 1988**

Region and State	Number of jails 1983	Number of jails 1988	Number of inmates 1983	Number of inmates 1988	Percent change, 1983-88	Inmates per 100,000 population in 1988[a]
U.S. total·	3,338	3,316	223,551	343,569	54%	144
Northeast	223	223	36,634	57,613	57%	126
Maine	14	15	560	669	19	56
Massachusetts	17	19	3,304	5,454	65	93
New Hampshire	11	11	475	789	66	73
New Jersey	32	28	5,971	11,124	86	144
New York	72	75	16,154	25,928	61	145
Pennsylvania	77	75	10,170	13,649	34	114
Midwest	972	964	39,538	50,646	28%	85
Illinois	98	95	8,849	9,891	12	85
Indiana	93	90	3,599	5,235	45	94
Iowa	90	90	839	1,036	23	37
Kansas	86	94	1,328	1,906	44	76
Michigan	87	85	7,637	9,404	23	102
Minnesota	67	71	1,954	3,227	65	75
Missouri	129	123	3,783	4,154	10	81
Nebraska	67	66	844	1,156	37	72
North Dakota	31	26	243	288	19	43
Ohio	121	122	7,116	9,160	29	84
South Dakota	31	29	316	522	65	73
Wisconsin	72	73	3,030	4,667	54	96
South	1,607	1,599	89,479	143,751	61%	171
Alabama	108	110	4,464	4,819	8	117
Arkansas	89	87	1,602	1,994	24	83
District of Columbia[b]	2	1	2,843	1,693	-40	274
Florida	103	102	14,668	28,236	93	229
Georgia	203	196	10,214	17,482	71	276
Kentucky	96	95	3,711	4,695	27	126
Louisiana	94	90	8,507	11,222	32	255
Maryland	30	35	4,608	7,486	62	162
Mississippi	91	96	2,498	3,501-	40	134
North Carolina	99	102	3,496	5,469	56	84
Oklahoma	104	100	2,215	2,595	17	80
South Carolina	58	55	2,690	3,497	30	101

Tennessee	108	108	6,005	10,858	81	222
Texas	273	275	15,224	29,439	93	175
Virginia	95	95	5,719	9,372	64	156
West Virginia	54	52	1,015	1,393	37	74
West	**536**	**530**	**57,900**	**91,559**	**58%**	**185**
Alaska[c]	5	5	37	27	-27	
Arizona	31	33	2,940	6,006	104	172
California	142	149	41,720	64,216	54	227
Colorado	60	61	2,747	4,882	78	148
Idaho	36	37	604	810	34	81
Montana	50	46	405	616	52	77
Nevada	23	19	940	2,343	149	222
New Mexico	35	34	1,346	2,188	63	145
Oregon	39	39	2,304	2,819	22	102
Utah	24	25	906	1,261	39	75
Washington	65	60	3,610	5,934	64	128
Wyoming	26	22	341	457	34	95

Note: Five States—Connecticut, Delaware, Hawaii, Rhode Island, and Vermont—had integrated jail-prison systems and were excluded from the report. Alaska had primarily an integrated jail-prison system; however, data from 5 locally operated Alaska jails were counted in the jail census and included in this report.

[a]Based on resident population estimates, July 1, 1988, U.S. Bureau of the Census Press Release CB89-47.

[b]The decline in the District of Columbia jail population reflects the reclassification of the Occoquan complex from a jail to a prison between 1983 and 1988.

[c]The number of inmates per 100,000 population could not be calculated.

More than 2 of every 5 local jail inmates were incarcerated in four States: California (19%), Texas (9%), Florida (8%), and New York (8%).

The largest rates of jail inmates per 100,000 State residents were for Georgia, (276 jail inmates per 100,000), Louisiana (255), Florida (229), California (227), Tennessee (222), and Nevada (222).

The smallest jail incarceration rates in 1988 were for Iowa (37), North Dakota (43), Maine (56), Nebraska (72), New Hampshire (73), and South Dakota (73).

Over the period 1983 to 1988, local jails in Nevada, New Jersey, and Texas reported the largest gains in the number of inmates per capita.

Percentage of women in jail increased

The 30,411 females accounted for nearly 9% of the Nation's jail inmates in 1988; women were 7% of the total in 1983. The female jail population nearly doubled (93%) during the 5-year period. The fastest growth in female population occurred in the Northeast, where their number rose 130% during 1983-88. In the South, where total jail population growth was greatest, the number of female inmates increased 108%.

Percentage of juveniles in adult jails declined

The percentage of juveniles in adult jails declined from 0.8% in 1983 to 0.5% in 1988. The decline was nearly the same for male juveniles (3%) as for female (4%). The reduction occurred in every region except the South, where the number of juveniles in jail increased 24%.

Average daily jail population rose markedly

Average daily population takes into account weekday to weekend variation in jail counts which can affect the population figures on a census date. The U.S. average daily population in jails was 338,017 during the annual period ending June 30,1988. This was 48% higher than the 1983 average and 113% higher than the 1978 average. The West had a 58% increase in its average from 1983 to 1988. The Northeast (52%) and the South (52%) followed. The Midwest's average daily count of jail inmates increased 20%.

Nevada led the States with a 127% increase in the average daily number of inmates, followed by Arizona (99%) and Texas (90%). Alaska and the District of Columbia had decreases. The smallest growth in average daily population occurred in Alabama (less than 0.5%) and in Illinois (2%).

White inmates outnumbered blacks by a small margin

About 43% of all inmates in local jails were white (non-Hispanic), according to facility records. Forty-one percent were black (non-Hispanic); 15% were Hispanics of any race; and 1% were other races — American Indians, Alaska Natives, Asians, and Pacific Islanders.

Representation of whites was highest in the Midwest (57%) and lowest in the Northeast (37%). Representation of blacks was highest in the South (51%) and lowest in the West (24%). The percentage of Hispanics ranged from 30% in the West to 4% in the Midwest, while the percentage of inmates of other races ranged from 3% in the West to less than 0.5% in the South.

Percentages of unconvicted and convicted inmates were unchanged

In 1983 and 1988 jails reported that they held about the same percentages of unconvicted (51%) and convicted (49%) inmates. The largest percentage of convicted inmates in 1988 was in the West (52%); the smallest percentage was in the Midwest and the South, both with 47%.

Admissions and releases Increased

Approximately 9.7 million admissions and 9.6 million releases of jail inmates occurred during the annual period ending June 30, 1988.

These transactions included intrasystem transfers within jail complexes. The entries and exits had increased 20% over the volume in 1983. By comparison, State prisons and other correctional facilities in 1988 had 681,300 admissions and releases.

There were 137 jail admissions per 1,000 civilian residents of the United States 18-34 years old—the predominant age group among incarcerated persons. The four regions in 1983 and 1988 compared as follows:

	Jail admissions per 1,000 civilian residents, age 18-34	
	1983	1988
Northeast	38	49
Midwest	78	89
South	170	196
West	158	181

Most jail detentions lasted a few days

Approximately two-fifths of all inmates released from jail during the week before the census had spent 1 day or less, and three-fifths had spent 4 days or less. Releases included arrested persons who left jail on bail before trial, persons found guilty, persons who had completed a sentence, and persons who had been transferred to other institutions. About 3% of the inmates released during the 7-day period had served more than 6 months, and 1% had spent more than a year. The median time spent was 3 days.

The number of jail deaths relative to releases was unchanged from 1983

A total of 667 inmates died while under the jurisdiction of jail authorities during the year ending June 30, 1988. This was 20% more than the number in 1983. However, deaths accounted for about the same fraction of releases from jail in both years. In 1988 there were nearly 2 million more releases than in 1983.

Men, who made up 91% of the average daily population, accounted for 95% of all inmate mortalities. There were deaths of 636 men, 26 women, 4 juvenile males, and 1 juvenile female.

Suicide was the leading cause of death (43%), followed by illness (41%). Acquired immune deficiency syndrome (AIDS), a new category in 1988, accounted for about 10% of jail deaths; homicide, 1%; and other causes, 5%. In the Northeast, illness, AIDS, and suicide each accounted for nearly a third of deaths. In the Midwest suicide was almost twice as frequent as illness; in the South illness and suicide were about equally common; and in the West illness caused about half the deaths.

The number of facilities decreased slightly

The number of jails decreased from 3,338 in 1983 to 3,316 in 1988. Net increases occurred in 17 States, net decreases in 23, and no change in 6.

The decline in the number of local detention facilities resulted in part from the merging of small jails into complexes, the changes in function as from a jail to a lockup, court-ordered closures, and closures for renovation. However, the number of new jails built between 1983 and 1988 nearly equaled the decline. Eleven percent of all jails operating in 1988 were less than 5 years old. Regional differences for new jails were as follows:

	Percent of facilities built after June 1983
U.S. total	11%
Northeast	13
Midwest	8
South	11
West	15

Most jails were small

Approximately 67% of all jails in 1988 held an average daily population of fewer than 50 inmates. The Midwest had the highest percentage (81%), and the Northeast, the lowest (30%).

The percentage of facilities holding fewer than 50 inmates decreased in every region from 1978 to 1988. The percentage of facilities for 50 to 249 inmates increased.

A majority of inmates were held in medium- or large-capacity jails

Large jails held a growing percentage of the Nation's inmates during the 1980s. Approximately 83% of all locally confined persons in 1988 were in facilities for 250 or more, including 28% in jails with capacities for 1,000 or more.

The number of inmates in jails for 1,000 or more increased 141% between 1983 and 1988, while the total number of jail inmates increased 54%. The number in facilities for 50 or fewer increased 9%.

Nearly 2 of every 5 bed spaces were added between 1978 and 1988

Jail space, as measured by rated capacity—the number of beds or inmates assigned by a State or local rating official—increased 7%, from 245,094 in 1978 to 261,556 in 1983. During the next 5 years the rated capacity increased 30% to 339,633 in 1988. Capacity may be increased by new jail construction, by renovation, or by more efficient use of space.

Jails require a greater reserve of bed space than prisons

Jails, like prisons, require a reserve of confinement space for protective custody, administrative segregation, disciplinary custody, sick or injured inmates, work release, and units under repair.

Unlike prisons, however, jails require space for unconvicted and convicted inmates with a wide range of security requirements:

- persons who were recently abusing alcohol or drugs
- juveniles and the mentally ill who should be separated by sight and sound from other inmates
- population surges from arrest sweeps by police
- weekday to weekend variation
- weekend sentencing.

For the decade 1978-88, 83% of the increase in U.S. jail capacity occurred during the last 5 years. Jails holding 1,000 inmates or more had a 283% increase in rated capacity during the decade, including an increase of 132% from 1983 to 1988. At the same time the rated capacity of jails holding fewer than 50 inmates fell 28%, including an 11% decrease during 1983-88.

Occupancy exceeded rated capacity

The 117% increase in jail population from 1978 to 1988 surpassed the 39% expansion in rated capacity. As a result, the amount of rated capacity that was occupied rose from 65% in 1978 to 85% in 1983 to 101% in 1988.

The West had the greatest increase in occupancy, from 69% of capacity in 1978 to 117% of capacity in 1988. The Midwest had the lowest increase, from 57% of capacity in 1978 to 86% in 1988. The South was the only region in which the occupancy level increased more from 1983 to 1988 (78% to 98%) than from 1978 to 1983 (63% to 78%).

In 1978 for every size category of jail, the inmate population was below capacity. By 1988, however, only jails intended for fewer than 50 inmates reported a population well below capacity — 64% occupancy. All other size categories of jails were near capacity or above.

One in every eight inmates was being held for other correctional authorities

Approximately 42,000 inmates (12% of the jail population) were being held for other correctional authorities on June 30, 1988. About 26,500 or 8% of all inmates in 1988, compared to 7,700 (3%) in 1983, were being held because of crowding in other institutions.

About two-thirds of all jail inmates held for other authorities in 1988 were State prisoners; a fifth were Federal prisoners; and the remainder were kept for other local jails. State jail inmates predominated in the Northeast and the South, where they accounted for about 75% of prisoners held for other authorities. Federal jail inmates were most common in the West (33%). Inmates from other local facilities were the largest group being held for other authorities in the Midwest (41%).

Approximately 54% of all jails held inmates for other authorities at midyear 1988. Twenty-nine percent of the jails held prisoners because of crowding in other institutions, compared with 17% in 1983.

Most jails charged fees to hold
inmates for other authorities

In 1988, 73% of jails charged a fee for holding inmates for other authorities. The fee varied by jurisdiction, region, and size of jail. Fourteen percent of all jails, as a general policy, did not hold inmates for other authorities; 13% held inmates for other authorities without charge.

Federal authorities paid an average of $34.05 per diem for each prisoner, about a third more than State authorities ($25.28) and a fourth more than local authorities ($26.67). Jails in the Northeast and those with 500-999 inmates charged the highest per diem fees, and jails in the South and those with fewer than 50 inmates, the lowest fees. Per diem charges may have varied according to whether the jails were located in major population centers. For example, the higher Federal per diem payment may reflect the need to hold prisoners near U.S. district courts.

Courts had ordered 1 of every 8 jails to
limit population or improve conditions

A total of 404 jails (12% of all facilities) were under State or Federal court order or consent decree to limit the number of inmates at midyear 1988. At the same time, 412 jails were under State or Federal court order or consent decree for specific conditions of confinement.

More than three-quarters of the jails that courts had cited for specific conditions were also under court order to limit the number of inmates. About 91% of all jails mandated to improve crowded living units were also under court order to limit inmate population. Other conditions that courts often cited together with population limits included inmate classification (83%), library services (81%), medical facilities or services (80%), food service (80%), and the totality of conditions (80%).

Staff growth kept pace with inmate increase

A record 99,631 jail payroll and nonpayroll employees, including 73,280 correctional officers, were at work during the 24-hour period of June 30, 1988. (Agencies other than jails paid the nonpayroll employees —for example, university employees staffing educational or counseling programs.) The 54% increase over the number of employees at work on June 30, 1983, was identical to the percentage rise in inmates during the period; however, the number of correctional officers, employees who directly monitor inmates, increased 65%.

There were regional variations in staff growth between 1983 and 1988. Staff and inmates increased at similar rates in the Midwest (31% and 28%) and in the West (82% and 58%). By contrast, the number of employees in Southern jails increased 46% while the number of inmates rose 61%. In the Northeast the number of employees increased 90% while the number of inmates rose 57%.

Sex and race/ethnicity representation of staff differed from that of inmates

In 1988 men comprised 73% of all paid jail employees, including 77% of the correctional officers. The percentage of correctional officers who were women was nearly 2 1/2 times greater than the percentage of inmates who were women.

Whites (non-Hispanic) made up an estimated 69% of all paid employees, including 68% of the correctional officers. They comprised 43% of all inmates. Blacks (non-Hispanic) were 23% of the payroll employees, including 24% of the correctional officers. Black inmates were 41% of the jail population. Hispanics accounted for 7% of the staff and 15% of the inmates.

Inmate-to-staff ratio rose among all occupational groups except correctional officers

There was an average of 3.4 inmates per employee in 1988. This ratio, obtained by dividing the average daily inmate population by the number of employees (excluding community volunteers), almost matched the 1983 ratio of 3.5 inmates per employee. There were more inmates per administrator in 1988 (50.0) than in 1983 (37.4). A similar increase occurred in the inmate-to-educational-staff ratio: 276.3 to 1 in 1988 versus 254.8 to 1 in 1983. But the ratio of inmates to each correctional officer declined from 5.1 in 1983 to 4.6 in 1988.

Annual jail spending exceeded $4.5 billion in 1988

Local jail expenditures throughout the United States totaled slightly more than $4.5 billion during the year ending June 30, 1988. This total (not adjusted for inflation) was 67% over the expenditures in 1983.

Gross salaries and wages, employer contributions to employee benefits, purchases of food, supplies, contractual services, and other current operating costs accounted for 78% of all expenditures. Construction costs, major repairs, equipment, improvements, land purchases, and other capital outlays accounted for the remaining 22%. In 1983 these percentages were nearly the same.

Excluding capital outlays, it cost an average of $10,639 to keep one inmate in jail for a year. In 1983 it cost $9,360. The Northeast had the highest average operating expenditure per inmate ($17,710), and the South, the lowest ($8,418). Excluding Alaska, average annual operating costs per inmate were highest in New York ($22,698) and lowest in Mississippi ($5,341).

Methodology

The 1988 Census of Local Jails was the fifth enumeration of local confinement facilities since 1970. As in previous censuses, the U.S. Bureau of the Census conducted the mail canvass for BJS.

The 1988 census included all locally administered jails that held inmates beyond arraignment (usually more than 48 hours) and that were staffed by municipal or county employees. Eight jails that were privately operated under contract for local governments were also included.

Excluded from the census were physically separate drunk tanks, lockups, and other holding facilities that did not hold persons after they had been formally charged, as well as all Federal and State facilities, including the combined jail-prison systems in Alaska, Connecticut, Delaware, Hawaii, Rhode island, and Vermont. Five locally operated jails in Alaska were included.

The facility universe was derived from the National Justice Agency List, maintained by the Bureau of the Census for BJS. Following revision of the 1983 questionnaire and pretests, the final census form was mailed to 3,448 facilities during the week of August 1, 1988. Forty-four jails were added to the initial mailout, and 176 were deleted, leaving a final count of 3,316 facilities. Extensive followup by the Bureau of Census staff and State Statistical Analysis Center directors resulted in a 100% response.

3

Report to the Nation on Crime and Justice
Sentencing and Corrections
U.S. Department of Justice, Bureau of Justice Statistics

Through Sentencing Society Attempts to Express Its Goals for the Correctional Process

The sentencing of criminals often reflects conflicting social goals. These objectives are—

- *Retribution*—giving offenders their "just deserts" and expressing society's disapproval of criminal behavior
- *Incapacitation*—separating offenders from the community to reduce the opportunity for further crime while they are incarcerated
- *Deterrence*—demonstrating the certainty and severity of punishment to discourage future crime by the offender (specific deterrence) and by others (general deterrence)

Source: *Report to the Nation on Crime and Justice—Sentencing and Corrections, Second Edition* (Washington, D.C.: U.S. Department of Justice, Bureau of Justice Statistics), March 1988, pp. 90-111.

- *Rehabilitation* — providing psychological or educational assistance or job training to offenders to make them less likely to engage in future criminality
- *Restitution* — having the offender repay the victim or the community in money or services.

Attitudes about sentencing reflect multiple goals and other factors. Research on judicial attitudes and practices in sentencing revealed that judges vary greatly in their commitment to various goals when imposing sentences. Public opinion also has shown much diversity about the goals of sentencing, and public attitudes have changed over the years. In fashioning criminal penalties, legislators have tended to reflect this lack of public consensus. Sentencing laws are further complicated by concerns for —

- *Proportionality* — severity of punishment should be commensurate with the seriousness of the crime
- *Equity* — similar crimes and similar criminals should be treated alike
- *Social debt* — the severity of punishment should take into account the offender's prior criminal behavior

Judges usually have a great deal of discretion in sentencing offenders. The different sentencing laws give various amounts of discretion to the judge in setting the length of a prison or jail term. In a more fundamental respect, however, the judge often has a high degree of discretion in deciding whether or not to incarcerate the offender at all. Alternatives to imprisonment include —

- probation
- fines
- forfeiture of the proceeds of criminal activity
- restitution to victims
- community service
- split sentences, consisting of a short period of incarceration followed by probation in the community.

Often, before a sentence is imposed a presentence investigation is conducted to provide the judge with information about the offender's characteristics and prior criminal record.

Disparity and uncertainty arose from a lack of consensus over sentencing goals. By the early 1970s researchers and critics of the justice system had begun to note that trying to achieve the mixed goals of the justice system without new limits on the discretionary options given to judges had—

- reduced the *certainty* of sanctions, presumably eroding the deterrent effect of corrections
- resulted in *disparity* in the severity of punishment, with differences in the sentences imposed for similar cases and offenders
- failed to validate the effectiveness of various rehabilitation programs in changing offender behavior or predicting future criminality.

Recent sentencing reforms reflect more severe attitudes and seek to reduce disparity and uncertainty. Reforms in recent years have used statutory and administrative changes to—

- clarify the aims of sentencing
- reduce disparity by limiting judicial and parole discretion
- provide a system of penalties that is more consistent and predictable
- provide sanctions consistent with the concept of "just deserts."

The changes have included—

- making prison mandatory for certain crimes and for recidivists
- specifying presumptive sentence lengths
- requiring sentence enhancements for offenders with prior felony convictions
- introducing sentencing guidelines
- limiting parole discretion through the use of parole guidelines
- total elimination of discretionary parole release (determinate sentencing).

States use a variety of strategies for sentencing. Sentencing is perhaps the most diversified part of the Nation's criminal justice process. Each State has a unique set of sentencing laws, and frequent and substantial changes have been made in recent years. This diversity complicates the classification of sentencing systems. For nearly any criterion that may be considered, there will be some States with hybrid systems that straddle the boundary between categories.

The basic difference in sentencing systems is the apportioning of discretion between the judge and parole authorities:

Indeterminate sentencing — the judge specifies minimum and maximum sentence lengths. These set upper and lower bounds on the time to be served. The actual release date (and therefore the time actually served) is determined later by parole authorities within those limits.

Partially indeterminate sentencing — a variation of indeterminate sentencing in which the judge specifies only the maximum sentence length. An associated minimum automatically is implied, but is not within the judge's discretion. The implied minimum may be a fixed time (such as 1 year) for all sentences or a fixed proportion of the maximum. In some States the implied minimum is zero; thus the parole board is empowered to release the prisoner at any time.

Determinate sentencing — the judge specifies a fixed term of incarceration, which must be served in full (less any "goodtime" earned in prison). There is no discretionary parole release.

Since 1975 many States have adopted determinate sentencing, but most still use indeterminate sentencing. In 1976 Maine was the first State to adopt determinate sentencing. The sentencing system is entirely or predominantly determinate in these 10 States:

California	Maine
Connecticut	Minnesota
Florida	New Mexico
Illinois	North Carolina
Indiana	Washington

The other States and the District of Columbia use indeterminate sentencing in its various forms. One State, Colorado, after changing to determinate sentencing in 1979, went back to indeterminate sentencing in 1985. The Federal justice system has adopted determinate sentencing through a system of sentencing guidelines.

Sentencing guidelines usually are developed by a separate sentencing commission. Such a commission may be appointed by the legislative, executive, or judicial branch of State government. This is a departure from traditional practice in that sentences are prescribed through an administrative procedure rather than by explicit legislation.

In some States the guidelines are prescriptive in that they specify whether or not the judge must impose a prison sentence and the presumptive sentence length. In other States the guidelines are advisory in that they provide information to the judge but do not mandate sentencing decisions.

States employ other sentencing features in conjunction with their basic strategies

Mandatory sentencing—Law requires the judge to impose a sentence of incarceration, often of specified length, for certain crimes or certain categories of offenders. There is no option of probation or a suspended sentence.

Mandatory sentencing laws are in force in 46 States (all except Maine, Minnesota, Nebraska, and Rhode Island) and the District of Columbia. In 25 States imprisonment is mandatory for certain repeat felony offenders. In 30 States imprisonment is mandatory if a firearm was involved in the commission of a crime. In 45 States conviction for certain offenses or classes of offenses leads to mandatory imprisonment; most such offenses are serious, violent crimes, and drug trafficking is included in 18 of the States. Many States have recently made drunk driving an offense for which incarceration is mandated (usually for relatively short periods in a local jail rather than a State prison).

Presumptive sentencing—The discretion of a judge who imposes a prison sentence is constrained by a specific sentence length set by law for each offense or class of offense. That sentence must be imposed in all unexceptional cases. In response to mitigating or aggravating circumstances, the judge may shorten or lengthen the sentence within specified boundaries, usually with written justification being required.

Presumptive sentencing is used, at least to some degree, in about 12 States.

Sentencing guidelines—Explicit policies and procedures are specified for deciding on individual sentences. The decision is usually based on the nature of the offense and the offender's criminal record. For example, the prescribed sentence for a certain offense might be probation if the offender has no previous felony convictions, a short term of incarceration if the offender has one prior conviction, and progressively longer prison terms if the offender's criminal history is more extensive.

Sentencing guidelines came into use in the late 1970s. They are—
• used in 13 States and the Federal criminal justice system
• written into statute in the Federal system and in Florida, Louisiana, Maryland, Minnesota, New Jersey, Ohio, Pennsylvania, and Tennessee
• used systemwide, but not mandated by law, in Utah
• applied selectively in Massachusetts, Michigan, Rhode Island, and Wisconsin
• being considered for adoption in other States and the District of Columbia.

Sentence enhancements—In nearly all States, the judge may lengthen the prison term for an offender with prior felony convictions. The lengths of such enhancements and the criteria for imposing them vary among the States.

In some States that group felonies according to their seriousness, the repeat offender may be given a sentence ordinarily imposed for a higher seriousness category. Some States prescribe lengthening the sentences of habitual offenders by specified amounts or imposing a mandatory minimum term that must be served before parole can be considered. In other States the guidelines provide for sentences that reflect the offender's criminal history as well as the seriousness of the offense. Many States prescribe conditions under which parole eligibility is limited or eliminated. For example, a person with three or more prior felony convictions, if convicted of a serious violent offense, might be sentenced to life imprisonment without parole.

Sources: Surveys conducted for the Bureau of Justice Statistics by the U.S. Bureau of the Census in 1985 and by the Pennsylvania Commission on Crime and Delinquency in 1986.

To determine whether a prison sentence should be imposed, the guidelines usually consider offense severity and the offender's prior criminal record. A matrix that relates these two factors may be used.

Sentencing matrix

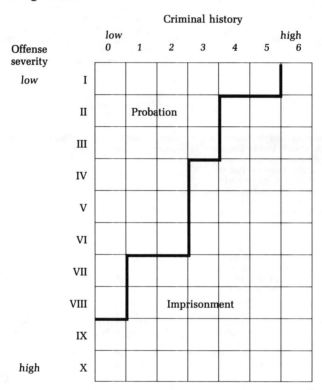

Adapted from *Preliminary report on the development and impact of the Minnesota sentencing guidelines*, Minnesota Sentencing Guidelines Commission, July 1982.

Sentencing guidelines used in the Federal justice system were developed by the United States Sentencing Commission. The guidelines provide for determinate sentencing and the abolition of parole. Ranges of sentence length are specified for various offense classifications and offender characteristics. The judge must provide written justification for any sentence that deviates from the guideline range; sentences that are less severe can be appealed by the prosecution, and sentences that are more severe can be appealed by the defense.

Changes in sentencing have brought changes in correctional practices. Many sentencing reforms have led to changes in the way correctional systems operate.

The proliferation of determinate and mandatory sentences during the past decade, together with dissatisfaction about the uncertainties of indeterminate sentencing (especially the linking of release decisions to rehabilitative progress or predictions of future behavior), have led to modifications in parole decisionmaking. Many States now use parole guidelines, and many have modified their use of "goodtime" and other incentives for controlling inmate behavior and determining release dates.

New administrative requirements, such as collection of victim restitution funds, operation of community service programs, and levying fees for probation supervision, room and board, and other services, have been added to traditional correctional practices.

Changes in sentencing laws and practices may be affecting the size of the correctional clientele. Such changes include—

- using determinate and mandatory sentencing
- limiting or abolishing parole discretion
- lowering the age at which youthful offenders become subject to the adult criminal justice system
- enacting in a few jurisdictions laws providing for life imprisonment without the possibility of parole.

Sanctions for Alcohol-Related Driving Offenses are Becoming More Severe

Alcohol-related driving offenses carry both criminal and administrative sanctions. Because States license drivers, sanctions against persons convicted of driving while intoxicated and driving under the influence of alcohol include revocation or suspension of drivers' licenses. In some States the administrative sanction may be imposed for a short period prior to conviction if there is sufficient evidence to believe the defendant was operating a motor vehicle while under the influence of alcohol. In 1986 the minimum period for license suspension or revocation for a first offense ranged from 21 days in one State to 36 months in another.

Criminal sanctions may involve incarceration, fines, community service, restitution, or alcohol treatment and education programs. In some States, criminal driving offenses are classified as felonies; in other

States, they are misdemeanors. The term of incarceration permitted by statute for a first offense ranges from a minimum of 1 day up to 2 years. First offense fines range from $100 to $5,000.

In almost all States both administrative and criminal sanctions may be imposed for a conviction of driving while intoxicated. The criminal court imposes criminal sanctions while the licensing agency imposes the administrative sanctions on notification of conviction by the court.

In most States possible sanctions for repeat alcohol-related driving offenders are progressively severe. In 1986 more than half the States had license suspension or revocation minimums of a few months for first offenders and 12 months for second offenders. In 43 States the fines that may be imposed also increased with the number of prior convictions. For example, Arizona law permits fines up to $1,000 for first offenses but up to $150,000 for third offenses. In 23 States repeat offenders may be subject to habitual offender laws resulting in enhancement of the term to incarceration.

Many States have resorted to mandatory sanctions:

Type of sanction and prior history	Number of States imposing mandatory sanctions	
	1982	1986
Imprisonment		
1st offense	12	16
2nd	22	42
3rd	19	40
Fines		
1st offense	9	15
2nd	10	13
3rd	9	12
License suspension or revocation		
1st offense	31	25
2nd	39	44
3rd	38	44

Source: *A digest of State alcohol-highway safety related legislation*, first edition and fifth edition, National Highway Traffic Safety Administration, U.S. Department of Transportation.

Many states have increased the severity of their mandatory sanctions against alcohol-related driving offenses. Between 1982 and 1986—

- 4 States increased their mandatory fines for at least one offense
- 8 States increased the length of mandatory imprisonment for at least one offense

- 11 States increased the term for license suspension or revocation

A few years after imposing severe mandatory sanctions, many States reduced the severity of their sanctions, particularly for first offenses.

Juveniles Receive Dispositions Rather Than Sentences

Juvenile court dispositions tend to be indeterminate. The dispositions of juveniles adjudicated to be delinquent extend until the juvenile legally becomes an adult (21 years of age in most States) or until the offending behavior has been corrected, whichever is sooner.

Of the 45 States and the District of Columbia that authorize indeterminate periods of confinement—

- 32 grant releasing authority to the State juvenile corrections agency
- 6 delegate it to juvenile paroling agencies
- 5 place such authority with the committing judges
- 3 have dual or overlapping jurisdiction.

Most juvenile cases are disposed of informally. In 1982 about 54% of all cases referred to juvenile courts by the police and other agencies were handled informally without the filing of a petition. About 20% of all cases involved some detention prior to disposition.

Of about 600,000 cases in which petitions were filed, 64% resulted in formal adjudication. Of these, 61% resulted in some form of probation, and 29% resulted in an out-of-home placement.

The juvenile justice system is also undergoing changes in the degree of discretion permitted in confinement decisions. Determinate dispositions are now used in six States, but they do not apply to all offenses or offenders. In most cases they apply only to specified felony cases or to the juveniles with prior adjudications for serious delinquencies.

California imposes determinate periods of confinement for delinquents committed to State agencies based on the standards and guidelines of its paroling agency. Four States have similar procedures, administered by the State agencies responsible for operating their juvenile corrections facilities.

As of 1981 eight States had serious-delinquent statutes requiring that juveniles who are either serious, violent, repeat, or habitual offenders be adjudicated and committed in a manner that differs from the adjudication of other delinquents. Such laws require minimum lengths of commitment, prescribe a fixed range of time for commitment, or mandate a minimum length of stay in a type of placement, such as a secure institution.

Dispositions for serious juvenile offenders tend to look like those for adults. Aggregate statistics on juvenile court dispositions do not provide an accurate picture of what happens to the more serious offenders because many of the cases coming before juvenile courts involve minor criminal or status offenses. These minor cases are more likely to be handled informally by the juvenile court.

An analysis of California cases involving older juveniles and young adults charged by the police with robbery or burglary revealed more similarities in their disposition patterns than the aggregate juvenile court statistics would suggest. For both types of offenses, juvenile petitions were filed and settled formally in court about as often as were complaints filed and convictions obtained in the cases against adults. The juveniles charged with the more serious offenses and those with the more extensive prior records were the most likely to have their cases reach adjudication. At the upper limits of offense and prior record severity, juveniles were committed to secure institutions about as frequently as were young adults with comparable records.

The outcomes of juvenile and adult proceedings are similar, but some options are not available in juvenile court. For example, juvenile courts cannot order the death penalty, life terms, or terms that could exceed the maximum jurisdiction of the court itself. In Arizona the State Supreme Court held that, despite statutory jurisdiction of the juvenile courts to age 21, delinquents could not be held in State juvenile corrections facilities beyond age 18.

Yet, juvenile courts may go further than criminal courts in regulating the lifestyles of juvenile offenders placed in the community under probation supervision. For example, the court may order them to —

- live in certain locations
- attend school
- participate in programs intended to improve their behavior.

The National Center for Juvenile Justice estimates that almost 70% of the juveniles whose cases are not waived or dismissed are put on probation; about 10% are committed to an institution.

Most juveniles committed to juvenile facilities are delinquents:

	Percent of juveniles
Total	100%
Delinquents	74
Nondelinquents	
Status offenders	12
Nonoffenders (dependency,	
neglect, abuse, etc.)	14

Source: BJS Children in Custody, 1985, unpublished data.

Current Sentencing Alternatives Reflect Multiple Objectives

What types of sentences usually are given to offenders?

Death penalty—In most States for the most serious crimes such as murder, the courts may sentence an offender to death by lethal injection, electrocution, exposure to lethal gas, hanging, or other method specified by State law.

- As of 1985, 37 States had laws providing for the death penalty.
- Virtually all death penalty sentences are for murder.
- As of yearend 1985, 50 persons had been executed since 1976, and 1,591 inmates in 32 States were under a sentence of death.

Incarceration—The confinement of a convicted criminal in a Federal or State prison or a local jail to serve a court-imposed sentence. Confinement is usually in a jail, administered locally, or a prison, operated by the State or Federal Government. In many States offenders sentenced to 1 year or less are held in a jail; those sentenced to longer terms are committed to a State prison.

- More than 4,200 correctional facilities are maintained by Federal, State, and local governments. They include 47 Federal facilities, 922 State-operated adult confinement and community-based correctional facilities, and 3,300 local jails, which usually are county-operated.
- On any given day in 1985 about 503,000 persons were confined in State and Federal prisons. About 254,000 were confined in local jails on June 30, 1985.

Probation—The sentencing of an offender to community supervision by a probation agency, often as a result of suspending a sentence to confinement. Such supervision normally entails specific rules of conduct while in the community. If the rules are violated a sentence to confinement may be imposed. Probation is the most widely used correctional disposition in the United States.

- State or local governments operate more than 2,000 probation agencies.
- At year end 1985, nearly 1.9 million adults were on probation, or about 1 of every 95 adults in the Nation.

Split sentences, shock probation, and intermittent confinement — A penalty that explicitly requires the convicted person to serve a brief period of confinement in a local, State, or Federal facility (the "shock") followed by a period of probation. This penalty attempts to combine the use of community supervision with a short incarceration experience. Some sentences are periodic rather than continuous; for example, an offender may be required to spend a certain number of weekends in jail.

- In 1984 nearly a third of those receiving probation sentences in Idaho, New Jersey, Tennessee, Utah, and Vermont also were sentenced to brief periods of confinement.

Restitution and victim compensation — The offender is required to provide financial repayment or, in some jurisdictions, services in lieu of monetary restitution, for the losses incurred by the victim.

- Nearly all States have statutory provisions for the collection and disbursement of restitution funds. A restitution law was enacted at the Federal level in 1982.

Community service — The offender is required to perform a specified amount of public service work, such as collecting trash in parks or other public facilities.

- Many States authorize community service work orders. Community service often is imposed as a specific condition of probation.

Fines — An economic penalty that requires the offender to pay a specified sum of money within limits set by law. Fines often are imposed in addition to probation or as alternatives to incarceration.

- The Victims of Crime Act of 1984 authorizes the distribution of fines and forfeited criminal profits to support State victim-assistance programs, with priority given to programs that aid victims of sexual assault, spousal abuse, and child abuse. These programs, in turn, provide assistance and compensation to crime victims.

- Many laws that govern the imposition of fines are being revised. The revisions often provide for more flexible means of ensuring equity in the imposition of fines, flexible fine schedules, "day fines" geared to the offenders daily wage, installment payment of fines, and the imposition of confinement only when there is an intentional refusal to pay.
- A 1984 study estimated that more than three-fourths of criminal courts use fines extensively and that fines levied each year exceed one billion dollars.

In Most Cases, a Felony Conviction Results in a Sentence that Includes Incarceration

Incarceration is most likely for serious crimes of violence:

Sentences imposed in nine jurisdictions in 1981[a]

| | Percent of convictions resulting in incarceration in prison or jail | |
	Any	More than 1 year
All felonies[b]	71%	37%
Homicide and manslaughter	86	70
Sexual assault	79	52
Robbery	83	58
Assault	64	24
Burglary	76	39
Larceny and auto theft	62	24
Stolen property	66	26
Fraud	60	23
Drugs	62	21
Weapons	60	26
Other[c]	63	21

[a] Indianapolis, Indiana; Los Angeles, California; Louisville, Kentucky; Borough of Manhattan, New York; New Orleans, Louisiana; State of Rhode Island; St. Louis, Missouri; Salt Lake City, Utah; San Diego, California.
[b] Indicted cases that resulted in conviction in felony court; a few of the convictions were for misdemeanors.
[c] Includes kidnaping, morals offenses, arson, unknown, and miscellaneous other felonies.

Source: Barbara Boland with Ronald Sones. INSLAW, Inc., *The prosecution of felony arrests*, 1981, BJS, 1986.

Confinement may be in State prisons or local jails. In most jurisdictions local jails are used to incarcerate persons with short sentences (generally less than 1 year), while longer sentences are served in State prisons. However, some jurisdictions use jail instead of prison more often as the sanction against convicted felons serving longer terms. For example, in both Baltimore City, Maryland, and Philadelphia, Pennsylvania, in 1983 two-thirds of convicted felons were sentenced to incarceration. In Baltimore, virtually all such persons went to State prisons, while Philadelphia sent half to State prisons and half to county institutions.

Many felons are sentenced to probation. A 1985 study of felony sentencing in 18 local jurisdictions revealed that more than a fourth of felony sentences were for probation alone. Almost another fifth of convicted felons were sentenced to a time in jail followed by probation (split sentence).

Sentences are more severe for offenders convicted of multiple charges than for those convicted of single charges. According to the 18-jurisdiction study—

- More than a fourth of the persons convicted of felonies were convicted of more than one charge.

- Persons convicted of multiple felony charges were more likely to go to prison and received longer sentences. Of those convicted of a single charge, 40% were sentenced to prison vs. 56% of those convicted of two charges and 69% of those convicted of four or more charges.

- About 11% of those convicted of multiple charges and sentenced to prison were given consecutive sentences; the individual sentences must be served in sequence. The rest were given concurrent sentences, allowing several sentences to be served at the same time.

The Death Penalty is Reserved for the Most Serious Offenses and Offenders

The death penalty was reaffirmed by the Supreme Court in 1976. In the 1972 decision *Furman* v. *Georgia*, the Supreme Court struck down on Eighth Amendment grounds (forbidding cruel and unusual punishment) State and Federal capital punishment laws that permitted wide discretion in the application of the death penalty. In response, many States revised their statutes to conform to the guidelines in *Furman*.

At the end of 1985, 37 States had death penalty laws in effect

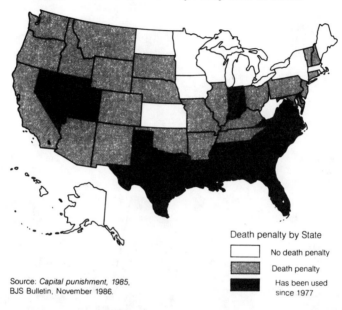

Death penalty by State

☐ No death penalty

▨ Death penalty

■ Has been used since 1977

Source: *Capital punishment, 1985,*
BJS Bulletin, November 1986.

The High Court clarified these guidelines in a series of five decisions announced on July 2, 1976. In *Woodson* v. *North Carolina* and *Roberts* v. *Louisiana*, the Court struck down State statutes that required mandatory imposition of the death penalty for specified crimes. As a direct consequence, mandatory death penalty provisions in 21 States were invalidated either through later court action or repeal by State legislatures. This resulted in the modification to life imprisonment of death sentences imposed on hundreds of offenders in these States.

In three other major cases, however, the Supreme Court upheld State death penalty laws that afforded sentencing authorities discretion to impose death sentences for specified crimes (*Gregg* v. *Georgia*, *Jurek* v. *Texas*, and *Proffit* v. *Florida*). The Court validated statutes that permitted the imposition of the death penalty after consideration of aggravating and mitigating circumstances.

A total of 3,909 people have been executed since 1930, including 50

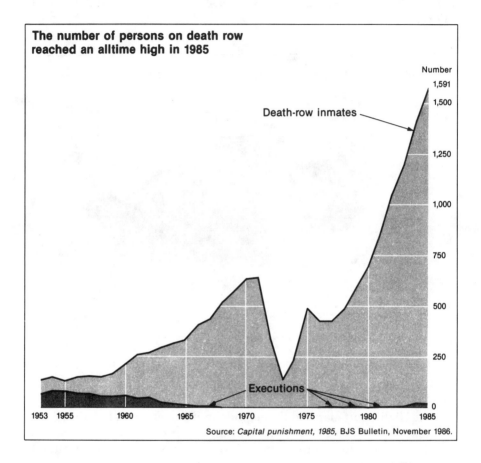

The number of persons on death row reached an alltime high in 1985

Number

1,591

1,500

Death-row inmates

1,250

1,000

750

500

250

Executions

0

1953 1955   1960   1965   1970   1975   1980   1985

Source: *Capital punishment, 1985*, BJS Bulletin, November 1986.

since 1977. In 1977 the first execution in a decade was carried out in Utah. Two more executions followed in 1979 (Florida and Nevada), 1 in 1981 (Indiana), 2 in 1982 (Virginia and Texas), 5 in 1983 (2 in Florida and 1 each in Alabama, Mississippi, and Louisiana), 21 in 1984 (8 in Florida, 5 in Louisiana, 3 in Texas, 2 each in Georgia and North Carolina, and 1 in Virginia), and 18 during 1985 (6 in Texas, 3 each in Florida and Georgia, 2 in Virginia, and 1 each in Indiana, Louisiana, South Carolina, and Nevada).

What Types of Murder are Most Often Cited in State Capital Punishment laws?

Type of murder for which death penalty is authorized	Number of States
Murder during another crime	
Sexual offense (such as rape)	35
Kidnaping	34
Robbery	33
Burglary	32
Arson	29
Murder of a certain type of victim	
Police or other law enforcement officer	34
Corrections employee	26
Firefighter	22
Murder by a person with a criminal history or criminal justice status	
Defendant was in custody	27
Defendant was previously convicted of murder	20
Murder carried out in a particular way	
Defendant created a grave risk of death to others	26
Murder was especially heinous, atrocious, cruel, vile, etc.	23
Murder carried out for a particular purpose	
For pecuniary gain (contract murder, murder for hire)	35
To effect an escape	26
To avoid or prevent an arrest	20
Other	
Multiple murders	22
Hiring another to kill	21

Source: BJS analysis of State capital punishment laws, 1986.

Who is on Death Row?

Of the 1,591 inmates on death row in 1985—

- All had been convicted of murder, 2 out of 3 had at least one prior felony conviction, 1 out of 11 had a prior murder conviction, and 2 out of 5 had a legal status (on bail, probation, or parole) at the time of the capital murder.

- 1,574 were male and 17 were female.

- 903 were white, 672 were black, 11 were American Indian, 5 were Asian, and 99 were of Hispanic origin.

- The median elapsed time since death sentence was imposed was 36 months.

What methods of execution are used by the various States?

Lethal injection	Electrocution	Lethal gas	Hanging	Firing squad
Arkansas[a]	Alabama	Arizona	Delaware	Idaho[a]
Idaho[a]	Arkansas[a]	California	Montana[a]	Utah[a]
Illinois	Connecticut	Colorado	New Hampshire	
Mississippi[a,b]	Florida	Maryland	Washington[a]	
Montana[a]	Georgia	Mississippi[a,b]		
Nevada	Indiana	Missouri		
New Jersey	Kentucky	North Carolina[a]		
New Mexico	Louisiana	Wyoming[a]		
North Carolina[a]	Nebraska			
Oklahoma[c]	Ohio			
Oregon	Pennsylvania			
South Dakota	South Carolina			
Texas	Tennessee			
Utah[a]	Vermont			
Washington[a]	Virginia			
Wyoming[a]				

[a]Authorizes two methods of execution.
[b]Mississippi authorizes lethal injection for persons convicted after 7/1/84; executions of persons convicted before that date are to be carried out with lethal gas.
[c]Should lethal injection be found to be unconstitutional, Oklahoma authorizes use of electrocution or firing squad.

Source: *Capital punishment, 1985*, BJS Bulletin, November 1986.

For Most Inmates, Prison Sentences Are Much Longer Than the Actual Time They Will Serve

Sentences to prison vary widely between minimum and maximum terms and are longer for violent crimes:

Admission offense	Percent of ad- missions	Average sentence of those admitted to prison	
		Minimum*	Maximum
All crimes	100%	40 mos.	72 mos.
Violent offenses	39%	62	100
Murder	4	177	281
Rape	3	82	117
Robbery	16	55	91
Assault	7	45	72
Property offenses	46%	27	58
Burglary	26	29	61
Auto theft	2	20	41
Forgery/fraud	5	26	53
Larceny	10	23	55
Drug offenses	8%	27	53
Public order offenses	5%	22	45
Other crimes	2%	27	27

*Defined as the estimated minimum time to be served prior to eligibility for release.

Source: *Prison admissions and releases*, 1983, BJS Special Report, March 1986.

Most prisoners are released before serving their maximum sentence. Release from prison generally occurs as the result of a decision of a paroling authority, mandatory release, or expiration of sentence. In 1984 half of all releases from prison were by a parole board decision.

Parole is the release of a prisoner by the decision of a paroling authority. The offender is placed under the supervision of a parole officer who monitors the offender's compliance with rules of conduct imposed by the paroling authority. Violations of these rules may result in reimprisonment for the balance of the unexpired sentence.

Mandatory release is based on earned "goodtime" (days earned for good behavior) or other statutory sentence-reduction measures and, though supervision is required after release, does not usually depend on the discretionary decision of a parole board. Supervision rules of conduct, if violated, may result in a return to prison for the time remaining on the sentence.

Expiration of sentence occurs when the maximum term imposed by the court is served and the offender must be released without further conditions or supervision.

The release-from prison process varies among jurisdictions. How long a prisoner will serve for a given offense usually depends on a long chain of decisionmaking processes that begin with the—

- types of sentencing standards set by State law
- degree of discretion allowed to a sentencing judge
- laws that govern goodtime earnings and eligibility for parole.

Goodtime is offered in nearly all jurisdictions as an incentive for good behavior while confined. In most jurisdictions inmates may earn credits against their sentences in two ways—automatic or earned goodtime. Automatic goodtime refers to credits defined by law or regulation based on the length of the sentence imposed, the length of time served, or the seriousness of the offense. For example, Colorado and Louisiana may credit up to 15 days per month while Minnesota and Oregon may credit 1 day for every 2 served. In the Federal system, automatic goodtime varies with the duration of the sentence:

Sentence length	Days credited per month
0-6 months	0 days
6 months to 1 year & 1 day	5
1 year & 1 day to 3 years	6
3 to 5 years	7
5 to 10 years	8
10 years or more	10

Earned goodtime, by contrast, is often given for participation in programs, such as education or vocational training, prison industry, or institutional work, and for exceptional conduct such as fighting forest fires and blood donations. Twenty States also have various kinds of early-release programs that may be invoked when institutions become crowded.

In 1983, more than half the persons released from State prisons served 19 months or less:

Conviction offense	Percent of releases	Time served by releasees	
		Average	Median
All offenses	100%	26 mos.	19 mos.
Violent offenses	34%	38	30

Murder	2	90	79
Manslaughter	3	36	32
Rape	2	54	47
Other sexual assault	2	34	29
Robbery	14	36	30
Assault	8	29	24
Kidnaping	1	41	33
Other violent offenses	1	19	14
Property offenses	47%	19	15
Burglary	24	21	17
Arson	1	25	21
Auto theft	2	17	15
Forgery/fraud	6	19	15
Larceny	12	16	12
Stolen property	2	18	13
Other property	2	16	12
Drug offenses	9%	19	15
Public order offenses	9%	13	10
Other crimes	1%	18	16

Note: Time served includes jail credits.

Source: *Prison admissions and releases, 1983.* BJS Special Report, March 1986.

The percentage of persons released from prison by parole-board decision has been declining. In 1977 nearly 72% of all prison releases were by a parole-board decision. By 1984 parole decisions accounted for 46% of all releases. This change illustrates the impact of the movement away from discretionary decisionmaking toward more fixed penalty systems both at the sentencing and release points in the justice system. Mandatory release has increased in significance, giving new importance to the role of goodtime provisions in determining the amount of time to be served.

How Many People are Under Some Form of Correctional Supervision?

An estimated 3.4 million adult men and women were under some form of correctional supervision at yearend 1987 — equivalent to 1 in 52 U.S.

residents age 18 and older. This total adult correctional population is 6.8% larger than in 1986 and 40% larger than in 1983.

Of the 3.4 million adults in correctional care or custody at yearend 1987, 3 of 4 were being supervised in the community:

Total	3,460,960	100.0%
Probation	2,242,053	64.8
Parole	362,192	10.5
Prison	562,623	16.2
Jail	294,092	8.5

From 1983 through 1987 the number of men and women under community supervision grew faster than the number of incarcerated adults:

- parolees increased by 47%
- probationers by 42%
- prisoners by 33%
- jail inmates by 33%.

In the first 6 months of 1988 the Nation's Federal and State prison population grew by 4%. This creates a continuing demand for about 900 new prison beds every week.

During 1925-86 the average annual growth rate for the prison population was 2.8%; from 1980 to 1986, the average annual percent increase was 8.8%.

On June 30, 1988, 5.1% of all prison inmates were women, the highest percent since recordkeeping began in 1926. In the first half of 1988 the female prison inmate population grew by 6.7% vs. 3.9% for males. Since 1980 the number of female inmates grew from 13,420 to 30,834, a 130% increase. The number of male inmates grew from 316,401 to 573,990, an 81% increase.

Why are prison populations growing?

State departments of corrections attribute the increase in prison population to changes in sentencing laws and practices that reflect greater interest in deterrence, incapacitation, and just deserts considerations; stricter law enforcement; growth in the number of persons in the high-risk age group (males ages 20-29); and, in some cases, economic conditions.

The number of admissions to prison annually has increased relative to both the number of serious crimes reported to the police and the number of adult arrests. Between 1980 and 1984, for example, prison population increased by 41%, commitments per 100 serious crimes increased by 50%, commitments per 100 adult arrests for serious crimes increased 25% and the number of commitments increased 19%. Over the same period, the number of adults in the resident population increased by 9%.

Since 1977 prison populations have grown by more than two-thirds. By yearend 1985 the Nation's prison population exceeded 500,000 and was growing by 750 new prisoners a week. During the preceding 5 years, Western States led the Nation, increasing their sentenced prison population by nearly 90%. In Southern States, many under Federal or State court orders to limit growth and control crowding, inmate growth was 37%. The prison populations growing most rapidly were in Alaska (160%), Hawaii (129%), Nevada (113%), New Hampshire (110%), California (108%), and New Jersey (104%).

Total admissions to prison reached an alltime high in 1984. Growth in admissions is due partly to the increase in conditional release violators returned to prison (mostly probation and parole violators). Among admissions to prison, conditional release violators made up 5% in 1930, 19% in 1970, and 23% in 1984.

Court commitment rates have not been shrinking. The highest rate of court commitments (101 per 100,000 adults in the population) was reached in 1983. In 1930 it was 70; in 1970 it was 50.

Between 1979 and 1984 the number of inmates in State-operated, community-based halfway houses grew half as fast as the number of inmates in State prisons. Many States operate halfway houses in local communities. They do so to ease the transition for State-sentenced prisoners from their confinement to their impending release. Between 1979 and 1984 the number of residents of such halfway houses grew by 2,300, even though, during the same period, the nationwide percentage of State-sentenced prisoners residing in such halfway houses declined from 4% to 3%.

In both 1979 and 1984 Southern States accounted for about half of the State-operated, community-based halfway houses and for more than 60% of the residents of such houses.

Between 1979 and 1984, while State prison populations grew by nearly 45%, the number of residents of halfway houses grew by about 21%.

An estimated 95% of State prison inmates are either convicted violent offenders or have a history of prior sentences to probation, jail, or prison. Major factors in the decision to impose a prison sentence are the gravity of the current conviction offense and the seriousness and extent of the prior criminal history of the offender.

In 1979—

- For an estimated 58% of State prison inmates, conviction for committing a violent crime led to their current incarceration.
- About a third of these violent offenders had previous convictions for a violent offense and 3 of 4 had at least one prior sentence to probation, jail, or prison.
- Nearly 9 of 10 of the prisoners convicted of a nonviolent offense had at least one prior sentence to probation, jail, or prison.

Overall, about 5% of State prison inmates had a current conviction for a nonviolent crime and had no previous sentences to probation, jail, or prison. Nearly half of these first-time, nonviolent offenders were in State prison for conviction offenses of burglary or drug trafficking and about a third had two or more current conviction offenses.

In What Type of Facilities Are Prisoners Held?

Confined offenders are housed in three types of facilities

- *Jails* are operated by local governments to hold persons awaiting trial or generally those sentenced to confinement for less than 1 year. In seven jurisdictions (Vermont, Rhode Island, Connecticut, Delaware, Alaska, Hawaii, and the District of Columbia), jails are operated by the same authority that administers the prison system. On June 30, 1983, 223,551 persons were held in 3,338 local jails. The Federal Bureau of Prisons operates Metropolitan Correctional Centers and Detention Centers that essentially function as Federal jails.
- *Prisons* are operated by States and the Federal Government to hold persons sentenced to confinement for generally more than 1 year; 4% of the Nation's prison inmates are serving sentences of less than 1 year or are unsentenced; nearly 63% of such inmates are housed in Federal institutions or the 7 jurisdictions with consolidated prison and jail systems. On June 30, 1984, 381,955 persons were confined in 694 State prisons.
- *Community-based* facilities are operated publicly or privately (under contract) to hold persons for less than 24 hours a day to

permit the offender limited opportunities for work, school, or other community contacts. Such facilities are used for a variety of purposes including specialized interventions or assistance (for example, drug or alcohol treatment), graduated release from prison—usually prior to parole—or as a sanction in lieu of prison or jail confinement. On June 30, 1984, 13,354 offenders were residing in 209 State-operated facilities and about 7,000 more beds were in use in privately operated facilities.

Most jails are quite small and hold small numbers of persons in custody. Two out of three local jails were built to hold fewer than 50 inmates, but only 1 of 8 jail inmates reside in such facilities. More than half of all jail inmates are in facilities built to house 250 or more inmates, but such places account for about 6% of all local jails.

Large jails are the most densely populated. The number of jail inmates often varies between weekends and weekdays and increases sharply after arrest sweeps by police. As a result, jail populations fluctuate more than those of prisons, so that jails typically need more reserve capacity than prisons. Nevertheless, unused bed space shrank between 1978 and 1983 as occupancy rose from 64% to 81%. Moreover, among large jails, where most inmates were housed, occupancy rose from 77% in 1978 to 96% in 1983. Among regions in 1983, occupancy in large jails peaked at 102% of capacity in the West, 97% in the Northeast, 96% in the Midwest, and 90% in the South.

Jails house diverse populations. Nationally, jails hold a mix of persons at various stages of criminal justice processing.

Among jail inmates are persons—

- awaiting arraignment or trial (the unconvicted)
- convicted but awaiting sentence
- sentenced to prison but awaiting transport
- held in jail because of prison crowding (there were more than 11,500 such persons in 1984)
- convicted of probation or parole violations

It is estimated that in 1984 49% of all jail inmates were convicted; the other 51% had not been convicted.

Annual jail admissions are nearly 36 times the average daily population. Perhaps the most important feature of local jails is the high volume of inmate turnover. In the year ending June 30, 1983, the 3,338 local jails reported a total of more than 16 million admissions and releases. In the Nation, nearly 44,000 jail transactions occur each day.

More than half the Nation's inmates live in large prisons. On June 30, 1984, the 694 State-operated prisons held 381,955 inmates. Southern States operated nearly 48% of these institutions, which held about 44% of all State inmates. Large prisons, housing more than 1,000 inmates, made up 15% of all prisons but held more than half the Nation's prisoners.

Prisons are often classified by the level of security:

- *Maximum- or close-custody prisons* are typically surrounded by a double fence or wall (usually 18 to 25 feet high) with armed guards in observation towers. Such facilities usually have large interior cell blocks for inmate housing areas. In 1984, according to self-reports of superintendents, about 1 in 4 State prisons was classified as maximum security, and about 44% of the Nation's inmates were held in these facilities.

- *Medium-custody prisons* are typically enclosed by double fences topped with barbed wire. Housing architecture is varied, consisting of outside cell blocks in units of 150 cells or less, dormitories, and cubicles. In 1984, according to self-reports of superintendents, 40% of all prisons were medium security and 44% of the Nation's inmates were held in such facilities.

- *Minimum-custody prisons* typically do not have armed posts and may use fences or electronic surveillance devices to secure the perimeter of the facility. More than a third of the Nation's prisons are graded by superintendents as minimum-security facilities, but they house only about 1 of 8 inmates. This is indicative of their generally small size.

What are the characteristics of State prisons?

Characteristics	Percent of prisons	Percent of inmates
Total	100%	100%
Region		
Northeast	15	17
Midwest	20	20
South	48	44
West	17	19
Size		
Less than 500 inmates	65	22
500-1,000	20	27
More than 1,000	15	51

Custody level		
Maximum security	25	44
Medium security	39	44
Minimum security	35	12
Sex of inmates housed		
All male	88	91
All female	7	3
Co-ed	5	5
Age of facility		
Over 100 years	5	12
50-99 years	16	23
25-49 years	22	18
15-24 years	14	13
5-14 years	23	20
5 years or less	20	15
Not known	—	—

Note: Totals may not add to 100% because of rounding.
—Less than 5%.

Sources: *Population density in State prisons*, BJS Special Report, December 1986. BJS *1984 Census of State Adult Correctional Facilities*, NCJ-105585, August 1987.

One in three prisons is at least 50 years old and 43% of all inmates live in such prisons. About one in five prisons is 5 years old or less. This is indicative of the rapid construction of new prisons in recent years. More than half of all prisoners are confined in prisons at least 25 years old; about 1 in 8 lives in a prison that is more than 100 years old.

Prisons employ about 1 staff member for every 3 inmates. In 1984 more than 135,000 persons were employed full-time in the Nation's State prisons. Custodial staff made up about two-thirds of all prison employees, with about four inmates per custodial officer. Prisons in Maine, New Mexico, Rhode Island, and Vermont reported the fewest inmates per staff member; prisons in Alabama, Arkansas, Nevada, and Ohio had the highest ratios of inmates to staff.

Since 1979 the number of full-time prison staff grew by nearly 45%. Custodial staff accounted for about 82% of the increase among all categories of employees. During the same period, prison population increased at about the same proportion as all staff.

About 3% of State inmates live in State-operated, community-based facilities. On June 30, 1984, 13,354 offenders residing in State correctional facilities were living in facilities that provided regular access to the community for selected offenders. These facilities, often referred to as halfway houses or prerelease centers, generally are used during the last 3-6 months of a State sentence to provide for gradual reentry to the community from prison. Female offenders make up about 4% of those in prisons and about 8% of those in community-based facilities.

The 209 community-based facilities are generally small—about half hold fewer than 50 inmates. About 1 in 7 of such facilities is designed to hold both male and female inmates.

Prison Crowding is a Major Issue in Nearly Every State

Recent growth in State and Federal prison populations has been substantial. Between 1980 and 1985, sentenced prison populations grew by 52%, adding more than 150,000 inmates over the period. The sentenced population of 34 States and the Federal prison system grew by 50% or more. Among the States with the fastest growth in prisoner populations were Alaska (160%), Hawaii (129%), Nevada (113%), New Hampshire (110%), and California (108%).

Growth of this magnitude has been difficult for many jurisdictions to accommodate. Planning, funding, siting, and building a facility and acquiring trained staff may require 5-7 years before the opening of a new facility. Between 1979 and 1984, 5.4 million square feet of housing space was built, an increase of 29% over the 1979 level. However, most States and the Federal Government continue to operate in excess of their capacities.

Various measures are used to assess crowding. Some of the most commonly used measures of crowding are—

- whether inmates are in single or multiple occupancy units
- the amount of space available per inmate (usually expressed in square feet)
- how long prisoners are confined in the housing unit and how long they spend, for example, in recreational or work areas
- the type of housing in which inmates are confined (general housing or special segregated housing that may be used for disciplinary confinement or protective custody).

The American Correctional Association's accreditation standards specify that inmates held in single occupancy cells should have at least 60 square feet in the cell and should not spend more than 10 hours per day in the cell. For inmates housed in multiple occupancy cells, the standards recommend 50 square feet per inmate and confinement for no more than 10 hours per day in a housing unit.

Other factors are often cited as being involved in crowding, such as the amount of privacy and security provided inmates and the ability of the facility to provide adequate food, basic health care, recreational opportunities, and other types of programs.

In what kind of space are prison inmates confined?

	Percent of inmates in general housing units with—		
	Less than 60 square feet	60 or more square feet	Total
Single occupancy	12%	18%	30%
Hours confined per day:			
Less than 10 hours	8	12	20
10 or more hours	5	5	10
Multiple occupancy	49	21	70
Hours confined per day:			
Less than 10 hours	32	15	47
10 or more hours	17	6	23
Total	62%	38%	100%

Note: Special housing is excluded because, by definition, inmates in such housing generally are kept in their housing units and are not eligible to participate in regular prison programs.

Source: *Population density in State prisons*, BJS Special Report, December 1986.

Prisons with the highest densities hold about a quarter of prison inmates. A prison is said to have the highest population density when more than 40% of its inmates in regular housing reside in less than 60 square feet for more than 10 hours per day. More than half of all prisons have no inmates in these conditions.

Population densities were highest in prisons in—

- the Southern and Western States
- larger institutions (more than 1,000 inmates)
- maximum security institutions
- male-only prisons
- the oldest prisons (more than 100 years old).

Many States hold prisoners in local jails because of prison crowding. At yearend 1985, 19 States reported more than 10,000 State-sentenced inmates in local jails because of prison crowding. Nationally, locally retained State prisoners accounted for about 2% of the total prison population. States with the largest percentage of prison inmates held in local jails were Louisiana (21%), Mississippi (15%), Kentucky (14%), and New Jersey (12%). Together, these States account for 62% of the prisoners backed up in local jails.

A number of States may release inmates earlier than usual to control prison populations. Generally, the three types of early release programs are—

- *Emergency release*—This permits jurisdictions to release inmates who are approaching the end of their sentences. Alaska, for example, allows early release of nonviolent offenders within 4 months of release. Wisconsin inmates may be discharged early if they are within 135 days of release.

- *Sentence rollback*—Nine States use sentence reductions to achieve population control. Generally, this approach requires a formal declaration that the prison system is above its authorized capacity and sentences of selected inmates (such as first offenders or non-violent offenders) may be reduced by up to 90 days. Some States permit reductions to be applied to the same offender more than once during a term of imprisonment.

- *Early parole*—Eight States allow parole release dates to be advanced for certain categories of offenders when the prison system is crowded.

Such programs may also entail a period of more stringent supervision by a parole officer or participation in special community-based programs.

During 1985, 19 States reported nearly 19,000 early releases under one or more of these approaches.

Juvenile offenders are housed in many kinds of facilities

More than 83,000 juveniles were in custody during 1984. They were held in 3,036 public and private juvenile custody facilities that were in operation in 1984. Such facilities include detention centers, training schools, reception or diagnostic centers, shelters, ranches, forestry camps or farms, halfway houses, and group homes.

The range of facilities and programs; the housing of delinquents, status offenders, voluntary admissions, and dependent and neglected children in the same facilities; and the participation of both the public and private sectors clearly distinguishes juvenile corrections from adult corrections.

Most juveniles in custody were being detained or were committed for a criminal offense. Of the 83,402 juveniles held in public and private facilities—

- 11% were being held for a violent offense of murder, forcible rape, robbery, or aggravated assault
- 23% were being held for the property crimes of burglary, arson, larceny-theft, or motor vehicle theft
- 4% were being held for alcohol or drug offenses.

Of the 25,451 nondelinquents held in juvenile facilities—

- 35% were status offenders
- 36% were being held for other reasons such as dependency, neglect, and abuse
- 28% were admitted voluntarily.

Public and private facilities generally hold different types of juveniles. Almost all (93%) of the juveniles in public facilities either are—

- detained pending adjudication
- have been committed after a finding of delinquency for a criminal offense (about a third of the juveniles in private facilities are in this classification).

Juvenile facilities are classified by the term of stay and type of environment:

Term of stay

- *Short-term*—facilities that hold juveniles awaiting adjudication or other disposition.
- *Long-term*—facilities that hold juveniles already adjudicated and committed to custody.

In 1985, 46% of public facilities and 9% of private facilities were short-term; 54% of public facilities and 91% of private facilities were long-term.

Type of environment

- *Institutional* — environments impose greater restraints on residents' movements and limit access to the community. Most detention or diagnostic centers, training schools, and ranches are classified as having institutional environments.
- *Open* — environments allow greater movement of residents within the facilities and more access to the community. Facilities with open environments mainly include shelters, halfway houses, group homes, and ranches, forestry camps, or farms.

Most public facilities (65%) have institutional environments, but most private facilities (86%) have open environments.

Most juvenile facilities are private, but about three-fifths of the juveniles are held in public facilities. Private facilities usually have open environments and are used for long-term custody. About 30% of all juveniles in custody are held in such facilities. Public facilities generally have institutional environments and are used for both short- and long-term custody. About 30% of all juveniles held are in long-term institutional public facilities; another 18% are in short-term institutional public facilities.

Most juvenile facilities are small; 80% are designed to house 40 residents or less:

Design capacity*	Number of facilities		
	Public and private combined	Public	Private
Total	3,036	1,040	1,996
Less than 10 residents	1,053	141	912
10-20	913	326	638
21-40	464	226	207
41-99	387	174	193
100-199	146	114	32
200 and over	73	59	14

*The number of residents a facility is constructed to hold without double bunking in single rooms or using areas not designed as sleeping quarters to house residents.

Source: *Children in custody: Public juvenile facilities, 1985,* BJS Bulletin, October 1986, and Chldren in Custody, 1985, unpublished data.

How Many Offenders Return to Criminal Activity After They Are Released?

Assessing postcorrectional performance depends on long-term follow-up of prison releases. Some indicator of a return to criminal activity is typically used to evaluate postcorrectional performance. Rearrest, reindictment, reconviction, and reimprisonment measured over some period of time after release from prison are generally used to gauge the extent of success and failure (recidivism) associated with correctional programs.

The unit of time selected and the level of criminal justice system penetration (that is, more persons are likely to be rearrested than reimprisoned) will substantially affect judgments about the proportion of releasees failing or succeeding after a correctional experience.

Moreover, conditionally released populations (parolees) are subjected to supervision requirements that, if violated, may result in a return to prison for noncriminal conduct (such as curfew violation or failure to report to a parole officer).

Most prison inmates
have prior convictions

Inmate criminal history	Percent of 1979 admissions to prison
Total	100%
Prior convictions	84%
1	19
2	17
3	11
4	9
5	6
6-10	15
11 or more	7
No prior convictions	16%

Source: *Examining recidivism*, BJS Special Report, February 1985.

Measures of recidivism vary; more offenders are rearrested than reconvicted and more are reconvicted than reincarcerated:

	Percent of young parolees who within 6 years of release from prison were—		
	Rearrested	Reconvicted	Reincarcerated
All parolees	69%	53%	49%
Sex			
Men	70%	54%	50%
Women	52	40	36
Race/ Ethnicity			
White	64%	49%	45%
Black	76	60	56
Hispanic	71	50	44
Other	75	65	63
Education			
Less than 12 years	71%	55%	51%
High school graduate	61	46	43
Some college	48	44	31
Paroling offense			
Violent offenses	64%	43%	39%
Murder	70	25	22
Robbery	64	45	40
Assault	72	51	47
Property offenses	73%	60%	56%
Burglary	73	60	56
Forgery/fraud	74	59	56
Larceny	71	61	55
Drug offenses	49%	30%	25%

Source: *Recidivism of young parolees*, BJS Special Report, May 1987.

Over a 20-year period, an estimated half of all releasees will return to prison, most in the first 3 years after release. A study based on prisoner self-reports of how long it took them to return to prison found that 49% of all males released from prison could be expected to return within 20 years. 60% of those returning reentered prison within the first 3 years after release. The highest risk of returning to prison was in the first year after release.

The number of prior arrests is strongly related to the probability of rearrest and reincarceration after release from prison:

Number of arrests prior to prison release	Percent of young parolees who within 6 years of release were—	
	Rearrested	Reincarcerated
1 arrest	59%	42%
2	64	45
3	70	49
4	77	57
5	82	52
6 or more	93	72
Total	69%	49%

Source: *Recidivism of young parolees*, BJS Special Report, May 1987.

Younger releasees have higher rates of returning to prisons:

Age at time of prison release	Cumulative rates of return to prison by years after release from prison						
	1 year	2 years	3 years	4 years	5 years	6 years	7 years
18–24 years old	21%	34%	41%	45%	48%	49%	50%
25–34	12	21	28	33	37	41	43
35–44	7	14	18	22	26	30	34
45+	2	4	6	8	10	11	12
All ages	14	23	29	34	37	40	42
Median age of those returning	23.5 yrs.	25.5 yrs.	26.3 yrs.	27.2 yrs.	27.8 yrs.	28.6 yrs.	32.4 yrs.

Source: *Examining recidivism*, BJS Special Report, February 1985.

4

Our Black Prisons
Scott Christianson

Everyone knows that blacks and other minorities are disproportionately represented in prison, but do we realize the real extent of that imbalance, its causes, and its effect on society?

As all of us are painfully aware, since the early 1970s expansion has been the dominant trend in correction. From December 31, 1971, to December 31, 1978, the population of state prisons in the United States rose from 177,113 to a record high of 276, 799, an increase of 64 percent.[1] From 1973-79, the median rate of incarceration for the fifty states and the District of Columbia increased from about 75 persons per 100,000 to about 112.[2] This growth has also been evident in the greatest prison-building program in American history, with 907 federal, state, and local institutions, having a total estimated capacity of 199,238 beds, presently listed as proposed or under construction.[3]

These developments are all the more striking when one considers that they have occurred amidst a campaign promoting so-called alternatives to incarceration, at a time when virtually everyone has agreed that imprisonment has failed to achieve its old stated goal of rehabilitation.

Many people may be unaware, however, that not only has the prison

Source: *Crime and Delinquency,* "Our Black Prisons," Vol. 27, No. 3 (July 1981), 364-375. Reprinted with the permission of the publisher.

system gotten bigger, but it also has gotten blacker. Analysis of national prison statistics for 1973 and 1979 reveals that the number of blacks in state correctional institutions increased from about 83,000 to about 132,000, and that the black share of the state prison population rose from about 46.4 percent to 47.8 percent.[4] Considering that blacks account for a minority of the total United States population — an estimated 11.5 percent in 1976[5] — this overrepresentation is very striking, indeed. Whereas the incarceration rate for whites increased from about 46.3 per 100,000 to about 65.1 from 1973 to 1979, the black incarceration rate rose from about 368 to 544.1 per 100,000 during that period.[6]

The gravity of the problem is compounded by the fact that these upsurges, both in the overall use of imprisonment and in racial disproportionality, have been close to nationwide. Rather than being concentrated in a particular region or a few states, overrepresentation of blacks in prison is pervasive throughout the United States.

In 1973 and 1979, for example, strong racial disproportionality was found in every region (see Table 1). In 1973 the white incarceration rates ranged from a low of 23.1 in the Northeast to a high of 66.6 in the South, while the black rates ranged from 340.3 in the Northeast to 452.5 in the West. Six years later the white rates had climbed to levels ranging from 36.7 in the Northeast to 100.5 in the South, but the black rates were up to 484.1 in the Northeast and 580.4 in the North Central states.[7]

Table 1

Incarceration Rates in the United States by Region and Race, 1973 and 1979*

	1973			*1979*		
	White	*Black*	*All Races*	*White*	*Black*	*All Races*
Northeast	23.1	340.3	50.5	36.7	484.1	88.7
North Central	35.1	365.3	64.9	59.5	580.4	108.5
South	66.6	367.0	131.5	100.5	558.1	194.9
West	65.0	452.5	86.1	61.6	497.5	106.5
United States	46.3	368.0	88.0	65.1	544.1	106.5

*Prisoners in state correctional facilities, per 100,000 civilian population.

For several years, the federal government's National Prisoner Statistics series has indicated significant regional differences in the use of incarceration, such as the fact that the South accounts for about one-third of the total United States population but nearly one-half of all state prisoners. When the results of the surveys for 1973 are ranked according to race by jurisdiction, they indicate that the white incarceration rates for the fifty states and the District of Columbia ranged from 19.5 in Hawaii to 110.8 in North Carolina, with a majority of jurisdictions reporting a rate of 42.4 or more. By 1979 these figures had risen to between 28.0 per 100,000 in Hawaii and 191.7 in North Carolina. Both surveys reported six of the top ten jurisdications in the imprisonment of whites as located in the South.

Perhaps contrary to expectation, this pattern did not apply to the imprisonment of blacks. In 1973, for example, the black rates ranged from 39.9 per 100,000 persons in New Hampshire to 825.3 in Iowa, with a majority of jurisdictions reporting a rate of 366.9 or more. In 1979 they ranged from 50.0 in North Dakota to 1,341.8 in Washington, with a median rate of 600.0. In both years, only one of the top ten jurisdictions was located in the South.

Comparison of the data for 1973 and 1979 reveals some disturbing trends:

Incarceration rates for both races increased substantially in every region, the white rate going up by 40.6 percent and the black rate by 47.9 percent.

Disparities between rates of imprisonment for blacks and whites also went up significantly. In 1973 the difference between the rates was 321.7 for the entire United States — quite a substantial gap. Yet in 1979 the difference amounted to 479.0 persons per 100,000, an increase in disparity of 157.3 in only six years.

The widening gap between blacks and whites was almost nationwide, with forty-seven of fifty-one jurisdictions reporting an increase in disparity (see Table 2). (Only Colorado, Alabama, Indiana, and North Dakota registered decreases.)

The Problem is Actually Much Worse

Such statistics only begin to convey the nature and scope of the problem. When one considers that about 96 percent of all prisoners in state correctional institutions are males, even though males comprise only about 48.5 of the United States general population, the question of disproportionality takes on additional meaning.

In 1978, for example — the most recent year for which comprehensive prisoner statistics by race and sex are available — black males accounted for only 5.4 percent of the general population. Yet a staggering 45.7 percent of the prisoners were black males.[8]

By region, the imprisonment rates for black males that year ranged from 1,031.7 in the Northeast and 1,032.7 in the West to 1,108 in the

Table 2
Jurisdictions Ranked by Change in Disparity between
Black and White Incarceration Rates, 1973-79

1.	Idaho	850.4	27.	Tennessee	146.7
2.	South Dakota	657.6	28.	North Carolina	120.2
3.	Washington	611.2	29.	Illinois	118.9
4.	Delaware	598.4	30.	Rhode Island	117.2
5.	Nevada	569.0	31.	New Hampshire	106.9
6.	District of Columbia	471.2	32.	Missouri	94.6
7.	Connecticut	469.0	33.	Maryland	92.5
8.	West Virginia	456.4	34.	New Jersey	91.6
9.	Vermont	429.7	35.	Arkansas	89.8
10.	New Mexico	424.1	!36.	Massachusetts	84.9
11.	Oregon	401.9	37.	Mississippi	83.2
12.	Arizona	400.0	38.	Alaska	74.5
13.	Wisconsin	393.5	39.	Georgia	58.2
14.	Michigan	344.9	40.	Wyoming	42.7
15.	Iowa	311.0	41.	Montana	33.6
16.	Ohio	283.1	42.	Oklahoma	32.8
17.	Utah	263.8	43.	Pennsylvania	27.5
18.	Virginia	246.9	44.	Nebraska	22.8
19.	Hawaii	229.0	45.	California	11.3
20.	Texas	222.8	46.	Kentucky	3.6
21.	Maine	215.9	47.	Minnesota	0.2
22.	Louisiana	190.2	48.	Colorado	− 6.1
23.	Florida	184.9	49.	Alabama	− 18.4
24.	Kansas	155.7	50.	Indiana	− 19.7
25.	South Carolina	155.2	51.	North Dakota	− 77.2
26.	New York	148.9			

South and 1,192.4 in the North Central region. At the end of 1978, the rate of imprisonment of black males nationwide was approximately 1.1 per 100 black men.

Ranked by jurisdiction, the 1978 incarceration rates for black males show three states (Washington, Arizona, and Alaska) with a shocking one of every fifty in prison; and several other jurisdictions were close behind (see Table 3).

The nature of these so-called rates of incarceration makes interpretation difficult, to be sure. After all, they are based on the number of prisoners in custody on a particular date (usually December 31), and thus simply reflect rates of commitment to prison. Since long-term prisoners (blacks more often than whites) are counted year after year,

Table 3
Incarceration Rates per 100,000 for Black Males, 1978

1.	Washington	2408.6	27.	Minnesota	1114.8
2.	Arizona	2210.3	28.	Massachusetts	1107.7
3.	Alaska	2200.0	29.	New York	1076.5
4.	Iowa	1972.2	30.	Georgia	1039.7
5.	Nevada	1963.2	31.	New Jersey	1006.3
6.	Delaware	1961.1	32.	South Dakota*	1006.0
7.	Nebraska	1834.8	33.	Missouri	1002.9
8.	Utah	1775.0	34.	Louisiana	975.0
9.	Michigan	1734.7	35.	South Carolina	954.5
10.	Wisconsin	1734.2	36.	Pennsylvania	879.2
11.	New Mexico	1720.0	37.	California	870.1
12.	Florida	1577.0	38.	Tennessee	845.7
13.	Oregon	1520.0	39.	Indiana	819.0
14.	Maryland	1509.8	40.	Illinois	810.3
15.	Texas	1438.9	41.	Maine	800.0
16.	Ohio	1399.6	42.	Arkansas	736.7
17.	Connecticut	1378.6	43.	Alabama	661.6
18.	Oklahoma	1372.3	44.	Kentucky	644.2
19.	Idaho*	1301.7	45.	New Hampshire	600.0
20.	Rhode Island	1266.7	46.	Montana	500.0
21.	North Carolina	1246.5	47.	Mississippi	463.8
22.	Virginia	1233.1	48.	North Dakota	400.0
23.	Colorado	1211.4	49.	Hawaii	350.0
24.	Kansas	1208.2	50.	Vermont*	225.7
25.	West Virginia	1200.0	51.	Wyoming	0.0
26.	District of Columbia	1118.0			

*No estimates for the number of black males in the civilian population of these states were available for 1976. Therefore, these rates were computed from 1970 census figures. In all other cases, the source for general population statistics was Bureau of the Census, "Demographic, Social and Economic Profile of States: Spring 1976," *Current Population Reports* (Washington, D.C.: Govt. Printing Office, 1979), Series P-20, No. 334, pp. 10-18.

the rates cited actually reflect as well the length of time served in prison. To that extent, incarceration rates also reflect the jurisdictions' sentencing and release policies.

Even when we take into account that many inmates are repeat offenders and prisoners serving long terms of incarceration, it is obvious the percentage of black males who are imprisoned at some point in their lives is much greater than the percentage of white men imprisoned. Specific figures, from cohort studies or otherwise, are not available. However, there can be no doubt that a significant portion of black males—and very probably an even larger percentage of urban black males—are imprisoned at one time or another in their lives.

These figures only suggest the extraordinary impact of imprisonment upon the black community. This being so, it is all the more puzzling that no one has studied that impact in detail.

A Record of Neglect

Historians and sociologists still write in great volumes about the legacy of slavery, an institution that was officially abolished over a century ago—some of them arguing, for example, for or against Daniel Patrick Moynihan's controversial thesis that enslavement wrecked the structure of black families and left a "tangle of pathology" that has persisted well into the twentieth century.[9] Many writers of various colors and persuasions have depicted welfare programs as a modern equivalent of slavery (or Reconstruction). Yet, surprisingly, no one has examined imprisonment in similar terms.

"Benign" or otherwise, this neglect represents an astonishing admission on the part of the intellectual community and society as a whole. Is there no one willing to confront this hideous reality? How many black Americans have a husband, son, brother, cousin, nephew, lover, friend, or neighbor behind bars? What effect does that experience have on the black family, the black community, the black individual, and the white?

This inattention seems even more striking when we recall that it was only a decade ago that the black prisoner was one of the most powerful symbols on the American political scene. Malcolm X, Eldridge Cleaver, George Jackson, and Angela Davis rattled the society to its foundations with their disturbing observations, Malcolm X going so far as to state, "That's what America means: prison."[10] In Soledad Brother, readers were told, "Black men born in the U.S. and fortunate to live past the age of eighteen are conditioned to accept the inevitability of prison. For most of us, it simply looms as the next phase in a sequence of humiliations."[11] A few months later, Attica exploded.[12]

Today there are no such voices being heard, and sometimes it seems that black prisoners have been abandoned in their cages by almost everyone, including most blacks. The old visions of "rehabilitation" have drowned under a wave of pragmatism that has killed any pretense of justification for reform. Most of the bright-eyed reformers have either burned out or succumbed to the sedatives of job security. Intended reforms, such as the abolition of parole, tend to have backfired, and hoped-for alternatives have turned out to be supplements to the traditional system, with "new" criteria that still serve to restrict clientele to those close in image to the program designers. The public wastes little sympathy on prisoners, particularly black prisoners.

The Legacy of Slavery

The usual response to statistics showing racially disproportionate incarceration rates is a very simple one. More blacks are sent to prison, we are told, because they commit more crimes than whites. Blacks receive longer sentences because their crimes are more serious or because they have heavier prior records. Black prisoners serve more time because they have committed more infractions inside the institution or because their lack of job qualification makes them unsuitable for release.

This line has become more sophisticated over the years, but essentially it has remained the same from one generation to the next. Positivist criminologists now refrain from describing themselves as such, and no one would ever explicitly state that black people are "born criminals" or suggest that their criminality is attributable to "degraded character" or other such "racial deficiencies." Officials who administer the criminal justice system have been cautioned by counsel not to admit that they are stopping suspects or excluding jurors simply because those persons happen to be black.[13]

The new style may be more subtle, but it produces the same result. The message is that blacks, because of the criminal acts they have committed, somehow deserve to be imprisoned more than whites.

These arguments are by no means persuasive, however. Dozens — perhaps hundreds — of studies suggest that racial discrimination in the criminal justice process is a significant factor in determining racially disproportionate rates of incarceration.[14] Indeed, the relationship between crime and incarceration rates is a matter of much dispute. William Nagel, writing in these pages a few years ago, found no significant correlation between a state's crime rate and the percentage of nonwhites in the population, or between its crime rate and incarceration rate. However, he did find, and subsequent tests by a competent (albeit blood-related) methodologist confirmed, a very strong positive correlation between a state's racial composition and its incarceration rate.[15] James Garofalo has reported finding a correlation between racial composition and rate of imprisonment that was too strong to be accounted for by indirect relationships (i.e., by types of crimes committed).[16] Richard Quinney and others have raised serious questions about the definitional biases of white-dominated legislatures.[17] Obviously, space constraints prevent a recounting of the litany against the criminal justice system and society at large in this regard. Yet the debate over race and crime is sure to continue to occupy the attention of criminologists for years to come.

Students of the matter might do well to consider for a moment the historical record. David Brion Davis, the Pulitzer Prize-winning historian, recently observed that "[w]e seldom think of black slavery as a penal institution. Yet throughout history enslavement has been used as a form of punishment, while some penal systems have acquired many of the characteristics of chattel slavery."[18] Davis reminds us that for centuries, slavery was regarded as a form of punishment for original sin. Some European apologists insisted that the Atlantic slave trade performed a beneficent service by rescuing many African heathens from savagery, and American plantation owners defended their system as a Biblically inspired instrument of rehabilitation.[19]

Thorsten Sellin has examined the links between slavery and imprisonment from antiquity to modern times, but his work scarcely scratches the surface with regard to the American experience.[20] Lest we forget, it was as prisoners — slaves — that African men, women, and children were transported to the Caribbean and America; and the majority of blacks continued to live and die in a state of bondage until emancipation during the nineteenth century. The state prison as we know it arose in part as a replacement for slavery, in order to control newly freed blacks.[21]

When Alexis de Tocqueville toured the United States, gathering material for what would later become *Democracy in America,* his official mission was actually to study America's developing industrial penal system.[22] Tocqueville's and Gustave de Beaumont's impressions were published in 1833 as the classic report *On the Penitentiary System in the United States and Its Application in France,* in which they observed that the great majority of black persons residing in the American South were kept as slaves, while "in those states in which there exists one Negro to thirty whites, the prisons contain one Negro to four white persons."[23] Numerous reports since the early nineteenth century have documented heavy overrepresentation of blacks in American prisons.[24]

Legal Implications

Racially disproportionate rates of incarceration have been part of criminal justice in this country for more than a century, and the high rate of imprisonment for blacks has surely had tremendous social and political implications. As Tocqueville himself put it, "Scarcely any political question arises in the United States that is not resolved, sooner or later, into a judicial question."[25] In the case of slavery, it took as long as 200 years for the courts to find the practice illegal. Sooner or later, judges will have to confront the unconstitutionality of racially disproportionate incarceration rates.

The recent experience of constitutional attacks on the death penalty offers many valuable lessons in this regard. By the early 1970s, social scientists and members of the bar were working closely in mounting challenges to the imposition of capital punishment. One of the important issues addressed was the strong overrepresentation of blacks among those sentenced to death and executed by state governments.[26] The result has been a series of Supreme Court decisions, some successful and some not, in which alleged racial discrimination has been scrutinized.[27]

Notwithstanding fundamental differences between capital punishment and imprisonment, it would seem that many of the constitutional issues that have been raised for the death penalty can and should be applied to other forms of punishment, including incarceration. Comparable data are available, which depict a similar racial imbalance. Unlike death sentence statistics, the statistics for incarceration show a pattern of racial discrimination that is nationwide, that apparently is not concentrated in the South. Also, we have seen, this imbalance appears to be growing more pronounced.[28]

In order for such an effort to be successful, social scientists, lawyers, and members of the black community need to collaborate in a new and massive undertaking, involving intensive research and litigation.

Satisfactory judicial response is by no means assured. With many years of similar efforts in fighting the death penalty, Hugo A. Bedau expressed disappointment a few years ago over the way the Supreme Court had reacted, or failed to react, to social science research on capital punishment. This neglect, he cautioned, was particularly evident in the decision of *Gregg v. Georgia,* even though Chief Justice Burger had complained only a few years before about the "paucity" of evidence on such questions.[29] Rather than heed the findings of the social scientists, the Court went on to devise "remedies," such as guided discretion, which had already been shown to be ineffective in reducing racial disproportionality in capital sentencing.[30]

And yet, the nation and its highest court must be made to confront the nature of imprisonment in America. Until that happens, to paraphrase Thoreau, none of us can be free.

Footnotes

[1]The primary source of United States prison statistics is the series of the National Prisoner Statistics special reports, *Prisoners in State and Federal Institutions,* published by the United States Department of Justice, Law Enforcement Assistance Administration, National Criminal Justice Information and Statistics Service.

[2]Scott Christianson and Richard Dehais, *The Black Incarceration Rate in the United States: A Nationwide Problem* (Albanay, N.Y.: Training Program in Criminal Justice Education, Graduate School of Criminal Justice, State University of New York, August 1980).

[3]*Jericho* (Newsletter of the National Moratorium on Prison Construction, 324 C St., S.E., Washington, D.C. 20003), Spring 1980, p. 12.

[4]Christianson and Dehais, *Black Incarceration Rate*, pp. 9, 19, 43, 51.

[5]Ibid., p. 31.

[6]Ibid., pp. 10, 19.

[7]Ibid. The regional breakdowns are as follows: Northeast includes Maine, New Hampshire, Vermont, Massachusetts, Rhode Island, Connecticut, New York, New Jersey, Pennsylvania; North Central is Ohio, Indiana, Illinois, Michigan, Wisconsin, Minnesota, Iowa, Missouri, North Dakota, South Dakota, Nebraska, Kansas; South is Delaware, Maryland, District of Columbia, Virginia, North Carolina, South Carolina, Georgia, Florida, Kentucky, Tennessee, Alabama, Mississippi, Arkansas, Louisiana, Oklahoma, Texas; West is Montana, Idaho, Wyoming, Colorado, New Mexico, Arizona, Utah, Nevada, Washington, Oregon, California, Alaska, Hawaii.

[8]Ibid., p. 31. See Department of Justice, *Prisoners in State and Federal Institutions on December, 31, 1978*, National Prisoner Statistics Bulletin No. SD-NPS-PSF-6 (Washington, D.C.: Govt. Printing Office, 1980).

[9]See Daniel Patrick Moynihan, *The Negro Family in America: The Case for National Action* (Washington, D.C.: Office of Policy Planning and Research, Department of Labor, 1965); Herbert G. Gutman, *The Black Family in Slavery & Freedom, 1750-1925* (New York: Pantheon, 1976).

[10]El-Haj Malik Shabazz (Malcolm X), quoted in Haywood Burns, "The Black Prisoner as Victim," *Black Law Journal*, Summer 1971, p. 120.

[11]George Jackson, *Soledad Brother: The Prison Letters of George Jackson* (New York: Bantam, 1970), p. 9.

[12]For two contrasting views by participants, see Richard X. Clark, *The Brothers of Attica* (New York: Links Books, 1973); and Russell G. Oswald, *Attica — My Story* (Garden City, N.Y.: Doubleday, 1972). Clark was a young Muslim prisoner, Oswald was corrections commissioner.

[13]The literature on race and crime is reviewed in Carl E. Pope, "Race and Crime Revisited," *Crime & Delinquency*, July 1979, pp. 347-57; and in Scott Christianson and David Parry, *Black Crime: An Annotated Bibliography*, Education Project Monograph (Albany, N.Y.: Graduate School of Criminal Justice, State University of New York, March 1980). For commentary, see Charles E. Reasons, "Race, Crime and the Criminologist," in *The Criminologist: Crime and the Criminal*, Charles E. Reasons, ed. (Pacific Palisades, Calif.: Goodyear, 1974), pp. 89-97; Robert L. Woodson, ed., *Black Perspectives on Crime and the Criminal Justice System* (Boston: G.K. Hall, 1977); Charles E. Silberman, *Criminal Violence, Criminal Justice* (New York: Random House, 1978); Robert Staples, "White Racism, Black Crime, and American Justice: An Application of the Colonial Model to Explain Crime and Race," *Phylon*, March 1975, pp. 14-22.

[14]See, for example, on arrest decisions: Irving Piliavin and Scott Briar, "Police Encounters with Juveniles," *American Journal of Sociology*, September 1964, pp. 206-14; William M. Kephart, "The Negro Offender: An Urban Research

Project," *American Journal of Sociology*, July 1954, pp. 46-50; Guy B. Johnson, "The Negro and Crime," *Annals of the American Academy of Political and Social Science*, September 1941, pp. 93-104; Thorsten Sellin, "The Negro Criminal: A Statistical Note," *Annals of the American Academy of Political and Social Science*, vol. 140 (1928), pp. 52-64. On bail, jury selection, and sentencing, see, for example: Jules B. Gerard and T. Rankin Terry, Jr., "Discrimination against Negroes in the Administration of Criminal Law in Missouri," *Washington University Law Quarterly*, 1970, pp. 415-38; Bernice Just, "Bail and Pre-Trial Detention in the District of Columbia: An Empirical Analysis," *Howard Law Journal*, vol. 17 (1973), pp. 844-57; Hayward L. Alker, Carl Hosticka, and Michael Mitchell, "Jury Selection as a Biased Social Process," *Law and Society Review*, Fall 1976, pp. 9-41; Notes, "Voir Dire: The Due Process Clause of the Fourteenth Amendment Does Not Require That Prospective Jurors Be Questioned as to Possible Racial Prejudice When the Defendant Is Black unless Special Circumstances Are Present," *American Journal of Criminal Law*, vol. 4, issue 2 (1975-76), pp. 180-93; J.M. Gaba, "Voir Dire of Jurors: Constitutional Limits to the Right of Inquiry into Prejudice," *University of Colorado Law Review*, vol. 48 (1977), pp. 525-45; Steven H. Clarke and Gary G. Koch, "The Influence of Income and Other Factors on Whether Criminal Defendants Go to Prison," *Law and Society Review*, Fall 1976, pp. 57-92; James Drew, "Judicial Discretion and the Sentencing Process," *Howard Law Journal*, vol. 17 (1973), pp. 859-64. On alternatives to incarceration and on parole, see, for example: David M. Petersen and Paul C. Friday, "Early Release from Incarceration: Race as a Factor in the Use of 'Shock Probation,'" *Journal of Criminal Law and Criminology*, March 1975, pp. 79-87; A.R. Smith, "Black Perspective on Pretrial Diversion," *Urban League Review*, Fall 1975, pp. 25-28; John J. Berman, "Parolees' Perceptions of the Justice System: Black-White Differences," *Criminology*, February 1976, pp. 507-20; Leo Carroll and Margaret E. Mondrick, "Racial Bias in the Decision to Grant Parole," *Law and Society Review*, Fall 1976, pp. 93-107.

[15]See William G. Nagel, "On Behalf of a Moratorium on Prison Construction," *Crime & Delinquency*, April 1977, pp. 154-72. His findings were subjected to statistical tests by his son, Jack, who published his conclusions in *Crime and Incarceration: A Reanalysis* (Philadelphia: School of Public and Urban Policy, University of Pennsylvania, 1977).

[16]See James Garofalo, "Social Structure and Rates of Imprisonment: A Research Note" (Paper presented at the annual meeting of the Academy of Criminal Justice Sciences, Cincinnati, Mar. 15, 1979).

[17]See, for example, Richard Quinney, *The Social Reality of Crime* (Boston: Little, Brown, 1970).

[18]David Brion Davis, "The Crime of Reform," review of David J. Rothman, *Conscience and Convenience: The Asylum and Its Alternatives in Progressive America*, New York Review of Books, June 26, 1980, p. 14. See also David Brion Davis, *The Problem of Slavery in Western Culture* (Ithaca, N.Y.: Cornell University Press, 1965); David Brion Davis, *The Problem of Slavery in the Age of Revolution* (Ithaca, N.Y.: Cornell University Press, 1975).

[19]Ibid. See also Winthrop D. Jordan, *White over Black: American Attitudes toward the Negro, 1550-1812* (Chapel Hill: University of North Carolina Press, 1968).

[20]See Thorsten Sellin, *Slavery and the Penal System* (New York: Elsevier, 1976). For a review, see Scott Christianson, "Slavery and the Penal System," *Criminal Law Bulletin*, March-April 1977, pp. 168-70.

[21]The state of New York, for example, legislated both the emancipation of slaves and the creation of the first state prison on the same date in 1796.

[22]See George W. Pierson, *Tocqueville in America* (Garden City, N.Y.: Doubleday, 1959).

[23]Gustave de Beaumont and Alexis de Tocqueville, *On the Penitentiary System in the United States and Its Application in France*, Francis Lieber, trans. (Philadelphia: Carey, Lea & Blanchard, 1833), p. 93. This important study is available in a paperback edition from Southern Illinois University Press in Carbondale, with an introduction by Thorsten Sellin.

[24]See, for example, William Crawford, *Report on the Penitentiaries of the United States* (1835; rep. ed., Montclair, N.J.: Patterson Smith, 1969); Frederick L. Hoffman, *Race Traits and Tendencies of the American Negro* (New York: Macmillan, 1896); William T. Root, Jr., *A Psychological and Educational Survey of 1916 Prisoners in the Western Penitentiary of Pennsylvania* (Pittsburgh: Board of Trustees of the Western Penitentiary, 1927); Sellin, "Negro Criminal," *Annals;* Leon F. Litwack, *North of Slavery: The Negro in the Free States, 1790-1860* (Chicago: University of Chicago Press, 1961); Hans von Hentig, "The Criminality of the Negro," *Journal of Criminal Law and Criminology,* January-February 1940, pp. 662-80; Edward Byron Reuter, *The American Race Problem*, rev. ed. (New York: Thomas Y. Crowell, 1927); Margaret Cahalan, "Trends in Incarceration in the United States since 1880," *Crime & Delinquency,* January 1979, pp. 9-41; Frank M. Dunbaugh, "Racially Disproportionate Rates of Incarceration in the United States, *Prison Law Monitor,* vol. 1, no. 9 (1979), pp. 1-4.

[25]Quoted in *Democracy in America,* vol. 1, Phillips Bradley, ed. (New York: Vintage, 1945), p. 290.

[26]See, for example, Frank E. Hartung, "Trends in the Use of Capital Punishment," *Annals of the American Academy of Political and Social Science,* vol. 284 (1952), pp. 8-19; Charles S. Magnum, *The Legal Status of the Negro* (Chapel Hill: University of North Carolina Press, 1940); Elmer H. Johnson, "Selective Factors in Capital Punishment," *Social Forces,* vol. 36 (1957), pp. 165-69; Marvin E. Wolfgang, Arlene Kelly, and Hans C. Nolde, "Comparison of the Executed and the Commuted among Admissions to Death Row," *Journal of Criminal Law, Criminology and Police Science,* September 1962, pp. 301-11; Hugo Adam Bedau, "Death Sentences in New Jersey, 1907-1960," *Rutgers Law Review,* Fall 1964, pp. 1-64; Rupert C. Koeninger, "Capital Punishment in Texas, 1924-1958," *Crime and Delinquency,* January 1969, pp. 132-41; Thorsten Sellin, *The Death Penalty* (New York: Harper & Row, 1967); Hugo Adam Bedau, ed., *The Death Penalty in America* (New York: Anchor, 1967).

[27]The most famous was Furman v. Georgia, 408 U.S. 238 (1972). Some other important cases have been Gregg v. Georgia, 428 U.S. 153 (1976); Woodson v. North Carolina, 428 U.S. 280 (1976); Profitt v. Florida, 428 U.S. 267 (1976); Jurek v. Texas, 428 U.S. 267 (1976); Roberts v. Louisiana, 428 U.S. 325 (1976); and Coker v. Georgia, 433 U.S. 584 (1977). For an interesting behind-the-scenes account of the development of the constitutional attack, see Michael Meltsner, "Litigating against the Death Penalty," *Yale Law Journal,* May 1973, pp. 1111-39.

[28]See the author's inquiries into this legal dimension, "Legal Implications of Racially Disproportionate Incarceration Rates," *Criminal Law Bulletin*, January-February 1980, pp. 59-63; "Racial Discrimination and Prison Confinement,"*Criminal Law Bulletin*, November-December 1980, pp. 616-21.

[29]Hugo Adam Bedau, "New Life for the Death Penalty," *Nation*, vol. 223 (1976), p. 147. This disappointment is echoed by Professor Marvin Wolfgang in "The Death Penalty: Social Philosophy and Social Science Research," *Criminal Law Bulletin*, January-February 1978, pp. 18-33.

[30]Marc Riedel, "Discrimination in the Imposition of the Death Penalty: A Comparison of the Characteristics of Offenders Sentenced Pre-Furman and Post-Furman," *Temple Law Quarterly*, vol. 49, no. 2 (1976), pp. 261-87, pointed out, in fact, that the Court's remedies were proving counterproductive. However, his research was ignored, just as the Justices in *Gregg, Profitt,* and *Jurek* ignored the social science research published since *Furman.*

5

The Criminal Type
Jessica Mitford

Time was when most crimes were laid at the door of the Devil. The English indictment used in the last century took note of Old Nick's complicity by accusing the defendant not only of breaking the law but of "being prompted and instigated by the Devil," and the Supreme Court of North Carolina declared in 1862: "To know the right and still the wrong pursue proceeds from a perverse will brought about by the seductions of the Evil One."

With the advent of the new science of criminology toward the end of the nineteenth century, the Devil (possibly to his chagrin) was deposed as primary cause of crime by the hand of an Italian criminologist, one of the first of that calling, Cesare Lombroso. Criminals, Lombroso found, are born that way and bear physical stigmata to show it (which presumably saddles God with the responsibility, since He created them). They are "not a variation from a norm but practically a special species, a subspeicies, having distinct physical and mental characteristics. In general all criminals have long, large, projecting ears, abundant hair, thin beard, prominent frontal sinuses, protruding chin, large cheekbones." Furthermore, his studies, consisting of exhaustive

Source: From *Kind and Usual Punishment: The Prison Business,* by Jessica Mitford. Copyright © 1973 by Jessica Mitford. Reprinted by permission of Alfred A. Knopf, Inc.

examination of live prisoners and the skulls of dead ones, enabled him to classify born criminals according to their offense: "Thieves have mobile hands and face; small, mobile, restless, frequently oblique eyes; thick and closely set eyebrows; flat or twisted nose; thin beard; hair frequently thin." Rapists may be distinguished by "brilliant eyes, delicate faces" and murderers by "cold, glassy eyes; nose always large and frequently aquiline; jaws strong; cheekbones large; hair curly, dark and abundant." Which caused a contemporary French savant to remark that Lombroso's portraits were very similar to the photographs of his friends.

A skeptical Englishman named Charles Goring, physician of His Majesty's Prisons, decided to check up on Lombroso's findings. Around the turn of the century he made a detailed study of the physical characteristics of 3,000 prisoners—but took the precaution of comparing these with a group of English university students, impartially applying his handy measuring tape to noses, ears, eyebrows, chins of convicts and scholars alike over a twelve-year period. His conclusion: "In the present investigation we have exhaustively compared with regard to many physical characteristics different kinds of criminals with each other and criminals as a class with the general population. From these comparisons no evidence has emerged of the existence of a physical criminal type."

As the twentieth century progressed, efforts to pinpoint the criminal type followed the gyrations of scientific fashions of the day with bewildering results. Studies published in the thirties by Gustav Aschaffenburg, a distinguished German criminologist, show that the pyknic type (which means stout, squate, with large abdomen) is more prevalent among occasional offenders, while the asthenic type (of slender build and slight muscular development) is more often found among habitual criminals. In the forties came the gland men, Professor William H. Sheldon of Harvard and his colleagues, who divided the human race into three: endomorphs, soft, round, comfort-loving people; ectomorphs, fragile fellows who complain a lot and shrink from crowds, mesomorphs, muscular types with large trunks who walk assertively, talk noisily, and behave aggressively. Watch out for those.

Yet no sooner were these elaborate findings by top people published than equally illustrious voices were heard in rebuttal. Thus Professor M.F. Ashley Montagu, a noted anthropologist: "I should venture the opinion that not one of the reports on the alleged relationship between glandular dysfunctions and criminality has been carried out in a scientific manner, and that all such reports are glaring examples of the fallacy of *false cause*...to resort to that system for an explanation of criminality is merely to attempt to explain the known by the unknown."

Practitioners of the emerging disciplines of psychology and

psychiatry turned their attention early on to a study of the causes of criminality. Dr. Henry Goddard, Princeton psychologist, opined in 1920 that "criminals, misdemeanants, delinquents, and other antisocial groups" are in nearly all cases persons of low mentality: "It is no longer to be denied that the greatest single cause of delinquency and crime is low-grade mentality, much of it within the limits of feeble-mindedness." But hard on his heels came the eminent professor Edwin H. Sutherland of Chicago, who in 1934 declared that the test results "are much more likely to reflect the methods of the testers than the intelligence of the criminals" and that "distribution of intelligence scores of delinquents is very similar to the distribution of intelligence scores of the general population...Therefore, this analysis shows that the relationship between crime and feeblemindedness is, in general, comparatively slight." In *New Horizons in Criminology*, Harry E. Barnes and Negley K. Teeters go further: "Studies made by clinical psychologists of prison populations demonstrate that those behind bars compare favorably with the general population in intelligence. Since we seldom arrest and convict criminals except the poor, inept, and friendless, we can know very little of the intelligence of the bulk of the criminal world. It is quite possible that it is, by and large, superior."

Coexistent with these theories of the criminal type was one that declares the lawbreaker to be a deviant personality, mentally ill, of which more later.

It may be conjectured that prison people were not entirely pleased by the early explanations of criminality; perhaps they welcomed the rebuttals, for if the malfeasant is that way because of the shape of his ears, or because of malfunctioning glands, or because he is dim-witted, none of which he can help—why punish? In this context, George Bernard Shaw points out, "As the obvious conclusion was that criminals were not morally responsible for their actions, and therefore should not be punished for them, the prison authorities saw their occupation threatened, and denied that there was any criminal type. The criminal type was off." The perverse old soul added that he knows what the criminal type is—it is manufactured in prison by the prison system: "If you keep one [man] in penal servitude and another in the House of Lords for ten years, the one will shew the stigmata of a typical convict, and the other of a typical peer." Eugene V. Debs expressed the same thought: "I have heard people refer to the 'criminal countenance.' I never saw one. Any man or woman looks like a criminal behind bars."

Skull shape, glands, IQ, and deviant personality aside, to get a more pragmatic view of the criminal type one merely has to look at the composition of the prison population. Today the prisons are filled with the young, the poor white, the black, the Chicano, the Puerto Rican.

Yesterday they were filled with the young, the poor native American, the Irish or Italian immigrant.

Discussing the importance of identifying the dangerous classes of 1870, a speaker at the American Prison Congress said: "The quality of being that constitutes a criminal cannot be clearly known, until observed as belonging to the class from which criminals come...A true prison system should take cognizance of criminal classes as such." His examination of 15 prison populations showed that 53,101 were born in foreign countries, 47,957 were native-born, and of these, "full 50 percent were born of foreign parents, making over 76 percent of the whole number whose tastes and habits were those of such foreigners as emigrate to this country."

At the same meeting, J.B. Bittinger of Pennsylvania described the tastes and habits of these dissolute aliens: "First comes *rum*, to keep up spirits and energy for night work; then three fourths of their salaries are spent in *theaters and barrooms*...many go to *low concert saloons* only to kill time...they play *billiards* for *drinks*, go to the *opera*, to the *theater, oyster suppers* and *worse*...they have their peculiar litera- ture: dime novels, sporting papers, illustrated papers, obscene prints and photographs." Commenting on the large numbers of foreign-born in prison, he added: "The figures here are so startling in their dis- proportions as to foster, and apparently justify, a strong prejudice against our foreign population."

The criminal type of yesteryear was further elaborated on in 1907 by J.E. Brown, in an article entitled "The Increase of Crime in the United States": "In the poorer quarters of our great cities may be found huddled together the Italian bandit and the bloodthirsty Spaniard, the bad man from Sicily, the Hungarian, Croation and the Pole, the China- man and the Negro, the Cockney Englishman, the Russian and the Jew, with all the centuries of hereditary hate back of them."

In 1970 Edward G. Banfield, chairman of President Nixon's task force on the Model Cities Program, updated these descriptions of the lower-class slum-dweller in his book *The Unheavenly City: The Nature and Future of the Urban Crisis*, an influential book that is required reading in innumerable college courses. Since it is reportedly also recommended reading in the White House, presumably it reflects the Administration's conception of the criminal classes as they exist today. "A slum is not simply a district of low-quality housing," says Mr. Banfield, "Rather it is one in which the style of life is squalid and vicious." The lower-class individual is "incapable of conceptualizing the future or of controlling his impulses and is therefore obliged to live from moment to moment...impulse governs his behavior...he is there- fore radically improvident; whatever he cannot consume immediately he considers valueless. His bodily needs (especially for sex) and his taste for 'action' take precedence over everything else—and certainly over any work routine." Furthermore he "has a feeble, attenuated sense of self...

"The lower-class individual lives in the slum and sees little or no reason to complain. He does not care how dirty and dilapidated his housing is either inside or out, nor does he mind the inadequacy of such public facilities as schools, parks and libraries; indeed, where such things exist, he destroys them by acts of vandalism if he can. Features that make the slum repellent to others actually please him."

Most studies of the causes of crime in this decade, whether contained in sociological texts, high-level governmental commission reports, or best-selling books like Ramsey Clark's *Crime in America*, lament the disproportionately high arrest rate for blacks and poor people and assert with wearying monotony that criminality is a product of slums and poverty. Mr. Clark invites the reader to mark on his city map the areas where health and education are poorest, where unemployment and poverty are highest, where blacks are concentrated—and he will find these areas also have the highest crime rate.

Hence the myth that the poor, the young, the black, the Chicano are indeed the criminal type of today is perpetuated, whereas in fact crimes are committed, although not necessarily punished, at all levels of society.

There is evidence that a high proportion of people in all walks of life have at some time or other committed what are conventionally called "serious crimes." A study of 1,700 New Yorkers weighted toward the upper income brackets, who had never been arrested for anything, and who were guaranteed anonymity, revealed that 91 percent had committed at least one felony or serious misdemeanor. The mean number of offenses per person was 18. Sixty-four percent of the men and 27 percent of the women had committed at least one felony, for which they could have been sent to the state penitentiary. Thirteen percent of the men admitted to grand larceny, 26 percent to stealing cars, and 17 percent to burglary.

If crimes are committed by people of all classes, why the near-universal equation of criminal type and slum-dweller, why the vastly unequal representation of poor, black, brown in the nation's jails and prisons? When the "Italian bandit, bloodthirsty Spaniard, bad man from Sicily," and the rest of them climbed their way out of the slums and moved to the suburbs, they ceased to figure as an important factor in crime statistics. Yet as succeeding waves of immigrants, and later blacks, moved into the same slum area the rates of reported crime and delinquency remained high there.

No doubt despair and terrible conditions in the slums give rise to one sort of crime, the only kind available to the very poor: theft, robbery, purse-snatching; whereas crimes committed by the former slum-dweller have moved up the scale with his standard of living to those less likely to be detected and punished: embezzlement, sale of fraudulent stock, price-fixing. After all, the bank president is not likely to become a bank robber; nor does the bank robber have the opportunity to embezzle depositors' funds.

Professor Theodore Sarbin suggests the further explanation that police are conditioned to perceive some classes of persons (formerly immigrants, now blacks and browns) as being actually or potentially "dangerous," and go about their work accordingly: "The belief that some classes of persons were 'dangerous' guided the search for suspects...Laws are broken by many citizens for many reasons: those suspects who fit the concurrent social type of the criminal are most likely to become objects of police suspicion and of judicial decision-making." The President's Crime Commission comments on the same phenomenon: "A policeman in attempting to solve crimes must employ, in the absence of concrete evidence, circumstantial indicators to link specific crimes with specific people. Thus policemen may stop Negro and Mexican youths in white neighborhoods, may suspect juveniles who act in what the policemen consider an impudent or overly casual manner, and may be influenced by such factors as unusual hair styles or clothes uncommon to the wearer's group or area...those who act frightened, penitent, and respectful are more likely to be released, while those who assert their autonomy and act indifferent or resistant run a substantially greater risk of being frisked, interrogated, or even taken into custody."

An experiment conducted in the fall of 1970 by a sociology class at the University of California at Los Angeles bears out these observations. The class undertook to study the differential application of police definitions of criminality by varying one aspect of the "identity" of the prospective criminal subject. They selected a dozen students, black, Chicano, and white, who had blameless driving records free of any moving violations, and asked them to drive to and from school as they normally did, with the addition of a "circumstantial indicator" in the shape of a phosphorescent bumper sticker reading "Black Panther Party." In the first 17 days of the study these students amassed 30 driving citations—failure to signal, improper lane changes, and the like. Two students had to withdraw from the experiment after two days because their licenses were suspended; and the project soon had to be abandoned because the $1,000 appropriation for the experiment had been used up in paying bails and fines of the participants.

The President's Crime Commission Report notes that "the criminal justice process may be viewed as a large-scale screening system. At each stage it tries to sort out the better risks to return to the general population," but the report does not elaborate on *how* these better risks are sorted. Professor Sarbin suggests an answer: "To put the conclusion bluntly, membership in the class 'lawbreakers' is *not* distributed according to economic or social status, but membership in the class 'criminals' *is* distributed according to social or economic status...To account for the disproportionate number of lower class and black prisoners, I propose that the agents of law enforcement and justice engage in decision-making against a backcloth of belief that people can be readily classified into two types, criminal and non-criminal."

This point is underlined by Professor Donald Taft: "Negroes are more likely to be suspected of crime than are whites. They are also more likely to be arrested. If the perpetrator of a crime is known to be a Negro the police may arrest all negroes who were near the scene— a procedure they would rarely dare to follow with whites. After arrest, negroes are less likely to secure bail, and so are more liable to be counted in jail statistics. They are more liable than whites to be indicted and less likely to have their cases *nol prossed* or otherwise dismissed. If tried, negroes are more likely to be convicted. If convicted, they are less likely to be given probation. For this reason they are more likely to be included in the count of prisoners. Negroes are also more liable than whites to be kept in prison for the full terms of their commitments and correspondingly less likely to be paroled."

As anyone versed in the ways of the criminal justice system will tell you, the screening process begins with the policeman on the beat: the young car thief from a "nice home" will be returned to his family with a warning. If he repeats the offense or gets into more serious trouble, the parents may be called in for a conference with the prosecuting authorities. The well-to-do family has a dozen options: they can send their young delinquent to a boarding school, or to stay with relatives in another part of the country, they can hire the professional services of a psychiatrist or counselor—and the authorities will support them in these efforts. The Juvenile Court judge can see at a glance that this boy does not belong in the toils of the criminal justice system, that given a little tolerance and helpful guidance there is every chance he will straighten out by the time he reaches college age.

For the identical crime the ghetto boy will be arrested, imprisoned in the juvenile detention home, and set on the downward path that ends in the penitentiary. The screening process does not end with arrest, it obtains at every stage of the criminal justice system.

To cite one example that any observer of the crime scene—and particularly the black observer—will doubtless be able to match from his own experience: a few years ago a local newspaper reported horrendous goings-on of high school seniors in Piedmont, a wealthy enclave in Alameda County, California, populated by executives, businessmen, rich politicians. The students had gone on a general rampage that included arson, vandalism, breaking and entering, assault, car theft, rape. Following a conference among parents, their lawyers, and prosecuting authorities, it was decided that no formal action should be taken against the miscreants; they were all released to the custody of their families, who promised to subject them to appropriate discipline. In the very same week, a lawyer of my acquaintance told me with tight-lipped fury of the case of a nine-year-old black ghetto dweller in the same county, arrested for stealing a nickel from a white classmate, charged with "extortion and robbery," hauled off to juvenile hall, and, despite the urgent pleas of his distraught mother, there imprisoned for six weeks to wait for his court hearing.

Thus it seems safe to assert that there is indeed a criminal type — but he is not a biological, anatomical, phrenological, or anthropological type; rather, he is a social creation, etched by the dominant class and ethnic prejudices of a given society.

The day may not be far off when the horny-handed policeman on the beat may expect an assist in criminal-type-spotting from practitioners of a new witchcraft: behavior prediction. In 1970, Dr. Arnold Hutschnecker, President Nixon's physician, proposed mass psychological testing of six- to eight-year-old children to determine which were criminally inclined, and the establishment of special camps to house those found to have "violent tendencies." Just where the candidates for the mass testing and the special camps would be sought out was made clear when Dr. Hutschnecker let slip the fact he was proposing this program as an alternative to slum reconstruction. It would be, he said, "a direct, immediate, effective way of attacking the problem at its very origin, by focusing on the criminal mind of the child."

The behavior-predictors would catch the violence-prone *before* he springs, would confine him, possibly treat him, but in any event would certainly not let him out to consummate the hideous deeds of which he is so demonstrably capable. Their recurring refrain: "If only the clearly discernible defects in Oswald's psychological makeup had been detected in his childhood — had he been turned over to us, who have the resources to diagnose such deviant personalities — we would have tried to help him. If we decided he was beyond help, we would have locked him up forever and a major tragedy of this generation could have been averted." They refer, of course, to Lee Harvey Oswald, who allegedly gunned down President Kennedy, not to Russell G. Oswald, the New York Commissioner of Corrections who ordered the troops into Attica, as a result of which 43 perished by gunfire.

Part II

The Realities of Prison Life

Introduction

In *Rhodes v. Chapman*, a 1981 decision holding that, by itself, the double-celling of inmates for long periods of incarceration does not violate Eighth Amendment standards, the United States Supreme Court declared that "to the extent that (prison) conditions are restrictive and even harsh, they are part of the penalty that criminal offenders pay for their offenses against society." Emphasizing that facilities housing persons convicted of serious crimes "cannot be free of discomfort," the Justices concluded that "[t]he Constitution does not mandate comfortable prisons." This undoubtedly is a sentiment that enjoys widespread public approval. It is not uncommon to hear people who have never even visited a jail or prison refer to America's prisons as "country clubs" or "Holiday Inns."

Such stereotyping, of course, obscures the fact that no two prisons are exactly alike. There are some prisons, primarily federal prison camps specializing in white collar offenders, which come complete with modern recreational facilities, a variety of work and therapy opportunities, and expansive visiting hours. However, anyone who reads the evidence accrued in the hundreds of lawsuits brought to the courts by state prisoners in the past few years can only conclude that all too many American prisons—perhaps the majority—are depressing, rat-infested, heavily overcrowded fortresses that have created perverse societies in which violence, homosexual rape, and other assorted cruelties are everyday occurrences.

Scholars have carefully documented the fact that imprisonment inevitably leads to anxiety, pain, and stress. In his classic 1958 work, *The Society of Captives*, a detailed study of a large, maximum security prison in New Jersey, Gresham Sykes described the most severe psychological and social problems which accompany incarceration. These "pains of imprisonment" included the loss of liberty, autonomy, security, goods and services, and heterosexual relations. These deprivations, according to Sykes, arouse intense anxiety and bitter resentment in prisoners, and, ironically, they pressure prisoners to seek refuge in the anti-social values of the prison community, thus destroying any prospects of rehabilitation and provoking the very types of behavior prisons are supposed to suppress.

Just how violent, degrading, and emasculating is life in the prisons of the 1980s? To what extent are prisoners brutalized by their fellow prisoners, guards, and other staff members? What effects does prison life have on prisoners and how do those other prisoners—the guards— adapt to the stresses of daily confrontations with a hostile, abusive, and potentially violent inmate population? These are among the questions discussed in Part II.

Our first selection "Target Violence," is the third chapter of Daniel Lockwood's excellent book *Prison Sexual Violence*. This book examines the causes, consequences, and possible cures of sexual aggression in men's prisons. In "Target Violence," Lockwood focuses on the prisoner who reacts violently to men who make aggressive sexual approaches to him. Lockwood provides numerous horrifying examples of victim-precipitated violence as he explores the links between fear, anger, and sexual violence. It is especially interesting that most prisoners and most staff members support violence against sexual aggressors because they believe it to be the best self-defense available. This chapter speaks volumes about the prevalence of prison violence by both aggressors and targets, and it depicts the harsh realities of life in a cannibalistic society where the strong prey on the weak.

In some respects, the conditions and practices in women's prisons are similar to those found in men's prisons in that both male and female prisoners suffer the same losses of liberty and autonomy, and must find ways to cope with the "pains of imprisonment." However, women's prisons, though increasingly overcrowded, tend to be smaller in size than men's prisons, and female prisoners are less likely than are male prisoners to engage in acts of extreme physical and/or sexual violence against one another. Nevertheless, women's prisons are places where rehabilitation is rare, where health care usually falls well below accepted medical standards, and where rules and regulations seem designed to harass and humiliate rather than to correct. In particular, women prisoners are often treated as "girls," as children in institutions in which paternalism and infantilization are dominant features of everyday life. Women prisoners, as Jean Harris has deftly chronicled in her 1988 book "They Always Call Us Ladies": Stories from Prison, are reduced to infancy by petty, arbitrarily enforced rules that tell them to walk and talk like "ladies," to avoid cursing, and to "act like grown women" when they go "shopping" at the prison commissary.

Without doubt, the treatment of imprisoned women reflects sexist attitudes that are deeply entrenched in our culture and the myth and folklore that have pervaded the study of female offenders. This is one of the themes taken up by Robert G. Culbertson and Eddyth P. Fortune in "Women in Crime and Prison," the second article in Part II. After examining recent research on the increased involvement of women in crime, Culbertson and Fortune provide a demographic profile of incarcerated women, revealing that young, poorly educated minority women are overrepresented in prison populations. The authors also discuss why educational and vocational programs for women prisoners rarely succeed in preparing them for occupational opportunities after release from prison. Finally, and most importantly, Culbertson and Fortune explore the leading research studies on the realities of life in women's prisons. These studies reveal the existence of a prison subculture in which many female prisoners establish homosexual relationships and form pseudo-families in which such traditional family roles as "husband," "wife," "father," "brother," and "daughter" can be played. These and other social roles existing in women's prisons form an inmate subculture that new students of corrections may find shocking.

Correctional staff, of course, also become a major part of the prison community. Accordingly, our next article concerns staff-prisoner victimization in United States prisons. "The Victimization of Prisoners by Staff Members" is taken from Lee Bowker's Prison Victimization, a comprehensive overview of the sexual, social, psychological, and economic victimization of prisoners and prison staff. New students of corrections may be shocked by the many well-documented accounts of psychological mistreatment, physical torture, and sexual assaults against both adults and juveniles by sheriffs, deputies, guards, and other correctional officials. But as Bowker explains, there are at least two intriguing theoretical explanations—total institutions theory and role theory—that can help us understand why the dynamics of prison life bring out the very worst impulses in inmates and staff alike.

Prisoners and prison guards tend to view one another with distrust, suspicion, and hostility. Nevertheless, sociological research on the prison community has revealed that the custodial staff seek to attain discipline and order not by imposing an inflexible set of rules on prisoners, but by maintaining an elastic system of rewards and punishments in which the guards deliberately fail to enforce the full range of institutional regulations in exchange for the cooperation of inmate leaders in preventing widespread rulebreaking. In "Prison Guards and Snitches: Deviance Within a Total Institution," James Marquart and Julian Roebuck explain how the guards in a maximum security penitentiary were able to use the most prestigious, aggressive, and feared inmates as "rats" or "snitches." This study contradicts previous research portraying "rats" as weak, pitiful outcasts. Most intriguingly, Marquart and Roebuck show that it was the non-informing, ordinary prisoners and the lower ranking guards who came to be labeled as deviant and who were relegated to a lower status position in the prison under study.

Prison guards are sometimes referred to as a society's forgotten prisoners, and with good reason. In most states, correctional officers are underpaid, undertrained, and overworked in one of the most frustrating, stress-filled, and dangerous jobs imaginable. Accordingly, the last selection in Part II examines the plight of the prison guard. Ben Crouch's "Guard Work in Transition," offers an insightful and detailed examination of how changes in American prisons over the past two decades have created new and difficult problems for today's guards. Crouch, a nationally recognized expert on the sociology of guarding, explores such issues as guard stress, the dangerousness of guard work, the increasing racial and sexual integration of guard forces, the nature and extent of guard deviance on the job, and guard reactions to the growing professionalization and bureaucratization of American prisons.

6

Target Violence

Daniel Lockwood

Most prison violence involves inmates assaulting each other (Cohen et al., 1976). One reason is that violent men and men from violent subcultures live in prison. As violence behind the walls becomes acceptable behavior, prison itself becomes a "subculture of violence" (Conrad, 1966). When otherwise peaceful men live with prisoners who are dangerous or perceived to be dangerous, they become distrustful and fearful. These feelings of vulnerability cause those who have not been violent before to arm themselves and prepare themselves psychologically for fighting. Thus, in prison, sexual aggression results in two main types of violence: (1) Aggressors use violence to intimidate targets, and (2) targets of aggressors react violently to sexual approaches. This chapter examines the latter class of violent behavior, i.e., target violence precipitated by aggressive sexual approaches.

Hans Toch, as a member of the California Task Force on Institutional Violence, constructed a typology of prisoners in violent encounters (Toch, 1965). He calls the man whom I discuss here the "Homosexual Self-Defender." This prisoner, according to Toch, uses violence against men who make sexual approaches to him in order to be left alone.

Source: Reprinted by permission of the publisher from Chapter Three by Daniel Lockwood, *Prison Sexual Violence*, 38-58. Copyright 1980 by Elsevier Science Publishing Co., Inc.

According to Toch, "The effort here is to get out of a corner by eliminating whoever is blocking the exit" (1965).

> Following a heated altercation between inmates S and L, S obtains a razor blade, enters L's cell, and cuts L about the face and chest. S testifies that L had visited him to involve him in homosexual activities, and had been pressuring him. Other inmate sources point out that S has been under pressure from several homosexuals. (Toch, 1965)

Observers describe similar target reactions in a number of settings (Huffman, 1960; Thomas, 1967). Following the riot of 1971, the New York State Special Commission on Attica (1974) interviewed inmates in Attica, who frequently voiced their belief that violence is the only way to ward off sexual attacks. The Commission noted:

> The irony was not lost on the inmates. They perceived themselves surrounded by walls and gates, and tightly regimented by a myriad of written and unwritten rules; but when they needed protection, they often had to resort to the same skills that had brought many of them to Attica in the first place. (p. 101)

When targets fight aggressors, it reminds us of victim-precipitated homicide (Schultz, 1964). Offenders are incited to assaultive responses by the aggressive actions of their victims. Victims of targets (sexual aggressors), like many homicide victims in the street, often have been previously arrested for crimes of violence. Their patterns of conduct involve them in situations that provoke others to hostile reactions. In prison, a physical environment enforcing contact between antagonists, the probability of an aggressor provoking a violent response may be even greater than in the street. As Albert Cohen points out, prisons create "back-against-the-wall situations" because threatened men often lack the option of withdrawing (Cohen et al., 1976). When interactions contain potential for conflict, confinement itself hastens violence.

A study of violence in six California prisons in 1963 and 1964—one of the few sources classifying inmate assaults—indicates the kinds of contribution that sexual aggression can make to prison violence. The report breaks inmate-to-inmate assaults into the following categories.

Accidental, real, or imagined insult combined with hypersensitivity	35%
Homosexual activities	25%
Pressuring (for possessions)	15%
Racial conflict	12%
Informant activities	9%
Retaliation for past assaults	7%

Incidents attributed to homosexuality divide almost equally between homosexual rivalry (12 percent) and homosexual force (13 percent) (Toch, 1965). However, as we shall see in this chaper, it is possible for sexual aggression to play a role in the other categories listed above.

Prevalence

I define physical violence to include instances where one person was forcefully touched by another, this being marked by vehement feelings or the aim to injure or abuse. According to such a definition, 51 percent of 150 incidents in my study involved physical violence. About half of these were initiated by aggressors using force against unprovoking targets. Targets began the rest. These were clearcut violent responses to sexual approaches targets perceived as aggressive.

The Violent Transaction

We followed a method suggested by Toch, who states:

> In this type of approach, each move is seen as the rational response by one player to the play of another. The focus is on logical possibilities left open by preceding moves and on logical implications of each move for successive moves. These possibilities and implications can be conceptualized and qualified (1969, p. 35).

Diagramming 114 transactions (incomplete cases were left out), we grouped them according to the aggressor's first move. They fall into the following four categories:

1. Incidents begun by sexual overtures accompanied by offensive remarks and gestures $(N = 42)$
2. Incidents begun by polite propositions $(N = 36)$
3. Incidents begun by physical attacks $(N = 21)$
4. Incidents begun by verbal threats $(N = 15)$.

With an examination of the largest group, we see that over half of these transactions, begun by aggressors directing offensive remarks or gestures to targets, quickly escalated to violence. The moves in those sequences culminating in violence commonly follow this pattern:

1. a. Aggressor(s) makes offensive sexual overture.
   b. Target tries to withdraw or target responds with force or threats and a fight starts.
2. a. Aggressor repeats overture, accompanied by threats.
   b. Target uses physical force against aggressor and a fight starts or target answers with counterthreat and a fight starts.

I use an example of this transaction from Coxsackie, a prison housing 700 youths ranging in age from 16 to 21. The target is a white marijuana dealer from Florida. The aggressor is black, a violent offender from New York City. During an incident an officer looks on but is out of earshot:

C2-27: While I was taking a shower he said to me, "You're all right and you're going to be mine later." There was two or three saying it, but they had one spokesman.... They were in the shower and they were waiting to have me turn around so that they could see my ass.... They were saying that I was going to be theirs and they would take care of me and buy me cigarettes and that I would be their main squeeze.

And I said, "Well you can see me later, but we're going to fight about it, because you're not going to get anything out of me."

So he said, "Okay, Angel, that's okay, I'll play it rough with you and then after you break then you'll be mine."

So I rinsed off and then I got the fuck out.... So I'm over there by the door and as he was going out he put his arm around me and as he did that, I pushed his arm away and I said, "I don't play that, man."

And he said, "Well, you're going to play what I want you to play."
And I said, "Definitely not—I don't want to hassle."

And he said, "You're going to be mine." And he leaned over and said that he was going to whisper something in my ear and I told him to back off, gave him a shove and he came back fighting. I hit him a couple of times and then the guards broke it up and then we were both locked up for the same amount of time.

An important feature of this fight is that before the violence, the target tries to withdraw, but cannot. As he tells us:

C2-27: I figured that he would want to hassle, so I got my clothes on and I went away from his group of people and then I went out the door and stayed away from him and I thought that maybe he would keep away from me that way and go on to somebody else. And I noticed that he was talking to some other people and giving them the same thing. I thought, if he's hassling somebody else, I'm not any hero and I'm not going to go defend somebody else.

Cornered, his back against the wall, the target starts the fight (i.e., by shoving the aggressor)—only after his antagonist has repeatedly propositioned him, threatened him, and attempted to whisper endearments in his ear. Because prison restricts movement, the transaction escalates to violence, even though one of the participants wants to retreat.

Why does the target finally shove the aggressor, thereby changing a verbal encounter to a physical one? Mindful that an officer is supervising the shower area, why can't the target limit himself to verbal responses? Whether his reaction springs from panic or the cool decision to make a preemptive strike, the root cause is fear. Following the aggressor's initial move, the target's thoughts are a mixture of fear and self-doubt.

C2-27: I was saying, "What could I do if all three of these guys came and jumped me?" I could probably hit a couple of them but I'm thinking of all these martial arts that I'm going to break into and all I've seen is Kung Fu on T.V. And there was nothing to pick up and I didn't have any shoes that I could kick them with.

If this target had felt safe, the fight might have been avoided. But prisons are places of fear where violence feeds on itself and breeds more violence. If this target had been able to withdraw, the fight might have been avoided. But prison prohibits free movement and men in antagonistic transactions lash out when cornered. If the target had been separated from abusive and threatening comments, the incident would never have occurred. But society deposits its bullies and exploiters in prison. Inevitably, behind the walls, they continue these patterns of behavior, directing their aggression against weaker prisoners instead of free citizens.

Forty-two incidents, like the above example, began with propositions accompanied by offensive remarks or gestures. Twenty-four (or 57 percent) ended in violence. Many incited sharp target reactions from the very first: 12 targets, for example, fought with aggressors immediately following their offensive overtures.

Does target violence work? Or is it senseless, an overreaction to a situation that could be resolved by talking over the problem? To examine this question, let us compare, still within the category of incidents begun by offensive remarks or gestures, targets responding violently to targets trying to ignore or respond politely to these sexual overtures. Only one target who responded without violence succeeded in ending this type of incident. In the other transactions in this category, the nonviolent target response was met in the following ways:

1. Seven aggressors repeated the offensive remark or gesture;
2. Four aggressors leveled sexual threats at targets; and
3. Four aggressors attacked targets.

Polite refusals, thus, tended to encourage aggressors to continue their offensive behavior. We know violent responses to unwanted sexual overtures are normative expectations of the convict community. Unfortunately, in some instances, they may actually be necessary for surviving incarceration with dignity.

We also grouped 36 incidents sequentially that opened with requests for sex — propositions. Twelve of these incidents evolved into physical violence. This escalation usually occurred in one of two ways. In the first, the target replied to the request for sex with a polite refusal, or ignored the request. Following this response, the aggressor reacted violently or accompanied a renewed request with threats. In the second sequence, the target, hearing the request, reacted with the use of force. In one-third of these incidents, targets responded with threats of their own before propositioners made violent or threatening moves. These threats ended half of these incidents, while the others escalated to higher levels of force.

The messages being communicated — that the propositioner wanted sex with the target, and that the target wanted the aggressor to stay away — tended to be confused by threats on both sides. In this scenario, threats often escalated into physical violence. Some targets heard a proposition and snarled back. Others attempted to reason with propositioners and ended up snapping back when their reasoning failed. Aggressors, beginning their approaches with requests for sex, were drawn into conflict for varying reasons. For example, a refusal might suggest the necessity for developing threats or violence. On the other hand, a refusal might be perceived as insulting. In these cases of violence, the sexual motive changes into a reaction to the sting of wounded pride.

We also grouped 21 incidents beginning with sexual attacks and 15 that began with extreme threats. Following these expressions of force, six targets submitted to sexual assault, because of the level of force exerted. Many immediately began to fight with their assailants. Officers then appeared and the incidents ended short of sexual penetration. Completed rapes depended more on the presence or absence of security than on any type of target response. Most incidents that began with immediate threats moved directly into physical violence. In four cases, violence occurred because aggressors used force when their threats were met with target attempts to withdraw peacefully. In nine cases, targets initiated the violence by responding to the threats with physical force. This set of incidents exemplifies both patterns of sequences resulting in physical violence. Aggressors escalate from threats to physical force, and targets escalate from being the objects of threats to being the initiators of physical violence.

In conclusion, the results of diagramming 150 incidents of sexual aggression may be stated simply. Attacks and threats are often answered by physical violence or threats. Targets tend to answer propositions with threats and aggressors tend to threaten or employ force when propositions have been declined. Thus, dialogue escalates to threats and threats escalate to violence. We could expect little less when violent men enter such transactions.

Fear, Anger, and Violence

We coded the psychological impact of sexual aggression, tabulating the incidence of specific emotions in each interview. The results of this laborious process showed *fear* and *anger* to be the feelings most often associated with the experience. These are concomitants of violent behavior in both animal and human interactions.

We will first examine the contribution of anger to target violence. By our definition, targets are recipients of unwanted sexual approaches. Because these approaches are unwanted — obnoxious and offensive — they cause frustration. Targets must often suffer frustration for long periods of time, while aggressors, who play the prison "pimp" role, take pride in their persistence. Because sexual problems are often unshareable problems, men do not talk about them, and they are sometimes afraid to vent their true feelings to aggressors. Frustration, having no release, dams up until it breaks in a flood of aggression. A prisoner tells us:

ARE-4:   And when he sat down, he had a cup of coffee in his left hand and he put his right arm around my whole shoulders.... And I got so irritated. Nothing would stop him, nothing. Neither threats nor making just sense, or trying to show him my point of view in the situation. Nothing. Nothing would deter it. So he sat down and put his arm around my shoulders and I realized that this was it. I had come to the end of my rope and put up with this crap for long enough. It all happened so fast. I had just come to the end of my rope. And when I jumped up he stood up immediately. I poked at him with that fork, and he backed up because he really thought that I was going to stab him. I was so angry, but I really wasn't going to stab him. I just wanted to make him realize that I could become violent. And like I said, "Back up and if you ever touch me I'll kill you." And I was just ready to enact it. I was at the end. All this pressure just came out at one time.

Aggressors often select targets who seem to have emotional problems that make them more vulnerable. This strategy backfires where targets have difficulty managing aggressivity and hostile feelings. Such men may be locked up because temper control is one of the components of their criminal behavior.

C2-29:   The guys were fooling around and grabbing me by the ass. He said I was a pussy and he is going to break me. So I picked him up and I threw him against the wall. When he come off the wall I just beat the pulp out of him. I kind of just lost my head and I know that if I get in that state I am really going to break because, you know, after a while it builds up. You can't take it no longer.

AR-16:   He will make a false move and that is when my whole body starts shaking. Like I have got a bad temper and I don't take no shit from nobody. I was close enough to kill one of these dudes around here. I am all nervous and anything could happen.

Of course, confinement can make any prisoner, regardless of his personality, unduly sensitive to irritations. Sexual approaches may impinge on a man already troubled by family worries, resentments over authority, or any of the other possible difficulties of confinement. Sexual pressure in some cases caps a sediment of accumulated aggravations. A target who killed his aggressor tells us:

B-6:   At that certain time, I had a whole lot on my mind. He caught me at the wrong time to talk to me about that stuff. If it was another time, I don't believe that I would have tried to kill him or would have tried to do anything to him. I had a whole lot of little things on my mind. It was the time. When I finished, I felt sorry for him. I really shouldn't have done that, but I did it.

Rationales for Violence

While some target violence relates to unscheduled explosions of rage, in other cases prisoners say they fight aggressors to carry out calculated aims. Violence, men tell us, becomes the medium for a message and a cool strategy for self-defense.

Defining Sexual Identity

Some targets say they become violent to show others they are straight and mean to stay that way. Most targets dread the gay label. When approached for sex, some avail themselves of the opportunity to attack aggressors so they can publicly demonstrate their disdain of homosexuality. While part of targets' fear revolves around anxiety about being stigmatized, men also feel that if others believe they are gay they will be open to further victimization. This fear relates to the tendency for prisoners to think of targets as "sissies" or "squeeze."

C2-30: It was mostly the same guy and I had to take it out on him because it was getting to a point, you know, everybody in the institution was thinking I was a punk or squeeze or a pussy and stuff like that. I had to to something about it in order to stop it. I had to prove to these other people that I wasn't a pussy or punk or anything else. I had to prove to these other people in my way and their way that I wasn't what he thought I was.

C2-29: And people was thinking, the people that was looking on at that time, that this guy—well, maybe this guy is a pussy or something. This guy is fooling around with his ass. There must be something wrong with him. He must be a pussy.
        So I turned around and I caught him fooling around. So I told him, "Do it once more and I am going to bust you in the face." The people,

that is the worst thing in this place, the people look on and they always have their ratings. And they have to gossip. They are like ladies and they really build it up and it runs around the institution.

CR-28: The guy right next to me, they grab his ass. He just lets it go by and so they call him a squeeze. I told him, "The next time that they touch your ass, you turn around and swing, or otherwise they are going to think that you are a squeeze."

Showing You Believe in the Convict Code

Those identifying with the convict code feel they must answer threat with threat. Such men cannot discuss the problem with the staff, for that shows they are rats. Similarly, the subcultural inmate sometimes cannot reason with an aggressor because he sees talk as a sign of weakness, uncoolness, or as an unacceptable attribute of straight society. Self-respect for prisoners upholding the convict code means favoring private solutions. The correct course of action calls for facing the challenge and responding to it forcefully.

AUI-2: See, when a guy first comes in a lot of guys will say, "Well, I don't want to hit the guy because I am thinking about the parole board." But, really, that is the very best way to deal with it. You could report the incident but that is snitching and I feel myself that if you have to knock the guy's head off to handle the problem, knock the guy's head off. You have to establish yourself as a man and you have to live with yourself. You have to look at yourself every morning in the mirror.

• • •

I: Did you think of any other ways to solve this problem?

AR-41: No, not really. Because what he said was already out in the open. If I talked to him, then everybody else would say I'm trying to cop out. So the only way I seen to solve the problem was to actually get out and fight, prove to him that I ain't going to go to no police and inform on anybody.

Showing You are Tough

Targets sometimes assert that they are violent because they wish to show others they are tough. Fighting is a way of communicating to all other potential aggressors—not just the men in the immediate incident—that one is not to be messed with. Discouraging the immediate approach becomes secondary to raising one's status. The assumption is that a violent demeanor is necessary for survival in prison, and that an aggressive image is a positive and worthwhile attribute of one's public personality, which must be consciously cultivated.

ARE-2: Now, if you were to go out and hit somebody across the head with a pipe and almost kill them, then people would think twice again. They would

say, "That dude is crazy and he might try to kill me if I ask him that."
And, so, then you know you can go where you want to go.

C2-23: Now, each and every inmate goes through a trial period here where
someone is going to say, "I want your ass." But if he straightens it out
himself and he gets into a fight with the guy, it will show everyone that
he is not going to take that kind of shit. He will be all right.

AR-41: I felt kind of different because, like, when I walked through the yard
there was people in it that went to school also and they were telling
their friends, "This little guy will cut you if you even attempt to do anything to him. He's a dude to stay away from." And you see people
looking at you as you're walking by, like saying, "Should I approach
him, will he cut me too?" Stuff like this going through their minds.

C2-27: I wanted to protect myself and the only way that you can protect yourself is with violence. And it was getting to the point where after a while
I was starting to do pushups every night. And then as I would get tired,
I said that I would kick that guy's ass as I got stronger. I noticed that
there was a bunch of them around, I thought when he hit me, "This is it,
that will show the other guys when I get into a fight with this one that
I'm not going to quit." So I fight and get punched a few times and I
punch him a few times and they see that I'm a man.

Violence as a Means of Curbing Violence

Violence can be a simple matter of using preemptive self-defense. At
a certain point the target begins to believe that the aggressor is on a
course escalating toward a forceful attempt at sexual assault. He then
fights to alter this self-conceived prediction. Even men who are approached with nonviolent propositions may project into the future, see
themselves as probably victims, and react violently.

C2-43: I was going to grab a bench or a piece of pipe or something and I figured
if I hit one of them and they got to bleeding or something they might stop
monkeying around.

A-1:   A lot of times fear will make you do things like that. The first time that
somebody gives you some lip, you stab him. It's a warning: "Look, I
don't want to be pushed around." If somebody comes to you, they can
say a word wrong and if you don't react to that one word in the right
way, you lose something and then they will test you a little further. If
you fail then you're in trouble.

Documenting Violence Effectiveness

Violence as a pragmatic solution is a formula upheld by most
inmates. But how does this theory work in actual practice? Is violence,
in fact, a successful way to meet the violence problem? On one level,
the answer is "yes." In concrete incidents, some men have found
violence to be a satisfactory ploy. Targets can report violent responses

that have curbed aggressive approaches, and some men who try reasoning with aggressors find them unresponsive until these targets project a more aggressive stance. The effectiveness of protective aggression in certain cases strengthens the norms supporting violence as a solution to forceful sexual approaches.

AR-1:   I stood my ground right then and there and I said, "Look, you just stay clear or else I am going to put a pipe right across your head." And I wasn't fooling. And that is the last time he has ever bothered me.

AR-41:   The Spanish dude, after I cut him, he comes back and he says, "Listen, I'm sorry for what I did."
         I said, "Do you really mean that? Then I'm sorry for cutting you."
         I had to put it straight right then, "I'll do it again if you try it again."
         And he says, "No, no, everything's all right."

C2-23:   He hit me and then I went after this guy, I beat him—I beat him real good. So about a week later he came back downstairs and all of a sudden he shook my hand and said, "Let's be friends." The only way to get respect from them is to put a foot in their ass.

AR-7:   He went to the hospital and I got locked up. I got a two-day keep-lock even though the administration knew basically that he was behind it. And after that, we more or less became friends, I suppose. We were talking to each other.

ARE-2:   A dude pushed a guy and cut him with a knife. And ever since then people don't do nothing. They talk about it among themselves but whenever he's around, people want to be friends with him.

Negotiating from Weakness

At the same time forces pull men toward violent solutions, other drives push them away from resolving the conflict by verbal negotiation. Especially for those on the brink of feeling powerless, the willingness to negotiate may be seen as an additional symbol of weakness, a further step toward vulnerability. Targets also feel that verbal sparring with aggressors can sink them into deeper trouble than they are in already. Lacking confidence in their bargaining ability, some targets fear that fast-talking "players" will easily manipulate any conversation to serve their ends.

C2-29:   You talk to the guy and he bullshits his way out and says this and that and tries to twist your words and throws them back to you. And it doesn't work. He doesn't listen. And the only way he is going to listen at this point is to punch him in the mouth. You can't do anything else.

A-1:   I think they can talk themselves into it deeper. I think that you can talk yourself out of it if you're very slick and if you're mean and have a mean rap. If you have the right eyes, and the right look in your eyes, and the right way of how anger should appear in your eyes, and how hate should appear, and malice, and how to project fear into somebody else's eyes, if you can do that, you can do it, you can talk your way out of it. But the thing is that if you're too scared, then you lose.

C2-23:   You try to talk to them—you try to talk sense to them and say, "Now, look, I am an inmate and you are an inmate."
         And they will say, "Ah—don't tell me that pussy shit." They will tell you that, you know. So, I figured that talking was no good with this guy. There is only one way to handle him and that is to fight with him.

A-1:   I hadn't even tried to talk them out of it, because I wasn't that good at expressing myself and I couldn't project fear into someone. I couldn't project hostility. There was something that I couldn't do.

Peer and Staff Support

The attitudes and behaviors associated with target violence are in part social behavior, learned in prison from other inmates and staff. Targets are generally new to the prison where they are harassed by sexual aggression; they may look to others for guidance. Peers, often men who have been targets themselves, may advise new men to consider violence favorably. Men who have never used weapons are supplied with "shanks" and "pipes" by their more experienced friends. Others are supplied with arguments through which guilt is neutralized. The target's violent response is an explicit normative expectation of the prison community. This is passed on to new men by experienced inmates as part of the process of "prisonization."

AR-23:   And I went out in the yard and I told my brother what was happening. The next thing you know one of my brother's friends came up and gave me a shank and told me that if a guy come up at me to stick him.

C2-52:   He just told me to grab anything that I can and just beat them. Whether it is a chair or whatever and just go after them.

C2-22:   This black dude was going to jump a friend of mine and so I talked to him and I said, "Look, man, the knife drawer is open. Grab one of them butcher knives and bring it upstairs. That is all." He took the knife out of the drawer and put it in the back of his pants and went upstairs and stuck it in the pillow and sewed the pillow back up. And if this dude come over, he would have got stabbed.

C2-28:   I just said, "Look-it, you just pick up something and you hit that dude. Or else you go and you make yourself a blade and you stab the dude—do anything." I says, "If the dude is going to rip you off, you kill the dude— that is all."

AR-36:   He was the water man and he was pretty straight. He came right out and he told me, "You are a little guy and you can expect trouble, you know, but if anything happens, don't even question it, just crack their skull and it will be over with — that is all.''

C2-30: I go over and pull him over in the corner and talk to him right then and there and tell him, "These guys are trying to get over on you. The best thing for you to do is to hang out with the white guys and try and get to know people. Lift weights. Try boxing and do what you can. Learn how to fight if you can't fight.''

C2-23: I told him that the best thing to do, in front of everyone, while this guy was popping shit to him, is to hit the guy. There is no other way that this thing is going to be resolved unless you hit the guy.

C2-44: I don't know how many times I told him, "If a dude run up on you, popping you some shit, just hit him in his face. If you lose, you lose — so what? You get locked up for seven days and you come downstairs and the dude will think twice before running up on you again. Because they are going to know that you will hurt him.''

AR-6: So I tried to talk about it with some of the white guys that was here. They was living on this tier with me. And they tried to give me solutions. The majority of them told me to hit this guy, anybody that come up to you, just hit him.

The advocacy of violence is spread by the old to the young and by the experienced to the inexperienced. Thus, in observing how targets are readied to behave violently, we see a process whereby a subculture upholding violence spreads its message. Moreover, the learning that occurs in these peer groups is not academic. It answers an immediate problem of pressing concern to the learner.

Staff

Staff members also support target violence so that the square or isolate inmate who identifies with officialdom can learn violent norms just as well as the group member who identifies with his peers. Why do staff uphold violent solutions? Some staff members have cultural origins similar to those of many inmates in the prison. They are working-class men themselves and hold norms supporting "masculine" responses to intimidation. In addition, staff, like inmates, belong to the prison community. This community, as a norm of its own, holds that a violent response is one of the simplest and most effective ways of handling an aggressive sexual approach. Finally, staff, especially officers, sometimes can think of no options that they know to work as well as a violent response.

C2-20: And the C.O. came in and asked what had happened and I told him that this guy had tried to take me off and I was just protecting myself. So then the C.O. said, "I'll shut the door and you do what you think is the best." And so I fucked the guy up and sent him to the hospital.

AR-46: In Attica, they told me to take a pipe to them if they bother you sexu
       ally. Take a pipe to them—that was the officers. I was told that in '65
       and so I started using one.

C2-51: The officer with me in the hall—he said, "You should have hit him in
       the nuts." And I said, "I am not a dirty fighter." He said, "That don't
       make no difference, man, you just do that." And I guess after a while
       I found out that he was right. So after a while, after I took it under
       deep study, I had the trouble and I hit him in the nuts.

AR-36: He [lieutenant] said, being a little guy, if anything like that should
       happen, hit the guy with the first thing available and try and knock him
       down. Try and do it in front of a hack or somebody and then he will
       come down and break it up. Once they do, you will go to the box. And
       once you get to the box, tell the hacks that you want to see me. I will
       come up, see what I can do. That is about the only thing that I can tell
       you.

●   ●   ●

I: So you spoke to the priest about this sex pressure, too? Did he offer
      you any advice?

C2-52: He just told me to do what I think is best and just fight if I have to.

●   ●   ●

I: You went to your company officer?

C2-23: Right, I went and said, "Look, this guy is bothering me, man. He keeps
       coming out with these sexual remarks and I want somebody to do some
       thing about this guy—tell him something." He said, "Well, there is
       nothing that we can do about it, and there is nothing that the brass can
       do about it, so hit him." He came right out and told me just like that.

During informal conversations, as when an officer on his rounds
pauses to discuss an inmate's problem with him, the staff advise
targets to be violent. Staff also offer this advice as part of the formal
delivery of counseling services. Administrators, counselors, and even
chaplains participate in giving such advice. The message that is communicated through official channels is essentially the same message as
the men receive from their peers. Its content mirrors the themes we
have reviewed: Violence will win you respect; it will deter future
approaches; it will cause the aggressor bothering you to back off.
Prison records show staff pleased with such advice, convinced of its
effectiveness. When one inmate applied for transfer, his counselor
wrote:

> Because of his youthful appearance, other inmates saw him as a
> prime material for homosexual activities. Through counseling and
> an individually tailored body building program, John has developed
> self-confidence and asserted his individuality. Having made his ad
> justment here, he should be able to hold his own in a camp setting.

When prisoners fight, they face stiff discipline. Formal procedures can remove privileges and sentence men to solitary confinement. In some cases of sexual aggression, however, informal arrangements suspend disciplinary proceedings, enabling staff to back up their advice with supportive leniency. When staff view inmate violence as justified and practical, formal measures to stop violence may be suspended. Staff may make private arrangements to overlook a fight provided it is in the service of survival. Staff thus monitor and even encourage instrumental inmate assaults on other inmates.

C2-37: I said, "Well, there is a nigger wanting to make me a kid." I says, "Before I give my ass up to any nigger, I would fucking kill him." So he [staff] says, "Well, you have got a point there." He says, "Yeah, all right, I am going to let you go." I said, "Any keep-lock or anything?" And he says, "You have got one day keep-lock and the next time any nigger or anything comes up on you, you do the same thing."

C2-31: One sergeant told me, "Put a bat across this dude's head and I will go to court and testify that you told me about this shit."

AR-36: When I went through my orientation, the senior lieutenant told me that if anything like that should happen, "Hit him, and when you go to the box, send the word and I will come up and talk to you. I will do what I can to get you out of trouble."

C2-30: I asked Sergeant Brown. And he told me to go ahead. "Pick up the nearest thing around you and hit him in the head with it. He won't bother you no more." I went over to another sergeant and I asked him and he said, "Pick up the nearest damn thing to you and just hit him with it, that is all." I looked at him and I said, "All right. If I do this I ain't going to get locked up for it, am I?" He looks at me and he says, "No." Because I am using self-defense.

Problems with Violent Solutions

The violent response to sexual approaches may be effective for some, but not for others. As Bartollas et al. (1976) point out, such values, in institutions, are "functional for aggressive inmates...the code clearly works to the disadvantage of the weak" (p. 69). Such men take into prison ideas opposed to violence while others have limited experience with violence. Men may also have types of personality that make violent behavior a difficult—or impossible—solution for them. According to Toch (1977) norms that prescribe violence create a difficult situation for inmates to whom violence is "ego alien."

A-7: The minute I think about what to do to a guy and how they butcher them and this and that, all that runs through my mind is blood. That scares the hell out of me. I don't like this. I wouldn't want to cut up anybody just like I wouldn't want them to cut me up....I am not a fighter, man, that's not my bag and I won't do it. I hardly did any fighting out on the streets. And they just told me to take a guy, take a club, and club him. And I never did that to a guy.

APC-14:   If you are an aggressive person, like a bigmouth, you stand a chance of people steering away from you. But if you're reserved, they'll run all over you. But I'm quiet and I don't think that I have got to adjust to them people. In other words, if I have got to be getting up and saying, "Hey, motherfucker," and make up lies that I did this and that, just to keep them away from me, then I could do it. But it's not my thing.

APCC-4:   It wasn't easy because I felt that he would see through me. Because I'm not that way naturally. And I thought that he would see through me and laugh at me.

While some violent reactions to sexual approaches are informally tolerated by officials, fear of institutional discipline restrains many men. They want to avoid punishment, losing good time, or being sentenced anew. Such repercussions are particularly likely when the target exceeds the limits of violence tolerated by authorities. For example, the man who murdered the aggressor who propositioned him received a sentence of five years. Another target sliced a man across the face, giving him a wound requiring 22 stitches, and he received a sentence of 22 years. This man also received a wide range of punishments available to the prison administration. He tells us:

AR-35:   They took me to special housing unit called the guard house and they put me in a stripped cell. No bed. No nothing. Just a toilet bowl and a sink. They left me there 38 days—just feeding me—took all my clothes and everything. I didn't have anything except for a toilet bowl and a sink and after a while I had an inmate sneak me a blanket and when the officers come by I would have to sneak it back to him. Then they took me to court and prosecuted me—assault in the first degree. They gave me 22 years. Before I went to trial, I was placed in a security cell for 38 days and taken to the superintendent's hearing and was prosecuted. And I had been punished about four or five times for that crime.

The fear of disciplinary infractions or of new charges puts some targets in a dilemma. Should they consider their long-term welfare or fight to alleviate an aggressor's pressure? Peer and staff support may facilitate personal aggression but cannot grant immunity to consequences. This means that the fear of punishment may outweigh the perceived benefits of violence.

Fear of punishment complicates the problem "solved" by the norm of violence. Similarly, the norms are no "solution" for those unable to fight because they are unprepared, socially and psychologically, to

meet tough urban sexual aggressors. These men are in especially difficult positions. Unable to avail themselves of the escape provided by the
convict culture, they are plagued by feelings of inadequacy. Knowing
that violence is the "correct" course of action but not being able to
implement it, they are failures in the convict world. The normative
advice cannot help them, and they must seek other, perhaps less
attractive, solutions to the problem. These are the men who often go to
the solitary confinement of protective custody — "protection
companies" — men who may live in fear throughout their stay in prison
(Lockwood, 1977a).

Conclusion

About half of 152 incidents of sexual aggression I examined involved
physical violence. Half of this violence came from aggressors who
attempted to coerce targets; the rest came from targets who reacted to
threats or perceived threats. Violent reactions are instrumental for
targets in the sense that they end more incidents than any other
reactions. After fights, targets tell us, aggressors leave them alone.
They move around the prison with less fear and feel better about
themselves.

Most men we interviewed had attitudes and values supporting
violent solutions to the problem of being a target. Prisoners see
violence as the medium for the message that one is straight, uninterested in sexual involvement, or that one is tough, not a prospect to "get
over on." Others say that violence is the best self-defense available.
Reacting with force unambiguously lets the aggressor know the
consequences of his behavior if he persists. In prison, target violence
usually leads to an improved self-image and a more favorable status
among other prisoners. Fellow inmates, looked to for guidance, school
new inmates to accept this solution. Staff support target violence and
back up their counsel with a flexible disciplinary process, exempting
some inmates from punishment when they fight to uphold their
manhood.

Other psychological factors complement these ideas supporting
inmate violence. Anger characterizes the target emotional response.
The irritation caused by aggressors can itself lead to targets exploding
in unpredictable and uncalculated ways. As in ethology, fear and
anger are linked to aggression. Threatened men, angered men, become
aggressive and turn aggressors into victims.

References

Bartollas, C., Miller, S.J., and Dinitz, S. 1976. *Juvenile Victimization.* New York: Sage Publications.

Cohen, A.K., Cole, G.F., and Bailey, R.G. 1976. *Prison Violence.* Lexington, MA: Lexington Books.

Conrad, J.P. 1966. "Violence in Prison." *Annals of the American Academy of Political and Social Sciences.* 364: 113-119.

Huffman, A. 1960. "Sex Deviation in a Prison Community." *Journal of Social Therapy.* 6: 170-181.

Lockwood, D. 1977a. "Living in Protection." In *Survival in Prison.* Toch, H., ed. New York: The Free Press.

New York State Special Commission on Attica. 1974. *Attica.* New York: Praeger.

Schultz, L.G. 1964. "The Victim-Offender Relationship." *Crime and Delinquency* 14: 135-141.

Thomas, P. 1967. *Down These Mean Streets.* New York: New American Library.

Toch, H. 1965. "Institutional Violence Code, Tentative Code of the Classification of Inmate Assaults on Other Inmates." Unpublished Manuscript, California Department of Corrections Research Division.

Toch, H. 1977. *Living in Prison.* New York: The Free Press.

7

Women in Crime and Prison
Robert G. Culbertson
Eddyth P. Fortune

A significant body of knowledge concerning female criminality is emerging as we proceed through the 1980s. For the most part, female criminality and women's prisons have been ignored by writers in the field of criminal justice. The current flurry of research activity reflects years of neglect and reveals considerable bias and myth in much of the early research concerning the female offender. Problems in regard to bias have been articulated by Smith (1965), who contends that issues in female criminality have been neglected or glossed over by sentiment and unreliable male intuition. Other writers link the absence of research on female criminality to the fact that women comprise less than five percent of the prison population in the United States. Historically, female

Source: From "Order Under Law": Readings in Criminal Justice, 2/E, by Robert G. Culbertson and Eddyth P. Fortune. Published 1984 by Waveland Press, Inc.

criminality has not been viewed as "dangerous." Rather, the criminal behavior which has brought women to court has been considered socially offensive.

Feinman (1980) and others point out that women traditionally have been placed in subordinate roles and, until recent times, considered property of the male because of what Feinman refers to as the "Madonna/Whore Duality." The "Madonna/Whore Duality" is a concept which has governed societal attitudes throughout the centuries. It places the female in the role of the bearer of legitimate heirs (the Madonna) and states she needs to be protected and properly controlled in order to assure she maintains this role. On the other hand, the female can inflame men's passions (the Whore). Women who strictly maintained their purity and their maternal roles were held in high esteem; those who went beyond the limits of purity (i.e., acted in deviant ways) were dealt with severely.

Because of these and related contradictory attitudes, intensive study of female behavior, especially deviant behavior, has not been accomplished. To complicate matters, researchers have preferred to focus on the male because of greater numbers, easier accessibility of information, and perceived dangerousness of the male offender.

It is important to note that the traditional role of the criminologist has been to maintain a close relationship with corrections policy-making bodies and officials. As a result, research has focused primarily on those issues which officials who distribute grants and consulting monies have defined as problematic. Historically, major management problems have been centered in maximum security prisons for men. Policy issues have tended to focus on these types of institutions; therefore, women's prisons have been ignored.

Significant changes began to occur in the late 1960s, and the focus of research shifted dramatically in the direction of female criminality and women in prison. Some contend the attention was the result of the emergence of the Women's Rights Movement, which became an increasingly powerful force in American society in the late 1960s and the 1970s. However, it is rarely mentioned that the Women's Movement actually began in the early 1800s and, despite the lack of scientific research, great strides were made in the treatment of female offenders. While these early reformers did not breach societal concepts of the traditional roles of females, as did later reformers, they were able to accomplish beneficial results, including separate facilities for housing convicted female offenders and treatment programs designed specifically for females.

The reformers of the 1960s and 1970s began the push for equity in the treatment of females in all areas of the criminal justice system. These modern-day reformers asserted there were many inequities in the system and, because of the lack of research, there was really very little known about the female offender. Their efforts are the foundation for those who claim the Women's Rights Movement was responsible for the current attention given to female criminality (Feinman, 1980; Price and Sokoloff, 1982; Feinman, 1979; Smart, 1979).

Others claim increased involvement of women in serious crime produced the new attention to female criminality. Many of these theories are founded in Uniform Crime Report data, which indicate female arrests for index crimes increased drastically in the 1960s and 1970s. Although many theorists during the 1970s did focus on the "new breed" of female offender, conscientious researchers were careful to point out that, while the data indicated increases in female arrests, there were several other factors which might have influenced these theories.

First, the Uniform Crime Reports were relatively new, and reporting procedures during that time have changed and improved. Second, societal attitudes toward women had begun to change drastically, which might have indicated a change in the way the criminal justice system was dealing with female criminality. Third, societal changes had occurred which found women leaving the home more frequently in order to pursue employment. Finally, the "Baby Boom" population of the 1950s had entered the "crime-prone" age (Adler, 1975; Simon, 1975; Smart, 1979).

Still others contend the myth and bias which pervaded much of the earlier research on female criminality enhanced the potential for new efforts reflecting less bias and prejudice in research strategies. Much of the early research on female criminality focused on theories that females were deviant due to biological differences. Lombroso (1958; originally published in 1895) asserted the female was biologically inferior to the male, with inferiorities including a "less active cerebral cortex," physiological immobility, and psychological passivity. Therefore, the female was more child-like and had a greater propensity towards deviance because of these inferiorities. Despite criticisms of this theory, many biologically-based theories emerged during the next several decades, and many of these theories were based on concepts presented by Lombroso (Klein, 1973).

Regardless of the reasons for the current interest in female criminality, there has been a recent flurry of new theories, many based on sociological perspectives. Some are based on "emancipation theories," which suggest women are becoming an increasingly dominant force in America and refuse to play subordinate roles linked to the traditional sex roles.

Women are aggressively pursuing constitutional rights in a variety of settings. At the same time, as opportunities increase for women in employment, opportunities increase in the area of crime. Because positions of financial trust historically were restricted to men, women were rarely charged with embezzlement or related offenses. However, as women overcome employment barriers and assume positions in the fields of finance and banking, it is no longer uncommon to find women charged with the same offenses as the men who hold these positions.

Some of the leading proponents of "opportunity" theory suggest that as women become equal to men their crime patterns will be more like those of males (Adler, 1975). Also, as women become actively involved in the work force they will become more actively involved in crime, especially property crimes (Simon, 1975). Although these theories appear to have some elements of substance, they frequently have been criticized because subsequent research has indicated that "emancipation" has really only affected the middle-class female. A large proportion of female offenders come from the lower socioeconomic strata.

Further, arrest data indicate that, although there was an overall increase in arrest rates for females during the late 1960s and 1970s, the rates of increase for violent offenses were not much different from the rates of increase for males committing violent offenses. The major increases in female arrests were for property offenses, primarily in the larceny category. Steffensmeier (1982) points out that "the percentage of all female arrests which were for violent crimes was 7.8 percent in 1965, compared to 8.4 percent in 1980, while, for males, it was 8.1 percent in 1965 and 11.5 percent in 1980" (p. 122). To continue, Steffensmeier indicated that larceny and fraud, larceny accounted for 10.6 percent of adult female arrests in 1965 compared to 19.4 percent in 1980. Arrests for fraud rose from 2.3 percent in 1965 to 9.6 percent in 1980. The Uniform Crime Reports for 1981 show that female arrests accounted for 19 percent of all arrests for serious crime, which represent 10 percent of violent crime and 21 percent of property crime. There also appears to be a leveling off or even a decrease in some offense categories (Price and Sokoloff, 1982; Smart, 1979).

Widom and Stewart (1977) concluded that "social disorganization" theories provided more support for explaining increases in female criminality seen during the 1960s and 1970s. Social disorganization theory is based on the concept that disruptive social conditions (be they familial, marital, economic, environmental, or educational disruptions) have some association with crime causation (Bloom, 1969; Sutherland and Cressey, 1974). According to Widom and Stewart, "the Social Disorganization Theory in general, then, would lead to the hypothesis that: Female criminality will increase as a function of rapid social change and social disorganization'' (p. 7). One need only look at the events of the time to find some credence for this perspective—increased school dropout rates, while, at the same time, greater female involvement in post-secondary education; higher population density; employment and economic instability; higher divorce rates and more females becoming heads of households; intensive pushes for civil rights for both minorities and women; and the Vietnam Era.

The following discussion summarizes a number of perspectives on female criminality and incarcerated women, relying extensively on the work of Glick and Neto (1977). Because it represents the most comprehensive study of female offenders and women's prisons at a national level, a profile of incarcerated women is presented.

A Profile of Incarcerated Women

Demographic data provided by Glick and Neto indicate women in prison are young. Two-thirds of those incarcerated were under thirty years of age; the median age for unsentenced women and misdemeanants held in jails was twenty-four. While Blacks comprise approximately 10 percent of the adult female population in the United States, studies indicate about 50 percent of incarcerated women are black (Goetting and Howsen, 1983). Other minorities, Indians and Hispanics, are also over-represented in prison populations. Glick and Neto also found that over half the incarcerated women had received welfare, with whites receiving benefits to a lesser extent than other ethnic groups. It is difficult to develop conclusions from these data, although it should be noted that minorities also tend to be over-represented in men's institutions.

It is important to realize that many minority groups often live within the lower socioeconomic level. Unemployment data during the past several years indicate the highest levels of unemployment are found among minorities, especially the young, both male and female. The 1980 Census revealed that more women were heads of households than ever before. These data may lend some element of credence to economic and social disorganization theories attempting to explain the increase in female criminality as well as the increases in some types of male criminality.

When compared to females in the national population, incarcerated women tend to be less educated. It is important to note that educational attainment levels are generally related to ethnic group status. That is, black women tended to be less educated than white women, and Indians and Hispanics had significantly lower levels of educational attainment when compared to other ethnic groups. Data concerning marital relationships revealed that 60 percent of the women in the Glick and Neto study had been married at least once, but only 20 percent reported they were currently married, and only 10 percent reported living with their husband immediately prior to incarceration. Twenty-seven percent of the women indicated they were single; another 19 percent were reportedly not married but indicated they were living with a man. Finally, 78 percent of the incarcerated women indicated they were separated or divorced, and 7 percent claimed to be widowed.

1975 Census Bureau data indicated incarcerated women tended to have more children than did non-incarcerated women: 2.4 children, compared to an average of 2.0 children for all families reported in the Census Bureau data. A profile of incarcerated mothers (Baunach, 1982) reveals these women tend to be "black more often than white. . ., under 35 years old, most likely divorced or never married and, like most incarcerated women, poorly educated and poorly skilled" (p. 156). Over half of these mothers lived with their children prior to arrest, and Baunach found that over 60 percent of the children had never been separated from their mothers before incarceration. Indications are that separation from their children is one of the most problematic areas for the incarcerated woman.

Sack, Seidler and Thomas (cited in Haley, 1977) point out that men incarcerated for felonies leave behind an average of 1.3 children. Further, men tend to assume a wife or female relative will care for their children. Glick and Neto found that arrangements for care of the children varied with ethnic groups and with the woman's living arrangements immediately prior to incarceration. Blacks were more likely to have their children living with them just prior to incarceration than were other ethnic groups, and they depended upon their own parents or other relatives to care for the children, rather than depending on husbands or non-relatives. The same arrangements were used predominantly by Hispanics; Whites and Indians depended more on husbands or non-relatives, including foster homes. A woman who had been residing with her husband prior to incarceration depended on him or his parents; a woman who had been living alone or with non-relatives was more likely to have her children placed in foster care.

Offense data compiled by Glick and Neto revealed that, while most arrests did not result in incarceration, there were some distinct differences between misdemeanants and felons when comparing arrests and incarcerations. While over half the women were arrested for misdemeanors, only 18 percent were jailed for those offenses. Data revealed that while only seven percent of female arrests were for violent crimes such as murder, manslaughter and armed robbery, 43 percent of incarcerated women had been convicted of violent offenses. The remainder were incarcerated for property offenses such as forgery, fraud, larceny, and drug-related crimes. Data concerning offenders' histories show nearly one-third of the incarcerated women had been arrested before their seventeenth birthday, and one-third had been previously incarcerated in a juvenile institution. Glick and Neto concluded property offenders were most often recidivists, while murderers were most likely to be first-time offenders. Habitual offenders tended to be prostitutes, drug offenders and petty thieves.

While Glick and Neto noted data collection for female offenders is difficult to carry out because of a lack of information, some conclusions can be drawn as to what the data tell us about women offenders. First, there is some evidence the criminal justice system may be discriminatory in the processing of women offenders. Second, family histories of incarcerated women often indicate family instability. Third, women arrested for violent crimes appear to be incarcerated more frequently than those arrested for property offenses.

Educational and Vocational Programs for Women Offenders

Educational and vocational programs for women in prison appear to have been randomly introduced over time, with little consideration to planning and relevancy. The development of programming in women's prisons, much like the development of programming in men's prisons, was initially designed to relieve boredom. Administrators often failed to develop educational and training programs which would prepare women for occupational roles after release from prison. Vocational programs in women's prisons have reinforced traditional sex roles and have typically consisted of cooking, cleaning, sewing, cosmetology and clerical training (Feinman, 1983). Women in the general population, in increasing numbers, are entering industrial positions previously restricted to men. There is little evidence that incarcerated women are being prepared for these opportunities.

A number of issues and problems in this area tend to confuse and complicate the development of educational and vocational programming for women offenders. Some problems reflect institutional constraints, including institutional size, location, budget, and the philosophical perspective of the administrator. All these ultimately affect programming for incarcerated women. In some women's prisons it is impossible to differentiate between those programs designed for vocational training and those designed for prison industries which serve the institution and perhaps other institutions in the system. For example, programs in the area of sewing may consist of an assembly line operation where women participate in very specific tasks. As a result, they do not learn the skills necessary to enhance employment potentials after release. Prison maintenance is often the purpose of the ''program.'' Much of what might be provided may be based on budget constraints and availability of services.

Another issue which tends to complicate the establishment of educational programs is that no two women's prisons are identical, and the educational needs of a particular institution's population may vary greatly from one area of the country to another. Glick and Neto found that educational attainment varied strongly both statewide and geographically, as well as by age and by ethnic group. Overall, about 40% of incarcerated women had at least a high school education, but the percentage of women with a high school education varied from 14% in some states to 50% in others. Therefore, the need for adult basic education and secondary education may be great in some institutions, whereas the need for post-secondary education or vocational programs may be more relevant in other institutions.

Vocational training programs within women's prisons are often criticized for being oriented toward traditional female sex roles (Feinman, 1983). The Glick and Neto study revealed that about two-fifths of the women reported having some vocational training. The majority of such training took place in the community prior to incarceration, and the majority of the training was in the area of traditional female occupations—the same type of training as that provided in the institutions. Several factors may offer some insight and possible explanation for the lack of serious efforts to incorporate non-traditional occupational training into programs for incarcerated women. First, while Glick and Neto found many women did aspire to higher occupations, only a small number (3.3%) aspired to the traditionally male, higher paying crafts. Additionally, a majority of the women saw working as an acceptable female role and supported traditional sex roles. They felt it was important for women to have children and for the man to be the main supporter of the family, with the woman providing secondary financial support.

Similar attitudes toward occupational choice have been reported in other studies. Sorensen (1978) found women incarcerated in a midwestern prison preferred, if given the choice, traditional female occupations or white-collar jobs over the higher paying, male-oriented crafts. In a study of women incarcerated in a southern institution, Fortune (1978) found the women showed the same preference for traditional female occupations as did those studied by Glick and Neto (1977) and Sorensen (1978). Fortune also reported that incarcerated women tended to pursue business-related training at a higher rate than did women in the general population. Further, data revealed those women who had completed high school pursued vocational training more often than did those with lower educational attainment, suggesting that the need for academic education prohibited many women from pursuing vocational training.

In a study conducted with female offenders in a community-based setting in which women were to be trained in non-traditional occupations, Fortune and Balbach (in press) found women participating in the project did not respond well to training for landscaping and horticulture. However, when an adjustment was made in one area of training there was a remarkable change in the women's level of enthusiasm and participation. The change made was to convert landscaping training to flower arranging and greenhouse work involving learning how to grow and pot plants, then having the women teach this skill to mentally deficient adults.

Another complication in providing what is perceived as more beneficial occupational opportunities for women after release is the failure to understand the criminal subcultures of drugs and prostitution. These subcultures provide important financial incentives for the newly released offender. In these subcultures, a woman is accepted and rewarded for those skills which may have contributed to her incarceration in the first place.

The Prison Experience: A Sociological Perspective

Research on the role taking process in women's prisons seems to focus on two areas: the psychological needs of the women involved in the role taking process and the social roles women play in the institutional context. Some theory and research in the area of psychological needs has been labeled sexist. The emphasis has been on the differences between men and women, as reflected in the division of labor in our society. Some theories are based on the premise that men come to prison as husbands, fathers and wage earners, while women come to prison as wives, mothers and homemakers. As a result of this perspective, it has been assumed that the man's position of leadership in the family setting differentiates men from women. Furthermore, it is assumed that this differentiation is reflected in the role structure in the prison setting. The self-concepts of men, then, reflect occupational roles which those men held before incarceration. Women, on the other hand, suffer primarily from separation from their families.

There are two basic theories on the development of prison subcultures. The deprivation theory asserts the prison subculture develops as the result of imprisonment preventing the inmate from fulfilling basic physical and psychological needs which normally would be met outside the prison setting (Sykes, 1958). Importation theory, developed by Irwin and Cressey (1962), suggests the subculture is originated by the values and beliefs the inmates bring into the prison setting when incarcerated. Bowker (1981) explains that both theories provide partial explanations for the development of prison subcultures, but the "evidence seems to indicate that the deprivation theory applies more fully to male institutions than female institutions, while the reverse is true of the importation theory" (p. 411). He argues males are socialized to be more independent and not to rely on others, whereas females are socialized to be more dependent on interpersonal support systems.

Research conducted by Cassel and VanVorst (1961) supports the notion that women bring to the prison identities and self-concepts which are linked to family roles such as wife, mother or daughter. This classic study is supported by subsequent studies (Burkhart, 1973; Chandler, 1973; Lockwood, 1980) which place women in a prison kinship system reflecting traditional family roles. As a result, it has been assumed that women are more dependent on family relationships than are men. This perspective suggests that women subordinate themselves to the economic interests of the husband and thereby tend to accept a limited range of activity.

Dependency is then continually reinforced, contributing to further power differentials. As a result, women tend to utilize physical attractiveness and seductivity as techniques in meeting needs and in manipulating authority structures. The social behavior of women in prison reflects psychological deprivation. Cassel and VanVorst (1961) and Heffernan (1972) found that psychological deprivation manifests itself in the taking of argot roles in the prison setting. Cassel and VanVorst have identified three types of personal needs which women bring to prison and which have a significant impact on their behavior during the incarceration process.

The first of these needs is "affectional starvation," which Cassel and VanVorst define as "the need for ego status among a very small group of intimate peers and some degree of sympathetic understanding for their personal problems by such intimate friends" (p. 28). The second need reflects the exaggeration of certain symbolic needs. That is, incarcerated women may engage in behaviors which are mutually advantageous and provide symbolic satisfaction to both partners in the relationship. The need to suckle a baby, for example, may manifest itself in the form of an intimate relationship, which provides symbolic satisfaction but which would not be socially approved outside the prison walls. Finally, the need for psycho-sexual gratification is identified as a "need for continuous interaction with the male member of the species or some surrogate symbol" (p. 28).

Cassel and VanVorst also identified a number of argot roles which exist in the institutional context and which are adopted to lessen the impact of psychological deprivation. "Argot" is a special language developed by a specific group to express the group's unique experiences. By using the special language of the prison, the inmate demonstrates allegiance to the inmate subculture which reflects the conflicts and tensions in prison. When this special language is applied to a pattern of behavior, the result is what has come to be referred to as an "argot role" (Sykes, 1958). Argot roles in women's prisons include the "femme," the female role in the homosexual relationship and the "butch," the male role in the homosexual relationship. Role determination in these homosexual relationships is based on the degree of dependence the incarcerated woman experiences. The greater the degree of dependence, the greater the likelihood that the woman will play the role of "femme." In male institutions, what is referred to as "homosexual" behavior is often coerced. Violent sexual activity is usually conducted for power or for economic transactions. In female institutions, "homosexual" behavior is more in the context of a loving relationship based on interpersonal desire for love, as opposed to overt sexual activity (Bowker, 1981).

Heffernan (1972) has identified three argot role adaptations. Each argot role carries major goal orientations and characteristics. In characterizing the "square," Heffernan notes adaptation to this role is largely concerned with the preservation of "squareness." This involves the maintenance of a conventional way of life while incarcerated. The "life" role is characterized by the conscious belief that prison has become a way of life. The prison is seen as a world separate and distinct from the "real" world, with a unique set of social norms, values and interaction patterns. The "life" role is the antithesis of the "square" role. Adaptation to the "life" role involves a conscious effort to break prison rules for personal gain, without regard to the costs of rule violation. The third role identified by Heffernan is that of the "cool." Women playing the "cool" role stay out of trouble and, at the same time, acquire the amenities that make for a more pleasant prison life. These women are exceptionally manipulative in the prison setting, yet they maintain an orientation external to the institution. Confinement is considered a temporary experience in the life cycle.

The data collected through the research efforts cited earlier clearly support the development of a pseudo-family in the prison setting, with relationships quite similar to those found in the traditional American nuclear family. Roles of "wife," "daddy," "husband," "brother," and "sister" are the most common. It is important to note these roles and relationships emerge as a result of the need to adapt to the deprivation of incarceration. A single-sex prison in which female inmates are deprived of interaction with family members and men facilitates the development of homosexual relationships in which traditional roles can be played and which meet psychological needs.

Culbertson and Paddock (1980) completed a study at the correctional facility for women in Illinois. In the data collection process, women were observed as they came to the dining areas from their respective living units. It was noted that "families" sat together, and each "family" had a table which was considered its own. "Husbands" sat at the head of the table, while other "family members" took their respective places. "Femmes," "grandmothers," and "children" showed respect to the "husband" by sharing their food. Newly incarcerated women were isolated and ignored because they had not yet become "family" members. It was clear that if an incarcerated woman was to enjoy the benefits of interpersonal communication, she could only participate in accord with the subcultural norms previously identified.

Giallombardo (1966) utilized a different perspective in the examination of the roles incarcerated women play in the institutional setting. In addition to pseudo-family roles, Giallombardo found that roles reflect reactions of peers, and, over time, the labeling process creates a social system for inmates and staff. Roles define certain behaviors as a part of the interaction process in the prison setting. For example, the role of "snitch" reflects disloyalty to other women and has serious implications for the role-player. Some "snitches" engage in the behavior routinely, while others are more sporadic. Motivation for this behavior is often related to the need to settle an economic dispute or homosexual conflict. One who systematically provides custody staff with information in the role of "snitch" is referred to as the "good girl" by staff who use the needed information to control behavior. Anonymous "snitching" is rare. While "snitching" occasionally results in violence, there may be other negative sanctions. One sanction is "panning" or gossiping about the inmate when she is not present. Another sanction is "signifying," which is done in the inmate's presence and which takes the form of a degradation ceremony.

The role of "inmate cop" is played by one who is in a position of authority because of her work assignment. Inmates resent taking orders from other inmates; therefore, the "inmate cop" is excluded from a number of important relationships. Giallombardo's (1966) argot role of "square" is not totally dissimilar from the role of "square" described by Heffernan (1972). Giallombardo's "square" is oriented toward the prison administration. There are both "cube squares" and "hip squares." The "cube square" tends to be quite loyal to prison officials, while the "hip square" is somewhat sympathetic to the inmate culture. The "jive bitch" is a troublemaker whose deviance is a deliberate, calculated strategy to cause conflict in the prison setting. The "jive bitch" stands in contrast to the "rap buddy," one with whom an inmate finds herself compatible because personal communications can be considered confidential. A similar role is that of the "homey," a person who comes from the same community as another inmate and who is considered to be as close as a "blood" relation. There is a bond of reciprocity in this relationship which includes mutual aid but generally excludes homosexual demands.

Inmates in women's prisons can obtain items such as extra cigarettes, contraband, candy and clothing through the "connect." The "connect" is an inmate who has a "good job" and can deliver valued information or scarce goods. The "booster," on the other hand, is a thief whose behavior consists solely of stealing from institutional supplies. "Petty boosters" are small time thieves and are differentiated from "boosters" who steal regularly and take items of considerable value. The "pinner" is a lookout who is placed as a sentry in key locations to prevent other inmates and institutional staff from learning about illicit activities such as homosexuality. A "pinner" is an admired person who is trusted and can tolerate institutional pressure without disclosing information. Bowker (1981) presents two reasons for these types of roles in both male and female institutions. First, in both institutions certain elements are characterized by a considerable opposition to staff. Second, there are "sub rosa" economic structures, although less developed in female institutions, which develop as a means for the inmates to acquire desirable, hard to obtain, or illegal commodities.

Giallombardo (1966) also identified a number of homosexual roles. A "penitentiary turnout" turns to homosexuality in the prison context because heterosexual relationships are not available. The "lesbian" prefers homosexual relationships in the free community and has little difficulty adapting to the single-sex society of the women's prison. The "femme" or "mommy," the female role in the homosexual relationship, is a role most women prefer to play. The "stud broad" or "daddy" is the male role in the homosexual relationship. The "stud broad" has considerable prestige in the prison setting because she provides a masculine image and plays the male role. Research in the women's prison in Illinois (Culbertson and Paddock, 1980) revealed a number of "stud broad" role types. These role types were characterized by distinctly male-looking hair styles parted to one side and cropped in the back. A number of women playing the "stud broad" role smoked pipes and wore slacks and shirts. On closer observation, one could see that these women had strapped their breasts back in such a way as to negate any exposure of their busts. On a number of occasions, women playing the role of "stud broad" were referred to as the "main man around here." The role is difficult to sustain over long periods of time because the stud is expected to internalize external symbols of sex differentiation and incorporate behaviors which are socially expected of males. It is interesting to note that some women identified as "stud broads" had made written requests for sex change operations.

When a "stud" and a "femme" establish a homosexual relationship, they are said to be "making it" or "being tight." In the inmate subculture they are recognized as "married," a "sincere" relationship based on romantic love. The relationship is in contrast to that which exists between the "commissary hustler" and the "trick." The "commissary hustler" may establish a "sincere" relationship in her cottage or living unit, but she also has a number of relationships with "tricks" for economic reasons. The "chippie" role is unique in that the "chippie" exploits each situation for its unique possibilities, be they sexual or economic. She does not establish "sincere" relationships, and she is often seen as a prison prostitute. Finally, the role of "cherry" is reserved for the uncommitted woman who has not been initiated into a homosexual relationship and is generally a young, first offender.

It is important that further research be developed to increase our understanding of female criminality, inmate subcultures and women's prisons. It is clear that family-type roles found in women's prisons generally do not exist in men's prisons, although there is considerable homosexuality in those institutions. Also, the level of violence in women's prisons is less than that in men's prisons. At the same time, we cannot assume that women's prisons constitute a static environment. As societal perspectives on women continue to change, we can anticipate that there will be changes in inmate subcultures. At the same time, it is important to understand argot roles in women's prisons and the features of the inmate subculture. If a woman is to survive incarceration, both physically and psychologically, it is important that she develop interpersonal relationships in the prison setting. These relationships and the roles she plays are determined by the social norms and rules of the prison community. In this regard, the prison community is a unique and artificial environment. Women adjust to the demands of this environment in ways that may shock the unknowing observer. Adjustments made by these women reflect the realities of prison life.

Bibliography

Adler, F. *Sisters in Crime*, Prospect Heights, IL: Waveland Press, Inc., 1975, reissued 1985.

Baunach, P.J. "You Can't Be a Mother and Be in Prison . . . Can You? Impacts of the Mother-Child Separation. "In *The Criminal Justice System and Women: Women Offenders/Victims/Workers*. B.R. Price and N. J. Sokoloff (Eds.). New York: Clark Boardman, 1982.

Bloom, B.L. "A Census Track Analysis of Socially Deviant Behaviors," *Multivariate Behavioral Research*. 1966, 1, 307-320.

Bowker, L.H. "Gender Differences in Prisoner Subcultures." In *Women and Crime in America*, Bowker, L.H. (Ed.). New York: Macmillan, 1981.

Burkhart, K.W. *Women in Prison*. New York: Doubleday, 1973.

Cassel, R.N. and VanVorst, R.B. "Psychological Needs of Women in a Correctional Institution.: *American Journal of Corrections*. 1961, 23, 22-24.

Chandler, E.W. *Women in Prison*. Indianapolis: Bobbs-Merrill, 1973,

Culbertson, R.G. and Paddock, A.L. "The Self Concept of Incarcerated Women and the Relationship to Argot Roles." Paper presented at the Annual Meeting of the Academy of Criminal Justice Sciences, Oklahoma City, OK, March, 1980.

Feinman, C. "Sex Role Stereotypes and Justice for Women," *Crime and Delinquency*, January 1979, pp. 87-94.

Feinman, C. *Women in the Criminal Justice System*. New York: Praeger, 1980.

Feinman, C. "An Historical Overview of the Treatment of Incarcerated Woman: Myths and Realities of Rehabilitation," *The Prison Journal*, Autumn-Winter, 1983, pp. 12-24.

Fortune, E.P. "Educational and Vocational Profiles of Female Offenders Incarcerated in a Southern Correctional Institution." Paper presented at the Annual Meeting of the American Society of Criminology, Dallas, TX, November, 1978.

Fortune, E.P. and Balbach, M. "Project MET: A Community Based Educational Program for Women Offenders." In *The Changing Roles of Women in the Criminal Justice System* by I.L. Moyer. Prospect Heights, IL: Waveland Press, Inc., 1985.

Giallombardo, R. *Society of Women: A Study of Women's Prison*. New York: John Wiley and Sons, 1966.

Glick, R.M. and Neto, V.V. *National Study of Women's Correctional Programs*. Washington, DC: U.S. Government Printing Office, 1977.

Goetting, A. and Howsen, R.M. "Women in Prison: A Profile," *The Prison Journal*, Autumn-Winter, 1983, pp. 27-46.

Haley, K. "Mothers Behind Bars: A Look at the Parental Rights of Incarcerated Women," *New England Journal of Prison Law*. Fall, 1977, 4, 141-155.

Heffernan, E. *Making it in Prison*. New York: John Wiley and Sons, 1972.

Irwin, J. and Cressey, D. "Thieves, Convicts and the Inmate Culture," *Social Problems*. Fall, 1962, 10, 142-155.

Klein, D. "The Etiology of Female Crime: A Review of Literature," *Crime and Social Justice: Issues in Criminology*. Fall, 1973, 3-30.

Lockwood, D. *Prison Sexual Violence*. New York: Elsevier, 1980.

Lombroso, C. and Ferrero, W. *The Female Offender*. New York: The Wisdom Library, 1958.

Price, B.R. and Sokoloff, N.J. (Eds.). *The Criminal Justice System and Women: Women Offenders/Victims/Workers*. New York: Clark Boardman, 1982.

Simon, R.J. "The Contemporary Woman and Crime," *Crime and Delinquency Issues*. Rockville, MD: National Institute of Mental Health, Center for Studies of Crime and Delinquency, 1975.

Smart, C. "The New Female Offender: Reality or Myth?" *British Journal of Criminology*. 1979, 19:1, 50-59.

Smith, A.D. *Women in Prison*. London: Stevens, 1962.

Smith, A.D. "Penal Policy and the Woman Offender." *The Sociological Review*. Monograph 9. Sociological Studies in the British Penal Services, University of Keele Press, 1965.

Sorensen, V. *Women in Prison — Educational and Vocational Needs Assessment*. Master's Thesis, Governor's State University, 1978.

Steffensmeier, D.J. "Trends in Female Crime: It's Still a Man's World." In *The Criminal Justice System and Women: Women Offenders/Victims/Workers*, B.R. Price and N.J. Sokoloff (Eds.). New York: Clark Boardman, 1982.

Sutherland, E.H. and Cressey, D.R. *Criminology*. Philadelphia: Lippincott, 1974.

Sykes, G. *The Society of Captives: A Study of A Maximum Security Prison*. Princeton, NJ: Princeton University Press, 1958.

U.S. Department of Justice. *Crime in the United States, 1981*. Uniform Crime Reports. Washington, DC: U.S. Government Printing Office, 1982.

Widom, C.S. and Stewart, A.J. "Female Criminality and the Changing Status of Women." Paper presented at the Annual Meeting of the American Society of Criminology, Atlanta, GA, November, 1977.

8

The Victimization of Prisoners by Staff Members

Lee H. Bowker

The documentation on staff-prisoner victimization in America's prisons is extensive but shallow. Most of this material describes victimization in prisons for men, with a smaller amount of documentation for institutions containing delinquent boys and very little information on staff-prisoner victimization in institutions for females. The treatment of the subject is superficial in that incidents tend to be mentioned only in passing (or as part of a polemical piece of writing), and they are not presented or analyzed in any great detail. Like other prison victimization reports, they tend to be recorded factually and not related to any general theoretical framework. Another general problem with documentation on staff-prisoner victimization is that the quality of the reporting of incidents is often difficult to determine. Reports are almost always limited to the views of one of the participants or observers, with no corroboration from others. Even when reports are written by social scientists, they usually consist of second- and third-person accounts derived from interviews rather than direct observation by the scientists.

Source: Reprinted by permission of the publisher from Chapter Seven by Lee H. Bowker, *Prison Victimization*, 101-127. Copyright 1980 by Elsevier Science Publishing Co., Inc.

Material on the victimization of prisoners by staff members is also beset by definitional problems. How does one separate the victimization of prisoners by individual staff members from the "fair" application of institutional policies by correctional officers?

This problem is particularly severe when dealing with historical material for which institutional standards of appropriate treatment are not available. Victimization is generally thought of as consisting of acts committed by individuals and groups that go beyond the conditions imposed upon prisoners by official institutional policies and state laws. In the modern prison, this definitional problem is not such a serious one because the official policies of the state and federal correctional systems are generally quite humane. Excessively victimizing behavior by staff members is usually clearly against the regulations of the institution. This is not the same as saying that offenders against these institutional regulations will be punished. In many correctional systems, it is probable that a careful staff member can engage in extensive victimizing behavior toward prisoners before he or she will be officially reprimanded for it. Even then, it is extremely unlikely that a staff member will ever be terminated for such behavior.

Definitional problems still exist in those jurisdictions that continue to use physically harsh means of punishing prisoners, and also in any correctional institutions where "goon squads" are used. The goon squads are groups of physically powerful correctional officers who "enjoy a good fight" and who are called upon to rush to any area of the prison where it is felt that muscle power will restore the status quo. If a prisoner is ripping up things in his cell and refuses to be quiet, the goon squad may be called and three or four of these correctional officers will forcibly quiet him, administering a number of damaging blows to the head and body. If there is a fight between two prisoners, the goon squad may break it up. Should a prisoner refuse to report to the hospital when he is ordered to do so, he may be dragged from his cell and deposited in the hospital waiting room. Mentally ill prisoners who are acting out are almost always initially dealt with by goon squads rather than by qualified therapeutic personnel or even by orderlies under the direction of such personnel. It is difficult to draw the line between the necessary application of force where human life or the social order are extensively threatened, and the misuse of violence by goon squad members.

Aside from goon squads and the few states that officially permit physically harsh means of punishment, we can define the behavior of a correctional officer as victimizing or nonvictimizing by comparing questionable incidents with the body of official regulations and policies that is usually summarized in a handbook distributed to all correctional officers. If the behavior goes beyond the regulations and policies, then it is victimizing. If it does not, then it is difficult to accuse the officer of being an aggressor in all but the most extreme cases.

However clear we may be able to make the definition of victimization by line staff members, there is no way to create a similarly precise definition for wardens and other top-level correctional administrators. When they implement a policy or regulation that is victimizing or potentially victimizing, they must take responsibility for having created a definition of the situation within which correctional officers may carry out what amounts to victimizing behavior as they perform their duties in conformance with institutional regulations. Few of these regulations are proclaimed by correctional administrators simply out of sadism. Instead, these administrators balance one evil against another, and decide to implement a potentially victimizing regulation because they feel that this regultion will solve more problems than it creates. This means that, except for cases at the periphery of reasonable judgment, we cannot easily judge an administrative action to be victimizing unless we know the rationale behind that action and have some objective set of data about conditions in the institution that informed the administrative decision. Since this kind of information is almost never available, we are left with a murky situation in which administrative responsibility for prisoner victimization can usually be assigned in only the most tentative fashion. With these qualifications in mind, we will proceed to examine the documentation on staff-prisoner victimization in correctional institutions.

Physical Victimization

However unpleasant prisons may be today, historical materials make it clear that they were infinitely worse in the past. Clemmer tells us that it was once common for correctional officers to assault prisoners with clubs and their fists, but by the late 1930s, perhaps in response to a new state law, the frequency of these attacks had declined to the point at which they occurred "only rarely."[1] Conley shows how the emphasis on custody and industrial productivity encouraged brutality and corruption in the Oklahoma prison system from the early 1900s through the 1960s. In addition to the usual beatings, officers used deliberate tortures such as forcing the men to eat in the hot sun during the summer when shade was nearby and handcuffing prisoners to the bars in their cells (with knotted rags in their mouths) so that when their legs collapsed, their body was suspended only by the handcuffs. When wardens ordered that physical victimization of prisoners by correctional officers be suspended, these officers adapted by moving to techniques of psychological victimization.[2]

The decrease in brutality by correctional officers that Clemmer describes as having occurred in Illinois in the 1930s did not reach some southern prisons until the 1970s. The mistreatment of prisoners in the Arkansas prison system has been documented in books such as *Killing Time, Life in the Arkansas Penitentiary*[3] and *Inside Prison U.S.A.*[4] The latter includes a description of the infamous "Tucker telephone," as well as blow-by-blow accounts of beatings. In the Tucker telephone, a naked prisoner was strapped to a table and electrodes were attached to his big toe and his penis. Electrical charges were then sent through his body which, in "long distance calls," were timed to cease just before the prisoner became unconscious. Murton and Hyams state that in some cases, "the sustained current not only caused the inmate to lose consciousness but resulted in irreparable damage to his testicles. Some men were literally driven out of their minds."[5] In testimony under oath, a 15-year-old prisoner accused the superintendent of an Arkansas institution of kicking and hitting him in the back and stomach while another staff member held him on the ground. The superintendent did not confirm this allegation, but he admitted driving a truck at 40 miles per hour with three prisoners draped over the hood and then jamming on the brakes to catapult them to the ground as a unique method of punishment.[6]

Reports from Louisiana,[7] Mississippi,[8] Virginia[9] and Florida[10] confirm that the habitual mistreatment of prisoners is not limited to the Arkansas prison system. The brutalization of prisoners by correctional officers outside of the south seems to be less extensive and also less statistically innovative. Some of the incidents reported from northern prisons make little sense, such as the prisoner who was killed by the use of chemical gassing weapons when he was locked in a solitary security cell[11] or the three prisoners who were handcuffed to overhead pipes as punishment for being too "noisy" during sleeping hours.[12] Most of the incidents reported from these facilities seem to be associated with unusual occurrences such as prison riots, protests and punitive transfers. These incidents all involve some sort of prisoner challenge to the authority of prison staff members, and the challenge is sometimes met with violence as a way of reestablishing administrative authority. For example, prisoners being transferred from one Ohio penitentiary to another after a period of considerable unrest alleged severe guard brutality. One prisoner asserted that he was handcuffed and chained, taken into a bus, and then beaten on the head by a correctional officer with a blackjack and left unconscious. Another prisoner alleged that while handcuffed, he was dragged into the bus where he suffered kicks and other blows about the back, legs, hips and groin. The worst incident described by the prisoners told the story of a prisoner who first had Mace sprayed in his face while he was still in his cell, and then was beaten with chains, blackjacks and fists by five correctional officers who then spit on him, slammed his head against the cell door, and took him to the bus, where he was subjected to further assault.[13]

When 500 prisoners at the Pendleton Reformatory in Indiana refused to return to their cells on a winter day in 1972, the correctional officers used tear gas and shotguns to force them back. None of the prisoners was shot because the shotguns were discharged into the air rather than at the prisoners. This change in policy was probably due to an earlier incident at the Reformatory in which "46 men [prisoners] were wounded, many critically, from shots in the head, in the back, through the chest, in the legs, feet, thigh, through the groin, in the side — in fact some who tried to throw up their hands in the traditional gesture of surrender had their hands shattered and are minus fingers."[14] In a related incident, a group of black prisoners refused to return to their cells, and one black prisoner raised his hand in the black power salute. A guard was heard to say, "That one is mine!" and the young man was fatally riddled with five bullets. Testimony before the United States Senate later revealed that approximately 50% of the correctional officers involved in the incident belonged to the Ku Klux Klan.[15]

Excessive violence used during a prisoner altercation may not be legitimate, but it is understandable. There are few parents who have not gone too far in punishing their children when they were angry. A more serious problem occurs when prisoners are brutalized for an extended period of time after a riot as punishment for having participated. A classic example of this occurred after the disaster at Attica in New York. Correctional administrators, in violation of a court order, refused to admit a group of doctors and lawyers to the prison as observers on the pretext that they needed to have an opportunity to assess the prison's condition. During the time that the observers were deliberately excluded, extreme violence occurred, involving the vanquished prisoners. The Second Circuit Federal Court of Appeals finally issued an injunction against further reprisals and physical abuse and found that in the four days beginning with the recapture of Attica, the state troopers and correctional personnel struck, prodded and assaulted injured prisoners, some of whom were on stretchers. Other prisoners were stripped naked and then forced to run between lines of correctional officers who beat them with clubs, spat upon them, burned them with matches, and poked them in the genitals — among other things.[16]

The Attica reprisals are well documented, but Toch is generally skeptical of other prisoner reports of organized brutality by correctional officers. He takes a different approach, looking at official records of officer-prisoner violence in New York State for the year 1973. A total of 386 incidents were recorded in the official file, and these involved 547 prisoners and 1,288 employees. The relative number of officers and prisoners in these incidents is meaningful in itself in that it indicates the more than two-to-one odds that prisoners face in these altercations. One might argue that with odds such as these, there is little excuse for causing excessive injury to the prisoners. In fact, there were no injuries at all in one-third of the reports. The most common action cited was a "hold," which included such maneuvers as half-nelsons, pulls and choking. Toch believes that correctional officer violence is routinely justified by formulas similar to those used to justify police brutality, and that it is really based on correctional officer subcultural norms favoring violence against prisoners. These norms develop because of the pervasive fear of prisoners that is part of the correctional officer subculture. This same subcultural phenomenon makes it almost impossible to convince a correctional officer to testify against one of his fellow employees, so corroborating testimony is rarely obtained in investigations of officer brutality, except from other prisoners. Toch also links officer violence to official regulations that forbid the forming of meaningful inter-personal relationships between officers and prisoners. Such regulations leave officers with only naked force as a way of enforcing order and also create what Toch characterizes as a "trench warfare climate" in prisons.[17] Whether one concentrates on the day-to-day routinized violence or the extreme brutality that is sometimes associated with prison disturbances and transfers, the conclusion is the same. It is that although most correctional officers in most prisons do not engage in any form of brutality and are only concerned with defending themselves against attack, there are enough officers who have values and beliefs that favor brutality and enough incidents that seem to require some sort of a show of force by officers so that there is a steady stream of minor unnecessary or excessive acts of violence in America's prisons, punctuated by occasional acts in which officers go far beyond any reasonable standard of the application of necessary force.

If an officer who favors the brutalization of prisoners is careful, he or she can limit the application of excessive force to incidents that fit the prison's definition of the appropriate use of force to maintain prison discipline or prevent escapes. Complaints lodged against such a correctional officer will invariably be dismissed by the warden who will rule that the violence was appropriately applied within institutional regulations. In fact, it may be claimed that had officers not used violence in the incident, they would have been delinquent in the performance of stated duties and subject to dismissal. This kind of rationale also makes it difficult for a prisoner to receive a fair hearing in court, where the warden's testimony carries considerable weight with judges and juries. As an example of this, I was close to a case in which a mentally ill prisoner was climbing a fence separating two prison yards and was fatally shot in the head by a prison officer who had commanded him to stop. The officer, who was stationed in a tower, probably was unaware of the mental condition of the prisoner and might not have taken that into account in any case. More importantly, he did not need to shoot the prisoner, as going from one prison yard to another does not constitute a risk of escape. Since the prisoner was unarmed, a shot in the leg rather than the head would have been more than sufficient even had he been climbing a fence on the boundary of the prison compound. The warden chose to ignore these arguments and immediately supported the action of the officer, saying that it was appropriate and required by institutional regulations. The local officials outside of the prison also accepted the judgment of the warden and declined prosecution in the case. There is nothing more serious than murder, and if this can be so easily justified by correctional officials one can appreciate the wide variety of possibly victimizing acts that are similarly justified annually in the United States.

The Involvement of Correctional Officers in Sexual Aggression

There are three ways that correctional officers can be involved in sexual aggression against prisoners. The first is to carry out the aggression themselves. This is occasionally hinted at, but has been well documented only for isolated cases that involved female and adolescent male victims. The second type of involvement is for correctional officers to permit a sexual attack in their presence and then to enjoy the spectacle. Although occasionally mentioned in passing, the best example of this sort of behavior in the literature comes from an institution for the retarded rather than from a prison.[18] The final form of correctional officer involvement in sexual attacks on prisoners is passive participation by deliberately failing to carry out one's custodial responsibilities. In this behavior, the officer does not adequately control an area or deliberately stays away from a site in which it is known that sexual assaults regularly occur. Although seemingly less severe than the first two forms of staff participation in sexual assaults, this third type is the most important because its occurrence is much more common than the first two types. As Sagarin and MacNamara conclude, prison rapes hardly seem possible "without the connivance, or at least deliberate inattention, of prison authorities.[19]

Cole[20] and Wooden[21] cite numerous examples of sexual assaults on juveniles by correctional officers. Boys and girls may be forced to submit to sexual advances by threats of violence or they may be manipulated to cooperate by promises of favors. Bartollas et al. quote a youthful prisoner:

> He had intercourse with me about every two weeks. I did not want to do it, but he talked about getting me out of [here] faster and I wanted to get out because I had been here a long time. I think the reason I did it was I just came back from AWOL and I thought I had a long time to go so I thought I would get out of here.[22]

These authors also show how a staff member can subtly approach the topic of participation in sexual relations with a prisoner so that they can not be quoted as having made a direct overture or threat. Another prisoner that they interviewed told them how a staff member began to talk to him about people they knew in common and then switched to the prisoner's homosexuality in what appeared at first to be an attempt to help him. Then the staff member began to talk about the sexual acts that he enjoyed himself and linked that to sexual acts that the prisoner enjoyed. At this point it was clear to the prisoner that he was being manipulated into committing homosexual acts although the staff member had not made a specific quotable overture.[23]

The occasional reports of sexual assaults carried out against girls and women by jailers, sheriffs, deputies and other correctional officials[24] were taken more seriously after the national publicity given to the case of Joanne Little.[25] Like many other county jails and understaffed correctional facilities, the Beaufort County Jail in North Carolina employed no female staff members to care for its occasional female prisoners. The autopsy report of the Beaufort County Medical Examiner made clear that the 62-year-old jailer had been killed by Ms. Little while he was forcing her to engage in sexual relations with him. Little stabbed him seven times with an icepick and then escaped, only to turn herself in to the police at a later date.[26] It is unlikely that Little was the first prisoner to be sexually approached by this jailer. Unfortunately, professional standards in rural local jails are so variable and documentation so completely lacking that it is impossible to make even "a ball park estimate" of the national incidence of this form of sexual victimization.

The only documented case of a correctional staff member forcing prisoners to engage in sexual behavior with one another is contained in Cole's book, *Our Children's Keepers*. He quotes a 15-year-old boy as saying that two counselors forced a friend of his to go into another room and have sexual intercourse with a known homosexual prisoner. When the friend refused to do so, he was taken into another room and beaten. The counselors then came out and brought in the homosexual prisoner, following which the two prisoners had sexual relations for the amusement of the counselors. In the words of the observer, "They get a kick out of somebody going through it — then they make fun of him in front of everybody else."[27] We cannot give too much credence to this report in view of the way in which it was obtained. It is included here merely as an example of how such events may occur in correctional institutions.

The contribution to sexual assaults between prisoners that is made by correctional officers who fail to carry out adequately their duties is legendary. There are relatively few prisons that are so poorly constructed and so greatly understaffed that it is absolutely impossible for staff members to keep prisoners under sufficient surveillance to prohibit sexual aggression. When Davis asked 26 correctional employees to take polygraph tests, 25 refused, presumably because they felt they were guilty of failing to carry out their assigned duties in situations that led directly to the sexual assault of prisoners in documented cases. Davis describes sexual assaults that were made possible because the officers in charge did not adequately patrol their areas. It is easy for skeptics to dismiss many of the reports of correctional officer complicity in prisoner sexual assaults, but the kind of documentation provided by Davis convinces us of this complicity beyond the shadow of a doubt. In one incident, a prisoner was reported as having screamed for over an hour while he was being gang-raped in his cell within hearing distance of a correctional officer who not only ignored the screams but who laughed at the victim afterward. Prisoners who reported this incident passed polygraph examinations while the accused officer refused to take the test.[28]

Extreme examples of officer involvement in inmate sexual behavior include a southern institution in which a prisoner could buy a homosexual partner from a correctional officer or even from the deputy warden[29] and the use of homosexual prisoners as "gifts" from staff members to prisoner leaders who helped them keep the institution quiet.[30] One ex-prisoner claims to have been presented to "an entire wing of the prison, as a bonus to the convicts for their good behavior. In this wing, any prisoner who wanted his services, at any time and for any purposes, was given it; the guards opened doors, passed him from one cell to another, provided lubricants, permitted an orgy of simultaneous oral and anal entry, and even arranged privacy."[31]

It is easy to see why some authors place heavy blame on correctional officers for their contribution to prison sexual assaults.[32] The only objective observer who defends them is Lockwood, who feels that the combination of sexually aggressive prisoners, overcrowded conditions, management and program needs that require prisoners to intermingle, and legal limitations imposed by the courts creates a situation in which the ability of correctional officers to prevent sexual victimization is sharply attenuated.[33]

Brutality in Children's Institutions

Professional standards in institutions for delinquent youth appear to be much more variable than professional standards in state correctional systems for adults. Although there are many exemplary institutions in which not even the slightest hint of staff brutality would ever be tolerated, these exist close by other institutions in which a wide range of staff aggression toward prisoners is not only tolerated but encouraged. It is impossible to estimate accurately a national rate of staff-prisoner victimization in juvenile institutions, but the impression one gets from reading the literature is that this form of victimization is probably more prevalent in juvenile institutions than in adult institutions. Cole tells about a staff member in a Louisiana institution who assaulted prisoners with a hosepipe and big sticks. The staff member combined the beatings with economic victimization when he extracted a portion of all the gifts received by prisoners through the mail.[34] Quoting descriptions of beatings derived from accounts collected by James,[35] Chase concludes that there are more American children being mistreated in institutions than in their homes.[36] The severity of this indictment is accentuated by the most recent report on American child abuse, which presents 507,494 incidents of child abuse reported to official agencies in 1977, a reporting rate of 2.3 cases per 1,000 population.[37]

The John Howard Association's report on the Illinois Youth Centers at St. Charles and Geneva provides rare detail on the physical abuse of youngsters by staff members. Of 46 youths between the ages of 14 and 19 whom they interviewed at St. Charles, 23 stated that they had been slapped, kicked, punched, had their arms twisted or were struck with an object by a staff member. About half of the youths stated that they had witnessed staff members committing such acts against other youngsters. Many of the staff members also admitted the use of extensive corporal punishment, and there were several staff members who were consistently named as physical abusers of children. One staff member admitted striking youngsters on different occasions with a stick, a fishing pole and his hands. These situations did not involve the use of necessary restraint to subdue a youth who was attacking a staff member or another youth. Instead, it was a matter of general brutality when staff members were in bad moods.[38] This kind of grutuitous punishment differs in degree, but not in kind, from the vicious brutality suffered by youngsters in reformatories more than a century ago.[39]

Reports of beating of institutionalized children are from all parts of the nation, from the deep south[40] to the relatively well-funded institutions that are found in Massachusetts. A Harvard student posing as a delinquent at a Massachusetts institution observed an incident in which a youngster's hair was used to mop up urine from the floor.[41] Feld showed that staff brutality was higher in custody-oriented institutions than in treatment-oriented institutions. The former institutions were characterized by acts such as choking and physical beatings, whereas the more benign treatment-oriented staff members limited themselves to beatings with a plastic baseball bat and other minor physical punishments.[42]

The most detailed analysis of staff-prisoner victimization in juvenile institutions was carried out by Bartollas et al. in their study of an Ohio reformatory. A number of forms of staff-prisoner victimization at this institution were actually supported by the informal staff normative code, a code analogous to the convict code among the prisoners. The "acceptable" forms of staff exploitation were psychological and social in nature, although physical victimization was not supported by the staff normative code. For example, direct physical brutality was defined as unacceptable when a leader was intoxicated, upset because of a personal problem, using weapons against the youth or deliberately trying to seriously injure a youngster. It was also unacceptable to encourage directly (as opposed to passively) the victimization of one prisoner by another, to aid escapes (which led to increased punishment for the escapee when he was caught), and to sexually exploit the boys for one's own pleasure. The tie-in of homosexual gratification to rewards such as cigarettes, protection from peers, or promise of early release was defined as particularly offensive behavior under the staff normative code and was dealt with informally by staff members whenever a rumor about sexual exploitation was substantiated. Informal sanctions usually led to the resignation of the offending staff member.[43]

Psychological Victimization

We have already mentioned Conley's observation that correctional officers in the Oklahoma State Penitentiary who were temporarily forbidden to physically brutalize prisoners switched to psychological forms of victimization. For example, officers conducting shakedowns would deliberately break open little boxes that contained a prisoner's personal trinkets instead of asking him for the key. They would also harass the prisoners by "making noise in the cell house so they couldn't sleep, refusing personal requests, failing to respond to an inmate's call for help if he was ill or a victim of an assault, and otherwise constantly hounding the individuals."[44] These forms of psychological victimization can be perpetrated on individual prisoners who have been marked for special mistreatment or on all prisoners as a matter of personal policy.

The author once observed the classic example of psychological victimization in which the sergeant placed letters to a prisoner where the prisoner could see them but not reach them, and then claimed that there were no letters for that prisoner. The prisoner became quite agitated as a result and eventually developed considerable paranoia about his mail. In each incident, the officer tormented him throughout the day and then gave him the letters in the evening saying that he had just discovered them. Eventually, the prisoner lost control completely and was cited for a disciplinary infraction, which may well have been the officer's goal in the manipulation. A more elegant form of the game is described by Heise as "The Therapeutic 'No.'" In this game, staff members deliberately say "no" to a prisoner who has come with a legitimate request in an attempt to force an explosive or angry response.[45]

A very sophisticated form of the psychological victimization of prisoners by staff members occurs when correctional officers use their special knowledge of the outside world to heighten prisoner anxieties about their loved ones, their release date or other subjects of paramount importance. An example of this, reported from a women's institution, involved a prisoner whose son was in foster care while she was incarcerated. The officer she worked for would wait until she was within hearing distance and then begin a conversation with a second correctional officer about how commonly foster children were mistreated. These discussions went on endlessly, concentrating on subjects such as starvation, corporal punishment and sexual victimization. The prisoner was not allowed to speak, nor could she report the incidents to the administration. How could she prove that the officers were deliberately practicing psychological victimization against her? These incidents, along with the mishandling of a medical condition by the prison physician, almost agitated her enough to attempt an escape.[46]

Staff members are also privy to another source of potentially victimizing information about prisoners—the data in their central files. Information in these files contains not only the complete criminal records of prisoners but also material from social investigations, institutional reports and other items revealing the most intimate details of their lives—details that are often irrelevant to any criminal prosecution. It is common in some institutions for correctional officers to uncover this material to embarrass prisoners. Homosexual behavior, low-status crimes such as sexual offenses against minors, self-destructive acts and bouts with mental illness are examples of the kinds of subjects that officers sometimes extract from central files to use against prisoners. This method of psychological victimization is not confined to correctional institutions, for Goffman also observed it in a mental hospital.[47] A variation on the game occurs when officers pass on derogatory labels that have been affixed to unlucky prisoners by their colleagues in crime, such as "rat," "snitch," and "punk."[48]

The number of forms that psychological victimization of prisoners by staff members can take is almost limitless. New examples are constantly being reported in the literature or revealed in testimony given in the nation's courts. In Nevada, a warden put a pistol to the neck of a prisoner and said, "Move or I'll kill you," when it was not necessary for him to do so because the deputy warden was already walking the prisoner down the corridor to solitary confinement.[49] An officer in a California penitentiary who had been asked for help by a prisoner who was coughing blood gave him a note that said, "Yell for help when the blood is an inch thick, all over the floor, and don't call before that."[50] It is likely that if the officer had judged the prisoner's condition to be serious, he would have summoned medical help. The psychological victimization in this incident occurs because the officer deliberately pretends that he will never summon help while the prisoner is alive. An injunction was granted in New York State against the assignment of male guards at a women's prison, which occurred as a result of testimony that these officers deliberately came into shower rooms to watch the women as they were naked and also deliberately watched them when they were on the toilet.[51] In one of the most gruesome incidents revealed in a Senate subcommittee hearing, an Ohio correctional officer collected pet cats from the prisoners and then "dashed their brains out in sight of the whole prison population."[52] Being deprived of their children, prisoners often invest fatherly and motherly emotion in their pets so that this act of brutality symbolized multiple infanticide to many of the prisoners who could not avoid seeing it.

In the history of prisons in America, groups of prisoners sometimes mutilated themselves in protest against mistreatment by staff members. The mass cuttings of heel tendons described by Keve[53] are no longer common on the American prison scene. Likewise, the self-mutilations accomplished by Peruvian prisoners as a result of severe beatings administered by criminal justice personnel are not replicated in this country.[54] Today, self-destructive behavior by prisoners is much more likely to be an individual act than an act of group protest. Mattick is probably correct that self-destructive behavior is declining as a percentage of all prison violence.[55] The highest rate of self-mutilations known in contemporary American prisons occurred at Angola Prison in Louisiana in a ten-month period in 1974. A total of 107 self-mutilation cases were heard by the disciplinary board during this period, an average of about ten per month.[56] The despair felt by prisoners who damaged themselves has been well documented in the literature.[57] This has been linked to physical victimization by correctional officers,[58] but there has been little recognition in the literature of the ways in which psychological victimization by prison officers can also contribute to suicidal and other self-damaging acts. One occasionally hears comments to the effect that psychologically disturbed and inadequate prisoners are more likely to be "picked on" by staff members than well-adjusted, highly prisonized inmates. In institutions where this is true, the deliberate mistreatment by staff members of prisoners who are already highly disturbed may be sufficient to precipitate self-destructive incidents.

Occasions in which prisoners harm themselves primarily because of psychological victimization by correctional officers are probably relatively rare in the United States. A more common contribution to prisoner self-destruction that is made by correctional officers is the lack of sensitivity to the needs of prisoners who are approaching potentially self-destructive personal crises. Because correctional officers are usually poorly trained in interpersonal relations, most of them neither recognize nor are sufficiently motivated to assist prisoners undergoing psychological breakdowns. For every officer who sadistically torments such prisoners, there are hundred who fail to give adequate support or to call in qualified medical personnel in a situation that is gradually deteriorating. This is not a matter of victimization at the individual level but is instead a reflection of policies and funding priorities in state legislatures and other funding bodies.

Economic Victimization

Prisoner officers and other staff members in correctional institutions may be involved in economic victimization of a very direct sort, such as eating a prisoner's food or wearing his or her clothing. Most institutions guard against this sort of direct economic victimization. It is probably more common for prisoner officers to victimize economically their charges *indirectly* by being involved in contraband operations and loansharking. For example, the director of the Omaha Urban League alleged in 1974 that prisoner officers were regularly bringing in drugs and reaping profits from the drug traffic in a midwestern penitentiary.[59] The warden of the federal penitentiary in Atlanta said that nothing could be done to halt the alleged staff corruption in that institution unless the culprits were actually caught in the act. At the same hearing, one of his prisoners testified that 95% of all marijuana in the prison was provided by staff members.[60] A Tampa newspaper, investigating the homosexual attack and murder of a 19-year-old prisoner, mentioned that the prisoners who assaulted the victim were middlemen for a loan racket run by the officer who was supervising the area in which the prisoner was raped and killed. Testimony revealed that the victim had been subjected to sexual assault before his death as punishment because the correctional officer believed that he was "snitching" on him for selling ham from the kitchen for private profit. In addition to the assault by prisoners, it was alleged that the victim had been beaten by several correctional officers four days before he died and had begged to be placed in the isolation unit but that his request was denied.[61]

When a staff member is involved in a sub rosa economic system of the prison, it is possible to "burn" prisoners with impunity because they cannot possibly report the crime to the administration without revealing their own involvement in the illegal activity. If the prisoner is a member of a powerful gang or clique, pressures can be brought to bear on correctional officers to keep them from this sort of economic victimization. On the other hand, sophisticated officers are careful never to burn any prisoner who has this kind of backing. Instead, they victimize only the isolated prisoners who enlist their help in sub rosa economic transactions. Such a prisoner, who gives an officer some money to smuggle out of the prison for his wife, may find out that the officer has pocketed it instead of delivering it, or perhaps that a portion of it was subtracted as an additional payment for delivery beyond the amount already agreed upon.

The definition of victimization becomes contorted out of all recognition in the case of the officer who regularly participates in sub rosa smuggling activities with prisoners but who keeps his record clean by occasionally reporting unsophisticated prisoners to the administration for attempting to bribe him. Victimization in this instance consists of enforcing the regulations that the officer should *have been enforcing* in a setting in which the regulations were habitually ignored. One officer who allegedly charged up to $300 a trip to "pack" contraband in and out of the prison made enough money over his career to establish an independent business in the free community. This "horse" (a slang term for prison officers who smuggle contraband into the institution) was probably able "to stay in business" for such a long time because he only "packed" for powerful, trustworthy prisoners and systematically wrote infraction tickets on every other prisoner who approached him.

We cannot leave the subject of the economic victimization of prisoners by staff members without mentioning drug testing, industrial victimization and the suppression of prisoner unions. These topics do not fit our definition of victimization because they refer to institutional policy and, in some cases, enacted law. Many prison industries are operated under less than safe conditions in order to maximize productivity. Once a major problem in America's prisons,[62] this lingers on today in industrial programs that continue to use equipment that is antiquated and unsafe.

The testing of dangerous drugs by prisoners, which has been rapidly declining in recent years, is another form of institutional victimization that is outside our technical definition. Beginning with a 1904 study of bubonic plague by Colonel R.P. Strong,[63] prisoners were paid a pittance (if anything) but offered minor administrative favors in return for participating in highly dangerous experiments. Even these small rewards were more than sufficient motivation to recruit prisoners for medical-and drug-testing experiments because the prisoners were artificially economically disadvantaged by polices and laws that forbade them to be paid more than a few cents an hour. Was it really necessary to apply radiation to the testicles of prisoners so that later they would become sterile? Prisoners, whom I know personally, were involved in such an experiment, claiming they were not adequately informed of the consequences at the time that they agreed to participate. Some of them would now like to lead normal married lives and have children, but their criminal records largely rule out adoption and their participation in the radiation experiment leaves them unable to conceive their own children. In an excellent treatment of the subject, Meyer shows how the pharmaceutical companies and the general public have benefited over the years from low-cost prisoner experiments. The victimizing nature of these experiments has been given credence by their abolition under contemporary federal standards for drug-testing experiments.[64]

The substandard wages that are generally paid to men and women working in prison industries are also economically victimizing, although such wages do not constitute victimization under our definition of the subject. However, technical victimization creeps into this situation when prisoners attempt to organize unions, following the model that is accepted in free society, and they are prevented from doing so when administrative actions such as punitive ransfers, punitive segregation and unjust parole board "flops" (parole board decisions to increase sentence length) are used to suppress the formation of prisoner unions.[65] Although prisoner unions are permitted in some European nations (such as KRUM, organized in Sweden in 1966), the only way for prisoner unions to survive in the United States is if they have a power base outside of the institution. The San Francisco-based Prisoners' Union, which was co-founded by John Irwin, is an example of this kind of an organization. Whether it will have any significant national impact remains to be seen.

Social Victimization

The most blatant form of social victimization carried out against prisoners by correctional officers is racial discrimination. Two other forms of victimization that are essentially social in nature are the non-performance of stated duties and the deliberate handing over of super-visory responsibilities to prisoners who then use their staff-sanctioned power to abuse others. Reports of correctional officer discrimination against black prisoners abound in the literature.[66] These reports include evidence of discrimination in job assignments[67] and disciplinary hearings.[68] Racial discrimination becomes mixed with reli-gious discrimination when groups such as the Black Muslims are denied their religious rights.[69] Carroll describes an incident in which kissing between a prisoner and a visitor, which was officially prohib-ited but always permitted for uniracial couples, resulted in the abrupt termination of a visit when a black prisoner kissed his white visitor.[70] Carroll also observed correctional officers admitting white visitors to inmate organizations without searches, but systematically searching visitors to black organizations and conducting bodily postvisit searches of black prisoners three times as often as similar searches of white prisoners.[71] All of these reports pale in comparison with the allegations of virulent racism by correctional officers at Soledad prison in California.[72]

When a staff member turns over supervisory activities to a prisoner, all of the other prisoners in that jurisdiction are subject to a potential victimization. We have already seen some examples of sexual victimi-zation that occurred because of this form of staff behavior. I cite only two additional examples here. Testimony in a federal court alleged that a prisoner in a Texas institution had been set up as a "prison enforcer" for which he was rewarded with special privileges such as a homosexual in his cell to service his sexual needs and the authority to assault other prisoners at any time in the service of maintaining insti-tutional order.[73] The other example comes from the juvenile institution studied by Bartollas et al. Staff members in this institution often catered to the needs of "heavy" (physically powerful) prisoners in return for their cooperation in running the reformatory. These favored prisoners were permitted to unlock the doors of their fellow prisoners with the staff's keys. This gave the "heavies" license to victimize other prisoners in return for their allegiance to staff members.[74]

The social victimization of prisoners as a class of individuals occurs when correctional officers and other staff members neglect to carry out their stated duties. Bartollas and his associates described staff members who stayed in their offices, perhaps taking naps, thus leaving the weaker prisoners open to all sorts of victimization by their peers.

Other staff members discriminated directly against scapegoats by giving them all the menial work details in the cottage, seldom talking with them, or permitted other youths to victimize them openly in the presence of staff.[75]

Prisoners are beginning to realize that they can file legal actions against correctional staff members who refrain from carrying out their duties in ways that lead to prisoner victimization. A recent issue of *Corrections Compendium* reports several such cases filed under 42 U.S.C. 1983. One of the complainants had suffered sexual abuse and alleged a history of incidents over a period of two years because of inadequate supervision by institutional staff members. The other alleged that one prisoner had been killed and another injured by a fire that broke out in an Arkansas jail while the sheriff had gone to a basketball game, leaving the jail unattended.[76] There is increasing recognition that such actions by correctional staff members constitute a serious form of victimization.

Two theoretical explanations for the victimization of prisoners by correctional officers have been advanced in the literature. These are the total institutions theory and the role theory. Actually there is very little difference between these two approaches. Total institutions theory looks at institutions as a whole and emphasizes the similarities between prisons, mental hospitals and other total institutions. In contrast, role theory emphasizes the role played by correctional officers and argues that citizens can be rapidly socialized to play the role of correctional officer.

The creation of total institutions theory is generally credited to Goffman in his book, *Asylums*, in which he discusses social and psychological assaults upon inmates by staff members. In Goffman's conception, the psychological victimization of inmates by staff members is part of the overall process of mortification, in which the inmates' attachment to civilian life is stripped away. The exasperating thing about much of the unnecessary psychological victimization that goes on is that the staff justifies the victimization in terms of institutional needs.[77] Following this same line of analysis, Hartmann has identified the existence of the staff role of the "key jingler" for persons who deliberately use power in a manner that is debilitating to the inmates. These individuals are concerned with "throwing their weight around" rather than promoting the welfare of the inmates under their control.[78]

The maximum security prison is conceptualized as a miniature totalitarian state by Burns. The six basic features of a totalitarian regime—totalitarian ideology, a single party typically led by one person, a terroristic police, a communications monopoly, a weapons monopoly and a centrally directed economy—are systematically applied to maximum security prisons in Burns' analysis. In this model, staff members who are in a position of great authority will be sorely tempted to practice brutality, blackmail, bribery and favoritism. Terroristic police practices are part of the social control mechanism for keeping inmates in line.[79] If Burns' conception of the maximum security prison as a totalitarian regime is correct, then we would expect that those correctional officers who are better integrated with the culture of the prison and more socially involved in it would be more brutal and totalitarian than those officers who exist at the periphery of the staff subculture. An exploratory investigation by Shoemaker and Hillery suggests that this may be true in some institutions. However, the correlations they found were significant in only one of three institutions (and that was a boarding school rather than a maximum security prison),[80] so their evidence does not lend more than minimal support to the theory advanced by Burns.

Role theory as applied to the victimization of prisoners by officers received support from the Stanford Prison Experiment conducted by Haney et al.[81] In this experiment, college students who had been authenticated as psychologically normal were paid to role-play guards and inmates in a pseudoprison in the basement of a Stanford building. Everyone involved was aware of the fact that the experiment was artificial, although it was very well staged. Commenting on this experiment, Zimbardo says:

> At the end of six days we had to close down our mock prison because what we saw was frightening. It was no longer apparent to most of the subjects (or to us) where reality ended and the roles began. The majority had indeed become prisoners or guards, no longer able to clearly differentiate between role-playing and self. There were dramatic changes in virtually every aspect of their behavior, thinking, and feeling. In less than a week the experience of imprisonment undid (temporarily) a lifetime of learning: human values were suspended, self-concepts were challenged and the ugliest, most base, pathological side of human nature surfaced. We were horrified because we saw some boys (guards) treat others as if they were despicable animals, taking pleasure in cruelty, while other boys (prisoners) became servile, dehumanized robots who thought only of escape, of their own individual survival and of their mounting hatred for the guards.[82]

In the Stanford experiment, approximately one-third of the staff members became tyrannical in their arbitrary use of power over the inmates. They developed creative ways of breaking the spirit of the prisoners who were in their charge. Although the other two-thirds of the staff members were not tyrannical, there was never a case in which one of them interfered with a command given by any of the tyrannical guards. They never even tried to pressure the other staff members into behaving more reasonably. The experiment was called off because of the possibility that some of the subjects were being severely damaged by their experiences. Three of them had had to be released in the first four days because they had severe situational traumatic reactions, such as confusion in thinking, severe depression and hysterical crying.

This experiment devastates the constitutional sadism theory of staff brutality, which is, in any case, not represented in the serious literature on staff-inmate victimization. The realization that any normal human being can take on the negative characteristics commonly associated with the worst of prison officers leads us to look more carefully at how roles are structured in the prison situation. A study of mine shows that even civilian volunteers who become quasistaff members of a correctional institution can engage in types of behavior that are psychologically victimizing. In a volunteer program administered by me in which all but two of the staff members were volunteers from the external community, there were many cases of power-tripping and sexual enticement by the staff members, with power-tripping being primarily engaged in by males, and sexual enticement by females, although the reverse was true in some cases. The power-tripper enjoys a feeling of control over the lives of prisoners and manipulates them in therapy groups and in administrative situations so as to make them more dependent and more anxious than they would otherwise be. Power-trippers are sure that inmates should do what they are told, and they imply that they have a great deal more power over the inmates' release date than is actually the case.

Sexual enticement occurs when the volunteer staff member dresses, talks and acts in a sexually suggestive way while within the prison. Pseudoromances are encouraged in which the prisoners are led to believe that the staff members have a real interest in them, while the staff members in actuality are merely gratifying themselves by being admired and sought after. When the relationship goes too far, the prisoners are often subjected to disciplinary actions because the victimizing staff member claims that it was "all the prisoner's fault." In addition, some prisoners become so emotionally involved that when the relationship falls apart, they become suicidal. Others come looking for thier "lovers" when they are released from prison, only to find out that these staff members have no intention of following up on the promises they made while the prisoners were safe behind bars.[83]

Is the role of the prison guard so compulsive that a certain percentage of the people who play it will be invariably motivated to abuse prisoners in one way or another. The comments by Zimbardo and my experiences say yes, and this idea is also consistent with a report by Jacobs and Kraft, that suggests the possibility that racial differences among guards are suppressed by the "master status" of the prison officer.[84] However, an obscure publication on correctional institutions in Wisconsin offers contrary evidence. This report by Ross describes what happened during a 16-day period when members of the Wisconsin State Employees Union went on strike and National Guard Units took over the administration of the prisons. The National Guardsmen were in the prisons for more than twice the period of time of Zimbardo's experiment, yet they were not institutionalized by the experience. Instead of becoming brutal and mistreating the inmates, they treated them like decent human beings. They relaxed the disciplinary regime and at the same time reduced the number of incidents of violence among inmates.[85]

It is probable that the reason the National Guardsmen's behavior did not deteriorate during their time as correctional officers was that they never conceived of themselves as playing the role of prison officers. They had a different role to play—the role of National Guardsmen acting in an emergency. In addition, they had a network of relations with each other that existed before they had entered the prison and that strengthened their resistance to the negative process of institutionalization. With these kinds of social supports, it is possible that the National Guardsmen could have had tours of duty of one or two years in length without ever adopting the more negative aspects of the role of the prison officer. International studies of prison camps in which the prisoners are able to live rather normal lives under the supervision of military units also offer some evidence in support of the idea that the military role can take precedence over the prison officer role and minimize the appeal of engaging in behavior that is at least psychologically victimizing if not physically brutal.

Footnotes

[1] Donald Clemmer, The Prison Community (New York: Holt, Rinehart and Winston, 1940), p. 204.

[2] John A. Conley, "A History of the Oklahoma Penal System, 1907-1967," Ph.D. dissertation, Michigan State University, 1977.

[3] Bruce Jackson, Killing Time, Life in the Arkansas Penitentiary (Ithaca, NY: Cornell University Press, 1977).

[4] Tom Murton and Joe Hyams, Inside Prison, U.S.A. (New York: Grove Press, 1969).

[5] Ibid., p. 7.

[6] Prison brutality revealed during the federal hearing, The Freeworld Times 1 (January 1972): 2.

[7] Fear, Angola's punishment camp terrorizes prisoners, Southern Coalition Report on Jails and Prisons 5 (Spring 1978): 3.

[8] Stephen Gettinger, Mississippi: Has come a long way but it had a long way to come, *Corrections Magazine* 5 (June 1979): 8; *Corrections Digest* 4 (December 12, 1973): 3.

[9] Philip J. Hirschkop and Michael A. Millemann, The prison life of Leroy Jones, in Burton M. Atkins and Henry R. Glick (Eds.), *Prisons, Protest, and Politics* (Englewood Cliffs, NJ: Prentice-Hall, 1972), pp. 55-59.

[10] Jessica Mitford, *Kind and Usual Punishment* (New York: Random House, 1971), pp. 41-42.

[11] Oklahoma prison guards indicted for inmate gassing incident, *Corrections Digest* 6 (February 5, 1975): 2.

[12] Federal jury convicts prison guards of brutality, *Corrections Digest* 5 (March 6, 1974): 2-3.

[13] 'Dedicated' with violence, *The Freeworld Times* 1 (August 1972): 8-9.

[14] Rioters killed, *The Freeworld Times* 1 (February 1972): 6,9.

[15] Ibid., p. 6.

[16] Mitford (1971), p. 290.

[17] Hans Toch, *Police, Prisons, and the Problem of Violence* (Washington, DC: U.S. Government Printing Office, 1977), pp. 65-67.

[18] Robert Bogdan and Steven J. Taylor, *Introduction to Qualitative Research Methods* (New York: Wiley, 1975).

[19] Edward Sagarin and Donal E. J. MacNamara, The homosexual as a crime victim, *International Journal of Criminology and Penology* 3 (1975): 21.

[20] Larry Cole, *Our Children's Keepers: Inside America's Kid Prisons* (New York: Grossman, 1972).

[21] Kenneth Wooden, *Weeping in the Playtime of Others: America's Incarcerated Children* (New York: McGraw-Hill, 1976).

[22] Clemens Bartollas, Stuart J. Miller and Simon Dinitz, *Juvenile Victimization: The Institutional Paradox* (New York: Wiley, 1976), p. 214.

[23] Ibid., p. 214.

[24] Gene Kassebaum, Sex in prison, violence, homosexuality, and intimidation are everyday occurrences, *Sexual Behavior* 2 (January 1972): 39-45.

[25] The case of Joanne Little, *Crime and Social Justice* 3 (Summer 1975): 42-45. For a more recent case, see Women press for change at Tutwiler, *Southern Coalition Report on Jails and Prisons* 5 (Fall 1978): 3.

[26] Woman's killing of jailer raises inmate abuse questions, *Corrections Digest* 5 (December 11, 1974): 11-12.

[27] Cole (1972), p. 8.

[28] Alan J. Davis, Sexual assaults in the Philadelphia prison system and sheriff's vans, *Trans-Action* 6 (December 1968): 11.

[29] Jack Griswold, Mike Misenheimer and Art Powers, *An Eye for an Eye* (New York: Holt, Rinehart and Winston, 1970), pp. 42-43, cited in Anthony M. Scacco Jr., *Rape in Prison* (Springfield, IL: C.C. Thomas, 1975), p. 32.

[30] Sagarin and MacNamara (1975).

[31] Ibid., pp. 21-22.

[32] See, for example, Davis (1968) and Scacco (1975).

[33] Daniel Lockwood, *Prison Sexual Violence* (New York: Elsevier, 1980), p. 140.

[34] Cole (1972), p. 64.

[35] Howard James, Children in trouble, *Christian Science Monitor* (April 5, 12, 19, 26, and May 10, 24, 1969), cited in Naomi F. Chase, *A Child Is Being Beaten* (New York: McGraw-Hill, 1976), pp. 154, 160.

[36] Chase (1976), p. 151.

[37] National Analysis of Official Child Abuse and Neglect Reporting (Washington, DC: Government Printing Office, 1969).

[38] John Howard Association, *Illinois Youth Centers at St. Charles and Geneva* (Chicago: John Howard Association, 1974).

[39] See, for example, Cliff Judge and Roma Emmerson, Some children at risk in Victoria in the 19th century, *Medical Journal of Australia* 1 (1974): 490-495.

[40] John Vodicka, Louisiana warden indicted for beatings of juveniles, *Southern Coalition Report on Jails and Prisons* 5 (Summer 1978): 1.

[41] Wooden (1976), p. 108.

[42] Barry C. Feld, *Neutralizing Inmate Violence* (Cambridge, MA: Ballinger, 1977).

[43] Bartollas et al. (1976).

[44] Conley (1977), p. 237.

[45] Robert E. Heise, *Prison Games* (Fort Worth: privately published, 1976).

[46] Kenneth Dimick, *Ladies in Waiting Behind Prison Walls* (Muncie, IN: Accelerated Development, 1977), pp. 46-47.

[47] Erving Goffman, *Asylums* (Garden City, NY: Doubleday, 1961).

[48] Heise (1976).

[49] *Corrections Digest* 3 (November 1, 1972), pp. 11-12.

[50] Mitford (1971), p. 148.

[51] Injunction granted against assignment of male guards at Bedford Hills, *Corrections Compendium* 2 (October 1977), p. 3.

[52] Mitford (1971), pp. 268-269.

[53] Paul W. Keve, *Prison Life and Human Worth* (Minneapolis: University of Minnesota Press, 1974).

[54] H. H. A. Cooper, Self-mutilation by Peruvian prisoners, *International Journal of Offender Therapy* 15 (1971): 180-188.

[55] Hans Mattick, The prosaic sources of prison violence, in Jackwell Susman, *Crime and Justice, 1971-1972* (New York: A.M.S. Press, 1974): 179-187.

[56] A. Astrachan, Profile/Louisiana, *Corrections Magazine* 2 (September-October 1975): 9-14.

[57] See, for example, R. S. Esparza, Attempted and committed suicide in county jails, in Bruce Danto (Ed.), *Jailhouse Blues* (Orchard Lake, MI: Epic Publications, 1973), pp. 27-46; James L. Claghorn and Dan R. Beto, Self-mutilation in a prison hospital, *Corrective Psychiatry and Journal of Social Therapy* 13 (1967): 133-141; Robert Johnson, *Culture and Crisis in Confinement* (Lexington, MA: D. C. Heath, 1976); Hans Toch, *Men in Crisis* (Chicago: Aldine, 1975); *Living in Prison: The Ecology of Survival* (New York: Free Press, 1977).

[58] R. J. Wicks, Suicide prevention — A brief for corrections officers, *Federal Probation* 36 (September 1972): 29-31.

[59] Nebraska prisoners speak-out, *The Freeworld Times* 3 (January-February 1974): 7.

[60] Danger, death, corruption at Atlanta federal prison detailed in Senate testimony, *Corrections Digest* 9 (October 6, 1978): 3-4.

[61] Inmate death linked to guard rackets, *The Freeworld Times* 2 (May 1973): 15.

[62] See Conley (1977) for historical examples of excessive industrial accidents caused by deliberate administrative inattention to matters of safety.

[63] Gilbert F. McMahon, The normal prisoner in medical research, *Journal of Clinical Pharmacology* 71 (February-March 1972): 72.

[64] Peter B. Meyer, *Drug Experiments on Prisoners, Ethical, Economic, or Exploitative?* (Lexington, MA: D. C. Heath, 1976).

[65] C. Ronald Huff, Unionization behind the walls, *Criminology* 12 (1974): 175-193; Prisoners' union: A challenge for state corrections, *State Government* 48 (1975): 145-149.

[66] Haywood Burns, The black prisoner as victim, in Michele G. Hermann and Marilyn G. Haft (Eds.), *Prisoners' Rights Sourcebook* (New York: Clark Boardman, 1973), pp. 25-31.

[67] Ronald Goldfarb, *Jails: The Ultimate Ghetto of the Criminal Justice System* (Garden City, NY: Doubleday, 1976), p. 405.

[68] Erik O. Wright, *The Politics of Punishment: A Critical Analysis of Prisons in America* (New York: Harper & Row, 1973), p. 127.

[69] James B. Jacobs, *Stateville: The Penitentiary in Mass Society* (Chicago: University of Chicago Press, 1977), p. 59.

[70] Leo Carroll, *Hacks, Blacks, and Cons* (Copyright © 1974) reissued 1988 by Waveland Press, Inc., Prospect Heights, IL), pp. 123-124.

[71] Ibid., pp. 127-128.

[72] George Jackson, *Soledad Brother: The Prison Letters of George Jackson* (New York: Bantam, 1970).

[73] This week: Texas prison faces federal court test, *Corrections Digest* 9 (October 6, 1978): 2-3.

[74] Bartollas et al. (1976), pp. 208-209.

[75] Ibid., pp. 207-209.

[76] Sheriff may be liable for acts of his subordinates, and Leaving prisoners unattended can lead to civil rights violation, *Corrections Compendium* 2 (June 1978): 5.

[77] Goffman (1961).

[78] Carl Hartman, The key jingler, *Community Mental Health Journal* 5 (1969): 199-205.

[79] Henry Burns, Jr., A miniature totalitarian state: Maximum security prison, *Canadian Journal of Criminology and Corrections* 11 (July 1969): 153-164.

[80] Donald J. Shoemaker and George A. Hillery, Jr., "Violence and Commitment in Custodial Settings," paper presented at the annual meeting of the American Sociological Association, 1978.

[81] Craig Haney, Curtis Banks and Philip Zimbardo, Interpersonal dynamics in a simulated prison, in Robert G. Leger and John R. Stratton (Eds.), *The Sociology of Corrections* (New York: Wiley, 1977), pp. 65-92.

[82] Philip Zimbardo, Pathology of imprisonment, *Society* 9 (6) (1972): 4.

[83] Lee H. Bowker, Volunteers in correctional settings: Benefits, problems, and solutions, in *Proceedings of the American Correctional Association* (Washington, DC: American Correctional Association, 1973), pp. 298-303.

[84] James B. Jacobs and Lawrence J. Kraft, Integrating the keepers: A comparison of black and white prison guards in Illinois, *Social Problems* 25 (1978): 304-318.

[85] Beth Ross, *Changing of the Guard: Citizen Soldiers in Wisconsin Correctional Institutions* (Madison: League of Women Voters of Wisconsin, 1979).

9

Prison Guards and Snitches
Social Control in a Maximum Security Institution

James W. Marquart
and
Julian B. Roebuck

In prison vernacular "rats," "snitches," "stool pigeons," "stoolies," or finks refer to inmates who "cooperate" with or discretely furnish information to staff members. By and large, the popular imagery and folk-beliefs surrounding these inmates are particularly negative. Typically, prison movies present "rats," as the weakest, most despicable and pitiful creatures in the prisoner society. "Rats" are usually depicted as outcasts or isolates that undermine the solidarity of the cons by breaking the inmate "code" of silence (see Sykes, 1958). Whenever a "rat" appears in a movie scene, groups of inmates stop

Source: Prepared especially for *The Dilemmas of Corrections* by James W. Marquart and Julian B. Roebuck. Some of the substantive findings herein are discussed in an article in the British Journal of Criminology (forthcoming) entitled "Prison Guards and Snitches: Deviance Within a Total Institution."

145

talking, disband, or mumble obscenities.[1] Some prison reseachers, like McCleery (1960), contend that uncovering snitches is an obsession for the majority of inmates. This may be true in many correctional institutions because "rats" are often the victims of "accidents" or savage reprisals from other prisoners, as evidenced by the New Mexico prison riot in 1980. The inmates in many other prisons have developed an inmate society, enabling them to define, label, and punish "rats" as deviants.

The sociology of confinement, especially prison role research, has for decades noted the negative perception of "rats" by the other inmates (see Bowker, 1977). Yet, despite the fascination with and knowledge of "rats," prison researchers (unlike police researchers) have offered little systematic research on snitches.[2] Johnson (1961) and Wilmer (1965) are the only prison investigators who have examined informing, but their work focuses on the types and personal attributes of "rats" rather than informing as a mechanism of social control. Perhaps the best descriptions of the exchange relationships between staff members and stool pigeons come from former inmates (see Bettelheim, 1943; Solzhenitsyn, 1975; and Charriere, 1970). Nevertheless, little is known about how officials use inmate-intelligence as a management strategy.

This paper examines a southwestern state penitentiary control system wherein a network of "paid" inmate informants functioned as surrogate guards. Although known "rats" may be typically loathed and disparaged by the staff and captives in most institutions, the "rats" in the prison under study were hated, but also envied, feared, and respected. No stigma was attached to their deviant role. We focus on the snitch recruitment process, the types of intelligence gathered, the informers' payoff and the use of this intelligence to maintain social order — in short the dynamics of this guard-surrogate guard society.

Setting and Method of Study

The data were collected at the Johnson Unit[3], a maximum security recidivist prison within the Texas Department of Corrections (TDC), that housed nearly 3200 inmates over the age of twenty-five (47% black, 36% white, and 17% hispanic). Many of these hard-core offenders had been convicted of violent crimes. Johnson had a system-wide reputation for tight disciplinary control, and inmate trouble-makers from other TDC prisons were sent there for punishment. Structurally, the prison had eighteen inside cell blocks (or tanks) and twelve dormitories branching out from a single central hall — a telephone pole design. The Hall, the main thoroughfare of the prison, was a corridor almost one quarter of a mile long, measuring sixteen feet wide by twelve feet high.

The data for this paper are derived from field research conducted from June 1981 through January 1983. The first author entered Johnson as a guard, a role which enabled him to observe and analyze first-hand the social control system. A number of established field techniques were used: participant observation, key informants, formal and informal interviews, and the examination of prison and inmate documents and records. The investigator directly observed and participated in the daily routine of prison events (work, school, meals, sick call, cell and body searches, counts, etc.) as well as various unexpected events (fights, stabbings, suicide attempts, drug trafficking). He also observed and examined officer/officer and officer/inmate (snitch) interaction patterns, inmate/officer transactions, leadership behavior, rule violations, disciplinary hearings, and the administration of punishment. With time, he established rapport with guards and inmates, gaining the reputation of a "good officer." (He was even promoted to sergeant in November 1982).

During the fieldwork, the observer developed, as did most ranking guards, a cadre of "rats" and channelled their information to supervisors (sergeants, lieutenants, captains, majors). These inmates routinely brought him information about prisoners (e.g., weapons, gambling, stealing) and even other officers (e.g., sleeping on the job, drug smuggling, having sex with inmates). The vast majority of snitches were shared, but the "rats" dealt primarily with officers who had the reputation of using good judgment (not overreacting, keeping cool) when handling sensitive information. Enmeshed in the intelligence network, the researcher frequently discussed these matters with the officers and "rats."

The Snitch System

Johnson employed 240 officers and housed nearly 3,200 inmates. One guard was generally assigned to supervise four cell-blocks totalling 400 prisoners. Obviously this situation obviated individual inmate supervision. Therefore, to facilitate control and order, staff members enlisted the "official" aid of the inmate elites as informers and surrogate guards. These snitches, called building tenders (BTs) and turnkeys, in turn cultivated their own inmate snitches. Johnson was managed via a complex information network facilitating a proactive as well as a reactive form of prisoner management. These surrogate guards acted with considerable authority.

Structure and Work Role

The BT system involved four levels of inmates. The top of the hierarchy consisted of the "head" building tenders. In 1981, each of the eighteen cell blocks had one building tender designated by the staff as the "head" BT. These BTs were responsible for all inmate behavior that occurred in "their" particular block. Block "ownership" was recognized by inmates and staff members alike who referred informally but meaningfully, for example, to "Watson's tank" or "Robinson's tank." Head BTs were the block's representatives to the staff and were held accountable for any problems that occurred therein. Besides procuring information (described in the next section), head BTs mediated problems (e.g., lover's quarrels, petty stealing, gambling, fighting, dirty or loud cell partners) within the living areas. They listened to and weighed each inmate's version of an argument or altercation. In most cases, the head BT warned the quarrelers to "get along with each other" or "quit all the grab-assing around." In some cases, they even let two antagonists settle their differences in a "supervised" fistfight. However, those inmates who could not or would not get along with the others were usually beaten and then moved to another cell block. BTs unofficially and routinely settled the mundane problems of prison life in the blocks without the staff's knowledge but with their tacit approval (see Marquart and Crouch, 1983).[4]

The second level of the system consisted of the rank and file building tenders. In every block (or dormitory), there were generally between three and five inmates assigned as BTs, totalling nearly 150 in the prison. BTs "worked the tank" and maintained control in the living areas by tabulating the daily counts, delivering messages to other inmates for the staff, getting the other inmates up for work, procuring information, and protecting the officers from attacks by the ordinary inmates. BTs also socialized new inmates into the system; that is, they educated them to "keep the noise down, go to work when you are called, mind your own business, stop "grab assing around," and tell us [BTs] when you have a problem." BTs broke up fights, issued orders to the other inmates, protected weak inmates from exploitation, protected the officers, and passed on information to the head BT and staff members.

Finally, the BTs unofficially disciplined erring inmates. For example, if an inmate was found stealing another's property, he was apt to receive a slap across the face, a punch in the stomach, or both. If the erring inmate continued to steal, he was summarily beaten and, with the staff's approval, moved to another cell block. The BTs were "on call" twenty-four hours a day and the head BT assigned the others to shifts (morning, evening, and night). It was an unwritten rule that cell block guards were not to order the BTs to sweep the floors, wash windows, or perform other menial tasks. Those officers who violated this "rule" were informed on and frequently disciplined (e.g., reassigned to gun towers, never assigned to that particular block again). This further underscores the building tenders' proprietorship of the tanks as well as their ability and power to curtail the lower ranking guards' authority and behavior.

The third level consisted of inmate runners or strikers. Runners were selected and assigned to work in the blocks by BTs on the basis of their loyalty, work ability, and willingness to act as informants. They also worked at regular jobs throughout the prison (e.g., laundry, shops, kitchen). Runners performed the janitorial work of the block such as sweeping, cleaning windows, and dispensing supplies to the cells. More importantly, runners, who were also called hitmen, served as the physical back-up for the BTs by assisting in breaking up fights and quelling minor disturbances. As a reward for their services, runners enjoyed more mobility and privileges within the block than the other inmates (but less than the BTs). Many runners were also friends or acquaintances of the BTs in the free world, and some were their consensual homosexual partners. Some blocks had three or four runners, while others had seven, eight, or even nine. Altogether, there were approximately 175 to 200 runners.

The fourth level of the BT system consisted of turnkeys, numbering 17 in 1981. The Hall contained seven large metal barred doors, riot barricades that were manned by turnkeys in six hour shifts. Turnkeys shut and locked these doors during fights or disturbances to localize and prevent disturbances from escalating or moving throughout the Hall. These inmates actually carried the keys (on long leather straps) which locked and unlocked the barricades. Every morning, turnkeys came to the central picket (a room containing all the keys for the prison and riot gear) and picked up keys for "their" barricades. Turnkeys routinely broke up fights, provided assistance to the BTs, and physically protected the officers from the ordinary inmates. These doorkeepers passed along information to the BTs about anything they heard while "working a gate." When off duty they lived in the blocks where they assisted the BTs in the everyday management of inmates. Turnkeys occupied a status level equal to that of the BTs.

Selection of BTs and Turnkeys

As "managers" of the living areas and Hall, these inmate-agents obviously performed a dangerous task for the staff. Vastly outnumbered, BTs and turnkeys ruled with little opposition from the ordinary inmates. In fact, most of the ordinary inmates feared their "overseers" because of their status and physical dominance. They were formally selected by the staff to perform an official job within the living areas. Unwritten but "official" departmental policy existed on the appointment of inmates to BT and turnkey positions. The staff at Johnson (and other Texas prisons) recommended certain inmates as BTs/turnkeys to the Classification Committee (a panel of four TDC officials all with prison security backgrounds).[5] This committee then reviewed the inmate records and made the final selections. Recommendations to the Classification Committee from the staff were not always honored and less than half of those recommended were selected for BT/turnkey jobs. One supervisor, an active participant in the recruitment process at Johnson, expressed a typical preference:

> I've got a personal bias. I happen to like murderers and armed robbers. They have a great deal of esteem in the inmate social system, so its not likely that they'll have as much problem as some other inmate because of their esteem, and they tend to be more aggressive and a more dynamic kind of individual. A lot of inmates steer clear of them and avoid problems just because of the reputation they have and their aggressiveness. They tend to be aggressive, you know, not passive.

The BTs and turnkeys were physically and mentally superior inmates, "natural leaders" among their peers. All were articulate and had physical presence, poise, and self-confidence. Generally, they were more violent, prisonized, and criminally sophisticated than the ordinary inmates. Of the eighteen head BTs, eight were in prison for armed robbery, five for murder (one was an enforcer and contract-style killer), one for attempted murder, one for rape, one for drug trafficking, and two for burglary. Their average age was thirty-nine and they were serving an average prison sentence of thirty-two years. Of the seventeen turnkeys, three were murderers, three were armed robbers, six were burglars, two were drug traffickers, one was a rapist and one was doing time for aggravated assault. Their average age was thirty-one and they were serving an average sentence of twenty-two years. All were physically strong, rugged, prison-wise, and physically imposing. BTs and turnkeys were older than most prisoners and often they were violent recidivists similar to the inmate leaders noted by Clemmer (1940) and Schrag (1954). In contrast, the average TDC inmate in 1981 had been given a twenty-one year sentence and was between twenty-two and twenty-seven years old. Almost half.(48%) were property offenders or petty thieves.

Information Acquisition

The most important means of controlling inmates' behavior in the cell blocks was the presence of BTs. These inmate-agents, while carrying out their other duties, spent most of their time sitting around the entrance to the block talking with other inmates, especially the runners. Conversations with and observations of other prisoners enabled the BTs to gather a variety of intelligence about inmates' moods, problems, daily behaviors, friends, enemies, homosexual encounters, misbehaviors, plans, plots and overall demeanor.

The runners, who worked throughout the prison had more contact with the ordinary inmates than did the BTs. This contact facilitated eavesdropping and the extracting of information. For example, while mopping the runs (walkways on each tier), runners talked to and observed the inmates already in their cells. At work, these inmates listened to, watched, talked to, and interacted with the others. Runners secured and relayed to the BTs information on work strikes, loan-sharking, stealing of state property, distilling liquor, tatooing, homosexual acts, and escape and revenge plans.

Information Sources in the Cell Blocks

Though informing was expected from runners, they were not formally instructed to inform. A head BT explains this situation:

> You don't pick these people and tell them now you've got to go in there and tell me what's going on inside the dayroom [a TV and recreation area in each living area]. By becoming a runner it is expected that you will tell what's going on; it's an unspoken rule that you will inform on the rest of the people in here. If you hear something you are going to come to me with it.

With the runners' information, the BTs penetrated the tank social system. Ordinary prisoners knew they were under constant surveillance and thus were amenable to the prisoner social control system — a system based on inmate intelligence reports, regimentation, strict rules, and certain punishments. For example, when the BTs found out that two or more inmates were "cliquing up" for any purpose, they immediately told the staff who disbanded the group through cell changes.

Atomized and lacking solidarity, the ordinary inmates "ratted" on each other, especially when they felt the need for protection. Ordinary inmates rarely, if ever, sought out the staff to solve a block problem because this brought punishment from the BTs. Instead they sought the counsel and help of the BTs, the power block they were forced to deal with. From the ordinary inmates, the BTs learned about a variety of things such as gambling pools, illicit sex, petty thievery, tatooing paraphernalia, liquor making, weapons, and numerous other forms of contraband, misbehavior, and planned misbehavior (e.g., plots of revenge, possible attacks on an overbearing guard). This knowledge enabled the guards to take a proactive stance, thereby preventing rule violations. Not all block residents were informers. Those who snitched did so for several reasons.

Like anyone else, prisoners react negatively to certain repugnant behaviors and situations. Most were followers and refrained from taking action themselves. Citizens often call the police, for example, about a neighbor's barking dog or loud stereo rather than complain directly to the neighbor. Inmates took similar action. They told the BTs about various illegalities (especially those that threatened them in any way) because they knew the problem would be resolved in the block without involving themselves or attracting official intervention. The BTs usually took swift action when resolving problems. For example, one inmate told the BTs in his block that his cell mate was making sexual advances to him. After investigating the claims, the BTs solved this problem by beating the sexually aggressive inmate and, with staff approval, moving him to another block. In another cell block, an inmate told the head BT that his cell partner was scaring him by turning off the cell's light bulb. The BT struck the pranking inmate on the head with a pipe and threatened to have him moved to another block. The prankster "got his message."

Inmates were not always straightforward and sometimes informed for revenge. For example, some inmates informed on those they desired to see the BTs punish and/or move to another cell block. Some inmates "planted" contraband in their enemies' cell and then "tipped off" the BTs. Some inmates gave the BTs false information about other inmates, a variety of snitching called "dropping salt" or "crossing out." However, revenge-informing was restricted because the BTs were especially aware of this maneuver—and severely punished the disclosed instigator. Those who gave spurious information of any kind (or who deceived the BTs in any way) played a dangerous game. If discovered, they were beaten. The BTs (like the guards) weighed and checked the informer's information, considered his motive, and noted the relationship between him and the one informed upon before taking action.

Some ordinary inmates reported illegalities to the BTs in return for favors and to get on their good sides. For example, when an inmate told the BTs about someone who was fashioning a weapon, he expected something in return. Favors assumed many forms such as selection as a runner or maybe even a job recommendation. BTs often recommended "helpful" inmates to the staff for jobs in the garment factory, shops, laundry, or showrooms—and these allies served as additional snitches.

A number of ordinary inmates "ratted" on other inmates as a sort of game playing device. They planned a scenario, informed, and then sat back and enjoyed the action and reaction. Several inmates told me that this kind of game playing relieved their boredom at others' expense. The BTs received most of their information from regular legitimate snitches. However, in some cases when the regular channels did not suffice, they resorted to threats and the terrorization of ordinary inmates to gather information.

BTs, like guards, could not be everywhere at once and therefore relied on stool pigeons. For example, BTs could not observe homosexuality in the cells, but their snitches could. Bob, a head BT, sums up the situation: "The tanks are run through an information system. Whether this information comes from runners or even other inmates, this is how trouble is kept down." The BTs' snitching system was officially recognized as part of the prisoner control system whereas their snitches' behavior was informal, though expected.

Information Gathered Outside the Block

Runners and ordinary inmates worked throughout the prison and routinely informed the BTs about activities in the work areas, school, hospital, laundry, dining rooms, and showerrooms. Gary, a head BT, described this activity:

> We [BTs] all have our people, but we don't fuck with each other's people. If you walk down the Hall and hear somebody say "he's one of mine" that means that that particular inmate owes some type of allegiance to a particular BT. The reason he owes that allegiance or loyalty is perhaps he [a BT] got him a job someplace, got him out of the field and into the Garment Factory. These people are loyal to me. I put them there not for me but for the Man [the warden] and they tell me what's going on in that particular place. If you don't help me then I'll bust you. I got Bruce the job in the Issue Room [clothing and supply room]. I own Bruce because I got him that job. He tells me if clothing is being stolen or if inmates are trying to get more than they deserve.

Misbehavior, plots, and plans were not confined solely to the living areas and the BTs had extended "ears" in all areas where inmates interacted. Consequently, they kept abreast of developments everywhere and relatively little happened without their knowledge.

Turnkeys were not isolated from this spy network because they too had snitches. The turnkeys worked in the prison corridor and therefore gathered much information about illegal behavior outside the cell blocks. They acquired information about weapons, drugs, or other contraband being passed in the Hall, a vital area in the prison because large numbers of inmates were in constant movement there from one point to another. The turnkeys had to keep a constant vigil in the Hall to keep out unauthorized inmates and to maintain order in a very fluid and potentially explosive situation. The Hall was divided into the north and south ends and inmates who lived on the north end were forbidden to walk to the south end and vice versa. No inmates were permitted in the Hall who were not enroute to an official designation. Turnkeys generally knew in which end of the building inmates lived and vigorously watched for "trespassers." Holding down the illegal inmate Hall traffic suppressed contraband peddling as well as general disorder.

Efficiency of the System

At first glance, this snitching system appears cumbersome and inadequate because (apparently) BTs' and Turnkeys' snitches could end up snitching on one another and the guards, creating an amorphous situation without accuracy, consistency, or legitimacy. However, the system worked effectively because the BTs and turnkeys, for the most part, knew "whose snitch was whose." Loyalty to key individuals and reciprocity were the key conditions underpinning the snitch system. BTs and turnkeys interacted amongst themselves and generally knew whose "people" were working where, and their grapevine facilitated the necessary communication. Some snitches were "shared" or owed allegiance to several BTs (or turnkeys). The snitches did not owe their allegiance to the guards or to the BTs as a group, but rather to a particular BT or the BTs who ran their cell block or who were in close supervisory contact with them. When a BT's snitch was "busted," he was expected to intervene with the staff to help his snitch get off or obtain light punishment. The snitches were not completely immune from the rules, but they had an edge over other inmates in circumventing certain rules and in receiving lighter punishments when caught in rule breaking.

Types of Information

The major organizational role of the BTs and turnkeys was to gather information on ordinary inmates' behavior, but they did not report every rule violation and violator. They screened all information and passed to the staff only intelligence about actual or potentially *serious* rule infractions. As Jerry, a head BT, says:

> Look, we don't tell the Man [Warden] about everything that goes on in the tanks. That makes it look bad if I'm running down to the Major's office[6] and telling somebody, old so and so, he's playing his radio too loud, or so and so, he's got an antenna that goes from his cell up to the window. That shows the Man up there that I don't have

control of that tank and I can't let that happen. That makes me look bad.

The BTs handled "misdemeanors" or petty rule violations themselves in the blocks. The BTs and turnkeys regularly informed the staff about five types of serious rule violations, commonly called "Major's Office Business."

"Major's Office Business"

First and foremost, the Bts and turnkeys were constantly on guard to detect escape plans because TDC considered escape the most serious of all violations. For example, one night when the first author was on duty, a cell block officer found several saw marks on the bars of a cell's air vent which provided access to the cell house plumbing area and ceiling fans. Should an inmate stop the fan, he could conceivably climb to the roof and perhaps escape. When a shift supervisor arrived to examine the marks, the block's Bts were assembled and asked about the situation. They knew of no hacksaw blades in the block and doubted that the two suspected inmates were the types to be preparing for an escape. They suggested that the cell's previous occupants were the most likely culprits. In any event, the BTs assisted several officers (including the researcher) in searching the inmates' belongings for escape tools. Nothing was found and everyone was allowed to go back to bed.

Second, BTs informed the staff about ordinary inmates' homosexual behavior. The staff considered this behavior serious because it frequently led to envy, fights, lover's quarrels, retaliation, stabbings, as well as to the buying and selling of "punks." Homosexuality also went against the legal and moral rules of the prison system. The guards, a moralistic conservative group, despised homosexuality and punished it severely, officially or otherwise. BTs were very adept at discovering this form of illicit behavior. For example, one night while I was on the third shift (9:45 to 5:45 a.m.), the head BT on 13-block informed a captain that one well-known homosexual (or "bitch") had entered the wrong cell on the second tier. I accompanied the shift supervisor and head BT as they slowly crept along the walkway and caught the inmates "in the act." Both were charged and punished. The BTs made sure the inmates entered their own cells and not someone else's, thus also keeping stealing to a minimum.

Third, the inmate-agents told the staff about inmates who strong-armed weaker-inmates into paying protection, engaging in homosexual acts, or surrendering their property. Extortion or strong-arming was considered serious because of the potential for violence and the prison's legal obligation to protect inmates from exploitation and physical harm. In most cases, these problems were handled informally within the blocks (i.e., a warning). If the behavior persisted, the offending inmate was generally beaten up ("tuned up") and reported to the staff. Staff members usually gave the erring inmate a few slaps across the face or kicks in the buttocks and transferred him to another cell block.

Fourth, BTs and turnkeys informed the staff about drug trafficking. The introduction of drugs into the population was extremely difficult but occasionally small quantities were smuggled inside. Again, the inmate-agents kept this activity to a minimum and assisted the staff in making "drug busts." For example, one head BT and a turnkey briefed the staff about an inmate who worked outside the prison compound (farm operation) and who was supplying marijuana cigarettes to a certain block. Plans were devised to catch the inmate with his supplies. As he came in from work the next day, another guard and the investigator detained and searched him. Although no marijuana was found, it was later reported to us that the "dealer" quit trafficking because he knew he was being watched.

The BTs and turnkeys also told ranking staff members about guards who brought in drugs. In fact, one head BT was notorious for convincing (or entrapping) officers, especially new recruits, to smuggle narcotics into the institution. If the officer agreed, and some did, the staff was informed, and plans were made to catch the unsuspecting officer. Officers caught bringing in drugs (or any other contraband such as pornography) to the inmates were immediately dismissed. The BTs in one block even assisted the staff in apprehending an officer who was homosexually involved with an inmate. This officer was promptly terminated.

Last, the BTs and turnkeys informed staff members about inmates who manufactured, possessed, or sold weapons, especially knives. Inmates with weapons obviously placed the officers and their inmate-agents in physical jeopardy. One day, John, the head BT on 18-block, came to the Major's Office and told the captain about a knife in the eighth cell on the first row of "his" block. Two officers, two BTs, and the researcher searched the cell and found a knife wedged in between the first bunk and the cell wall. The owner of the weapon received a disciplinary hearing, spent fifteen days in solitary confinement, and was then moved to another cell block. It was common for the BTs to help the guards search suspected inmates' cells because they knew the tricks and places that inmates used to conceal weapons. Many officers learned how to search cells from the BTs. On another occasion a turnkey told the first author that an inmate, who had just exited a dining hall, was carrying a knife in his ankle cast. The cast was searched and a small homemade knife was found. The turnkey later revealed to the investigator that one of his snitches spotted the inmate putting the "shank" in his cast just prior to leaving the block for the dining hall.

Routing of Information

The actual passage of information did not always follow a formal chain of command. Though runners and ordinary inmates "reported" directly to the BTs and turnkeys, these latter inmates relayed informamation only to those ranking officers (sergeants, lieutenants, captains, majors, wardens) with whom they had developed a personal relationship. Some guards were trusted by few if any inmate-snitches and were essentially left out of the informer process. Others who had displayed sufficient consistency and common sense in handling sensitive information were trusted, respected, and admired by the inmate elites. Inmate-agents actively sought alliances with these officers. Indeed, only a "man" could be trusted with confidential information. Such officers were briefed each day about events on and off their work shifts. Some of these inmate-agents were so loyal to a particular staff member that they refused to "deal" with other officers in that particular staff member's absence.

Staff members who had a cadre of inmate-agents "working" for them were in a better position to anticipate and control problems in the prison. Somewhat ironically, therefore, inmates were in a position to confer status on officers and even to affect indirectly their promotions. Some officers often gave their favorite BT or turnkey special jobs generally performed only by staff members. These jobs included stake outs, shadowing, or entrapping a suspected inmate or officer to gather evidence about rule violations or plans of wrongdoing. These special assignments brought the staff member and inmate together in an even tighter, symbiotic relationship, leading sometimes to mutual trust and friendship. Some of these snitches were so fanatical in their loyalty that they openly stated they would kill another inmate if so ordered by "their" officer.

An Open System of Informing

Unlike "rats" in prison movies, BTs and turnkeys did not hide the fact that they were snitches. It was not uncommon to see some of these inmate-agents point out the misdeeds of another inmate to a guard in the presence of other inmates. It was quite common to see Bts and turnkeys "escort" their officer "friends" as companions and bodyguards while these guards were making their rounds. While accompanying "his" officer, the inmate-agent openly informed the staff member about what was "going on" in a particular cell block or work area. The "betrayer-betrayed" relationship was not hidden and when the guards searched an inmate's cell or body, the suspected inmate knew full well in most cases who had "tipped off" the staff. One could argue that the BTs and turnkeys were not "rats" because they officially, voluntarily, and openly worked for the staff. Following this reasoning, the only "real" snitches were the BTs' and turnkeys' informers who were ordinary inmates. These inmates were mildly stigmatized by other inmates, but rarely punished because all inmates feared the BTs' presence and wrath.

Although informing occurred throughout the prison, the Major's Office was the official focal point of such activity. This office, located directly off the main corridor, was the place BTs-turnkeys conducted their "business;" that is, turned in intelligence reports and discussed plans of action. This site was divided into two rooms; the front part (off the Hall) housed the inmate bookkeepers and the back room contained two desks for the major and captains. Disciplinary court was convened in the back room where such punishments as slapping, punching, kicking, stomping, and blackjacking were administered.

The staff and their "inmate-guards" socialized here as well as conducted the daily "convict business." Throughout the day, BTs and turnkeys came in to visit their bookkeeper friends and mingle with the ranking guards. Together, in this office area, the guards and their inmate-agents drank coffee, smoked, discussed the point spreads for sporting events, joked, chatted, engineered practical jokes, roughhoused, and ate food from the prison canteen. Whenever a captain, major, or warden entered, these inmates (sometimes there were eight or nine) would, if sitting, stand and say "hello sir." However, all was not fun and games. These inmates also kept the staff abreast of what was "going on," especially in terms of Major's Office business. All day, a steady stream of these inmate-agents filed in and out. BTs and turnkeys entered this office at will. However, the Major's Office was off-limits to the ordinary inmates except for official reasons. It was a status symbol for the "rats" to hang around this office and interact with the guards.

The Informer's Payoff

Skolnick (1966: 124), in his account of police informants, maintains that "the informer-informed relationship is a matter of exchange in which each party seeks to gain something from the other in return for certain desired commodities." Similarly, BTs and turnkeys expected to receive rewards for the information they proferred beyond a sense of accomplishment for a job well done.

In addition to status and influence, BTs and turnkeys also enjoyed a number of privileges which flowed from and defined their position. Some of these privileges appear relatively minor, yet they loomed large in a prison setting. The privileges included such scarce resources as specially pressed clothes and green quilted jackets. Ordinary inmates, meanwhile, wore white, ill-fitting coats. Some BTs possessed aquariums and such pets as cats, owls, rabbits, and turtles. BT cell block doors were rarely closed, permitting BTs to move freely about the block and to receive "visits" in their cells from friends and homosexuals. The latter were not threatened or forced to engage in sexual behavior; they voluntarily moved in to share the benefits. Head BTs roamed the halls and spent considerable time in and around the Major's Office.

Furthermore, BTs were able to eat whenever they desired and often ate two or three times in one meal period. Part of this special freedom stemmed from the fact that BTs and turnkeys were on call 24 hours a day. Nonetheless it was viewed by them and others as a special privilege. These inmate-agents were permitted to carry weapons with which to protect themselves and the guard force. These weapons, usually kept concealed, included wooden clubs, knives, pipes, blackjacks, "fistloads," and hammers. A special privilege was relative immunity from discipline. For example, if a fight occurred between a BT (or turnkey) and another inmate, the non-BT might receive several nights in solitary or ten days in cell restriction; the BT might receive a reprimand or, more likely, no punishment at all. This differential treatment reflected the understanding that the BT was probably "taking care of business." The BTs also used their influence to persuade the staff to "go lightly" on their runners who faced disciplinary cases for "helping the Man." In short, the BTs and turnkeys did "soft" time. Because of their position and privileges, the BTs-turnkeys were hated, but also feared, envied and respected by the other prisoners.

On an interpersonal level, many of the BT-turnkey-officer relationships transcended a simple *quid pro quo* of exchange of favors for instrumental purposes. That is, upper level staff members called their favorite BTs and turnkeys by their first names. Sometimes, they even took the word of a head BT over that of a cell block officer. In this way, the status differential between the staff members and their inmate-agents was decreased. As one supervisor put it:

> Look, these guys [BTs-turnkeys] are going to be here a while and they get to know the cons better than us. I can't depend on some of these officers, you know how they are, they're late, they're lazy, they want extra days off, or just don't show up. Hell, you've got to rely on them [BTs and turnkeys].

This preferential treatment of a subset of inmates caused frustration

and low morale among many low ranking officers, contributing to a
high turnover rate among the guard staff, especially weak guards.[7]

Inmates, Information, and Social Control

The prison staff's primary duty is to maintain social order and
prevent escapes. Although Johnson's barb-wire fences, lights, alarm
system, perimeter patrol car, and rural isolation reduced the
possibility of escapes and mass disorder, routine control and order
were achieved proactively by penetrating and dividng the inmate population. Walls, fences, and alarms were the last line of defense as well
as symbolic forms of social control. Moreover, the staff's guns, tear
gas, and riot gear were also an end of the line means of control and
were infrequently utilized. The prison guards, like police officers,
rarely employed weapons to achieve order.

The day-to-day maintenance of order at Johnson depended on the cooptation of inmate elites, a snitching system, and the terrorization of
the ordinary inmates. The constant surveillance and terrorization of
ordinary inmates prevented them from acquiring the solidarity
necessary for self-protection and the cohesion needed for organized
resistance. Although the ordinary inmates were atomized, they lived in
a regimented and predictable environment. The staff's power,
authority, and presence permeated the institution.

The role and identify of the inmate-agents was not hidden and they
did not suffer from role strain or spoiled identities. Even though the
ordinary inmates surreptitiously called the BTs-turnkeys "dogs"
among themselves, they avoided physical confrontations with the
"dogs" at all costs. They lacked the influence, prestige, power and
organization necessary to stigmatize the BTs'-turnkeys' status or
define their roles as deviant (see Lofland, 1969). To compound
deviancy, one must be caught committing an inappropriate act, and
snitching by the BTs and turnkeys was not considered inappropriate
(see Matza, 1969: 148-9). At Johnson, informing was a means to
enhance one's status and well-being. The inmate-agents were pro-staff
and openly sided with and protected the guards. As one building tender
stated: "I'm proud to work for the Man [Warden] because I know who
butters my bread." They rationalized away their snitching behavior by
denigrating and dehumanizing the ordinary inmates, referring to them
as "scum" and "born losers." Ordinary inmate-snitches were looked
down upon but rarely punished.

The guard staff used this snitch system to penetrate the inmate population and thereby act proactively to reduce the likelihood of such
breaches of prison security as escapes, murders, rapes, narcotic rings,

mob violence, loansharking, protection rackets, excessive stealing, and racial disruption. The officers, protected by the elites, were rarely derogated or attacked and never taken hostage or murdered. The staff was rarely caught off guard. This totalitarian system virtually destroyed any chances among the ordinary inmates (as individuals or groups) to unite or engage in collective dissent, protests, or violence. Those ordinary inmates who were docile and went along with the system were generally protected and left alone. This proactive system was so successful that only two inmate murders and one riot occurred from 1972 through 1982.

The aggressive use of co-opted snitches was not, however, without problems. Ordinary inmates under this system were non-persons who lived in continuous fear, loneliness, isolation, and tension. They never knew when they might be searched or, for that matter, disciplined on the basis of another inmate's accusation. BTs and turnkeys were not above occasionally falsely accusing "insubordinate" inmates of wrongdoing. The staff routinely backed up their allies. Some "unruly" inmates were "set up" by the BTs (e.g., having a knife thrown in their cell while they were at work) and then reported to the staff. Every ordinary inmate was suspect and even lower ranking guards were sometimes terminated solely on the word of a head BT. Furthermore, a federal judge, as part of the class action civil suit *Ruiz v. Estelle* (1980), stated that this form of prisoner control at TDS was corrupt and deviant in terms of progressive penology. The snitch system at Johnson is now defunct and the staff no longer uses BTs and turnkeys (see Marquart, 1984).

Conclusion

This paper examined the structure and workings of an informer-privilege system within a penitentiary for older recidivists. At Johnson, the official informers, called BTs and turnkeys, worked for and openly cooperated with the staff. These snitches, the most aggressive, older, and criminally sophisticated prisoners, were not deviants or outcasts. In turn, they cultivated additional snitches and, with the staff's help, placed these allies in jobs or positions throughout the institution. Ordinary inmate behavior as well as that of lower ranking guards was under constant scrutiny. Therefore, the staff knew almost everything that occurred within the institution, permitting proactive control and thereby preventing in many instances, violent acts, group disturbances, and escapes.

The ordinary inmates considered the inmate-guards "rats." However, they lacked the influence, prestige, and power to define and label them as such—to impute deviancy to the BT-turnkey role. Selection as a BT or turnkey was not assignment to a deviant category, but rather to an elite corp of pro-staff inmates. Within this system, the only deviants were the unruly ordinary inmates and weak lower ranking guards. Both of these groups were stigmatized and labelled deviant by the staff and their inmate-agents within the prison. From the standpoint of progressive penologists and reform-minded citizens, this entire system would be considered deviant, inhumane, ahd morally corrupt. Although the system described in this paper may be unusual, it remains to be seen if and how other prison staffs co-opt elite inmates to help maintain social order. Past prison research has demonstrated some informal alliances between prison staffs and inmate elites. However, the form of this alliance may vary widely from prison to prison.

Footnotes

[1]Perhaps the epitome of the hatred of "rats" was in the movie "Stalag 17" (1952) wherein William Holden was falsely accused of being a "plant" in a German POW camp during World War II.
[2]The use of informants in police work, especially in vice and narcotic operations has been well-documented (see Greeno, 1960; Skolnick, 1966; Westley, 1970).
[3]Johnson is a pseudonym.
[4]For a more thorough analysis of the BT/turnkey system see Marquart (1983).
[5]The exact format or guidelines used by the Classification Committee is not known. However, this committee was composed primarily of security personnel and these members probably exerted the greatest voice in the selection process.
[6]The Major's Office is simply an office area where the ranking guards (sergeants, lieutenants, captains, majors and wardens) conducted disciplinary hearings and other forms of prison "business."
[7]Weak guards were easily bullied by the inmates, could not or would not enforce order, failed to break up fights, failed to fight inmates, and were basically ignored and laughed at by the other guards and inmates.

References

Bettelheim, B.
    1943   "Individual and mass behavior in extreme situations." Journal of Abnormal and Social Psychology.
Charriere, H.
    1970   Papillon. New York: Basic Books.
Clemmer, D.C.
    1940   The Prison Community. New York: Holt, Rinehart and Winston.
Greeno, E.
    1960   War on the Underworld. London: John Long.

Johnson, E.H.
  1961   "Sociology of Confinement: Assimilation and the prison 'rat.'"
          The Journal of Criminal Law Criminology, and Police Science. 51:
          528-533.
Lofland, J.
  1969   Deviance and Identity. Englewood Cliffs, NJ: Prentice Hall.
Marquart, J.W.
  1984   The Impact of Court-Ordered Reform in a Texas Penitentiary: The
          Unanticipated Consequences of Legal Intervention. Paper pre-
          sented at the Southern Sociological Society Annual meetings in
          Knoxville (April).
Marquart, J.W. and B.M. Crouch
  1983   Coopting the Kept: Using Inmates for Social Control in a Southern
          Prison. Paper presented before the American Society of Crimin-
          ologists Annual meetings in Toronto.
Matza, D.
  1969   Becoming Deviant. Englewood Cliffs, NJ: Prentice Hall.
McCleery, R.
  1960   "Communication patterns as bases of systems of authority." in
          Theoretical Studies in Social Organizations of the Prison. New
          York: Social Science Research Council.
Ruiz v. Estelle, 503 F. Supp. 1265 (S.D. Texas) 1980.
Schrag, C.
  1954   "Leadership among prison inmates," American Sociological
          Review. 19: 37-42.
Skolnick, J.H.
  1966   Justice Without Trial: Law Enforcement in Democratic Society.
Solzhenitsyn, A.I.
  1975   The Gulag Archipelago II. New York: Harper and Row.
Sykes, G.
  1958   The Society of Captives. Princeton, N.J.: Princeton University Press.
Westley, W.
  1970   Violence and the Police. Cambridge, MA: MIT Press.
Wilmer, H.A.
  1965   "The role of a 'rat' in prison." Federal Probation 29 (March): 44-49.

10

Guard Work in Transition
Ben M. Crouch

Prior to the 1970's, two conceptions of prison guards prevailed. First, the popular media pictured guards as brutal or dull white males dividing their time between manning towers and harassing inmates. Second, the social science conception cast guards as non-entities, mere background contributors to the inmates' "pains of imprisonment." In both, guards and guard work are simple and seemingly inconsequential to prison dynamics. Just the opposite is true, however. Guards make up approximately two-thirds of any prison staff, have the closest and most influential interaction with inmates, and can significantly influence the success of prison policies. Although media portrayals of guards have changed little over time, corrections researchers have come to recognize that guards constitute a significant presence behind the walls (see Crouch, 1980).

My purpose in this chapter is to examine the guard role and work environment, especially as they have been affected by fundamental transitions in institutional corrections over the past three decades or so. I begin by identifying the changes which seem most to affect guard work.

Source: Prepared especially for *The Dilemmas of Corrections, Second Edition* by Ben M. Crouch.

Then I examine some of the more significant problems guards face on the job, problems often exacerbated by rapid change. And finally, I consider how prison personnel accommodate an altered work environment.

Guard Work in Context

Contemporary accounts of prison guards frequently depict guards as relatively isolated workers in a tense and uncertain environment. Some observers even invoke an incarceration imagery, characterizing guards as "imprisoned" (Lombardo, 1981) or as "society's professional prisoners" (Wicks, 1980); men who feel "rejected, shunned and even despised. . ." (Jacobs and Zimmer, 1983:145). This sense of embattlement among guards became especially apparent as external pressures and reforms rocked the prison world (Irwin, 1980). The most consequential changes for guards have been: (1) an emphasis on rehabilitation, (2) changes in the size and composition of inmate populations, and (3) judicial intervention. Since these changes serve as the backdrop for the following discussion of guards, each will be considered briefly.

The reemergence of rehabilitation as a major prison goal in the late 1950s had direct implications for guards. The introduction of rehabilitation meant prison workers were to reform as well as control inmates. For security staff this often led to role conflict and to conflict with treatment personnel. Although studies purporting to show that correctional treatment programs were generally ineffective eventually led to a deemphasis on rehabilitation, the initial push toward treatment fostered a greater concern for humane treatment of inmates. Consequently, prison officers felt pressured somehow to combine treatment with custody.

The second broad change affecting guard work involved shifts in the size and composition of inmate populations. Prison populations surged in the early 1970s and again in the late 1970s; the latest upward trend continues into the late 1980s. Population growth strains prison personnel as well as housing and support services. Consequently, officers must supervise and control many more inmates on a very tight daily schedule. As the growth of inmate populations outstrips the hiring of new officers, the existing staff may find itself spread too thin. At the same time, changes in the composition of prison populations exacerbate the overcrowding situation. As corrections officials divert less serious offenders to community corrections programs, those who actually do time are more apt to be violent as well as young and from a minority group (Toch, 1976). Such population shifts add tensions to guard work.

The third, and perhaps most consequential, change in the prison environment has been court intervention to guarantee the civil rights of inmates (see Alpert, Crouch and Huff, 1984). Prior to the mid-1960s, judges adhered to a "hands off" policy, accepting the notion that convicted felons lost their rights. At that time, changes in legal philosophy and case law led to a much greater willingness by judges to hear prisoner petitions. As judicial activism increased, prisoners gained for the first time a source of relief other than their keepers (see Haas, 1977; 1981). Court decrees to reform unconstitutional practices and conditions altered standards of prisoner care and custody, and, in turn, changed traditional power relations between the keepers and the kept (Crouch and Marquart, 1989).

Problems on the Line

These and related changes have increased problems guards face in relating to inmates, administrators, and co-workers. In the following sections, I will examine six of these problems in some detail: (1) role conflict and ambiguity, (2) danger on the job, (3) loss of control, (4) stress, (5) racial and sexual integration of guard forces, and (6) deviant behavior on the job.

Role Conflict and Ambiguity

While officers have generally accepted the legitimacy of prisoner rehabilitation as a prison objective, they have often had trouble combining treatment expectations with custody routines. Specifically, the juxtaposition of security and rehabilitation can create role conflict for guards.

Role conflict among guards is particularly likely when prison administrators rapidly introduce treatment objectives, as Carroll's (1974) analysis of the Eastern Correctional Institution (ECI) illustrates. After years of operation as a custody-oriented prison, a new manager took over at ECI and called for a strong commitment to treatment goals. Guards saw this shift in emphasis as jeopardizing security and prisoner control. In turn, they experienced considerable role ambiguity and conflict in trying to meet both traditional custody demands and new, ill-defined treatment demands.

Role conflict is also likely if officers take the title "correctional officer" quite literally and try, through some form of social work, to reform inmates. This orientation ensures some level of role conflict for security officers since the realities of their job limit the extent to which guards can actually treat or reform prisoners. If they remain in security, these officers will likely reduce role conflict by adopting a modest definition of treatment. They may move from trying to change lives to helping prisoners each day in situation-specific ways.

Danger

While prisons have always been potentially dangerous places to work, prisoner assaults on staff were relatively infrequent three decades ago. Then, prisoners were apparently more accepting of the prison status quo, more willing to accept both their time in prison and the authority of their keepers. But as reforms altered the prison world and as prisoner aggressiveness and gangs grew, risks to officers grew as well. Through the 1970's, evidence from several state prisons indicated that the proportion of altercations involving guards and prisoners increased, with assaults on staff becoming more deliberate and even status-conferring for some prisoners (Toch, 1976).

Although being taken hostage in an escape attempt or riot is certainly less likely than being assaulted by an inmate, it is nevertheless a source of danger for officers. A 1974 escape attempt in a Texas prison provides an illustration. To force prison officials to free them, three inmates took 11 people hostage, including several women teachers and one uniformed officer. The correctional officer hostage was singled out for special attention during the 11 days of negotiation. Several times one of the three rebels placed a gun barrel to the head of the officer and squeezed the trigger, letting the hammer fall on what only the inmate knew to be an empty chamber. The officer assumed each time he was about to die (House, 1975).

Being held hostage in a riot situation may be even more dangerous, if only for the number of inmates involved. Officers taken hostage in a riot are at risk at three points. The first is when prisoners take over parts of the prison and attempt to subdue or eliminate opposition from officers. The second point is when prisoners gain control over the building or cell block area and of the officers who have not gotten away in the takeover. Officers taken hostage at best may be blindfolded, herded about and threatened and, at worst, physically abused or even killed. During the Santa Fe prison riot in February, 1980, for example, one young officer was repeatedly sodomized, an experience that has left long-term psychological scars. Finally, officer hostages are at risk if the authorities retake the institution by force, as occurred during the Attica riot. Regardless of the circumstances, being a hostage is a traumatic event, and survivors may suffer prolonged anxiety along with loss of sleep, appetite, and sexual potency (Donovan, 1983).

Fear and uncertainty are daily realities for many guards. They see inmate-inmate violence and know that it could be directed at them. It is thus not surprising that guards in New York (Lombardo, 1981: 114) and Illinois (Jacobs, 1981: 45) named danger as the major disadvantage or source of dissatisfaction on the job.

How do officers deal with danger? Some simply leave. The possibility of injury certainly contributes to the high turnover among guards, especially those in the lower ranks. Most, however, adjust in some other manner, perhaps by having a private plan for staying out of harm's way. An informant in the Texas system told me, for example, that all the officers on one of the more tense prison units had identified a hiding place to be used "when it came down." Others may rely on their relations with particular inmates. Just prior to the Santa Fe riot, friendly inmates told several officers and treatment staff to "be sick" and not show up the day before the riot. Probably the most common method of handling fear, however, is to deny it, to present to self and others a "manly" front.

Loss of Control

Twenty-five years ago prisons were politically and legally isolated from the societal mainstream. Officials frequently operated according to self-determined and unquestioned policies which made guarding and doing time predictable, if not always constitutional. The subordinate status of prisoners was clearly defined, and role expectations were unequivocal. Officers maintained dominance over inmates by whatever means they found practical and were typically supported by their superiors. But as political, social, and legal activists criticized prison conditions and operations, inmates gained power relative to their keepers. Media attention and litigation especially called into question or eliminated many traditional methods of inmate control and punishment. While most officers today probably would not favor a wholesale return to the control devices and strategies of the past, most feel that inmates have too much freedom and that guards have lost much authority and control (Hepburn, 1983).

Guards have been concerned not only about diminished control, but about reduced support from prison administrators as well. This sense of being forsaken by the "front office" stems in part from court intervention. As the number of suits grew and the range of issues subject to litigation widened, administrators readily complied with court rulings, sometimes even welcoming court intervention as a means of improving prison conditions (Haas and Champagne, 1976). Administrative sensitivity to inmate plaintiffs, however, convinced many line officers that their administrators were more interested in inmates than in them. The frequent turnover of administrators in many prisons also undermined guard-administrator relations. That is, to protect their jobs administrators sometimes became more attuned to political and judicial pressures than to the frustrations of their staffs. This situation limited front-office support for guards and, in turn, eroded guard confidence in their own authority in dealing with prisoners. A New York officer's statement reflects the frustration of having limited support in a hostile work setting (Lombardo, 1981: 122):

> With our job today we really don't have authority like we used to. You're restricted. The state doesn't back you if something happens. They don't want to know right from wrong. Now when there's a mob situation, you just stand there and observe. Years ago you would disperse them, persuade them to move. Today they're hesitant. We just let things boil longer and things develop into confrontations.

Guards have reacted to this apparent erosion of authority and control in several ways. One reaction is alienation (Poole and Regoli, 1981), the feeling that traditional norms are no longer appropriate or acceptable and that control over one's work has diminished. To combat alienation and restructure their work setting, guards may become more punitive and thus more likely to invoke disciplinary procedures against inmates (Poole and Regoli, 1980a). Other officers may adopt a very cynical attitude toward their work and the prison organization generally, especially if they believe that they do not have the support of the front office (Poole and Regoli, 1980b).

Most officers, however, probably try to disguise the toll taken by the job and make the best of what is an often a frustrating situation. Though not immune to the pressures of the workplace these officers project a tough, steady image which precludes sharing frustrations with either co-workers or family members. Some of these officers may be particularly vulnerable to stress.

Stress

The problems just examined—role conflict, danger, and diminished control—may produce considerable stress for individual officers (Cullen, et al., 1985). Stress as experienced by correctional workers has received considerable research attention in recent years on the assumption that current prison conditions exacerbate it. If inordinate stress is present within a guard force, it can be costly to both individual officers and to the institution. Among officers it can promote heart attacks, hypertension, ulcers, and hypoglycemia (Dahl, 1980). Organizational costs of stress include reduced work efficiency as officers become more negative, caustic, and inclined to perform "by the book." At the same time, increases in sick leave and resultant overtime pay can be very expensive.

Stress among correctional officers has several sources. An immediate stressor is the perception that the workplace is increasingly dangerous and that guards cannot lawfully retaliate in kind to violence by inmates. Long term stress is particularly likely when the following conditions, all characteristics of prisons today, are present: (1) contradictory goals, objectives, and limited support from superiors; (2) role ambiguity; (3) uncooperative consumers of the worker's service; (4) felt vulnerability; and (5) inability to leave the job (Brodsky, 1977). Recent work on correctional stress suggests that a particularly significant source of stress among guards is a kind of "double bind" (Cheek and Miller, 1982). Specifically, officers want to respond to both intractable inmates and overcrowding by "putting the lid on," by "cracking down." Yet their superiors, fearing litigation, call for officers to limit their control efforts, to be "loose." The bind is further felt by officers when they realize that to maintain control, rules must be bent. In today's prison world, officers who do bend rules may find administrators unwilling to support them.

Integration of the Guards

Guarding in prison has traditionally been the occupational domain of white males. Security forces have included black officers, but they have been relatively few in number, even where the inmate population has been predominantly black. Women officers in men's prisons have been even more rare. Despite some resistance, however, the proportion of black and women officers has grown in recent years. The result has been increasingly heterogeneous and fragmented guard forces.

Racial integration: by the late 1960s, blacks and other minorities began to enter guard work in greater numbers than ever before. The civil rights movement which opened prisons to black employment coincided with a growing need for correctional manpower. As courts required prison administrators to increase the ratio of officers to inmates, many officials found it necessary to look beyond the local, white manpower pools from which they had traditionally drawn officers. Pressure from inmate groups also prompted administrators to hire more minority officers (Jacobs and Kraft, 1978).

Veteran white officers have been at best suspicious of this growing contingent of black officers. In Illinois the "old guard" felt that this "new breed" of typically non-white, urban guards was more pro-inmate and less trustworthy (Irwin, 1977). Not surprisingly, black officers often see race and racism as barriers to recruitment, co-worker relations, and promotion (Beard, 1975).

Racism is particularly pernicious when it has an institutional character. Institutional racism exists when almost no minority officers hold upper level security positions and few can qualify for those posts. Such a situation existed in New York in 1972 (Jacobs and Zimmer, 1983: 146). When only two black officers made the sergeant's list in the New York Department of Corrections, a group of minority officers challenged the department's promotion process. Subsequent litigation led to a non-discriminatory promotional system and a racial quota for promotions. White officers then sued, claiming reverse discrimination. An appellate court ultimately struck down the quota system but found the original examination to be valid. Such confrontations may not be characteristic of race relations among officers in all prisons, nor is race as divisive among officers as it is among inmates. Nevertheless, it remains a significant factor in guard relations on and off the job.

Sexual integration: Though still a fairly small minority, the number of women guards in adult male prisons has grown considerably (Jurik, 1985). In state and federal prisons they constitute six and 18 percent, respectively (Morton, 1981; Ingram, 1980). Not surprisingly, these women are usually in the lower ranks of the guard hierarchy.

Title VII of the 1964 Civil Rights Act removed legal barriers to the employment of women officers, but their entry has been resisted by both prison administrators and male officers. Indeed, they have probably been more resistant to female officers than to minority male officers. After all, the latter at least meet the size and gender criteria guards have long believed to be unquestionable requisites for the job. Just to get hired, would-be women officers have had to overcome through litigation the argument that being male is a "bona fide occupational qualification" for working in male institutions (Alpert, 1984).

Yet getting hired is only the first step; women still have to perform the tasks guard work requires. Traditional objections to women guards have involved their ability to relate to, supervise, and control male prisoners. One matter regularly at issue in litigation, and relevant to the women officer's success on the job, is inmate privacy (Jacobs, 1983). Women can apparently learn, however, to deal effectively with situations where they are in close proximity to inmates. One female officer, for example, stated: "I've stood at a cell door and talked to a man using the toilet. I just looked the other way. When they're in the shower, they might wave their thing at you. You just ignore it'' (Potter, (1980: 33). Other evidence (Kissel and Katsampes, 1980: 220) indicates that most inmates may not be particularly troubled by the privacy issue.

Another question raised about women guards concerns their ability to establish personal authority in dealing with inmates and thereby maintain order. Again, women appear to perform well. Inmates report women officers are generally no more easily conned or manipulated than men (Peterson, 1982: 451). Moreover, women officers do not promote prisoner aggression or violence through their sexuality or presumed greater vulnerability to being taken hostage. Indeed, women officers may even facilitate order by bringing about a more relaxed and normal atmosphere (Potter, 1980). The only shortcoming women appear to have is handling violence once it is initiated; inmates as well as male officers prefer males in such situations (Peterson, 1982). Women officers thus appear to be as capable as their male counterparts on the job. For individual women officers, the initial difficulties with inmates tend to wane with time; gender apparently becomes less of an issue as female officers and inmates become used to each other.

Although it too may improve with time, the most persistent problem women officers appear to face is non-acceptance by their male co-workers. Women working in male prisons enter a masculine world and encounter a more specific occupational subculture; they must accommodate the normative expectations of both (Crouch, 1985). General masculine norms demand toughness, confidence, and aggressiveness, while the guard subculture proscribes being friendly to inmates, getting conned, snitching on other officers (solidarity), and trusting the "front-office" (Bowker, 1982: 176-184). If women are generally less physically aggressive, less apt to take formal action, more nurturing, and have a higher need to affiliate (Peterson, 1982), then they will contravene both sets of norms. To the extent these norms prevail among their male counterparts, women officers in men's prisons are going to be at a disadvantage.

Deviant Behavior on the Job

Guard deviance is the failure to comply with laws and the legal policies of the prison administration. So defined, the range of deviance can be broad. A study of security employee offenses within the Florida Department of Corrections (1981) between 1967 and 1980 suggested an illustrative, though certainly not exhaustive, list of deviant acts: (1) introduction of or trafficking in contraband; (2) grand theft; (3) warehouse sabotage; (4) homosexual relations with inmates; (5) bartering with inmates; (6) inappropriate use of force; (7) horseplay leading to injury of inmates; (8) assisting in an escape; and (9) theft of .38 caliber revolvers. Such acts have an important impact on institutional safety, inmate control, and the economic efficiency of the prison organization.

One of the few studies to address systematically the distribution of guard deviance is by McCarthy (1981). He examined 122 cases of serious misconduct referred to the Internal Affairs Unit of one prison system during the period from October, 1978 to December, 1979. McCarthy found that misuse of authority by guards accounted for 44 percent of the offenses, theft (over $50) accounted for another 20 percent, and embezzlement and trafficking in contraband accounted for 16 percent each; miscellaneous offenses accounted for the remainder.

Officers abuse their authority when they use their position for personal gain such as accepting gratuities to secure privileges for prisoners. For example, an officer managing a work release program solicited a fee from an inmate for finding him a job. Another officer asked an inmate to pay him for transfer to a less secure facility. Similarly, officers may solicit payoffs from inmates to foster or overlook illicit activities. This would include "selling" the rights or franchises to illicit businesses such as drugs, gambling, or prostitution within the prison. In one case reported by McCarthy, an officer told an inmate he would leave a gate open for an escape if the inmate would pay him $6000. Extortion is an even more blatant misuse of authority. The personal gain here is typically money or a percentage of illicit profit. One female inmate, however, alleged that a male supervisor threatened to place her on restriction if she did not grant him sexual favors. A final misuse of authority noted by McCarthy is mismanagement, usually involving illicit skimming or other profiteering from the work area, warehouse, or industry the employee supervises.

These examples of guard deviance are probably best understood in individual rather than organizational terms. Theft, extortion, and homosexuality appear to stem from "bad guards" — individuals who either brought their penchant for misconduct into the prison with them or developed it essentially on their own in response to an opportunity to exploit a work situation. Other types of officer deviance, however, stem more from the expectations of prisoners, peers, and superiors about how the job is to be done. This latter type of deviance may be more pernicious than theft since it may undermine prison order and/or promote widespread unjust treatment of inmates. Three types of deviance stem primarily from organizational factors: corruption of authority, questionable disciplinary actions, and patterned guard violence.

Corruption of authority. As Sykes (1958) noted in an early study, the authority of prison custodians may easily be corrupted or eroded due to two fundamental realities of guard work. First, guards lack total power. Since they cannot completely impose their will upon inmates, some negotiation is always required. Secondly, guards must work in close, daily proximity to inmates, and thus come to know at least some of them as individuals. Together these two occupational realities can compromise an officer's authority in several ways.

Yielding to cultural pressures to be a "good guy," the officer may begin to interact with inmates on a personal basis, joking or working out with them. Interaction leading to such a relationship may often be initiated by an inmate who astutely picks out a likely officer, observes his moods, and then offers him support and a sympathetic ear. The officer over time comes to depend on this support, expect it and, in turn, feels obligated to the inmate. The result can be not only loss of authority but the officer's trafficking in contraband at the inmate's request or demand. As reforms lead to larger, more diverse guard forces and break down informal controls within the guard subculture, such acts may increase dramatically (see Crouch and Marquart, 1989).

Authority may also be corrupted if the officer, being overly busy or perhaps just lazy, permits an inmate to carry out some of the officer's own duties. In time the officer may discover that his control in the work area has slipped away. Finally, an officer may lose authority by engaging in trade-offs with powerful inmates under his supervision; they ensure order on his cell block, and he grants them special privileges. In addition to cell block order, the officer gets a good rating from his superiors. But here, as in each of these circumstances of authority corruption, the officer may find that when he seeks to invoke his authority over these "special" inmates, his authority may be severely eroded. As Sykes puts it, authority, like virtue, is difficult to retrieve after it has been lost.

Deviance in formal disciplinary actions. The misuse of authority in the formal disciplining of inmates for rule violations is another broad area of guard deviance. Prisons have unique and extensive sets of rules, all ostensibly designed to protect or maintain inmates, officers, and the general order. This plethora of rules means that it is extremely difficult for inmates to avoid violating some minor rule daily and that officers have many opportunities to put inmates on report. Yet in practice officers actually use their authority to formally sanction inmates in a very selective manner.

This selective sanctioning involves two types of deviance: (1) non-enforcement of prison rules when a violation has clearly occurred, and (2) enforcement for personal reasons. First, officers overlook much inmate misconduct, especially of a minor nature. They may not "write him up" because the rule violated seems inappropriate in a given setting, because of personal relations with the violator, or because the cost of invoking sanctions seems too high in terms of the resultant inmate hostility. Second, officers may engage in selective sanctioning to establish or confirm their personal authority in dealing with particular inmates. That is, formal disciplinary actions are often not just impersonal, even-handed applications of organizational rules but means of communicating a message to inmates, of establishing an officer's reputation as one deserving respect (Crouch and Marquart, 1980). Technically, the practice of selective sanctioning is deviant; the organizational rules presumably have a purpose, and officer failure to enforce them violates that purpose. Although officially deviant, the practice is nonetheless not only widespread but normative in terms of the informal expectations of inmates, officers, and administrators. Indeed, some selective sanctioning is necessary and even functional for the smooth operation of prisons.

Selective sanctioning becomes much more significantly deviant, however, when officers use the formal disciplinary process to discriminate systematically against a category of inmates (Flanagan, 1983). The question is whether the fact that black inmates have a disproportionately higher rate of prison rule infractions than whites demonstrates discrimination against black inmates in the disciplinary process. Evidence on this question is mixed, although most points to at least some degree of discrimination by officers. White officers constitute the bulk of most guard forces and often do not like non-whites (Irwin, 1980: 125). Typically from rural backgrounds, these officers not only often misunderstand the perspective and culture of minority prisoners but feel superior to them. These attitudes make non-whites more likely to be written up and formally sanctioned. Indeed, Held, Levin and Swartz (1979) report that in those infraction categories where guards do not have to substantiate their charges with evidence (i.e., "disrespect" by inmate), blacks are significantly overrepresented. Apparently, unencumbered by the need to produce evidence, guards give discriminatory tendencies freer rein. In a study of race and severity of prison discipline, however, I found that a generally prejudiced and overwhelming white guard force did not give minority inmates more severe punishments than white inmates for comparable infractions (Crouch, 1983). Clearly, the extent of this type of deviance by officers, its consequences, and the conditions under which it exists require further research.

Patterned guard violence. A final area of officer deviance involves physical punishment of inmates instead of or in addition to, formal, legal disciplinary action. Because prisons can be violent places, physical control of inmates by officers is sometimes necessary as in the case of self-defense or of an unbalanced inmate who needs restraint. The problem emerges when officers employ physical force unnecessarily and excessively.

The use of force as a control mechanism may be so routine in some prison settings that abuse of inmates reflects organizational expectations and is best understood in those terms. Punitive violence by guards may not only be encouraged by the informal guard subculture but tacitly supported by the administration. Marquart (1986) reports, for example, that in one prison the willingness to fight an inmate reflected positively on an officer's manhood; those who exhibited this behavior were rewarded, sometimes with promotion. In the prison Marquart investigated, physical punishment of inmates was institutionalized to the point that guards understood two levels of action, the "tune up" and the "overhaul." A "tune up" involved slapping an inmate around for a persistent bad attitude or a minor transgression. An "overhaul" was more serious, often prompted by an inmate striking or merely attempting to strike an officer; here the objective was to hurt the inmate severely.

Officers may also use excessive violence during a riot situation, especially during its quelling and immediately thereafter. The obvious motivation for collective guard violence in such situations is a desire to punish inmates and to ensure that the riot is not repeated. There may, however, be a less obvious motivation, namely a desire to redress lost occupational esteem. In his analysis of the unauthorized participation by guards in the retaking of the Attica prison in 1971, Stotland (1980) argues that guards at Attica, for many of the reasons discussed above, felt a reduced importance on the job. Their excessive violence in the retaking of the prison and the harsh treatment of inmates in the riot's aftermath were efforts to recapture their own self-esteem.

The extent of staff violence is difficult to determine. Some evidence, however, suggests that there is less guard brutality in prisons today than in the past (Toch, 1976). May (1981: 33), for example, reports that in Connecticut, the prison ombudsman handled 1,062 inmate complaints in a three year period in the early 1970s, and only 15 involved inappropriate use of force by guards. The primary reason for less physical coercion is that prison staff behavior today receives much closer scrutiny from the courts and media.

Regaining Control

Prison security forces today are much more diverse than they were two or three decades ago. Officers of different sexes, races, and backgrounds work together. Differences in organizational goals or in personal orientations to the job lead some to be institutional cops and others to be overtly concerned with prisoner welfare. Even at the same prison, solidarity within the officer force may be more apparent than real. Despite this diversity, however, officers who experience the problems considered above tend in time to reflect similar attitudes and perspectives on the job (Crouch and Alpert, 1982; Jacobs and Kraft, 1978). One of the most commonly shared perceptions among officers today is that they have less control both over prisoners and over their jobs, and, as a result, feel dissatisfied.

While there are many means through which officers may regain some measure of control on the job and, in the process, improve their morale, three seem particularly significant: unionization, professionalization, and bureaucratization. Each represents a restructuring of prison relations and has a different potential for improving the officers' lot.

Unionization

Concerned in recent years about their loss of power on the job, guards have increasingly expressed their general dissatisfaction through sick-outs, slow-downs, strikes, and a heightened push toward unionization (Irwin, 1980: 221). The most formal of these actions, the unionization movement, is relatively new. While a few states have had unionized guard forces for decades, most correctional staffs which have turned to collective bargaining have done so only during the 1970s (Flanagan, van Alstyne and Gottfredson, 1982: 138-39). Until relatively recently officers saw little need for unionization, feeling comfortable with their relations with prisoners and especially with prison managers. Reforms, however, created a rift between officers and those managers. Feeling forsaken by the front-office, under judicial, media and even legislative scrutiny, many officers turned to the apparent power of unions.

But while union pressure can help improve wages and working conditions, limit management arbitrariness, and promote management-union interaction, there are limitations on the extent to which unions can improve control or morale. In a study of the New York guard union, Jacobs and Zimmer (1983) found that while collective bargaining helped with problems of wages, benefits, and some specific grievances, it was not able to address the most fundamental problems facing officers in New York and elsewhere—loss of control, loss of status, and racial tension. At the same time, guard unions may limit job mobility by stressing seniority and by generally preserving and extending the status quo (Wynne, 1978).

Thus, as an occupational strategy for accommodating current and anticipated changes in institutional corrections, unionization may not be sufficient. It may be that more fundamental changes in guard work will be called for in the future than unionization may foster or permit.

Professionalization

Whereas unionization is initiated primarily by the officers themselves, professionalization must be initiated and supported by prison administrators. Professionalization connotes, among other things, the hiring of better educated people, more sophisticated and protracted training, and the enlargement or diversification of the guard role. Its goal is to improve staff qualifications so that officers can project a humane treatment orientation, can reduce prison tensions, and can experience greater occupational self-esteem by having more control over decision making. Unfortunately, professionalization efforts have not been especially productive in achieving these objectives.

A number of factors limit the professionalizing of guard forces (Jurik and Musheno, 1986). First, despite much rhetorical support for creating a professional force, there is still public, legislative, and even administrative opposition to professionalizing programs and expenditures, as they might appear to "coddle" prisoners (see Cohen, 1977). Thus, formal efforts to expand the job beyond custodial duties are often thwarted. Second, resources are typically insufficient to attract many skilled people to corrections work through high salaries or to develop the sophisticated pre- and in-service training that professionalization requires. A third barrier, beyond informal resistance from "custody-oriented" staff and administrators, is the fact that the formal, para-military organization of prison security is structurally incompatible with professional autonomy. Guard force hierarchies have been, and largely remain, uninterested in input from the bottom, preferring tight control of information flow and of the actions of rank-and-file officers. Thus, when well-trained and professionally-oriented officers do find their way to the cell blocks, they are often particularly frustrated and dissatisfied.

Litigated reform may also limit the on-the-job autonomy which professionalism requires. Court intervention into prison operations typically occurs when policies and practices in some way abuse prisoners. Since guards put those policies into practice, it is the guards and their supervisors that the courts have been particularly keen to monitor. To ensure that guards act legally, the prison administration, following court directives, carefully spells out what officers can or must do. This accountability to strict, imposed rules limits autonomy and the enlargement of the officer role. When litigated reforms restrict guard actions, low morale is a predictable by-product (Crouch and Marquart, 1989).

Bureaucratization

Reforms of the past 25 years have left prison organizations more specialized, centralized, and formalized — in short, more bureaucratic. The fundamental objective of this trend has been to restructure prison organizations and operations so they will be more constitutional and humane. As suggested above, reform very often involves redirecting and then closely controlling guards to ensure their compliance with new policies. The most effective type of staff control is bureaucratization, and it has significantly altered traditional guard work. Specialization reduces the scope of line officers' influence on prisoners' lives, centralization shifts power from supervisors and wardens to top administrators, and formalization proliferates rules and the paperwork to hold officers accountable to them. That prisoners seem to gain freedoms and that courts and top administrators seem bent on taking away officers' discretion is disheartening to officers.

Yet, bureaucratization, which seems to have so tied the hands of officers, has actually become a tangible means for regaining control, if not satisfaction. That is, many guards have learned to use the rules and not to fight them. In time, the new, more formal guidelines for doing work become routine; guards become accustomed to new ways of relating to prisoners and to superiors. In the process, officers discover that even if they have relatively less discretion, they can still control prisoners by holding them to the "letter of the rule" or by using the initially abhorred rules and paperwork to punish, deprive, or harass inmates.

Prison Guards in the 1990s

Through the 1970s and 1980s state prison guards frequently claimed they had lost the ability to control prisoners and to maintain order. But this was more lament than an accurate description of guard work. Guards today do have control; they just use somewhat different means. Recognizing that the arbitrary and abusive control techniques of the "old days" are taboo, officers have learned to use strict rule enforcement and the threat of long-term lockdown in an "administrative segregation" cell — methods that are technically in accord with due process — to deal with problem prisoners. Bolstering this bureaucratic order is the fact that officers may have less to fear from prisoners who would attack them through the courts. In the 1980s, numerous Supreme Court decisions curtailed the availability of judicial relief for prisoners, thus making it more difficult for inmates to bring suits against their keepers (Haas and Alpert, 1989).

But if officers today have control over prisoners, they are still frequently frustrated and dissatisfied. A major reason is the loss of traditional intrinsic rewards on the job, both from relationships with prisoners below and administrators above. Until the 1960s and, in some prisons through the 1970s, guards enjoyed unquestioned dominance and related to prisoners in a very paternalistic manner. At the same time, relatively small, all-male and largely white security forces could sustain considerable subcultural solidarity, bolstered by support from powerful, sometimes charismatic, administrators. These aspects of guard work were intrinsic rewards which helped compensate for low pay and the "dirty work" the job often entails. Yet, these aspects of guard work have been eroded, primarily by the prisoners' rights movement and by other humanitarian reforms of the last two decades. Among other things, reforms extended the rights of prisoners, made guard forces larger and more heterogeneous, and attenuated traditional front-office support, especially for questionable guard actions. Many officers thus feel they have lost some major sources of job status and self-esteem — clear dominance over prisoners, broad discretion on the job, inclusion in a closed masculine subculture, and loyalty rewarded by administrative support — that in the past provided gratification on the job.

This analysis suggests a peculiar problem facing prison security forces in the 1990s. In the turmoil of American prisons from the late 1960s through the 1980s, guards have frequently felt powerless and dissatisfied. While unionization and professsionalization have generally failed to redress these grievances, bureaucratization, somewhat ironically, has at least provided legal means of prisoner control. But none of these has been able to offer career officers much in the way of job status and satisfaction. In the more structured prison environment of today, guards lack the trappings of professionalism and are not often expected to contribute either to treatment or to policy. Predictably, some officers respond by simply going through the motions, by just "putting in their eight." Many officers, however, despite endemic problems and frustrations, are able on their own to find meaning on the job and to carry out their tasks with dedication and humanity.

References

Alpert, G. 1984. "The Needs of the Judiciary and Misapplications of Social Research: The Case of Female Guards in Men's Prisons." Criminology 22 (August): 441-56.

Alpert, G., B. Crouch and C. Huff. 1983. "Prison Reform by Decree: The Unintended Consequences of Ruiz v. Estelle." The Justice System Journal 9 (Winter): 291-305.

Beard, E. 1975. Final Report: The Recruitment and Retention of Minority Correctional Employees Research Project. Washington, DC: Institute for Urban Affairs and Research, Howard University.

Bowker, L. 1982. Corrections: The Science and the Art. New York: Macmillan Publishing Co., Inc.

Brodsky, C. M. 1977. "Long-term Work Stress in Teachers and Prison Guards." Journal of Occupational Medicine. 19 (February): 133-38.

Carroll, L. 1974. Hacks, Blacks and Cons. Prospect Heights, IL: Waveland Press, Inc. (reissued 1988 with changes).

Cheek, F. and M. Miller. 1982. "Reducing Staff and Inmate Stress." Corrections Today. (October): 721-78.

Crouch, B. (ed.) 1980. The Keepers. Springfield, IL: Charles C Thomas Publishers.

_____. 1983. "Inmate Deviance and Formal Prison Discipline: The Relevance of Minority Status to Punishment Severity." Sociological Focus. 18 (August): 221-34.

_____. 1985. "Pandora's Box" Women Guards in Men's Prisons," Journal of Criminal Justice. 13: 535-48.

Crouch, B. and G. Alpert. 1982. "Sex and Occupational Socialization: A Longitudinal Study of Prison Guards." Criminal Justice and Behavior. 2 (June): 159-76.

Crouch, B. and J. Marquart. 1980. "On Becoming a Prison Guard," pp. 63-109 in B. Crouch (ed.) The Keepers: Prison Guards and Contemporary Corrections. Springfield, IL: Charles C Thomas Publishers.

_____. 1989. An Appeal to Justice: Litigated Reform of Texas Prisons. Austin, TX: University of Texas Prisons.

Cullen, F. T., et al. 1985. "The Social Correlates of Correctional Officer Stress." Justice Quarterly. 2 (December): 505-34.

Dahl, J. J. 1980. "Occupational Stress in Corrections," pp. 207-22 in Proceedings of the 110th Annual Congress of Corrections. Association. College Park, Maryland.

Donovan, E. 1983. "Responding to the Prison Employee-Hostage as a Crime Victim," pp. 17-24 in Correctional Officers: Power, Pressure and Responsibility. American Correctional Association, College Park, Maryland.

Flanagan, T. 1983. "Correlates of Institutional Misconduct Among State Prisoners." Criminology. 21 (February): 29-39.

Flanagan, T., D. van Alstyne and M. Gottfredson (eds.). 1982. Sourcebook of Criminal Justice Statistics-1981. Washington, DC: U.S. Department of Justice, Bureau of Justice Statistics.

Florida Department of Corrections. 1981. "Response to the Findings and Recommendations of the AD HOC Sub-committee of the House Committee on Corrections, Probation and Parole."

Haas, K. C. 1977. "Judicial Politics and Correctional Reform: An Analysis of the Decline of the 'Hands-Off' Doctrine." *Detroit College of Law Review* (Winter): 795-831.

———. 1981. "The 'New Federalism' and Prisoners' Rights: State Supreme Courts in Comparative Perspective," *Western Political Quarterly* 34 (December): 552-71.

Haas, K. C. and G. Alpert. 1989. "American Prisoners and the Right of Access to the Courts" in L. I. Goodstein and D. L. McKenzie (eds.) *The American Prison: Issues in Research and Policy*. New York: Plenum.

Haas, K. C. and A. Champagne. 1976. "The Impact of *Johnson v. Avery* on Prison Administration." *Tennessee Law Review*. 43 (Winter): 275-306.

Held, B. D. Levine and V. Swartz. 1979. "Interpersonal Aspects of Dangerousness." *Criminal Justice and Behavior*. 1 (March): 45-58.

Hepburn, J. 1983. "The Prison Control Structure and Its Effects on Work Attitudes: A Study of the Attitudes of Prison Guards," paper presented at the American Society of Criminology meeting, Denver.

House, A. 1975. *The Corrasco Tragedy*. Waco, TX: The Texian Press.

Ingram, G. 1980. "The Role of Women in Male Federal Correctional Institutions," pp. 275-81 in the *Proceedings of the 110th Congress of Correction of the American Correctional Association*. College Park, Maryland.

Irwin, J. 1977. "The Changing Social Structure of the Men's Correctional Prison," pp. 21-40 in D. Greenberg (ed.) *Corrections and Punishment*. Beverly Hills, CA: Sage Publications.

———. 1980. *Prisons in Turmoil*. Boston: Little, Brown and Co.

Jacobs, J. 1981. "What Prison Guards Think: A Profile of the Prison Force," pp. 1-53 in R. Ross (ed.) *Prison Guard/Correctional Officers: Uses and Abuses of the Human Resources of Prisons*. Toronto: Butterworth.

———. 1983. *New Perspectives in Prisons and Imprisonment*. Ithaca: Cornell University Press.

Jacobs, J. and L. Kraft. 1978. "Integrating the Keepers: A Comparison of Black and White Prison Guards in Illinois." *Social Problems*. (25): 304-318.

Jacobs, J. and L. Zimmer. 1983. "Collective Bargaining and Labor Unrest," pp. 145-59 in J. Jacobs *New Perspectives in Prisons and Imprisonment*. Ithaca: Cornell University Press.

Jurik, N. 1985. "An Officer and a Lady: Organizational Barriers to Women Working as Correctional Officers in Men's Prisons" *Social Problems* 32 (April): 375-88.

Jurik, N. and M. Musheno. 1986. "The Internal Crisis of Corrections: Professionalization and the Work Environment" *Justice Quarterly*. 3 (December): 457-480.

Kissel, P. and P. Katsampes. 1980. "Impact of Women Corrections Officers on the Functioning of Institutions Housing Male Inmates." *Journal of Offender Counseling Services and Rehabilitation*. 4 (Spring): 213-31.

Lombardo, L. 1981. *Guards Imprisoned*. New York: Elsevier.

McCarthy, B. 1981. "Patterns of Prison Corruption." Paper presented at the American Society of Criminology annual meeting, Philadelphia.

Marquart, J. 1986. "Prison Guards and the Use of Physical Coercion as a Mechanism of Social Control" *Criminology*. 2 4: 347-66.

Marquart, J. and B. Crouch. 1984. "Coopting the Kept: Using Inmates for Social Order in a Southern Prison," *Justice Quarterly*. 1 (December): 491-509.

May, E. 1981. "Prison Guards in America—The Inside Story," pp. 19-40 in R. Ross (ed.) *Prison Guard/Correctional Officer: The Use and Abuse of the Human Resources of Prisons*. Toronto: Butterworth.

Morton, J. 1981. "Women in Correctional Employment: Where Are They Now and Where Are They Headed?", pp. 7-15 in *Women in Corrections*. College Park, MD: American Correctional Association.

Petersen, C. 1982. "Doing Time with the Boys: An Analysis of Women Correctional Officers in All-Male Facilities," pp. 437-60 in B. Price and N. Sokoloff (eds.) *The Criminal Justice System and Women*. New York: Clark Boardman Co., Ltd.

Poole, E. and R. Regoli. 1980a. "Role Stress, Custody Orientation and Disciplinary Actions: A Study of Prison Guards." *Criminology*. 18 (August): 215-26.

_____. 1980b. "Work Relations and Cynicism Among Prison Guards." *Criminal Justice and Behavior*. 7 (Sept.): 303-314.

_____. 1981. "Alienation in Prison: An Examination of Work Relations Among Prison Guards," in *Criminology* 19 (Aug.): 251-70.

Potter, J. 1980. "Should Women Guards Work in Prisons for Men?" *Corrections Magazine*. 5 (October): 30-38.

Stotland, E. 1980. "Self-Esteem and Violence by Guards and State Troopers at Attica," pp. 291-301 in B. Crouch (ed.) *The Keepers*. Springfield, IL: Charles C Thomas Publishers, Inc.

Sykes, G. 1958. "The Corruption of Authority and Rehabilitation." *Social Forces*. 34 (March): 257-62.

Toch, H. 1976. *Peacekeeping: Police, Prisons and Violence*. Lexington: Lexington Books.

Wicks, R. J. 1980. *Guard: Society's Professional Prisoner*. Houston: Gulf Publishing Co.

Wynne, Jr., J. M. 1978. *Prison Employer Unionism: The Impact on Correctional Administration and Programs*. National Institute of Law Enforcement and Criminal Justice.

Part III

The Courts and Corrections

Introduction

Prior to the 1960s, the vast majority of courts refused to hear cases in which prisoners complained of cruel punishments or harsh conditions of confinement. In declining jurisdiction over litigation involving prisons, the courts relied upon a policy generally referred to as the "hands-off doctrine." This approach to inmate lawsuits reflected the views that a convicted prisoner was a "slave of the state" without enforceable rights and that the courts lacked the authority and expertise to intervene in correctional affairs. In practice, the hands-off doctrine made it virtually impossible for prisoners to seek judicial relief from alleged mistreatment at the hands of prison officials.

In the 1960s, many federal courts and a few state courts began to relax their traditional hands-off attitude toward the legal rights of prisoners, and the early 1970s were years of growth and development in prison litigation. Federal court decisions enlarged the scope of the prisoner's right of access to the courts and expanded (but did not totally recognize) inmate rights to religious freedom, uncensored mail correspondence, decent medical care, and procedural due process during prison disciplinary hearings. Although most cases were decided in favor of prison authorities, prisoners nevertheless won significant victories protecting them from arbitrary beatings and tortures, contaminated and nutritionally inadequate food, poor sanitation, severe overcrowding, and

185

prolonged confinement in isolation cells which were covered with the bodily wastes of previous cell inhabitants and which were lacking light, ventilation, and any means of maintaining bodily cleanliness.

These victories for prisoners, however, have now given way to what legal scholars are calling a "modified hands-off doctrine." Since 1976, the Supreme Court has sanctioned strict limitations on prisoners' rights to visitation, free speech, and freedom of expression. The Court has minimized due process protections when prisoners are disciplined or transferred to more punitive facilities, and it has imposed a series of troublesome and time-consuming procedural obstacles to the access of state prisoners to federal courts.

Such setbacks have tempered earlier enthusiasm over the role courts can play in bringing about correctional reform. This is not to say that recent decisions should be read as the death knell for prison litigation. Rather, it seems likely that prisoners' rights have reached a status quo that is likely to remain static for the next decade or so. Moreover, a good case can be made that federal court decisions on behalf of prisoners during the past fifteen to twenty years have spurred more improvements in American corrections than all other types of reform efforts over the preceding 200 years. The readings in Part III are intended to give students a broad perspective of what the judiciary has and has not accomplished in the area of penal reform.

In the first article in this section, Judge Frank Johnson, a federal district judge in Alabama, graphically details the brutal and degrading conditions that existed in Alabama's prisons in the 1970s. He does so to explain his controversial prisoners' rights decisions mandating broad improvements in staffing, physical facilities, medical care, rehabilitation programs, inmate classification, and many other aspects of Alabama prison management. Judge Johnson argues that the intolerability of life in Alabama's prisons had reached such a critical state that it was his constitutional duty to take measures to defend prisoners from barbaric and inhumane conditions. He makes a convincing case that concerns about excessive judicial activism and the increasing volume of prison litigation must never prevent the courts from preserving the rights of prisoners or any other minority group that must resort to the courts to secure protection against abuses perpetrated or tolerated by the executive and legislative branches of government.

Legal scholars generally recognize the right of access to the courts as the most important constitutional protection accorded prisoners, primarily because it is the right upon which all other rights turn. Without the right of access, prisoners would have no way to vindicate other constitutional rights such as their right to freedom of religion and their right to be protected against cruel and unusual punishments. As a federal court declared in 1966, "A right of access to the courts [is] of incalculable importance to the protection of other precious rights" [*Coleman v. Peyton*, 302 F. 2d 905, 907 (4th Cir. 1966)]. In "American Prisoners and the Right of Access to the Courts: A Vanishing Concept of Protection," Ken Haas and Geoffrey Alpert, the editors of this volume, analyze recent trends in this area of law. They demonstrate that the U.S. Supreme Court has made it increasingly difficult for prisoners to seek judicial redress of their grievances, and they discuss the implications of the Court's retrenchment for correctional practitioners and correctional researchers.

The Supreme Court's declining solicitude toward the rights of prisoners in various areas of correctional law was compellingly demonstrated during the Court's 1988-89 term. All six prisoners' rights cases decided in that term were resolved in favor of correctional officials and against prisoners. Our next selection offers a brief review of three particularly important cases from that term. "The Supreme Court's Retreat From the Protection of Prisoners' Rights" is adapted from the *Correctional Law Reporter*, a bi-monthly journal edited and published by William C. Collins and Fred Cohen, two of the nation's leading authorities on prison law.

Two of the cases highlighted here expand the authority of prison officials to place limits on the inmate's right to receive correspondence (*Thornburgh v. Abbott*) and visitors (*Kentucky v. Thompson*). The third case (*Murray v. Giarratano*) holds that death-row inmates seeking state post-conviction relief do not have a right to greater legal assistance than do prisoners who are not facing the death penalty. The holdings in these cases and the Court's willingness to defer to the judgments of correctional administrators and other state officials indicate that judicial involvement in correctional affairs will continue to diminish in the foreseeable future.

Despite the Supreme Court's retreat from the protection of prisoners' rights, lawsuits arising from prison disciplinary hearings remain common. William C. Collins offers readers an insightful analysis of recent judicial activity in this sphere of law in "Disciplinary Hearings: Something Old, Something New, but Always Something," a chapter taken from his book, *Correctional Law: 1986*. The years 1985 and 1986 were especially noteworthy in terms of Supreme Court and lower court treatment of prison discipline issues, and Collins shows how courts continue to struggle with issues left unsettled by the Supreme Court's landmark decision of *Wolff v. McDonnell* (1974).

Prison law is often perplexing and ambiguous. In this area—as in all areas of law—the Supreme Court simply cannot hear enough cases to clarify all of the corollary principles that may derive from its major decisions. The emotionally charged issues that are often present in major prisoners' rights cases and the difficulties inherent in writing majority opinions that must represent a compromise among the differing viewpoints of individual Justices add considerably to the likelihood that the Supreme Court's corrections law decisions will be inexact and uncertain. Jack Call's "Recent Case Law on Overcrowded Conditions of Confinement" provides an excellent example of how the Supreme Court's major decisions on prison overcrowding—Bell v. Wolfish and Rhodes v. Chapman—have provoked intriguing variations and disagreements among lower courts as to when prison crowdedness rises to the level of "cruel and unusual punishment" prohibited by the Eighth Amendment. Call demonstrates that by holding that confining two inmates to a cell built for one (double-celling) is unconstitutional only when it inflicts severe harm on inmates or when it exists within a plethora of inhumane conditions, the Supreme Court has made it extraordinarily difficult to predict with confidence the outcome of prison overcrowding suits.

Our next two selections assess the impact of prison litigation. First, Geoffrey Alpert, Ben Crouch, and Ronald Huff investigate the latent or unintended consequences of Ruiz v. Estelle (1980)—a case in which a federal district judge declared the operations of the Texas prison system to be in violation of the Eighth Amendment and entered an extensive remedial order affecting virtually every aspect of Texas prison management. Applying "rising expectations" theory to their analysis of events immediately following the Ruiz decision, Alpert, Crouch, and Huff contend that while mandating many desirable changes, the remedial decree set in motion a chain of events that led to at least a temporary increase in prison disturbances and riots. In 1982, a federal appeals court affirmed the district court's finding of unconstitutional prison conditions, but modified some of the relief, particularly the orders relating to overcrowding. However, much of the original decree remains in effect, and only time will tell whether the Ruiz decision will result in a long-term reduction of violence and meaningful improvements in institutional conditions.

More positive findings concerning the impact of court decisions on inmate behavior have been reported elsewhere. For example, some of the studies cited in Chapter 12 of this book show that improved prison legal assistance programs mandated by court decisions have promoted values conducive to rehabilitation by convincing inmates that they are being treated fairly. The finding that legal aid programs can be rehabilitative may surprise some readers. But by reducing the tensions that inevitably accompany unresolved legal problems and decreasing feelings of vulnerability and powerlessness, litigation can sometimes have a beneficial effect upon a prisoner's mental health. A dramatic example of this phenomenon is provided in the final chapter in Part III. Richard Korn's "Litigation Can Be Therapeutic" tells the fascinating story of Bobby Hardwick's legal struggles against the Georgia prison system. Bobby Hardwick's victory over his keepers in the courtroom was remarkable, but even more remarkable was his triumph over mental illness.

11

The Constitution and the Federal District Judge

Frank M. Johnson

Modern American society depends upon our judicial system to play a critical role in maintaining the balance between governmental powers and individual rights. The increasing concern paid by our courts toward the functioning of government and its agencies has received much comment[1] and some criticism[2] recently. As governmental institutions at all levels have assumed a greater role in providing public services, courts increasingly have been confronted with the unavoidable duty of determining whether those services meet basic constitutional requirements. Time and again citizens have brought to the federal courts, and those courts reluctantly have decided, such basic questions as how and when to make available equal quality public education to all our children;·how to guarantee all citizens an opportunity to serve on juries, to vote, and to have their votes counted equally; under what minimal living conditions criminal offenders may be incarcerated; and what minimum standards of care and treatment state institutions must provide the mentally ill and mentally retarded who have been involuntarily committed to the custody of the state.

Source: Published originally in 54 Texas L. Rev. 903, (1976). Copyright © 1976 by the *Texas Law Review*. Reprinted by permission of the *Texas Law Review*.

The reluctance with which courts and judges have undertaken the complex task of deciding such questions has at least three important sources. First, one of the founding principles of our Government,[3] a principle derived from the French philosophers of the eighteenth century, is that the powers of government should be separate and distinct, lest all the awesome power of government unite as one force unchecked in its exercise. The drafters of our Constitution formulated the doctrine of separation of powers to promote the independence of each branch of government in its sphere of operation. To the extent that courts respond to requests to look to the future and to change existing conditions by making new rules, however, they become subject to the charge of usurping authority from the legislative or executive branch.

Second, our Constitution and laws have strictly limited the power of the federal judiciary to participate in what are essentially political affairs. The tenth amendment[4] reserves any power not delegated to the United States to the individual states or to the people. Reflecting the distrust of centralized government expressed by this amendment, courts and citizens alike since the Nation's beginning have regarded certain governmental functions as primarily, if not exclusively, state responsibilities. Among these are public education;[5] maintenance of state and local penal institutions;[6] domestic relations;[7] and provision for the poor, homeless, aged, and infirm.[8] A further limitation on the role of federal courts with respect to other governmental bodies lies in the creation and maintenance of these courts as courts of limited jurisdiction.

Last, federal judges properly hesitate to make decisions either that require the exercise of political judgment[9] or that necessitate expertise they lack.[10] Judges are professionally trained in the law—not in sociology, education, medicine, penology, or public administration. In an ideal society, elected officials would make all decisions relating to the allocation of resources; experts trained in corrections would make all penological decisions; physicians would make all medical decisions; scientists would make all technological decisions; and educators would make all educational decisions. Too often, however, we have failed to achieve this ideal system. Many times, those persons to whom we have entrusted these responsibilities have acted or failed to act in ways that do not fall within the bounds of discretion permitted by the Constitution and the laws. When such transgressions are properly and formally brought before a court—and increasingly before federal courts—it becomes the responsibility of the judiciary to ensure that the Constitution and laws of the United States remain, in fact as well as in theory, the supreme law of the land.

On far too many occasions the intransigent and unremitting oppo-

sition of state officials who have neglected or refused to correct unconstitutional or unlawful state policies and practices has necessitated
federal intervention to enforce the law. Courts in all sections of the
Nation have expended and continue to expend untold resources in
repeated litigation brought to compel local school officials to follow a
rule of law first announced by the Supreme Court almost twenty-two
years ago.[11] In addition to deciding scores of school cases, federal
courts in Alabama alone have ordered the desegregation of mental
institutions,[12] penal facilities,[13] public parks,[14] city buses,[15] interstate
and intrastate buses and bus terminals,[16] airport terminals,[17] and
public libraries and museums.[18] Although I refer to Alabma and
specific cases litigated in the federal courts of Alabama, I do not intend
to suggest that similar problems do not exist in many of our other
states.

The history of public school desegregation has been a story of
repeated intervention by the courts to overcome not only the threats
and violence of extremists attempting to block school desegregation[19]
but also the numerous attempts by local and state officials to thwart
the orderly, efficient, and lawful resolution of this complicated social
problem.[20] Desegregation is not the only area of state responsibility in
which Alabama officials have forfeited their decisionmaking powers
by such a dereliction of duty as to require judicial intervention. Having
found Alabama's legislative apportionment plan unconstitutional,[21] the
District Court for the Middle District of Alabama waited ten years for
State officials to carry out the duty properly imposed upon them by the
Constitution and expressly set out in the court's order. The continued
refusal of those officials to comply left the court no choice but to
assume that duty itself and to impose its own reapportionment plan.[22]
State officers by their inaction have also handed over to the courts
property tax assessment plans;[23] standards for the care and treatment
of mentally ill and mentally retarded persons committed to the State's
custody;[24] and the procedures by which such persons are committed.[25]

Some of these cases are extremely troublesome and time consuming
for all concerned. I speak in particular of those lawsuits challenging
the operation of state institutions for the custody and control of citizens
who cannot or will not function at a safe and self-sustaining capacity in
a free society. Ordinarily these cases proceed as class actions seeking
to determine the rights of large numbers of people. As a result, the
courts' decisions necessarily have wide-ranging effect and momentous
importance, whether they grant or deny the relief sought.

A shocking example of a failure of state officials to discharge their
duty was forcefully presented in a lawsuit tried before me in 1972,
Newman v. Alabama,[26] which challenged the constitutional sufficiency
of medical care available to prisoners in the Alabama penal system.

The evidence in that case convincingly demonstrated that correctional officers on occasion intentionally denied inmates the right to examination by a physician or to treatment by trained medical personnel, and that they routinely withheld medicine and other treatments prescribed by physicians. Further evidence showed that untrained inmates served as ward attendants and X-ray, laboratory, and dental technicians; rags were used as bandages; ambulance oxygen tanks remained empty for long periods of time; and unsupervised inmates without formal training pulled teeth, gave injections, sutured, and performed minor surgery. In fact, death resulting from gross neglect and totally inadequate treatment was not unusual.

A nineteen-year-old with an extremely high fever who was diagnosed as having acute pneumonia was left unsupervised and allowed to take cold showers at will for two days before his death. A quadriplegic with bedsores infested with maggots was bathed and had his bandages changed only once in the month before his death. An inmate who could not eat received no nourishment for the three days prior to his death even though intravenous feeding had been ordered by a doctor. A geriatric inmate who had suffered a stroke was made to sit each day on a wooden bench so that he would not soil his bed; he frequently fell onto the floor; his legs became swollen from a lack of circulation, necessitating the amputation of a leg the day before his death.[27]

Based on the virtually uncontradicted evidence presented at trial, the district court entered a comprehensive order designed to remedy each specific abuse proved at trial and to establish additional safeguards so that the medical program in Alabama prisons would never again regress to its past level of inadequacy.[28] The State was ordered to bring the general hospital at the Medical and Diagnostic Center (now Kilby Corrections Facility) up to the minimum standards required of hospitals by the United States Department of Health, Education, and Welfare for participation in the medicare program.[29] The court also directed the Alabama State Board of Health to inspect regularly for general sanitation all the medical and food processing facilities in the prison system.[30] Finally, the court decreed that all inmates receive physical examinations by physicians at regular intervals of not more than two years.[31]

One of the most comprehensive orders that I have entered concerning the operation and management of state institutions relates to the facilities maintained by the Alabama Department of Mental Health for the mentally ill and mentally retarded. Plaintiffs in *Wyatt v. Stickney*[32] brought a class action on behalf of all patients involuntarily confined at Bryce Hospital, the State's largest mental hospital, to establish the minimum standards of care and treatment to which the civilly committed are entitled under the Constitution. Patients at Searcy

Hospital in southern Alabama and residents at the Partlow State School and Hospital in Tuscaloosa joined the action as plaintiffs, thereby compelling a comprehensive inquiry into the entire Alabama mental health and retardation treatment and habilitation program.

At trial plaintiffs produced evidence showing that Bryce Hospital, build in the 1850's, was grossly overcrowded, housing more than 5000 patients.[33] Of these 5000 people ostensibly committed to Bryce for treatment of mental illness, about 1600—almost one-third—were geriatrics neither needing nor receiving any treatment for mental illness. Another 1000 or more of the patients at Bryce were mentally retarded rather than mentally ill. A totally inadequate staff, only a small percentage professionally trained, served these 5000 patients. The hospital employed only six staff members qualified to deal with mental patients—three medical doctors with psychiatric training, one Ph.D. psychologist, and two social workers with master's degrees in social work. The evidence indicated that the general living conditions and lack of individualized treatment programs were as intolerable and deplorable as Alabama's rank of fiftieth among the states in per patient expenditures[34] would suggest. For example, the hospital spent less than fifty cents per patient each day for food.[35]

The evidence concerning Partlow State School and Hospital for the retarded proved even more shocking than the evidence relating to the mental hospitals. The extremely dangerous conditions compelled the court to issue an interim emergency order[36] requiring Partlow officials to take immediate steps to protect the lives and safety of the residents. The Associate Commissioner for Mental Retardation for the Alabama Department of Mental Health testified that Partlow was sixty percent overcrowded; that the school, although it had not, could immediately discharge at least 300 residents; *and that seventy percent of the residents should never have been committed at all.*[37] The conclusion that there was no opportunity for habilitation for its residents was inescapable. Indeed, the evidence reflected that one resident was scalded to death when a fellow resident hosed water from one of the bath facilities on him; another died as a result of the insertion of a running water hose into his rectum by a working resident who was cleaning him; one died when soapy water was forced into his mouth; another died of a self-administered overdose of inadequately stored drugs; and authorities restrained another resident in a straitjacket for *nine years* to prevent him from sucking his hands and fingers. Witnesses described the Partlow facilities as barbaric and primitive;[38] some residents had no place to sit to eat meals, and coffee cans served as toilets in some areas of the institution.

With the exception of the interim emergency order designed to eliminate hazardous conditions at Partlow, the court at first declined to devise specific steps to improve existing conditions in Alabama's mental health and retardation facilties. Instead, it directed the Department of Mental Health to design its own plan for upgrading the system to meet constitutional standards.[39] Only after two deadlines had passed without any signs of acceptable progress did the court itself, relying upon the proposals of counsel for all parties and amici curiae, define the minimal constitutional standards of care, treatment, and habilitation[40] for which the case of *Wyatt v. Stickney* has become generally known.

During the past several years conditions at the Partlow State School for the retarded have improved markedly. It was pleasing to read in a Montgomery newspaper that members of the State Mental Health Board (the *Wyatt* defendants) recently met at Partlow and agreed that "what they saw was a different world" compared to four years ago; that "things are now unbelievably better," with most students "out in the sunshine on playground swings or tossing softballs [,]...responding to a kind word or touch with smiles and squeals of delight"; and that "enrollment has been nearly cut in half, down from 2,300 to just under 1,300 while the staff has tripled from 600 to 1,800."[41]

Persons incarcerated in state and local prison and jail facilities around the Nation increasingly have attacked the conditions of their confinement as unconstitutional. In recent years, federal courts in Alabama,[42] Arkansas,[43], Florida,[44] Maryland,[45] Massachusetts,[46] and Mississippi,[47] among others, have been forced to declare that the constitutional rights of inmates are denied by the mere fact of their confinement in institutions that inflict intolerable and inhuman living conditions. In Texas a federal judge has held unconstitutional the detention of juveniles in certain facilities maintained by the Texas Youth Council because of the extreme brutality and indifference experienced in these institutions.[48] In fashioning appropriate remedies in these cases, the courts have exhibited sensitivity to the real but not the imagined limitations imposed on correctional officials forced to operate penal facilities with the meager sums appropriated by legislators who see few or no political rewards in supporting constitutional treatment of prisoners. Some courts have ordered that entire institutions be closed and abandoned;[49] others have required substantial improvements in facilities and services as a precondition to their continued operation.[50]

Knowing firsthand the considerable time, energy, and thought that must precede any decision affecting mental hospital or prison conditions, I seriously doubt that any judge relishes his involvement in such a controversy or enters a decree unless the law clearly makes it his duty to do so. The Fifth Circuit adheres to the well-settled rule that federal courts do not sit to supervise state prisons or to interfere with their internal operation and administration.[51] The American system of justice, however, equally acknowledges that inmates do not lose all constitutional rights and privileges when they are confined following conviction of criminal offenses.[52]

James v. Wallace,[53] a recent class action tried before me objecting to conditions in Alabama's state penal facilities, presents another graphic example of how a state's irresponsibility in carrying out an essential governmental function necessitated federal judicial intervention to restore constitutional rights to citizens whose rights were systematically disregarded and denied. Preserving prisoners' rights is no less vital than safeguarding the liberties of school children, black citizens, women, and others who have found it necessary to resort to the courts to secure their constitutional rights.[54] The James trial began last August following extensive pretrial discovery, which included more than 1000 facts stipulated to by all parties and filed with the court. At the close of the defendants' case, the lead counsel for the Governor and the State Board of Corrections acknowledged in open court that "the overwhelming majority of the evidence...shows that an Eighth Amendment violation has and is now occurring to inmates in the Alabama prison system."[55]

Plaintiffs in James demonstrated the intolerability of life in Alabama's prisons by proof of both general living conditions and commonplace incidents. Fighting, assault, extortion, theft, and homosexual rape are everyday occurrences in all four main institutions. A mentally retarded twenty-year-old inmate, after testifying that doctors had told him he had the mind of a five-year-old, told in open court how four inmates raped him on his first night in an Alabama prison.[56]

The evidence showed that most prisoners found it necessary to carry some form of homemade or contraband weapon merely for self-protection. One prisoner testified that he would rather be caught with a weapon by a prison guard than be caught without one by another prisoner.[57] Seriously dilapidated physical facilities have created generally unsanitary and hazardous living conditions in Alabama's prisons. Roaches, flies, mosquitoes, and other vermin overrun the institutions. One living area in Draper prison housing over 200 men contained one functioning toilet.

A United States public health officer, testifying as an expert witness after having inspected the four major prisons, pronounced the facilities wholly unfit for human habitation according to virtually every criterion used for evaluation by public health inspectors. He testified that as a public health officer, he would recommend the closing of any similar facilities under his jurisdiction because they presented an imminent danger to the health of the exposed individuals.[58] Moreover, all the parties to the lawsuit agreed that severe overcrowding and understaffing aggravated all these other difficulties. At the time of trial over 3500 prisoners resided in facilities designed for no more than 2300. The Commissioner of the Alabama Board of Corrections testified that although the prison system required a minimum staff of 692 correctional officers, it then employed 383.[59] Correctional experts testified that such an overflow of prisoners, coupled with the shortage of supervisory personnel, precludes any meaningful control over the institutions by the responsible officials. The facts bore out that conclusion. Prison guards simply refused to enter some dormitories at night,[60] and one warden testified that he would not enter a certain dormitory at his institution without at least four guards by his side.

Understaffing and lack of funds have deprived nearly all the inmates who are confined twenty-four hours a day of meaningful activity; usually they lie around idle. Most live in dormitories or barracks that afford them neither privacy nor security for their personal possessions. The defendants stipulated that over half of the prison population possessed no skills, and that in the first quarter of 1975 the average entering inmate could not read at the sixth-grade level. The few vocational training and basic education programs offered can accommodate only a tiny fraction of the inmates, and the entry requirements for the programs are highly restrictive. Alabama prisons do not have a working classification system, an essential ingredient of any properly operated penal system. A functioning classification system enables officials to segregate for treatment and for the protection of other prisoners not able or willing to function in any social setting. Currently, mentally disturbed inmates receive no special care or therapy, and are housed and treated like the general prison population. Consequently, violent and aggressive prisoners live together with those who are weak, passive, or otherwise easily victimized. For example, when the twenty-year-old inmate I spoke of earlier reported the rape to prison officials, the warden of the institution told him that he, the warden, could do nothing about it.

Since the final order in *James*, new reports have revealed other instances of what at best constitute questionable management practices. A committee of the Alabama Legislature investigating prison operations disclosed that financial records reflect the use of prison funds to purchase cases of caviar, evidently consumed in the course of entertaining legislators.[61] The committee also questioned a recent transaction in which the Alabama Board of Corrections approved the bartering of fifty-two head of beef cattle owned by the Board in exchange for three Tennessee walking horses. The Commissioner of Corrections publicly explained that the horses were acquired for breeding purposes.[62] It later developed that the horses obtained for breeding purposes were geldings.[63]

Based on the overwhelming and generally undisputed evidence presented at trial, the court granted immediate partial relief to plaintiffs in the form of two interim orders,[64] which remain in effect. One order enjoined the State from accepting additional prisoners, except escapees and parole violators, until each State prison facility decreases its population to its design capacity. The second ruling banned the use of isolation and segregation cells that fail to meet minimum standards. Before this order, as many as six inmates were confined in four-by-eight foot cells with no beds, no lighting, no running water, and a hole in the floor for a toilet that only a guard outside could flush.

The final opinion and order entered in *James* in January 1976 established a broad range of minimum standards[65] designed to remedy the broad range of constitutional deprivations proven at trial and conceded to exist by the State's lawyers. The standards govern staffing; classification of prisoners; mental and physical health care; physical facilities; protection of inmates; and educational, vocational, recreational, and work programs.

The fourteenth amendment,[66] which generates much of the litigation discussed above, forbids a state to "deprive any person of life, liberty or property, without due process of law" or to "deny to any person within its jurisdiction the equal protection of the laws."[67] The Supreme Court has interpreted the due process clause to require that the states fulfill most of the obligations toward citizens that the Bill of Rights imposes on the federal government.[68] Each state in all its dealings with its people must recognize and preserve their guaranteed freedoms. Nevertheless, state officials have frequently raised the tenth amendments's reservation of powers to the states as a defense to the exercise of federal jurisdiction over actions alleging state violations of constitutional rights. While the tenth amendment clearly preserves for the states a wide and important sphere of power, it does not permit any state to frustrate or to ignore the mandates of the Constitution. *The tenth amendment does not relieve the states of a single obligation imposed upon them by the Constitution of the United States.* Surely the concept of states' rights has never purported to allow states to abdicate their responsibility to protect their citizens from criminal acts and inhumane conditions. I find it sad and ironic that citizens of Alabama held in "protective custody" by Alabama had to obtain federal court orders to protect themselves from violent crimes and barbaric conditions.

The cornerstone of our American legal system rests on recognition of the Constitution as the supreme law of the land,[69] and the paramount duty of the federal judiciary is to uphold that law.[70] Thus, when a state fails to meet constitutionally mandated requirements, it is the solemn duty of the courts to assure compliance with the Constitution. One writer has termed the habit adopted by some states of neglecting their responsibilities until faced with a federal court order "the Alabama Federal Intervention Syndrome," characterizing it as

> the tendency of many state officials to punt their problems with constituencies to the federal courts. Many federal judges have grown accustomed to allowing state officials to make political speeches as a prelude to receiving the order of the district court. This role requires the federal courts to serve as a buffer between the state officials and their constituencies, raising the familiar criticism that state officials rely upon the federal courts to impose needed reforms rather than accomplishing them themselves.[71]

As long as those state officials entrusted with the responsibility for fair and equitable governance completely disregard that responsibility, the judiciary must and will stand ready to intervene on behalf of the deprived. Judge Richard T. Rives of the Court of Appeals for the Fifth Circuit, in joining a three-judge panel that struck down attempts by state officials to frustrate the registration of black voters, eloquently expressed the reluctance with which the vast majority of federal judges approach intervention in state affairs:

> I look forward to the day when the State and its political sub-divisions will again take up their mantle of responsibility, treating all of their citizens equally, and thereby relieve the federal Government of the necessity of intervening in their affairs. Until that day arrives, the responsibility for this intervention must rest with those who through their ineptitude and public disservice have forced it.[72]

We in the judiciary await the day when the Alabama Federal Intervention Syndrome, in that State and elsewhere, will become a relic of the past. To reclaim responsibilities passed by default to the judiciary—most often the federal judiciary—and to find solutions for ever-changing challenges, the states must preserve their ability to respond flexibly, creatively, and with due regard for the rights of all. State officials must confront their governmental responsibilities with the diligence and honesty that their constituencies deserve. When lawful rights are being denied, only the exercise of conscientious, responsible leadership, which is usually long on work and short on complimentary news headlines, can avoid judicial intervention. The most fitting Bicentennial observance I can conceive would be for all government officials to take up the constitutional mantle and diligently strive to protect the basic human rights recognized by the founders of our Republic two hundred years ago.

Footnotes

[1]See, e.g., L. Levy, *Judgments* 33-57 (1972); Mason, *Judicial Activism: Old and New*, 55 Va. L. Rev. 385, 394-426 (1969).

[2]See, e.g., Griswold, *The Judicial Process*, 31 Fed. B.J. 309, 321-25 (1972).

[3]See *The Federalist* Nos. 47, 48 (J. Madison).

[4]*U.S. Const.* amend. X.

[5]Cumming v. Richmond County Bd. of Educ., 175 U.S. 528, 545 (1899); Crews v. Cloncs, 432 F.2d 1259, 1265 (7th Cir. 1970).

[6]Hoag v. New Jersey, 356 U.S. 464 (1958); Threatt v. North Carolina, 221 F. Supp. 858, 860 (W.D.N.C. 1963).

[7]Ohio *ex rel.* Popovici v. Agler, 280 U.S. 379, 383 (1930); Morris v. Morris, 273 F.2d 678, 682 (7th Cir. 1960); Ainscow v. Alexander, 28 Del. Ch. 545, 550, 39 A.2d 54, 56 (Super, Ct. 1944).

[8]Adkins v. Curtis, 259 Ala. 311, 315, 66 So. 2d 455, 458 (1953); Beck v. Buena Park Hotel Corp., 30 Ill. 2d 343, 346, 196 N.E.2d 686, 688 (1964); Collins v. State bd. of Social Welfare, 248 Iowa 369, 375, 81 N.W.2d 4, 7 (1957).

[9]See, e.g., Marbury v. Madison, 5 U.S. (1 Cranch) 137, 170 (1803).

[10]See, e.g., Brotherhood of Locomotive Firemen v. Chicago, R.I. & P.R.R., 393 U.S. 129, 136-37 (1968).

[11]Brown v. Board of Educ., 347 U.S. 484 (1954).

[12]Marable v. Mental Health Bd., 297 F. Supp. 291 (M.D. Ala. 1969).

[13]Washington v. Lee, 263 F. Supp. 327 (M.D. Ala. 1966), *aff'd*, 390 U.S. 333 (1968).

[14]Gilmore v. City of Montgomery, 176 F. Supp. 776 (M.D. Ala. 1959), *modified*, 277 F.2d 364 (5th Cir. 1960), *rev'd in part*, 417 U.S. 556 (1974).

[15]Browder v. Gayle, 142 F. Supp. 707 (M.D. Ala.), *aff'd*, 352 U.S. 903 (1956).

[16]Lewis v. Greyhound Corp., 199 F. Supp. 210 (M.D. Ala. 1961).

[17]United States v. City of Montgomery, 201 F. Supp. 590 (M.D. Ala. 1962).

[18]Cobb v. Library Bd., 207 F. Supp. 88Q (M.D. Ala. 1962).

[19]United States v. United Klans of America, 290 F. Supp. 181 (M.D. Ala. 1968).

[20]Harris v. Board of Educ., 259 F. Supp. 167 (M.D. Ala. 1966); Lee v. Board of Educ., 231 F. Supp. 743 (M.D. Ala. 1964).

[21]Sims v. Frink, 208 F. Supp. 431 (M.D. Ala. 1962), *aff'd sub nom.* Reynolds v. Sims, 377 U.S. 533 (1964).

[22]Sims v. Amos, 336 F. Supp. 924 (M.D. Ala.), *aff'd*, 409 U.S. 942 (1972).

[23]Weissinger v. Boswell, 330 F Supp. 615 (M.D. Ala. 1971) (per curiam).

[24]Wyatt v. Stickney, 324 F. Supp. 781 (M.D. Ala. 1971), *enforced*, 344 F. Supp. 373 (M.D. Ala. 1972) (mentally ill) *and* 344 F. Supp. 387 (M.D. Ala. 1972), *modified sub nom.* Wyatt v. Aderholt, 503 F.2d 1305 (5th Cir. 1974) (mentally retarded).

[25]Lynch v. Baxley, 386 F. Supp. 378 (M.D. Ala. 1974).

[26]349 F. Supp. 278 (M.D. Ala. 1972), *aff'd in part*, 503 F.2d 1320 (5th Cir. 1974), *cert. denied*, 421 U.S. 948 (1975).

[27]*Id.* at 285.

[28]*Id.* at 286-88.

[29]*Id.* at 286.

[30]*Id.* at 287.

[31]*Id.*

[32]325 F. Supp. 781 (M.D. Ala. 1971), *enforced,* 344 F. Supp. 373 (M.D. Ala. 1972) *and* 344 F. Supp. 387 (M.D. Ala. 1972), *modified sub nom.* Wyatt v. Aderholt, 503 F.2d 1305 (5th Cir. 1974) (affirming constitutional "right to treatment").

[33]*Id.* at 782.

[34]*Id.* at 784.

[35]Wyatt v. Aderholt, 503 F.2d 1305, 1310 (5th Cir. 1974).

[36]Wyatt v. Stickney, Civil No. 3195-N (M.D. Ala., Mar. 2, 1972) (emergency order). This order preceded the final order.

[37]Wyatt v. Aderholt, 503 F.2d 1305, 1310 (5th Cir. 1974).

[38]See Wyatt v. Stickney, 344 F. Supp. 387, 391 n.7 (M.D. Ala. 1972).

[39]Wyatt v. Stickney, 325 F. Supp. 781, 785-86 (M.D. Ala. 1971).

[40]344 F. Supp. at 395-409 (Partlow State School); 344 F. Supp. at 379-86 (Bryce Hospital).

[41]Reese, *Things Unbelievably Better at Partlow, Director Says,* Alabama Journal, Feb. 20, 1976, at 13, cols. 3-4.

[42]McCray V. Sullivan, Civil. No. 5620-69-H (S.D. Ala., Feb. 10, 1976); James v. Wallace, 406 F. Supp. 318 (M.D. Ala. 1976).

[43]Holt v. Sarver, 309 F. Supp. 362 (E.D. Ark. 1970), *aff'd,* 442 F.2d 304 (8th Cir. 1971).

[44]Costello v. Wainwright, 397 F. Supp. 20 (M.D. Fla. 1975), *aff'd,* 525 F.2d 1239, *rehearing in banc granted,* 528 F.2d 1381 (Mar. 3, 1976) (No. 75-2392).

[45]Collins v. Schoonfield, 344 F. Supp. 257 (D. Md. 1972).

[46]Inmates of Suffolk County Jail v. Eisenstadt, 360 F. Supp. 676 (D. Mass. 1973), *aff'd,* 494 F. 2d 1196 (1st Cir.) *cert. denied,* 419 U.S. 977 (1974).

[47]Gates v. Collier, 349 F. Supp. 881 (N.D. Miss. 1972), *aff'd,* 501 F.2d 1291 (5th Cir. 1974).

[48]Morales v. Turman, 383 F. Supp. 53 (E.D. Tex. 1974).

[49]*Id.*

[50]James v. Wallace, 406 F. Supp. 318 (M.D. Ala. 1976); Costello v. Wainwright, 397 F. Supp. 20 (M.D. Fla. 1975), *aff'd,* 525 F.2d 1239 (5th Cir. 1976).

[51]Novak v. Beto, 453 F.2d 661, 671 (5th Cir. 1971); Newman v. Alabama, 349 F. Supp. 278, 280 (M.D. Ala. 1972), *aff'd in part,* 503 F.2d 1320 (5th Cir. 1974), *cert. denied,* 421 U.S. 948 (1975).

[52]Washington v. Lee, 263 F. Supp. 327, 331 (M.D. Ala. 1966), *aff'd per curiam,* 390 U.S. 333 (1968).

[53]406 F. Supp. 318 (M.D. Ala. 1976).

[54]Recently courts have recognized that prisoners retain all their constitutional rights except those necessarily diminished as an incident of incarceration. See Pell v. Procunier, 417 U.S. 817, 822 (1973); Jackson v. Godwin, 400 F.2d 529, 532 (5th Cir. 1968); James v. Wallace, 406 F. Supp. 318, 328 (M.D. Ala. 1976).

[55]Record, vol. II, at 357. The eighth amendment prohibits "cruel and unusual punishments." *U.S. Const.* amend. VIII.

[56]406 F. Supp. at 325.

[57]*Id.*

[58]*Id.* at 323-24.

[59]*Id.* at 325.

[60]*Id.*

[61]Montgomery Advertiser, Feb. 6, 1976, at 1, cols. 5-8.

[62]*Id.*

[63]Alabama Journal, Feb. 6, 1976, at 13, cols. 5-6.

[64]406 F. Supp. at 322, 327.

[65]*Id.* at 332-35.

[66]*U.S. Const.* amend. XIV.

[67]*Id.*

[68]Duncan v. Louisiana, 391 U.S. 145 (1968).

[69]See *U.S. Const.* art VI, §2.

[70]See Mitchum v. Foster, 407 U.S. 225, 238-39 (1972); Zwickler v. Koota, 389 U.S. 241, 248 (1967); England v. Louisiana State Bd. of Medical Examiners, 375 U.S. 411, 415 (1964).

[71]McCormack, *The Expansion of Federal Question Jurisdiction and the Prisoner Complaint Caseload,* 1975 Wis. L. Rev. 523, 536 (footnotes omitted).

[72]Dent v. Duncan, 360 F.2d 333, 337-38 (5th Cir. 1966).

12

American Prisoners and the Right of Access to the Courts
A Vanishing Concept of Protection

Kenneth C. Haas and Geoffrey P. Alpert

Introduction

In 1987, Americans celebrated the 200th anniversary of the United States Constitution. It is from this document that our basic rights and responsibilities have been developed. These rights, however, have never been distributed equally to all segments of the population. For example, the rights enumerated in the Constitution have never been fully extended to those who are incarcerated. Although the rights of free citizens have been generally preserved during this 200-year period, the history of prisoners' rights is a history of indifference and neglect.

Source: From *The American Prison: Issues in Research and Policy*, edited by Lynne Goodstein and Doris Layton MacKenzie (Plenum Publishing Corporation, 1989). Reprinted by permission of the publisher.

Prisoners have always been the forgotten Americans in the United States Constitution. The original document of 1787 affirmed the fundamental right of habeas corpus (the right to challenge the legality of one's confinement) but did not specifically mention prisoners. Two years later, the Bill of Rights—the first 10 amendments to the Constitution—provided safeguards for those accused of crime. However, it would take nearly two centuries for the Bill of Rights to emerge as a major weapon in securing rights for those already convicted of crimes. And it would take the courts equally as long to recognize that "a right of access to the courts is one of the rights a prisoner clearly retains" (*Coleman* v. *Peyton*, 1966: 907).

The purposes of this chapter are to examine the prisoner's right of access to the courts and to comment on how changes in this area of law may affect research on prisons and on the role of the courts in spurring prison reform. The right of access is the most important of all prisoners' rights because it is the right upon which all other rights turn. Without it, prisoners would have no way to appeal their convictions or to vindicate their rights in such areas of law as the First Amendment's protections of speech, religion, and peaceable assembly; the Eighth Amendment's ban on cruel and unusual punishments; and the right to Fifth and Fourteenth Amendment due process in prison disciplinary proceedings.

We will explore the right of access by examining the two major types of cases that make up this body of law. First, we will focus on cases that involve the constitutionality of various prison policies that allegedly interfere with inmate efforts to seek judicial relief. Second, we will analyze recent trends in cases dealing with the availability of judicial remedies frequently sought by prisoners. These cases involve procedural and jurisdictional questions that can either make judicial remedies easier to obtain or place severe restrictions on the right of access.

Prison Policies and Practices Affecting the Right of Access to the Courts

U.S. Supreme Court Decisions

Until the past 20 years, federal and state courts followed a policy of declining jurisdiction in nearly all suits brought by prisoners. Generally known as the "hands-off" doctrine, this policy reflected the traditional view of the prisoner as a "slave of the state" (*Ruffin* v. *Commonwealth*, 1871: 796) without enforceable rights. As a practical matter, the judiciary's extreme reluctance to become involved in the internal operations of prisons made it virtually impossible for prisoners to seek judicial relief from alleged mistreatment and needlessly harsh conditions of confinement (Haas, 1977). Generally, the courts based their refusals to hear prisoner complaints on one or more of five rationales:

1. The separation of powers doctrine
2. The low level of judicial expertise in penology
3. The fear that judicial intervention would undermine prison discipline
4. The fear that opening the courthouse doors to prisoners would result in a deluge of inmate litigation
5. The view that considerations of federalism and comity should preclude consideration of the claims of state prisoners by federal courts (Haas, 1977).

A strict version of the hands-off doctrine prevailed among most courts until the late 1960s and early 1970s. Nevertheless, it was in 1941—a time when the hands-off doctrine remained strong—that the U.S. Supreme Court first recognized that the due process clauses of the Fifth and Fourteenth Amendments guarantee all Americans—even prisoners—the right of access to the courts. In the case of Ex Parte Hull, the Court struck down a Michigan prison regulation that required inmates to submit all their legal petitions to prison officials for approval. Whenever prison authorities felt that inmate petitions were frivolous, inaccurate, or poorly written, they would refuse to mail them to the courts. The Supreme Court held that this procedure amounted to an impermissible denial of the fundamental right of access to the courts. In no uncertain terms, the Justices told prison officials: "Whether a petition for a writ of habeas corpus addressed to a federal court is properly drawn and what allegations it must contain are questions for that court alone to determine" (Hull at 549).

Despite the Hull ruling, most courts remained extremely reluctant to interfere with prison policies restricting inmate access to the courts. In the 1950s and 1960s, many courts approved such prison practices as refusing to allow prisoners to purchase law books, prohibiting correspondence with law book publishers, allowing the confiscation of an inmate's legal documents found in another inmate's cell, refusing to permit a prisoner to type his or her own legal papers, and censoring or withholding legal correspondence between prisoners and attorneys (Edwards, 1968). Moreover, even when prison regulations were more accommodating to the right of access, ignorance, illiteracy, and poverty kept prisoners with arguably meritorious claims from filing their complaints.

Like their counterparts of yesteryear, today's prisoners often discover that legal barriers and personal handicaps can make court access very difficult. The right to a state-supplied attorney does not extend to inmate actions attacking prison conditions or to discretionary appeals of a criminal conviction (*Ross* v. *Moffitt*, 1974). Prisoners lack the money to hire attorneys, and they rarely possess the literacy needed to write and interest attorneys who might take a case without fee. As a result, the large majority of cases brought by prisoners originate from either the petitioning prisoner or from a "jailhouse lawyer" or "writ-writer" — a prisoner who claims to have expertise in law and prepares legal documents for fellow inmates. Thus it is not surprising that the first major right of access case after *Hull* involved the limitations that prison officials could place on jailhouse lawyers.

In *Johnson* v. *Avery* (1969), the Supreme Court invalidated prison regulations that prohibited jailhouse lawyers from helping other prisoners with their legal problems. The Court conceded that jailhouse lawyers may burden the courts with frivolous complaints and undermine prison discipline by establishing their own power structure and taking unfair advantage of gullible prisoners (*Johnson* at 488). Nevertheless, the Justices declared that these concerns were outweighed by the importance of insuring that prisoners have reasonable access to the courts and "the fundamental importance of the writ of habeas corpus in our constitutional scheme" (*Johnson* at 485). Because most prisoners possess neither the necessary funds to hire their attorneys nor the necessary educational background to write their own appeals, their only recourse in most cases, reasoned the Justices, was to seek the help of a jailhouse lawyer (*Johnson* at 488-490). Consequently, the High Court concluded that prison officials could no longer enforce no-assistance rules unless the prison itself provided some type of legal services program that was reasonably effective in assisting prisoners with their petitions for post-conviction relief (*Johnson* at 490).

At first glance, the *Johnson* holding may seem to be rather narrow. However, the *Johnson* precedent, more than any other decision, paved the way for more effective efforts by prisoners seeking access to the courts. In the aftermath of *Johnson*, it became increasingly difficult to escape the logic that if inmates have the right to the assistance of another inmate in the preparation of legal documents, they cannot be absolutely restrained from acquiring the requisite legal materials and due process protection needed to assist in the preparation of petitions or to acquire an attorney or some other type of competent assistance to help them seek an appropriate and speedy judicial remedy (see Haas, 1982: 728).

However, the *Johnson* decision lacked precision. It provided prison officials with only the basic parameters of the right of access. Since 1969, the Supreme Court has resolved several important issues left unsettled by *Johnson*. In *Younger* v. *Gilmore* (1971), the Court affirmed a lower court ruling that required prison officials to provide inmates with a law library that contained a sufficient collection of books and materials to assure that prisoners were able to file petitions that demonstrate at least some legal proficiency. Three years later, the Court struck down a California prison policy that barred law students and legal paraprofessionals from working with prisoners (*Procunier* v. *Martinez*, 1974: 419-422). Also in 1974, the Justices invalidated a Nebraska regulation stating that prisoners could seek legal assistance only from a single "inmate legal adviser" who was appointed by the warden and who was permitted to provide assistance only in preparing habeas corpus petitions (*Wolff* v. *McDonnell*, 1974: 577-580). Finally, in *Bounds* v. *Smith* (1977), the Court held that even when prison policies allow jailhouse lawyers to operate, prison officials nevertheless must provide prisoners with either an adequate law library or adequate assistance from persons trained in the law.

Like the *Johnson* opinion, the *Bounds* opinion was far from specific in explaining what it would take to provide "adequate" legal services and materials for prisoners. The *Bounds* Court simply noted:

> While adequate law libraries are one constitutionally acceptable method to assure meaningful access to the courts, our decision here . . . does not foreclose alternative means to achieve that goal. . . . Among the alternatives are the training of inmates as paralegal assistants to work under lawyers' supervision, the use of paraprofessionals and law students, either as volunteers or in formal clinical programs, the organization of volunteer attorneys through bar associations or other groups, the hiring of lawyers on a part-time consultant basis, and the use of full-time staff attorneys, working either in new prison legal assistance organizations or as part of public defender or legal services offices. (*Bounds* at 828)

Thus there is still confusion after *Bounds* as to what prison officials must do to guarantee inmates meaningful access to the courts. Questions involving the adequacy of particular prison law libraries or legal services programs must be answered by the state and federal courts on a case-by-case basis. In states with small, homogenous prison populations, it may be sufficient to provide adequate law libraries and access to materials with some quasi-professional help. But in large, multilingual prison populations that are found in larger states, licensed attorneys may be necessary to guarantee access to the courts (Note, 1983; Alpert and Huff, 1981). A federal district court in Florida adopted that view in 1982 (*Hooks* v. *Wainwright*), holding that the state's plan to provide prisoners with law libraries staffed by inmate law clerks and librarians was insufficient to guarantee prisoners access to the courts. Accordingly, the court ordered the Florida Department of Corrections to provide some form of attorney assistance as part of its legal services plan.

However, on appeal, this decision was reversed by the Eleventh Circuit Court of Appeals (*Hooks* v. *Wainwright*, 1985). The court of appeals held that the lower court had interpreted *Bounds* too broadly and that attorneys were not required. In other words, a combination of law libraries and inmate law clerks will meet the *Bounds* mandate. The Ninth Circuit also approved the use of inmate law clerks rather than lawyers (*Lindquist* v. *Idaho Board of Corrections*, 1985) but indicated that the clerks must have received at least some sort of organized training.

Thus the issue of what must be done for illiterate inmates remains unsettled. But at a minimum, it appears that most courts will require both an adequate law library and assistance from persons who have some demonstrable understanding of the legal process. We now look at some of the available programs that provide legal services to inmates in state prisons, and we assess the impact of such programs.

Prison Legal Assistance Programs and Their Impact

Two frequently found types of prison legal aid programs are (1) institutionally supported networks of jailhouse lawyers, and (2) resident counsel programs staffed by actual attorneys. Among the states that have institutionalized the jailhouse lawyer as a source of legal assistance to other prisoners are Nebraska and Pennsylvania (Bluth, 1972; Rudovsky, Bronstein, and Koren, 1983). Although the participating jailhouse lawyers are not permitted to collect fees or special favors for their work, they are commonly awarded "good time" credits that earn them earlier release from prison. Under the Pennsylvania system, a group of writ-writers offers free legal services to other prisoners, with work credit, supplies, and office space provided by prison officials. There is no definite answer as to whether or not such writ-writer programs are truly successful in meeting the complex legal needs of prisoners. But many legal scholars believe that to be effective, jailhouse lawyers should be supervised by an attorney who can make sure that the writ-writers are capable of competent work and do not encourage frivolous or repetitious suits (Gobert and Cohen, 1981: 31).

The second type of legal assistance program, resident counsel, may be designed to include jailhouse lawyers and law students or paralegals under the supervision of lawyers at the prison (Alpert and Huff, 1981: 339). Early examples of such programs can be found in Washington, Texas, and Massachusetts. These programs, and others like them, provide legal assistance in non-fee-generating cases through the use of licensed attorneys and trained paralegals. It seems likely that resident counsel programs are generally superior to jailhouse lawyer-run programs in providing competent and comprehensive legal assistance to prisoners. Attorneys with some background in prison law are usually familiar with the technical aspects of drafting pleas and practical matters of legal strategy.

As to possible disadvantages, resident counsel programs can be very costly, depending upon the number of attorneys required. Moreover, problems may develop in the relationships among attorneys and correctional officials. On the other hand, the fact that these lawyers are state employees may cause inmates to stay away from the service—seeing it as a "cop-out to the man" or as a token program designed merely to co-opt prisoners. If inmates fail to use state-funded attorneys for these or other reasons, access to the court has not been provided.

What affects the use of resident counsel programs by prisoners? In a study of such a program in the state of Washington, 120 out of 198 surveyed prisoners (61%) acknowledged that they had legal problems (Alpert, 1976). Ninety-one out of the 120 (76%) sought recourse to the legal aid project. Twenty-nine prisoners who had legal problems decided not to use the project. Out of these 29, five (17%) stated that they were retaining private counsel, 4 (14%) just "didn't give a damn," and 20 (69%) said that state funding discouraged their use of the Legal Services Project. Of those using the service, 63% felt that the project served the prisoners, whereas 37% felt it served the needs and goals of the state.

Research on resident counsel programs in Texas and Massachusetts also found that most of the inmate clients had positive attitudes toward the service (Alpert, 1980: 14-15). The research showed that for inmates in Texas

> participation in the legal aid project is a significant factor in producing positive changes in prisonization and in prisoners' attitudes toward police, lawyers, law and the judicial system. . . . A second significant finding which moves beyond attitudinal changes concerns the number of institutional infractions committed by members of our cohorts. The finding that users of legal aid experience fewer convictions for institutional infractions is significant in that it uses a behavioral measure as an independent variable. Providing legal services to prisoners is one step to reduce

tension and anxiety, and reduce hostility among inmates. (Alpert, 1978: 44, 46-47)

The assertion that prison legal service programs can effectively reduce institutional tensions may seem surprising. However, this is a conclusion with which correctional administrators overwhelmingly concur. Two nationwide surveys of prison officials found that a large majority of the respondents believe that the inmate legal assistance programs mandated by court decisions have led to a decrease in disciplinary problems and have facilitated rehabilitation efforts. For example, Cardarelli and Finkelstein (1974) reported that over 80% of a large sample of state corrections commissioners, prison wardens, and treatment directors agreed that legal services provide a safety valve for inmate grievances, reduce inmate power structures and tensions from unresolved legal problems, and contribute to rehabilitation by showing the inmate that he or she is being treated fairly.

A second nationwide survey of prison officials (Haas and Champagne, 1976) disclosed that the prison systems that had hired attorneys to supervise legal aid programs had experienced a marked decline in problems with jailhouse lawyers and in friction between staff and inmates concerning alleged violations of rights. This study concluded that legal services programs supervised by attorneys help to maintain an atmosphere of discipline by undermining the power of the more unscrupulous jailhouse lawyers and by providing inmates with an outlet for their grievances and frustrations. Clearly, this is one area of correctional law that has contributed measurably to positive changes in American prisons.

Procedural and Jurisdictional Obstacles to Inmate Access

Section 1983 of the Civil Rights Act of 1871

We have just shown that over the past 20 years, the U.S. Supreme Court has broadened the prisoner's right of access to the courts by striking down prison regulations barring the activities of jailhouse lawyers and by requiring prison officials to establish reasonably adequate law libraries and/or legal assistance programs. However, it is important to understand that the right of access also encompasses questions involving judicial policies affecting the availability of the various judicial remedies sought by prisoners. Cases dealing with procedural and jurisdictional issues are of great importance because such cases can either limit or expand the availability of judicial relief for prisoners. And in this area of law, prisoners have not fared very well in recent years, for the Supreme Court has made it increasingly difficult for prisoners to secure full judicial review of their grievances.

Because over 90% of America's nearly 700,000 state and federal prisoners are housed in state prisons (Bureau of Justice Statistics, 1989), the large majority of lawsuits attacking allegedly unconstitutional prison practices are brought by state prisoners. Most of these suits are filed in federal court under Section 1983 of the Civil Rights Act of 1871 (hereinafter Section 1983). Although some state courts are more inclined to support civil rights and liberties than they were in the past (see generally Tarr and Porter, 1987), state prisoners generally believe that federal judges, as a group, are more sympathetic to their claims than are state judges. Indeed, research on comparative judicial behavior suggests that prisoners are correct in this regard. State courts that have been quite vigorous in protecting the rights of other minority groups generally have been less vigilant than the federal courts in safeguarding the rights of prisoners (Haas, 1981).

This state of affairs may change as an increasing number of President Reagan's appointees assume their duties on the federal bench. But there are important institutional and structural factors that militate against change. For example, whereas all federal judges enjoy lifetime appointments, the majority of the nation's state trial and appellate judges must stand in periodic elections and thus are more susceptible to public sentiments against prisoners. Moreover, federal court rules and procedures in such critical areas as pleading, fact finding, immunities, attorneys' fees, pretrial discovery, and class actions are more hospitable to prisoners' cases than the rules used by most state courts (Neuborne, 1981).

Section 1983 has been by far the most effective device for redressing the grievances of state prisoners (see generally Turner, 1979). Originally passed in an effort to combat the Ku Klux Klan in the aftermath of the Civil War, Section 1983 provides that any person acting under color of state or local law who violates the federal constitutional or statutory rights of another "shall be liable to the party injured in an action at law, suit in equity, or other proper proceeding for redress." Under Section 1983, state prisoners may challenge violations of their First Amendment freedoms of speech, religion, and association, or, for that matter, unconstitutional prison policies that deny or restrict their right of access to the courts. Most inmate Section 1983 cases, however, focus on allegedly unconstitutional conditions of confinement, covering such issues as privacy, unsanitary conditions, inadequate medical and dental care, overcrowding, nutritionally inadequate food, lack of exercise opportunities, inadequate heating, ventilation, and lighting, and unprovoked physical attacks by prison staff. Due process violations also are frequently litigated under Section 1983. Such cases may involve the rights of prisoners in disciplinary hearings, reclassification proceedings, interprison transfers, and parole eligibility hearings. Section 1983 actions also are commonly brought by probationers and parolees who claim that they were denied constitutionally mandated protections before or during revocation proceedings.

Monroe v. *Pape* (1961) and Its Progeny

Section 1983 was rarely invoked by prisoners or anyone else for nearly a century. But in a landmark 1961 case (*Monroe* v. *Pape*), the U.S. Supreme Court interpreted Section 1983 as giving federal courts original jurisdiction over any claims alleging violations of federal constitutional rights by state or local officials. This meant that petitioners suing state or local officials would not have to worry about the delays and expense involved in meeting the traditional requirement of exhausting all state judicial remedies before bringing suit in a federal court. They could instead bypass the state courts and go directly to the federal court with their Section 1983 claims. Three years later (*Cooper* v. *Pate*, 1964), the High Court made it clear that state prisoners could bring allegations of unconstitutional prison policies and conditions against state correctional employees under the provisions of Section 1983, thus creating a readily available and effective judicial remedy for prison abuses.

To be sure, there are other statutes, state and federal, under which prisoners can file legal claims. These include the federal Habeas Corpus Statute, the federal Tort Claims Act, state habeas corpus statutes, and state tort claims acts. However, for a variety of reasons, state prisoners and their attorneys prefer Section 1983 as the fastest and potentially most advantageous device for advancing claims against prison officials (see generally Manville, 1983: 163-220). Section 1983, for example, clearly is an appropriate vehicle for challenges to a prisoner's conditions of confinement. By contrast, many state habeas corpus statutes allow prisoners to challenge the legality of their conviction but not to challenge the conditions of confinement. Whereas Section 1983 is phrased in terms that permit the awarding of both compensatory and punitive damages to a victorious plaintiff, most state tort claims acts do not provide for punitive damages. The federal Habeas Corpus Act allows no monetary damages of any kind and strictly requires the exhaustion of all state remedies. The federal Tort Claims Act can be a useful remedy for some kinds of suits, but the Tort Claims Act does not allow prisoners to sue governmental bodies for assault and battery claims or other intentional (as opposed to negligent) torts.

Because Section 1983 is the major device by which state prisoners seek to protect their rights to fair treatment and humane conditions, any new laws or court decisions that limit the usefulness of Section 1983 pose a major threat to prisoners. And, indeed, from the perspective of prisoners and the advocates of prison reform, there have been disturbing signs that Section 1983 may not survive into the twenty-first century. In a series of recent cases, the U.S. Supreme court has begun to diminish the effectiveness of Section 1983 as a means by which to combat violations of inmate rights.

Space limitations preclude a discussion of all of the Supreme Court decisions that have affected the use of Section 1983 by state prisoners (see generally Nahmod, 1986). Furthermore, it should be noted that a few of the Court's decisions have benefited inmate Section 1983 litigants. For example, inmates in city and county jails have profited from recent decisions establishing that local municipalities can be sued for compensatory damages under Section 1983 (*Monell* v. *Department of Social Services*, 1978) and that municipalities are unprotected by any kind of qualified immunity (*Owen* v. *City of Independence*, 1980).

The High Court also upheld the traditional scope of Section 1983 liability in a case involving a young inmate who suffered a night of rape and torture because a guard needlessly placed him in a cell with two prisoners known to have violent tendencies (*Smith* v. *Wade*, 1983). By a 5-4 vote, the Court affirmed that a prison employee may be held liable for punitive damages in a Section 1983 action alleging violations of the Eighth Amendment's cruel and unusual punishment clause. The *Wade* Court also determined that a Section 1983 plaintiff with Eighth Amendment claims is entitled to punitive damages if he or she can show that the defendant acted with reckless or callous disregard for the plaintiff's health or safety. The plaintiff, in other words, does not have to show that the defendant acted with malicious intent to injure the plaintiff, a more demanding standard.

Despite these victories for prisoners, most of the Supreme Court's jurisdictional pronouncements have sent a clear signal to the lower federal courts to cut back the availability of Section 1983 relief for state prisoners. For example, in 1973, the Court's decision in *Preiser* v. *Rodriguez* placed significant limitations on inmate use of Section 1983. *Preiser* established that whenever a state prisoner files a claim that, if successful, would result in a reduction in the length of his or her sentence (for example, a due process challenge to the fairness of a prison disciplinary committee's decision to take away an inmate's "good time" or early release credits), the prisoner can no longer sue under Section 1983. Instead, he or she will have to file the suit as a habeas corpus action, thus necessitating the time-consuming and often futile exhaustion of all state judicial and administrative remedies.

The *Preiser* majority conceded that the "broad language" of Section 1983 made it applicable to actions in which prisoners challenge prison practices that may unfairly lengthen their sentences (*Preiser* at 488-489). Nevertheless, the majority Justices held that the history of habeas corpus, the specific wording of the federal Habeas Corpus Statute, and the importance of allowing state courts the first opportunity to correct unfair state prison practices justified their decision to declare habeas corpus to be the sole remedy for state prisoners challenging the length of their confinement (*Preiser* at 477-490). In dissent, Justice Brennan asserted that the majority's effort to distinguish between prisoner challenges to prison practices affecting the conditions of confinement (where Section 1983 can be used) and prison practices affecting the duration of confinement (where habeas corpus, with its exhaustion requirement, must be used) was historically incorrect, analytically unsound, and certain to create unnecessary confusion that would inevitably thwart the fair and prompt resolution of legitimate inmate grievances (*Preiser* at 506-511).

More recent decisions have also narrowed the scope of liability under Section 1983. The Supreme Court has declared that states are not considered "persons" subject to suit under Section 1983 (*Quern v. Jordan*, 1979) and that local governments cannot be sued for punitive damages in Section 1983 cases (*City of Newport v. Fact Concerts*, 1981). State legislators have long enjoyed absolute immunity from Section 1983 liability (*Tenney v. Brandhove*, 1951), and the Court has made it clear that prison officials are protected by the affirmative defense of qualified or "good faith" immunity (*Procunier v. Navarette*, 1978).

In 1980, Congress passed legislation intended to curtail the use of Section 1983 by state prisoners. Section 1997e of the Civil Rights of Institutionalized Persons Act (hereinafter Section 1997e) requires state prisoners to exhaust state *administrative* remedies before they can file a section 1983 suit in a federal court. This requirement, however, applies only when either the attorney general of the United States or the federal court in which the suit is filed has certified that the state administrative remedy—some kind of inmate grievance system—meets minimally accepted standards of fairness. Section 1997e further states that a federal court must continue the case for no more than 90 days in order to require exhaustion of the administrative remedy.

In *Patsy* v. *Florida Board of Regents* (1982), the Supreme Court held that nonprisoner Section 1983 plaintiffs cannot be required to exhaust state administrative remedies. However, the Justices bestowed their approval on Section 1997e's special filing requirements for prisoners, noting that it was reasonable to carve out an exception to the general no-exhaustion rule in order to relieve the burden of inmate complaints on the federal courts (*Patsy* at 509). It can be argued that a 90-day delay is not unreasonable and that Section 1997e may have the beneficial effect of motivating state prison administrators to improve their internal grievance systems (see McCoy, 1981). Nevertheless, prisoners can only find it unsettling to be singled out as the only class of Section 1983 litigants who cannot proceed directly to a federal court to seek relief from possible violations of their constitutionally protected rights.

From *Parratt* (1981) to *Daniels-Davidson* (1986)

In *Parratt* v. *Taylor* (1981), the Supreme Court announced the first of a series of decisions that have considerably weakened Section 1983 as a vehicle by which state prisoners can go to federal court to challenge prison policies. *Parratt* involved a Section 1983 suit brought by a Nebraska prisoner seeking $23.50 from prison employees for their alleged negligence in failing to follow the normal prison procedure for receiving mailed packages and thereby losing a mail-order hobby kit for which he had paid $23.50. The lower courts had determined that the loss of the prisoner's property was properly construed as a violation of the due process clause of the Fourteenth Amendment and thus was cognizable in a Section 1983 suit.

The Supreme Court, however, disagreed, holding that when a plaintiff asserted the loss of *property* because of the *negligent* action of a state employee, the existence of a state postdeprivation remedy precludes a Section 1983 claim based on the due process clause. In this case, according to Justice Rehnquist's majority opinion, the prisoner must bring his suit under the Nebraska Tort Claims Act—a state law that Justice Rehnquist conceded to be less efficacious than Section 1983 in that it contained no provisions for trial by jury or for punitive damages (*Parratt* at 543-544). Nevertheless, in Justice Rehnquist's view, a state remedy that may not be as advantageous as Section 1983 but that can potentially compensate a prospective Section 1983 plaintiff for his or her losses is "sufficient to satisfy the requirements of due process" (*Parratt* at 544). Therefore, the negligent conduct that had led to the loss of the prisoner's property had occurred with due process of law—the possibility of postdeprivation relief in the state courts—and was not actionable in the federal courts under Section 1983 (*Parratt* at 543-544).

Legal commentators were quick to point out that the implications of *Parratt* were ominous for state prisoners (see, for example, Friedman, 1982; Blum, 1984), and they turned out to be absolutely correct. Three years later, the logic of *Parratt* was extended to *intentional* deprivations of property. In *Hudson* v. *Palmer* (1984), a state prisoner in Virginia brought a Section 1983 action against a prison guard who allegedly had conducted a "shakedown" search of the prisoner's cell and had intentionally destroyed his *noncontraband* personal property including legal papers, a letter from his wife, and a picture of his baby. The suit was based on two legal theories: (1) the assertion that prisoners retain some reasonable expectation of privacy in their cells and are thus constitutionally entitled to some minimal Fourth Amendment protections against unreasonable searches and seizures (i.e., the right to be present during cell searches); and (2) the contention that the guard's intentional destruction of the inmate's personal property should be actionable as a due process claim in federal court under Section 1983 regardless of whether an adequate state postdeprivation remedy was available.

In an opinion authored by Chief Justice Burger, the *Palmer* Court decided both of the previously mentioned issues in favor of the guard and against the prisoner. First, a 5-4 majority held that prisoners possess absolutely no recognizable expectations of privacy in their cells (*Palmer* at 529-530). Therefore, according to the majority, prisoners enjoy no Fourth Amendment protection against arbitrary searches or unjustified confiscation of their personal property, even if the sole purpose of the search and seizure is to harass the inmate (*Palmer* at 529-530).

Second, the Court voted unanimously to apply the reasoning behind *Parratt* v. *Taylor* to intentional deprivations of property by state employees. Pointing out that the destruction of the prisoner's property was a random, unauthorized act by a state employee rather than an established state procedure (in which case Section 1983 arguably could still be used), Chief Justice Burger argued that predeprivation due process was "impractical" because the state court "cannot predict when the loss will occur" (*Palmer* at 532). Therefore, according to the Chief Justice, the underlying rationale of *Parratt* must be applied to intentional deprivations of property because there is "no logical distinction between negligent and intentional deprivations of property insofar as the 'practicality' of affording predeprivation due process is concerned" (*Palmer* at 533).

Perhaps the weakest aspect of the Chief Justice's majority opinion is his failure to offer any explanation as to why prisoners who suffer unjustified, egregious, and humiliating property losses at the hands of state employees must use the arguably less efficacious state postdeprivation remedy rather than the federal postdeprivation remedy — Section 1983 — that Congress has established as the means by which to redress wrongs committed by state employees. Nevertheless, the result of *Palmer* is that when the state provides an "adequate" postdeprivation remedy by which abused prisoners can seek compensation for their losses, they are barred from seeking compensation under Section 1983 in a federal court — even if they lose their state court lawsuit. Chief Justice Burger acknowledged that under the Virginia Tort Claims Act, a prisoner "might not be able to recover . . . the full amount he might receive in a Section 1983 action" (*Palmer* at 535). However, the Chief Justice embraced Justice Rehnquist's *Parratt* argument that a state remedy need not be as efficacious as Section 1983 in order to satisfy the due process requirements of the Fourteenth Amendment (*Palmer* at 535).

In the aftermath of *Palmer*, one legal commentator accused the Supreme Court of "reviving the era of near total deference to prison administrators" (Leading Cases, 1984). Others speculated that the outlook for inmate litigants could become even worse if the rationale of *Parratt* and *Palmer* were to be applied to deprivations of liberty as well as to deprivations of property (Levinson, 1986). But this is precisely what the High Court did in two cases decided in January 1986 — *Daniels v. Williams* and *Davidson v. Cannon*.

In *Daniels*, a county jail inmate had slipped on a pillow negligently left on the stairs by a guard. The inmate then brought a Section 1983 suit seeking compensation for his alleged back and ankle injuries on the grounds that the guard's negligence had deprived him of his *liberty* interest under the Fourteenth Amendment to be free from bodily injury caused by government employees. Writing for a unanimous Court, Justice Rehnquist (who would be confirmed as Chief Justice later in 1986), argued that the Fourteenth Amendment's guarantee that no state shall "deprive any person of life, liberty, or property, without due process of law" was originally intended to apply only to *intentional* deprivations of life, liberty, or property by government officials (*Daniels* at 331). Justice Rehnquist offered no evidence to support the contention that the 1868 Congress that enacted the Fourteenth Amendment held such a narrow view of the due process clause. However, he asserted that the history of the Supreme Court's handling of due process cases supported his argument:

> No decision of this Court before *Parratt* supported the view that negligent conduct by a state official, even though causing injury,

constitutes a deprivation under the due process clause. (*Daniels* at 331)

The practical impact of Justice Rehnquist's extraordinarily brief examination of the history of the Fourteenth Amendment was devastating for state prisoners and local jail inmates. In one swift stroke, Justice Rehnquist overruled the one aspect of *Parratt* that had allowed prisoners any legal recourse when they had suffered losses at the hands of negligent state or local officials:

> Upon reflection, we . . . overrule *Parratt* to the extent that it states that mere lack of due care by a state official may 'deprive' an individual of life, liberty, or property under the Fourteenth Amendment. (*Daniels* at 330-331)

Thus state prisoners are not only barred from bringing negligence claims to federal courts under Section 1983; as a result of *Daniels*, they are not even constitutionally entitled to an adequate state postdeprivation remedy when they have suffered losses of life, liberty, or property at the hands of negligent state or local employees. In other words, under *Daniels*, negligent acts, however stupid or harmful, can never violate the Fourteenth Amendment. If the state has not enacted some kind of tort claim act under which the victim of negligent conduct can seek redress (and this was indeed the plight of plaintiff Roy Daniels), he or she simply will have no right to go to any court—state or federal—to seek relief.

One of the nation's leading authorities on tort law described *Daniels* as "novel," "far-reaching," and as a "reinterpretation of the Fourteenth Amendment" (Mead, 1986: 27). But the damage done to the prisoner's right of access to the courts is perhaps best demonstrated by showing how the *Daniels* precedent was applied to the facts of *Davidson v. Cannon* (1986). Whereas *Daniels* was a simple slip-and-fall case that could arguably be called "insipid," *Davidson* involved egregious and inexcusable negligence on the part of state prison officials. After another prisoner had threatened him, Robert Davidson, the plaintiff, reported the threats both orally and in writing to the appropriate prison officials. His written request for protection found its way to the assistant superintendent of the prison who read it and sent it to the cellblock's corrections sergeant on December 19, 1980. But the sergeant, though informed of the note's contents and the identity of the threatening prisoner, forgot about the note and left it on his desk unread when he left the prison some 8 hours later. Because both the assistant superintendent and the sergeant did not work on December 20 or 21, the guards on duty knew nothing about the threat. On December 21, the inmate who had threatened Robert Davidson attacked him with a fork, breaking his nose and inflicting severe wounds to his face, neck, head, and body.

Without question, the facts of Robert Davidson's case are far more compelling than those of Roy Daniels' case. Surely Justice Rehnquist could not conclude that judicial willingness to consider Robert Davidson's claims "would trivialize the centuries-old principle of due process of law" (*Daniels* at 332). But in a four-page majority opinion, Justice Rehnquist, in effect, did just that. This was nothing more than a simple case of negligence, declared Justice Rehnquist, and therefore "the principles enunciated in *Daniels* [are] controlling here" (*Davidson* at 347-348)

It is notable that three justices dissented in *Davidson*. The three dissenters—Justices Blackmun, Marshall, and Brennan—expressed the belief that the conduct of the prison officials in *Davidson* arguably reached the level of *deliberate* or *reckless indifference* to the prisoner's safety (*Davidson* at 349-360). Thus they would have remanded the case to the lower courts to consider whether the actions of the prison officials should be treated as a "reckless indifference" claim under the Eighth Amendment's cruel and unusual punishment clause as in *Smith* v. *Wade* (1983). In Justice Blackmun's words:

> When the state incarcerated Daniels, it left intact his own faculties for avoiding a slip and a fall. But the state prevented Davidson from defending himself, and therefore assumed some responsibility to protect him from the dangers to which he was exposed. In these circumstances, I feel that Davidson was deprived of liberty by the negligence of prison officials. Moreover, the acts of the state officials in this case may well have risen to the level of recklessness. I therefore dissent. (*Davidson* at 350)

For prisoners and the supporters of prison reform, the implications of *Daniels* and *Davidson* are foreboding. The Supreme Court's next step could very well be to decide that *intentional* deprivations of *liberty* can no longer be litigated in federal courts when state remedies are available. For that matter, the Court may eventually go even further and apply the logic of *Daniels* to intentional deprivations of liberty, thus allowing the states to decide whether or not to provide remedies for such violations. Also in doubt is the continued vitality of *Smith* v. *Wade* (1983). Few legal scholars would be surprised if the Court were to hold that Eighth Amendment claims of reckless indifference to state prisoners' health or safety can no longer be brought under Section 1983 to the federal courts when adequate state remedies are available.

As a result of the Supreme Court's narrowing of Section 1983 jurisdiction, prisoners increasingly find themselves in a classic "Catch

22'' situation. In *Johnson* v. *Avery* (1969), *Bounds* v. *Smith* (1977), and other cases, inmates won the right to challenge prison policies that violate their right of access to the courts and other substantive constitutional rights. But these hard-earned rights are rapidly becoming ''rights without remedies'' because of Supreme Court decisions that establish formidable and inflexible procedural and jurisdictional barriers to bringing suit in a federal or state court.

Implications for Research on the Courts and Corrections

Since *Monroe* v. *Pape* (1961), American prisoners have been transformed from ''slaves of the state'' to individuals with significant constitutional rights. The courts agreed to consider the complaints of prisoners only after years of neglect and the failure of prison administrators to manage their institutions appropriately. One consequence of the judiciary's willingness to review prison conditions was the raising of the iron curtain that had been drawn between the courts and prisoners. For a window in time, the pendulum was swinging toward the advantage of those who were incarcerated. As the previous analysis has demonstrated, the pendulum has reached its most advanced degree and is now moving rapidly in the opposite direction, toward the return of what can be termed a ''modified hands-off doctrine.'' In particular, the Supreme Court's recent decisions curtailing the availability of Section 1983 relief for state prisoners have, in effect, closed the federal (and, in some cases, the state) courthouse doors to prisoners who may have verifiable and meritorious claims.

The major justification for this trend is that inmate petitions — especially Section 1983 filings — are placing increasing burdens on the time and resources of judges and correctional officials. Several Supreme Court justices, notably Chief Justice Rehnquist and Justice O'Connor, have charged that inmate Section 1983 suits waste scarce judicial resources and create financial hardships for state and local governments (see *Monell* v. *Department of Social Services* (1978) at 724 (Rehnquist, J., dissenting; O'Connor, 1981: 808-815). Even judges who are generally more sympathetic to the need for federal protection of civil rights through Section 1983 have expressed concerns about the burdens that Section 1983 imposes on the federal courts (Coffin, 1971; Friendly, 1973: 87-107).

These concerns suggest that it is important to conduct a great deal more research on the financial and social costs of inmate Section 1983 claims and other types of lawsuits brought by prisoners. Is there really a deluge of prison litigation? Is the Section 1983 caseload a problem of crisis dimensions for court personnel and correctional employees? Or is it possible that the so-called flood of litigation is a largely illusory problem, created by the hyperbole of those who are simply hostile to prisoners as a class of litigants?

To answer the preceding questions will require increasingly sophisticated research on how the courts process prisoner petitions and how correctional personnel respond to inmate complaints. So far, the few empirical studies of how Section 1983 cases are handled by the federal courts tend to undermine the assertion that these cases are overburdening the federal docket (see, for example Bailey, 1975; Eisenberg, 1982; McCoy, 1981; Turner, 1979). It is especially interesting that most of these studies have indicated that the burden on the federal courts may be exaggerated by those who advocate limits on inmate Section 1983 cases. For example, Turner (1979: 637) discovered that "a large proportion of [Section 1983] cases are screened out and summarily dismissed before they get under way, . . . court appearances and trials are rare, and . . . prisoner cases are not particularly complex as compared to other types of federal litigation."

On the other hand, Roger Hanson (1987: 224) recently pointed out that the burdens of screening and disposing of Section 1983 cases especially the typically inarticulate *pro se* complaints drafted by inmates without benefit of counsel should not be underestimated. His study of four federal district courts revealed that the major workload of a majority of Section 1983 cases falls not on federal judges, but "on the shoulders of federal magistrates and *pro se* law clerks" (1987: 224). Moreover, Hanson stresses that we do not know and thus need more research on such important factors as:

(1) The cost to state attorneys general (or private counsel) in defending state officials.
(2) The cost to federal magistrates and their staff in the time spent handling cases through the pretrial stages.
(3) The time spent by federal district court judges and their staff in preparing for and conducting trials.
(4) The time spent by federal circuit court judges and their staff in hearing appeals.
(5) The administrative costs to the federal district and circuit courts in the maintenance and processing of court documents.
(6) The costs in time and money to correctional officials in attending hearings, preparing answers, submitting to depositions, and transporting inmates to and from the courthouse. (1987: 225)

Even without additional research on the costs of prisoner litigation, it would not be premature to conclude that the costs are indeed significant. This is not to say that the costs necessarily outweigh the benefits. Some of the benefits are precious and priceless. For example, there is no way to put a dollar value on the importance of upholding the principle that all Americans—even those who have shown no respect for the law—are entitled to humane treatment, fundamental fairness, and due process of law. But if these values could be preserved while decreasing the social and economic costs of inmate litigation, everybody would benefit.

This intuitively appealing idea suggests the desirability of developing and refining inmate grievance systems that can resolve inmate complaints in a fair and prompt manner while reducing the caseloads of the federal and state courts. It was presumably with this intention that Congress passed the Civil Rights of Institutionalized Persons Act in May, 1980. This Act, discussed earlier, was designed specifically to reduce the Section 1983 caseload. It allows prison officials who have had their institutional grievance systems approved by either the United States Attorney General's Office or the federal court of jurisdiction to delay Section 1983 cases for up to 90 days in order to attempt to resolve inmate grievances internally. In other words, the Act provides for a period of negotiation in which a determination of the accuracy and importance of the allegations can be made, and a fair and just resolution can be negotiated.

Unfortunately, the states have shown an unwillingness to request certification for inmate grievance procedures and a reluctance to take advantage of the provisions of the Act. Only four states—Virginia, Wyoming, Iowa, and Louisiana—have certified grievance mechanisms in place, and only Virginia has had a certified procedure in place long enough to allow study of the effects of the Institutionalized Persons Act. Preliminary research by Hanson (1987: 227) indicates that "Virginia has experienced a substantial decrease in filing rates after gaining certification whereas adjoining states in the same federal circuit that have not been certified have experienced much smaller changes in litigation rates." This suggests that there is a compelling need for additional research on the effectiveness of certified grievance procedures and on how internal grievance systems generally affect the rights of both prisoners and correctional staff. Among the questions that need to be answered are:

1. What kinds of grievance systems are most effective in resolving inmate complaints?

2. Are certain kinds of grievance systems more effective than others in reducing Section 1983 litigation?

3. Is inmate participation (in a decisional capacity) in a grievance system helpful or counterproductive in settling disputes?

4. Can grievance systems offer fair compensation to prisoners who have suffered losses that are no longer compensable in the courts as a result of *Daniels, Davidson,* and other Supreme Court decisions?

5. Do grievance systems reduce—or merely postpone—frivolous and nonmeritorious Section 1983 suits?

6. How satisfied are prisoners and correctional staff with various kinds of grievance procedures?

Answers to these and other questions about the impact of internal grievance mechanisms on the courts and on the prisons may encourage the states to establish new and better dispute resolution procedures. However, it would be naive to be overly optimistic about this possibility. As Christopher Smith (1986: 149) warned, "[r]elying on the states for the development of remedies means [that the] implementation of protections for prisoners' rights is placed squarely in the hands of the elected legislatures and governors who fostered the unconstitutional prison conditions in the first place."

Thus it remains vitally important to continue earlier research on the realities of American prison conditions (see, e.g., Bowker, 1980; Toch, 1977) and to carry out new research on how these conditions affect the character, content, and number of suits filed by prisoners. In addition, it will be necessary to update earlier studies focusing on the impact of court decisions on prison policies and practices (Alpert, 1978; Haas and Champagne, 1976). Accordingly, our initial research agenda includes the following:

1. Comparative and longitudinal analyses of the conditions under which prisoners seek and are either provided or denied access to the courts.

2. Comparative and longitudinal analyses of how prisoners achieve access to the courts by type of prison and jurisdiction.

3. Studies on how the provision of legal assistance affects the attitudes and behavior of prisoners and staff.

4. Studies on how specific court decisions affect the attitudes and behavior of prisoners and staff.

The changing scope of the prisoner's right of access to the courts over the past century has reflected evolving judicial philosophies about the meaning of justice, the limits of punishment, and the proper role of the courts in a free society. It is our hope that a philosophy of humanitarianism, informed by carefully crafted and skillfully executed research, will shape correctional policies and provide guidance for the courts of the future.

References

Alpert, G. P. Prisoners' right of access to courts: planning for legal aid. *Washington Law Review*, 1976, 51, 653-675.

Alpert, G. P. *Legal rights of prisoners*. Lexington, MA: Lexington Books, 1978.

Alpert, G. P. Prisoners and their rights: An introduction. In G.P. Alpert (Ed.), *Legal rights of prisoners*. Beverly Hills, CA: Sage Publications, 1980.

Alpert, G. P., and Huff, C. R. Prisoners, the law and public policy: planning for legal aid. *New England Journal on Prison Law*, 1981, 7, 307-340.

Bailey, W. S. The realities of prisoners' cases under U.S.C. Section 1983: A statistical survey in the northern district of Illinois. *Loyola University of Chicago Law Journal*, 1975, 6, 527-559.

Blum, K. M. The implications of *Parratt v. Taylor* for Section 1983 litigation. *The Urban Lawyer*, 1984, 16, 363-386.

Bluth, W. Legal services for inmates: Coopting the jailhouse lawyer. *Capital University Law Review*, 1972, 1, 59-81.

Bowker, L. H. *Prison victimization*. New York: Elsevier, 1980.

Bureau of Justice Statistics. *Prisoners in 1988*. Washington, DC: U.S. Government Printing Office, 1989.

Cardarelli, A., and Finkelstein, M. M. Correctional administrators assess the adequacy and impact of prison legal services programs in the United States. *Journal of Criminal Law and Criminology*, 1974, 65, 91-102.

Coffin, F. M. Justice and workability: Un essai. *Suffolk University Law Review*, 1971, 5, 567-587.

Edwards, J. A. The prisoner's right of access to the courts. *California Western Law Review*, 1968, 4, 99-114.

Eisenberg, J. Section 1983: Doctrinal foundations and an empirical study. *Cornell Law Review*, 1982, 67, 482-556.

Friedman, L. *Parratt v. Taylor*: Closing the door on Section 1983. *Hastings Constitutional Law Quarterly*. 1982, 9, 545-578.

Friendly, H. I. *Federal jurisdiction: A general view*, New York: Columbia University Press, 1973.

Gobert, J. L., and Cohen, N. I. *Rights of prisoners*. Colorado Springs: Shepard's/McGraw-Hill, 1981.

Haas, K. C. Judicial politics and correctional reform: An analysis of the decline of the "hands-off" doctrine. *Detroit College of Law Review*, 1977, 4, 796-831.

Haas, K. C. The "new federalism" and prisoners' rights: State supreme courts in comparative perspective. *Western Political Quarterly*, 1981, *34*, 552-571.

Haas, K. C. The comparative study of state and federal judicial behavior revisited. *Journal of Politics*, 1982, 44, 721-746.

Haas, K. C., and Champagne, A. The impact of *Johnson v. Avery* on prison administration. *Tennessee Law Review*, 1976, *43*, 275-306.

Hanson, R. A. What should be done when prisoners want to take the state to court? *Judicature*, 1987, *70*, 223-227.

Leading cases of the 1983 term. *Harvard Law Review*, 1984, *98*, 151-165.

Levinson, R. B. Due process challenges to governmental actions: The meaning of *Parratt* and *Hudson*. *The Urban Lawyer*, 1986, *18*, 189-208.

Manville, D. E. *Prisoners' self-help litigation manual*. New York: Oceana Publications, 1983.

McCoy, C. The impact of Section 1983 litigation on policymaking in corrections. *Federal Probation*, 1981, *45*, 17-23.

Mead, S. M. Evolution of the "species of tort liability" created by 42 U.S.C. Section 1983: Can the constitutional tort be saved from extinction? *Fordham Law Review*, 1986, *55*, 1-62.

Nahmod, S. *Civil rights and civil liberties litigation*. Colorado Springs: Shepard's/McGraw-Hill, 1986.

Neuborne, B. Toward procedural parity in constitutional litigation. *William and Mary Law Review*, 1981, *22*, 725-787.

Note. A prisoner's constitutional right to attorney assistance. *Columbia Law Review*, 1983, *83*, 1279-1319.

O'Connor, S. D. Trends in the relationship between the federal and state courts from the perspective of a state court judge. *William and Mary Law Review*, 1981, *22*, 801-819.

Rudovsky, D., Bronstein, A. I., and Koren, E. I. *The rights of prisoners*. New York: Bantam, 1983.

Smith, C. E. Federal judges' role in prisoner litigation: What's necessary? What's proper? *Judicature*, 1986, *70*, 141-150.

Tarr, G. A., and Porter, M. C. State constitutionalism and state constitutional law. *Publius*, 1987, *17*, 1-12.

Toch, H. *Living in prison: The ecology of prison survival*. New York: The Free Press, 1977.

Turner, W. B. When prisoners sue: A study of prisoner Section 1983 suits in the federal courts. *Harvard Law Review*, *1979*, 92, *610-663*.

Cases

Bounds v. Smith, 430 U.S. 817 (1977).

City of Newport v. Fact Concerts, 453 U.S. 247 (1981).

Coleman v. Peyton, 302 F.2d 905 (4th Cir. 1966).

Cooper v. Pate, 378 U.S. 546 (1964).

Daniels v. Williams, 474 U.S. 327 (1986).

Davidson v. Cannon, 474 U.S. 344 (1986).

Ex parte Hull, 312 U.S. 546 (1941).

Hooks v. Wainwright, 536 F. Supp. 1330 (M.D. Fla. 1982), rev'd, 775 F.2d 1433 (11th Cir. 1985).

Hudson v. Palmer, 468 U.S. 517 (1984).

Johnson v. Avery, 393 U.S. 483 (1969).

Lindquist v. Idaho Board of Corrections, 776 F.2d 851 (9th Cir. 1985).

Monell v. Department of Social Services, 436 U.S. 658 (1978).

Monroe v. Pape, 365 U.S. 167 (1961).

Owen v. City of Independence, 445 U.S. 622 (1980).

Parratt v. Taylor, 451 U.S. 527 (1981).

Patsy v. Florida Board of Regents, 457 U.S. 496 (1982).

Preiser v. Rodriguez, 411 U.S. 475 (1973).

Procunier v. Martinez, 416 U.S. 396, 419-422 (1974).

Procunier v. Navarette, 434 U.S. 555 (1978).

Quern v. Jordan, 440 U.S. 332 (1979).

Ross v Moffitt, 417 U.S. 600 (1974).

Ruffin v. Commonwealth, 62 Va. (21 Gratt.) 790 (1871).

Smith v. Wade, 461 U.S. 30 (1983)

Tenney v. Brandhove, 341 U.S. 367 (1951).

Wolff v. McDonnell, 418 U.S. 539, 577-580 (1974).

Younger v. Gilmore, 404 U.S. 15 (1971).

13

The Supreme Court's Retreat From the Protection of Prisoners' Rights

Three Major Cases From the Court's 1988-89 Term

Correctional Law Reporter

Rules for Publication and Letter Rejection Eased, Early Precedent Overruled

Thornburgh v. Abbott
109 S.Ct. 1874 (1989)

With this decision, the Supreme Court has taken perhaps its most dramatically conservative shift since it began deciding prisoners' rights cases in the early 1970s.

The issue in the case was one of censorship under the First Amendment: under what circumstances could a prison or jail censor or reject publications coming to an inmate from the outside? Specifically under attack was a comprehensive set of regulations of the federal Bureau of Prisons.

Source: *Correctional Law Reporter*, Vol. 1, No. 3 (August 1989), pp. 37-41. Reprinted with the permission of the co-editors, William C. Collins and Fred Cohen.

The Court of Appeals for the District of Columbia had thrown out substantial portions of the rules on the grounds they allowed rejection of a publication which didn't go so far as to "encourage" a breach of security or some impairment of rehabilitation. (The regulations at issue are reproduced in their entirety at the end of this article). The appeals court thus held that publication which merely depicted or described such things as escapes from prison could not be rejected, 824 F.2d at 1166.

The Court of Appeals decision seemed on solid ground since it relied on one of the earliest Supreme Court prisoners' rights cases, and the first case which dealt directly with First Amendment rights, *Procunier v. Martinez*, 416 U.S. 396 (1974).

The Supreme Court reversed, upheld the regulations, and (surprisingly) rejected *Martinez* as a basis for evaluating the case. The Court simply overruled a substantial part of *Martinez*. Instead of *Martinez*, the Court said the 1987 case of Turner v. *Safley*, 482 U.S. 78, provides the basis for reviewing challenges to publication denials:

> In sum, we hold that *Turner's* reasonableness standard is to be applied to the regulations at issue in this case, and that those regulations are facially valid under that standard, 109 S.Ct. at 1884.

The Court went on to extend the *Turner* reasonableness test (under which the proper inquiry is whether the challenged regulations are "reasonably related to legitimate penological interests") to review of incoming correspondence of all sorts, not just publications. The *Martinez* standard (which requires a greater showing of need on the part of prison officials) was held to apply only to outgoing correspondence, which the Court felt presents a security concern of a "categorically lesser magnitude" than material entering the prison, 109 S.Ct. at 1881.

The Court also held that when a portion of a particular publication or letter is properly rejected, the *entire document* may be rejected. Correctional officials do not have to cut and paste materials. This part of the case, which also reversed the lower court, should bring a sigh of relief from staff involved in handling of inmate mail.

What is startling about the decision in *Abbott* is the Court's specific overruling of its earlier decision in *Martinez* when, even in the judgment of Justice Blackmun who wrote the majority opinion, the Court could have simply interpreted *Martinez* to reach the result the majority wanted.

Abbott then marks a major milestone in correctional law not only for its specific holding but, perhaps even more significantly, because it is the first time the Court has had the opportunity to review one of its own precedents in this field and, some would say, gut that precedent almost entirely.

What then does *Abbott* mean for those running prisons or jails?

Most obviously, it lowers the requirements which must be met in order to reject a publication. Although the majority of the Court believes the *Turner* standard is not "toothless," 109 S.Ct. at 1882, one must question the sharpness of the teeth the test possesses and whether the new standard is strong enough to overturn the rejection of almost any sort of publication even remotely connected with security or rehabilitation, at least where the inmate has access to other, alternative sources of reading material. Unfortunately, the test may encourage or allow rejection of material which in fact presents no meaningful threat to security.

By lowering the legal requirements for rejection of materials, the case may also suggest agencies review and revise the policies and procedures or regulations under which they presently operate, since odds are that those regulations were adopted to meet a more demanding legal standard than now prevails. (Again, the BOP regulations challenged and upheld in *Abbott* are offered as a model. Note that all the Court did in *Abbott* was to approve these rules *as written*. The *Abbott* case has gone back to the lower courts to see if the actual censorship decisions made by the BOP and attacked in the case were made properly under the new testa adopted by the Court.)

By rejecting *Martinez* as the foundation for reviewing publication and incoming correspondence rejection claims, *Abbott* implicitly reverses virtually every existing case in this area, since virtually all of those cases relied on *Martinez*. Thus the law of publication censorship in corrections begins anew, as of May 15, 1989, the date of the *Abbott* opinion.

Abbott may allow (but clearly doesn't require) the censorship of many publications which have been coming into many prisons and jails for years. But the administrator who begins censoring and rejecting publications with a vengeance, perhaps trying to test the limits of the *Abbott* decision, invites a shift of this type of litigation into state court and before judges not nearly as conservative as those now making up a majority of the Supreme Court. Prudence would suggest that before every publication which "depicts or describes" escapes, criminal activity, or other possible security breaches is rejected (which would include most editions of the daily newspaper and even many editions of *Reader's Digest*), a realistic examination be made of what publications currently are allowed in facilities around the country and what problems in fact are created by them.

Due Process Doesn't Protect Visiting—
Plus Blueprint To Avoid Creating Liberty Interests

Kentucky v. *Thompson*
109 S.Ct. 1904 (1989)

While *Thompson* will be known as the "visiting case," its far greater significance lies in the area of Due Process and the confusing concept of "state created liberty interests." This article will discuss both the visiting and Due Process aspects of the decision. First, visiting:

The six Justice majority said:

> "Respondents do not argue—nor can it seriously be contended, in light of our prior cases—that an inmate's interest in unfettered visitation is guaranteed directly by the Due Process Clause," 109 S.Ct. at 1909.

So visiting isn't inherently protected by the Fourteenth Amendment. But in a concurring opinion Justice Kennedy warns:

> "Nothing in the Court's opinion forecloses the claim that a prison regulation permanently forbidding all visits to some or all prisoners implicates the protections of the Due Process Clause in a way that the precise and individualized restrictions at issue here do not," 109 S.Ct. at 1911.

In other words, *Thompson does not* say a prison or jail could ban visits altogether for some or all inmates. Such complete bans would face serious constitutional challenge.

Next, State Created Liberty Interests
And How To Avoid Them

What the opinion *does* say is that the Fourteenth Amendment (Due Process) does not inherently require some sort of hearing as part of the decision to ban or terminate visiting for a particular inmate or visitor in a particular situation.

After this point, the opinion becomes considerably more complex and significantly more important, for what it says goes far beyond questions of just visiting.

Although the Fourteenth Amendment doesn't inherently require some sort of a hearing as part of the visiting denial process, state rules and regulations could be written in such a way as to create Due Process protections. This is the concept of *state created* liberty interests.[1] The Court in *Thompson* decided that two sets of visiting rules used by

Kentucky (one applicable just to the Reformatory) did not create liberty interests. Thus, in the pessimistic words of Justice Marshall's dissent:

> "Corrections authorities at the . . . Reformatory are free to deny prisoners visits from parents, spouses, children, clergy members, and close friends for any reason whatsoever, or for no reason at all. Prisoners will not even be entitled to learn the reason, if any, why a visitor has been turned away," 109 S.Ct. at 1911.

Justice Marshall's rhetoric aside, his point is accurate: by interpreting Kentucky's rules as not creating a liberty interest, the majority opinion removes a constitutional protection for the visiting denial decision AND provides a model for writing other institution rules in ways which do not create liberty interests.

The state created liberty interest concept says, in essence, that whenever an agency imposes a limitation on its own discretion in making some type of decision-making through rules, policies, etc., it creates a "liberty interest" which in turn means that some from of due process must accompany the decision to assure that proper grounds exist for making the decision. Thus rules which say the institution "shall" place someone in administrative segregation "only" upon finding the person is a threat to security, an escape risk, or meets some other specific condition, create a liberty interest. The liberty interest then demands that some level of Due Process accompany the decision, even if the amount of process due may be slight. If the same rule said the institution "may" put someone in administrative segregation whenever it is felt appropriate, no liberty interest would be created.

Without Due Process Protections, Will Decisions Be Made Properly?

The goal of procedural due process is to enhance the quality of the decision being made by trying to assure (through procedures) that facts exist to warrant making the decisions and that the decisions are something the agency is legally authorized to make.

Due process then is the court's way of preventing abuse of agency power. For the agency, other means may exist to reach this goal, through various forms of supervision, audits, and other reviews of decisions. The effect of *Thompson* is to put the burden on the institution administration to assure that such supervisory techniques, in whatever form, are used to assure that decisions, such as those denying visits are made fairly, with good reason.

The dissent notes the virtually universal agreement among correctional professionals that visiting is important for inmates and that visits shouldn't be denied without "good cause shown," 109 S.Ct. at 1912. The *Thompson* opinion may open the legal door to allow denial of visits without good cause. The challenge for correctional leaders then is, through enforced policy, to prevent this from taking place.

No Special Access To Court Rights
For Death Row Inmates

Murray v. Giarrantano
45 CrL. 3155 (1989)

In *Bounds* v. Smith[2] the Supreme Court reaffirmed the view that inmates possessed a federal constitutional right of access to the courts and that government had some minimal obligation to affirmatively assist inmates in gaining "meaningful access." An earlier decision, *Johnson* v. *Avery*[3] had determined that states could not punish inmates who gave fellow inmates legal-type assistance in the absence of some meaningful alternatives.[4] Where *Johnson* may be seen as a "thou shalt not discriminate" decision, *Bounds* is the "affirmative action" decision of inmate access to the courts.

Ah, but the question is: what affirmative action is required? In *Bounds*, the Court plainly stated that prison authorities must "assist inmates in the preparation of meaningful legal papers by providing prisoners with adequate libraries or adequate assistance from persons trained in the law." *Murray* v. *Giarratano* takes on the question of whether Virginia's death-row inmates have a right to greater legal assistance than generally guaranteed by *Bounds*.

A 5 to 4 Court overruled the federal district court and an en banc Fourth Circuit and held that neither Due Process nor Equal Protection required the State to appoint counsel for indigent prisoners seeking state post-conviction relief.

After the *Bounds* decision, the Court decided in *Pennsylvania* v *Finley*[5] that the Constitution simply did not require the State to appoint counsel in post-conviction proceedings.[6] The Court found no reason to apply *Finley* differently in capital cases and, thus, death row inmates must look to state programs and mandates or a diminishing supply of volunteer lawyers.

Certainly any question about whether *Bounds* might be more liberally applied—for example, taking account of the low education and frequent illiteracy of most inmates—has been laid to rest in *Giarratano*. The choice remains: law libraries or legal assistance.

The four dissenters focus on the uniqueness and finality of the death penalty; the fact that some claims (new evidence, prosecutorial misconduct, e.g.) are relegated to post-conviction review; and the greater difficulty for the death row inmate to wage the often complex post-sentence battle.

An ABA study showed that lawyers invest 992 hours on each capital post-conviction proceeding in Virginia. Ironically, the success rate in federal habeas corpus in capital cases ranges from 60 percent to 70 percent.[7] What this decision portends is that success—life or death— may well depend on the roll of the attorney dice.

There is a great deal of constitutional law that applies only to capital cases—bifurcated trials, enhanced discovery, mandated appeals, and more—but here the Court says, in effect, no more. The Chief Justice, in response to a policy argument, wrote that "this 'mother knows best' approach should play no role in constitutional adjudication."

Lawyers For Illiterate Inmates?

The question which *Giarratano* doesn't answer, but certainly seems to point toward a likely answer, is whether the duty to provide "meaningful" access to the courts requires provision of lawyers for inmates who can't read well enough to be able to use a law library. This issue has been addressed by various courts, with conflicting results, see *Hadix v. Johnson*, 694 F. Supp. 259 (E.D. Mich., 1988), *Hooks v. Wainwright*, 775 F.2d 1433 (11th Cir., 1985).

In light of the Court's sharp rejection of the idea that special circumstances for death row inmates might expand the scope of the right of meaningful access to the courts to include lawyers, it seems likely the Court would reach the same conclusion for inmates unable to read. At the same time, it seems hard to conclude that giving an illiterate inmate access to a library provides meaningful anything, let alone meaningful access to the courts.

Even if the right of access to the courts doesn't ever require the state to provide lawyers for inmates instead of just law libraries, it may well be that something more than just libraries will ultimately be required if the "meaningful" part of the right is to mean anything. The "something" could perhaps be access to other inmates ("jailhouse lawyers"), in which case a question will arise as to whether these would-be Clarence Darrows must have any sort of training.

The issue of what must be provided inmates unable to use a library by reason of intelligence and/or education is one which is certain to receive continuing attention from the courts and which should ultimately reach the Supreme Court.

Footnotes

[1] The Fourteenth Amendment prohibits deprivations of "life, liberty or property without Due Process of law." Thus if an individual has an "interest" in life, liberty, or property, that interest is protected by Due Process. Through the language of its rules, the state can create a liberty interest.

[2] 430 U.S. 817 (1977).

[3] 393 U.S. 483 (1969).

[4] E.g., providing lawyers, law students working out of a supervised law school clinic.

[5] 481 U.S. 551 (1987).

[6] Without going into great detail, the Court has guaranteed at-trial counsel in "serious" criminal cases and on the first appeal of right. It has refused to mandate the appointment of counsel in further discretionary review — say, to a state's supreme court — and consistently denied counsel claims in habeas corpus or other so-called collateral proceedings.

[7] See Mello, Facing Death Alone: The Post-Conviction Attorney Crisis on Death Row, 37 *Am. U.L. Rev.* 513, 520-21 (1988).

Appendix

Mail Censorship Regulations Approved By Supreme Court In *Abbott*, from 28 CFR Ch. V, Subpart F, Sec. 540.70, *et seqs* (7-1-88 ed.)

Subpart F—Incoming Publications

Authority: 5 U.S.C. 301; 18 U.S.C. 4001, 4042, 4081, 4082, 5006-5024, 5039; 28 U.S.C. 509, 510; 28 CFR 0.95-0.99.

540.70 Purpose and scope.

(a) The Bureau of Prisons permits an inmate to subscribe to or to receive publications without prior approval and has established procedures to determine if an incoming publication is detrimental to the security, discipline, or good order of the institution or if it might facilitate criminal activity. The term publication, as used in this rule, means a book (for example, novel, instructional manual), or a single issue of a magazine or newspaper, plus such other materials addressed to a specific inmate as advertising brochures, flyers, and catalogues.

(b) The Warden may designate staff to review and where appropriate to approve all incoming publications in accordance with the provisions of this rule. Only the Warden may reject an incoming publication.

[44 FR 38260, June 29, 1979, as amended at 47 FR 55129, Dec. 7, 1982] 540.71 Procedures.

(a) An inmate may receive hardcover publications and newspapers only from the publisher, from a book club, or from a bookstore. An inmate may receive other softcover material (for example, paperback books, newspaper clippings, or magazines) from any source. The Warden may have all incoming publications inspected for contraband.

(b) The Warden may reject a publication only if it is determined detrimental to the security, good order, or discipline of the institution or if it might facilitate criminal activity. The Warden may not reject a publication solely because its content is religious, philosophical, political, social or sexual, or because its content is unpopular or repugnant. Publications which may be rejected by a Warden include but are not limited to publications which meet one of the following criteria.

(1) It depicts or describes procedures for the construction or use of weapons, ammunition, bombs or incendiary devices;

(2) It depicts, encourages, or describes methods of escape from correctional facilities, or contains blueprints, drawings or similar descriptions of Bureau of Prisons institutions;

(3) It depicts or describes procedures for the brewing of alcoholic beverages, or the manufacture of drugs;

(4) It is written in code;

(5) It depicts. describes or encourages activities which may lead to the use of physical violence or group disruption;

(6) It encourages or instructs in the commission of criminal activity;

(7) It is sexually explicit material which by its nature or content poses a threat to the security, good order, or discipline of the institution, or facilitates criminal activity.

(c) The Warden may not establish an excluded list of publications. This means the Warden shall review the individual publication prior to the rejection of that publication. Rejection of several issues of a subscription publication is not sufficient reason to reject the subscription publication in its entirety.

(d) Where a publication is found unacceptable, the Warden shall promptly advise the inmate in writing of the decision and the reasons for it. The notice must contain reference to the specific article(s) or material(s) considered objectionable. The Warden shall permit the inmate an opportunity to review this material for purposes of filing an appeal under the Administrative Remedy Procedure unless such review may provide the inmate with information of a nature which is deemed to pose a threat or detriment to the security, good order or discipline of the institution or to encourage or instruct in criminal activity.

(e) The Warden shall provide the publisher or sender of an unacceptable publication a copy of the rejection letter. The Warden shall advise the publisher or sender that he may obtain an independent review of the rejection by writing to the Regional Director within 15 days of receipt of the rejection letter. The Warden shall return the rejected publication to the publisher or sender of the material unless the inmate indicates an intent to file an appeal under the Administrative Remedy Procedure, in which case the Warden shall retain the rejected material at the institution for review. In case of appeal, if the rejection is sustained, the rejected publication shall be returned when appeal or legal use is completed.

(f) The Warden may set limits locally (for fire, sanitation or house-keeping reasons) on the number or volume of publications an inmate may receive or retain in his quarters. The Warden may authorize an inmate additional storage space for storage of legal materials in accordance with the Bureau of Prisons procedures on personal property of inmates.

[44 FR 38260, June 29, 1979, as amended at 47 FR 55130, Dec. 7, 1982: 50 FR 411, Jan. 3, 1985]

14

Disciplinary Hearings
Something Old, Something New,
But Always Something

William C. Collins

Judicial activity in the area of prison discipline remains active at the Supreme Court level as well as in the lower courts. In the last two years, (1985-1986), the Supreme Court has decided three cases involving prison disciplinary issues. At the lower court level the rights clearly established in 1974 with the Supreme Court's landmark decision of *Wolff* v. *McDonnell*, 94 S.Ct. 2963 remain the subject of continuing litigation. In *Wolff*, the Court held that the due process clause of the Fourteenth Amendment obligates prison officials to give a prisoner accused of serious misconduct the opportunity to appear before an impartial prison hearing board to rebut the charges against him. The prisoner must be given written notification of the charges against him at least 24 hours prior to his appearance before the hearing tribunal. The prisoner also may present documentary evidence and call witnesses in his defense at the hearing unless this jeopardizes institutional safety or other

Source: Reprinted from William C. Collins, *Correctional Law 1986*, 39-46. Reprinted with the permission of the authors.

correctional goals. Further, the prisoner is entitled to the assistance of a "counsel substitute" (either a fellow prisoner, if permitted, or a staff member) when the inmate is illiterate or the issues are unusually complex. Finally, *Wolff* requires the hearing board to provide the prisoner with a written statement of the evidence supporting its decision and the reasons for any disciplinary action taken. It is equally important to note that the *Wolff* Court held that inmates are not entitled to retained or appointed counsel and that they have no constitutional right to confront or cross-examine hostile witnesses (although the hearing board has the discretion to permit confrontation and cross-examination).

Since *Wolff*, the courts have continued to struggle with questions such as what restrictions should apply when information from anonymous informants is used in a disciplinary hearing and how much due process must be afforded for minor infractions. While there will always be litigation about prison disciplinary proceedings, much current litigation could have been avoided by closer adherence to rules and procedures which have been in effect for years.

Supreme Court: Judicial Review of the Evidence, Reasons for Denying Witnesses, and No Judicial Immunity

Sufficiency of the Evidence

Federal courts usually are not interested in whether an inmate was guilty or innocent of a disciplinary infraction. Instead the courts are interested in whether proper procedures were followed.

This trend received a sharp boost from the Supreme Court in *Superintendent v. Hill*,[1] a 1985 case in which the Court decided how much evidence is required by the Fourteenth Amendment to support a finding of guilty. The answer? "Some Evidence." The Court's precise holding:

> We conclude that where good time credits constitute a protected interest, a decision to revoke such credits must be supported by some evidence," 105 S.Ct. at 2770.

What the Court was saying becomes clearer when one examines other statements from the opinion and when one considers the facts of the case, which the Court found sufficient to support a guilty finding from a disciplinary hearing in a Massachusetts hearing.

> "We hold that the requirements of due process are satisfied if some evidence supports the decision. . . to revoke good time credits. This standard is met if 'there was some evidence from which the conclusion of the administrative tribunal could be deduced. . .' (citation

omitted). Ascertaining whether this standard is satisfied does not require examination of the entire record, independent assessment of the credibility of witnesses, or weighing of the evidence. Instead, the relevant question is whether there is any evidence in the record that could support the conclusion reached by the disciplinary hoard," 105 S.Ct. at 2774.

In other words, a court reviewing the evidence in a disciplinary hearing under the Fourteenth Amendment will not be able to weigh the evidence. Once the court finds there is some evidence which, if believed, would support a conclusion of guilt, due process is satisfied.

The evidence in the case was described by the Supreme Court as "meager," but still was sufficient. An officer reported he had heard an inmate twice say in a loud voice "What's going on?" Upon investigating, the officer found another inmate lying bleeding. Dirt was strewn about, suggesting a scuffle had occurred. Three inmates, including the two inmates who were respondents in the case at the Supreme Court, were seen jogging away down a walkway. Testimony was given at the hearing supporting that the inmate had been beaten. Both inmates denied beating anyone and the victim stated in writing that the two had not beaten him. There was no direct evidence linking the two inmates with the beating.

One of the more significant aspects of *Superintendent* may be its clear statement that credibility will not be an issue for review under the Fourteenth Amendment. Thus hearings which boil down to swearing contests between staff and inmate ("He did it." "No I didn't, I was asleep in my cell when it happened.") should not be subject to federal court review.

The results in this case should be taken with a grain of salt. They apply only to Fourteenth Amendment reviews of evidence in disciplinary hearings. They do not necessarily apply to reviews conducted under applicable state laws or constitutional provisions. It is entirely possible that stiffer review standards will be imposed under these criteria. It is certainly likely that "sufficiency of the evidence" issues will be presented to state courts, since clearly the federal Constitution is no longer an attractive source of review for inmates.

Reasons For Denying Witnesses

In *Wolff* in 1974, the Court held that an inmate in a disciplinary hearing has the right to call witnesses unless "unduly hazardous to institutional safety or correctional goals."[2] The issue before the Court 11 years later in *Ponte v. Real*[3] was "when must the institution tell the inmate its reasons for denying witnesses in a given case?"

Although the reasonable time to state such reasons would be at the hearing, when the reasons are fresh in the minds of the hearing committee and when they can be reviewed by other institution officials, the Supreme Court held that due process does not require that reasons for denying a witness be given at that time. Instead, the Court held that the reasons need not be given until the inmate challenges the denial in court. In other words, nowhere in the administrative process (in the hearing, during any administrative appeals, etc.) must the reasons for denying a witness be given. Only if the inmate pursues the denial by filing a lawsuit must the reasons be stated.

While there may be situations where it is necessary to not state a reason for denying a requested witness in a hearing before the inmate who called him, it does not appear wise to postpone stating the reason in any or all administrative contexts in favor of waiting to see if the inmate files a lawsuit over the question. This delay creates several potential problems: It invites more litigation and court involvement in the disciplinary process. It increases the likelihood that the hearing committee members may not remember why the denial was made, or even that the members may no longer work for the institution. It means that there is no administrative review of denial decisions, even though these decisions are obviously of constitutional significance.

The more prudent practice would be to require, by administrative rule, that the committee state its reason for denying inmate witnesses at the hearing, in writing. If there are security-related justifications for not telling the inmate the reason, then a record still should be made which then could be reviewed either in the context of an inmate appeal of the decision or independently of the appeal process, simply as a regular administrative review of the disciplinary process.

In its opinion in *Ponte* the Court also noted that in judicial reviews of denial decisions, the reviewing court should examine the reasons in chambers, away from the inmate, "if prison security or other paramount interests appear to require" such examination.[4]

While it has always appeared that disciplinary hearing officers should have the inherent right to limit witnesses for other that security reasons, simply as a part of running an orderly hearing, there has remained some question about this power since *Wolff* spoke only in security and "correctional goal" terms. This uncertainty probably has been laid to rest by a comment in Justice Marshall's dissent in *Ponte*. In calling for a requirement that reasons be given at the hearing, Justice Marshall states:

> "To include (in the statement of reasons for the final decision in the hearing) a brief explanation of the reasons for refusing to hear a witness, such as why proffered testimony is "irrelevant" or "cumulative" could not credibly be said to burden disciplinary boards in any meaningful way. . .," 105 S.Ct. at 2207.

This statement recognizes that "correctional goals" include the goal of running efficient disciplinary hearings, with some ability to control the inmate who may request an inordinate number of witnesses, or demand to call witnesses who clearly could not offer information relevant to the question of guilt or innocence. This ability was applied and upheld in a 1985 Virginia case.[5] The inmate requested to call witnesses, but the request was denied on the basis that there was only one witness who had already been interviewed in the investigation and whose testimony would have made no difference to the outcome of the hearing. The Court agreed with this result.

Hearing Officers Ain't Judges. Hold Onto Your Pocketbooks. Maybe.

In a 1986 case, *Cleavinger v. Saxner*,[6] the Court rejected an argument that prison disciplinary hearing officers should enjoy a quasi-judicial (absolute) immunity. Instead, the Court limited the hearing officers to only qualified immunity, the same enjoyed by other government officials. Had the case gone the other way, hearing committee members would have been completely immune from having to pay damages in Civil Rights cases, even though their actions in the hearing may have violated the rights of the inmate.

Complete immunity could have provided some comfort to hearing officers, because the area of rights with which such officers are concerned are, for the most part, clearly established. As such, their violation subjects a defendant to liability for damages. For example, damages of $25 per day for each day an inmate was held in segregation following a constitutionally defective disciplinary hearing were imposed in one case, along with $78 for the inmate's loss of pay. Total bill: $1203 actual damages, plus a small sum for nominal damages, and an unspecified amount of attorneys' fees.[7]

Lower Court Activity: Review of Clearly Established Rights Means Potential Damages

The primary issues in lower court litigation which arise out of the disciplinary process are those relating to the application of existing rights which were originally stated by the Supreme Court in *Wolff*. However, some issues seen with some regularity in the lower courts still have not reached the Supreme Court.

Do It Right or Pay the Price.

The likelihood that any violation of an inmate's rights in the disciplinary process will result in damages of some amount, along with whatever injunctive relief the court may feel appropriate (expungement of records, etc.), makes it even more important that hearings are conducted in accordance with applicable rules. This means that staff conducting the hearing and involved in the hearing process should be trained to know inmate due process rights, know applicable state/institution rules and policies, and know how to conduct a hearing.

It still seems that correctional staff often do not have an understanding of the importance courts place on procedural rights. Instead, staff tends to focus on what is perceived as probable guilt and on expediency. The guiltier an inmate appears to be, the less important are the procedural due process rights which are part of the disciplinary process, in the minds of at least some staff. In the case cited in footnote 7, the inmate was charged with possessing marijuana which was found in his cell. The inmate denied possessing the marijuana, and offered information from other inmates suggesting it had been left by a prior occupant of the cell known only as "Bo." The inmate asked the officer appointed to assist him in the hearing to search records to see when the cell had last been searched and to find Bo and take a statement. The officer did not check the records. Limited investigation by the hearing committee did not identify Bo and the committee chair finally indicated:

> "Alright. I am not going to try to identify the inmate and. . .(even) if we could identify him, which is doubtful, then we'd have to take the time and the expense to track him down; and, like I say, it is very,very doubtful that the man would admit to making such a statement, anyway, even if he did make it."[8]

The court concluded that the help from the staff assistant was inadequate in light of the failure to carry out the inmate's requests which were, under the facts of the case, reasonable on their face. These problems were continued by the actions of the hearing committee in refusing to pursue the inmate's requests and totally rejecting the inmate's defense, without affording the inmate the opportunity to fully prepare the defense.

Experienced correctional staff reading the facts above may quickly come to the conclusion that the defense was one commonly contrived by inmates in whose cell contraband is found and that to pursue the claim of the inmate would have indeed been a waste of time and money. A reviewing court cannot and will not make these assumptions, particularly when they are used to deny the inmate due process rights.

Participants in the hearing process—investigators, staff appointed to assist the inmate and most certainly the hearing committee itself—must be sure that the required procedural steps are taken. To ignore them for expediency reasons or because "everybody knows the inmate is guilty" only invites the result in the New York case: damages, expungement of the records, and prohibitions against any further disciplinary action based on the original incident.

The chair of the hearing committee is in a particularly important position by being able to check that rights are properly afforded and to correct any errors which may have crept into the process,even if this means starting the hearing process over again. Knowledge of what rights the inmate has and knowledge of how to conduct a hearing, particularly how to make a solid record, can avoid a great deal of litigation. Cases which are filed should be far easier to defend when they challenge hearings presided over by officers who (to reverse the usual complaint) "know more about the rules than the inmates do."

Any appellate review of the hearing process also must be sensitive to violations of procedural rights if the appellate process is to play a litigation prevention function.

The rights of inmates in the disciplinary process are not that long or complex. One need not be a judge to understand or apply the rights in question. Virtually every correctional system in the country has rules and regulations which comply with the rights the courts have defined. The problem then is simply assuring that these rights are followed in the disciplinary process and that any mistakes that might be made are identified and corrected at the earliest possible opportunity. Proper training and review of the disciplinary process should result in few, if any, errors getting to court.

Use of Anonymous Informants.

Under what circumstances and in accordance with what procedural protections may information from an informant whose identity is not disclosed to the inmate be used against the inmate in a disciplinary hearing? Several courts have addressed this issue over several years. While the results are not all identical, the use of anonymous testimony has uniformly been approved. Indeed, the Supreme Court in *Wolff*, by refusing to impose a right to confront and cross-examine witnesses in a prison disciplinary hearing implicitly recognized and approved the use of anonymous testimony. Where the courts have differed is on the question of what steps must the institution go through to establish the reliability and credibility of the missing witness.

Late in 1985 the 7th Circuit addressed the anonymous witness issue in a case coming from the federal prison at Marion.[9] Anonymous informants had implicated inmate Mendoza in the stabbing death of another inmate. Mendoza sought to overturn the results of the disciplinary hearing (where he was found guilty of murder and lost one year of good time and was given disciplinary segregation for 60 days) for various reasons, all relating to the use of informant testimony.

The court quickly ruled that use of informant testimony was generally acceptable and the hearing committee has discretion to decide whether to reveal the names of witnesses. However, the committee must make a determination as to the reliability of the informant and that determination is subject to review by the court. The committee need not state in any public record what the factual basis is for its determination (citing to Ponte, the court emphasized that the reasons need not be presented to anyone prior to litigation. Obviously, the reasons should be set down somewhere prior to going to court, if the reasons are to be recalled in any detail).

The court's review may be "in camera," i.e., in chambers and in the presence of only the judge. Even the inmates' counsel may be excluded. The court said that judicial review must give a good deal of deference to the decisions of the committee. A reference to Superintendent v. Hill suggests that if the review by the court shows some evidence on which the committee could have based a finding of reliability, the committee's decision must be upheld.

Even if a stricter standard than "some evidence" is required to uphold the decision to withhold the informant's identity from the inmate, the decision of the 7th Circuit is notable for its approval of "in camera" examination of the documentation which is used to support the committee's decision. The court approved a review by the judge alone, allowing what the dissent criticizes as a "secret trial,"[10]

In a later case, the 7th Circuit approved a process for using anonymous inmate testimony in disciplinary hearings:[11]

- The report of an investigative officer (if such an officer was involved) had to be under oath.
- Guilt normally would have to be based on more than one reliable confidential source or one source plus other corroborating factual evidence. A single confidential source could suffice if

peculiar circumstances existed convincing the committee that the informant must be reliable.

- Informant reliability must be established. Past reliability as well as other (unspecified) factors will suffice to establish reliability. These should be given to the committee. Staff had an affirmative duty to determine if there was any basis for the informant providing false information.

- All confidential information coming to the committee must be in writing, stating facts and the manner in which the informant arrived at knowledge of those facts.

- The chair of the committee, at least, must know the identity of the informant. The entire committee must know the substance of the informant information. The record of the hearing should state the basis for the committee's finding that the information given by the informant was reliable. (Note, this means the committee must decide both that the informant is reliable and the specific information provided is also reliable.)

- The committee must at least incorporate the informant's statements into the record by reference. Normally the hearing report should document the finding of reliability. Where this information cannot be shared with the inmate, a separate report should be prepared.

A process which allows the hearing committee to rely on a third party's conclusion about informant reliability may exceed the limits of due process. From the perspective of being able to defend committee decisions in court, clearly the better procedure is for the committee to receive sufficient information (which can be heard outside the presence of the inmate) to allow the committee to decide for itself that the informant is generally reliable and the specific information being provided is believable. The more specific, factual information the committee has, the more defensible its decisions will be.

Must the Reporting Officer be Present?

The disciplinary process begins with a report prepared by an officer, often indicating that the officer was a witness to an infraction by the inmate. Must the officer be present at the hearing, or may simply the written report by introduced as evidence? Relying on *Wolff's* statement that inmates do not have the right to confront and cross-examine witnesses, the inmate does not have a right to have the officer present.[12]

But there is a catch to this issue. While the inmate lacks the right to confront and cross-examine a witness against him, the inmate does have a limited right to call witnesses. What then if the inmate chooses to call the reporting officer as a witness? Then the refusal to call the witness must be based on the conclusion that calling the witness would be "unduly hazardous to institutional safety or correctional goals."[13] Unless it appears the inmate has no purpose in calling the officer except for harassment, refusals should be limited to grounds of "undue hazard . . . ."

Assistants Should be of Assistance.

In the *Wolff* decision, the Supreme Court held that inmates do not have the right to counsel in disciplinary hearings, but also noted that when an illiterate inmate is involved in a hearing or the issues are so complex that the inmate can't reasonably be expected to collect and present information for a defense, the inmate should be allowed to have the assistance of a fellow inmate or designated staff member to assist in preparation for the hearing.

While the illiteracy test is relatively objective, the complexity test may depend on the circumstances. For instance, the otherwise intelligent inmate probably cannot adequately prepare for a hearing if locked in pre-hearing detention pending the hearing. However, this same inmate may be quite capable of presenting information at the hearing, assuming someone has gathered it for him.

It is not clear if the role of the assistant is that of an advocate or something more neutral. Caselaw does not address this issue to any degree, although it appears that many states see the role as non-adversarial. Given that the Supreme Court in *Wolff* chose not to require counsel in disciplinary hearings because they would increase the adversary cast of the proceedings, it would appear that a non-adversarial role is consistent with *Wolff*.

A couple of recent cases suggest the problems with assistants is not defining the role as adversarial or non-adversarial, but is somewhat more basic: simply having it recognized that the assistance must be meaningful in quality and quantity to meet the requirement of *Wolff*. An apparent lackadaisical attitude on the part of one appointed assistant contributed to a violation of a New York inmate's rights, see footnote 7. In another case, a summary judgment in favor of the institution was reversed by a court of appeals in part because the record showed the inmate had been given all of five minutes to confer with a fellow inmate allowed to assist in a disciplinary hearing.[14]

Where an inmate is permitted assistance from either staff or inmate, the hearing committee should assure itself that there has been sufficient contact between the two and that the assistant has done what the inmate requested, or has at least made a good faith attempt to fulfill the inmate's requests. Where there are problems apparent to the committee, steps should be taken to remedy the problems, including temporarily recessing the hearing. Similarly, any appellate review should be sensitive to this issue and be ready to remand cases back for new hearings when there is doubt about the adequacy of the assistance provided an inmate.

Is *Wolff* The Last Word in Disciplinary Due Process?

After the decision in *Wolff* v. *McDonnell* in 1974, it appeared that the question of how much process was due an inmate in a disciplinary hearing was settled. Although the bulk of the opinion in *Wolff* focuses on the loss of good time as the sanction which triggered the due process protections required in the opinion, most people interpreted the holding as also applying to other serious sanctions, including disciplinary segregation. The result is that most disciplinary rules are broken into major and minor categories, with very minor sanctions being attached to the latter category.

A recent Supreme Court decision concerning due process and administrative segregation raises the question as to whether the line between major and minor disciplinary proceedings must be drawn where it is or whether stiffer sanctions could be included for so-called "minor" infractions without requiring the full *Wolff* due process procedures.

Whether due process is required in most prison contexts depends on whether a "state-created liberty interest" exists.[15] In other words, due process protections may not be inherently required by the Fourteenth Amendment in a given context (i.e., the decision to place someone in administrative segregation), but the state, by the way it writes its statutes, rules, or policies, can create a liberty interest which then is protected by some level of due process under the Fourteenth Amendment. The state creates a liberty interest when it chooses to voluntarily place limits on circumstances under which it will exercise its discretion. A rule which says that a specific action will be taken by the institution (such as placing someone in administrative segregation) will take place only upon a finding of certain facts or conditions (e.g., a finding that the individual is a threat to the security of the institution) creates a liberty interest. A rule which does not impose such limits ("an inmate may be placed in administrative segregation in the discretion of the superintendent") does not.

Applying this somewhat confusing concept to the administrative segregation placement decision, the Supreme Court in the *Hewitt* case decided that placing someone in administrative segregation under the state regulations involved in *Hewitt* did require limited due process protections. Even though the Court assumed conditions in administrative segregation were no different than conditions in disciplinary segregation, the Court chose not to require *Wolff* protections. Instead, the Court required only an informal, non-adversary review:

> An inmate must merely receive some notice of the charges against him and an opportunity to present his views to the prison officials charged with deciding whether to transfer him to administrative segregation. Ordinarily, a written statement by the inmate will accomplish this purpose, although prison administrators may find it more useful to permit oral presentations in cases where they believe a written statement would be ineffective.[16]

In other words, no in-person hearing, no limited right to call witnesses, no limited right to assistance are required. Only a notice and an opportunity to respond in writing. Although the Court did not specify that the decision maker had to be impartial, this can be assumed.

The reasons the Court differentiated the administrative segregation procedures from disciplinary procedures largely had to do with the judgmental, predictive nature of the administrative segregation decision, as contrasted with the relatively factual nature of the disciplinary decision.

It is common for prison discipline to have two levels, with minor infractions being handled with less than *Wolff* due process. But these minor proceedings are truly minor, with very limited sanctions available. Does the result in *Hewitt* suggest that the level of minor infractions could be raised, with more severe sanctions still available with process less than that required by *Wolff*? Can *Wolff* be limited to only those situation where good time is at stake? At least one court has recently recognized that "the process due may decrease as the severity of the punishment decreases," without suggesting where *Wolff* due process leaves off and something less may begin.[17]

Before administrators leap to amend disciplinary codes, it must be emphasized that the hypothesis suggested above has little or no specific caselaw to support it, other than the general sort of comment quoted above. Therefore, the hypothesis may be nothing more than idle legal speculation.

Even assuming the legal risk is worth taking, there is a question as to whether any change would be worth it administratively. A procedurally simpler disciplinary process would probably save some time and money. It could also reduce liability exposure. Various questions would have to be addressed in developing such a system. For instance, what infractions would be included in which level? Could a "minor" infraction be referred to the "major" committee to allow a sterner sanction and if so, according to what standards?

Would the actual fairness of the expanded minor procedure decrease as the inmate's procedural protections were decreased? Certainly inmates and many observers of prison administration would perceive a decrease in fairness.

Such a restructuring, which perhaps could limit *Wolff* requirements to those cases where time loss was involved, should only be undertaken after close consultation with counsel both as to the probable legality of such a change and as to how such a change could be initiated with minimal liability exposure. For instance, it can be assumed such a change would be challenged in court. But if the revised process were allowed to run during the pendency of the challenge, the institution could be faced with having to undo easily two years or more worth of disciplinary infractions should the rules be found unconstitutional.

Comment

Due process and prison disciplinary systems have come a long way from the days when the thought of imposing some sort of procedural requirements on the process threatened life as we knew it. But there are still a significant number of lawsuits arising from prison disciplinary hearings, which usually allege that the hearing committee failed to follow the institution's own rules and in so doing violated a mandate of *Wolff* or some other court decision. Many of these suits can be avoided — or at least won easily — if those involved in the hearing process paid greater attention both to following applicable rules and to understanding more about what the rules are intended to produce: a hearing process which is fair both to the inmate and the institution.

Footnotes

[1] 105 S.Ct. 2769 (1985).
[2] 418 U.S. at 566.
[3] 105 S.Ct. 2192.
[4] 105 S.Ct. at 2197.

[5] *Cook v. Robinson*, 612 F. Supp. 187 (D.Va., 1985).

[6] 106 S.Ct. 496 (1986).

[7] *Pino v. Dalshiem*, 605 F. Supp. 1305 (S.D. N.Y., 1984).

[8] 605 F. Supp. at 1312.

[9] *Mendoza v. Miller*, 779 F.2d 1287 (7th Cir., 1985).

[10] 779 F.2d at 1304, n. 9.

[11] *McCollum v. Williford*, 793 F.2d 903, 907, n. 3(7th Cir., 1986). *McCollum* and *Mendoza* are the latest in a series of anonymous witnesses cases the 7th Circuit has been dealing with over the last several years, all coming from Marion. Given the attention the 7th Circuit has been giving to this issue, the results in these cases probably deserve special attention. Other circuits have consistently approved use of informant testimony where the committee makes a determination as to the reliability of the informant, although these opinions are not as exhaustive as those of the 7th Circuit in the Marion series of cases, *Helms v. Hewitt*, 655 F.2d 487 (3rd Cir., 1981), *Smith v. Rabalais*, 659 F.2d 539 (5th Cir., 1981), *Kyle v. Hanberry*, 677 F.2d 1386 (11th Cir., 1982).

[12] *Harrison v. Pyle*, 612 F. Supp. 850 (D. Nev., 1985).

[13] *Ponte v. Real*, 105 S.Ct. at 2197.

[14] *Grandison v. Cuyler*, 774 F.2d (3rd Cir., 1985).

[15] *Hewitt v. Helms*, 459 U.S. 460, 103 S.Ct. 864, 74 L.Ed.2d 675 (1983).

[16] 103 S.Ct. at 874.

[17] *Gibbs v. King*, 779 F.2d 1040, 1044 (5th Cir., 1986).

15

Recent Case Law on Overcrowded Conditions of Confinement

An Assessment of Its Impact on Facility Decisionmaking

Jack E. Call

The past decade has been marked by unprecedented increases in prison populations, and concomitant increases in the level of overcrowding in our Nation's correctional institutions (Mullen and Smith, 1980). Moreover, during the same decade the courts have become far more active in accepting and deciding cases concerning conditions of confinement, including the issues of overcrowding and double-bunking (American Civil Liberties Union, 1982).

In order to accommodate the increasing volume of inmates, many jails and prisons have added a second bunk (or a third, even) or a floor mattress to cells that had been designed originally to house one inmate. In other instances, new jails or prisons have been constructed to solve

Source: *Federal Probation*, Vol. 47, No. 3 (September 1983), 23-32.

but also because of their effect on the precedential value of previous lower court decisions concerning conditions of confinement. Because the Court overturned the lower courts' findings of unconstitutionality in *Wolfish* and *Chapman*, and because the conditions of confinement in those cases were not substantially better than the conditions found unconstitutional in some prior cases, it is difficult to assess the present the problem. Because of the austere fiscal policies that have characterized the public sector in recent times, governmental bodies considering the latter alternative must determine whether to build a facility with single cells, double cells, or dormitories. Since many authorities prefer to avoid the security problems associated with dormitories, the decision for corrections officials often boils down to a choice between double-bunking single cells or building a new facility with single or double occupancy cells. However the problem is approached, the growing body of case law on jail and prison conditions is an important factor which must be taken into account.

Traditionally, courts had assumed a "hands off" approach in cases involving prison administration (Gobert and Cohen, 1981). By the late 1960's, however, this approach began to change as courts were called upon to decide cases involving rather appalling conditions of confinement. In 1974, the Supreme Court provided some support for this interventionist movement when it declared that:

> though his rights may be diminished by the needs and exigencies of the institutional environment, a prisoner is not wholly stripped of constitutional protections when he is imprisoned for crime. There is no iron curtain drawn between the Constitution and the prisons of this country (*Wolff* v. *McDonnell*, pp. 555-56).

Indeed, the 1970's witnessed a virtual explosion of court cases dealing with the constitutionality of conditions of confinement (Fair, 1979; Gobert and Cohen, 1981). In most of these cases, a particular physical condition or the "totality of conditions" were declared unconstitutional. In many cases the courts issued remedial orders which required governmental bodies to take extensive, and usually expensive, steps to rectify the constitutional violations.

A rather abrupt change in this interventionist approach occurred in 1979 when the Supreme Court issued its opinion in *Bell* v. *Wolfish*. The tone of the Court's opinion in this case, and in *Rhodes* v. *Chapman* decided 2 years later, was obviously antagonistic to the activist approach taken by the lower courts. In both cases, the Federal district court had found overcrowded conditions unconstitutional and the circuit court of appeals had upheld the district court, yet the Supreme Court overturned these decisions, declaring that the conditions of confinement were not unconstitutional.

Wolfish and *Chapman* are clearly landmark decisions. They represent the Supreme Court's first (and to date, only) pronouncements on the question of when physical conditions of confinement in correctional institutions (as opposed to institutional practices) violate the Constitution. The fact that the Supreme Court found the conditions of confinement constitutional in these cases is significant not only because of the hostility shown to the activist posture of lower courts validity of cases decided prior to *Wolfish*. Indeed, it would appear that we are entering a new era of case law with respect to conditions of confinement.

Because of this change in judicial reaction, this article will concentrate on court cases decided since *Wolfish*. However, a brief treatment of case law on conditions of confinement prior to *Wolfish* is provided to place the subsequent discussion in proper historical and legal perspective. Following that, the opinion in *Wolfish* and lower court treatment of *Wolfish* are analyzed in detail. Then the opinion in *Chapman* and lower court reaction to that case are analyzed. The discussion concludes with an assessment of the effect of this case law on the issue of double-bunking cells designed for single occupancy and on the construction of facilities with cells designed for double occupancy.[1]

Case Law Prior to Wolfish

Most conditions of confinement cases prior to *Wolfish* dealt with two common issues: (1) the constitutionality of double-bunking cells designed for single occupancy (or the closely related issue of operating a jail or prison in excess of its "rated" capacity) and (2) whether the Constitution requires some minimum amount of living space per inmate, usually expressed in terms of square footage.

Pre-*Wolfish* cases were fairly evenly split as to whether double-bunking cells designed for single occupancy was constitutional, but most pre-*Wolfish* cases did not consider whether double-bunking alone was unconstitutional. Similarly, some pre-*Wolfish* cases held that allowing the inmate population to exceed the facility's design capacity was unconstitutional *per se*, but most cases did not frame the constitutional issues in these terms or found overcrowding unconstitutional because in combination with other substandard conditions it resulted in unconstitutional conditions.

Pre-*Wolfish* cases addressing the question of amount of living space per inmate also divided into two basic camps. A minority of the decisions insisted that the Constitution demanded a minimal amount of living space per inmate, and these decisions established a specific square footage requirement based on correctional standards (Commission on Accreditation for Corrections, 1977). However, most of the pre-*Wolfish* cases, while demonstrating concern for the amount of living space per inmate, declined to focus exclusively on this issue.

Increasingly the pre-*Wolfish* cases did not look to a single condition or factor related to overcrowding in reaching judgment on the constitutionality of the conditions of confinement. Instead, the courts examined a variety of conditions to determine if a combination of inadequate conditions rose to the level of unconstitutionality. Robbins and Buser (1977) suggest that these cases focused on 11 factors:

(1) Health and safety hazards created by the physical facilities
(2) Overcrowding
(3) Absence of a classification system
(4) Conditions in isolation and segregation cells
(5) Medical facilities and treatment
(6) Food service
(7) Personal hygiene and sanitation
(8) Incidence of violence and homosexual attacks
(9) The quantity and training of prison personnel
(10) Lack of rehabilitation programs
(11) The presence of other constitutional violations

In addition to focusing on the combination or totality of conditions, pre-*Wolfish* cases developed a distinction, for purposes of constitutional analysis, between convicted offenders and pretrial detainees. Pre-*Wolfish* cases dealing with convicted offenders agreed that the conditions in which these inmates were confined could not be so harsh as to constitute cruel and unusual punishment, which is prohibited by the eighth amendment. The cases disagreed, however, as to the test to be employed in making that determination. Fair (1979) has identified four tests that the pre-*Wolfish* cases used: (1) the "shock the conscience" test under which the court asked if the proved conditions shocked its conscience; (2) the "totality of circumstances" test under which the courts asked if the cumulative effect of conditions amounted to cruel and unusual punishment; (3) the "evolving standards of decency" test under which the courts asked if the conditions exceeded "the evolving standards of decency that mark the progress of a maturing society" (quoting from *Trop* v. *Dulles*); and (4) the "balancing" test under which the courts compared the severity of the conditions with the need for those conditions in order to achieve legitimate penal goals.

The pre-*Wolfish* cases involving pretrial detainees generally agreed that the constitutional prohibition against cruel and unusual punishment did not apply. Rather, the due process clauses of the fifth and 14th amendments, which prohibit any punishment of pretrial detainees because they have not been convicted, were viewed as the appropriate standard. These cases generally required either that correctional authorities employ the least restrictive means necessary to insure the security of the facility and to assure the detainee's presence at trial or that any condition of confinement imposed upon a pretrial detainee be demanded by some compelling penal necessity (*U.S. ex rel. Wolfish* v. *U.S.*; Fair, 1979).

The Supreme Court and Pretrial Detainees

Prior to *Wolfish*, the U.S. Supreme Court seldom had occasion to address constitutional issues relating to the conditions of confinement in American jails and prisons. The issues which the Court had addressed dealt more with correctional practices, such as mail censorship or extent of medical care, rather than general conditions of confinement, such as double-bunking or overcrowding. In *Bell* v. *Wolfish*, however, the Court examined these issues directly.

Inmates at the Federal Metropolitan Correctional Center (MCC), a short-term facility primarily housing pretrial detainees, challenged the constitutionality of a number of practices and conditions including the double-bunking of a number of cells to accommodate a population 16 percent greater than MCC's design capacity. The lower courts in *Wolfish* had determined that since pretrial detainees are presumed innocent and are detained only to insure their presence at trial, it was unconstitutional to subject them to conditions which were not necessary to confinement alone, unless those conditions were justified by some compelling governmental necessity.

The Supreme Court rejected this relatively stringent test and held that the due process clause of the Constitution only prohibited the government from subjecting pretrial detainees to punishment. Under this approach, inmates can demonstrate that they are being punished by proving an intent to punish on the part of corrections officials, by showing that the challenged condition is not rationally related to some purpose other than punishment, or by showing it is excessive in relation to that alternative purpose. In particular, the Court indicated that there is no "'one man, one cell' principle lurking in the Due Process Clause of the Fifth Amendment" and that the overcrowding at MCC did not amount to punishment of the pretrial detainees housed there.

In arriving at this conclusion, the Court seemed to stress several facts concerning the situation at MCC. First, the Court pointed out that detainees were required to spend only 7 or 8 hours in their cells, during which time they were presumably sleeping, and the 75 square foot cells provided "more than adequate space for sleeping," even when double-bunked. Second, the detainees were exposed to these conditions for relatively short periods of time—85 percent of the detainees were released from MCC within 60 days. And third, the Court noted that unlike other lower court cases in which courts had established minimum space requirements, *Wolfish* did not involve a traditional jail in which inmates were locked in their cells most of the day. It is unclear whether by this implied reference to MCC as a nontraditional jail the Court meant to suggest that the modern design of MCC and its cells with doors rather than bars, carpet rather than bare floors, and windows rather than solid walls also militated in favor of its decision.

Lower Court Treatment of Wolfish

Undoubtedly, groups concerned with prison reform feared that *Wolfish* sounded the death knell for their movement in the courts. However, the reaction of the lower courts to *Wolfish* suggests that the reformers' fears were largely unfounded. Most lower court decisions in overcrowding cases after *Wolfish* (and before *Chapman*) have still found the conditions of confinement unconstitutional. In light of the response of the lower courts, it would appear that they did not find *Wolfish* persuasive. A surprising number of lower courts only mentioned *Wolfish* briefly and made little effort to analyze the effect of *Wolfish* on the case at hand. In some instances the courts may simply have decided that the conditions at issue were intolerable and either ignored or thought it superfluous to distinguish *Wolfish*.

It is important to note than in most post-*Wolfish* cases, the plaintiffs consisted solely of, or included, convicted inmates and that the conditions were found unconstitutional as to the convicted inmates. In order to reach a finding of unconstitutionality, the courts had to determine that the conditions constituted cruel and unusual punishment, which is prohibited by the eighth amendment. Once the conditions were found to constitute cruel and unusual punishment as to convicted inmates, the conditions were obviously punishment as to the pretrial detainees. Since the conditions satisfied the more stringent standard of cruel and unusual punishment, the courts may have seen no need to distinguish or discuss *Wolfish*. Nevertheless, *Wolfish* should have been discussed and distinguished because if double-celling and overcrowding did not constitute punishment in *Wolfish*, the courts should have explained why these conditions would meet the more stringent criterion of cruel and unusual punishment in the case at hand.

Thus, it is difficult to arrive at a clear and precise statement of the effect of *Wolfish* on subsequent, and even current, cases concerning overcrowding and double-bunking. Some courts explicitly relied on

Wolfish in their opinions, other seemed to ignore or give rather short shrift to *Wolfish*, while still others attempted to distinguish between *Wolfish* and the instant case. It is to the latter cases that we now turn so as to examine the factors that may still lead to a finding of unconstitutionality even in light of the Supreme Court's ruling in *Wolfish*.

From the written opinions of courts which (1) found overcrowded conditions unconstitutional and (2) explained the effect of *Wolfish*, five factors seem particularly important. The factor most often cited was the inability of inmates to escape the pressures of overcrowded cells. Typically, this conclusion was based upon the relatively brief periods of time that inmates spent outside their cells or dormitories. In a few cases inmates spent over 22 hours a day in their cells. But even in an instance when they normally spent as little as 7 to 12 hours per day in their cells, the practice was questioned because the overcrowding had so taxed prison activities that inmates were often forced to spend more than 7 to 12 hours in their cells (*Capps v. Atiyeh*, 1980). Another court was concerned because inmates' access to day rooms was limited to several points during the day (*Lareau v. Manson*, 1981). In two instances courts were even willing to permit the overcrowded conditions to continue so long as inmates were given significantly greater periods of time outside their cells (*Lock v. Jenkins; Campbell v. Cauthron*).

A second distinguishing factor was the smaller size of the cells or less square footage per inmate (which is usually the concern where a case involves overcrowding in general rather than double-celling *per se*). Only one court specifically mentioned this as a distinguishing factor and there the cells were 60-65 square feet (*Lareau v. Manson*, 1981). However, several of the courts which did not specifically distinguish *Wolfish* were dealing with cells of square footage significantly less than in *Wolfish*. In one case the space per inmate was reported to be only seven square feet during some periods of the day (*Jones v. Diamond*).

A third distinguishing factor was the longer period of incarceration experienced by inmates. One court was considering a long-term confinement facility in which the mean sentence served was 24 months (*Capps v. Atiyeh*, 1980). But even in cases where only 17 percent of the inmates were confined for more than 60 days (*Lareau v. Manson*, 1981) or where the average length of confinement was 60 days (*Lock v. Jenkins*), courts found these differences from *Wolfish* significant.

A fourth distinguishing factor was the difference in quality of the institutional facilities. This can be implied from the courts' descriptions of dirty, unsanitary conditions, poor ventilation, and inadequate food, or their reference to a facility as "a traditional jail."

The fifth distinguishing factor was increased security problems and inadequacies in classification methods (*Lareau* v. *Mason*, 1981; *Lock* v. *Jenkins*; *West* v. *Lamb*; Capps v. *Atiyeh*, 1980). The two are included as one factor because they are closely related. Courts have stated that overcrowding often results in a "climate of tension, anxiety, and fear among both inmates and staff" (*Capps* v. *Atiyeh*, 1980), and that assaultive behavior may increase as a result of overcrowding. The failure to establish a careful method of classifying inmates, so as, for example, to avoid placing passive inmates in cells with aggressive inmates, is also seen to exacerbate these security problems.

In *Wolfish*, the Supreme Court held that double-bunking of cells designed for single occupancy was not unconstitutional *per se* and seemed to be suggesting to lower courts that they should be more restrained in their willingness to find overcrowded conditions of confinement unconstitutional. Nevertheless, in most decisions of the lower courts subsequent to *Wolfish*, overcrowded conditions of confinement were still found unconstitutional and the decision in *Wolfish* was either distinguished on the basis of different facts or was largely ignored. The factors most often used to distinguish *Wolfish* were: length of confinement per day, cell size, length of incarceration, the quality of the institution and increased security risks.

The Supreme Court and Convicted Inmates

If *Wolfish* had been the Supreme Court's only pronouncement on the constitutionality of overcrowded jails or prisons, lower court decisions would apparently have continued on a rather uninterrupted course. But within 2 years of *Wolfish*, the Court decided *Rhodes* v. *Chapman*. Whereas *Wolfish* had dealt with constitutional requirements concerning conditions of confinement for pretrial detainees, *Chapman* dealt with convicted offenders. *Wolfish* established that the constitutional standard for pretrial detainees is whether the conditions amount to punishment; *Chapman* confirmed that cruel and unusual punishment is the constitutional standard for convicted offenders. Moreover, for the first time the Supreme Court interpreted that standard in the context of crowded prison or jail conditions.

In *Chapman*, the Court summarized the law on cruel and unusual punishment that had developed in other contexts by indicating that "conditions must not involve the wanton and unnecessary infliction of pain, nor may they be grossly disproportionate to the severity of the crime warranting punishment" (101 S.Ct. 2399). Applying these standards to the double-bunked cells at the Southern Ohio Correctional Facility (SOCF), Ohio's only maximum security prison, the court found no constitutional violations.

Like the MCC in *Wolfish,* SOCF is a modern facility (built in the early 1970's) consisting primarily of cells designed for single occupancy, but which had been double-bunked to accommodate an unanticipated increase in convicted offenders. Cells were 63 square feet, well-heated and ventilated, and day rooms equipped with television, card tables, and chairs were accessible by most inmates between 6:30 a.m. and 9:30 p.m. Food was adequate, cells did not smell, noise was not excessive, inmates were allowed contact visits, medical and dental needs were being reasonably met, a number of recreational and educational opportunities were available to most inmates, and the rate of violent behavior had not increased since double-bunking had been instituted. Those who believed that double-bunking should be permitted as a means of housing the spiraling increase in incarcerated offenders could not have hoped for a better factual situation for the Supreme Court to consider.

These rather felicitous conditions at SOCF would have made *Chapman* an easily distinguishable case for courts considering subsequent conditions of confinement cases, but the tone of the Court's opinion would appear to be difficult to sidestep by lower courts bent on finding prison or jail conditions unconstitutional. For example, in its determination that the conditions of confinement at SOCF were unconstitutional, the District Court had specifically relied on five considerations: "the long terms of imprisonment served by inmates at SOCF; the fact that SOCF housed 38 percent more inmates than its 'design capacity'; the recommendation of several studies that each inmate have at least 50-55 square feet of living quarters; the suggestion that double-celled inmates spend most of their time in their cells with their cellmates; and the fact that double-celling at SOCF was not a temporary condition" (101 S.Ct. 2399). However, the Supreme Court found that "these general considerations fall far short in themselves of proving cruel and unusual punishment, for there is no evidence that double-celling under these circumstances either inflicts unnecessary or wanton pain or is grossly disproportionate to the severity of the crimes warranting imprisonment" (101 S.Ct. 2399). As we have seen, three of these considerations were important factual distinctions which lower courts had used to distinguish *Wolfish* from the cases before them. The language in *Chapman,* however, will make it more difficult for courts anxious to find conditions of confinement unconstitutional to distinguish between *Chapman* and subsequent cases.

In addition, the Court was careful to stress that "the Constitution does not mandate comfortable prisons" and that prisons like SOCF "CANNOT BE FREE OF DISCOMFORT" (101 S.Ct. 2400). Furthermore, the Court reiterated a theme from *Wolfish,* that problems of prison administration are quite complex and require the special expertise of legislative and executive officials rather than judicial intervention (101 S. Ct. 2401, FN 16). The clear message was one that the Court had tried to communicate in *Wolfish* and perhaps felt that it had failed to express with enough force: Federal courts had become too enmeshed in the administration of America's jails and prisons.

The tone of the concurring opinion of three of the justices implies that they may have been concerned that the majority's message to the lower courts of disengagement was expressed with too much force. The concurring justices recounted the history of judicial involvement in conditions of confinement cases, reminding readers that much of this admittedly regrettable judicial intervention occurred in response to appalling circumstances in which a failure to respond would have resulted in great injustice. With this reminder as background, the concurring justices stressed three points: (1) SOCF is an unusually fine correctional institution—"one of the better, more humane large prisons in the Nation" (101 S. Ct. 2409). (2) Judicial scrutiny of conditions of confinement under constitutional standards must be conducted on the basis of the "totality of circumstances" at the institution, a test which the concurring justices believed the majority adopted in *Chapman* (101 S.Ct. 2407). (3) The touchstone of when conditions of confinement become cruel and unusual punishment is "the effect upon the imprisoned" (101 S.Ct. 2408). If the District Court had found that the overcrowded conditions at SOCF had seriously harmed the inmates confined there, the concurring justices apparently would have found a violation of the Constitution.

Lower Court Treatment of Chapman

In spite of the Court's clear desire to decrease judicial intervention in the administration of jails and prisons, it is the more equivocal spirit of the concurring justices that characterizes the lower court decisions since *Chapman*. The response of the lower courts has been somewhat similar to their response to *Wolfish*. In many instances, the treatment of *Wolfish* and *Chapman* by lower courts has been perfunctory. For example, in a jail overcrowding case in the Western District of Virginia involving primarily pretrial detainees, the court determined that the overcrowded conditions were unconstitutional without citing *Chapman* and cited *Wolfish* only to establish that the constitutional standard regarding pretrial detainees is whether the conditions of confinement constitute punishment (*Gross v. Tazewell County Jail*).

The court's slighting of *Chapman* and *Wolfish* could be explained on the basis that the defendants in *Gross* did not seriously question that the jail was unconstitutionally overcrowded. But even in more strenuously contested cases, the courts' treatment of *Chapman* and *Wolfish* has sometimes been unexpectedly brief. For example, the District Court for the Northern District of Indiana ruled that the Admissions and Orientation cells at the Indiana State Prison were so small that they violated the eighth amendment. These cells were only 38 square feet, but they housed one inmate who thus had more space than the two inmates who shared a 63 square foot cell in *Chapman*. The court disposed of *Chapman* and *Wolfish* by indicating that:

> The facilities at issue in *Wolfish* and *Rhodes* present quite a different perspective to the prisoners confined there than does the prospect faced daily by the inmates on A&O. The inmates on A&O at the I.S.P. are in much smaller cells and are not free to move about. The evidence shows the confinement in the A&O unit subjects the inmate to genuine privations and hardships (*Hendrix* v. *Faulkner*, p. 524).

Thus, the court distinguished *Chapman* and *Wolfish* on the basis of cell size and the amount of time spent in cells per day. Yet these two factors are virtually the same as two of the factors that the District Court in *Chapman* had relied upon and which the Supreme Court indicated were "insufficient to support the District Court's) constitutional conclusion" (101 S.Ct. 2399).

Four courts have declared overcrowded conditions of confinement unconstitutional since *Chapman* and carefully explained why their cases differed from *Chapman* and *Wolfish*. They focused on the effects of overcrowding as the distinguishing factor (*Fairman* v. *Smith; Villanueva* v. *George; Union County Jail Inmates* v. Scanlon; *French* v. *Owens*). All four courts pointed to smaller cells and briefer periods of time afforded inmates outside their cells as important factors in their decisions, but they also emphasized other aggravating matters.

In *Villanueva* v. *George*, the Eighth Circuit Court of Appeals, sitting *en banc*, considered the constitutionality of the conditions to which a pretrial detainee had been subjected while incarcerated at the St. Louis Adult Correctional Institution. The plaintiff had been housed for 19 days in a six-foot by six-foot cell, furnished with a bed, combination toilet-sink, and light bulb. Every second or third day, he was allowed out of the cell for about 15 minutes to shower or walk in the hallway. The cell was infested with insects and the inmate was bitten once by a rodent. He found hair and roaches in his foot at least twice and was permitted no more than one phone call and one noncontact visit each week. In ruling that the inmate had produced enough evidence to permit a jury to find that his conditions of confinement were excessive, the circuit court explained that:

> our decision is not based solely on the fact that [plaintiff] was confined in a cell measuring six feet by six feet [citing *Chapman*]. It is

rather based upon the totality of the circumstances, including cell size, time spent in cell, lack of opportunity for exercise or recreation, general sanitary conditions, and the fact that plaintiff's past behavior demonstrated an ability to be confined under less restrictive conditions without incident (659 F.2d 854).

In *Smith* v. *Fairman*, the District Court for the Central District of Illinois declared unconstitutional the overcrowded conditions at the Pontiac Correctional Center, a maximum security prison constructed in 1871. The prison's population was 33 percent above design capacity with inmates double-celled in approximately 400 cells, which ranged in size from 55.3 to 64.5 square feet. The court distinguished this case from *Wolfish* because the cells at Pontiac were much smaller, inmates could "escape" their cells only 4-6 hours a day, and the length of confinement for inmates was measured in years rather than days. *Chapman* was distinguished since the ameliorating conditions at SOCF, namely, the adequate ventilation, absence of offensive odors, well-controlled temperature, low noise level, adequate library resources and school rooms, and inmates' ability to leave their cells during nearly two-thirds of the day were absent at Pontiac. The court concluded that the conditions at Pontiac constituted cruel and unusual punishment because the prison:

> is overcrowded, antiquated, and has inadequate facilities to provide significant and constructive correctional programs to the inmates. The confinement for years on end of two adult males for periods of eighteen to twenty hours a day in a cramped, ill-ventilated, noisy space designed a century ago for one person is contrary to every recognized modern standard of penology and is in conflict with minimum standards established by the Illinois legislature (528 F. Supp. 201).

In *Union County Jail Inmates* v. *Scanlon*, the New Jersey District Court declared unconstitutional the overcrowded conditions in a county jail that was housing pretrial detainees and convicted offenders, many of whom were state prisoners that the state refused to accept because of the overcrowded conditions in the state prisons. The population of the jail had been as much as 60 percent in excess of design capacity and cells of 39 square feet were being double-bunked by placing a mattress on the floor. The court distinguished *Wolfish* because the county jail was a traditional jail, the cells were much smaller, inmates lacked access to large dayrooms, and recreational and visitation opportunities had been severely impacted by the overcrowding. The court indicated that the Constitution does not condone such "spatial starvation" and "[e]ven the incarcerated are entitled to something more than a walk-in closet" (537 F.Sup. 1004). The court was not as careful in distinguishing *Chapman*, but it did point out that the Union County Jail was more like the older prisons which the Supreme Court described in *Chapman* as deplorable and sordid (537 F. Supp. 1007).

In *French v. Owens*, convicted offenders at the Indiana Reformatory were double-bunked in cells of 44 or 47.6 square feet. The court distinguished the Indiana Reformatory from the jail in *Wolfish* and the prison in *Chapman* because the two latter facilities were "new, clean, and relatively comfortable" (p. 936) whereas the Indiana Reformatory was "a 59 year old structure with inadequate ventilation, erratic heating, no cooling, and archaic electric wiring" (id.). All witnesses at the trial agreed that the severe overcrowding at the Indiana Reformatory had "caused the confined persons unusual stress, discomfort, aggravation, and pain" (p. 937).

The conditions cited by these courts as establishing cruel and unusual punishment in the aggregate do not include references to an atmosphere of violence. However, there is considerable case law to support the principle that the eighth amendment requires correctional institutions to provide inmates reasonable protection from harmful assaults by other inmates (see cases cited in *Madyun v. Thompson*). These cases require a pattern of violence and not simply a few isolated instances of inmate assaults. Although this condition alone, even in an uncrowded jail or prison, would violate the Constitution, it seems probable that the likelihood of such an atmosphere is enhanced by overcrowded conditions. Some courts have found that this duty to protect inmates also gives rise to a duty to classify inmates so that a reasonable effort is made to prevent inmate assaults (Gobert and Cohen, 1981).

Although post-*Chapman* cases discussed above are arguably at odds with the Supreme Court's apparent desire to reduce judicial involvement in jail and prison cases, five decisions of Federal circuit courts of appeal have been more responsive to that concern. In *Ruiz v. Estelle*, the Fifth Circuit Court of Appeals stayed a district court injunction ordering the Texas Department of Corrections (TDC) to single-cell its facilities. The majority of the TDC cells were 45 square feet and many double-celled inmates were not free to move about outside their cells. Nevertheless, the court of appeals noted that the factors which the district court relied on in *Ruiz* (the district court rendered its decision before *Chapman*) were very similar to those relied on by the district court in *Chapman* and were expressly repudiated by the Supreme Court. Although the cells in *Ruiz* were substantially smaller than those in *Chapman*, the court of appeals did "not believe that there is any constitutionally mandated square footage requirement per prisoner so long as the totality of conditions does not constitute cruel and unusual punishment" (650 F.2d 568). Consequently, the court of appeals granted Texas' request for a stay of the district court's injunction because it believed that "the State has made a substantial case on the merits respecting the serious legal question whether single-celling of inmates at TDC is constitutionally required under the district court's findings of fact" (650 F.2d 567).

When the Fifth Circuit subsequently decided the *Ruiz* overcrowding issue, it upheld the district court's finding that the overcrowded conditions at TDC violated the eighth amendment. However, the Fifth Circuit overruled the district court's order that all TDC inmates be single-celled. The appellate court noted the Supreme Court's admonition in *Chapman* that courts not substitute their judgment for the policy decisions of prison officials and determined that some of the other remedial orders issued by the district court might eliminate the harmful effects of overcrowding without the necessity of single-celling every inmate.

In *Nelson* v. *Collins,* the Fourth Circuit Court of Appeals decided three consolidated cases involving overcrowding in the Maryland prison system. Maryland had decided to solve temporarily its unanticipated increase in inmates by double-celling the new Jessup Annex and double-bunking some dormitories at another institution. The court of appeals saw no significant differences between Jessup Annex and SOCF.

> The facilities and conditions of confinement at the Jessup Annex are as good, if not better than those at SOCF. The cells are roughly the same size; there is no significant difference in the recreational opportunities; the provision for food, medical, dental, and psychiatric services are comparable; the facilities in the cells are practically the same; all in all, both facilities...are in line with the facilities in the most modern penal institutions (659 F.2d 428).

The double-bunking of the dorms was also held to be constitutional. In four dorms all beds in excess of 75 were removed and the 75 beds were double-bunked. As a result, each dorm housed nearly 40 additional inmates, but no inmate was assigned to a double-bunked dorm for more than 120 days. In an interesting approach to the space problem, however, the court reasoned that with fewer beds actually touching the floor the addition of new inmates still left "the actual space available to each inmate...substantially the same" (659 F.2d 429).

In *Hoptowit* v. *Ray,* the district court had found the overcrowded conditions at the Washington State Penitentiary unconstitutional. The prison had a rated capacity of 872 inmates but a population of 1,000 to 1,100. Some cells, ranging in size from 102.5 square feet to 130 square feet, were housing three and occasionally four inmates. The Ninth Circuit Court of Appeals overturned the district court's decision because the latter court had made no findings as to whether the overcrowded conditions had resulted in harmful effects on inmates. Citing *Wolfish*, *Chapman*, and other cases, the Ninth Circuit was careful to point out that "[c]ourts must recognize that the authority to make policy choices concerning prisons is not a proper judicial function...The Eighth Amendment is not a basis for broad prison reform" (682 F.2d 1246).

In *Smith* v. *Fairman*, discussed earlier, the Seventh Circuit Court of Appeals overturned the lower court decision, finding that Pontiac inmates received adequate food and medical care and lived in reasonably sanitary conditions. The appellate court was particularly concerned that the district court had been inattentive to uncontroverted evidence at trial that physical violence at the prison had been on the decline. The Seventh Circuit noted that while the Supreme Court had established that "the eighth amendment prohibition of cruel and unusual punishment is a fluid concept which 'must draw its meaning from the evolving standards of decency that mark the progress of a maturing society...,'" the Supreme Court had also made it clear in *Chapman* that "this standard did not mean judges are free to substitute their subjective views on this subject for those of society" (690 F.2d 125).

As stated previously, the response of the lower courts to *Chapman* has been similar to the response to *Wolfish*. It should be apparent, however, that *Chapman* has proven to be more difficult for the lower courts to distinguish, even though they have still frequently made the distinction. Increasingly, the lower courts appear to be recognizing the need to find that some condition relating to the basic necessities of life and resulting from the overpopulation is inadequate. Such a finding has been appearing more frequently in the opinions since *Chapman*, although the courts have not always been careful to point to this finding as a fact which distinguishes *Chapman*.

The cases just discussed that upheld, or leaned toward upholding, crowded prison conditions against constitutional challenges are particularly significant. First, they carry considerable weight since they are appellate court decisions while nearly all the post-*Chapman* decisions finding overcrowded conditions unconstitutional are trial court decisions. Second, the cases are carefully considered, well-reasoned opinions which are likely to influence future appellate court decisions. Of course, *Chapman* is still a "new" case and the "early returns" are too inconclusive to permit confident prediction as to the eventual judicial response to *Chapman*.

Double-Celling in the Post-Chapman Era

The preceding discussion of the law relating to overcrowded jails and prisons is intended to provide a basis for answering two important questions: (1) What legal problems are likely to arise from construction of a jail or prison with cells designed for double occupancy? (2) What legal problems are likely to arise from double-bunking cells originally designed to house only one inmate?

The construction of a jail or prison with double occupancy cells poses few legal problems. It is clear that the size of such cells do not have to comply with published correctional standards, although state and local facilities may have to abide by a state law or regulation which establishes a minimum cell size. Constitutionally, there is surely some "critical size" which would be so small as to constitute cruel and unusual punishment. Prior to *Wolfish* and *Chapman*, a reasonably good estimate of this critical size would have been a size smaller than the smallest size espoused by any of the professional standards. It is impossible to hazard even a reasonable guess as to the critical size now. One can only say with confidence that based on *Chapman*, if all other conditions of confinement meet constitutional minima, a double occupancy cell of 65 square feet or more is constitutionally acceptable.

Of course, this hypothetical new jail or prison must be constructed and maintained so as to provide inmates the basic necessities of life: adequate food, habitable living conditions, adequate plumbing and sanitation, attention to serious medical needs, and a resonably secure environment. It is this latter duty—to provide a reasonably secure environment—that is most likely to create potential legal problems for a new facility with double occupancy cells.

As indicated previously, several courts have held that the eighth amendment requires jails and prisons to take reasonable steps to protect inmates from attack by other inmates. In a facility consisting largely of double occupancy cells, this duty to protect places a significant burden on the facility to devise a reasonable method for making cell assignments so as to minimize the likelihood of placing a passive, "victim-prone" inmate in a cell with an aggressive one. The duty to protect would also suggest that staffing levels and the structural design of the institution be such that the double occupancy cells can be adequately monitored. For example, one would certainly want to avoid the situation that existed at the Hartford Community Correctional Center where double-bunked cells had solid doors with a glass window that did not open and there was no way for inmates inside the cell to contact guards. As a result, "if an inmate is being victimized by his cellmate, his only recourse is to slip pieces of paper or other narrow objects through the crack between the door and the doorjamb until the guard happens to look in his direction and notice" (*Lareau v. Manson*, 1981, p. 100).

Double-bunking of single cells is more likely to result in legal problems than constructing a facility with double occupancy cells. It is clear from *Wolfish* and *Chapman*, however, that double-bunking is not in itself unconstitutional. It would also appear from *Chapman* that double-bunking is constitutionally permissible for convicted offenders even though the double-bunking is permanent, the duration of confinement is lengthy, and the inmates in the double-bunked cells spend most of their time in their cells. As mentioned earlier, however, the lower courts are not consistently viewing *Chapman* this way. In addition, it is not clear that these conditions would be constitutionally permissible if the affected inmates are pretrial detainees.

Nearly all the courts that have cited *Chapman* and addressed the issue of double-bunking have concluded that *Chapman* requires courts to consider all the circumstances relating to the conditions of confinement in determining whether the eighth amendment has been violated.[2] The greatest legal danger created by double-bunking is that as the double-bunked facility becomes more overcrowded, the quality of other conditions of confinement is likely to deteriorate.[3] It becomes more difficult to keep the facility clean, to provide adequate and properly prepared food, to keep the plumbing in good working order, to permit sufficient exercise, to provide adequate health care, and even to allow inmates adequate time out of their double-bunked cells. The duty to protect inmates from each other will also become more difficult, creating the potential legal problems discussed earlier with respect to double occupancy cells. This analysis suggests that as double-bunking becomes more prevalent in an institution, the likelihood of a lawsuit based on overcrowded conditions will increase with the age of the institution and the degree to which the institution is unable to expand its resources, particularly size of staff.

Conclusion

The law, its interpretation, and the prediction of its future interpretation and application are obviously an inexact science. Officials with responsibility for the administration of a jail or prison who are concerned about being sued for overcrowded conditions are faced with a dilemma. A careful reading of *Wolfish* and *Chapman* would suggest to such officials that they can constitutionally operate penal institutions with populations greater than the institutional design capacity so long as they continue to meet adequately the inmates' basic necessities of life. However, the lower court decisions since *Wolfish* and *Chapman* suggest that at least some courts are still appalled by the conditions of confinement brought to their attention and are disposed to distinguish or even ignore those decisions. As a result, when correctional facilities become crowded the likelihood of a lawsuit still must be considered substantial and the court's resolution of the dispute cannot be predicted with confidence.

Note: Tables corroborating information presented in this article are available upon request from the author.

Footnotes

[1]This article focuses on the case law that would relate to a decision as to the most desirable celling arrangements in correctional institutions. The legal research has centered on conditions of confinement cases in which overcrowding was an issue or was closely related to the issues resolved by the cases. In the strict sense of the term, conditions of confinement cases include cases involving the legality of institutional practices, such as search procedures, visitation practices, classification systems, and disciplinary procedures. However, legal issues concerning institutional practices are not ordinarily relevant to celling arrangements except where such practices are affected by overcrowding. For the most part, the overcrowding cases have focused on the overcrowding itself or the effects of overcrowding on other physical or environmental conditions, such as sanitation, ventilation, and quality of medical care. Consequently, use of the term "conditions of confinement" in the article will refer to physical and environmental conditions rather than institutional practices.

[2]The Ninth Circuit Court of Appeals is an exception (*Hoptowit* v. *Ray*). Note also that *Chapman* does not prevent a court from basing a finding of cruel and unusual punishment on a single condition, such as inadequate medical care (*Estelle* v. *Gamble*). *Wolfish* also seems to call for the application of a totality of the circumstances test in determining whether the conditions of confinement of pre-trial detainees constitute punishments.

[3]See *Lightfoot* v. *Walker* for an example of a case which was decided on the basis of the adequacy of the health care provided inmates. The court's decision was not based on the overcrowded conditions that existed, but it is clear that the overcrowding was a primary cause of the inadequate health care.

References

American Civil Liberties Union, "Status Report: The Courts and Prisons," March 8, 1982

Commission on Accreditation for Corrections, *Manual of Standards for Adult-Correctional Institutions* (Rockville, Md.: American Correctional Association, 1977).

Daryl R. Fair, "The Lower Federal Courts as Constitution-Makers: The Case of Prison Conditions," *The American Journal of Criminal Law*, Vol. 7, p. 119 (1979).

James J. Gobert and Neil P. Cohen, *Rights of Prisoners* (Colorado Springs: Shepard's/McGraw-Hill, 1981).

Joan Mullen and Bradford Smith, *American Prisons and Jails, Vol. III: Conditions and Costs of Confinement* (Washington, D.C.: U.S. Government Printing Office, 1980).

Ira P. Robbins and Michael B. Buser, "Punitive Conditions of Prison Confinement: An Analysis of Pugh v. Locke and Federal Court Supervision of State Penal Administration Under the Eighth Amendment," *Stanford Law Review*, Vol. 28, p. 893 (1977).

Table of Cases

Adams v. Mathis, 614 F.2d 42 (5th Cir. 1980)
Atiyeh v. Capps, 101 S.Ct. 829 (1981) (Rehnquist, Circuit Justice)
Batton v. State Government of North Carolina, 501 F.Supp. 1173 (E.D.N.C. 1980)
Bell v. Wolfish, 441 U.S. 520 (1979)
Benjamin v. Malcolm, 495 F.Supp. 1357 (S.D.N.Y. 1980)
Bono v. Saxbe, 620 F.2d 609 (7th Cir. 1980)
Burks v. Teasdale, 603 F.2d 59 (8th Cir. 1979)
Campbell v. Cauthron, 623 F.2d 503 (8th Cir. 1980)
Campbell v. McGruder, 32 Cr.L. 2084 (D.D.C. 1982)
Capps v. Atiyeh, 495 F.Sup. 802 (D. Ore. 1980)
Chapman v. Rhodes, 101 S.Ct. 2392 (1981)
Chavis v. Rowe, 643 F.2d 1281 (7th Cir. 1981)
Dawson v. Kendrick, 527 F.Supp. 1252 (S.D. W.Va. 1981)
Epps v. Levine, 480 F.Supp. 50 (D. Md. 1979)
Estelle v. Gamble, 429 U.S. 97 (1976)
Feliciano v. Barcelo, 497 F.Supp. 14 (D.P.R. 1979)
French v. Owens, 538 F.Supp. 929 (S.D. Ind. 1982)
Gross v. Tazewell County Jail, 533 F.Supp. 413 (W.D. Va. 1982)
Heitman v. Gabriel, 524 F.Supp. 622 (W.D. Mo. 1981)
Hendrix v. Faulkner, 525 F.Supp. 435 (N.D. Ind. 1981)
Hoptowit v. Ray, 682 F.2d 1237 (9th Cir. 1982)
Hutchings v. Corum, 501 F.Supp. 1276 (W.D. Mo. 1980)
Johnson v. Levine, 588 F.2d 1378 (4th Cir. 1978)
Jones v. Diamond, 636 F.2d 1364 (5th Cir. 1981)
Jordan v. Wolke, 615 F.2d 749 (7th Cir. 1980)
Lareau v. Manson, 651 F.2d 96 (2d Cir. 1981)
Lareau v. Manson, 507 F.Supp. 1177 (D. Conn. 1980)
Lightfoot v. Walker, 486 F.Supp. 504 (S.D. Ill. 1980)
Lock v. Jenkins, 641 F.2d 488 (7th Cir. 1981)

Madyun v. Thompson, 657 F.2d 868 (7th Cir. 1981)

McElveen v. County of Prince William, 31 Cr.L. 2446 (E.D. Va. 1982)

McMurry v. Phelps, 33 F.Supp. 742 (W.D. La. 1982)

Nelson v. Collins, 659 F.2d 420 (4th Cir. 1981)

Ramos v. Lamm, 639 F.2d 559 (10th Cir. 1980)

Ruiz v. Estelle, 679 F.2d 1115 (5th Cir. 1982)

Ruiz v. Estelle, 666 F.2d 854 (5th Cir. 1982)

Ruiz v. Estelle, 650 F.2d 555 (5th Cir. 1981)

Ruiz v. Estelle, 503 F.Supp. 1265 (S.D. Tex. 1980)

Smith v. Fairman, 690 F.2d 122 (7th Cir. 1982)

Smith v. Fairman, 528 F.Supp. 186 (C.D. Ill. 1981)

Trop v. Dulles, 356 U.S. 86 (1957)

Union County Jail Inmates v. Scanlon, 537 F.Supp. 993 (D.N.J. 1982)

United States Ex.rel. Wolfish v. U.S., 428 F.Supp. 333 (S.D.N.Y. 1977)

Vazquez v. Gray, 523 F.Supp. 1359 (S.D.N.Y. 1981)

Villanueva v. George, 659 F.2d 851 (8th Cir. 1981, en banc)

West v. Lamb, 497 F.Supp. 989 (D. Nev. 1980)

Wickham v. Fisher, 629 P.2d 896 (Utah, 1981)

Withers v. Levine, 449 F.Supp. 473 (D. Md. 1978), aff'd 615 F.2d 158 (4th Cir. 1980)

Wolff v. McDonnel, 418 U.S. 539 (1974)

Wright v. Rushen, 642 F.2d 1129 (9th Cir. 1981)

16

Prison Reform by Judicial Decree

The Unintended Consequences of *Ruiz v. Estelle*

Geoffrey P. Alpert
Ben M. Crouch
C. Ronald Huff

Introduction

The history of the world is in part a history of revolutions. As societies evolved from simple, agrarian, and homogeneous to complex, industrial and heterogeneous, the level of social conflict (violence, rebellion, and revolution) increased markedly. One major theoretical perspective which has been formulated to explain collective responses by those seeking relief or freedom is the theory of rising expectations. James Davies (1962), in an influential article, outlined such a theory as

Source: *The Justice System Journal*, Vol. 9, No. 3 (1984), 291-305. Reprinted with the permission of the publisher.

applied to revolutions, and we believe that his ideas and propositions may usefully be extended to the phenomena of prison riots — not at the "grand theory" level, but at least as a useful framework for understanding many prison disturbances.

To summarize briefly, Davies (1962) argued that two ideas set forth in the writings of Marx and Engels and Tocqueville have explanatory and predictive value when juxtaposed and placed in proper temporal sequence. Marx and Engels (1959) noted that progressive social degradation could reach a point of despair, with revolution likely to follow. In a modifying statement, they added that even an increase of benefits, when disproportionate to the increased enjoyments of the capitalists, must be included as a precondition of unrest. This same conclusion was reached by Tocqueville (1955) in his study of the French Revolution. Both theoretical statements emphasize that the loss of something already gained will trigger dissatisfaction, and it is a state of mind (*relative* deprivation), rather than a tangible level of deprivation, which serves as a catalyst for rioting. In light of these observations, it is interesting to note that the National Advisory Commission on Criminal Justice Standards and Goals (1976: 19-20) found that: "... (M)ass violence and terrorism more frequently occur during a time of improvement than during social deterioration. They appear to be stimulated by rising expectations, or, more specifically, by the disappointment in them." Similarly, Gurr (1970) advocated a "relative deprivation" theory of civil strife.[1]

Historically, the courts were reluctant to intervene in prison policy and management.[2] However, such intervention has grown significantly during the past three decades (Alpert and Huff, 1981).[3] Such intervention, especially mandated changes in basic institutional policies and practices (Baker, Blotky, Clemens, and Dillard, 1973), has formalized and legitimated prison conflict. The implementation of court-ordered change has virtually assured us that prisoners will eagerly anticipate improvements in the general conditions of confinement and in many specific areas, such as personal living space, medical care, access to the courts, and working conditions. In addition, court orders have provided prison administrators with unparalleled power if such orders are reversed on appeal or if only lip-service is paid to the mandates. This creation of a "win-loss" situation for one side could end up as a "no-win" situation for the prisons and for society.

Research Questions and Sources of Data

The central purpose of this study is to describe the consequences, both intended and unintended, of court-ordered reform in a major case

(*Ruiz v. Estelle*, 1980) affecting an entire state prison system (Texas). Our purpose here is not to provide "just another case study," but rather to assess the applicability of rising expectations theory in understanding the dynamics of prison conflict, riots, and disturbances.

In the correctional context, the theory of rising expectations must, of course, be adapted in order to serve as a framework for analyzing such impact. We are mindful that our study focuses on a micro, rather than macro (societal revolutions) level. Nonetheless, the *Ruiz* case provides us an opportunity to seek answers to the following research questions:

1. What, if any, observable impact did the decision have on the behavior of inmates (individual and collective)?
2. What, if any, observable impact did the decision have on the behavior of management and line staff?
3. What were the consequences of *Ruiz* on the social control system which had been established in the Texas prisons?
4. What policy and management implications may be derived from this research?

These questions are as sensitive as they are important. Where the prison environment is relatively unstable, collecting data to address these issues is particularly problematic. Consequently, for the analysis presented here we have relied on several sources of information. Reliance on multiple sources was also advantageous because that strategy permitted us to check one source against another. Our sources included:

1. newspaper accounts, particularly over the three years following the court order;
2. official Texas Department of Corrections (TDC) information releases;
3. information from periodic reports on compliance and resistance of the TDC;
4. our collective knowledge of prisoner behavior based on prior research and extant literature in the field; and
5. informal interviews with key actors in the system (management, correctional officers, and inmates).[4]

Texas: A Case Study

The Texas Department of Corrections is both a typical and an atypical example of the impact of court-ordered change. It is typical in that it is only one of many state prison systems which have experienced change and uncertainty due to judicial decisions over the past decade (Bowker, 1982: 282-289; Gettinger, 1977). This commonality makes Texas a useful case study. At the same time, Texas is atypical. That is, this prison system had, until the Ruiz case, a history of stability inside and a remarkable degree of insularity from external social and political forces. The TDC's insularity and stability also enhance its value as the locus of this case study, because major changes can be attributed more confidently to the court decision, rather than to other variables operating at the same time.

Procedural History of the Ruiz *Case.* The Ruiz case was almost nine years old by the time Federal District Judge William Wayne Justice handed down his decision in a memorandum opinion which consumed 248 legal-sized pages (Cohen, 1981). The civil action was initiated in June 1972, when David Ruiz filed suit against the director of the TDC, pursuant to 42 U.S.C. 1983, seeking declaratory and injunctive relief for alleged constitutional violations. The Ruiz case subsequently was consolidated with the suits of seven other TDC inmates into a single civil action, Ruiz v. Estelle (1980). The case eventually evolved into a class action, and damage issues were considered for all TDC inmates. After more than three years of pre-trial issues, the case finally reached the trial stage. Finally, after 159 days of trial (October 1978 to September 1979), the testimony of 349 witnesses, and the presentation of 1,565 exhibits, the Court issued its opinion.

The Opinion. Judge Justice found the TDC in violation of inmates' constitutional rights in six major areas: (1) overcrowding; (2) security; (3) fire safety; (4) medical care; (5) discipline; and (6) access to the courts. The order granted relief in each of these areas and included, *inter alia,* the following (Ruiz v. Estelle, 1980):

1. The TDC must end the practice of putting three inmates in one cell, end the practice of routinely housing two inmates in 45 and 60 square foot cells, and reduce the overcrowding in dormitories;
2. The TDC must end guard brutality, increase the number of guards, improve the selection and training procedures for guards, and eliminate the building-tender system;
3. The TDC must improve its methods of fire safety, its water supply, plumbing, wastewater, and solid waste disposal;
4. The TDC must increase its medical staff, restrict inmates performing medical and pharmacological functions, improve unit infirmaries, substantially renovate the main prison hospital, establish diagnostic and sick-call procedures that eliminate non-medical interferences with medical care, and improve the pharmaceutical operations;
5. The TDC must provide all inmates accused of disciplinary infractions with notice of charges, consider literacy and mental capacity and provide representation for those unable

to represent themselves, inform inmates of their right to call witnesses, and have sufficient evidence before ordering a "lock-up"; and

6. The TDC must desist blocking prisoners' access to the courts.

The order called for a meeting of attorneys from both sides to work out compromises on some issues and to determine a timetable for change on others. When this attempt at negotiation failed, Judge Justice, in March 1981, ordered the TDC to effect the changes ordered by the opinion and announced that he would appoint a special master to oversee the implementation of the decree.[5]

The TDC Prior to Ruiz. According to the theory of rising expectations, either a disproportionate increase or a decrease in benefits can lead to unrest, as can the real or imagined loss of something already gained. Because one must understand the "baseline" historical conditions which existed before one can assess the impact of change, it is therefore necessary to characterize briefly the philosophy and organizational structure of the TDC prior to *Ruiz* so that the impact and consequences of the court order may be more clear.

Traditional TDC philosophy consisted of three major tenets: (1) an emphasis on inmate control at all times; (2) strong support of the conventional work ethic; and (3) the efficient use of human and material resources. Every aspect of TDC's extensive operations reflected these principles. The prison's agricultural program illustrates the extent to which these principles have been integrated in practice. TDC has long required all inmates to work and, at least during the early part of their sentences, all inmates participate in some aspect of the TDC's extensive (100,000 acre) agricultural program. The TDC's rationale for this has been as follows: first, it provides a critical and direct introduction to the work ethic; second, it introduces inmates to the TDC's officer-inmate relationship (Crouch, 1980); and third, it makes use of this inmate labor to reduce the costs of incarceration. Over the past three decades, adherence to this philosophy has created a controversial prison system seen by some as a "paragon of prisons" and by others as a "slave plantation" (*Corrections Magazine*, 1978).

Organizationally, the structure of the TDC has reflected each tenet of this basic philosophy, especially the emphasis on inmate control. The TDC's tradition of stability and relatively low rates of violence (Sylvester *et al.*, 1977) stem largely from the effectiveness of (1) mid-level security personnel and (2) "building tenders" (inmates who work closely with custody officials to maintain order). Mid-level officers (those holding the rank of lieutenant, captain, major, or warden) without exception entered the security hierarchy at the bottom (there is no lateral entry)—in many cases more than twenty years ago—and have risen through the ranks. Because there is considerable turnover at the lowest ranks, these mid-level officers, by virtue of rank and experience, are the control mainstays of the relatively isolated TDC prison units. Their commitment to the traditional definition of inmate subordination and control stems both from the rural, east Texas background of most of these men[6] and from the TDC's preference for promoting to mid-level security positions those men who develop reputations for effective personal control over prisoners (Crouch and Marquart, 1980).

The building tender system officially employs inmates to keep the cellblocks clean and to aid officers with such menial tasks as helping with the count. Unofficially, building tenders actually represent an extension of the security and control machinery directed by the guards.[7] Building tenders administer sanctions to fellow inmates both with and without the knowledge of the authorities (Gettinger and Krajick, 1978; Marquart and Crouch, 1982). Mid-level officers and building tenders have in common the desire and the ability to enforce the TDC's general philosophy — especially inmate control. The extent to which this philosophy has been implemented is reflected in the title of one account of the TDC: "They Keep You In, They Keep You Busy, and They Keep You From Getting Killed" (Krajick, 1978). Although some inmates and outside observers view the TDC as a neocolonial slave system, the official intent of the TDC's philosophy of inmate control is perhaps best summed up in the comments of an inmate who did time in two other state prison systems before being committed to the TDC (Krajick, 1978: 21).

> Everything here is predictable. You know what to expect. You don't have to worry about getting stabbed or raped by other inmates, or what's going to happen from one day to the next, because it's the administration that's totally in control. After a short time here, you realize that if you go to your cell, go to mess, wash up, go to work quietly, all will go well. It's almost more like the service than the penitentiary, except for the bars.

The Impact of the Decree

It did not surprise us to learn that the weight of the federal judiciary rests heavily on the TDC and that its employees are afraid of losing a great deal of the power and influence they have gained over the years. The TDC's power and influence have benefitted from rapid growth in the inmate population (it has risen from 16,000 in 1975 to about 37,000 in 1983, for example) and a corresponding increase in the size of the organization and its budget (Bureau of Justice Statistics, 1983; Corrections Magazine, 1978). This shift has also affected the general conditions of confinement and overcrowding. Lawsuits have been filed and won, and these have, to some extent, altered the TDC's operations. The *Ruiz* case did not fall upon a pristine system; however, because of the nature of the *Ruiz* order, the legal complexities involved, and the massive media coverage, *Ruiz v. Estelle* (1980) brought about a concrete realization, by inmates and staff alike, that changes in the status quo were not far away. It is our contention that *Ruiz*, while mandating many desirable improvements in the administration of the TDC, has also set in motion a chain of events that has undermined the traditional stability, safety, and regularity within the TDC and has created a serious crisis of control, with all of the usual dysfunctions which accompany anomic social conditions. Such unanticipated consequences often follow interventions aimed at reforming established social institutions and systems. It is likely that any prison system in which significant change is anticipated will experience major problems of social control. In Texas the contrast, and the effects, are most dramatic.

Impact on Inmates and Guards. An initial and crucial impact of the court order was a generalized sense of rising expectations among inmates. One correctional officer observed: "....They think it's an emancipation proclamation. They expect (Judge) Justice to pull up in his long, black Cadillac, open the gates and turn 'em all loose" (Crouch, 1981b). Although clearly an exaggeration and oversimplification revealing his own emotional reaction to the court order as much as anything else, this officer's comment concerning heightened inmate expectations is supported by other sources. According to our sources inside the TDC and its prisons,[8] many inmates sensed that the conditions of their total subordination were about to be improved measurably. Heightened inmate expectations of improvement, along with notions that official control would diminish, led to increased conflict between guards and inmates. This discord manifested itself in three specific ways. First, guards reported an increase in verbal and physical abuse from inmates. Feeling less constrained by traditional rules and control mechanisms, many inmates were more willing to voice resentment to orders and, in some cases, to disobey them. Second, there was an increase in lawsuits filed by inmates alleging official misconduct. Legal services attorneys reported an increase in requests for assistance, while guards reported that more investigators were asking more questions than ever before. A building captain who had been employed by the TDC for nine years stated that he had talked to more U.S. Department of Justice personnel in the prior year than in all the previous years since he had joined the TDC (Crouch, 1981a). Finally, there was a marked increase in the number of disturbances and riots. During the *Ruiz* trial, the TDC experienced a number of

minor inmate disturbances, some of which were intended to demonstrate inmate solidarity for the cause being litigated.[9]

The *Ruiz* order, requiring massive changes, was finalized in March
1981, and as required, each inmate received a copy of the order via the
prison newsletter, *The Echo*. This notification was viewed by inmates
as evidence of concrete and significant changes, further escalating
among inmates the expectation that change would be rapid. Inmate
emotions and excitement seemed to be on display in collective violence,
with 11 riots taking place between June and November, 1981. In just six
months, there were twice as many riots as had occurred in the
preceding eight years![10]

Increases in control problems are further reflected in a report
recently released by the TDC (*Houston Chronicle*, 1983), which showed
that in the first six months of 1983 there had been 13 escape attempts,
as compared with only two during the same period in 1982. Moreover,
in the early months of 1983, four TDC inmates had been killed by other
prisoners, the greatest number in nearly a decade. Finally, the number
of offenses committed within TDC prisons increased by 17% over the
previous year. The elevated level of prison disturbances appears to be
linked to the court order and its effects on the social system of the TDC.

The court order prompted two important changes in life at the TDC.
First, the inmates began challenging their status quo and reaching for
more freedom. Second, the ruling markedly altered traditional TDC
control mechanisms. Because of the shroud of uncertainty, officers
were less likely to enforce some rules and to carry out their duties, and
a growing number of experienced officers resigned, apparently
deciding that they wanted no part of the direction in which the "new
TDC" was being moved by the federal court.

Rapid Change and Organizational Anomie. Although TDC's unrest
appears to have been stimulated by the rising inmate expectations
created by judicial alteration of the old status quo, several related
factors exacerbate that unrest. Foremost among these is the serious
problem of overcrowding. TDC houses approximately 37,000 prisoners
and vies with California as the nation's largest prison system. Another
important factor is the loss of information once provided by those elite
inmates who worked as building tenders, floormen, or turnkeys. Most
TDC officials agree that the demotion of once powerful convicts has
caused a significant reduction in both the amount and the quality of
information coming to officers about activities within the inmate population. Finally, to comply with the court order and to fill many of the
jobs formerly held by inmates, the TDC must increase the number of
uniformed security personnel.

The need to increase personnel creates, in turn, at least two conditions which may further diminish the TDC's traditional control and

stability. First, although the TDC unit wardens actually removed inmates from old positions and, where necessary, regained control of keys during May and June, 1982, it will take considerable time to find, hire, and train sufficient officers to fill those positions vacated by inmates and those vacancies attributable to normal attrition and resignations. Meanwhile, the TDC continues to be understaffed and its officers have less information than was formerly available to them.

Second, when large numbers of new officers must be hired at one time, the limited selectivity dictated by the available labor pool, along with the often abbreviated training which accompanies wholesale infusion of personnel into an organization in crisis, may create as many problems with "officer control" as with inmate control. There is fairly widespread concern within the TDC about the quality of the current (and probably future) new officers. Where mid-level officers have only marginal trust in line personnel, not only will there be uncertainty among the ranks, but the critical informal socialization process may be hampered as well.

In short, the *Ruiz* decision set in motion an interrelated chain of events which has had the unintended consequence of creating a crisis of control within the Texas prison system. The decision caused the expectations of inmates to rise rapidly, created uncertainty among TDC staff, and, in the new environment characterized mainly by anomie, inmate/guard conflict rose markedly and rioting occurred at a rate which appears to be linked to the court's decision and its effects on the prison system.

Policy and Management Implications

A central thesis of this article has been that externally-imposed reform may induce both intended and unintended consequences. Our focus has not been on the social desirability of the specific reforms ordered by the Court; rather, we have been concerned with an analysis of the effects of the court's order on the Texas prison system. Our primary conclusion is that the *Ruiz* decision led to a number of unanticipated consequences, many of which were dysfunctional. We further argue that one of the mechanisms by which this unanticipated change occurred was through the rising expectations of inmates, linked closely with the organizational anomie which prevailed after the decision. The collective violence which seems to have been associated with the decision (or, more precisely, with the conditions which followed the decision) suggests that serious crisis of control did in fact ensue.

Perhaps the most important implication flowing from this study is the obvious need for greater coordination and cooperation in implementing judicial decrees in complex organizations such as prisons and prison systems. Those familiar with the extant research and theory on complex organizations will undoubtedly find it surprising that so little attention is paid to the implementation of a far-reaching court order after nearly nine years of considering evidence in the case. Likewise, in the *Ruiz* decision there is every indication that the federal judge was fully aware that the TDC had a strongly established set of policies and management practices, not to mention a clear stratification of management, staff, and inmates (perhaps the clearest in the Western world!). It was, in fact, many of those policies and practices which served as the focal point for the decision. Therefore, it would seem self-evident that the iimplementation of change in such a system should be informed by organizational theory. However, this seldom has occurred in the history of institutional legal reform, and it certainly did not occur in *Ruiz*.

As we have argued, serious organizational conflict, including collective violence, can result from externally-induced reform which has certain effects on the social structure of and personal relationships within the organization targeted for change. Therefore, to minimize the possibility of such problems, judges should seek to understand complex organizations in general and the particular organization they seek to reform. Because organizations share some characteristics in common, knowledge of organizational theory and research would greatly benefit judges seeking to restructure or reform them in certain ways. However, every organization is also unique in some ways, and more detailed information is necessary to assess the probable impact of court orders on each one. It is likely, from our point of view, that the same judicial decree would have differential effects across organizations. We further assert that the implementation strategy best suited to each case should be identified only after careful analysis of the organization has been completed.

Although the need for evaluation of court-ordered reform is great (Huff and Alpert, 1982), we can say with reasonable certainty that those judges who understand complex organizations and their behavior are much more likely to formulate and implement successful decrees. (This, of course, presumes a view of legal reform as a substantive, rather than merely symbolic, activity). As another observer has commented: "...If a remedy is to be effective, then a judge designing relief must take into account the nature of the organizations whose policies and processes he seeks to alter" (Note, 1980: 513).

Introducing change in a prison or prison system inherently is more difficult and more risky than changing most other types of organizations. Issues of personal safety (both inside and outside the walls) must be considered carfully and given great weight in formulating an implementation strategy. With respect to the TDC, for example, many policy and management issues were raised in the *Ruiz* case and the judge, finding many of them objectionable, ordered them changed and hired a special master to ensure that change occurred, without giving careful consideration to the functions served by each policy or practice and how these functions might be effectively addressed in a more constitutionally acceptable manner.

One of the most pervasive problems which characterizes the implementation of judicial decrees in prison systems has to do with intergovernmental relations. Specifically, because prisons are part of the executive branch of government, judicial decrees requiring change must be viewed within the perspective of judicial and executive governmental relations. As such, cooperation is often less than satisfactory. In *Ruiz*, of course, this was complicated by the fact that the case involved state/federal, as well as judicial and executive conflicts. Duffee (1980) has provided a useful discussion of the problems of managing change in corrections and the additional difficulties posed by intergovernmental conflict. One of the major problems, of course, is that those responsible for implementing the change are seldom involved in its formulation, and thus have little or no sense of "ownership" in the change to be effected. A participatory model of formulating and implementing change should be considered whenever possible, even though special structural barriers to such a model may exist. Certainly insofar as determining specific strategy for implementing change, it is desirable to involve management whenever possible (and management, in turn, should involve staff whenever possible). The judiciary should identify specific targets to be met (e.g., a shift from reliance on inmate building tenders to greater security staff) and then work closely with the organization, as well as objective experts, in formulating specific strategies and timetables for implementing change.

Greater knowledge of complex organizations would enable judges to structure institutional reform in much more effective ways. As judges juxtaposed their legal reform goals with each organization's mission, goals, current power structure, and other factors, they would have a much greater chance of identifying implementation strategies that could work. Consider, for example, the applicability of the following observation when applied to the *Ruiz* case (note, 1980:524):

> ...(C)hanging tasks is even more difficult when the reward system is closely intertwined with task performance, that is, when employees accustomed to being rewarded for performing certain tasks have those tasks changed as a result of court action. Courts must induce organizational actors to perform the tasks necessary for compliance with the court order. Usually, judges will be most effective when the

actors perceive that compliance will not diminish their professional rewards.

Our study of the impact of *Ruiz* on the TDC has demonstrated that an almost purely adversarial climate evolved around the case, with the judge, the TDC, and the special master involved in open conflict just as much as the inmates and the guards. Under such circumstances, it is little wonder that the fragile social system of the prison erupted in violent conflict.

In conclusion, we believe that judges, prison managers, and all students of organizational behavior can learn a great deal from the difficulties which have surrounded the implementation of the *Ruiz* decision. Judges must become more familiar with complex organizations if they are to improve their record of decree implementation, and prison managers should be more closely involved in designing implementation strategy. Greater weight must be given to the prevention of dysfunctional, unintended consequences such as collective violence. The incremental introduction of change, carefully based on organizational analysis and knowledge of organizational behavior, would represent a more productive approach to decree implementation.

Footnotes

[1] See Piven and Cloward (1979: 1-40) for a useful discussion of the structuring of protest, including a critique of relative deprivation theory.

[2] Historically, the control of prisons and prisoners was left up to the administrator. Only limited activities were subject to external review. The role of the judiciary in corrections was confined to the interpretation of statutes and limited review of administrative actions. Prior to the early 1960s, any attempt at intervention by the judiciary which might go beyond these narrow bounds was met with severe objections. The "hands-off" doctrine established by the Supreme Court in *Banning v. Looney* (1954) effectively curtailed the viability of litigation initiated by inmates and directed at prison officials. This historic reticence to intervene has been based on three principles: (1) the separation of powers doctrine; (2) the low level of penological expertise among the judiciary; and (3) the fear that judicial intervention would undermine prison administrators and their methods of discipline.

[3] Since the 1960s, the judiciary has gone beyond its traditional role and has become increasingly willing to intervene in cases involving prisons and prisoners (Rudovsky et al., 1983). This shift in juridical theory was encouraged by the Supreme Court in *Monroe v. Pape* (1961), which held that the 1871 Civil Rights Act, 42 U.S.C., 1983, vested federal courts with the jurisdiction to hear cases involving parties alleging that they were deprived of their constitutional rights. Although the availability of recourse to the federal courts was created in *Monroe v. Pape* (1961), many circuits remained reluctant to hear civil rights cases brought by state prisoners, citing federalism and comity. It was not until

Cooper v. Pate (1964) that prisoners were able to enjoy fully the protections of 1983. This trend in civil rights protections continued to expand during the late 1960s and 1970s (Alpert, 1980; Alpert and Huff, 1981; Calhoun, 1977; Haas and Champagne, 1976; Turner, 1979). These rulings, decisions, and orders continue to have an unparalleled impact on prison policy and management throughout the United States.

[4]One of the authors has for the past decade conducted research within the TDC, focusing especially on security personnel and the problem of order maintenance in general (see Crouch, 1980). The contacts made and maintained over this period of time on many different TDC units regularly provided information (via informal interviews) on change in the system. Approximately forty interviews were conducted with a wide range of respondents on the impact of the court order. Much additional information came from J.W. Marquart who, as a graduate sociology student and TDC prison guard, contributed valuable inter-view data and participant observation documentation of inmate and official perceptions of and reactions to *Ruiz* (see Marquart and Crouch, 1982).

[5]Mr. Vincent Nathan was appointed as special master. The role of special master in institutional reform litigation is complex and not, in general, well understood. Two articles which provide thoughtful analyses of this role are Nathan (1979) and Levinson (1982).

[6]Prison officers in many states typically have rural backgrounds, usually due in part to the rural location of prison sites. Jacobs (1977) and March (1978) are among those who have contributed useful discussions to the literature on prison guards. In Texas, a large proportion of mid-level officers, especially, have rural backgrounds (Crouch, 1977). Having grown up in a setting where respect for authority (saying "sir" comes naturally) and hard work are highly valued facilitates socialization into the TDC, because these values are very consistent with the TDC's philosophy.

[7]Limited evidence available to us suggests that building tenders are typically selected on the basis of long sentences, toughness, and the ability to control other inmates.

[8]This conclusion rests primarily on observations of inmate behavior (see note 4) and staff interviews. Virtually all respondents believed that inmates perceived a rise in their own status and power relative to that of their keepers.

[9]Although very difficult to document precisely, guard informants agreed that inmate responsiveness to work orders, as well as inmate productivity, became problematic as the trial and resultant court order became widely known.

[10]The TDC experienced only six major riots from 1973 to 1981.

Cases

Banning v. Looney, 348 U.S. 859 (1954).
Cooper v. Pate, 378 U.S. 546 (1964).
Monroe v. Pape, 365 U.S. 167 (1961).
Ruiz v. Estelle, 503 F.Supp. 1265 (S.D. Tex. 1980); 679 F2d 1115 (5th Cir. 1980);
    cert. denied, 103 S.Ct. 452 (1983); Modified on reh'g, 688 F2d 266 (5th Cir.
    1982); cert. denied, 103 S.Ct. 1438 (1983).

References

Alpert, Geoffrey P. (1977) "Collective Violence Behind Bars," in M. Riedel and P.A. Vales (eds.) *Treating the Offender: Problems and Issues.* New York: Praeger. (1980) *Legal Rights of Prisoners.* Lexington, MA: D.C. Heath.

Alpert, Geoffrey P. and C. Ronald Huff (1981) "Prisoners, the Law, and Public Policy: Planning for Legal Aid," 7 *New England Journal on Prison Law* 307.

American Correctional Association (1981) *Riots and Disturbances in Correctional Institutions.* College Park, MD: American Correctional Association.

Baker, Donald P., Randolph Blotky, Keith Clemens, and Michael Dillard (1973) "Judicial Intervention in Corrections: The California Experience — An Empirical Study," 20 *UCLA Law Review* 452.

Bowker, Lee H. (1982) *Corrections: The Science and the Art.* New York: Macmillan.

Bureau of Justice Statistics (1983) "Prisoners at Midyear 1983," *BJS Bulletin.* Washington, DC: U.S. Department of Justice, Bureau of Justice Statistics.

Calhoun, Emily (1977) "The Supreme Court and the Constitutional Rights of Prisoners: A Reappraisal," 4 *Hastings Constitutional Law Quarterly* 219.

Cohen, Fred (1981) "The Texas Prison Conditions Case: Ruiz v. Estelle," 17 *Criminal Law Bulletin* 252.

Corrections Magazine (1978) Volume 4, front cover.

Crouch, Ben M. (1977) "A Profile of the Typical Correctional Officer in the Eastham, Ellis, Ferguson, and Huntsville Units," *Technical Note #5 Research and Development Division.* Huntsville, TX: Texas Department of Corrections.

_____ (1980) "The Book vs. the Boot: Two Styles of Guarding in a Southern Prison," in Ben M. Crouch (ed.) *The Keepers: Prison Guards in Contemporary Corrections.* Springfield, IL: Charles C Thomas.

Crouch, Ben M. and James W. Marquart (1980) "On Becoming a Prison Guard," in Ben M. Crouch (ed.) *The Keepers: Prison Guards in Contemporary Corrections.* Springfield, IL: Charles C Thomas.

_____ (1981a) Field notes, interview with building captain, Eastham Unit.

_____ (1981b) Field notes, interview with correctional officer, Ferguson Unit.

Davies, James C. (1962) "Toward a Theory of Revolution," 27 *American Sociological Review* 5.

Duffee, David (1980) *Correctional Management: Change and Control in Correctional Organizations.* Reissued 1986 by Waveland Press, Inc. Prospect Heights, IL.

Garson, G. David (1972a) "The Disruption of Prison Administration: An Investigation of Alternative Theories of the Relationship Among Administrators, Reformers, and Involuntary Social Service Clients," 6 *Law and Society Review* 531.

_____ (1972b) "Force Versus Restraint in Prison Riots," 8 *Crime and Delinquency* 411.

Gettinger, Steve (1977) "Cruel and Unusual Prisons," 3 *Corrections Magazine* 3.

Gettinger, Steve and Kevin Krajick (1978) "Are 'Building Tenders' the Key to Control?" 4 *Corrections Magazine* 22.

Gurr, T. Robert (1970) *Why Men Rebel.* Princeton: Princeton University Press.

Haas, Kenneth C. and Anthony Champagne (1976) "The Impact of Johnson v. Avery on Prison Administration," 43 Tennessee Law Review 275.

Heaps, William (1970) Riots, U.S.A., 1765-1970. New York: Seabury Press.

Houston Chronicle (1983) "Violence Peaks at 9-year High," July 6, 1983.

Huff, C. Ronald (1983) "Prison Violence: Sociological and Public Policy Implications," (in Hebrew) 11 Crime and Social Deviance 65.

Huff, C. Ronald and Geoffrey P. Alpert (1982) "Organizational Compliance with Court-Ordered Reform," in Merry Morash (ed.) Implementing Criminal Justice Policies. Beverly Hills, CA: Sage Publications.

Jacobs, James B. (1977) "Macrosociology and Imprisonment," in David Greenberg (ed.) Corrections and Punishment. Beverly Hills, CA: Sage Publications.

Krajick, Kevin (1978) "They Keep You In, They Keep You Busy, and They Keep You From Getting Killed," 4 Corrections Magazine 4.

Levinson, Marc R. (1982) "Special Masters: Engineers of Court-Ordered Reform," 8 Corrections Magazine 7.

March, Ray (1978) Alabama Bound: Forty-Five Years Inside a Prison System. University, AL: The University of Alabama Press.

Marquart, James W. and Ben M. Crouch (1982) "Cooptation of the Kept: Maintaining Order in a Southern Prison,": Paper presented at the 1982 meeting of the American Society of Criminology, Toronto, Ontario, Canada.

Marx, Karl and Frederick Engels (1959) "Manifesto of the Communist Party," in L.S. Feuer (ed.) Marx and Engels: Basic Writings on Politics and Philosophy. Garden City, NY: Doubleday.

McKay, Robert B. (1983) "Prison Riots," in Sanford H. Kadish (ed.) Encyclopedia of Crime and Justice. New York: Free Press.

Nathan, Vincent M. (1979) "The Use of Masters in Institutional Reform Litigation," 10 The University of Toledo Law Review 419.

National Advisory Commission on Criminal Justice Standards and Goals (1976) Disorders and Terrorism. Washington, DC: Government Printing Office.

Note (1980) "Judicial Intervention and Organizational Theory: Changing Bureaucratic Behavior and Policy," 8 The Yale Law Journal 513.

Piven, Francis F. and Richard A. Cloward (1979) Poor People's Movements. New York: Random House.

Rudovsky, David, Alvin Bronstein, and Edward Koren (1983) The Rights of Prisoners. New York: Bantam Books.

Sylvester, Sawyer, John Reed and David Nelson (1977) Prison Homicide. New York: Spectrum Publications.

Tocqueville, Alexis de (1955) The Old Regime and the French Revolution. Garden City, NY: Doubleday.

Turner, William B. (1979) "When Prisoners Sue: A Study of Prisoners' Section 1983 Suits in the Federal Courts," 42 Harvard Law Review 610.

17

Litigation Can Be Therapeutic

Richard R. Korn

Soviet psychiatrists claim to have discovered certain forms of delusion not yet recognized by Western medicine. One of these is "litigation mania," in which a patient continually claims that his confinement is a violation of his civil rights. American psychiatry has generally rejected "litigation mania" as a diagnosis. But, in one case at least, psychiatric and correctional authorities had no problem with it at all. In prisoner Bobby Hardwick they found a patient who fitted the Soviet diagnosis perfectly.

On January 22, 1970, a Georgia psychiatrist found Hardwick, a newly admitted 39-year-old inmate serving a ten-year sentence for armed robbery, to be suffering from paranoid schizophrenia with hallucinations and delusions of persecution. Hardwick spent the next eight years being shuttled back and forth from solitary cells in prison to solitary rooms in mental hospitals. All the while he deluged authorities with complaints about his treatment. Although Hardwick's attacks on the Georgia penal system were purely literary—he presented no behavioral threat—the prison authorities finally lost patience with him, and in 1974 he was transferred from Reidsville

Source: *Corrections Magazine*, Vol. 7, No. 5 (October 1981), inside cover, 45-48.
Reprinted with the permission of the publisher.

prison to a unit for "incorrigibles and security risks" located in H-House of the Georgia Diagnostic and Classification Center (GDCC) at Jackson.

In setting forth his reasons for requesting Hardwick's removal, Reidsville Warden Joseph Hopper unwittingly paraphrased the essential elements of the "litigation mania" diagnosis: "He has written so many writs that it has taken an extra, separate file to hold his legal papers. He has continuously complained about mistreatment. Hardwick has chosen an antisocial path.... Therefore it is recommended that he be transferred to GDCC to participate in their behavior modification program in the hope that this will change his devious trend."

Hardwick's new location, a solitary confinement block, did not modify his litigious behavior. In August 1974 he filed suit in the U.S. District Court of Georgia, claiming several violations of his constitutional rights. Named as defendant in the suit was Dr. Allen Ault, who had participated in the design of the H-House program. Dr. Ault was, at the time the suit was filed, commissioner of the Department of Offender Rehabilitation.

Late in 1975 Judge Wilbur T. Owens, Jr. consolidated Hardwick's suit with 25 other cases which had been filed at Hardwick's instigation. The trial in the case of *Hardwick vs. Ault* was set for March 1977, at which point I was called in as an expert witness by the ACLU of Georgia. Given the relative positions and reputations of the two litigants, the outcome hardly seemed in doubt.

But on Jan. 12, 1978, Judge Owens shattered expectations. In a landmark decision, the judge ruled that the totality of conditions in H-House were in violation of the 8th and 14th Amendments. The word of a certified psychotic had prevailed over the diagnosis of his keepers. But something even more remarkable had happend. Throughout the lengthy preparation for the trial, the state's psychiatrists had continued to monitor Hardwick's mental condition. During the same period they also checked frequently on the mental health of his fellow litigants, who were not all mentally ill. After four years in solitary confinement in H-House, the condition of most of the other plaintiffs had deteriorated. But Hardwick, whose diagnosis of schizophrenia had predated his entry to H-House, was clearly getting better in a situation in which normal prisoners were getting worse. Each new report confirmed the trend. By 1978, at the moment of his victory, Hardwick was unmistakably sane. Today he is out of prison and running a successful business in the Southwest.

Under what conditions was Hardwick living during his four year struggle? In his decision, Judge Owens described life in H-House with numbing specificity: "Inmates are kept in their small individual cells almost all the time....The typical prisoner...is out of his cell only slightly over six hours per week. Prisoners...are constantly subject to severe security measures. In addition to being constantly under surveillance...they are strip searched for any movement out of H-2. During the search two correctional officers keep 'stun guns' trained on the prisoner. The prisoners are fed by the guards who deliver the food in carts while another guard watches with a stun gun. No guard ever goes alone down on the range in front of the prisoners. Almost all of the prison staff's communication with inmates occurs through the porthole in the top of the cell."

The "porthole in the top of the cell" is one of the stranger features of isolation in H-House. It allows prison officials to see and hear without being seen or heard. Prior to his confinement there, Hardwick had already been described as "hearing voices." In H-House, being watched by invisible onlookers and talked to by disembodied voices was part of the program. The porthole was reached by an overhead catwalk. Judge Owens described its use: "The catwalk allows guards to monitor constantly...and because [they] follow no set routine the surveillance through the hole in the ceiling...is always unexpected. The catwalk is used...for nearly all communications with prisoners in H-2. Thus the fate of an H-2 inmate is determined in large part by his conversations with people talking to him through a metal grate. Other than through this grate the H-House inmate has very little contact with other human beings."

But by far the most stressful impact of H-House was the sheer duration of the time spent there. "Punishment in H-House is disproportionate in the sense that it has no proportion with respect to time..." wrote Judge Owens. "Because the passage of time is in part a function of space and activity, time truly appears to slow down for the inmate in H-House. This slowing of time is made worse by the indefiniteness of the duration. Without hope or promise as to when the punishment will end, H-House inflicts considerable mental anguish. This anguish was described and testified to by almost everyone who had contact with H-House, including guards, prison counselors, and prison administrators."

Summarizing his assessment of conditions in H-House, Judge Owens concluded: "There can be little doubt that H-House constitutes punishment beyond the original, ordinary incarceration of inmates in the Georgia prison system....Long periods of lock-up in a confined space, limited contact with others, continued and unexpected surveillance and limited exercise eventually take a serious toll on the mental health of the inmates."

Judge Owens' decision was a stinging rebuke to the state's attempt to redefine traditional solitary confinement as a modern form of behav-

ioral treatment. But Hardwick's apparent recovery during the course
of his attempts to fight his confinement is an even more fundamental
affront to classical psychiatric theory. According to accepted therapeutic doctrine, a paranoid person ought not to be encouraged to
believe that his delusions of persecution are valid. Moreover, those
who seek to help a paranoid person are supposed to help him realize
that his problems are internal rather than environmental, and that his
task is to change himself, not his circumstances.

As a former prison psychologist and director of treatment at the New
Jersey State Prison at Trenton (1952-1955) I at one time accepted these
principles, without question. And I saw it as my professional responsibility to do what I could to dissuade inmates from evading responsibility by merely blaming their environment. One of my duties at the
state prison was to monitor the condition of inmates confined to indefinite administrative segregation. As I watched inmate after inmate
succumb to the rigors of unrelieved solitary confinement, I described
with clinical detachment their struggles to preserve their sanity by
fighting back. One of my observations was to be strikingly appropriate
to Hardwick 30 years later:

> At the outset the segregated offender typically occupies himself
> with an ambitious program of protest. Intensive legal activity fre-
> quently characterizes this period; the offender busies himself with
> the search for an effective way to combine the expression of his
> resentment with a method of obtaining his release. Following the
> failure of legal appeals, there are attempts to deluge all manner of
> public officials with a lengthy recital of complaints. As a matter of
> sound correctional administration, these complaints should be fully
> and routinely investigated. In addition to providing a precaution
> against actual injustice, the investigation of unfounded complaints
> serves a therapeutic purpose. Once again the inmate is provided a
> demonstration of the failure of his manipulative techniques.

What had not occurred to me, of course, was that indefinite solitary
confinement was in itself an injustice, made all the more intolerable by
the official belief or pretense that it was for the inmates' own good.

Why, then, did Hardwick not break down under it? One thing was
clear not only to me but to others who had observed and interviewed
him prior to the trial: Hardwick had recovered his wits even before his
legal success. Is it conceivable that it was his struggle, rather than its
positive outcome, that was decisive? Or is it possible that Hardwick
was never psychotic in the first place?

As an expert witness I was privy to Hardwick's psychiatric reports,
which became part of the public record of the trial. I have obtained his
permission to reproduce relevant portions of the reports here.
Hardwick was first seen by a psychiatrist, Dr. Julius Ehik, in January

1970, shortly after his admission as a new inmate. Dr. Ehik reported: "This inmate...will not eat and has not eaten anything for the past three days. He also will not let anybody come close to him and will beg not to be touched. He thinks that he is in the service. He has conversations with a Captain Whitehead who is, according to him, telling him things to do, and keeps him locked up. He stated that he won't eat because he had been told that the food is poison, and that they were trying to get rid of him....From my brief contact with this prisoner, it would appear to me that he is acutely psychotic, that he is paranoid and is hallucinating."

Hardwick's next psychiatric examination took place in September 1974, soon after he had been transferred to H-House. The report, made by another psychiatrist, Dr. J.F. Casey, reflects an unmistakeable concern and sensitivity: "He seems to be hallucinating at the time of the interview. From time to time he would turn his head as if listening to someone, and then when he was asked about this would be very suspicious and insisted that I had heard the same thing that he had heard....He tells at great length of this conspiracy which is not definitely organized other than that it is against him primarily because he is a highly intelligent person and since he is black 'they' whom he would never identify resent his being as intelligent as he is and are taking various steps to suppress him. These steps include his being sent out of the Army and then arrested and having been sent to prison in order to put him away so that he couldn't participate in the take-over of the world which he insists is going to occur in any event....During the interview he tells about hidden microphones in the examining room with us.

"This is a 30-year-old black inmate who is obviously quite hallucinated and delusional and apparently has been for some time. I feel he is suffering from schizophrenia of a paranoid type with relatively little deterioration."

At no point in his assessment does the psychiatrist note the fact that Hardwick is living in a solitary confinement cell where his contact with other human beings is largely limited to communication with their disembodied voices. This omission is consistent with the conventional view that paranoid schizophrenia can best be understood as an internal problem. This same lack of reference to the patient's environment characterizes the psychiatric reports about Hardwick's fellow inmates in H-House. The second point to be stressed is this: While the condition of most of his colleagues was deteriorating, Hardwick's was apparently improving.

Hardwick next saw Dr. Casey two years later, in March 1976. By this time Hardwick was deeply involved in organizing his massive class action suit. He had enlisted the aid of the ACLU of Georgia, and he was in frequent contact with some of the most prestigious attorneys in the state. And he had earned a respect approaching awe by his fellow sufferers. When speaking to him or about him, they rarely used his name. They called him "Lawyer."

In his report of his 1976 interview, Dr. Casey noted an impressive change in Hardwick: "This inmate appears considerably improved from a mental point of view over what he was when last seen. He seems to have fewer ideas of a typical paranoid nature. Some are still with him but not nearly to the extent they were present on the previous exam....Emotionally he is certainly not depressed. He doesn't appear flattened emotionally as when last seen....At the present time he denies any actual hallucinations, which is in some contrast to the previous time when he didn't actually admit it but his nonverbal communication certainly would intimate so. When informed that he thought previously he had had hidden mikes in the room he was quite doubtful and couldn't remember this and it was obvious that he didn't believe it."

By the time I interviewed Hardwick prior to the trial in 1977, a year after his last examination, there was no evidence whatever of any symptomatology. He was resilient, cheerful, without hostility, and his conversation crackled with wit and good humor. When I first saw him I had not yet read his psychiatric reports. When I saw them I was amazed. My impression of his excellent mental health was shared by all those who worked with him and by those who watched and heard his testimony. One reporter, Marcia Kunstel, wrote: "After watching Bobby Hardwick testify in a confident, contained manner before a federal judge, it was hard to believe a psychiatrist characterized him as 'delusional, schizophrenic, paranoid and definitely psychotic' only a few years ago."

Conventional psychiatric theory does not have an explanation for Hardwick. According to classical psychiatric doctrine, paranoids remain ill by continuing to blame their environment for their troubles. Their only hope for improvement is to begin to realize that their problems are internal. In a situation well calculated to drive sane people mad, Hardwick had, to all intents and purposes, made himself well. He accomplished this feat in a way that violated every canon of psychiatric treatment. Instead of permitting people to persuade him that his beliefs were delusional, he had succeeded in persuading others that they were valid. This alone should have been enough to confirm and exacerbate his illness. Instead of submitting to his circumstances, he had attacked them. Worse, he had attacked them successfully, which according to accepted doctrine amounts to little more than shifting the burden of his madness onto the world.

Conventional psychiatric theory does have the beginning of an explanation for Hardwick's "symptomatic" improvement. The noted psychiatrist Silvano Arieti has written: "There are persons who, because of unusual circumstances...or because of their ability to organize, succeed in changing and manipulating their environment according to their bizarre wishes, and therefore have no need to develop *overt* paranoid symptoms. These are cases of 'acted out' or 'externalized' psychoses. For instance, people like Nero or Hitler were able to alter the environment in accordance with their wishes, no matter how bizarre these wishes were. As long as they were able to do so on a realistic level, they had no need to become psychotic in a clinical or legal sense."

Dr. Arieti's concept presents some internal difficulties. Is an idea still "bizarre" after many people finally come to believe it? Was Hardwick's wish to change his circumstances irrational? His psychiatrists thought so, but many other rational people, including a federal judge, did not agree. These people found H-House rather bizarre. They found it hard to accept a treatment program which somehow managed to fulfill almost every condition of paranoia itself, including conversations with invisible people who appeared and disappeared unexpectedly.

Some years ago the late psychiatrist J.L. Moreno, creator of psychodrama and sociometry, recalled his frustrating work as a young resident in the disturbed wards of the main mental hospital in Vienna. One of Moreno's patients was a former bank clerk who was convinced that he was actually a general being held in captivity as a prisoner of war. Another was an elderly lady who was positive that the ragged doll she constantly clutched to herself was actually her infant.

After spending his day in the wards, fruitlessly trying to convince his patients to give up their delusions, Moreno would gratefully descend into the streets of Vienna. On his way home he would pass young boys playing at being soldiers, and young girls pushing their toy baby carriages and talking with great seriousness about their "children." Moreno then posed for himself a question: Why are the adult fantasists in the hospital wards thought to be insane, while children acting out fantasies in the street are considered normal? And why were the children willing and able to put their fantasies aside when they returned home, while the adults in the wards were not?

Moreno pushed his questioning one step further. Why, he asked, do people, adults and children alike, need to have fantasies in the first place? Why isn't "reality" enough? His answer to his first question provided a clue to the second. Peole obviously need to relieve themselves with dreams and fantasies when their reality frustrates their inner needs, or violates their inner sense of who they actually are and need to be. Later studies of dream deprivation would confirm Moreno's insight. Waking up experimental subjects when they are about to start dreaming is seriously disturbing. It follows that the ability to indulge in dreams and fantasies, and to believe in them at some level, is essential for coping with stresses of a refractory and frustrating reality. In effect, to be denied the relief and release of dreaming is to be crippled in one's ability to cope on any level.

An indulgent adult world gives children permission to act out their fantasies in play. Children grant each other's fantasies the essential element of credibility by confirming them in vivid and convincing role-playing. A little boy who needs to act out a fantasy of power can mobilize other children to confirm him as a "general" by taking the role of his soldiers. Having satisfied his inner need by expressing it in emotionally authentic action, the boy can relinquish it. He can content himself with playing ordinary soldier to another child's "general," or he can go back to his assigned role of little boy.

Unlike a child, an unhappy adult is not given permission to suspend an accepted but frustrating social identity by acting out his fantasies in the real world. Nor, unless he is a Hitler or a Nero, will he ordinarily find other adults who are willing to confirm his secret self by acting out the counterpart roles of his fantasy with him.

The tragedy of conventional mental hospital treatment is that it intensifies the process that compelled the individual to take on his compensatory fantasy role in the first place. It was to counteract a treatment process that essentially mimicked the disease that Moreno created his system of psychodramatic therapy. Recognizing the metaphorical validity of the patient's fantasies, he also understood that one can relinquish an essential wish only after one has fulfilled it on some psychologically authentic level. So he encouraged his clients to confirm each other's aspirational identities as children do, in dramatic action.

Inmates of prisons and mental hospitals have been drastically "disconfirmed" by their social environments. Like children, their identities are subject to the definitions of others; they are in the clutch of circumstances they cannot control. They have few good choices. To accept their dependency is to accept their neutralization as self-directing human beings. To act out against their circumstances, to try to transform them or to escape from them, is to risk further restriction and neutralization.

All of these conditions are exacerbated in indefinite solitary confinement. There the choices are even more bleak. Inmates can resist by violence. They can retreat into a world of fantasy from which they may not emerge. They can sink into vegetative apathy, or permit themselves to be tranquilized into a state of mindlessness. They can try to escape by self-destruction. The high rates of assault, self-inflicted injury, suicide and psychosis testify to the prevalence of these doomed attempts to transcend the horrors of immobility, isolation and sensory and social deprivation in prolonged solitary confinement.

Litigation offers a striking promise of a better alternative. By persuading outsiders to acknowledge their terrible circumstances, prisoners can obtain confirmation that their difficulties are not merely "internal." By enlisting the aid of these outsiders—attorneys, expert witnesses, judges—they can participate in an attempt to change their circumstances, or to procure their release from them. Whether they are successful or not, the activity of litigation offers an alternative to self-destructive acceptance of a pathological environment, or equally self-destructive violence against it.

There may well be other advantages. Litigation changes the offender's relationship to the law. As a predator, the offender looked at the law and its agents as enemies to be defied or evaded. By definition, the successful criminal is a successful law-breaker. In turning to litigation as his last hope, the offender must enlist the law as his friend. If he is serious, he must take the role of the law, and he must look at himself and his pleadings with a critical eye for their defects. In effect, he must, for perhaps the first time, look at himself as a judge and jury might look at him. The chance exists that he may internalize these attitudes as criteria for his future conduct.

Psychotic or not, Hardwick seems to have succeeded in doing all these things. If he was truly delusional, he was delusional only when he was unable to do anything about his situation in fact. One may not need to feel that he must save the whole world if he can save at least his part of it. The moment Hardwick began to use the law on his behalf, and on behalf of his fellow prisoners, his grander projects were less and less necessary or useful. What was useful now were his powers of observation, his rationality, his ability to persuade. These abilities are pre-eminently the abilities of a sane human being.

Hardwick was, of course, an exception to the rule. As a result of Judge Owens' court order, H-House was closed and its inmates dispersed in the general prison population. It is now Georgia's death row, and is the subject of a new inmate/ACLU lawsuit charging that confinement there constitutes cruel and unusual punishment.

Part IV

The Rehabilitation Debate
What Works?

Introduction

For most of the past 200 years, the dominant purposes of corrections have gradually moved from a strictly punitive philosophy toward the ideal of rehabilitation. This rehabilitative ideal—the belief that criminal offenders can be reformed and taught to live socially productive, crime-free lives—became a major goal of correctional policy in the 1950s and 1960s. By the early 1970s, however, the public's increasing fear of crime and widespread perceptions that both crime rates and recidivism rates were rising led many to view rehabilitation programs as well-intentioned, but misguided efforts that simply do not work.

The critics of rehabilitation were bolstered by Robert Martinson's 1974 article in *The Public Interest*, "What Works?—Questions and Answers About Prison Reform." In that highly publicized piece and in a subsequent book, *The Effectiveness of Correctional Treatment*, Martinson and his colleagues Douglas Lipton and Judith Wilks assembled evidence pointing to the conclusion that "nothing or almost nothing works" in criminal rehabilitation. Martinson and his colleagues reviewed over 200 evaluative studies of such correctional treatment programs as vocational training, education programs, work opportunities, group counseling, individual counseling, and psychotherapy. All of the studies had been done between 1945 and 1967, and Martinson's review convinced him that "with few and isolated exceptions, the rehabilitative efforts that have been reported so far have had no appreciable effect on recidivism."

Martinson's conclusions were highly compatible with the "get tough" approach to the crime problem increasingly embraced by Americans and their elected representatives. Indeed, the contention that "nothing works" is still widely promulgated by many federal and state criminal justice officials. However, a growing number of correctional scholars and practitioners have come forward to refute the assertion that treatment programs are ineffective. The defenders of rehabilitation argue that prison treatment programs rarely have been given a fair and fully-funded opportunity to produce positive results. The cost of prison rehabilitation projects amounts to less than five percent of the billions of dollars spent annually on state and federal prison operations. The vast majority of correctional employees do nothing in the way of treatment; they merely guard prisoners. When supported by reasonable budgets and carried out by well-trained staff, treatment efforts, say the supports of rehabilitation, will prove successful in reforming criminal behavior. Up to now, it is asserted, many correctional officials have mastered the rhetoric of rehabilitation programs while actually using such programs to suppress inmate dissent and maintain the punitive practices of the past.

The advocates of rehabilitation also have criticized Martinson's methods of evaluating the findings of earlier correctional treatment studies. For example, Martinson has been chastised for limiting his review to studies done in the 1945 to 1967 time period, thereby ignoring the more optimistic findings of studies that were done in the 1967-1974 time period. In an influential 1975 article, "Martinson Revisited," published in the *Journal of Research in Crime and Delinquency*, Ted Palmer criticized Martinson for refusing to judge a treatment program as successful unless it had generated almost exclusively positive results. Palmer's reassessment of the studies included in the Martinson survey indicated that nearly half of them had yielded at least "partly positive results." According to Palmer, the effectiveness of correctional treatment depends upon a variety of factors, including the type of offender, the type of rehabilitation program, and the skills brought to the task by staff members. Thus, although no single method of treatment will benefit all offenders, some offenders will respond positively to some types of treatment programs.

In the late 1970s, Martinson published several articles [See, for example, "Save Parole Jurisdiction" in Part V of this book] recognizing that certain correctional programs had demonstrated measurable success in curbing recidivism rates. Today, the debate over the efficacy of rehabilitation is by no means finished. But there seems to be an emerging consensus among scholars that we should redirect our efforts toward developing better research methods that may help us discover which, if any treatment strategies will work best for which types of offenders and under what conditions. For that matter, it has been pointed out— perhaps most eloquently in Francis Cullen and Karen Gilbert's book, *Reaffirming Rehabilitation*—that there are other reasons why it would be a mistake to abandon rehabilitation as a major goal of our correctional system. Most importantly, even if rehabilitation programs do not change most criminals into model citizens, the ideal of rehabilitation can serve as a valuable resource for those who are striving to improve conditions and increase humanitarianism in America's prisons.

The possibility that "[c]orrectional intervention can operate in a framework of humane interaction" is among the ideas discussed by Ted Palmer in "The 'Effectiveness' Issue Today: An Overview." Palmer shows that the combatants who took extreme positions for and against correctional treatment programs in the 1960s and 1970s have been replaced by two somewhat more moderate "camps." On the one hand, a relatively "sanguine" camp of scholars believes that many treatment efforts have proved successful with various offender populations and thus should be refined and expanded. On the other hand, a more "skeptical" camp of researchers contends that although a small number of treatment projects may have achieved slight reductions of recidivism, rehabilitation programs have failed to demonstrate enough potency to deserve to play a major role in the future of corrections.

The next two essays in Part IV represent positions taken by the "sanguine" and "skeptical" camps respectively. Embracing an optimistic outlook, Paul Gendreau and Robert Ross argue that there no longer can be any serious doubt that many criminal offenders are capable of learning new attitudes and acquiring new behaviors. They believe that the most important questions still to be answered in the rehabilitation debate concern why some programs work and some do not. Their analysis of how successful treatment programs differ from unsuccessful programs contains valuable advice for anyone interested in working with juvenile or adult offenders.

In the first edition of his highly influential 1975 book, *Thinking About*

Crime, political scientist James Q. Wilson took a very pessimistic view of correctional rehabilitation programs:

> It requires not merely optimistic but heroic assumptions about the nature of man to lead one to suppose that a person, finally sentenced after (in most cases) many brushes with the law, and having devoted a good part of his youth and young adulthood to misbehavior of every sort, should, by either the solemnity of prison or the skillfulness of a counselor, come to see the error of his ways and to experience a transformation of his character (p. 190).

By 1980, Wilson, though not ready to jump on the rehabilitation bandwagon, was willing to acknowledge the possibility that certain offenders ("amenables") may become less criminal in response to certain rehabilitation programs. In "What Works?" Revisited: New Findings on Criminal Rehabilitation," reprinted from the Fall 1980 issue of *The Public Interest*, Wilson also points out that some treatment projects may contribute to an increase in law-breaking among certain offenders ("non-amenables"). The rehabilitation debate, he cautions, is more complex than earlier commentators may have realized, and no clear answers can be expected until researchers utilize more sensitive and realistic measures of the success or failure of treatment programs.

This is just what Dale K. Sechrest does in our next selection, "Prison 'Boot Camps' Do Not Measure Up." This article takes a close look at a correctional program that has been widely publicized as a way to respond to the needs of young offenders. Prison "boot camps," technically called "shock incarceration," have been praised as cost-effective and successful alternatives to other punishments, especially by politicians and media representatives who subscribe to the "get tough" ideology of criminal justice. Students of correctional history, however, are well aware that the "boot camp" bandwagon may turn out to be an example of the so-called "panacea phenomenon"—the tendency to embrace and exaggerate the effectiveness of simplistic, "cure-all" approaches to correctional rehabilitation that do not prove to be especially effective upon closer examination.

In his 1982 book, *Scared Straight and the Panacea Phenomenon*, James Finckenauer skillfully debunked the dramatic and exaggerated claims of success for "Scared Straight" or "juvenile awareness" programs in which juvenile offenders are brought to a prison where they meet with hardened, long-term prisoners who tell them prison horror stories and counsel them to lead a "straight" life. While such programs may be helpful for some youngsters (for example, those who do not already have an extensive history of delinquency) as part of a larger treatment effort, there is no evidence that serious young offenders can be turned around simply by "Scared Straight" or similar short-term programs. Will prison boot camps prove to be more successful than previous efforts to rehabilitate young offenders? According to Professor Sechrest, the answer almost certainly is "no." He examines some of the early evaluations of these shock incarceration programs and finds no evidence that they constitute a major breakthrough in correctional rehabilitation. At most, he concludes, boot camps may be useful for some types of offenders and thus should be viewed as "another of many tools for use in helping selected offenders."

The two remaining contributions to our discussion of the role of rehabilitation in American corrections have been authored by two men who recently retired from the bench after distinguished careers as federal judges. First, we are pleased to publish David L. Bazelon's thought-provoking address to the 1972 Conference of the American Association of Correctional Psychologists. In this piece, Judge Bazelon, who served as Chief Judge of the United States Court of Appeals for the District of Columbia from 1962 through 1978, poses a question that still has not been satisfactorily resolved: "Have we, perhaps, been focusing our attention on the wrong part of the problem—on the offender and his mental condition instead of on the [social] conditions that produced him?" Second, Warren E. Burger, who retired as Chief Justice of the United States Supreme Court in 1986, made the sorry state of the nation's prisons the subject of his commencement address to Pace University's Class of 1983. As readers will quickly realize, the former Chief Justice presents a persuasive, if empirically unsupported, case that substantially improved prison programs that emphasize vocational training and meaningful work experiences could salvage a good many prisoners from a life of crime.

18

The "Effectiveness" Issue Today
An Overview
Ted Palmer

In 1974, a wide-ranging debate regarding the effectiveness of rehabilitation was launched by Robert Martinson's assertion that nothing
or almost nothing works. [18] Since then, rebuttals and counter-
rebuttals have been exchanged and, in the process, some light has been
shed though considerable heat and haze remain. This process has been
difficult but necessary; and, though "sides" are still sharply drawn,
the justice system may soon reap some benefits from the exchange.
What, then, is the current status of this debate, and what are its
emerging trends?

The overview that follows derives primarily from several major
works conducted during 1966-1980. Chief among these are reviews and
evaluations by: Adams; Bailey; Empey; Gendreau and Ross; Greenberg;
Lipton, Martinson, and Wilks (LMW); Martinson; the National
Academy of Sciences Panel; Palmer; Romig; Wilson; Wright and Dixon.
[1; 3; 6; 7; 10; 14; 18; 20; 21; 23; 24; 26; 27] These efforts focused on
experimental studies of juvenile and adult offenders in institutional as

Source: *Federal Probation,* Vol. 47, No. 2 (June 1983), 3-10.

well as community settings. Each such category of offender and setting was well-represented in the studies reviewed, as were the major, traditional, rehabilitation methods (individual and group counseling; vocational and educational training; etc.); other, less common interventions were also included. Most such methods were implemented under non-voluntary conditions and—in the case of institutional programs—in an indeterminate-sentence context. Though the studies which were reviewed related to minor as well as serious or multiple offenders, the present overview will emphasize the implications of those reviews for the latter individuals. Throughout, the central question will be: Does rehabilitation work?

To address this question we will focus on programs that were judged successful or unsuccessful because—whatever else they did or did not accomplish with their target group—they either did or did not reduce recidivism. Use of recidivism is consistent with our view that the ultimate goal of rehabilitation is increased public protection. Clearly, rehabilitation efforts may also produce successful or desireable outcomes with respect to attitude-change, skill development, and various aspects of community adjustment, and these as well as other outcomes often do—but often do not—relate to recidivism. Nevertheless, for present purposes, the central criterion of success or effectiveness will be the reduction of illegal behavior—arrests, convictions, and related actions. This criterion was also used in the reviews mentioned above.

As discussed in this overview, rehabilitation or habilitation includes a wide range of interventions whose principal as well as ultimate goal is the increased protection of society. This, the *socially centered* goal of rehabilitation, is achieved when the offender's behavior is modified so that it conforms to the law. It is promoted but not in itself achieved by modifying given attitudes, by strengthening the offender as an individual, by reducing various external pressures and increasing given supports or opportunities, and/or by helping him or her become more satisfied and self-fulfilled within the context of society's values. Attitude-change, increased coping ability, etc., comprise the secondary or *offender-centered* goal of rehabilitation. Though this goal has absolute value in itself, it is—from the perspective of the overall justice system and this system's function in society—chiefly a "means" to the socially centered "end" of public protection. [20]

Before proceeding, let us briefly indicate what we mean by the phrase "rehabilitation program or approach." The following is not a formal, exhaustive identification of rehabilitation or habilitation; however, for present purposes, it will suffice.

The primary and secondary goals of rehabilitation are achieved by focusing on such factors and conditions as the offender's present adjustment techniques, his interests and skills, his limitations, and/or his life-circumstances, in ways that affect his future behavior and adjustment. Rehabilitation efforts are thus focused on particular factors or conditions and are directed toward particular future events. Insofar as they involve specific components or inputs (e.g., counseling or skill-development) that are organized, interrelated, and otherwise planned so as to generate changes in those factors and conditions (e.g., skills or life-circumstances) that may in turn help generate the desired future events, those efforts can be called rehabilitation programs or approaches. Such efforts—"interventions"—may involve what has been called treatment, external control, or both. Under some conditions, what has been called punishment may be considered an adjunct approach to rehabilitation.[1] However, methods such as electroshock treatment, psycho-surgery, etc., are not included under rehabilitation despite the factors or conditions on which they may focus and despite the specific effects—e.g., reduced illegal behavior—they may produce or be designed to produce.[2]

We now turn to the overview of "effectiveness."

Current Status of "Effectiveness"

Martinson's conclusion that "nothing works," which was widely accepted during the middle and later 1970's, is increasingly seen as a faulty synthesis of the findings from recidivism studies previously described by Lipton, Martinson, and Wilks. [14, 18] Palmer's critique of Martinson's method of synthesizing those findings showed that the latter's conclusion was valid only in the following sense: No single, broadly categorized treatment *method*, e.g., group counseling or vocational training (each of which, of course, has many variations[3]), is guaranteed to reduce the recidivism of its target group. [21] The critique ("Martinson Revisited") showed that several group counseling *programs* (in effect, variations or types of group counseling) did reduce recidivism either for the target group as a whole or for various subgroups within the total target group. This was observed in high-quality and acceptable-quality research studies alike. Because of this and subsequent critiques, Martinson, in 1978 and 1979 explicitly repudiated his highly pessimistic conclusion that nothing or almost nothing works. Instead, he recognized the difference between evaluative statements concerning *individual* programs and those relating to *groups* of programs, i.e., broadly categorized methods. [2; 8; 17; 20]

Though extreme pessimism no longer prevails regarding the effectiveness of rehabilitation or habilitation programs, the pendulum is by no means swinging rapidly toward the opposite extreme. Nor is it even approaching the rather optimistic position that *most* treatment efforts (broadly categorized or not) have substantially reduced recidivism with many or perhaps most offenders, even in certain settings only (e.g., institutions). Moreover, what might be considered today's officially sanctioned position—that taken by the National Academy of Sciences in 1979—is very guarded: No single correctional program (and, therefore, no broadly categorized method) has been unequivocally proven to reduce the recidivism of its target group; that is, using very strict standards of evidence, none has been shown to work beyond almost all doubt. At any rate, none can be guaranteed to work. [24]

Despite its extreme scientific caution and stringent methodological standards, the NAS Panel indicated the following (these views were based on what it acknowledged as the "suggestions...concerning successful rehabilitative efforts" that were reported by LMW, and partly on the above and subsequent critiques):

1. A few approaches may perhaps be working for some subgroups within the total target group; however, the quality and especially quantity of evidence do not allow for definite conclusions regarding the subgroup-success of these approaches.

2. Though no specific approaches have been proven to work, neither have they been disproven; instead, it is simply unclear which approaches have and have not been "given a fair trial." [24]

3. Many programs might have proven effective if they had been better implemented, if they had operated more intensively (i.e., had more treatment-input per client), etc.

In sum, the NAS Panel's position was very guarded and carefully qualified, but contained some glimmers of hope. In 1981, the Panel reaffirmed its position and further discussed these glimmers. [15]

The Panel's marked caution seemed to closely parallel the position taken by Empey in 1978, both as to the "inconclusive" nature of most research studies and the extreme difficulty of scientifically sorting-out precisely what works. [6] (That is, sorting-out is difficult even when good-quality research designs exist and certainly when program operations are only sketchily described.) Yet Empey was less restrictive than the Panel in one respect. He apparently did not believe that the results from all research studies which, methodologically, had been somewhat less than flawless but which were still relatively strong, should be discounted as a basis for correctional policy recommendations. Rather than insist that the results from any given study be demonstrated with almost absolute certainty, e.g., beyond the shadow of a doubt, he seemed to accept what amounted to a preponderance-of-evidence standard in this regard. As a result, he believed that some programs, though probably not many, *had* been adequately shown to be successful with serious offenders; at least, they seemed promising enough to have positive policy implications.

Beyond this, Empey—like the NAS Panel after him—believed that some programs might have produced better results if they had been directed, not at the full range of offenders, but at certain subgroups only. This view reflected the already existing "differential intervention" position, summarized below.

Several researchers and scholars—chiefly Palmer and Warren; Romig; Gendreau and Ross—have expressed a more sanguine view than that offered by the NAS Panel, by Greenberg, and, more recently, by Conrad [4; 7; 10; 23; 24; 25]. To be sure, these individuals, like the Panel and Conrad, believe that *much* criminal justice research has been mediocre and that *most* rehabilitation efforts have probably been unsuccessful thus far, relative to their overall target group. Nevertheless, they believe that many programs, often well-researched programs by *LMW*'s detailed standards and those of others, have been shown to work with specified offenders (subgroups) under specific conditions. Their view—with the partial exception of Romig's—is generally known as the differential intervention (DI) position.[4],[5] This view, which mainly grew from the early efforts of Warren, et al., in California's Community Treatment Project [25] goes beyond another well-known view—that which focuses on "amenability" alone.

In contrast to DI (see below), what might be termed the basic treatment-amenability (BTA) position only minimally distinguishes among types of offenders. The BTA position generally asserts that (1) certain offenders (e.g., the "bright, verbal, and anxious") will respond to many treatment approaches, presumably under most conditions or settings, and (2) most remaining offenders will respond to few if any approaches, again, regardless of conditions or settings. In contrast, the differential intervention view suggests that some offenders (BTA's amenables included) will respond positively to given approaches under very similar conditions; other combinations of offender, approach, setting—and resulting outcome—are also implied. Finally, DI also suggests that many offenders who in the BTA view are generally described as nonamenables may in fact respond positively to certain approaches under particular conditions, e.g., close structuring within institutional settings. [7; 20; 25]

> In short, overly simplified, DI asserts that certain categories of offenders (e.g., the Conflicted) but not others (e.g., the Power Oriented) will respond positively to certain approaches only, at least under specified conditions—and that the opposite may occur in response to other approaches or conditions. There are no all-around amenables and nonamenables, even though some individuals do usually perform better than others.

Thus, compared with BTA, the DI view is both more and less "optimistic" about so-called amenables; it is more optimistic about offenders who are often considered non-amenables, as well.

The "basic treatment amenability" and "differential intervention" positions have both been supported by Glaser, Adams, and others. [1; 8] The *amenability* view has, in addition, recently been supported by Wilson, a long-time critic of rehabilitation who also accepts the NAS Panel's overall caution regarding the validity of research findings to date. [26] All in all, there is increasing agreement among researchers, academicians, and practitioners as to which offenders are most likely to respond positively to standard—and, to a lesser extent, more specialized—rehabilitation approaches. *DI* has further been supported by Jesness, Hunt, Quay and Parsons, Megargee, et al., Wright and Dixon, and others. [11; 12; 13; 19; 22; 27] By 1979, Martinson himself was essentially supporting differential intervention:

> ...no treatment program now used in criminal justice is inherently either substantially helpful or harmful. The critical fact seems to be the *conditions* under which the program is delivered. For example, our results indicate that a widely-used program, such as formal education, is detrimental when given to juvenile sentenced offenders in a group home, but is beneficial (decreases reprocessing rates) when given to juveniles in juvenile prisons. Such startling results are found again and again in our [recent] study for treatment programs as diverse as individual psychotherapy, group counseling, intensive supervision, and what we have called "individual/help" (aid, advice, counseling). [17]

Finally, as indicated, both Empey and the Panel believe there may be something to this view.

In sum, both the BTA and DI positions have received moderate but clearly growing support within the justice system community; quantitatively, this applies to their empirical support as well. Nevertheless, as the Panel indicated, this evidence—while suggestive—is neither overwhelming nor entirely consistent.[9; 24]

Whether *many* programs or only a *small percentage* of programs have reduced recidivism is unclear. (Here, it makes little difference whether numbers or percentages are considered. However, by "many" we mean at least 30% of the sample-of-programs reviewed by such authors as *LMW*, Bailey, and Adams, respectively—recognizing that many programs were included in more than one such sample.) The many-programs position is found not just among reviewers who have questioned the effectiveness of rehabilitation efforts. The small-percentage view—with no specific percentage or percentage-range having been stated—is that implied by the Panel, by Empey, and by Greenberg.[7] Though the truth (objective reality) may well lie between these positions, the available evidence favors the former—assuming that "small" means less than 15 percent. More specifically, direct

counts (Bailey's included, e.g., for "experimental studies") suggest that
—conservatively—at least 20-25 percent of all experimental
programs reviewed have reduced recidivism for their total target
groups, while at least an additional 10-15 percent have done so for one
or more subgroups only. [1; 3; 20; 21] However, the exact percentages
may not be too important. What may matter in the long-run is whether
knowledge has been and can be gathered regarding the nature of (1)
those programs which work and (2) offenders whom those programs
apparently serve best. Such information could make it possible to
reproduce, improve, and more efficiently utilize those and similar
programs, and to discard whatever approaches seem to accomplish
little for the preponderance of their clients. In this way, the percentage
of successful programs could increase—whether from today's small or
more substantial level.

Long-range considerations aside, percentages—or at least terms
such as "most," "many," and "few"—have nevertheless played a
large and often confounding role in the effectiveness literature. For
instance, DI proponents believe that many individuals who consider
rehabilitation programs ineffective consistently overlook or ignore a
basic fact, whether or not recidivism is involved as the sole outcome-
measure: Although *most* programs have probably not worked well and
most research was probably not done well, this still leaves numerous
programs—i.e., from among the several hundred that were experi-
mentally studied—that did work well or moderately well, that were
researched satisfactorily, or both. Moreover, even if only 10 percent of
those several hundred were found to work, this would still leave
"many."

> In short, proponents feel that, by overlooking this fact, these ef-
> fectiveness-critics erroneously conclude or at least imply that since
> most programs—literally hundreds of programs—have not done
> well, rehabilitation efforts are obviously a failure and claims of
> effectiveness can be dismissed. Yet, in context, most is far from *all*.

DI proponents also believe that the dozens of programs mentioned
above have, collectively, provided not only very strong evidence that
something, in fact several things, work, but substantial converging
evidence as to *what* works for many offenders. Thus, given these
numerous positive-outcome programs, they consider it immaterial that
the *general* quality of research-to-date, and even program-implementa-
tion-to-date, may have been far from satisfactory, or perhaps even
lamentable. Meanwhile, however, effectiveness-critics suggest that DI
and perhaps BTA proponents greatly exaggerate the importance or
implications of what they, the critics, consider the *few* programs that
may possibly have worked. In any event, effectiveness critics usually
emphasize the atypical—and, by implication, the probably-difficult-to-

replicate—nature of these few. [4]

Apart from *how many* programs reduce recidivism, there is the question of how sizable that reduction is. *LMW* indicated that although some programs did indeed work, "corrections has not yet found satisfactory ways to reduce recidivism by significant amounts." [14] They neither defined significant nor presented a percentage-reduction figure. In addition, Martinson, in 1976, suggested that the reduction in question was probably trivial—meaning, 5-to-15 percent. [16] (In 1979, however, he stated: "...contrary to my previous position, some treatments *do* have appreciable effect on recidivism." [17] The NAS Panel was silent on this point, and, at present, only one percentage-reduction figure seems to exist. Focusing on all programs reported in *LMW* which reduced recidivism by at least 10 percent,[8] Palmer found an average reduction of 32 percent, the mean followup being 19 months; from a public-protection as well as cost perspective, even half this figure might often be considered important. [20] At any rate, since this is the only available figure, it is perhaps best to conclude that little is presently known regarding the average recidivism-reduction of positive-outcome studies—i.e., of *all* such studies (not just *LMW's*), and using varying definitions of success. Nevertheless, we suspect that the average reduction is substantial, e.g., over 20 percent. (The problem of defining successful programs is independent of the fact that *LMW* and Martinson may have made their estimates by combining successful and unsuccessful programs. At any rate, much depends on how success is operationally defined.)

The following question is closely related to the issue of percentage reduction in recidivism. For what percentage of the total target group, i.e., all offenders combined, have programs been "appropriate"? That is—in terms of the presently considered criterion—how often have they reduced recidivism? Here, no specific answer is known, and no average figure exists. Despite this absence of information, certain principles and related implications can be stated: Clearly, if a program and all its offender-subgroups are matched, the percentage reduction that may result will be larger than if unmatched, in this case "inappropriate," subgroups are included. To date, few programs or even major program components have been designed for defined offender subgroups only—more specifically, for only those individuals who would presumably or theoretically be matched to those particular approaches. However, where program/offender matching *has* been used—as in California Youth Authority institutions during the 1960's —it has shown considerable promise. [12] Of course, the ideal program would perhaps be one that is flexible enough or contains enough relevant components to successfully work with *all* major subgroups, even though that program might not quite maximize the percentage reduction in recidivism for all its offenders combined.

Such programs — in effect, near-panaceas — are nowhere on today's horizon; in fact, as indicated, the NAS Panel believes that no approach has been decisively shown to work even for *specific subgroups*. To be sure, the Panel's view with respect to demonstrated subgroup success is shared by neither differential intervention nor treatment-amenability proponents. Yet, despite this disagreement, both sets of individuals agree as to the existence of two major preconditions to effective rehabilitation or habilitation:

1. Single-modality approaches may be too narrowly focused to deal with the complex or multiple problems of most serious offenders. Instead, combinations-of-methods, e.g., vocational training *and* individual counseling, may be required.
2. Program input may have to be considerably greater ("More intense") than it has typically been — that is, if, as in (1) above, one wishes to generate lasting behavioral or other forms of change in most serious offenders.

These preconditions would apply regardless of the program components or specific input involved, provided, of course, that the latter do bear on the particular offenders' problems. As indicated, the Panel believed that — with improved research designs — many approaches might have been shown to work if they had met pre-conditions such as these.

This agreement among otherwise differing observers is important, particularly in light of their further agreement regarding the value (or, in the case of the Panel, the directly implied value) of matching offenders with programs. Together, these preconditions/principles suggest that concentrated efforts, and perhaps greater individualization than in the past, are needed in order to effect substantial change in serious offenders. These suggestions may comprise some of the more constructive or at least potentially constructive products of the effectiveness-debate thus far. At any rate, they would have policy implications regardless of *how many* programs have been successful, and exactly *how* successful they have been.

Finally, it should be added that differential intervention proponents largely agree among themselves on two additional points (here, the Panel took no public stand):

1. Some offenders probably require, not so much the standard rehabilitation inputs such as counseling, vocational training, etc. They may require — primarily, or perhaps on an equal footing — external controls, heavy structuring, and, with respect to community programs, considerable surveillance.

2. Staff characteristics and staff/offender matching are probably major factors in successfully implementing given approaches, at least for many offenders.

Though the evidence for these points is neither overwhelming (quantitatively) nor entirely consistent, it is by no means insubstantial and has grown considerably in the past several years. At any rate, the present author would add a different and perhaps broader point, one that focuses on likely preconditions to effective rehabilitation and applies across the board:

3. Fairness or fair treatment by the justice system, and humane interactions overall, can help create a tolerable, believable, sometimes supportive atmosphere for involvement and decision-making by offenders, especially but not exclusively in institutions.

Yet the following might be kept in mind. Fair treatment, etc., like just deserts and standardized dispositions by themselves, do not supply the direction, do not arouse the motivation, and do not provide the feedback or personal reward that probably must exist before realistic, satisfying decisions are generated and maintained by those individuals. That is, unlike many rehabilitation efforts, they do not address the specifics of the offenders' future—their concrete needs and opportunities within an often demanding environment. Nor do they address the often complex task of motivating or realistically helping them come to grips with that environment and, in many cases, with themselves. Thus, for many offenders, fairness and humane interactions without programmed assistance can be empty, in a sense blind, and programs without fairness can be futile, even pathetic. [20]

Review and Conclusion

An unsettled atmosphere exists regarding the effectiveness of rehabilitation or habilitation. Neither the global optimism of the 1960's nor the extreme pessimism of the middle and later 1970's seem justified, and neither view in fact prevails. Two slightly more moderate "camps" have replaced them, and a sizable but not entirely unbridged gap exists between these two.

Within the "skeptical" camp, some individuals believe it is clear— based on what they consider enough adequately conducted research— that relatively few rehabilitation programs work; moreover, those which work probably reduce recidivism by fairly small amounts. These individuals feel that rehabilitation, while not a total loss, therefore holds little promise and should be given a minor role. The remaining individuals within this group believe that *very little* is clear: Because of (1) minor or major research flaws in almost all studies, (2) poorly implemented programs, or (3) both, we don't really know whether given approaches do or do not—can or cannot—work, for their target groups as a whole. In this respect, rehabilitation has not been "given a fair trial." Though some approaches may possibly have worked for at least some offenders, the picture is again unclear because the findings are neither ironclad for any one study nor entirely consistent across various studies. These individuals believe that rehabilitation may well have promise—and a major role—but that no specific approaches can be recommended right now, at least not widely.

The more "sanguine" camp agrees that most programs have not been particularly effective thus far, certainly with their overall target groups. However, it believes that many programs and approaches have been shown—with reasonable scientific assurance—to work for specified portions of their target group. Some such proponents believe that certain offenders ("amenables") will respond positively to many approaches under a wide range of conditions and that many or most remaining offenders will probably respond to very few. Other proponents partly accept this view but believe that almost all offenders will respond positively, neutrally, or negatively depending on the *specific* approach and the external conditions or setting. The objective evidence, while neither vast in quantity nor flawless in quality, tends to support the latters' position while not negating the formers'. Both groups believe that successful programs often reduce recidivism by substantial amounts; they also feel that various approaches can be recommended right now for some offender-groups, even though these recommendations would reflect knowledge that is still largely "atheoretical" or at least not systematically and explicitly linked to a carefully defined set of underlying mechanisms and principles which have themselves been largely validated or seem quite plausible. Moreover, whether few or many programs have worked thus far (however those terms are defined), those and similar programs can perhaps be built upon and the remaining programs or approaches can eventually be discarded. In addition, whether recidivism reductions are considered moderately large or relatively small within typical programs to date, those reductions—like the percentage of successful programs itself—can probably be increased through program/ offender matching in future rehabilitation efforts.

The differences between the more skeptical and more sanguine individuals are complex and can only partly be traced to technical factors such as differing units of analysis,[9] differing standards of evidence, differing approaches to synthesizing as well as generalizing various findings from within and across studies, etc. They seem to be partly experiential and philosophical as well. For the most part, these differences — especially the latter two — will probably long remain, even though the former (the technically centered) will doubtlessly be narrowed quite a bit. Beyond this, disagreement exists as to when the results from a given study or group of studies should be used for various types and levels of policy recommendation, espeically if those results are positive. At a more basic yet related level, disagreement has clearly emerged as to what constitutes an adequately or well-researched study, one whose findings — whether positive or negative — can be considered valid and somewhat generalizable.

Given such differences and disagreements, it is significant that certain areas of agreement nonetheless exist. Basically, many "skeptics" and "sanguines" seem to believe that, to be effective with serious or multiple offenders, rehabilitation programs must be broader-based and more intensive than in the past. That is, given the often complex and interrelated problems, limitations, and attitudes of most such offenders, future programs will often have to use "multiple modality" approaches, e.g., simultaneous or successive combinations of vocational training, individual counseling, and perhaps others. Moreover, to achieve substantial rather than minimal impact, such approaches will have to be provided on a more intensive basis. One final area of agreement exists or is at least implied: program/offender matching. Here, a program's resources — multiple or otherwise, intensively provided or not — are organized and distributed according to the needs, interests, and limitations of the offender subgroups that are present; they are not applied to the *total* offender group in an indiscriminate, across-the-board manner. Taken together, these areas of agreement suggest that future programs should be more carefully adapted to the life circumstances and personal/interpersonal characteristics of offenders. This view has policy implications regardless of the exact content of those as well as present programs.

The truth regarding "effectiveness" may lie between the skeptical and more sanguine views — in fact, it probably does. Yet, however the effectiveness issue may finally devolve, the future of rehabilitation or habilitation programs will be neither dim nor dull; for one thing, not only direction but considerable room for improvement already exists. In any event, the above areas of agreement may reflect one important part of that truth, and future.

And regarding that future, three last points. First, rehabilitation need not be wedded to a medical model; it can proceed on the assumption that offenders, like nonoffenders, have positive potential which they can, should, and usually wish to use. Offenders need not be viewed as defective; and, like most nonoffenders, the vast majority are quite capable of recognizing the potenttal relevance to their lives of various forms of assistance, e.g., vocational training. To assume that offenders lack this ability or can seldom exercise or sustain it is to consider them defective or highly indifferent indeed—no less so, perhaps, than in a "medical model" itself. Along a related line, the fact that some or perhaps many offenders often play "treatment games" within or outside institutions does not mean that the majority do so or that they do so most of the time. [20]

Secondly, rehabilitation need not be linked to indeterminate sentencing; it can be implemented for—and by—offenders under conditions of determinate sentencing, with or without written contracts.

Finally, rehabilitation or correctional intervention need not demean its participants or interfere with given reform movements. It can disassociate itself from the more questionable or undesirable practices of the past and can be integrated with numerous justice system concerns and legitimate strivings of the present and future. Correctional intervention can operate in a framework of humane interaction and exchange despite the unavoidable need, outside and inside the system, for some degree of social control. By building on its past *successes*, be these "many" or "few," it can eventually regain its place and recognition (this time on more solid grounds) as one more useful tool—another option for society and offenders alike. [5; 20]

Footnotes

[1]Though punishment—temporary confinement, withdrawal-of-privileges, added restrictions, etc.—may well affect future behavior and adjustment, it is not part of a rehabilitation effort if used as an end in itself or as a means to such ends as revenge. However, if used in the context of focused, directed, and organized activities such as the above, e.g., if occasionally used to bolster given components by gaining the individual's attention, it may be considered part of rehabilitation. Nevertheless, the distinguishing features of most rehabilitation programs are those which have been designed to (1) change/modify the offender mainly through positive incentives and rewards, subtle and otherwise, or to (2) change/modify his life-circumstances and social opportunities by various pragmatic means.

[2]Perhaps arbitrarily, we are including only those methods whose "humaneness" is not open to serious, certainly widespread, question. At any rate, we are focusing on methods that basically utilize, develop, or redirect the powers and mechanisms of the individual's mind, not reduce, physically traumatize, disorganize, or devastate them, whether or not by mechanical means; the former may be called positive treatment programs (PTP's), the latter, drastic or traumatic rehabilitation approaches (DRA's). We are also excluding various methods—not infrequently used in other times and/or places—such as: mutilation or dismemberment; sterilization or castration; physical stigmatization (e.g., branding); public humiliation (e.g., via stock and pillory).

[3]That is, each *individual program* which is categorized as, say a "group counseling" *method* represents a variation within the method.

⁴These individuals believe that the conclusions which were drawn from several hundred studies conducted during 1945-1978 (mainly 1960-1975) were justified either in terms of a preponderance-of-evidence standard or, somewhat more strongly, beyond a reasonable doubt; at least, this applied to the conclusions from numerous studies that yielded positive results. In any event, they regard the latter conclusions as scientifically supportable even though the individual study designs were indeed far from flawless and the conclusions were therefore not justified with almost absolute certainty (as the NAS Panel would have preferred), i.e., virtually beyond the *shadow* of a doubt. Moreover, they believe it would be inappropriate and certainly peculiar to dismiss the similar or converging evidence regarding given program approaches and program components that was observed *across* many such positive-outcome studies — studies which they feel had defensible research designs and that involved at least adequate program implementation.

⁵Romig, while accepting this view, believes one should go beyond it — to "truly individualized treatment." [23] Thus, he supports but does not identify with DI per se. (It might be noted that individualization is a relative term.)

⁶Regarding the question of (1) which offenders are usually more amenable than others? and (2) which approaches seem to work for whom? BTA and/or DI proponents and supporters generally believe that results from various studies, i.e., *across* studies, are more consistent than inconsistent and show greater convergence than scatter. At any rate, they believe the consistency and convergence is substantial and revealing, and that it — in some respects, an expression of partial replication — partly compensates for less-than-flawless research designs. On this latter point, "the importance of scientific replication does not negate that of unusually impressive [e.g., virtually flawless] individual studies. However, the latter value can hardly substitute for the former..." Thus, for example, one unusually impressive study which, say, "focused on particular treatment inputs and involved specific operating conditions" would not necessarily be seen, by most DI proponents, as outweighing "several acceptable [or perhaps high-quality] studies which, collectively, may have covered a wider range of treatment inputs and operating conditions."[20]

⁷The reason for substantially differing estimates is somewhat unclear. At any rate, the many programs-estimates generally range from 30% to 55% and were obtained not just from reviews which did, but from others which did not, include the following among their sample-of programs: those for which positive results were reported either for the total target group or only for a major subgroup within the total group. When the latter were included, estimates were only slightly higher than when they were not. An explanation for the differing estimates may partly lie in the fact that the various reviewers seldom focused on an identical or even nearly identical set of programs. Beyond that, they used somewhat different definitions of success.

⁸Included, here, was 42% of *LMW's* pool of positive- and negative-outcome studies combined. These 42% comprised four-fifths of all programs which — based on a behavioral, not just a policy-related index such as revocation or discharge — had reduced recidivism by *any* amount, i.e., by 1% or more. (Again, programs that reduced recidivism by less than 10% — via, by 1-9% — were *not* considerred positive-outcome studies in this as well as in most reviews and

evaluations; if these programs *had* been included in the present analysis, the 32% recidivism-reduction figure would have dropped to 26%). Most of the 42% showed a statistically significant difference (.05 level) between the total target group and its control or comparison group. *LMW* had categorized many studies from within this 42% group as high-quality, not just adequate-quality. [14; 20]

[9]For example, an emphasis on either (1) broadly categorized treatment methods only (in effect, treatment-*types* or types of individual programs—as in Martinson, pre-1978). (2)'overall programs, i.e., individual programs, viewed as undifferentiated entities, (3) program components within the overall program, or (4) similar program components or common factors that are found *across* numerous overall programs.

References

[1] Adams, S. "Evaluative research in corrections: status and prospects." *Federal Probation, 38(1),* (1974): 14-21.

[2] Allinson, R. "Martinson attacks his own earlier work," In: *Criminal Justice Newsletter, 9,* (December, 1978): 4.

[3] Bailey, W. "Correctional outcome: An evaluation of 100 reports." *J. Criminal Law, Criminology, and Police Science.* 57, (1966): 153-160.

[4] Conrad, J. "Research and developments in corrections: A thought experiment," *Federal Probation, 46(2),* (1982): 66-69.

[5] Cullen, F. and Gilbert, K. *Reaffirming Rehabilitation.* Cincinnati, Ohio: Anderson Publishing Co. 1982.

[6] Empey, L. *American Delinquency: Its Meaning and Construction.* Homewood, Ill.: Dorsey, 1978.

[7] Gendreau, P. and Ross, R. *Effective Correctional Treatment.* Toronto: Butterworths. 1980.

[8] Glaser, D. "Achieving better questions: A half-century's progress in correctional research." *Federal Probation, 39,* (1975): 3-9.

[9] Gottfredson, M., Mitchell-Hersfeld, S., and Flanagan, T. "Another look at the effectiveness of parole supervision." *J. of Research in Crime and Delinquency, 19(2),* (1982): 277-298.

[10] Greenberg, D. "The correctional effects of corrections: A survey of evaluations." In: Greenberg, D. (ed.) *Corrections and Punishment.* Beverly Hills, Calif.: Sage Publications. 1977. 111-148.

[11] Hunt, D. *Matching Models in Education.* Toronto: Ontario Institute for Studies in Education. 1971.

[12] Jesness, C. *The Preston Typology Study: Final Report.* Sacramento: California Youth Authority. 1969.

[13] Johnson, S. "Differential classification and treatment: The case against us." *The Differential View, 11,* (1982): 7-18.

[14] Lipton, D., Martinson, R., and Wilks, J. *The Effectiveness of Correctional Treatment: A Survey of Treatment Evaluation Studies.* New York: Praeger. 1975.

[15] Martin, S., Sechrest, L., and Redner, R. *New Directions in the Rehabilitation of Criminal Offenders.* Washington, D.C.: The National Academy Press. 1981.

[16] Martinson, R. "California research at the crossroads." *Crime and Delinquency, 22,* (1976): 180-191.

[17] _____. "Symposium on sentencing. Part II." *Hofstra Law Review, 7(2),* Winter, 1979): 243-258.

[18] _____. "What works? — questions and answers about prison reform." *The Public Interest, 35,* (Spring, 1974): 22-54.

[19] Megargee, E., Bohn, M. Jr., Meyer, J. Jr., and Sink, F. *Classifying Criminal Offenders: A New System Based on the MMPI.* Beverly Hills, Calif.: Sage Publishers, Inc. 1979.

[20] Palmer, T. *Correctional Intervention and Research: Current Issues· and Future Prospects.* Lexington, Mass.: Lexington Books, 1978.

[21] _____. "Martinson revisited." *J. of Research in Crime and Delinquency, 12,* (1975): 133-152.

[22] Quay, H. and Parsons, L. *The Differential Behavior Classification of the Juvenile Offender.* Morgantown, West Virginia: Robert F. Kennedy Youth Center. 1970.

[23] Romig, D. *Justice for Our Children.* Lexington, Mass.: Lexington Books. 1978.

[24] Sechrest, L., White, S., and Brown, E. *The Rehabilitation of Criminal Offenders: Problems and Prospects.* Washington, D.C.: The National Academy of Sciences. 1979.

[25] Warren, M. "Classification of offenders as an aid to efficient management and effective treatment." *J. Criminal Law, Criminology, and Police Science, 62,* (1971): 239-258.

[26] Wilson, J. "What works?" revisited: New findings on criminal rehabilitation." *The Public Interest, 61,* (Fall, 1980): 3-17.

[27] Wright, W., and Dixon, M. "Juvenile delinquency prevention: A review of evaluation studies." *J. of Research in Crime and Delinquency, 14(1),* (1977): 35-67.

19

Correctional Treatment
Some Recommendations for Effective Intervention
Paul Gendreau
Robert R. Ross

Martinson's well-publicized conclusion that in correctional rehabilitation "almost nothing works" (Martinson, 1974) touched off a debate
that preoccupied the criminal justice system for more than a decade.
Although there were a few dissenters who rejected the validity of
Martinson's castigation of correctional treatment programs, there
appeared to be a widespread endorsement of the view that treatment
of the offender is an ineffective response to delinquent or criminal
behavior. Proclamations about the apparent lack of evidence of the
efficacy of correctional treatment undoubtedly have had major
repercussions throughout the field of criminal justice (cf. Empey, 1979).
Correctional managers, faced with dwindling budgets, have been
loathe to expend funds on treatment programs which, they were told,

Source: *Juvenile and Family Court Journal*, Vol. 34 (Winter 1983-1984), 31-39.
Reprinted with the permission of the publisher.

had little likelihood of success. Academicians and policy-makers disenchanted with correctional rehabilitation models or "medical" models which, they were told, had failed to live up to their extravagant promises, became enamoured with alternative models. Radical nonintervention (Schur, 1973), justice-as-fairness (Fogel, 1979), and deterrence (Tullock, 1974) along with a succession of others attracted loyal disciples eagerly seeking new panaceas. Perhaps the most significant effect of the "nothing works" proclamation was the promotion of a pervasive cynicism and feeling of hopelessness among correctional workers who were reminded again and again that their efforts at offender rehabilitation were of no value.

A further consequence of Martinson's "almost nothing works" assertion was that it motivated some researchers to reexamine the evidence for and against treatment effectiveness. Notable among these researchers was Ted Palmer (1975: 1978) who rejected Martinson's broad indictment of correctional programs by reference to evidence that Martinson himself had reported (and disregarded). Many of the programs that Martinson had reviewed actually were quite successful! Palmer's "revelation" was given short shrift in the debate on treatment effectiveness which unfortunately deteriorated into polemic and name-calling, becoming little concerned with more substantive matters, and less objective (Gendreau & Ross, 1979).

Recently, however, there appears to be a growing recognition that the "almost nothing works" credo is invalid. The evidence continues to mount that some programs do work and work well (Andrews, 1980: Gendreau & Ross, 1979, Peters, 1981). Even the most vociferous and persuasive proponent of the anti-treatment camp, Martinson recently acknowledged publicly that he could have been in error in his conclusion that correctional treatment was impotent (cf. Serrill, 1975; Martinson & Wilks, 1977). In our recent review of the published literature between 1973 and 1979 we found convincing evidence that some correctional programs significantly reduce recidivism (Gendreau & Ross, 1979). A number of these programs have been presented with additional follow-up data in a recent book (Ross & Gendreau, 1980).

In our view, the debate on correctional effectiveness should no longer focus on whether treatment programs are effective. That should now be viewed as an overly simplistic question. A more meaningful question which should now be addressed is which programs work. Equally important, questions should be asked about why some programs work and some do not.

The question of which programs work was addressed in previous publications which identified a substantial number of effective treatment programs (Gendreau & Ross, 1979; Ross & Gendreau, 1980). In this paper, we present a preliminary answer to the second question by discussing the characteristics of effective programs and suggesting some of the reasons why other programs fail.

It is not yet possible to speak with absolute assuredness about the essential ingredients of effective correctional programs but our examination of successful programs does suggest some guidelines which may help managers and policy-makers in the field of delinquency.

Effective Programs

Evaluation

The first characteristic of an effective program is not really a characteristic of the program per se, but of the evaluation of the program. Most of the recent successful programs we identified, were conducted in methodologically impressive research. Of the studies, 33 percent employed true experimental designs with random assignment of subjects. Twenty-three percent employed a variety of baseline comparisons. Twenty-five percent used matched comparison groups. Clearly there has been a major improvement in the quality of research on the outcome of correction intervention. Hackler's (1972, p. 346) "well-known law" of delinquency program research asserts that "the more carefully you evaluate a program, the greater the probability that it will show little effect" is simply incorrect. The quality of program evaluation in the correctional treatment area is now in many cases far superior to the evaluation of other correctional approaches including deterrence (Gendreau & Ross, 1981).

Magnitude and Persistence of Effects

The effectiveness of programs has been demonstrated in a wide variety of correctional areas with both juvenile and adult offenders. Whereas the majority are community-based, remarkably successful programs have also been conducted in various institutional settings. The type of offenders involved range from pre-delinquents to sophisticated hard-core offenders and recidivistic adult criminal heroin addicts. Major reductions in recidivism have been demonstrated ranging in well controlled studies from 30-60 percent (e.g., Alexander & Parsons, 1973; Chandler, 1973; Lee & Haynes, 1980; Phillips et al., 1973; Ross & McKay, 1976; Walter & Mills, 1979). These are by no means short-term effects. Substantial beneficial results have been reported in follow-ups as much as three to 15 years after treatment! (e.g., Blakely, Davidson, & Saylor, 1980; Sarason, 1978; Shore & Massimo, 1979).

Program Conceptualization

The successful programs appear to share a number of characteristics that distinguish them from their less successful counterparts. We found no evidence of the effectiveness of programs which were derived from the medical (disease) or the clinical sociology model of criminology. Rather the majority of successful programs were based on a social learning model of criminal conduct (cf. Bandura, 1979; Nettler, 1978; Nietzel, 1979). In some instances, the intervention was in accord with specific assumptions of Differential Association Theory (Andrews, 1980; Burgess & Akers, 1966), developed not from assumptions about delinquents' psychopathology, but from assumptions about their clients' cognitive or social skills. Most attempted to broaden their social perceptions or their repertoire of adaptive behaviors rather than attempting to cure some underlying emotional disorder.

Program Types

Disappointing, of course, to panacea-seekers is the fact that no one therapeutic modality can be associated with success. The intervention techniques of successful programs vary greatly. They include family therapy, contingency contracting, behavioral counseling, role-playing and modeling, vocational and social skills training, interpersonal cognitive problem-solving training, and peer-oriented behavioral programs. All effective programs are, in fact, multi-facetted. The superiority of any one technique is yet to be demonstrated.

Program Components

Although the identification of the essential parameters of successful intervention is still in its infancy, much has been learned from some of the successful intervention research programs. In particular, the studies of Andrews & Kiessling (1980, p. 445, 446) are exemplary in this regard. They examined factors associated with effective supervision and counseling of probationers and identified five sets of conditions which influence the outcome of intervention: (a) authority—where rules and or formal legal sanctions are clearly spelled out; (b) anti-criminal modeling and reinforcement—where the development of pro-social and anti-criminal attitudes, cognitions and behaviors are engendered and reinforced by appropriate modeling of pro-social behavior; (c) problem-solving—the client is assisted in coping with personal or social difficulties, particularly in the instances where they relate to fostering attitudes which have led him to experience pro-social behavior; (d) use of community resources; (e) quality of interpersonal relationship—an effective relationship consists of empathy, and the establishment of open communication and trust.

Our examination of successful programs suggests that each incorporates at least some of the factors identified by Andrews & Kiesling. As would be expected, there does exist considerable variation among successful programs in terms of the factors they emphasize. For example, Platt, Perry, & Metzger (1980) focussed on interpersonal problem-solving, whereas Lee & Haynes (1980) stressed the quality of interpersonal relationships and Ross & McKay (1976) emphasized an anti-criminal modeling and reinforcement approach.

Unsuccessful Programs

As we develop our knowledge about the types of programs that have a reasonable guarantee of success we also are acquiring insight as to the characteristics of programs and practices which are likely to fail.

Andrews (1979) has critically reviewed the studies of counseling programs in the correctional area. He found that counseling procedures which depend primarily on open communication "friendship" models, are non-directional, or involve self-help groups in which the offenders themselves are in charge of the program, typically have either had negligible effects or actually increase illegal behavior. A number of studies support this conclusion (e.g., Craft, Stephenson, & Granger, 1964; Fenton, 1960; Grant & Grant, 1959; Kassebaum, Ward, & Wilner, 1971). One implication of this observation is that with offender populations, trust, positive regard, warmth and empathy, though they may be necessary are simply not sufficient in themselves to effect change. Anti-criminal program components (verbalizations, contracting or modeling, etc.) must be an integral part of the successful intervention, or else the "good relationship" will be less than effective. The Ross & McKay (1976) study illustrates this point. Their program clearly communicated respect and trust for their institutionalized chronic delinquents and utilized a peer therapist procedure. However, central to the intervention and a key to its success was a programmatic structure which was deliberately established to yield pressure towards pro-social behavior rather than anti-social behavior. The delinquents were directed towards responsible behavior which persuaded them that they were, in fact, pro-social individuals. Attempts to replicate this program by providing only the peer self-help aspects of the program were dramatically unsuccessful (Ross & McKay, 1979).

Behavior modification programs have enjoyed both impressive success and dramatic failure in corrections. The differences between those which have "worked" and those which have not are relatively clear. Reviews of this literature (Ross & McKay, 1978; Emery &

Marholin, 1977) pointed out that many programs should never have been expected to succeed because they really never operationalized behavioral principles in their practices. They were operant conditioning programs in name only. Others completely distorted or bastardized the behavioral principles or attempted to change behaviors which had little relevance to the clients' anti-social or delinquent behavior. Ross & McKay's (1978) review revealed that unsuccessful programs had the following features: (a) they were imposed on the offenders who were never involved in the development of the program; (b) the target behavior; (c) they failed to neutralize or utilize in a positive way the offenders' peer group. The successful behavior modification programs behavior; (c) they failed to neutralize or utilize in a positive way the offenders peer group. The successful behavior modification programs (cf. Hoefler, 1975; Davidson & Robinson 1975) avoided or minimized these negative elements.

As we noted earlier, programs based on a "medical-model" disease conception of anti-social behavior (cf. Balch, 1975) have not been fruitful. Whether the disease is some form of psychopathology or biological deficit (e.g., extra chromosomes), we have not found one well controlled positive report (Ross & Gendreau, 1980), although Hippchen (1976), among others, states that alleviating nutritional chemical deficiencies of delinquents, reduces anti-social behavior. Unfortunately, studies purporting to support this view (e.g., Von Hilsheimer, Philpott, Buckely & Klotz, 1977) have been lacking in adequate controls.

Intervention programs based on a deterrence model were once proclaimed quite frequently (cf. Martinson, 1976) to be the "cureall" for combating crime but the most recent evidence has provided a very sobering experience for deterrence proponents. Although there is the occasional study attesting to effective deterrence on a large societal scale for the short-term (Gendreau & Surridge, 1978) or for a certain crime in a specific area (Schnelle, Kirchner, McRae, McNees, Eck, Snodgrass, Casey, & Uselton, 1978), there are many more studies showing mixed, if not negligible effects (cf. Blumstein, Cohen, & Nagin, 1978; Gendreau & Ross, 1981). Moreover, some studies indicate that deterrence programs were associated with increased offending (Critelli & Crawford, Jr., 1980; Erickson, 1977; Hart, 1978). The lack of evidence of effective deterrence may not entirely reflect the inadequacy of the deterrence model per se but shortcomings in its application. Attempts at applying the deterrence model have generally been so poorly conceptualized that no firm conclusions about the efficacy of deterrence could be reached (cf. Zimring, 1978). Moreover, there are profound and, perhaps, unresolvable methodological problems in deterrence research (cf. Gendreau & Ross, 1981) mitigating against finding easy, simplistic answers in the near future. Nevertheless, deterrence research should not be abandoned as there may be payoffs in considering how specific deterrence and treatment techniques can interact to produce effective intervention. The Hayes (1973) and Walter & Mills (1979) studies are two examples of this type of approach to intervention.

Confronting the Issues

Our review of the treatment research literature has confirmed that there are programs which can and have reduced recidivism and some which have not and probably cannot. However, we are not naive enough to assume that correctional agents and agencies will rush to replicate these successful programs nor will there be a marked modification of correctional policy in light of this recent positive evidence. There are any number of reasons for this despairing reality, one of these being that we are far from being an experimenting society (cf. Campbell, 1969; Tavris, 1975) at least in the criminal justice system. We seem neither to learn from our successes or failures, which is one characteristic we appear to share with the offenders we deal with — the failure to profit from experience. As we have documented previously (cf. Gendreau & Ross, 1981; Ross & McKay, 1978) pana-ceaphalia and negativism run rampant throughout the field. Fads are too enthusiastically embraced.

These characteristics are not, of course, indigenous to the criminal justice system; elements of this kind of thinking can be found in other applied fields where ready answers to complex problems have not been forthcoming. Likely, as the criminal justice system matures these characteristics will gradually extinguish. However, presently there are four issues that we feel are particularly crucial and must be urgently addressed. Failure to take a comprehensive view of the behavioral literature, the lack of therapeutic integrity, the neglect of differential treatment, and the failure to assess and examine the system itself can only lead to negative consequences.

Comprehensive View of the Literature

While the study of criminology purports to be a multi-disciplinary endeavor, in actual fact, the proponents of various positions have rarely taken the broad, well-informed view. The debate over rehabilitation centered on literature published before 1967 and various reviews (purportedly to settle the issue) have been highly selective and/or ignored large bodies of relevant material (Gendreau & Ross, 1979, p. 464-465). As Andrews (1980) incisively noted, the popularity of clinical sociology (Cressey, 1955) has never undergone any kind of thorough scrutiny whatsoever, as proponents of the model failed to test their assumptions and remained blind to the behavioral evolution that occurred outside their discipline. We have reported on a similar phenomenon occurring amongst deterrence proponents who have virtually ignored the fact that weaknesses in their model and theory building are in part due to a profound ignorance of basic experimental psychology (e.g., Carroll, 1978; Walters & Grusic, 1977) that directly touches upon their concerns.

In our opinion, the long term consequences of failing to take an informed view has led to some of the barren theorizing that has characterized the criminal justice field. Only by ignoring the relevant literature, could one comfortably arrive at the policy positions characterized by the radical criminology, or radical non-intervention (Schur, 1973) or just desert models (Fogel, 1979). The former demands a wrenching radical change in Western society; the second (in some cases) suggests programs that have a good chance of increasing recidivism (Andrews, 1980, p. 449) and the latter theory besides demanding "justice-as-fairness" sounds the cheerful note that outside of killing people we cannot stop people from committing crimes (e.g., Fox, 1974).

Therapeutic Integrity

The major issue in service delivery has centered about the lack of quality and intensity of the service delivery systems developed to date. For example, "to what extent do treatment personnel actually adhere to the principles and employ the techniques of therapy they purport to provide? To what extent are the treatment staff competent? How hard do they work? How much is treatment diluted in the correctional environment so that it becomes treatment in name only?" (Gendreau & Ross, 1979, p. 467). As Quay (1977) and Sechrest et al. (1979) have reported, the above questions are rarely answered positively in delinquency intervention research.

This sort of problem, unfortunately, is not one of history. It still occurs. In the recent review of behavioral contracting programs with delinquents, Peters (1981) reported that "the single most important contributing factor to the success or failure of the programs is that quantity and quality of supervision provided to the therapists as they implement the programs..."

Differential Treatment

The potential of treatment programs has also been dismissed by those who naively require that in order for program effectiveness to be established, it must be demonstrated across-the-board with *all* offenders. It seems reasonable to think that in correctional programming, as in every other human enterprise, the effect of an action will depend upon the individual to whom the action is applied and the situation in which it occurs. A program which is effective with some offenders may not be so with other offenders. There are no cure-alls nor should we expect there ever will be. Thankfully, the failure to consider differential treatment effects is becoming less common in the delinquency literature (cf. Glaser, 1975; Warren, 1977). The majority of the effective programs examine individual differences and their interactions with treatment variables. They are crucial to assessing the value of employment programs (e.g., Andrews & Kiessling, 1980; Andrews, Wormith, Daigle-Zinn, Kennedy & Nelson, 1980: Jessness, 1975) and community-based and family therapy programs (e.g., Alexander, Barton, Schiavo & Parsons, 1976; O'Donnell & Fo, 1976).

Differential tretment is not a mere "will of the wisp" phenomenon as Martinson (1976) argued.

System Variables

Chaneles (1976) has noted that a very small percentage of cor-rectional budgets are spent on offender programs. Berk & Rossi (1976) have pointed out that so many bureaucratic and political constraints have been placed on programs that their potential effectiveness is often neutralized. A great deal of the criticism of treatment programs should more properly be directed to criticizing the failure of program managers to attend to how system variables impinge on the program to influence its impact. There have been a few individual accounts (e.g., Rappaport, Seidman & Davidson, 1979; Reppuci, Sarata, Saunders, McArthur & Michlin, 1973) of how program policies in and of them-selves can affect outcome. But we need more concentrated efforts at systems analysis linking (a) setting factors—the physical and social structure of the program, (b) process and content of intervention, (c) intermediate targets, e.g., attitude change and (d) recidivism and cost-benefit (e.g., Andrews & Kiessling, 1980, p. 443). We need to examine how variables affecting the implementation of service systems affect outcome.

Finally, correctional administrators have sensed for a long time that political expediencies often prevent the network of social service systems from functioning harmoniously so as to deliver services effi-ciently (e.g., McDougall, 1976). The extent to which this has happened has been ignored. Even in correctional and social service systems reported to be affluent and progressive, the system operates ineffi-ciently in service delivery. Very often few offenders and their families recieve services outside of the criminal justice system (Gendreau, Madden & Leipciger, 1979). A few successful intervention programs have bridged this gap (See Gendreau & Ross, 1979, p. 488), but in most cases the services are simply not there or are not oriented towards offenders (Peters, 1981)—a reality that has escaped proponents of the advocacy-broker model and "leave the children alone" approach (Dell'Apa, Adams, Jorgenson & Sigurdson, 1976) of service delivery.

The systems and operations research must be drastically increased if any of our successful programs are to be entrenched and we are to even remotely approximate our claims as the experimenting society.

Conclusion

There are correctional programs that are effective. They can be distinguished from unsuccessful programs. There are perfectly good reasons why, in spite of our knowledge of what kinds of programs work, only limited success has been achieved to date, and it is within our means to be constructive in this regard. Admittedly, there are crime problems that go beyond the pale of what is possible given our current acceptance of what is possible given our current acceptance of what we construe to be moral and ethical correctional intervention (Gendreau & Ross, 1980, p. 25). Nevertheless, the majority of offender problems are well within bounds of our means to implement programs that work.

References

Alexander, J.F., Barton, C., Schiavo, R.S., and Parsons, B.V. Systems—Behavioral Intervention with Families Behavior and Outcome. *Journal of Consulting—Clinical Psychology*, 1976, 44, 656-664.

Alexander, J.F. and Parsons, R.J. Short-term Behavioral Intervention with Delinquent Families: Impact on Family Process and Recidivism. *Journal of Abnormal Psychology*, 1973, 81, 219-225.

Andrews, D.A. The Friendship Model of Voluntary Action and Controlled Evaluations of Correctional Practices: Notes on Relationships with Behavior Theory and Criminology. Toronto: Ministry of Correctional Services, 1979.

Andrews, D.A. Some Experimental Investigations of the Principles of Differential Association Through Deliberate Manipulations of the Structure of Service Systems. *American Sociological Review*, 1980, 45, 448-462.

Andrews, D.A. and Kiessling, J.J. Program Structure and Effective Correctional Practices: A Summary of the CAVIC Research. In R.R. Ross and P. Gendreau (eds.) *Effective Correctional Treatment*. Toronto: Butterworths, 1980.

Andrews, D.A., Wormith, J.S., Daigle-Zinn, W.J., Kennedy, D.J., and Nelson, S. Low and High Functioning Volunteers in Group Counseling with Anxious and Non-Anxious Prisoners: The Effects of Interpersonal Skills on Group Process and Attitude Change. *Canadian Journal or Criminology*, 1980, 22, 443-456.

Balch, R.W. The Medical Model of Delinquency: Theoretical, Practical, and Ethical Implications. *Crime and Delinquency*, 1975, 21, 116-129.

Bandura, A. The Social Learning Perspective: Mechanisms of Aggression. In H. Toch (ed.) *Psychology of Crime and Justice* (Copyright (c) 1979) reissued 1986 Waveland Press, Inc., Prospect Heights, IL.

Berk, R.A. and Rossi, P.H. Doing Good or Worse: Evaluation Research Politically Re-examined. *Social Problems*, 1976, 23, 337-349.

Blakely, C.H., Davidson, W.S., Saylor, C.A., and Robinson, M.J. Kentfields, Rehabilitation Program: Ten Years Later. In R.R. Ross and P. Gendreau (eds.) *Effective Correctional Treatment*. Toronto: Butterworths, 1980.

Blumstein, A., Cohen, J., and Nagin, D. (eds.) *Deterrence and Incapacitation: Estimating the Effects of Criminal Sanctions on Crime Rates*. Washington, DC: *National Academy of Sciences*, 1978.

Burgess, R.L. and Akers, R.L. A Differential Association-Reinforcement Theory of Criminal Behavior. *Social Problems*, 1966, 14, 128-147.

Campbell, D.T. Reforms as Experiments. *American Psychologist*, 1969, 24, 409-428.

Carroll, J.S. A Psychological Approach to Deterrence: The Evaluation of Crime Opportunities. *Journal of Personality and Social Psychology*, 1978, 36, 1512-1520.

Chandler, M.J. Egocentrism and Antisocial Behavior: The Assessment and Training of Social Perspective-Taking Skills. *Developmental Psychology*, 1973, 9, 326-333.

Chaneles, S. Prisoners can be Rehabilitated Now. *Psychology Today*, 1976, 10, 129-133.

Cratt, M., Stephenson, G., and Granger, C.A. A Controlled Trial of Authoritarian and Self-governing Regimes with Adolescent Psychopaths. *American Journal of Orthopsychiatry*, 1964, 34, 543-554.

Cressey, D.R. Changing Criminals: The Application of the Theory of Differential Association. *American Journal of Sociology*, 1955, 61, 116-120.

Critelli, J.W. and Crawford, R.F. The Effectiveness of Court-Ordered Punishment: Fines Versus Punishment. *Criminal Justice and Behavior*, 1980, 7, 465-470.

Davidson, W.D. and Robinson, M.J. Community Psychology and Behavior Modification: A Community-Based Program for the Prevention of Delinquency. *Corrective and social Psychiatry*, 1975, 21, 1-12.

Dell'Apa, F., Adams, W.T., Jorgenson, J.D.D. and Sigurdson, H.R. Advocacy, Brokerage, Community: The ABC's of Probation and Parole. *Federal Probation*, 1976, 40, 37-44.

Emery, R.E. and Marholin II, D. An Applied Behavior Analysis of Delinquency: The Irrelevancy of Relevant Behavior. *American Psychologist*, 1977, 32, 860-873.

Empey, I.T. From Optimism to Despair: New Doctrines in Juvenile Justice. In C.A. Murry and I.A. Cox, Jr. *Beyond Probation: Juvenile Corrections and the Chronic Delinquent*. Beverly Hills, CA: Sage, 1979.

Erickson, M.L., Gibbs, J.P. and Jensen, G.F. The Deterrence Doctrine and the Perceived Certainty of Legal Punishments. *American Sociological Review*, 1977, 42, 305-317.

Fenton, N. Group Counselling in Correctional Practice. *Canadian Journal of Corrections*, 1960, 2, 229-239.

Fogel, D. *We Are the Living Proof: The Justice Model for Corrections*. Cincinnati: Anderson, 1979.

Fox, S.J. The Reform of Juvenile Justice: The Child's Right to Punishment. *Juvenile Justice*, 1974, 25, 2-9.

Gendreau, P. and Andrews, D.A. *Psychological Consultant*. New York: Grune & Stratton, 1979.

Gendreau, P., Madden, P., and Leipciger, M. *Norms and Recidivism* Rates for Social History and Institutional Experience of First Incarcerate: Implications for Programming. *Canadian Journal of Criminology*, 1979, 21, 416-441.

Gendreau, P., and Ross, R.R. Effective Correctional Treatment: Bibliotherapy for Cynics. *Crime and Delinquency*, 1979, 25, 463-489.

Gendreau, P., and Ross, R.R. Effective Corrections Treatment: Bibliotherapy for Cynics. In R.R. Ross and P. Gendreau (eds.) *Effective Correctional Treatment*. Toronto: Butterworths, 1980.

Gendreau, P., and Ross, R.R. Correctional Potency: Treatment and Deterrence on Trial. In R. Roesch and R. Corrado (eds.) *Evaluation Research and Policy in Criminal Justice*. Beverly Hills: Sage, 1981.

Gendreau, P., and Ross, R.R. Prescriptions for Successful Intervention. Manuscript under review, 1981.

Gendreau, P., and Ross, R.R. Getting Serious about the Deterrence of Offenders: Problems and prospects. Manuscript under review, 1981.

Gendreau, P., and Surridge, C.T. Controlling Gun Crimes: The Jamaican Experience. *International Journal of Criminology and Penology*, 1978, 6, 43-60.

Glaser, D. Achieving Better Questions: A Half-century's Progression in Correctional Research. *Federal Probation*, 1975, 39, 3-9.

Grant, J.D., and Grant, M.Q. A Group Dynamics Approach to the Treatment of Non-Conformists in the Navy. *Annals of the American Academy of Political and Social Science*, 1959, 322, 126-135.

Hackler, J.C. *The Prevention of Youthful Crime: The Great Stumble Forward*. Toronto: Methuen, 1978.

Hart, R.J. Crime and Punishment in the Army. *Journal of Personality and Social Psychology*, 1978, 36, 1456-1471.

Hayes, S.N. Contingency Management in a Municipally-Administered Antiabuse Program for Alcoholics. *Journal of Behavior Therapy and Experimental Psychiatry*, 1973, 4, 31-32.

Hippchen, L.J. Biomedical Approaches to Offender Rehabilitation. *Offender Rehabilitation*, 1976, 17, 115-123.

Hoetler, S.A., and Bornstein, Ph. H. Achievement Place: An Evaluative Review. *Criminal Justice and Behavior*, 1975, 2, 146-168.

Jeffrey, R., and Woolpert, S. Work Furlough as an Alternative to Incarceration: An assessment of its Effects on Recidivism and Social Cost. *Journal of Criminal Law and Criminology*, 1974, 65, 405-415.

Jessness, C.F. Comparative Effectiveness of Behavior Modification and Transactional Analysis Programs for Delinquents. *Journals of Consulting and Clinical Psychology*, 1975, 43, 758-779.

Kassebaum, G., Ward, D., and Wilner, D. *Prison Treatment and Parole Survival: An Empirical Assessment.* New York: Wiley, 1971.

Lee, R., and Haynes, N.M. Project CREST and the Dual-Treatment Approach to Delinquency: Methods and Research Summarized. In R.R. Ross and P. Gendreau (eds.) *Effective Correctional Treatment.* Toronto: Butterworths, 1980.

Martinson, R. "What works? Questions and Answers About Prison Reform. *The Public Interest,* 1974, 35, 22-54.

Martinson, R. California Research at the Crossroads. *Crime Delinquency,* 1976, 22, 180-191.

Martinson, R.,and Wilks, J. Save Parole Supervision. *Federal Probation,* 1977, 41, 23-27.

McDougall, E.C. Corrections has not been tried. *Criminal Justice Review,* 1976, 1, 63-76.

Nettler, G. *Explaining Crime.* New York: McGraw-Hill, 1978.

Nietzel, M.T. *Crime and Its Modification: A Social Learning Perspective.* New York: Pergamon, 1979.

O'Donnell, C.R., and Fo, W.S.O. The Buddy System: Mediator-Target Locus of Control and Behavioral Outcome. *American Journal of Community Psychology,* 1976, 4, 161-166.

Phillips, E.L., Phillips, R.A., Fixsen, D.L., and Wolf, M.W. Behavior Shaping Works for Delinquents. *Psychology Today,* 1973, 6, 75-79.

Palmer, T. Martinson revisited. *Journal of Research in Crime and Delinquency,* 1975, 12, 133-152.

Palmer, T. *Correctional Intervention and Research.* Lexington, MA: Heath, 1978.

Peters, R. Deviant Behavioral Contracting with Conduct Problem Youth: A Review and Critical Analysis. Department of Psychology, Queen's University, Kingston, Ontario, 1981.

Platt, J.J., Perry, G.M., and Metzger, D.S. The Evaluation of a Heroin Addiction Treatment Program Within a Correctional Environment. In R.R. Ross and P. Gendreau (eds.) *Effective Correctional Treatment.* Toronto: Butterworths, 1980.

Quay, H.C. The Three Faces of Evaluation: What Can Be Expected to Work. *Criminal Justice and Behavior,* 1977, 4, 341-354.

Rappeport, J., Seidman, E., and Davidson II, W.S. Demonstration Research and Manifest Versus True Adoption: The Natural History of a Research Project. In R.F. Munoz, L.R. Snowden, and J.G. Kelly (eds.) *Social Psychological Research and Community Settings.* San Francisco: Jossey-Bass, 1979.

Repucci, N.D., Sarata, B.P., Saunders, J.T., McArthur, A.V., and Michlin, L.M. We Bombed in Mountville: Lessons Learned in Consultation to a Correctional Facility for Adolescent Offenders. In I.I. Goldenberg (ed.) *The Helping Professions in the World of Action.* Boston: D.C. Heath, 1973.

Ross, R.R. and Gendreau, P. *Effective Correctional Treatment.* Toronto: Butterworths, 1980.

Ross, R.R. and McKay, H.B. A Study of Institutional Treatment Programs. *International Journal of Offender Therapy and Comparative Criminology,* 1976, 20, 165-173.

Ross, R.R. and McKay, B. Treatment in Corrections: Requiem for a Panacea. *Canadian Journal of Criminology*, 1978, 120, 279-295.

Ross, R.R. and McKay, B. *Self-Mutilation*. Boston: Lexington, 1979.

Sarason, I.G. A Cognitive Social Learning Approach to Juvenile Delinquency. In R.D. Hare and D. Schalling (eds.) *Psychopathic Behaviour Approaches to Research*. New York: Wiley, 1978.

Schnelle, J.F., Kirchner, R.E., McRaie, J.E., McNees, M.P., Eck, R.H., Snotdgrass, S., Casey, J.D., and Uselton, P.H. Police Evaluation Research: An Experimental and Cost-Benefit Analysis of a Helicopter Patrol in a High Crime Area. *Journal of Applied Behavior Analysis*, 1978, 11, 11-21.

Schur, E.M. *Radical Nonintervention: Re-thinking the Delinquency Problem*. Englewood Cliffs: Prentice-Hall, 1973.

Sechrest, L., West, S.G., Phillips, M.A., Redner, R., and Yeaton, W. Some Neglected Problems in Evaluation Research: Strength is Integrity of Treatments. In L. Sechrest, S.G. West, M.A. Phillips, R. Redner and W. Yeaton, *Evaluation Studies Annual Review* (Vol. 4). Beverly Hills: Sage, 1979.

Sechrest, L., White, S.O., and Brown, G.D. (eds.) *The Rehabilitation of Criminal Offenders*. Washington, DC: National Academy of Sciences, 1979.

Serrill, M.S. Is Rehabilitation Dead? *Corrections Magazine*, 1975, 11, 3-12, 21-26.

Shore, M.F. and Massimo, J.L. Fifteen Years After Treatment: A Follow-up Study of Comprehensive Vocationally-oriented Psychotherapy. *American Journal of Orthopsychiatry*, 1979, 49, 240-245.

Tayris, C. The Experimenting Society: To Find Programs That Work, Government Must Measure its Failures. *Psychology Today*, 1975, 9, 47-56.

Tullock, G. Does Punishment Deter Crime: *Public Interest*, 1974, 35, 103-111.

Von Hilsheimer, G., Philpott, W., Buckley, W., and Klotz, S.D. Correcting the Incorrigible: A Report on 229 Incorrigible Adolescents. *American Laboratory*, 1977, 101, 197-218.

Walter, T.L., and Mills, C.M. A Behavioral-Employment Intervention Program for Reducing Juvenile Delinquency. In J.S. Stumphauzer (ed.) *Progress in Behavior Therapy with Delinquents*. Springfield, IL: Thomas, 1979.

Walters, G.C., and Grusec, J.E. *Punishment*. San Francisco: Freeman & Co., 1977.

Warren, M.Q. Correctional Treatment and Coercion: The Differential Effectiveness Perspective. *Criminal Justice and Behavior*, 1977, 4, 355-376.

Zimring, F.G. Policy Experiments in General Deterrence: 1970-75. In A. Blumstein, J. Cohen, and D. Ngain (eds.) *Deterrence and Incapacitation: Estimating the Effects of Criminal Sanctions on Crime Rates*. Washington, DC: National Academy of Sciences, 1978.

20

"What Works?" Revisited
New Findings on
Criminal Rehabilitation
James Q. Wilson

Few articles appearing in this magazine have been as widely reprinted or as frequently cited as Robert Martinson's "What Works? —Questions and Answers About Prison Reform," published in 1974. Its major conclusion has become familiar to almost everyone even casually interested in crime control programs: *"With few and isolated exceptions, the rehabilitative efforts that have been reported so far have had no appreciable effect on recidivism."* For politicians as well as for scholars, the message seemed clear—nothing works. In fact, the article was careful to point out that there were, scattered through the 231 studies that were reviewed by Martinson and his co-workers, hints of *some* reductions in criminality for *some* kinds of offenders under *some* circumstances. But these hints did not constitute, even generously interpreted, a clear and consistent pattern of success on which a public policy might be based.

Source: Reprinted with permission of the author from *The Public Interest*, No. 61 (Fall 1980), 3-17, © 1980 by National Affairs, Inc.

There was little new in the 1974 article. In 1967, R.G. Hood had published in Europe a review that concluded that different ways of treating offenders generally led to similar, and not very encouraging, results. A year earlier, Walter C. Bailey published in this country a survey of 100 evaluations of correctional treatment programs that led him to the judgement that "evidence supporting the efficacy of correctional treatment is slight, inconsistent, and of questionable reliability." Indeed, such gloomy findings go back at least 30 years. In 1951, Edwin Powers and Helen Witmer reported on the results of the ambitious Cambridge-Somerville Youth Study, begun in 1939 as an effort to prevent delinquency by an intensive counselling program. Despite high hopes, they had to conclude that, by any measure, boys randomly assigned to counselling were as likely as similar boys left on their own to run afoul of the law.

Unlike these earlier studies, the Martinson article—based on a massive volume he had prepared in collaboration with Douglas Lipton and Judith Wilks—created a sensation. Partly it was the times: It appeared in the early 1970's, after the optimism of the Great Society had been dashed and the enthusiasms of the 1960's had moderated, but when politicians were still searching desperately for some response to the widespread public fear of street crime. Martinson did not discover that rehabilitation was of little value in dealing with crime so much as he administered a highly visible *coup de grace*. By bringing out into the open the long-standing scholarly skepticism about most rehabilitation programs, he prepared the way for a revival of an interest in the deterrent, incapacitative, and retributive purposes of the criminal justice system.

But it was not just the times. During the 1960's, there had developed in California a remarkable concentration of talent and energy devoted to finding and testing rehabilitation programs, especially ones designed to treat delinquents in the community. Marguerite Q. Warren, Ted Palmer, and others not only used advanced psychological testing to classify delinquents by personality type and employed skilled counsellors to provide intensive community supervision, they randomly assigned delinquents to the treatment and control groups in order to insure the best possible scientific evaluation of the results.

At first, these results were encouraging, so much so that the President's Commission on Law Enforcement and Administration of Justice, in its 1967 report to Lyndon Johnson, endorsed the Community Treatment Program (CTP) of the California Youth Authority, describing it as having reduced delinquency (as measured by parole revocation) from 52 percent among youth who were incarcerated before release to 28 percent among those given intensive counselling in the community.

The Martinson article was particularly critical of these claims. In their re-analysis of the California data, Lipton, Martinson, and Wilks concluded that Warren and her colleagues had substantially under-counted the number of offenses committed by the youth in the experi-mental community program. Apparently, probation officers assigned to these delinquents developed such close relations with their charges, and were so eager to see their program succeed, that they failed to report to the authorities a number of offenses committed by the exper-imentals, whereas youth assigned to the control groups had their offenses reported in the normal way by probation and parole authorities.

California Counterattacks

Given the resources devoted to the California project and the pub-licity it had received, it is hardly surprising that its leaders counter-attacked. Ted Palmer published in 1975 a rebuttal to the Martinson article, claiming that it overlooked or downplayed a number of success stories in the rehabilitation literature and that in particular it mis-represented the CTP. Palmer conceded that the youth in the experi-mental program had a number of offenses overlooked by counsellors, but argued that these were largely minor or technical violations, many of which were detected simply because the youth were under closer observation and some of which involved merely the failure to partici-pate regularly in the intensive supervision program. Moreover, the Martinson review ended in 1967; if it had continued through 1973, Palmer said, the differences between experimentals and controls, at least for serious offenses, would have been clear.

Martinson responded vigorously to this challenge, and the battle was joined. In the midst of the verbal pyrotechnics of Palmer and Martinson —they were nothing if not spirited adversaries—a new and, as it turned out, more weighty voice was heard. Paul Lerman, a Rutgers sociologist, published a book-length evaluation of the CTP (as well as of the California probation subsidy program) in which he concluded, after a painstaking analysis of the published data, that "the CTP did not have an impact on youth behavior that differed significantly from the impact of the control program."[1] Moreover, the "community" focus of the experimental program turned out to be somewhat exaggerated— in fact, the great majority of experimental youth were placed in detention at least once and many were detained repeatedly in order to maintain control over them. Indeed, the youth in the experimental "community" program were more likely to be sent to detention centers than the control group supervised by regular parole officers. Finally, Lerman found strong evidence that, though the CTP had·tried to match experimental and control groups by randomly assigning youth to each, over the many years the program operated the two groups began to differ markedly in their characteristics as persons dropped out of the program for one reason or another. In particular, the experimental group came to be composed disproportionately of persons who were older, had higher IQ's, and were diagnosed as "neurotic" (rather than as "power-oriented"). This intriguing finding, largely buried in an appendix to the Lerman book, raises issues to which we shall return presently.

Lerman had made many of these points earlier, in a 1968 article; he made them more elaborately in the 1975 book. Curiously, Palmer, who continued to protest against the Martinson article, appears to have taken little notice, at least publicly, of the Lerman criticisms. Palmer's book-length attack on Martinson and his reassertion of the claims of the CTP appeared in 1978; there is no mention of Lerman in it.[2]

Enter the National Research Council

While the debate in correctional journals raged, the public view, insofar as one can assess it from editorials, political speeches, and legislative initiatives, was that Martinson was right. Because of this widespread belief that "nothing works," the National Research Council, the applied research arm of the prestigious National Academy of Sciences, created in 1977 a Panel on Research on Rehabilitative Techniques, chaired by Professor Lee Sechrest, then of the Department of Psychology of Florida State University. The Panel was charged with reviewing existing evaluations of rehabilitative efforts to see if they provided a basis for drawing any conclusions about the effectiveness of these efforts. Its first report—on efforts to rehabilitate in correctional institutions—was issued in 1979; a second report, on community rehabilitation, will appear later.

Owing to the importance in the public debate of the review by Lipton, Martinson, and Wilks (LMW), that book was made the focus of the Panel's attention.[3] In addition, the report examined reviews that analyzed studies appearing after 1968, the cutoff date for the LMW review. Among the papers commissioned by the Panel was a detailed re-analysis of a sample of the studies analyzed by LMW, carried out by two scholars not identified with the on-going debate, Stephen Fienberg and Patricia Grambsch.

The conclusion of the Panel is easily stated: By and large, Martinson and his colleagues were right. More exactly, "The Panel concludes that Lipton, Martinson, and Wilks were reasonably accurate and fair in their appraisal of the rehabilitation literature." If they erred at all, it was in being overly generous. They were sometimes guilty of an excessively lenient assessment of the methodology of a given study. Moreover, the evaluations published since 1968 provide little evidence to reverse this verdict. For example, David F. Greenberg's 1977 review of the more recent studies comes to essentially the same conclusion as Martinson. S.R. Brody's survey in England on the institutional treatment of juvenile offenders agrees.

The Panel looked in particular at Palmer's argument that nearly half the studies cited by Martinson showed a rehabilitative effect. The Panel was not persuaded: "Palmer's optimistic view cannot be supported, in large part because his assessment accepts at face value the claim of the original authors about effects they detected, and in too many instances those claims were wrong or were over-interpretations of data...." In any event, "we find little support for the charge that positive findings were overlooked."

The conclusion that Martinson was right does not mean that he or anyone else has proved that "nothing works," only that nobody has proved that "something works." There is always the chance, as the Panel noted, that rehabilitative methods now in use but not tested would, if tested, show a beneficial effect and that new methods yet to be tried will prove efficacious. (One such method will be discussed in a moment.)

Are Some Offenders Amenable to Treatment?

One unresolved issue is whether certain kinds of offenders are more amenable to rehabilitation than others. If this is the case, and if the amenable subjects are mixed together in a treatment group with non-amenable ones, then any reductions in criminality among the former might be masked by increases in criminality among the latter; the average (and misleading) result would be, "no change."

This view has been vigorously advanced by Daniel Glaser, among others. Writing in 1973, a year before the Martinson article appeared, he pointed to evidence from a variety of evaluative studies suggesting that certain kinds of offenders were especially amenable to rehabilitation. They tended to be persons who could easily communicate, who had not found their prior criminal career to be especially rewarding, and who had not been greatly disappointed by their efforts to find legitimate alternatives to crime. The CTP, for example, made explicit use of a psychological classification scheme designed to differentiate among delinquents on the basis of their "interpersonal maturity level" and their particular mode of behavior. One such group was classified as having a relatively high level of maturity, by which is meant the members had an internalized set of standards and some regard for the opinions of others, but displayed as well neurotic tendencies—either feelings of guilt and anxiety or a proclivity to "acting-out." The interpretation of the CTP data by Glaser, Palmer, and others was that these anxious, neurotic, guilt-stricken delinquents benefitted substantially from intensive counselling. Recognizing the criticisms already levelled by Lerman (in his 1968 article) at the CTP, Glaser felt that even allowing for counsellor bias the neurotics did substantially better in the treatment groups than they did when left alone in the control groups. Moreover, Glaser has argued that Lerman himself neglected the long-term effects of treatment on different types of delinquents.

If this is true, then those studies which show no change among treated offenders may include not only some "amenables" who commit less crime *but some non-amendables who actually commit more crimes as a result of the treatment.* And this is exactly what Palmer believed he found in the CTP data. In his 1978 book, he showed the monthly arrest rates for two kinds of offenders—the "conflicted" (by which he apparently means "neurotic") and the "power-oriented" (by which he seems to mean those delinquents who lack an internalized set of conventional standards and either manipulate others or identify with the norms of a deviant group). Neurotic delinquents in the treatment group had a lower monthly arrest rate than neurotics in the control group, both during the early stages of the program and four years after discharge. "Power-oriented" offenders in the treatment groups, on the other hand, had a *higher* arrest rate than the power-oriented controls four years after discharge. Glaser had surmised that this increase in criminality among power-oriented delinquents in the treatment program arises because they learn from it how to manipulate their counsellors, obtain favors, win early release, and generally "con" the system. "Treating" such persons—at least by means of verbal therapy —apparently makes society worse off.

An earlier study by Stuart Adams provides some confirmation for this point of view. In 1961 he described the "Pilot Intensive Counselling Organizations" (PICO) in California, aimed at reducing delinquency among older juvenile offenders. The eligible youth were first classified as "amenable" or "non-amenable" by the persons running the project. (Exactly how they reached these judgments is not clear.) Once classified, they were then randomly assigned to either a treatment or control group. (The treatment consisted of individual counselling sessions, once or twice a week for about nine months, carried on inside a correctional institution). After nearly three years of observation, Adams discovered that the amenable delinquents who had been treated were much less likely than amenable delinquents who had not been treated to be returned to custody. On the other hand, delinquents judged non-amenable who were given counselling did much worse — indeed, they were *more* likely to be returned to jail than the non-amenables who had *not* been treated. *In short, if you are amenable, treatment may make you less criminal; if you are not, treatment can make you more criminal.* Adams found that the delinquents judged to be amenable were "bright, verbal, and anxious." These characteristics are similar to those of the neurotics in the CTP.

This conclusion is consistent with a good deal of evidence about the effects of psychotherapy generally. Changing delinquents is not fundamentally different from changing law-abiding people: "Crime," after all, is not a unique form of behavior; it is simply behavior that is against the law. The illegality of the behavior is no trivial matter, but illegality alone does not differentiate one action from many similar actions. For example, many (perhaps most) offenders tend to do poorly in school, to have emotional problems, to find it difficult to get along with parents and friends, and to drink a good deal of alcohol. They are generally a mess. But poor school work, strained peer relations, emotional stress, and drinking liquor are not illegal.

Psychologists have long argued over whether any form of therapy will help any kind of problem. H.J. Eysenck, in a famous pair of articles published in 1952 and 1965, claimed that there was little evidence that therapy did anybody much good. He was (and is) the Robert Martinson of psychotherapy. Of late, psychologists have questioned the sweeping nature of Eysenck's claim. Mary Lee Smith and Gene V. Glass published in 1977 a comprehensive review of nearly 400 controlled evaluations of therapy and counselling and concluded that the client was often better off being treated than not. However, they noted that the improvements were generally with respect to such matters as "adjustment" (under which heading, of course, one finds most criminal behavior). Smith and Glass also tried to measure what factors made some subjects more amenable to therapy than others. They were able to identify two statistically significant ones: whether the therapist resembled the client, and the IQ of the client. Brighter clients did better than duller ones.

Similarly, if we are to believe Lerman, the brighter (and more neurotic) delinquents remain in the CTP program longer than those with the opposite characteristics; thus, any improvement measured by Palmer in their law-abidingness may result either from their greater receptivity to therapy, or from their tendency over time to outnumber the more delinquent-prone youth, or both.

The possibility that some persons are amenable to criminal rehabilitation is intriguing but it is not yet clear how much to make of it. The National Research Council Panel took note of the issue but remains skeptical that we have any clear understanding of it. The CTP, the major source of claims about amenability, is methodologically flawed. The PICO project did not define amenability with any rigor. Classifying a criminal as "amenable" may only mean that a therapist has a good hunch as to who will cooperate with the program. But if the therapist cannot communicate to others the basis for that hunch or provide a clear explanation of its rationale, it is hard to see how it can be used routinely as the basis for classifying and treating offenders. Moreover, some difficult legal and ethical issues arise. Suppose we are able to differentiate, accurately, amenable from non-amenable offenders. Suppose further that the treatment from which the amenables will benefit is less restrictive, more benign, and shorter in duration than the conventional punishment to which non-amenables will be assigned. Should we allow the criminal justice system to be "nicer" to "amenable" offenders than to non-amenable ones, even though their offenses and prior records may be identical. (Of course, it may also turn out that the rehabilitative program is felt by the recipients to be more onerous than doing "straight time"; the issue, however, remains the same.)

Nevertheless, the possibility of identifying amenable subjects and aiming programs at them that work is sufficiently attractive as to merit intensive new research. Someone has even coined a shorthand term to describe what we now suspect are the amenable subjects of therapy: YAVIN (young, anxious, verbal, intelligent, neurotic).

Recidivism, Rates, and Restrictiveness

The most dramatic new argument in the continuing debate over rehabilitation, however, comes from two authors who do not, at first glance, appear to be writing about rehabilitation at all. Charles A. Murray and Louis A. Cox, Jr., members of a private research organization, were retained to find out what happens to chronic delinquents in Chicago who are confronted by sanctions of varying degrees of restrictiveness.[4]

The Chicago authorities wanted to know if any of the programs offered in that city—ranging from commitment to a conventional juvenile reformatory, to newer programs that left the delinquent in the community or sent him to a wilderness program—changed the rate at which delinquents committed offenses. Such studies have been done many times, usually with the negative results reported by Martinson. But Murray and Cox redefined the outcome measure in a way that seems to make a striking difference. Until now, almost all students of recidivism "rates" or rehabilitation outcomes have measured the success or failure of a person by whether or not he was arrested for a new offense (or was convicted of a new offense, or had his parole revoked) after leaving the institution or completing the therapeutic program. "Success" was an either-or proposition: If you did not (within a stated time period) get into trouble again, you were a success; if you did get into trouble—*even once*—you were a "failure." Though the evaluators of rehabilitation programs typically speak of "recidivism rates," in fact they do not mean "rate" at all—they mean "percent who fail." More accurately, they use "rate" in the sense of "proportion," as in the "birth rate" or the "tax rate." But there is a different meaning of rate: the *frequency* of behavior per unit of time. Even a cursory glance through the studies reviewed by Lipton, Martinson, and Wilks reveals that almost all of them use "recidivism rate" to mean "the proportion who fail."

It was Murray's and Cox's happy thought to use rate in the sense of frequency and to calculate how many arrests per month were charged against a given group of delinquents before and after being exposed to Chicago juvenile treatment programs, and to do so separately for each kind of program involved. They examined three groups of youth.

The first was composed of 317 serious delinquents. They had been arrested an average of 13 times prior to being sent to the Department of Corrections, which was when Murray and Cox first started to track them. They were young—the average age was 16—but active: They had been charged with 14 homicides, 23 rapes, over 300 assaults and 300 auto thefts, nearly 200 armed robberies, and over 700 burglaries. The boys entered the study by having been sentenced by the court to a state correctional institution where they served an average of about ten months. Murray and Cox followed them for (on the average) 17 months after their release.

By the conventional measure of recidivism, the results were typically discouraging—82 percent were rearrested. But the *frequency* with which they were arrested during the follow-up period fell dramatically—the monthly arrest rate (i.e., arrests per month per 100 boys) declined by about *two-thirds*. To be exact, the members of this group of hard-core delinquents were arrested 6.3 times each during the year before being sent away but only 2.9 times each during the 17 months on the street after release.

The second group consisted of 266 delinquents who were eligible to go to a state reformatory but who instead were diverted to one of several less custodial programs run by the Unified Delinquency Intervention Services (UDIS), a Cook County (Chicago) agency created to make available in a coordinated fashion non-institutional, community-based programs for serious delinquents. Though chosen for these presumably more therapeutic programs, the UDIS delinquents had criminal records almost as severe as those sent to the regular reformatories — an average of over 13 arrests per boy, of which eight were for "index" (i.e., serious) offenses, including nine homicides, over 500 burglaries, and over 100 armed robberies. Nonetheless, since these youth were specially selected for the community-based programs, one would expect that in the opinion of probation officers, and probably in fact, they represented somewhat less dangerous, perhaps more amenable delinquents.

Despite the fact the UDIS group may have been thought more amenable to treatment, the reduction in their monthly arrest rates was *less* than it had been for the group sent to the reformatories (about 17 percent less). In general, UDIS did not do as well as the regular Department of Corrections. Even more interesting, Murray and Cox found that *the more restrictive the degree of supervision practiced by UDIS, the greater the reduction in arrest rates.* Youths left in their homes or sent to wilderness camps showed the least reduction (though some reduction nonetheless); those placed in group homes in the community showed a greater reduction; and those put into out-of-town group homes, intensive-care residential programs, or sent to regular reformatories showed the greatest reduction. If this is true, *it implies that how strictly the youth were supervised, rather than what therapeutic programs were available, had the greatest effect on the recidivism rate.*

Ordinarily, we do not refer to the crime-reduction effects of confinement as "rehabilitation." Technically, they are called the results of "special deterrence" ("special" in the sense that the person deterred is the specific individual who is the object of the intervention, and not the general delinquent population). "Rehabilitation" usually refers to interventions that are "nice," benevolent, or well-intended, or that involve the provision of special services. A psychologist might say that rehabilitation involves "positive reinforcements" (such as counselling) rather than "negative reinforcements" (such as incarceration). Indeed, the National Research Council Panel defines rehabilitation as the result of "any planned intervention" that reduces further criminal activity, "whether that reduction is mediated by personality, behavior, abilities, attitudes, values, or other factors," provided only that one excludes the effects of fear or intimidation, the latter being regarded as sources of special deterrence.

Although the distinction has a certain emotional appeal, it makes little sense either scientifically or behaviorally. Scientifically, there is no difference between a positive and negative inducement; behavioral psychologists long ago established that the two kinds of reinforcements have comparable effects. (It is not generally true that rewards will change behavior more than punishments, or vice versa). Behaviorally, it is not clear that a criminal can tell the difference between rehabilitation and special deterrence if each involves a comparable degree of restriction. Rehabilitation can (and usually does) involve a substantial degree of coercion, even of intimidation ("be nice or you won't get out," "talk to the counsellor or stay in your cell," "join the group discussion or run the risk of being locked up"). Behavior-modification therapy can involve the simultaneous use of positive reinforcers ("follow the rules and earn a token") and negative ones ("break the rules and lose a token"). It might help the discussion of offender-oriented programs if the distinction between rehabilitation and special deterrence were collapsed.

Two Questions

The real issue raised by the Murray-Cox study is not, however, what to call the effect they observe, but whether they have actually observed any effect at all. A number of criticisms have been made of it, but two are of special importance. First, does the decline in arrests indicate a decline in actual criminality or merely an increase in skill at avoiding apprehension? Second, if there is an actual decline in criminality, might this not be explained by the maturation of youth—that is, growing out of crime as they become older? Andrew C. Gordon, Richard McCleary, and their colleagues made these and other criticisms in response to a preliminary report of the Murray-Cox findings. In their later, book-length treatment of the Chicago project, Murray and Cox responded.

The second criticism seems the easiest to answer. Murray and Cox were able to show that the decline in rearrest rates existed for all incarcerated serious delinquents regardless of age. As an additional check, the authors examined a third group—nearly 1,500 youth born in Chicago in 1960 and arrested at least once by the Chicago Police Department before their 17th birthdays. Since this group was chosen at random from all arrested youth of the same age, it naturally is made up primarily of less serious offenders. Indeed, only 3 percent of this group was ever referred to UDIS or the Department of Corrections. When the monthly arrest rates for this group were examined, the data showed a more or less steady increase throughout the teenage years. Being arrested or being placed on probation had no apparent effect on subsequent delinquency. By all the tests they used, therefore, the decline in arrest rates for those delinquents given strict supervision cannot be explained by the fact that they were simply getting older.

The other criticism is harder to answer. Strictly speaking, it is impossible to know whether arrest data are a reasonable approximation of the true crime rate. No one argues, of course, that every crime results in an arrest. All that is at issue is whether a more or less constant fraction of all crimes result in arrests. There are two possibilities — either having been arrested before draws police attention to the boy (he is "stigmatized" or "labeled", thus making him more likely to be arrested for subsequent crimes, or the arrest and subsequent punishment increases his skills at avoiding detection (the system has served as a "school for criminals"), thus making him less likely to be arrested for a given offense.

Now it is obvious that the first of these two possibilities — the "labeling" effect of being arrested — cannot be true, for, we have seen, delinquents who are placed under supervision have their subsequent arrest rates decline. If the police "pick on" previously arrested youth, they either do so without making an arrest (by keeping an eye on "troublemakers," for example) or they try harder to arrest them but find the youth are not committing as many crimes as before.

The other possibility — that boys become skilled at avoiding arrest — is impossible to disprove, but Murray and Cox raise some serious questions as to whether this gain in skills, if it occurs at all, could explain the decline in arrest rates. Perhaps their most telling argument is this: One must not only believe that correctional institutions are "schools of crime," one must believe they are such excellent schools that they produce a two-thirds gain in arrest-avoiding skills. This would make reformatories and group homes the most competent educational institutions in the country, since no one has yet shown that conventional schools, with the best available educational technology, can produce comparable gains in learning non-criminal skills. And all this must be accomplished within the ten-month period that is the average length of detention. It is still possible, of course, that the "schools of crime" hypothesis is true, but it requires one to make some heroic assumptions in order to sustain it: that large numbers of boys learn more during ten months in a reformatory than they learn in ten years on the street; that the great majority, despite their statements to the contrary made to interviewers, increase their commitment to crime as a way of life (rather than as an occasionally profitable activity) as a result of incarceration; and that the object of their efforts when back on the street is to employ their sharpened skills at avoiding apprehension while committing relatively unprofitable crimes rather than attacking more profitable (and riskier) targets.

Though Murray and Cox make a persuasive case for the validity of their findings, it cannot be taken as a conclusive study. For one thing, we would like to know what happens to these delinquents over a much longer period. Most studies of rehabilitation suggest that any favorable effects tend to be extinguished by the passage of time (though such extinction usually appears within the first year). We would also like to know more about the kinds of offenses for which these persons were arrested, before and after court intervention (perhaps they change the form of their criminal behavior in important ways). And above all, we would like to see such a study repeated in other settings by other scholars. It may even be possible to do this retrospectively, with data already in existence but never before analyzed using frequency of offending (rather than proportion of failures) as the measure of outcome.

In fact, long before the Murray-Cox study, LaMar T. Empey and Maynard L. Erickson had reported on the Provo Experiment in Utah, an effort to reduce delinquency that was evaluated by arrest rates before and after treatment — the same outcome measure used by Murray and Cox (indeed, the latters' book contains a foreword by Empey). The Provo Experiment was, in principle at least, an even better test of changing recidivism rates than the Chicago project because the former, unlike the latter, randomly assigned delinquent boys to either treatment or control groups and kept detailed records (in addition to before-and-after measures) of what actually happened to the boys in the treatment programs. The experimental program was community-based, but unlike conventional probation or even group homes, involved an intensive level of participation in a supervised group discussion program, absence from which was promptly penalized by being locked up. The program was in time killed by community opposition (many persons thought it excessively punitive, others quarreled over who should pay for it). The four years worth of data which could be gathered, however, indicate that there have been substantial reductions in arrest rates that cannot be explained by maturation or social class differences for all boys. This was true of both those incarcerated and those left in the community, with the greatest reductions occurring among boys in the experimental programs.[5] Though open to criticism, the Provo data provide some support for the view that, if one measures offense *frequency*, some kinds of programs involving fairly high degrees of restrictiveness and supervision may make some difference.

Thoughts for the Future

The Murray-Cox and the Empey-Erickson studies are important, not only because they employ rates rather than proportions as the outcome measure, or even because they suggest that something might work, but also because they suggest that *the study of deterrence and the study of rehabilitation must be merged — that, at least for a given individual, they are the same thing.* Until now, the two issues have been kept separate. It is not hard to understand why: Welfare and probation agencies administer "rehabilitation," the police and wardens administer "deterrence"; advocates of rehabilitation think of themselves as "tender-minded," advocates of deterrence see themselves as "tough-minded"; rehabilitation supposedly cures the "causes" of crime, while deterrence deals only with the temptations to crime; psychologists study rehabilitation, economists study deterrence. If Murray-Cox and Empey-Erickson are correct, these distinctions are artificial, if not entirely empty.

The common core of both perspectives is, or ideally ought to be, an interest in explaining individual differences in the propensity to commit crime, or changes in a single individual's propensity over time. The stimuli confronting an individual can rarely be partitioned neatly into things tending to produce pain and those likely to produce pleasure; most situations in which we place persons, including criminals, contain elements of both. If explaining individual differences is our object, then studying individuals should be our method. Studies that try to measure the effect on whole societies of marginal changes in aggregate factors (such as the probability of being imprisoned, or the unemployment rate) are probably nearing the end of the line—even the formidable statistical methodologies now available are unlikely to overcome the gross deficiencies in data that we shall always face.

Policy makers need not embrace the substantive conclusions of Murray and Cox (though it is hard to see how they could reasonably be ignored) to appreciate the need to encourage local jurisdictions to look at the effect of a given program on the rate of behavior of a given set of offenders. If they do, they may well discover, as Murray and Cox feel they have discovered in Chicago, that for the serious, chronic delinquent, the strategy of minimal intervention—probation, or loosely supervised life in the community—fails to produce any desirable changes (whether one calls those changes deterrence or rehabilitation), whereas tighter, more restrictive forms of supervision (whether in the community or in an institution) may produce some of these desired changes, or at the very least not produce worse delinquency through "labeling" or "stigmatization." It is hard to imagine a reason for not pursuing this line of inquiry.

Footnotes

[1]Paul Lerman, *Community Treatment and Social Control* (Chicago: University of Chicago Press, 1975), p. 67.
[2]Ted Palmer, *Correctional Intervention and Research* (Lexington, Mass.: D.C. Heath/Lexington Books, 1978).

[3]Douglas Lipton, Robert Martinson, and Judith Wilks, *The Effectiveness of Correctional Treatment: A Survey of Treatment Evaluation Studies* (New York: Praeger, 1975).

[4]Charles A. Murray and Louis A. Cox, Jr., *Beyond Probation: Juvenile Corrections and the Chronic Delinquent* (Beverly Hills, California: Sage Publications, 1979).

[5]LaMar T. Empey and Maynard L. Erickson, *The Provo Experiment* (Lexington, Mass.: D.C. Heath/Lexington Books, 1972).

21

Prison "Boot Camps" Do Not Measure Up

Dale K. Sechrest*

It pays to advertise, so they say, but is the product advertised the best product? Using available data, the principal objective of this paper is to lay to rest the idea that short-term "shock" incarceration, at least in its present form, is a valid response to the problems of young offenders. These types of programs are not the best response to the problem of improving offenders' lives or increasing the probability that they will not commit new crimes when they return to the community. They add to the fiction that short-term, "quick-fix" panaceas can solve significant social problems.

Prison "boot camps," technically called "shock incarceration," known variously as Basic Training (Florida), Special Alternative Incarceration (Georgia), Regimented Inmate Discipline (Oklahoma), are flourishing in the United States. At last eight states now have such programs and at least eight more soon will have them. The National Institute of Justice (NIJ) completed a major report on them in 1989, and the U.S. General Accounting Office (GAO) published an earlier report on them in 1988. New York State has the largest program (500 beds), followed by Georgia (200 beds), which, along with Oklahoma, was one

*Research assistance for this article was provided by Mr. Carmelo J. Cabarcas.

Source: *Federal Probation*, Vol. 53, No. 3 (September 1989), 15-20.

of the first to begin the programs in late 1938. The programs accept young offenders, aged 18 to 24 in most states, who have nonviolent criminal records. These convicted offenders are put through a program of strict discipline and military-style drills for a period of 90 to 120 days, although Louisiana and New York State operate 6-month programs. In New York State 180 days are seen as necessary to calm public fears about the early release of violent offenders and to do a better job of treatment. In exchange for completion of the program, the sentence, which could be up to 10 years, is reduced to the time served and the boot camp experience. In Florida this is an average of 245 days (8 months) and amounts to 20 percent of the sentence (an average of 3.5 years).[1] Four states have boot camp programs for women inmates—Oklahoma, Mississippi, South Carolina, and Orleans Parish and the State of Louisiana—with the largest having 60 beds (Mississippi).

The Florida profile of participants shows the typical offender to be under 20 at the time of prison admission, a user of illegal drugs, of average intelligence, convicted of a first- or second-degree felony (30- or 15-year maximum sentences, respectively). Participants may have no prior commitments to prison and their sentence must be 10 years or less. Selection for boot camp programs varies from state to state, although in most states the participants are convicted of felonies and sentenced to the department of corrections (DOC) and then selected for boot camp participation, often after several months in jail or prison. Judges are involved in the decision in about two-thirds of the program states. Most program descriptions do not point out the significance of the conviction, which precludes military service and carries with it all the problems of loss of rights subsequent to release.[2]

Shock Incarceration Techniques

Shock incarceration stresses discipline and purports to have the same results as military recruit training with respect to developing positive attitudes toward authority and providing physical conditioning. Official goals in Florida are "to divert offenders from long terms of imprisonment while at the same time deterring them from future criminal activity." Inmates "receive training in psychological methods that promote responsibility and improve decisionmaking."[3] Related goals that apply for most programs are providing inmates a chance for re-evaluation of their lives through working with others, learning to accept discipline, and improving their self-respect and ability to control their behavior; in the process they learn to seek realistic goals, and are taught how to live without committing crimes. While education and job training are not part of the Georgia and Florida programs, with vocational training part of none, some programs emphasize education and job skills to a limited extent. As opposed to "rehabilitation," the New York State shock incarceration program purports to "habilitate," or properly socialize these offenders.[4] For most states system goals include reducing prison crowding and system costs, and ultimately recidivism and its related costs.[5]

The primary technique, or "treatment tool" is teaching discipline through the use of military "boot camp" techniques. A new "recruit" in Georgia (of "both races") is shouted at and referred to as a maggot, scumbag, boy, a fool, or a nobody, and repeatedly threatened with transfer to the main facility where he may be sexually abused, he is told, if he fails the program.[6] In Florida the "pukes" must pull together or they are all punished as a group, which is standard recruit fare. The NIJ report points out that the Army no longer uses these types of abusive and degrading techniques as part of their training, preferring to use "voice commands" and other forms of motivation.[7] Motivation in the Florida program is provided by moving through stages marked with different colored hats leading to graduation.

Shock incarceration programs appear to have less appeal to corrections officials than to the public or its representatives.[8] The programs have great media appeal, and are widely publicized as meeting the need to "do something" about the crime problem. The public appeal is similar to that for the "scared straight" and "shock" probation and parole concepts of the early 1980s, none of which have proven effective on close examination. Corrections officials' arguments are more practical, including better prison management, reduced crowding, and expanded sentencing options.

The Success of Shock Incarceration

What are the successes and failures of these programs? As with the other shock and scare programs, as well as other highly touted social panaceas, such as methadone maintenance, deinstitutionalization, determinate sentencing, and the like, early media and program reports are glowing. Early reports from Georgia claimed 80 percent success rates for graduates "staying out of trouble."[9] In 1986, Mississippi reported a return to prison rate "35 percent lower than the normal return rate," which would be about 5 percent, since the national return rate is about 40 percent over a 3-year followup period.[10] Florida always claimed a success rate of 75 to 80 percent, which they can now document, as discussed below.[11]

In fact, about half the inmates selected for these programs complete them. Their return rates to prison are not better than the national average for most programs over a 3-year followup period. Georgia had a 23-percent return rate after 2 years (1986 figures) and the U.S. General Accounting Office reported a 39-percent return rate for Georgia inmates at 3 years compared with a 38-percent return rate for controls after 3 years (through July 1988).[12] The NIJ report cites the Georgia figure of 38.5 percent, indicating that those entering in their teens had a 46.8 percent return to prison rate. The NIJ report cites a study of Oklahoma's program in which return rates of shock incarceration (SI) graduates were compared with similar nonviolent offenders sentenced to their DOC; after 29 months almost half the SI graduates, but only 28 percent of the other group had returned to prison.[13] These data appear to indicate that the programs may have early successes, but in the long term they may not do any better than conventional methods. The real test, as always, is performance in the community. A recent NIJ 3-year followup study of released offenders nationally reported that 62.5 percent of former state inmates were rearrested for a felony or a serious misdemeanor within 3 years of their discharge from prison; 47 percent were convicted of new crimes, and 41 percent returned to prison.[14] Based on these findings, the GAO report conclusions concurred with those of the NIJ report in advising caution to states planning to move ahead with such programs, recommending further study.[15]

The Florida Study

Florida's recently completed study reports on a 1-year followup comparison of a "matched" group of (nonparticipant) offenders of the same age and general background as the boot camp graduates. Unfortunately, the "matched" sample had 257 more inmates than those graduating, a total of 400, which does not make it a truly matched group but more of a comparison pool of offenders with similar characteristics. And, since the possibility of any occurrence was greater in the larger group, comparisons of any kind will be flawed. Nonetheless, return-to-prison rates (probation revocations) after 1 year for the 143 graduates were 5.59 percent (8 graduates of 143) and 7.75 percent for the 400 "matched" offenders (31 of 400), a claimed "likelihood of returning to prison nearly 40 percent greater than that of Boot Camp graduates."[16] Since the size of these population was reported, some statistical tests were possible. A chi-squared test revealed no significant difference between the two groups on return to prison ($X_2 = .73$, p M .39).[17] In addition to returns to prison, postrelease failures of all kinds were reported—absconding, or a new felony, misdemeanor, or technical revocation; these figures revealed a different picture. There were 13 failures of graduates and 69 in the comparison group, which proved significant ($X^2 = 5.5$, p M .012), indicating that overall failure rates show graduates doing better than the comparison group. However, there were no technical violations for the graduates and 22 for the matched group, which had 257 more inmates. When technical violations are treated as successes there is no significant difference between the two groups ($X^2 = .76$, p M .38). The rate of absconders in the comparison group was also double that of the graduates (7.3% v. 3.5%). These comparisons make it difficult to pronounce the program a success on prison return rates or failures at this time. Florida officials are reluctant to pronounce the program a complete success even with these findings in hand, citing too many unanswered questions at this time.[18]

The Florida report also compared program graduates (successes) with nongraduates (failures). Graduates (54% of all admissions) were older (19.5 v. 18.7 years), in better physical condition at program onset, more likely to have completed high school (31% v. 10.2%), lacking full-time employment at arrest (32.2% v. 44.8%), twice as likely to be convicted of a first-degree felony for armed robbery, violent crime(s) or drug sale/manufacture (44.1% v. 20%), and more likely to have had a prior term of probation or community control (42.7% v. 33.3%).[19] Statistically significant differences between the groups are not provided in the report, only tendencies based on percentages. Chi-squared comparisons reveal that significant differences existed for high school completion (favoring graduates; $X^2 = 13.29$, p M .001), employment at admission (less for graduates; $X^2 = 4.1$, p M .04), and convictions for armed robbery (greater for graduates; $X^2 = 6.48$, p M .02). The question of seriousness of the crimes is an important one. While armed robberies are reported as significantly greater for graduates, total crimes for economic gain (see table 1 footnote for types) are not significantly different for either group, and *include armed and unarmed robbery*.[20] In fact, when armed and unarmed robbery are combined and compared for the two groups there are no significant differences ($X^2 = 2.2$, p M .13) For economic crimes, also, there are no statistically significant differences between the two groups—80.4 percent graduates, 85.7 percent nongraduates ($X^2 = 1.2$, p M .28). The report itself, in discussing differences between participants and other inmates, as shown in table 1, states that "Boot Camp admissions are also less likely to have had a term of probation and more likely to have been involved in a crime for economic gain."[21]

Table 1 is extracted from the Florida Department of Corrections report and compares the characteristics of boot camp admissions with males under 25 admitted in 1987-88 and the general population of males admitted in 1987-88. No actual numbers are reported for the latter two groups, so statistical comparisons are not possible. However, armed robberies and "economic crimes" are shown for each group, and again, even though armed robberies are shown as greater for boot camp admissions, economic crimes are the predominate criterion for admission to the Florida program. These comparisons appear to indicate that boot camp participants in Florida are, in fact, a less serious group of offenders.

Table 1: 7 Characteristics of Boot Camp Admissions in Florida*			
		All Admissions 1987-1988	
Offender Characteristic	Boot Camp Admissions	Males 24 & Younger	All Males 25 & Older
	Percent	Percent	Percent
Employed at Arrest	88.9	51.0	64.2
Prior Probation	25.9	61.7	86.3
Prior violation of Probation or Community Control	14.6	43.1	37.4
Primary Offense:			
Burglary	31.8	27.4	18.5
Armed Robbery	16.8	9.0	4.6
Narcotics	9.0	11.9	17.4
Physical Injury Crimes**	8.4	12.0	16.4
Economic Crimes***	82.2	71.2	61.1
Sentence Length in years	3.6	3.5	4.1

* Source: Bureau of Planning, Research, and Statistics, Florida Department of Corrections, *Research Report, Boot Camp Evaluation*, p. 5.

** Includes homicide, manslaughter, sexual crimes, assault, and battery.

*** Includes robbery (armed and unarmed), burglary, larceny, fraud, narcotics (sale), receiving stolen property, possession of burglary tools, and auto theft.

Interestingly, very few of the boot camp offenders in Florida have been tried on probation and, of those who have been, far fewer have violated community control. This concern is expressed in the NIJ report, which notes that many states have adopted the criteria used for shock probation sentences to target "persons believed most likely to be deterred—young, non-violent offenders who have not been confined before under sentence . . . most of whom would have gotten probation in the past."[22]

Space and Cost Factors

Costs are difficult when evaluating correctional programs. Institutions have fixed costs that do not vary a great deal when more inmates are added to the population. This is why the facilities can be crowded without major increases in costs; there are "economies of scale." Programs that claim great cost savings by reducing prison populations 200 to 400 inmates per year are not providing great savings. Georgia provides a cost of $3,523 per inmate/year for Special Alternative Incarceration (SAI), inclusive of probation supervision, compared to $13,450 per year for conventional incarceration.[23] An early report from New York State quoted a cost of $9,000 per inmate compared to $19,400 for regular prison inmates.[24] NIJ figures are for annual facility operations and simply do not support the notion that it costs less to operate these shock incarceration programs. Costs are at least the same.[25] In fact, New York State now reports higher costs for shock incarceration, which are no doubt indicative of the longer time spent in the program and the depth of the services provided. An early report from the Oklahoma program reported that the staff-inmate ratio was about four times greater than that for the general prison population.[26] The program acknowledges being most costly than a comparable living unit in the department, which could be due to its greater emphasis on educational and vocational programs.[27] A concern for Florida is that only 61.6 percent of the program beds are filled, on average, indicating that it is difficult to find inmates willing to undergo this type of program, especially when sentence reductions due to crowded prisons might make their sentence equally brief.[28] Still, shorter confinement times, even with more program expenditures, should produce some cost savings in the long term, but how much is unclear at this time. In fact, as the NIJ report points out, if these offenders had received probation, even greater savings could have been realized.[29] All factors must be carefully evaluated to really understand the savings possible—actual prison costs, not inflated daily figures based on original design capacities, the actual need for incarceration, and the effects of these programs on reduced crime and recidivism—the ultimate cost saving.

Problems With Boot Camps

Corrections officials do not appear to be as delighted with shock incarceration programs as are judges, law enforcement officers, legislators, and prosecutors.[30] Why is this? Perhaps the military emphasis makes them nervous. In one state the program was originally designed around programs of education, training, and the like. However, the director later became concerned that the military aspect had so much appeal that it became the rationale for the program, *not* providing emotional support, education, and job skills to these youngsters over the long term. It is further feared that the military style used by correctional officers may bring out their "dark-side," or sadistic tendencies. There are possibilities for abuse of authority, especially since conventional disciplinary procedures are waived by the inmates coming into these programs.

The NIJ report suggests that this "discipline therapy" or confrontation style, which the military has abandoned, can and has gotten out of control in some instances. Experience with confrontational "T-groups" and "haircuts" used in drug treatment programs in the 1960s and 1970s tells us that some individuals find confrontation and abuse emotionally damaging and unlikely to build self-esteem. Further, most evaluations of "shock" programs, whether jail, prison or probation, have shown that gains are most often short term unless followup is available. Sometimes even more hostility toward the system is engendered. The NIJ report notes that program inmates did not object to profanity by officers as long as it was not directed at them—if so, it angered them.[31]

Abuses do occur, although there have been no legal challenges to the practices used because it would be difficult to see this as cruel and unusual punishment when it is used by the military. Nonetheless, NIJ investigators found the use of racial slurs in one program that led to transfer of some employees to other duties. It has been demonstrated in other types of programs that rules can be enforced, physical stress used, and firm discipline applied in contexts that will build self-esteem. The "wilderness programs," such as Outward Bound, use these techniques which, along with scared straight, appear to make up the roots of the boot camp concept. VisionQuest, a program that places chronic juvenile delinquents in rustic wilderness camps and other settings, appears to show success in reducing recidivism, reducing arrests to 55 percent for program participants compared to 71 percent for those in a conventional treatment facility after one year.[32] The NIJ report contains an appendix section that discusses "challenge" programs, which have the goals of increasing self-esteem, self-control, and respect for authority through vigorous physical and mental challenges. In fact, Outward Bound was founded by two former merchant seamen who saw the value of building personal confidence through the learning of survival skills and transposed this concept to the civilian world.[33]

Conclusions

Shock incarceration programs—"boot camps"—should not be created as a public relations gimmick. They may be good politics, but they could become programs that will not be good for corrections or society in the long run. Over the past 15 years corrections officials have been criticized repeatedly and resoundingly for failed programs. The "rehabilitation" programs they sold the public in the past were pronounced to be failures, i.e., "nothing works." Most corrections officials fell back into the incapacitation role, augmented by voluntary program participation, as a matter of simple self-defense. It is now almost unbelievable that these same corrections officials would allow the media to tout these untested programs as they did the old "failed" programs.

The boot camp programs are often underfunded, sometimes underused or poorly implemented, clearly untested, and mostly incomplete efforts to provide full correctional programs for young offenders. Followup programs that may exist are never mentioned by the media, probably because they appear to be little used by shock incarceration programs anyhow. Surely they are not newsworthy. Some probation departments have special programs for these individuals, but these do not appear to be well-organized or well-funded. New York State claims to have a treatment program that is "more extensive" than others, lasting 6 months, and involving drug treatment, which is a sound direction for the future. The program provides early contact with parole officers in an "aftershock," or intensive parole supervision, phase, but no extensive evaluation of that appears to be planned. Many probation officers report that offenders released from these programs are easier to manage, so continuity appears to be important. What about the program dropouts? No program appears to take positive steps with dropouts, although Oklahoma appears to move them into other programs that will assist them upon their release.[34] The NIJ study did not address this issue.

Unfortunately, the emphasis lies with the military aspects of the program, the notion that we can shock or scare young people out of crime by drilling it out of them! The programs are not unlike scared straight in their emphasis on fear and intimidation to transform offenders into upstanding citizens. Grueling exercise and labor are the bywords, and punishment surely occurs. After all, it works for the military — but those aren't criminal offenders, either. Further, the boot camps are not like the military, which has entirely different purposes. Military boot camps train people to kill other people; their dropout rates are considerably lower than the prison programs; and, they provide followup, i.e., young men and women stay in the service long enough to realize the benefits of their initial experience. Prison boot camp graduates cannot get into the military because the military won't accept either a G.E.D. certificate or a convicted felon. In fact, this is exactly what they don't want! Curiously, no shock incarceration program appears to be attempting to break down this barrier to military service, which may now be possible in view of upcoming personnel shortages in the military.

What Does the Future Hold?

Regardless of the media hype, there is no evidence that shock incarceration "works" for the offenders that need to be reached any more than scared straight or shock probation worked to any great degree. None. Yet these types of "quick-fix" solutions linger on. Shock programs like scared straight and boot camps appear to be "right" methods based on our middle class understanding of how punishment works. The American Correctional Association notes that "This deeply-rooted social problem [of juvenile delinquency] cannot be eradicated by exposing juveniles to threats of force, intimidation, verbal abuse, or other practices that are meant to shock youths out of delinquent-prone behavior." Generally, programs like these will not erase the social conditions under which these people must live upon release. Where are the community programs that are required both before and after incarceration? Corrections officials must demand these resources before committing themselves to a program that may produce only limited benefits in its present form and again show that "nothing works."

Most experts agree that without the help of the family, and without addressing social problems emanating from poor schools, unemployment, poverty, and racial discrimination, there is little likelihood that the "scare" or the "drill" will last for any length of time. Young men and women require well-rounded, community-based programs which will assist them in growth at home, in school, and in finding and financing training for jobs. Frightening or "discipline drilling" people who have resorted to crime will not have a long-term deterrent effect if these people cannot get satisfaction through legitimate alternatives in society. Nor will determinate sentencing, methadone programs, selective incapacitation, more prison space, better law enforcement, or increased punishments solve deeply rooted social problems.

This is not to say that properly used and evaluated, these programs may not be successful for some types of inmates, although the possibilities of abuse are evident and the programs lack long-term commitments to the offenders involved. In the final analysis, properly run shock incarceration programs should be another of many tools for use in helping selected offenders. This may occur if they can be expanded to include education, job training, and skill development components starting in the facility and continuing into the community. Corrections staff may be learning how to evaluate offenders better for programs along some continuum of need. Now that corrections has the attention of its constituency, it would appear to be time to ask for sufficient resources to explore the full potential of this early intervention approach to young offenders. As Commissioner Coughlin of New York State says of shock incarceration, "It is a major step in recognizing that incarceration, on its own, is not necessarily the proper punishment for all offenders. Now we must look ahead to see if this alternative provides habilitation of inmates and protection of society."[35] But how will we know?

Footnotes

[1] Bureau of Planning, Research, and Statistics, Florida Department of Corrections, *Research Report, Boot Camp Evaluation*, March, 1989, p. ii.

[2] Cf. Velmer S. Burton, Jr., Lawrence F. Travis III, and Francis T. Cullen, "Reducing the Legal Consequences of a Felony Conviction: A National Survey of State Statutes," *International J. of Comparative and Applied Criminal Justice* 12:1, Spring 1988, pp. 101-109; same authors, "The Collateral Consequences of a Felony Conviction: A National Study of State Statutes," *Federal Probation*, September 1987.

[3] Florida Department of Corrections, p. 1.

[4] American Correctional Association, 1988 Winter Conference, November 24, 1988: 1.

[5] Dale G. Parent, *Shock Incarceration: An Overview of Existing Programs*, National Institute of Justice *Issues and Practices*, U.S. Department of Justice (undated advance copy, May 1989): 21.

[6] *People*, February 1, 1988, p. 25; *Life*, June 1988, p. 82.

[7] National Institute of Justice, *Shock Incarceration*, p. 21.

[8] Ibid., p. 3.

[9] *People*, February 1, 1988, p. 25; Carmelo J. Cabarcas, telephone interview with Lt. James Combs, Georgia Shock Unit Supervisor, November 1988.

[10] *Time*, August 11, 1986, p. 17.

[11] Carmelo J. Cabarcas, telephone interview with Jim Mitchell, Florida Department of Corrections, November 1988.

[12] *Prison Boot Camps, Too Early to Measure Effectiveness*, a Briefing Report to the Honorable Lloyd Bentsen, U.S. Senate, September 1987, p. 5.

[13] National Institute of Justice, 1989, p. 4.

[14] U.S. Bureau of Justice Statistics, April 1989. A useful benchmark for shock incarceration programs might be the 30 to 40 percent estimated lifetime recidivism rates for male offenders developed by the U.S. Bureau of Justice Statistics by Patrick A. Langan and Lawrence A. Greenfeld in "The Prevalence of Imprisonment," July 1985, p. 7.

[15] U.S. General Accounting Office, p. 4.

[16] Florida Department of Corrections, 1989, p. 26.

[17] All chi-squared statistics are four-fold tables, df = 1; continuity corrections were used where cell sizes warranted.

[18] *The Miami Herald*, April 12, 1989, p. 11A.

[19] Ibid., p. 1.

[20] Ibid., p. 9.

[21] Ibid., p. 4.

[22] National Institute of Justice, *Shock Incarceration*, 1989, pp. 3-4.

[23] David C. Evans, Georgia Department of Corrections Probation Division, Report on Special Incarceration Units, undated (c. 1988).

[24] *Corrections Today*, June 1988, p. 87.

[25] National Institute of Justice, 1989, p. 16.

[26] Al Pagel, "Doing a Tour of Duty in a 'Boot Camp' Prison," *Corrections Compendium*, November 1986, p. 10.

[27] National Institute of Justice, *Shock Incarceration*, 1989, p. 7.

[28] *The Miami Herald*, April 12, 1989; 11A; Florida Department of Corrections, 1989, p. 23.

[29] National Institute of Justice, *Shock Incarceration*, p. 16.

[30] Ibid., p. 3.

[31] Ibid., p. 22.

[32] *Criminal Justice Newsletter*, March 1, 1988, p. 5.

[33] National Institute of Justice, 1989, p. 57.

[34] Les Crabtree, "Military Discipline, Young Offenders Learn Accountability," *Corrections Today*, December 1985, pp. 38-39.

[35] Commissioner's Commentary, *D.O.C.S. Today*, New York State Department of Correctional Services, April, 1988.

22

Pyschology and Correctional Treatment

David L. Bazelon*

When President Johnson appointed the members of the Prsidential Commission to study crime in America, there was a great hue and cry over the failure to name to the Commission a single behavioral scientist. I joined in the criticism because I had been assured by men whose intellect and judgment I admired that the behavioral sciences could provide a significant input to the Commission's effort. In response to the uproar, the Commission indicated that it had no intention of insulating itself from behavioral science. And at my urging, a meeting was called to establish a procedure whereby the contributions of these scientists could be funnelled into the project. I proposed this meeting not because I was in a position to define the role these sciences could fill, but because I saw myself as a spokesman for men

*Senior Circuit Judge, United States Court of Appeals, Washington, D.C.

Source: This address was delivered at the American Association of Correctional Psychologists' Conference on "Psychology's Roles and Contributions in Problems of Crime, Delinquency and Corrections," on January 20, 1972 at Pinewood Estate, Lake Wales, Florida. Reprinted by permission of the author.

and women who could sit down with the Commission and hammer out a program. Representatives of some of the leading associations in the field were present at the meeting.

The meeting could only be described as a calamity. I had not expected instant results, but I was disappointed and embarrassed that some of the outstanding scholars in these areas could not even come up with helpful insights. In fact, to the best of my recollection, not a single significant idea or proposal emerged from the entire discussion. No one was able to describe the contribution these disciplines could make, or even to suggest a means of finding out what sort of contribution might be made. And worse, no one was prepared to commit himself or his organization to the formulation of a plan or course of action.

Regretfully, I must tell you that the papers prepared for this Conference on the role of psychology in corrections do nothing to allay my increasing doubts and uncertainties about what it is that psychologists or any other behaviorists can offer. All of the papers begin with the unexamined assumption that the correctional psychologist can make an important contribution, and the further assumption, which is thought to follow. logically, that we therefore need more psychologists. None of them examines critically the work that psychologists have done in the past, or even begins to inquire why they have failed to accomplish more. There is no mention of changes in the training, practice or employment of the correctional psychologist. None of the papers even asks whether there should be any such specialty.

It would be easy to dismiss my doubts, of course, if the scholars at the meeting I described or those who prepared these papers were second-rate representatives of their profession. But correctional psychology has no more able spokemen than these. I am not a psychologist and naturally I am not well qualified to evaluate their credentials. But from all accounts these men fully deserve their outstanding reputations. If these leaders have not yet established a role in this area for your profession, then there are difficult questions that must finally be confronted.

I certainly hope you will not draw the impression that I consider psychology a worthless discipline that ought to be abandoned. The issue is not whether psychology is good, but what it is good at. I think I can make my point by telling you a story about a mother who called a doctor and told him that her young son was suffering terribly from fever, nausea, and cramps. "Is he having fits?" the doctor asked. The mother said no. "That's too bad," the doctor replied. "I'm terrific on fits." I am afraid that I may be addressing a large group of the nation's leading specialists on fits, who have been asked to treat a patient that badly needs care, but that doesn't happen to be suffering from fits. There is no doubt that our correctional apparatus is gravely ill. The

question is, is your expertise—which no one questions—what we need
to solve this particular problem?

On the whole, it seems to me that the institution of correctional
psychology has had far too little outside evaluation or scrutiny. Psychologists have not produced any remarkable successes in the corrections field. But apparently that has never been considered a sufficient
reason to scrutinize your work closely. After all, our entire correctional process is a shambles, and it is hard to single out psychologists
for blame when none of the other participants has been able to
generate successful programs. Moreover, psychology is still widely
considered a fledgling discipline in the field of corrections, and it is
often assumed that it needs breathing room and time to establish itself
before it can make inroads on the problem. Demanding quick results
could smother the effort, or encourage programs that sacrifice long-
range promise for short-term pay-offs. And finally, even if we were
prepared to hold psychologists to a stringent standard of accountability, we dimply don't have any uniformly agreed upon standard to
measure your performance. To be sure, there are critics like Dr.
Thomas Szasz who tell you that you have no right to succeed. But no
one on the outside has been able to take psychology on its own terms
and ask whether it has moved the ball forward or provided data that
would enable others to begin understanding our problems. Accordingly, if any questioning is to be done, you are the ones who must do it.

In suggesting that you initiate a process of self-criticism and reexam-
ination, I cannot avoid the responsibility that I share with other judges
and law enforcement officials for having pressed you to assume your
present role in the correctional process. To a large extent you did not
volunteer—you were asked to come up with answers for problems that
seemed too difficult for us to solve. Perhaps I deserve a special share of
the responsibility, for I have devoted much of my career to the goal of
opening lines of communication between law and the social sciences.
And I hope you will not depreciate my questioning as the predictable
over-reaction of a disenchanted lover. We all have to learn some hard
truths about uncritical reliance on experts. Difficult problems will not
go away merely because we turn them over to experts. Throughout the
criminal process one can find distressing examples of just that kind of
uncritical reliance. In the area of civil commitment, for example, the
courts have frequently abandoned to behavioral scientists and doctors
the responsibility for deciding which persons should be subject to
involuntary treatment. These experts are unquestionably
knowledgeable about mental illness and various treatment modalities.
But the questions raised by civil commitment are primarily legal and
moral, not medical. And there is no reason to assume that the expertise
of these doctors and scientists extends to questions of law and

morality. Perhaps we should rely on these doctors, whatever their expertise, to make the legal and moral decisions. But we clearly should not stick our heads in the sand and pretend that we are only asking them medical questions.

In the same vein, the courts and law enforcement agencies have often tried to wash their hands of the correctional process, comforted with the notion that the experts—you—are minding the store. That may be the easy solution for us, and I am sure it has advantages for you, but it must not stop us from asking whether the questions raised by crime and punishment and corrections are really questions that psychologists or other behavioralists can and should be answering.

Because the related problems of crime and corrections are deeply disturbing to a large number of people, and because none of the attempted solutions shows any sign of success, there is an almost irresistible temptation to soothe the public by sweeping the problems under the rug. One method of accomplishing this is to treat the courts as a whipping boy, blaming them for a problem they did not create and they cannot solve. But a second method of camouflaging the real issues —and the one that should concern us here—is to divert the public's attention by calling on experts to provide a pill that will magically make all of our problems disappear. Instead of facing up to the true dimensions of the problem and admitting that violent crime is an inevitable by-product of our society's social and economic structure, we prefer to blame the problem on a criminal class—a group of sick persons who must be treated by doctors and cured. Why should we even consider fundamental social changes or massive income redistribution if the entire problem can be solved by having scientists teach the criminal class—like a group of laboratory rats—to march successfully through the maze of our society? In short, before you respond with enthusiasm to our plea for help, you must ask yourselves whether your help is really needed, or whether you are merely engaged as magicians to perform an intriguing side-show so that the spectators will not notice the crisis in the center ring. In considering our motives for offering you a role, I think you would do well to consider how much less expensive it is to hire a thousand psychologists than to make even a miniscule change in the social and economic structure. If your participation permits us to divert attention from the real problems, you must consider the costs of holding out your skills as pertinent to the solution of the problem.

The critical issue, it seems to me, is whether the fundamental postulates of your discipline make it impossible for you to reach the central problem. Your discipline invariably assumes, I think, that aberrant behavior is the product of sickness, and it brings to bear on the problem a medical or therapeutic model. That model assumes a white, middle-class, non-conforming subject whose anti-social conduct is attributable to mental disturbance. That type of subject may well be amenable to group therapy and the other rehabilitative techniques in your arsenal. It also assumes, and I think this emerges clearly from the papers prepared for this Conference, that criminals are more like other criminals than they are like other human beings. I am hard pressed to see how those assumptions can be applied to the problem of violent crime—the kind of crime that most alarms society. That kind of crime is committed by persons who are clearly at the bottom of society's barrel. They have usually been raised in deplorable and destructive conditions with few of the values and goals that are usually pushed on middle-class children. We should not be surprised, therefore, if a great many of them do not respond to the same pressures and stimuli that motivate middle-class children. I fear that we may be trying to rehabilitate these offenders with techniques that can work, if at all, only on the middle class. Poor, black offenders are not necessarily sick. They may simply be responding to an environment that has impoverished them, humiliated them and embittered them. Will group therapy help a black teenager who steals cars and peddles drugs, and who will be tossed at the end of his "rehabilitation" right back into the environment that nurtured him? Will the Rorschach or Bender-Gestalt tests tell us anything about an offender who steals, not because he suffers from kleptomania and gets his kicks from stealing, but because he wants money to buy goods and services that most of us can already obtain? Or who needs money to feed his addiction to narcotic drugs? Does it really make sense to treat such an offender as a sick person who can be cured? Have we, perhaps, been focusing our attention on the wrong part of the problem—on the offender and his mental condition instead of on the conditions that produced him?

The papers presented at this Conference carry the implication that these questions can be answered as soon as we have more programs, more of something labelled "rehabilitation," and, above all, more psychologists. But if these requests for more are predicated on an unrealistic picture of the problem, then more of anything is not going to solve the problem. I am convinced, at least, that more money will not provide an answer. When I was on the Advisory Council of the National Institute of Mental Health I saw hundreds of project proposals that were designed to deal with these problems, but I think I could count on one hand the number that offered anything resembling a promise of producing information useful to persons in the front lines of the criminal process. And if research money is being absorbed by unpromising projects, it is also clear that money is being squandered on action programs that have no connection with the real world. For example, we now have a federal penal institution in West Virginia that spends, and this was the figure several years ago, about $13,000 per year on each inmate. Don't we have to ask whether the problem could be better handled by letting the inmates out of the institution and just giving each one of them $13,000 per year? From what I understand about the theory that underlies that institution, it seems to me already outdated. I cannot think of any function for it except as a warehouse for those offenders who are least in need of help (and who would probably have been released if this impressive facility were not available). I think we have to ask whether elaborate and costly programs for research and rehabilitation serve any other function than providing staff — including correctional psychologists — with jobs and income. That is not an easy question for you to ask. But I do not see how — in good conscience — you can avoid it.

If I have given you the impression that I am convinced psychology has no role to play in this area, then I must clarify my own position. I don't know whether psychology should have a significant role, and I don't even know how to find out except by asking you. If you undertake the inquiry I am suggesting, you may reach the painful conclusion that you have completely misdirected your efforts in trying to solve the problems of crime and corrections. More likely, however, you will conclude that psychology does have a limited role, but that its potential abilities have been greatly overstated. That conclusion would be extremely important, for you cannot hold yourselves out as capable of solving the entire problem when you can have an impact, at best, on no more than a very, very small part of it — particularly as respects the kind of crime that causes governments and foundations to support meetings such as this one.

You may find, for example, that the therapeutic model does have application to certain kinds of white-collar crime, crimes of passion and mental illness rather than poverty and drug addiction. If that is your conclusion, then I urge you to pursue that aspect of the overall problem. Middle-class crime is a significant subject of inquiry, and your contribution will probably be important. But there should be no mistake that the crime problem which most alarms the public is not the problem of white-collar crime, but the problem of so-called violent street crime. And since the public is obsessed with fear of this kind of crime, it is willing to spend large amounts of money to ferret out a solution. If psychologists proclaim their inability to participate in the search, they will, of course, lose their share of the money. Conferences like this one probably could not take place without the financial support of a public that thinks you can help solve the problem of violent street crime. If you conclude that the problem is beyond your powers, we all may have to stay home more often. But I am sure you will agree that there is no justification for obtaining public money — even for worthy purposes—under false pretenses. More important, so long as you permit us to talk about a magic pill instead of the real problem, you will seriously impede the quest for a meaningful solution.

Alternatively, you may find that you can have a significant impact on the problem of violent crime by taking bitter and violent offenders and re-shaping them so that they learn to live with the devastating and ugly conditions of life that none of us could tolerate. If you can succeed in that endeavor, I am confident that the public will shower you with money and you will honestly have earned it. But whether you want to serve as high-priced janitors who sweep up society's debris so that our problems will be pushed out of sight but in no sense resolved, is a question that you yourselves must answer after you have squarely faced it.

23

Factories with Fences
Warren E. Burger*

The ancient and honorable American custom of commencement speeches is an innocuous one that has done very little harm to those who are graduating, and it may even have the beneficial consequence of teaching the graduates the virtue of patience. With the problems you are about to confront in the disturbed world of today, you will need patience. And the parents, who are now to be released from paying the high costs of keeping a student in college, are bound to be in such a happy mood that no speech could depress them.

I have no talent or inclination for framing cosmic remarks about the future, and I have never thought that even the most eloquent of speakers could make much out of "handing the torch" to those who have survived the rigors of a university education.

All of my training and experience, as a lawyer and as a judge, is to try to go to the heart of problems and to seek and frame solutions.

I discover, on reading about Pace University, that I am almost as old

*Chief Justice, Supreme Court of the United States.
Source: This address was delivered at the commencement exercises of Pace University on June 11, 1983, at Madison Square Garden, New York. It was first published in the *Pace Law Review*, Vol. 4, No. 1 (Fall 1983), 1-9. Reprinted with the permission of the publisher.

as the university itself and quite frankly I was astonished to find that you have an enrollment approaching 30,000 men and women. More important than either the age or the size of the university, is how it approaches its task. It is clear that Pace University is in the forefront of institutions that look to the future and to the enormous role that technology will play in our lives in the years ahead. In its systematic anticipation of the needs of the future, Pace University fulfills one of the great obligations of a university. I naturally have a particular affinity for night school graduates. And those who attended your *day* law school have a *special* benefit—they can always call on their more mature friends of the night section for help and advice and guidance!

Now to be serious—

Today I want to discuss with you a grave problem which my generation and those who went before me have failed to solve and as a result, you inherit the consequences of that failure. In one sense we can say that it is a "torch" you are being handed, one that will singe your pocketbooks and affect your lives from now on.

Since I have been a member of the federal judiciary I have thought and spoken on the subject of penal and correctional institutions and those policies and practices that ought to be changed. I see this as part of the administration of justice. People go to prisons only when judges send them there and judges should have a particular concern about the effectiveness of the prisons and the correctional process, even though we have no responsibility for their management. Based on my observations as a judge for more than twenty-five years and from visiting prisons in the United States and in most of the countries of Europe— and in the Soviet Union and The People's Republic of China—I have long believed that we have not gone about the matter in the best way.

This is one of the unresolved problems on your agenda and today I will propose some changes in our approach to prisons. But before doing that, let me suggest why the subject has a special relevance, even a special urgency, right now. Our country is about to embark on a multi-billion dollar prison construction program. At least one billion dollars of construction is already underway. The question I raise is this: are we going to build more "human warehouses" or should we change our thinking and create institutions that are training schools and factories with fences around them where we will first train the inmates and then have them engage in useful production to prepare them for the future and to help pay for their confinement?

One thoughtful scholar of criminal justice described the state of affairs in much harsher terms than I have ever used. Four years ago he wrote this:

> Criminal justice in the United States is in a state of spreading decay.
> ...The direct costs of crime include loss of life and limb, loss of

[earnings],...physical and mental suffering by the victims and their
families....[1]

These direct losses, he continued, run into many billions of dollars
annually. But indirect losses are vastly more and reach the astonishing figure of 100 billion dollars a year. These indirect costs include
higher police budgets, higher private security measures, higher
insurance premiums, medical expenses of the victims, and welfare
payments to dependents of prisoners and victims. In the immediate
future these astounding figures and the great suffering that underlies
them can be reduced. This can be done by more effective law enforcement which in turn will produce a demand for more and more prison
facilities. But more prisons of the kind we now have will not solve the
basic problem. Plainly, if we can divert more people from lives of crime
we would benefit those who are diverted and the potential victims. All
that we have done in improved law enforcement, in new laws for
mandatory minimum sentences, and changes in parole and probation
practices has not prevented thirty percent of America's homes from
being touched by crime every year.

Twenty years ago I shared with such distinguished penologists as the
late James V. Bennett, longtime Director of the Federal Bureau of
Prisons, Torsten Eriksson, his counterpart in Sweden, and Dr. George
K. Sturrup in Denmark and others, high hopes for rehabilitation
programs. These hopes now seem to have been based more on optimism
and wishful thinking than on reality. During that period of time we
have seen that even the enlightened correctional practices of Sweden
and other northern European countries have produced results that,
although better than ours, have also fallen short of expectations.

On several occasions I have stated one proposition to which I have
adhered to for the twenty-five years that I have worked on this problem
and it is this:

> When society places a person behind walls and bars it has an obli-
> gation—a moral obligation—to do whatever can reasonably be
> done to change that person before he or she goes back into the
> stream of society.

If we had begun twenty-five, thirty-five, or fifty years ago to develop
the kinds of correctional programs that are appropriate for an
enlightened and civilized society, the word "recidivist" might not have
quite as much currency as it does today. This is not simply a matter of
compassion for other human beings, it is a hard common sense matter
for our own protection and our own pocketbooks.

In just the past ten years the prison population in America has
doubled from less than 200,000 inmates to more than 400,000. This
reflects, in part, the increase in crime, better law enforcement, and the

imposition of longer sentences and more stringent standards of parole and probation. Budgets for law enforcement, for example, like the rates for theft insurance have skyrocketed.

If we accept the idea that the most fundamental obligation of government in a civilized society is the protection of people and homes, then we must have more effective law enforcement, but equally important, we must make fundamental changes in our prison and correctional systems. Just more stone, mortar and steel for walls and bars will not change this melancholy picture. If we are to make progress and at the same time protect the persons and property of people and make streets and homes safe from crime, we must change our approach in dealing with people convicted of crimes. Our system provides more protection and more safeguards for persons accused of crime, more appeals and more reviews than any other country in the world. But once the judicial process has run its course we seem to lose interest. The prisoner and the problem are brushed under the rug.[2]

It is predictable that a person confined in a penal institution for two, five or ten years, and then released, yet still unable to read, write, spell or do simple arithmetic and not trained in any marketable vocational skill, will be vulnerable to returning to a life of crime. And very often the return to crime begins within weeks after release. What job opportunities are there for an unskilled, functional illiterate who has a criminal record? The recidivists who return to our prisons are like automobiles that are called back to Detroit. What business enterprise, whether building automobiles in Detroit or ships in Norfolk, Virginia, or airplanes in Seattle, could continue with the same rate of "recall" of its "products" as our prisons?

The best prisons in the world, the best programs that we can devise will not totally cure this dismal problem for, like disease and war, it is one that the human race has struggled with since the beginning or organized societies. But improvements in our system can be made and the improvements will cost less in the long run than the failure to make them.

I have already said that today one billion dollars in new prison facilities is actually under construction. More than thirty states have authorized construction programs for new prison facilities that over the next ten years will cost as much as ten billion dollars.

If these programs proceed, and we must assume they will, it is imperative that there be new standards that will include the following:

A. Conversion of prisons into places of education and training and into factories and shops for the production of goods.
B. Repeal of statutes which limit the amount of prison industry production or the markets for such goods.

C. Repeal of laws discriminating against the sale or transportation of prison-made goods.

D. The leaders of business and organized labor must cooperate in programs to permit wider use of productive facilities in prisons.

On the affirmative side I have every reason to believe that business and labor leaders will cooperate in more intelligent and more humane prison programs. Of course, prison production programs will compete to some extent with the private sector, but this is not a real problem. With optimum progress in the programs I have outlined, it would be three to five years, or even more, before these changes would have any market impact and even then it will be a very small impact. I cannot believe for one moment that this great country of ours, the most voracious consumer society in the world, will not be able to absorb the production of prison inmates without significant injury to private employment or business. With the most favorable results, the production level of prison inmates would be no more than a tiny drop in the bucket in terms of the Gross National Product. Yet, we find prisons in the United States with limited production facilities which are lying idle because of statutory limitations confining the sale of their products to city and county governments within the state.

Amazingly enough, Congress recently dealt prison industry another blow in the form of a rider to the five percent gas tax, which prohibits the use of prison labor products in federally funded highway projects. This will damage state prison industries which were employing hundreds of prisoners in sign making, and may cost many millions of dollars in unsaleable inventory.

Happily this may be changed. The House of Representatives just passed a bill repealing the highway prohibition and increasing authorization for prison industry projects. It is now up to the Senate.

Prison inmates, by definition, are for the most part maladjusted people. From whatever cause, whether too little discipline or too much; too little security or too much; broken homes or whatever, these people lack self-esteem. They are insecure, they are at war with themselves as well as with society. They do not share the work ethic that made this country great. They did not learn, either at home or in the schools, the moral values that lead people to have respect and concern for the rights of others. But if we place that person in a factory, rather than a "warehouse," whether that factory makes ballpoint pens, hosiery, cases for watches, parts for automobiles, lawnmowers or computers; pay that person reasonable compensation, charge something for room and board, I believe we will have an improved chance to release from prison a person better able to secure gainful employment and to live a normal, productive live. If we do this, we will have a person whose self-esteem will at least have been improved so that there is a better chance that he or she can cope with life.

There are exceptions of course. The destructive arrogance of the psychopath with no concern for the rights of others may well be beyond the reach of any programs that prisons or treatments can provide. Our prison programs must aim chiefly at the others—those who want to change.

There is nothing really new in this concept. It has been applied for years in northern Europe, and in my native state of Minnesota there are important beginnings. Special federal legislation authorized pilot programs for contracts with private companies to produce and ship merchandise in interstate commerce. Even though Minnesota's pilot program involves only a fraction of the inmates it represents a significant new start. In that program prisoners were identified by tests to determine their adaptability for training. After that they were trained and now there are approximately fifty-two prisoners in one section of the Minnesota prison engaged in assembling computers for Control Data Corporation. These prisoners will have a job waiting for them when they leave prison. Is it not reasonable to assume that the temptation to return to a life of crime will be vastly reduced?

On my first visit to Scandinavian prisons twenty-five years ago, I watched prison inmates constructing fishing dories, office furniture, and other products. On my most recent visit six years ago, prisoners in one institution were making components for prefabricated houses, under the supervision of skilled carpenters. Those components could be transported to a building site and assembled by semi-skilled workers under trained supervision. Two years ago in a prison I visited in The People's Republic of China, 1000 inmates made up a complete factory unit producing hosiery and casual sport shoes. Truly that was a factory with a fence around it. In each case, prisoners were learning a trade and paying at least part of the cost of their confinement.

Today the confinement of the 500,000 inmates in American prisons cost the taxpayers of this country, including the innocent victims of crimes, who help pay for it, more than twelve million dollars a day! I will let you convert that into billions. We need not try in one leap to copy fully the Scandinavian model of production in prison factories. We can begin with the production of machine parts for lawnmowers, automobiles, washing machines or refrigerators. This kind of limited beginning would minimize the capital investment for plant and equipment and give prisoners the opportunity to learn relatively simple skills at the outset.

We do not need the help of behavioral scientists to understand that human beings who are taught to produce useful goods for the marketplace, and to be productive are more likely to develop the self-esteem essential to a normal, integrated personality. This kind of program would provide training in skills and work habits, and replace the sense of hopelessness that is the common lot of prison inmates. Prisoners who work and study forty-five to fifty-five hours a week — as you graduates have done — are also less prone to violent prison conduct. Prisoners given a stake in society, and in the future, are more likely to avoid being part of the "recall" process that today sends thousands of repeat offenders back to prisons each year.

One prison in Europe, an institution for incorrigible juvenile offenders from fourteen to eighteen years of age who had been convicted of serious crimes of violence, has on the wall at the entrance to the institution four challenging statements in bold script with letters a foot high. Translated they read approximately this way:

1. You are here because you need help.
2. We are here to help you.
3. We cannot help you unless you cooperate.
4. *If you don't cooperate, we will make you.*

Here is an offer of a compassionate helping hand coupled with the kind of discipline that, if missing in early life in homes and schools that ignored moral values,' produces the kind of maladjusted, incorrigible people who are found in prisons. Some voices have been raised saying that prisoners should not be coerced into work and training programs. Depending upon what these speakers mean by "coerced," I might be able to agree. But I would say that every prisoner should be "induced" to cooperate by the same methods that are employed in many other areas. Life is filled with rewards for cooperation and penalties for non-cooperation. Prison sentences are shortened and privileges are given to prisoners who cooperate. What I urge are programs in which the inmate can earn and learn his way to freedom and the opportunity for a new life.

Opportunities for rewards and punishments permeate the lives of all free people and these opportunities should not be denied to prison inmates. At the core of the American private enterprise system is the idea that good performance is rewarded and poor performance is not. So I say we can induce inmates to cooperate in education and in production. A reasonable limit is that they should not be made to study more or work longer hours, for example, than students at Pace University must work to earn a degree! Surely it would not be rational to settle for less. I can hardly believe that anyone would seriously suggest that prisoners should be treated with less discipline than the young men and women in the colleges of America.

With as much as ten billion dollars of prison construction looming, we are at a crossroad, deciding what kind of prisons we are to have. As we brace ourselves for the tax collector's reaching into our pockets for these billions we have a choice: we can continue to have largely "human warehouses" with little or no educational, training or production programs or we can strike out on a new course with constructive, humanizing programs that will in the long run be less costly. The patterns are there in our federal prisons and in states like Minnesota.

It is your future. You make the choice.

Footnotes

[1] J. Gorecki, *A Theory of Criminal Justice* at xi (1979).
[2] The Federal Bureau of Prisons under the leadership of the late James V. Bennett and now Norman Carlson, the present Director, has performed extremely well, given legislative restraints on production of goods in prisons and archaic attitudes of business and labor. But the Federal Bureau of Prisons deals with barely seven percent of the 400,000 prisoners now confined.

Part V

Corrections in the Community

Introduction

If, as many experts contend, the prison drill only hardens prisoners' antisocial tendencies and teaches them the skills they need to pursue a criminal career, what alternative punishments are available? Many penal authorities have criticized the courts for being too lenient with habitually violent felons and too harsh on non-violent offenders. Nearly half of the nation's inmates are serving time for non-violent offenses, and many of these offenders pose little or no threat to society. It is more humane, more effective, and far cheaper, many criminologists assert, to send nondangerous convicts to halfway houses and work release programs and to require them to perform community services and reimburse the victims from whom they stole.

The argument that the best way to remedy overcrowding is to channel non-violent offenders into community-based programs is not new. In 1967, the final report of the *President's Commission on Law Enforcement and the Administration of Justice* advocated a major shift to community correctional programs and far greater funding for probation and parole programs, halfway houses, work release centers, and other alternatives to imprisonment. Prisons, according to the *Commission*, should be used only as a last resort, preceded by many interim options designed to keep men and women as close as possible to their families and jobs — not caged, dehumanized, and deprived of all opportunities to learn self-reliance. Six years later, another President's Crime Commission — *The National Advisory Commission on Criminal Justice Standards and*

Goals—concluded a sober review of the scandals of incarceration with the recommendation that "[p]risons should be repudiated as useless for any purpose other than locking away persons who are too dangerous to be allowed at large in a free society."

In some states, the challenge of community-based corrections has been taken seriously. Minnesota, Oregon, Kansas and Mississippi, among others, have established community work programs in which offenders are given employment counseling, assigned to jobs in the community, and are required to make restitution to their victims. For that matter, as of December 31, 1988, approximately 2.4 million Americans were on probation, 400,000 were on parole, and probably another 100,000 were in halfway houses, work release centers, and other community corrections programs.

Community-based corrections, however, certainly has not succeeded in eliminating the most prominent and distressing features of the U.S. prison system. Prisons cost taxpayers $8 billion in operating costs each year to achieve a monumental record of failure. They are still underfunded, more overcrowded than ever, and run by an undertrained and underpaid staff who are unable to protect prisoners from other prisoners. Moreover, despite opposition from the supporters of community corrections, over $12 billion in federal, state, and local cell construction is planned over the next decade.

Those who advocate an accelerated campaign of prison construction have argued that although building more prisons is costly, the costs of not building more prisons may also prove expensive. Pointing to studies indicating that some hardened, habitual offenders can be one-person crime waves who single-handedly commit well over 100 crimes per year, a 1987 report issued by the National Institute of Justice (Edwin W. Zedlewski, "Making Confinement Decisions") took the position that the costs of building and running prisons may not be too expensive when weighed against the money saved by incapacitating and deterring those who would otherwise commit serious crimes that impose great monetary and social costs on crime victims and on society generally. Supporters of expanded prison construction also contend that community corrections has not been proven to be demonstrably effective in protecting the public and reducing recidivism rates. Indeed, although some community-based programs have been judged to be safe and effective, many evaluative studies have produced inconsistent and contradictory results, in part because of the methodological problems that are widespread throughout all corrections research (see Part IV).

Some detractors of community-based programs have claimed that many such programs actually increase the amount of control, punishment and surveillance to which offenders are subjected. Critics also have warned that expanded community corrections efforts will not necessarily lead to reduced prison populations. For example, in his 1980 book *Prisons in Turmoil*, John Irwin declares that "[i]nstead of dipping into the [prison population], community corrections and other diversion programs receive those who were formerly filtered out of the system through dismissal, reduction of charge, and probation."

With all of the controversy surrounding community-based corrections, it is fitting that the first article in Part V addresses the question of whether we should emphasize community-based rehabilitation programs in planning for the future of corrections. We really have little choice, says Charles W. Thomas in his thoughtful essay, "Corrections in America: Its Ambiguous Role and Future Prospects." After pointing out that some of the major goals of what we euphemistically call the "corrections" system have nothing to do with rehabilitation, Thomas explains why he is convinced that institutionally-based treatment programs are doomed to failure. Community-based programs, however, need not suffer from the same social and psychological pressures that inevitably subvert prison rehabilitation efforts. If we could introduce greater fairness and rationality in the sentencing of criminal offenders and devise community corrections programs to fit the needs of nondangerous offenders who sincerely want to change their behavior, there may at least be room for guarded optimism about the future of corrections.

Perhaps the most unyielding obstacles to more innovative and extensive use of community-based alternatives to imprisonment are the public's fear of crime and the willingness of some public officials to exploit that fear. Many politicians have discovered that it is easy to win votes by coming out in favor of doing away with probation and parole, closing half-way houses, and building more prisons. Maygene Giari, author of "In Oklahoma, Building More Prisons Has Solved No Problems," tells the story of how Oklahoma public officials systematically undermined a promising 1973 Master Plan for Corrections that called for the expanded use of parole and other community-based sentencing alternatives. In Oklahoma, she contends, some public figures actually set out to create a public demand for harsher sentencing by vigorously promoting the misconception that *all* convicted offenders are vicious felons. Her article is intended to convince readers that if Americans were told the truth about crime—that it is a complex problem not amenable to easy, quick solutions—they would be more supportive of community-based programs and less supportive of the seemingly endless proliferation of prison construction.

According to H.H. Brydensholt, General Director of Denmark's Prison and Probation Administration, and author of "Criminal Policy in Denmark: How We Managed to Reduce the Prison Population," Danish public officials are striving to reduce their already small (compared to the U.S.) prison population rather than build more prisons. Whereas the United States seems committed to using imprisonment more frequently and for longer periods of time, Denmark's "depenalization" laws—passed in 1973—were aimed at using imprisonment less frequently and for shorter periods. Such Danish penal policies as the greater use of probation and the adoption of shorter sentences for property offenders have proved to be remarkably successful in stemming the increased flow of offenders into the prisons. However, Denmark is not content with the status quo and is considering new alternatives to incarceration in the near future.

Danish criminal justice policies may astonish readers who are familiar with recent American correctional history: prison admissions up, parole releases down, and government leaders clamoring for more of the same. In fact, in the past decade, at least eight states have abolished parole, and most other states have greatly increased the range of crimes which carry minimum mandatory sentences without the possibility of parole. The movement toward the abolition of parole is often justified by reference to the "nothing works" findings reported by Robert Martinson and his colleagues in 1974 and 1975 (see Part IV). It is therefore ironic that in 1977, Martinson and Judith Wilks identified a correctional program that does seem to work. In "Save Parole Supervision," they report the results of a study in which they examined the arrest, conviction, and re-imprisonment rates of two statistically comparable groups of released prisoners—those released under parole supervision and those released without parole supervision. Their conclusions: "The evidence seems to indicate that the abolition of parole supervision would result in substantial increases in arrest, conviction, and return to prison."

As noted earlier, community corrections programs have generally failed to win support from politicians and the public. However, our next article offers evidence that this state of affairs may be changing. In "Alternatives to Incarceration: A Conservative Perspective," Charles Colson and Daniel W. Van Ness point out that an increasing number of conservative politicians have announced their support for expanding community-based alternatives to imprisonment. Colson, Chairman of the Board of Prison Fellowship Ministries, and Van Ness, President of Justice Fellowship (the criminal justice reform arm of Prison Fellowship Ministries), have worked on behalf of correctional reform with public officials across the United States. They argue that the time has come for men and women from every political perspective to support well-run community-based correctional programs that can benefit offenders, victims, correctional employees, and the taxpaying public. Equally important, Colson and Van Ness offer profiles of specific types of community programs that have been introduced in some states in recent years. As readers will see, there are a number of programs — including intensive probation supervision, house arrest, restitution, and community service — that may prove to be superior to imprisonment in dealing with non-violent offenders.

The final three selections in Part V provide insights into three types of community-based correctional programs that recently have been promoted as effective ways to punish criminals without punishing taxpayers. First, Billie S. Erwin and Lawrence A. Bennett summarize the results of a study of the effectiveness of Georgia's Intensive Probation Supervision program, one of a growing number of such programs across the country. As Erwin and Bennett point out, the evaluation evidence suggests that the program provides stronger controls than regular probation while costing considerably less than incarceration. Second, in "Experimenting with Community Service: A Punitive Alternative to Imprisonment," Richard J. Maher and Henry E. Dufour make the case for community service programs, contending that such programs can achieve the goals of punishment while avoiding the costs of imprisonment. Finally, in a National Institute of Justice report issued in 1989, Annesley K. Schmidt discusses the increasing use of electronic monitoring devices that signal authorities when the wearer — usually a non-violent offender — attempts to leave his or her home.

24

Corrections in America
Its Ambiguous Role and Future Prospects
Charles W. Thomas

More than a decade ago I wrote an article for *Federal Probation*, a journal that has a readership which includes large numbers of what we commonly refer to—whether accurately or only euphemistically—as correctional practitioners (Thomas, 1973). The article was entitled "The Correctional Institution as an Enemy of Corrections." The title was fairly descriptive of the primary point I sought to emphasize. Much as some have tried to inject rehabilitation into the list of goals that prisons are expected to pursue, I took the position that prisons have been, were, and would continue to be unable to promote rehabilitation. Without any intention whatsoever of being either facetious or simpleminded in dealing with such a serious and perplexing problem, I argued that a major reason for this rehabilitative impotence is to be found in the very nature of the prison rather than in any inherent characteristics of those we choose to confine in prisons.

My point was and is valid. Even a superficial understanding of prisons as a special type of formal or complex organization should convince any reasonable person that these are simply not

Source: Prepared especially for *The Dilemmas of Corrections* by Charles W. Thomas.

organizations that can transform the human raw material that they receive from our courts into a rehabilitated product (e.g., Etzioni, 1975; Thomas, 1977). This is not because people are such inflexible and rigid creatures that they cannot be changed. Changing people in one or more ways is possible (e.g., Brim and Wheeler, 1966; Kennedy and Kerber, 1973). Many of the "people processing" organizations we have created —public schools, colleges, mental hospitals, various components of the military, and so on—clearly have shown that people, including those who have reached adulthood, can be changed in some ways under some circumstances. Prisons of the type on which we rely today, however, lack the capacity to produce the particular kinds of lasting and positive changes in the attitudes, values, and behavior of offenders that many have in mind when they use the term "rehabilitation."

My less than positive assessment of the likelihood of successful prison-based rehabilitative efforts did not win me large numbers of friends among the readership of *Federal Probation*. Nevertheless, Professors Haas and Alpert have asked me to reconsider what I had to say in my earlier essay and also to move a bit beyond that essay by commenting on the likely viability of rehabilitative efforts which take place in community-based correctional programs. The scope of the underlying question Ken Haas and Geoff Alpert have posed to me is exceedingly broad. The question itself, however, is easily stated: Is rehabilitation possible? If so, in what general setting are rehabilitative efforts most likely to be effective?

Readers will certainly appreciate the impossibility of what is to be attempted here. A small library could be filled with volumes within which both the possibility and the impossiblity of rehabilitation have been addressed. We will be able to do little more than concern ourselves with the surface of these broad waters. However, there are some fundamental issues that deserve to be identified and discussed. Some are generic in the sense that they are of direct relevance to all types of rehabilitative efforts. Others are relevant to specific strategies for change.

Regardless, here is a sketchy outline of what is to follow. First, I will begin by distinguishing between the rehabilitative and non-rehabilitative goals of our correctional system. There is, but need not be, confusion over this distinction; thus this portion of our discussion will be simple and direct. Second, it is very important that we recognize some core problems which can and often do undermine all types of rehabilitative intervention. Perhaps the real issue we will have to confront has to do with whether we have reached the point at which we have become bright enough even to attempt to rehabilitate offenders. Third, we need to pose pointed questions regarding whether community-based and institutionally-based correctional efforts are equally effective (or ineffective) strategies.

What Rehabilitation Is and Is Not

Perhaps the most common mistakes one can make when considering the field of corrections are, first, to evaluate what takes place in corrections as though the primary objective of our correctional system is to prevent crime and, second, to equate successes or failures in the area of crime prevention with successes or failures in the area of rehabilitation. Such mistakes are a perfectly understandable by-product of our referring to all of our methods of dealing with offenders as falling within the field of corrections. However, the truth of the matter is that many if not most of the objectives of our so-called correctional system have little to do with crime prevention. Moreover, many if not most aspects of crime prevention have relatively little to do with rehabilitation.

The Retributive Purposes of Punishment

In the hope of avoiding such mistakes in this discussion, perhaps we can best begin by quickly distinguishing between *retributive* and *utilitarian* justifications for punishment. Doing so will allow us to establish that some important purposes of punishment are unrelated to either crime prevention or rehabilitation.

Those who adopt a retributive position regarding punishment concentrate their attention on two fundamental concerns: (1) the harm caused by a criminal act and (2) the culpability or blameworthiness of the person who caused the harm. They contend that punishment is deserved when one person harms another and when the person causing the harm did so without an acceptable justification or excuse (e.g., self-defense, insanity, and so on). The amount of punishment deserved is limited by what retributivists often refer to as the *principle of just desert* or the *doctrine of proportionality*. Both concepts urge us to look backward in time, make an assessment regarding harm done as well as the culpability of the person who caused the harm, and then impose a type or a degree of punishment on a blameworthy actor that is equal to what he or she deserves for what he or she did (e.g., Pincoffs, 1966; Hart, 1968). At the very core of a retributive position is a moral conviction that the offender must receive no more and no less punishment than what his or her blameworthy conduct deserves. What is deserved has nothing whatsoever to do with any future benefits — such as crime prevention — which may be gained by punishment.

Much of our attitude toward criminal law and legal sanctions reflects our acceptance of precisely such a view of punishment. We demand that the guilty be punished because of what they did and without regard to whether the punishment will benefit the offender or anyone else in the future. More and more often this commitment to punishment rather than to rehabilitation is set forth quite explicitly in our body of criminal law. In a recent modification of some features of its sentencing guidelines, for example, the Florida Supreme Court was very straight-forward in stating the secondary importance of any form of rehabilitation: "The primary purpose of sentencing is to punish the offender. Rehabilitation and other traditional considerations continue to be the desired goals of the criminal justice system but must assume a subordinate role" (451 So.2d. 825).

This commitment to punishment may seem harsh and punitive, but it is not a view that would be rejected by most of us. Consider criminal homicide or rape or aggravated assault or a host of other offenses that we regard as serious moral wrongs as well as violations of criminal law (which is crudely what we mean by the common distinction we draw between *mala in se* and *mala prohibita* offenses, for the former are wrongful in both a legal and a moral sense and the latter — perhaps as illustrated by violations of income tax laws, draft registration requirements, and many traffic laws — are wrongful in the limited sense that they involve legal but not moral guilt). Imagine, for example, that there was entirely persuasive evidence which showed that punishing those who committed such serious offenses had absolutely no effect on the future behavior of those who were punished or on anyone else. Would we then think of punishment as being without any justification? Would we think of punishment as being a pointless infliction of pain and suffering that we would wish to avoid?

Perhaps some of us would have affirmative answers for both of these questions, but I suspect the vast majority of us would still want and indeed demand that the murderer or the rapist or the perpetrator of assault be punished. We would do so because our basic conceptions of justice would be greatly offended were nothing to be done to such offenders simply because doing so would yield no future benefits whatsoever. We would do so because we knowingly or unknowingly have accepted some portion of the retributive perspective on punishment. This willingness to impose "pointless" punishment, moreover, clearly illustrates the point I want to make here. Punishment that is imposed within our correctional system — which certainly includes an involuntary commitment to an institutionally or non-institutionally based correctional program — has goals that have little or nothing to do with rehabilitation. Our demand for retribution is one such goal, and it is often true that we demand that the pursuit of this goal be given a higher priority than any other goals we may have for the field of corrections.

The Utilitarian Purposes of Punishment

The utilitarians take a very different approach to punishment. They think of punishment in terms of how it may be applied to blameworthy offenders in a way that permits us to realize future benefits in the form of broadly defined notions of crime prevention. Jeremy Bentham, a leading advocate of the utilitarian viewpoint whose work attracted much attention around the end of the eighteenth century, emphasized this commitment to future benefits in much of his writing. Punishment, he argued, is an evil that can only be relied upon when doing so can negate some other evil (e.g., preventing harm that would otherwise be caused by future acts of crime). Thus, in one of his more influential works, *Introduction to the Principles of Morals and Legislation*, he reasoned that we should never impose punishment if the evil we seek to prevent can be prevented in some way which does not require punishment, if the evil punishment produces is greater than the evil we seek to prevent, if punishment proves to be an ineffective way of preventing future evil, and, of course, if punishment is recommended as a response to some activity which is not morally blameworthy. Furthermore, utilitarians differ from retributivists with regard to the amount of punishment which should be imposed on offenders when punishment is deemed to be necessary. All other things being equal, the amount of punishment should be no less and no more than what is required if we are to achieve future benefits in the form of crime prevention. Otherwise, the utilitarians contend, the punishment would be pointless and, therefore, morally unjustifiable.

Clearly, then, there can be no presumption that a retributivist would favor either more or less punishment than would a utilitarian. A retributivist, for example, might encounter a blameworthy offender whose conduct had not caused significant harm and thereby demand no more than a modest degree of punishment. The utilitarian might favor harsher punishment than would the rebributivist if the nature of the harmful conduct proved to be difficult to prevent. Similarly, a utilitarian might favor a minimal punishment for a blameworthy offender whose behavior, while quite harmful, could be easily prevented by a type or degree of punishment that would strike a retributivist as being entirely too lenient given the harmfulness of the conduct being considered.

Despite the "future benefits" orientation of those adopting a utilitarian perspective on punishment, it would be inaccurate to conclude that there is a strong relationship between utilitarianism and commitment to the goal of rehabilitation. In fact, it would be fairly simple to argue that there is no true relationship of any kind between those adopting a utilitarian viewpoint regarding the purposes of punishment and feeling that the primary purpose of punishment should be rehabilitative. Utilitarians, after all, urge us to think of law violating behavior as a clear reflection of choices that have been made by rational, amoral human beings who are primarily motivated by self-interest and who have concluded that the risks associated with crime are acceptably lower than are the rewards of such conduct. The objective of punishment, therefore, becomes at least two-fold.

First, punishment can serve the goal of crime prevention by so altering perceptions of risks that rational actors will choose to avoid conduct prohibited by law. This can happen in no less than two ways: (1) punishment can convince those who have been punished that the risks associated with any future law violating behavior are unacceptably high (i.e., *specific deterrence*); and (2) punishment can convince those who are not themselves the objects of punishment that they should refrain from law violating behavior because the risks are too high (i.e., *general deterrence*).

Assume, for example, that we wish to lessen or eliminate altogether the incidence of various forms of harmful activities involving corporations and that we therefore define those activities as crimes. We make each violation of law punishable by the payment of a fine that is equal to some fixed percentage of the offending corporation's net profits. A violation is then detected and prosecuted successfully. If the punishment we impose on the corporation reduces or eliminates future violations on the part of that corporation, we might conclude that we had evidence of a specific deterrent effect of punishment. If it had such an effect on the behavior of other corporations, then we might conclude that there was evidence of a general deterrent effect of the punishment we imposed. (Naturally, you can imagine finding evidence of no effect, only a specific deterrent effect, or both a specific and a general deterrent effect.)

Second, utilitarians suggest that it is possible that some types of punishments will have crime prevention effects even if they have no influence whatsoever on risk perception. If the nature of a punishment is such that it deprives potential offenders of the opportunity to commit one or more types of crime, then the crimes such potential offenders otherwise would have committed will not be committed (i.e., the *incapactitative effects* of punishment) (e.g., Cohen, 1978). Imprisonment, for example, effectively deprives those who are confined of the opportunity to commit many types—though certainly not all types—of crime. Theoretically, therefore, the overall volume of criminal behavior can be reduced by confining those who would commit crimes were they to have the opportunity to do so.

Such utilitarian views on the potential benefits of punishment are almost totally contrary to most rehabilitative ideas. Rehabilitation is thought of as a strategy or set of strategies that correctional practitioners apply as they go about the business of making fundamental changes in the attitudes, values, personalities, skills, and behavior of those over whom they have been given control. But the rehabilitative approach has been constructed upon a quasi-medical foundation. Those who adopt it contend that people are driven to unlawful conduct by forces over which they have little or no control. Crime, in effect, is said to be a disease that requires treatment and certainly not a reflection of healthy actors freely choosing between lawful and unlawful conduct.

Summary

We need not labor over this set of issues much further. The points I wish to make should now be coming into focus. The most important of those points can be summarized concisely. We often claim that we are going to talk about the field of corrections, but the term "corrections" is both inaccurate and misleading. Much of what goes on within the field has nothing to do with either rehabilitation or crime prevention. It has instead to do with a desire to pursue the goal of retribution by punishing offenders for what they have done without any regard whatsoever for whether that punishment changes their conduct or that of others who might consider engaging in similar conduct. Furthermore, even those goals of our system of corrections that have a "future benefits" flavor often have little or nothing to do with rehabilitating offenders. They have to do with pursuing the goals of specific deterrence, general deterrence, incapacitation, and various other utilitarian objectives of punishment. Indeed, because of the emphasis we place on these utilitarian objectives, it would be foolish to suggest that those who are released from correctional supervision and who do not become reinvolved in criminal activities provide us with evidence of successful rehabilitative efforts. If the punishment a court imposes on an offender convinces him or her that the risks of punishment exceed the rewards of criminal conduct, then it is the punishment and not a rehabilitative effort that is responsible for such a "correctional success."

In short, it should now be abundantly clear that our search for an answer to questions regarding the viability of institutionally- or non-institutionally-based rehabilitative efforts poses difficult conceptual problems. We commonly think of correctional practices as being reflective of our intent to rehabilitate offenders. Our common thoughts are flatly incorrect. Our own choice of terms can and does mislead and confuse us. A major, and perhaps the primary, objective of those responsible for our correctional system is not to correct but to create a system within which retributive notions of just punishment are crudely —very crudely—translated into penological practice. Other objectives primarily reflect those utilitarian ideas that crime may be prevented via such mechanisms as deterrence and incapacitation. Rehabilitation thus remains nothing more than a secondary goal of our correctional system. Importantly, however, there is more than ample evidence in support of the contention that rehabilitation is essentially impossible when its pursuit is secondary to either retributive or utilitarian goals. There are similar reasons to believe that the retributive and utilitarian purposes of punishment are so different that emphasizing one of these purposes diminishes our ability to pursue the other. In our less than infinite wisdom, however, we foolishly claim that our correctional system can impose just punishment for past blameworthy conduct (i.e., be retributive), seek out the future benefits described by the utilitarians, and rehabilitate. A reasonable person would be forced to doubt the likelihood of our being able to achieve all these objectives at the same time.

Fundamental Flaws in the Rehabilitative Ideal

We must now turn our attention to quite a different topic. What has been said before suggests little more than that we have deceived ourselves into believing that we can rely on the field of corrections to pursue a set of inconsistent and often contradictory objectives. In and of themselves, such comments are of relevance to our primary topic only in the sense that they suggest that rehabilitation is an improbable consequence of what we are now doing in the field of corrections. They do not address what we might achieve were we to alter our priorities in such a way that rehabilitation became our primary or our exclusive objective. Assume, therefore, that you had total power over our correctional system and that you fully intended to use that power to do nothing other than rehabilitate offenders. Retribution thus would become an irrelevant concern, as would deterrence and incapacitation. Would you be more likely to be successful than those working in the field today who share your commitment to rehabilitation but whose efforts are undermined by the contradictory directives and purposes we have identified earlier?

The answer—at least my answer—is that your probability of success, while difficult to estimate in any realistic way, is quite likely to be low. There are, I think, some fundamental flaws in the foundation of the rehabilitative ideal that would thwart your best efforts. Here I will have an opportunity to do little more than present a sketchy overview of the most obvious of these flaws.

To begin, the rehabilitative or treatment model as we know it today did not begin to take form until roughly a century ago. This is not to say that nobody imagined that people could be changed until that point in human history. Plato, for example, expressed some interest in the possibility of reforming offenders more than two thousand years ago (e.g.,

Jenkins, 1984). Europeans began to seek changes in the behavior of institutionalized youthful and adult offenders by the sixteenth century (e.g., Barnes, 1972; Eriksson, 1976; McKelvey, 1977). Similar efforts were begun in this country, especially pioneer efforts in Pennsylvania and in New York, in the eighteenth century (e.g., Rothman, 1971; McKelvey, 1977; Adamson, 1984).

The rehabilitative model, however, involves far more than a belief that human beings can be changed. At its very core is the contention, which is quite unlike the core contention of such other change-oriented perspectives as those advanced by the early utilitarians, that those who violate the law are drawn to such unlawful conduct by forces over which they have little or no control. They are depicted not as persons who choose to violate the law because they perceive the risks of punishment to be acceptably low, but as people whose unlawful conduct is little more than a symptom of some underlying disease, defect, or disorder. Such persons, it was and still is said, should not be punished, for they are not morally blameworthy (thus blocking the efforts of retributivists) and they are not likely to respond favorably to any punishment that might be imposed (thus blocking the efforts of utilitarians). Instead, such persons deserve to have their cases examined on a highly individualized basis, to have qualified experts diagnose the root cause of their inappropriate behavior, and to be committed to a program of appropriate treatment and rehabilitation until the sought after cure has been achieved (e.g., Menninger, 1968; Cullen and Gilbert, 1982).

Offenders, in short, came to be thought of as sick people and not as people who knowingly and willfully violated the law. The roots of this idea can easily be traced to the writings of the Positive School of criminology, especially to the works of Lombroso (e.g., Vold and Bernard, 1981; Thomas and Hepburn, 1983: 146-162), but these efforts of the late nineteenth and early twentieth century provide us with only a portion of the real story. It must also be understood that the rise to power of a broad array of medical practitioners was taking place during precisely the same period of history. It has been observed, for example, that it was not until well after the beginning of this century that those seeking medical care from physicians had better than an even chance of coming away from such encounters in a better rather than a poorer state of health (e.g., Conrad and Schneider, 1980: 28-37). When conceptions of the causes of crime and deviance shifted away from identifying such conduct as sinful or as willful violations and to a view.that crime was a disease, the changing perspective on crime was not taking place in a social or a political vacuum. It was in many ways little more than a single illustration of what has been called the "medicalization of deviance" (Conrad and Schneider, 1980).

Here, then, is what clearly appears to be the initial flaw in the rehabilitative model, and it is a flaw quite without regard to the context
within which rehabilitative efforts are attempted. Is criminal behavior
symptomatic of some underlying disease, defect, or disorder which
would cry out for treatment rather than punishment were we to permit
expert correctional practitioners rather than judges to evaluate individual cases?

The question is far from easy to answer. There are surely those who
violate the law because they are deeply troubled people who in a
practical if not always in a legal sense lack a meaningful ability to
conform their conduct to the requirements of law. These people,
whether defined in the vernacular of everyday language or in
accordance with more or less accepted clinical terminology, are sick,
in need of supportive therapy, and in no way blameworthy. But the
rehabilitative model did not evolve to deal with this tiny category of
offenders. The rehabilitative model begins with the assumption that all
criminal acts are manifestations of some disease-like entity driving
otherwise healthy people toward unlawful conduct, and the tautolog-
ical proof of the claim is that their criminal acts unequivocally prove
that the disease entity is there to be found if only we are smart enough
to diagnose it.

The claim is flatly absurd. At one or more points in our lives, virtually all of us will engage in what could be defined as unlawful
conduct (e.g., Nettler, 1984: 81-97). To accept a perspective that would
define virtually all of us as being in need of therapy would be an
intelligent decision only if those making it were clinicians who sought
to profit from such an obvious con game. And by promoting such a
fraud, those clinicians would presumably provide us with an indication that they are themselves deserving of treatment. Thus, there are
compelling reasons to question the initial assertion of the rehabilitative
model which suggests that those who violate the law are in need of
treatment. While some certainly are, the vast majority certainly are
not.

Assume, in spite of all that I have said previously, that rehabilitation
is the major objective of our correctional system and that the vast
majority of those who violate the law do indeed require treatment.
Were this to be true, would your task become easier if you had the
power to do whatever was necessary to create a viable rehabilitative
system?

Again my answer is simple. The answer is, "No." The reason for the
answer is also simple. At the present time neither those in the
behavioral sciences nor those in the so-called clinical disciplines have
the means of screening offenders in a way that is capable of determining with certainty whether they are suffering from some underlying

problem which deserves treatment. Assuming such a problem does exist, it is extraordinarily difficult to determine with any degree of reliability or validity the diagnostic category into which the problem should be classified. Further, the magnitude of this general problem increases substantially with the complexity of the problem being considered. Persons suffering from very specifically focused phobic neuroses (a phobia being defined as 'an intense learned fear of specific objects, situations, or living organisms" (Adams, 1981: 206) are relatively easy to identify and to classify properly. However, more complex patterns of behavior defy being dealt with so neatly. Many studies have shown that clinicians have little ability to reach similar definitions of identical cases or even to distinguish perfectly normal persons from those with serious psychiatric problems (e.g., Rosenhan, 1973).

The second problem, therefore, is that we lack an ability to separate those who are in need of treatment from those who are not. Again, however, pretend that rehabilitation is the goal of corrections, that offenders do require rehabilitative efforts, and that the particular needs of particular offenders can be diagnosed with an acceptable level of accuracy. Were all of these assumptions to be true, would the rehabilitative approach then have some real potential?

Unfortunately, the answer to this question is also, "No." The reason is once again simple: Even if we rightly or wrongly convince ourselves that offenders are, by definition, in need of treatment, the state of our knowledge regarding how to deliver the needed "cure" is so poor that our efforts tend to be both inefficient and ineffective. Study after study reveals that the effectiveness of our rehabilitative efforts is not significantly better today than it was many decades ago and that we are often fortunate if our efforts benefit as much as they harm offenders (Bailey, 1966; Kassebaum et al., 1971; Lipton et al., 1975; Logan, 1977; Martinson, 1980).

True, there are many who look at this huge volume of research in which the ineffectiveness of rehabilitative efforts has been so thoroughly documented and who respond by saying that rehabilitation has not been given a fair chance (e.g., Cullen and Gilbert, 1982). Never, they contend, have we allowed the real correctional experts to pursue their therapeutic ends with sufficient support, time, resources, and so on. If we did all of these things, they argue, certainly we would become more effective. Perhaps the claim is correct. Nobody knows whether it would or would not be. However, the claim itself is very similar to that advanced by those who favor the death penalty. Though no evidence supports the hypothesis that executions deter murder any better than does lengthy imprisonment, many death penalty supporters remain convinced that if we would execute a far greater number of convicted murderers than we do now, then surely we would find that executions would have a strong deterrent effect on potential murderers. The question, of course, is how long are we willing to have faith in the assertions of those supporting either rehabilitation or executions before we, as more or less reasonable people, take the position that both of these emperors have been running around with no clothes for more years than we can count.

There is one final problem that is generic to the rehabilitative model, and it is a major problem even if you are once again ready to assume that all that I have said previously is false. Assume, in other words, that offenders do require rehabilitation, that we can identify the particular type of rehabilitative effort that is needed, and that we can use that particular strategy of change with great effectiveness. Fine. We know that change is needed and we have the means of producing the change. Into what are offenders to be changed? If they enter our correctional system as a sort of human raw material that we seek to transform into quite a different final product, what is that final product going to look like?

The answer is that we have only vague notions about what the characteristics of a rehabilitated offender should be. We thus know virtually nothing regarding when offenders have been rehabilitated and, therefore, when the time has come to return them to the larger society. Because we lack this important ability as well as any ability to predict who will or will not become reinvolved in criminal behavior after release from correctional supervision, we find ourselves in the very awkward and circular position of saying that those who do not recidivate were treatment successes and that those who do recidivate did not receive a sufficient "dose" of treatment (never saying, of course, that the assumptions regarding the need for treatment and our ability to deliver treatment were themselves deficient and defective).

This is foolish for at least two reasons. First, either we can predict future criminal conduct when dealing with those we have tried to rehabilitate or we cannot. The fact of the matter is that our predictions might as well have been drawn from a table of random numbers (e.g., Monahan, 1978). Second, there is every reason to believe that those who do not later become reinvolved in crime avoid criminality for reasons that have nothing to do with our rehabilitative efforts. Thus, any claim that low levels of recidivism are proof of the success of therapeutic efforts should be viewed with considerable skepticism, to say the least.

Summary

Before moving on to a discussion of the prospects for institutionally- and non-institutionally-based correctional efforts, it might be useful to pause for a moment to retrace some of the ground that has been covered already. In the initial section of this essay I tried to show that we run a considerable risk of confusing ourselves by a very misleading use of the terms one commonly encounters in commentaries on "corrections." Because our interest here is with the rehabilitative potential of correctional efforts, the risk of confusion is quite substantial. To the extent that our system for dealing with offenders has a strong retributive purpose, for example, it is entirely inappropriate to use the word "corrections" for the simple reason that it implies a quest for changing something about the future attitudes, values, and behavior of offenders. Such an emphasis on the future would be viewed as inappropriate by retributivists, especially if that commitment to the future led us to impose any more or any less punishment on offenders than they deserved given the harmfulness of their behavior. In some ways the confusion becomes greater when utilitarian purposes of punishment are emphasized. Those purposes, while involving efforts to change offenders, clearly do not fall within the scope of the change-oriented ideas of those who adopt a rehabilitative approach.

This confusion aside, there are fundamental problems in the rehabilitative model itself. Those problems are as pressing when rehabilitation is attempted within non-institutional settings as they are when they are attempted in institutionally-based programs. The rehabilitative model is defective to the extent that (1) offenders do not suffer from a type of problem which calls for therapeutic intervention, (2) we lack a meaningful ability to diagnose the particular underlying condition which manifested itself in criminal behavior, (3) we have failed to develop effective and efficient methods of treating those deserving of treatment, and (4) we have less than a clear image of the goals of rehabilitation. I have argued that each of these potential defects in the traditional rehabilitative model is also a real defect. Now, however, we need to shift our attention to the relative merits and limitations of institutionally-based and non-institutionally-based correctional efforts.

The Prospects for Rehabilitation

From reading what has been said already, it may appear that my views on the prospects for rehabilitative efforts are that such efforts are doomed to failure. In some ways the drawing of such an inference would be entirely correct. It is certainly my opinion that the sorts of efforts we are making today are at least as likely to produce harm as they are to yield any present or future benefits. However, the position in which we find ourselves is one that demands action. Sitting back and bemoaning the existing state of affairs, while a luxury that some aca-

demic criminologists certainly enjoy, is not an option that is available
to those who must deal with the problems of crime in the real world.
Thus, in this concluding section I will try to address myself to the sorts
of responses one might reasonably make to those who have engaged in
unlawful conduct and the contexts within which those responses might
have the greatest likelihood of being beneficial.

Rethinking Our Position on Crime and Punishment

The first step that probably must be taken in our efforts to use the
correctional system to reduce law-breaking behavior is to reconsider
why we have a body of criminal law, how we should apply that law,
and what we hope to gain through the exercise of law. Because this is
itself a broad and a complex topic, little can be said about it here.
However, the probable success of any efforts we make within the
context of our correctional system presupposes that we take a reasonable position regarding why we create and how we use criminal law.

Very briefly put, it seems to me and to many others that we create
criminal law in the hope that doing so will have future benefits.
Criminal law requires or prohibits particular forms of conduct with the
fairly obvious expectation that doing so will increase the likelihood of
required conduct (e.g., timely and accurate filing of income tax
returns) and decrease the likelihood of prohibited conduct (e.g.,
criminal homicide). In this sense it is obvious that the general purpose
of having law is utilitarian and not retributive (e.g., Hart, 1968). Applying the penalty provisions found in criminal law to particular instances
of law violation, however, presents us with considerably more complex
problems. Indeed, it is a problem that will defy resolution if we adhere
to the contradictory position that there is some type or degree of
punishment which our retributive purposes require us to impose on
blameworthy offenders and, at least in the vast majority of cases, some
very different type or degree of punishment that our utilitarian purposes require. Clearly, then, there must be some generally acceptable
compromise position that would have the practical consequence of
pleasing — or at least of not offending — retributivists and utilitarians.

A compromise position, I think, does exist. Unless retributive perspectives on punishment are reduced to exceedingly simple versions of
what is often referred to as "in-kind retributivism" — which is where
on finds such *lex talionis* notions as "an eye for an eye and a tooth for a
tooth" — determining an offender's just desert" can do no more than
define an upper and a lower limit to the punishment that retributivists
feel we must apply without any thought as to whether the punishment
will yield future benefits (e.g., Morris, 1982). A retributivist could thus
define a range of punishments as being justifiable. Though defining
such a range would certainly be very difficult to do, it would appear to

be within the range of possibility. Perhaps, for example, carefully conducted survey research might permit us to identify the range of punishments that those in our society view as being morally defensible on retributive grounds. Less punishment than what might be identified as the lower limit of a "just desert range" would be difficult to justify on any ground. Even a utilitarian would agree that a punishment which was so minimal that it undermined public respect for the law could be thought of as being a greater evil than the evil the punishment sought to prevent. The same limiting principle would apply to the upper limit of the range of just deserts.

Of what advantage would such a scheme be? Well, I think the advantage would be that we would be in a position to claim *both* that our system of punishment is just in a retributive sense of that term (i.e., no offender could receive any more or any less than what his or her culpable and harmful conduct was said to deserve) *and* that punishments falling within the retributively defined range could be chosen in accordance with our perceptions of utility. And here it is exceedingly important for the reader to appreciate the fact that I use the term utility to refer to a quest for future benefits that encompasses a combination of traditional utilitarian objectives (e.g., deterrence and incapacitation) and other types of benefits (e.g., treatment, rehabilitation, and so on). As I have noted previously, it is my firm opinion that the flaws in the traditional rehabilitative model are fundamental and fatal. Such a quasi-medical conceptualization of the causes of and appropriate responses to offenders has done grave damage both to the lives of countless thousands of offenders and to the larger society. However, the demonstrable failure of a traditional rehabilitative approach cannot and should not be taken to mean that our correctional system cannot justly and effectively promote meaningful change were that system to assume the role of a facilitator of change rather than a filler of pseudo-medical prescriptions.

Furthermore, such a system of allocating particular degrees of punishment, because it integrates a combination of retributive and utilitarian principles, could smooth the otherwise ragged edges we sometimes encounter when these justifications for punishment are employed separately. Offenders could not receive excessively lenient punishments because the lower limit of punishment would be fixed; offenders could not receive excessively harsh punishments because either (1) the maximum punishment would also be fixed or (2) because sentencing authorities would be free to select any punishment within a retributively defined range of just punishments and, therefore, could avoid the upper limit of the range when some lower degree of punishment was deemed to be appropriate.

The scheme outlined above, of course, is neither as simple as it may seem, nor perfect. One cannot answer questions regarding whether it would be "just" in some abstract sense. Much as we use the term "justice," we do so without ever having agreed on what the term means. It has no clear definition (e.g., Gross and von Hirsch, 1981). If, however, one thinks of justice as fairness and equity in the distribution of the suffering which punishment entails, then those who would be punished would be dealt with fairly and equitably. Similar offenders would be dealt with more or less similarly (though one might receive the lowest level of punishment permitted while another received the highest level). Similarly, if one thinks of justice in terms of certainty, then the policy recommended would meet that test (i.e., all who were convicted would be punished). Finally, if one thinks of justice in terms of retaining the ability to tailor the punishment to the individual characteristics of the offense and/or offender, the scheme also survives (i.e., the sentencing authority, in selecting a particular punishment within the range of permitted punishments, would still be free to individualize decisions so long as in doing so it did not go above or below the agreed upon limits).

Does all or any of this have some relevance to the prospects of institutionally- and non-institutionally-based rehabilitative efforts? Absolutely. A fundamental problem confronted in many if not most areas of the country today—and I certainly include those jurisdictions within which determinate sentencing schemes have been implemented—is that large numbers of offenders suffer almost irreparable damage as they move through our criminal justice system. Serious offenders receive trivial sentences. Trivial offenders receive excessive punishments. Men are dealt with more harshly than women. In situation after situation we find that the law tolerates, encourages, and sometimes flatly demands the imposition of punishments that are entirely devoid of fairness, equity, or any other ascertainable purpose. Offenders often and understandably come to the conclusion that the system is arbitrary and discriminatory. They enter correctional programs full of distrust, alienation, and hostility. The very best change-oriented efforts are thus doomed to failure. The system defeats itself. The rest of us tolerate and sometimes even encourage such self-defeating behavior. And the system fails. And we get no more and no less than what we deserve.

The Context for Change

Having covered much—perhaps too much—territory already, we must now turn our attention to the prospects that our correctional system could have a positive influence on offenders. While I will once again be guilty of painting with far too broad a brush, there are some ideas and recommendations that strike me as being ones that would be viable even were the discussion to be more thorough and detailed.

To begin with, much of the evidence available to us at this time indicates that efforts which rely exclusively on institutionally-based corrections (i.e., jails and prisons) are doomed to fail. This should not be interpreted to mean that those confined in institutions are likely to become worse rather than better. Much as criminologists have hypothesized that prisons do more to cause than to prevent crime, there are many reasons to believe that prison adaptations and experiences are poor predictors of either positive or negative postrelease conduct (e.g., Glaser, 1964, Kassebaum et al., 1971; Lipton et al., 1975). An interesting qualification or exception to this general rule is that those who adapt well and quickly to life within prison seem likely to adapt less well to the world they encounter on release from prison (e.g., Goodstein, 1979).

The primary reasons for the failure of institutions to promote prosocial change seem to be fairly clear. First, meaningful changes in attitudes, values, behavior, and so on presuppose some receptivity on the part of those who are the objects of change efforts. When the criminal justice system operates in such a way as to create or enhance opposition rather than cooperation via, for example, arbitrary, uneven, and discriminatory disposition of cases, offender receptivity to rehabilitation efforts is decreased if not eliminated altogether.

Second, our correctional system operates in a manner which reflects no appreciation for the commonsense notion that you can lead a horse to water but you cannot make him drink. Change, in other words, presupposes a voluntary involvement on the part of those who are the objects of change. The correctional system is obviously coercive rather than voluntary, and the chances of more than superficial change being a consequence of involvement in so coercive a system are low (e.g., Morris, 1974). Indeed, organizations like prisons are so inherently coercive that they spawn opposition, hostility, and alienation on the part of those they seek to change, thus making treatment efforts pointless (e.g., Morris, 1974; Thomas, 1977).

Third, while our terminology may encourage us to speak of correctional institutions rather than prisons, it would be foolish to be deceived by this largely cosmetic approach to making punishment more palatable. The single most important goal of those administering our prison system is that of maintaining custodial control. They evaluate themselves and are evaluated by others on the basis of how well they achieve this single objective. A prison warden who proves to be incapable of preventing escapes and prison violence — especially violence directed against members of the prison staff by inmates — will not keep his or her job. A prison warden whose rehabilitation efforts prove to be less than effective will never be noticed. This reality is reflected by the routine recording of numbers of escapes, assaults, and other disruptive activities and the remarkable infrequency with which any efforts of any kind are made to evaluate the success or failure of correctional programs (e.g., Lipton et al., 1975).

Fourth, only rather infrequently does one encounter programs being operated within prison that are targeted at a rehabilitative goal. To be sure, it is common to find such programs being operated within prison contexts. Practically speaking, however, many treatment programs operate as little more than safety valves which provide inmates with an acceptable outlet for expressing feelings that might otherwise threaten security. Similarly, vocational and educational programs commonly have two non-rehabilitative goals. One of these calls for inmates to be involved in activities that either directly or indirectly support the immediate objectives of the prison itself (e.g., doing work that maintains the institution—plumbing, food service, growing crops that are consumed by inmates, etc). The other goal is to maintain custodial control simply by keeping as many inmates occupied as possible.

Fifth, a voluminous literature on the origins and characteristics of what is often referred to as the "prison community," the "inmate society," or the "inmate subculture" clearly shows that prisons typically contribute to the development of an informally organized inmate society into which large numbers of inmates become assimilated (for a review of this large literature, see Bowker, 1977). This assimilative process, which is now commonly referred to as *prisonization,* encourages a broad spectrum of attitudes and values that tend to undermine responsiveness to rehabilitative efforts of all kinds. The negative consequences of prisonization are especially apparent in large maximum security prisons (e.g., Street et al., 1966; Cline, 1968; Feld, 1981).

These and many other factors interact with one another in such a way that prisons are especially unlikely contexts within which positive changes are likely to take place. Indeed, although some criminologists have argued that the odds of success might well increase if we could diminish the unfairness and arbitrariness of sentencing (e.g., by adopting determinant rather than indeterminant sentencing policies) and by making participation in prison programs voluntary rather than compulsory, we are beginning to see research reports that challenge the viability of these sorts of adjustments (e.g., Goodstein, 1979, 1982).

The question, of course, is whether community-based correctional efforts are likely to produce greater benefits than prison-based strategies. The answer to the question is that we really do not know. However, those of us who have special interests in penology are at least guardedly optimistic that community-based strategies have far more potential than do institutionally-based alternatives.

Imagine, for example, an integrated correctional system, the door to which has been created by something akin to the sentencing scheme I outlined previously. Imagine that sentences imposed by our courts could not be increased or decreased by such obviously arbitrary and/or discriminatory policies as those presently associated with parole. Imagine, at one end of the correctional continuum, a system of prisons which, while considerably smaller in terms of inmate population than many of those in use today, would be used to confine inmates whose crimes call for imprisonment even at the minimum end of our scale of deserved punishment and inmates who simply cannot be controlled in less secure facilities. The goal of these prisons would be to confine inmates efficiently, effectively, and humanely, but the objective would also be to make a broad array of treatment and training programs available to inmates on a purely voluntary basis. At the other end of the correctional continuum, imagine substantial numbers of offenders who would be left in their communities under the terms of an "unsupervised probation" agreement, an agreement that might, among other things, require that these offenders obtain or keep full-time jobs as a way of allowing them to make restitution to those harmed by their criminal conduct. And imagine between these two extreme points on our correctional continuum a whole series of intermediate points (minimum security facilities in community settings that would house offenders who were working outside these facilities in "normal" jobs, facilities within which offenders would be deprived of their liberty during only particular periods of time (e.g., weekends), sentences that would involve traditional types of probation supervision, and so on).

Could such a system work? Could it be both punitive enough to satisfy those primarily concerned with retribution and sufficiently nonpunitive that it could serve the sometimes unrelated goals of deterrence, treatment, and rehabilitation? Naturally, nobody knows for sure. It would certainly call for us to make far-reaching changes in both public attitudes toward crime and punishment as well as massive changes in both our body of criminal law and the operation of our criminal justice system. Indeed, each of the many pieces of the puzzle we would need to create are so interrelated with one another that a failure in one area could destroy the entire initiative.

Obvious and major problems aside, we really have little choice. To the extent that we hope to rely upon methods of responding to those who violate the law that will serve some purpose that is not immediately achieved by the very nature of the punishment (e.g., retribution and, sometimes, incapacitation), then virtually everything that we now know shows that imprisonment is pointless. It is not a context within which treatment efforts are likely to be successful. Neither is it a context within which less clinically-focused strategies will prove to be effective. Sometimes, of course, we will be forced to imprison some offenders simply because we either feel that doing so is a fundamental requirement of justice or because we know of no other way of dealing with them. However, many criminologists seem inclined to estimate that a relatively small proportion of offenders — perhaps no more than ten to fifteen percent — deserve or require confinement in the traditional kinds of prisons on which we rely so heavily today. Thus, if the term "correctional system" is to have any real meaning, then it seems obvious that its future is to be found in the community. The advantages would be many. The only question is whether we have the interest and the insight to think our way through this very difficult set of problems and to respond in a way that reflects reason rather than fear, disgust, vengeance, and petty politics.

References

Adams, Henry E. *Abnormal Psychology*. 1981, Dubuque, Iowa: William C. Brown Company.

Adamson, Christopher. "Toward a Marxian penology: Captive criminal populations as economic threats and resources." *Social Problems* 31 (April), 1984: 435-458.

Bailey, Walter C. "Correctional outcome: An evaluation of 100 reports." *Journal of Criminal Law, Criminology and Police Science,* 33 (Winter), 1966: 774-785.

Barnes, Harry E. *The Story of Punishment*. 1972, Montclair, New Jersey: Patterson-Smith.

Bowker, Lee H. *Prisoner Subcultures*. 1977, Lexington, Massachusetts: D.C. Heath.

Brim, Orville G., Jr. and Stanton Wheeler. *Socialization after Childhood: Two Essays*. 1966, New York: John Wiley.

Cohen, Jacqueline. "The incapacitative effect of imprisonment: A critical review of the literature." Pp. 187-243 in Alfred Blumstein, Jacqueline Cohen, and Daniel Nagin, editors, *Deterrence and Incapacitation: Estimating the Effects of Criminal Sanctions on Crime Rates*. 1978, Washington, D.C.: National Academy of Sciences.

Conrad, Peter and Joseph W. Schneider. *Deviance and Medicalization: From Badness to Sickness*. 1980, St. Louis: C.V. Mosby Company.

Eriksson, Torsten. *The Reformers: An Historical Survey of Pioneer Experiments in the Treatment of Criminals*. 1976, New York: Elsevier.

Etzioni, Amitai. *A Comparative Analysis of Complex Organizations*. 1975, New York: Free Press.

Glaser, Daniel. *The Effectiveness of a Prison and Parole System*. 1964, Indianapolis, Indiana: Bobbs-Merrill Company.

Goodstein, Lynne, "Inmate adjustment to prison and the transition to community life." *Journal of Research in Crime and Delinquency* 16 (July), 1979: 246-272.

"A quasi-experimental test of prisoner reactions to determinate and indeterminate sentencing." Pp. 127-146 in N. Parisi, editor, *Coping with Imprisonment*. 1982, Beverly Hills, California: Sage Publications.

Gross, Hyman and Andrew von Hirsch (editors). *Sentencing*. 1981, New York: Oxford University Press.

Hart, H.L.A. *Punishment and Responsibility: Essays in the Philosophy of Law*. 1968, New York: Oxford University Press.

Jenkins, Philip. *Crime and Justice: Issues and Ideas*. 1984, Monterey, California: Brooks/Cole Publishing.

Kassebaum, Gene, David A. Ward, and Daniel M. Wilner. *Prison Treatment and Parole Survival: An Empirical Assessment*. 1971, New York: John Wiley.

Kennedy, Daniel B. and August Kerber. *Resocialization: An American Experiment*. 1973, New York: Behavioral Publications.

Lipton, Douglas, Robert Martinson, and Judith Wilks. *The Effectiveness of Correctional Treatment: A Survey of Treatment Evaluation Studies*. 1975, New York: Praeger.

Logan, Charles. "Recidivism and the 'effectiveness' of prison and parole." 1977, *Intellect Magazine:* 424-426.

Martinson, Robert. "What works? Questions and answers about prison reform." Pp. 11-44 in Charles W. Thomas and David M. Petersen, editors, *Corrections: Problems and Prospects, 2nd Edition*. 1980, Englewood Cliffs: Prentice-Hall.

McKelvey, Blake. *American Prisons: A History of Good Intentions*. 1977, Montclair, New Jersey: Patterson-Smith.

Menninger, Karl. *The Crime of Punishment*. 1968, New York: Viking Press.

Monahan, John. "The Prediction of violent criminal behavior: A methodological critique and prospectus." Pp. 244-269 in Alfred Blumstein, Jacqueline Cohen, and Daniel Nagin, editors, *Deterrence and Incapacitation: Estimating the Effects of Criminal Sanctions on Crime Rates*. Washington, D.C.: National Academy of Sciences.

Morris, Norval. *The Future of Imprisonment*. 1974, Chicago: University of Chicago Press.

Madness and the Criminal Law. 1982, Chicago: University of Chicago Press.

Nettler, Gwynn. *Explaining Crime, 3rd Edition*. 1984, New York: McGraw-Hill.

Pincoffs, Edward. *The Rationale of Legal Punishment*. 1966, New York: Humanities Press.

Rothman, David. *The Discovery of the Asylum*. 1971, Boston: Little, Brown.

Thomas, Charles W. "The correctional institution as an enemy of corrections." *Federal Probation*, 37 (March), 1973: 8-13.

"Theoretical perspectives on prisonization: A comparison of the importation and deprivation models." *Journal of Criminal Law and Criminology*, 68 (Winter), 1977: 135-145.

Thomas, Charles W. and John R. Hepburn. *Crime, Criminal Law, and Criminology*. 1983, Dubuque, Iowa: William C. Brown.

Vold, George and Thomas J. Bernard. *Theoretical Criminology, 2nd Edition*. 1981, New York: Oxford University Press.

25

In Oklahoma, Building More Prisons Has Solved No Problems

Maygene Giari

In 1973, Oklahoma State Penitentiary exploded in a disastrous riot. Three prisoners were killed. Property damage totaled $20 million, making this the costliest riot in American prison history. Overcrowding was acknowledged to be a major factor in causing the riot. A legislative task force set up to study the riot reported that its single most significant finding was that Oklahoma had been imprisoning people at a rate twice the national per capita average. The task force recommended that immediate steps be taken to reduce the inmate population. That was in 1973.

One might suppose that the revelation of the extent of overincarceration would be of paramount importance to a state with a badly malfunctioning prison system. Obviously, sentencing practices would determine the financial outlay that would be required. Yet, in the months and years that followed, in spite of the desperate and deterior-

Source: *Crime and Delinquency*, Vol. 25, No. 4 (October 1979), pp. 450-462. Reprinted with permission of the publisher.

ating conditions in the penitentiary and the whole prison system, public discussion of the desirability of imprisoning so many people was minimal. No studies were undertaken to determine whether Oklahoma had a lower crime rate as the result of its hard-line policies. (As a matter of fact, Oklahoma County, which has the highest per capita rate of commitments, also has had the greatest increase in its crime rate.) No defense of harsh sentencing practices was offered. Presumably, public opinion was in support of the harsh form of justice meted out in Oklahoma. The extent of the overincarceration was largely ignored.

The National Clearinghouse for Criminal Justice Planning and Architecture prepared a Master Plan for Corrections in Oklahoma. The plan was—at least in theory—adopted by the state. Eventually, the author of the plan was appointed director of corrections. But over the years that followed, the recommendations of the Master Plan were effectively subverted. It would appear that, rather than making any attempt to educate Oklahoma residents, officials deliberately whipped up public opinion to gain support for that subversion.

The Master Plan and What Happened to It

Recognizing the extent of the overincarceration in Oklahoma, the Master Plan did not provide for expansion of the prison system. Rather, a top priority was a phased reduction in the number of inmates, to bring the size of Oklahoma's prison population into conformity with the prison populations of neighboring states. This was to be achieved in part through expanded use of parole and nonincarcerative, community-based sentencing alternatives. The penitentiary was to be rebuilt as the only maximum-security institution in the state, with the population reduced from the preriot total of 1,500 inmates to 300 inmates. The preferred option for the reformatory was to phase out its use over a five-year period, replacing it with one or more smaller institutions in more populated areas. The plan emphasized that its implementation could be carried out only through the cooperation of the judiciary, the legislature, and the parole board.

Reduction of Inmate Population

However, when it came to implementing the Master Plan, the recommendation for reducing inmate populations—supposedly a top priority—was not addressed. Instead, the new governor—who had campaigned on a platform of penal reform—in his first year in office concentrated only on appropriations to build a reception and assessment center. In his second year, the governor steam-rollered appropriations through the legislature for two medium-security prisons. (*Steam-*

rollered is an appropriate term. The appropriations bills were challenged on constitutional grounds and were forced through the
legislature three times.)

The only effort made by the governor to implement a nonincarcerative alternative was his support of the passage of a restitution statute.
Under this program, more than 2,500 offenders have continued to hold
jobs in the community; between October 1976 and April 1979 they
repaid almost three-quarters of a million dollars to the victims of their
crimes. But the restitution program did not check the rising influx of
prisoners into the institutions.

By 1977, instead of the inmate population of approximately 2,600
projected by the Master Plan, the inmate population had grown to
4,500. The designed capacity of the entire system was 2,300. The
critical capacity—defined by the director of corrections as the point
at which no more inmates could be crammed into the institutions—
was 4,570. The attorney general ruled that the Corrections Department must continue to accept prisoners after the critical capacity had
been reached. With the opening of the first of the new institutions still
nearly a year away, it was becoming apparent that the completion of
the new prisons not only would not relieve overcrowding in the old
ones; the new prisons would also be overcrowded the day they opened.

Location of New Institutions

The new institutions were to be built in major metropolitan areas.
But, after months of stormy debate over site selection, the criterion of
"in or near a major metropolitan area" was revised to "within fifty
miles of a major metropolitan area." Not one of the three new prisons
is in or near a major city. All are in areas only slightly less remote than
the existing institutions. The governor engineered the compromises
that resulted in the final site selections.

Use of Parole

The Master Plan called sentencing "a vital issue to Oklahoma's
correctional system" and advised against mandatory sentences. But
the governor endorsed a mandatory minimum sentence proposal.

The Master Plan called for wider use of parole and for nonincarcerative options for parole violators whenever possible. In previous years,
the parole board had been recommending a smaller percentage of
inmates for parole than the national average, or even than neighboring
states. But now the governor encouraged the parole board to tighten up
even more on parole recommendations. Furthermore, Oklahoma is one
of only three states in which the governor has the final responsibility
for granting or denying parole. As a candidate, the governor had said

he favored taking the governor out of the parole process. As governor, he granted fewer paroles than his predecessor and instituted a new policy of revoking parole for technical rule violations even when no new crime had been committed. The governor denied 43 percent of the paroles recommended by the parole board.

Use of Community-Based Alternatives

The governor announced he had adopted the Master Plan "with minor modifications." His early statements sounded as though the modifications were minor. The Master Plan called for a gradual reduction of the inmate population through pretrial diversion and wider· use of probation as well as shorter prison sentences and more extensive use of parole; it also called for the establishment of eight new community treatment centers. The governor said the success of the plan depended on an expanded community treatment program that would provide more nonincarcerative options for judges.

The only measure for reducing the inmate population supported by the governor during his entire term of office was the restitution program. He vetoed a measure to liberalize bonding procedures, although he had earlier promised to support it.

The 1978 legislature authorized alcohol education programs to divert some of the drunken drivers from the prison system. It also appropriated funds for the Department of Corrections to contract for treatment of about twenty prisoners in facilities other than those administered by the department. Such treatment was to include rehabilitation aimed at alcohol or drug abuse, mental health services, and nursing home care. Except for the community treatment centers, that is about the full extent of the community-based facilities.

The governor endorsed the expansion of the community treatment program, but called for a one-year evaluation of the performance of the five existing prerelease centers before developing any of the eight additional centers called for by the Master Plan. The first new center did not open until more than two years after the governor took office. Five of the eight recommended centers eventually were opened during the governor's term in office, but only after long delays resulting from problems in selecting sites. The governor announced that two of the new centers would provide work or study release for first-sentenced offenders sent directly to those centers from reception; but he did nothing to gain public acceptance of any of the centers·.

What he did do encouraged resistance to finding sites for the centers. Theoretically, the Board of Corrections has the sole authority for site selection, but the governor overruled the board's choices. At one point, a group of concerned citizens was advised that he was having a count made of the "pro" and "con" letters about a Tulsa site as a means of determining whether or not he should veto that site. That is to say, the governor selected the sites on the basis of minimal resistance from local residents, not on the basis of their adequacy for the work of the institution.

The Quality of the Institutions

When the legislature authorized funds for the new construction, it also slashed operating expenses, with the governor's blessing. Some of the improvements eliminated were required by a court order in 1974: improved medical care throughout the whole system, more guards and better guard training, and better access to the courts for prisoners. Additional personnel were authorized in one budget, but the line-item appropriation did not include salaries for all the new positions. One food budget was nearly half a million dollars short of the requirements of the expanding prison population (a supplemental appropriation had to be passed in the next session). Other casualties were a unit for approximately 150 "functionally disabled" (ailing geriatric, mentally retarded, and physically handicapped) prisoners and a unit for the care of almost an equal number of severely mentally disturbed or criminally insane prisoners.

The need to improve living conditions for prisoners was challenged. Public figures protested that the court was trying to force the state to "coddle criminals," to create a "Holiday Inn" atmosphere for convicted felons. Yet, in 1977, a federal judge had ordered monthly reductions in the populations of the penitentiary and the reformatory, specifying that prisoners were being deprived not of luxuries but of the basic necessities of life: pure water, sanitary sewer facilities, hygienic food preparation areas, protection from fire, adequate personal hygiene, minimum living space. About 2,100 prisoners were living in areas ranging from less than 3 by 6 feet of space to 5 by 8 feet. Over 1,400 of these inmates were spending more than twenty-one hours a day in enforced idleness in this cramped, poorly lighted, poorly ventilated space.

Manipulation of Public Opinion

Aside from the restitution bill, no executive action was taken to enlist the cooperation of the judiciary, the parole board, or the legislature to reduce overincarceration. A public ignorant of the extent of overincarceration in Oklahoma did not demand a reduction in the inmate population.

It was not only the public that was ignorant of the extent of overincarceration in Oklahoma. Five years after the legislative task force reported how many more people Oklahoma was sending to prison than were even neighboring states, a member of one of the legislative penal committees was "surprised" to learn of the situation. He had been on that committee for several years.

The site-selection process for new community treatment centers was no less acrimonious than that for the medium-security prisons. The people who crowded the site-selection hearings to protest the establishment of centers in their neighborhoods were terrified of being exposed to "dangerous criminals." One would have thought the intent of the Corrections Department was to establish convenient lairs for vicious criminals to go forth and prey on law-abiding citizens.

A few public officials sought to reassure these frightened citizens. Others found the temptation to pose as "protectors of the public" irresistible and further inflamed the fears of their panicky constituents by defending their opposition to the proposed sites.

When the judge ordered the monthly reductions in inmate population, the governor declared the state would not release "dangerous criminals" to prey on law-abiding citizens. When the Tenth District Court upheld the population-reduction order, the governor complained about the courts' "callous disregard" for the safety of Oklahoma's citizens.

These pronouncements were as inflammatory as they were demagogic. The court order specified that the ruling could be stayed any time the state could demonstrate any threat to the public safety. (As a matter of fact, the ruling was temporarily stayed from February to September, 1978, on the state's claim that no more prisoners could safely be transferred from the penitentiary.)

The Corrections Department said that from 500 to 600 prisoners could be released without threat to the public. The judge said he was perplexed about why Oklahoma found it necessary to imprison more than twice as many people as did neighboring states. But the hard-liners, including much of the media, were not listening.

Parole board members said they were confident the people of Oklahoma would not favor the release of murderers, rapists, and thugs —though no one knew better than the parole board how small a percentage of murderers, rapists, and thugs are included in the parole dockets.

The tightening up on parole, incidentally, occurred after the major newspaper in Oklahoma City ran a nineteen-part series of articles about people who had been paroled. Only a few of the parolees discussed in the articles (five or six parolees were named in each one) had committed new crimes. The effect of the articles on the parolees was disastrous. One parolee was fired both from his regular job and from a second, moonlighting job. His employers had known about his record when hiring him, but they now said that so many customers had threatened to take their business elsewhere that they could not afford to continue to employ the parolee.

The attorney general, who was a gubernatorial candidate, said he was not going to apologize for the overcrowded prisons. The overcrowding only showed that law enforcement, district attorneys, courts, and juries were doing a good job, he said. The attorney general neglected to mention that the kind of job they were doing included a five-year sentence (all but ninety days suspended) meted out to an elderly, senile man who ran up a $100 motel bill he could not pay, a two-year sentence for bogus checks totaling $17.50, and another two-year sentence for theft of a $26 tool kit. The attorney general did not mention ten-year sentences for possession with intent to distribute for growing a dozen marijuana plants, ten years for theft of a calf, or five to ten years for joyriding. He did not mention the "habitual offenders" sent back to prison for stealing $1.75 worth of candy from a vending machine or for taking a dime in someone else's change from a vending machine. Nor did he mention the twenty-five-year sentence imposed on a prior offender for $150 worth of bogus checks, or the ninety-nine-year sentence given to an offender for stealing $11 from a relative's piggy bank.

Nondangerous, petty offenders such as these are overcrowding Oklahoma's prisons. A monthly analysis of new prison admissions issued by the Department of Corrections gives a breakdown of the number of people sentenced for crimes regarded as violent and nonviolent by the Oklahoma State Bureau of Investigation. The nonviolent category regularly comprises about 80 percent of the new admissions. Some are sent to the overcrowded state institutions to serve sentences as short as thirty days. The media receive the monthly analysis as a press release, but almost never use the material.

After the Master Plan — Back to Square One

The governor protested federal intervention in the affairs of a state that was making a "good faith" effort to improve its penal system, citing the new institutions to be opened within a year or so. Yet for months before the 1977 court order, the Corrections Department and a handful of conscientious legislators had been telling anyone who would listen that unless something was done to check the rate of commitment, the $38 million worth of new prisons under construction would be overcrowded the day they opened.

It was not until *after* the court order that the parole board began to recommend more inmates for parole and the budget for correction was increased enough to provide any immediate relief of overcrowding. It took the pressure of the court order to produce the "good faith" effort that received so much publicity. But these facts were not generally known.

After the 1977 court order, the Board of Corrections commissioned an architectural study to determine what measures would be necessary to bring the penitentiary and reformatory into compliance with court-ordered requirements. The study recommended that the state adopt one of two options: either replace both prison and reformatory entirely, or carry out a renovation-rebuilding program such that substandard units would be demolished as adequate ones were completed.

The study did what it was commissioned to do. It focused on how to make the prison system constitutionally adequate. The study demonstrated convincingly that continued use of the two prisons in their present condition would be impractical from every point of view. Reducing the number of inmates to meet court-ordered space requirements would greatly increase the maintenance and operating expenses per inmate. Other court-ordered improvements could only be provided at exorbitant cost. The prisons are extravagantly wasteful to operate and maintain now, and they provide inadequate safety and security for staff as well as inmates. Nevertheless, the study also showed that construction alone would provide no lasting solution. On completion of either the replacement or the renovation-rebuilding option, the entire prison system would provide constitutionally adequate spaces for from 3,600 to 3,800 inmates. For these reasons among others, the Master Plan had called for only 2,200 inmates by 1979.

The number of people sentenced to prison has continued to increase at a rate estimated by a special legislative committee to vary from 3 to 8 percent per year. Throughout 1978 and 1979, the inmate population has been held to approximately 4,200, with some fluctuation; but recently it has been rising. With little or no provision being made to reduce the number of inmates by developing alternatives to prison, keeping the population at the 4,200 level has been achieved by more liberal parole policies. The earlier warnings that increasing the number of parolees would threaten the public safety have for the most part died down. But, at the present rate of incarceration, the third prison, scheduled to open in October 1979, will still be unable to accommodate the burgeoning inmate population. Other new or renovated facilities will be overcrowded as fast as they are finished.

The special legislative committee reported in 1978 that, at the present rate of commitment, Oklahoma would need to open one new prison or two smaller institutions every year to keep up with the influx of prisoners. The same committee warned again in 1979 that Oklahoma must either develop more alternatives or plan to build more prisons. That is at the present rate of commitment; but the present rate may well increase.

In November 1978, Oklahomans adopted a constitutional amendment permitting the legislature to set mandatory maximum and minimum sentences for habitual criminals and to fix the period of time that must be served before parole consideration. The measure gives the impression that the mandatory sentence and the fixed period of time to be served before parole eligibility will ensure that serious criminals will be imprisoned.

The new provisions could also ensure lengthy imprisonment for a large number of very petty offenders. The lower limit defining a felony offense in Oklahoma is $20. Other trivial offenses, comparable to a $20 property offense, are also felonies in Oklahoma. Present habitual offender statutes (which have no limitation on parole eligibility) make no distinctions as to the seriousness of the crimes, past or current, which are subject to the habitual offender designation.

In 1978, six escapees left a trail of death across Oklahoma and neighboring states. With an eye to the impending compliance hearings on court-ordered prison improvements, some candidates found in the bloody incidents a politically expedient way to endorse more prison construction. One gubernatorial candidate declared, "The people of Oklahoma are scared to death," and went on record in favor of constructing a maximum-security facility. Another said that if the choice were to build more prisons or turn prisoners loose, he would choose more prisons. He specified they would not be luxury prisons.

In September 1978, a federal court ruled that if funds had not been provided to rebuild four of the five cellblocks at the penitentiary and the reformatory by July 1, 1979, those cellblocks must be "closed to further habitation." The ruling further specified that groundbreaking for the cellblocks must take place by November 1, 1979, and the old cellblocks must be permanently closed by May 1, 1981.

The court order also called for closing wooden barracks of World War II vintage and setting up a health service plan in conformity with court-adopted standards by December 1, 1978; housing only one inmate per cell at the penitentiary and reformatory by April 1, 1979; meeting Health Department standards for water, sewage, plumbing, and electrical systems at all facilities by July 1, 1979; and conforming with environmental standards at state facilities other than the penitentiary and reformatory by December 1, 1979.

The cost of the improvements was estimated at between $30 and $50 million. The governor (subsequently elected to the Senate) ordered an appeal of the rulings. He said he was confident that most Oklahomans share his belief that a federal judge should not be able to "tell the taxpayers and their elected representatives how to write a state budget." The governor reiterated his earlier comments about the state's "good faith" efforts," the safety of the lawabiding public," and his determination not to release prematurely any prisoners who would be a threat to the public.

Comment — the Myths and the Realities

Statements such as these obscure the basic issue and are a disservice to the public. The basic issue is not whether a federal judge should be able to tell the state how to spend its money — the chairman of a special legislative committee on criminal justice pointed out that the improvements would be needed even if there were no court order. The basic issue is not, as supposed, the safety of the public — not when Oklahoma imprisons twice as many nondangerous offenders as do neighboring states. The basic issue is whether it is really necessary to send as many people to prison as are presently being committed, whether it is desirable to send even more people to prison in the future. To continue sentencing minor offenders to long terms in prison while failing to provide the bare essentials of life and health in those prisons is an abdication of responsibility by the state.

Overcrowding is the result of overincarceration, and the two problems are inseparable. Oklahoma has been discovering that just building more prisons without at the same time developing more alternatives to prison is no solution. Prison construction simply cannot keep pace with the rate of commitment — nor can the taxpayers afford the staggering costs of prison construction and overincarceration. But selling alternatives to the public will not be easy. The myths that all convicts are dangerous criminals and that improvement of prison conditions means luxurious living will continue to be believed. Public fears have been inflamed and reinforced for years, both by public figures and by the media.

A harsh law-and-order press has played a major role in influencing decisions about the Oklahoma prison system. As an example, immediately after the sweeping court order in 1978, a major metropolitan daily featured a front page article with the headline "Prison Order Stirs Cold Fear among Crime Victims." People whose relatives had been killed in violent crimes were interviewed. One protested that the state would be required to give murderers what amounts to "a poolside home," and expressed fear that violent prisoners would be released on parole sooner than they should be. Another interviewee worried about "endangering the innocent population."

Even so, for several months after the November 1978 election it looked as if a concerted effort would be made to resolve the twin problems of overincarceration and overcrowding. The newly elected governor said the state would have to make its prisons humane and to develop alternatives to prison. His budget included nearly $34 million to bring the prison system into compliance. Other officials warned that an appeal of the court order was not likely to be successful and advised the 1979 legislature to consider alternatives to prison for nonviolent offenders.

A number of bills providing nonincarcerative options were introduced in the 1979 session. Although the mandatory sentencing with parole restrictions for habitual offenders has yet to be implemented, what kind of habitual offender statute will eventually emerge is still uncertain. A bill that was defeated would have required prisoners to serve at least ten years before parole consideration. While its author believed that the bill would increase the prison population by "only" 10 to 14 percent, the Corrections Department said it would double the population at the penitentiary and reformatory. A bill to make anyone convicted of any felony ineligible for nonincarcerative options was defeated.

Instead of pressing the appeal to Tenth District, the state presented a compromise plan for coming into compliance with the court order. Legislative leaders testified that they believed the plan would put Oklahoma's prisons into "substantial compliance." The new governor appeared before the court voluntarily and pledged his determination to carry out the court order. In May 1979, the court accepted the compromise plan, extending most of the deadlines by six months. The court accepted postponement of the decision to renovate or close the cellblocks at the reformatory and a proposal to spread appropriations to fund the required improvements over a two-year period instead of funding all of them in 1979. The court noted, appreciatively, that "for the first time" state officials were moving toward compliance.

Some of the same newspapers that in 1973 denounced the National Standards and Goals recommendations for reducing incarceration began to editorialize favorably about wider use of probation, parole, and restitution and developing weekend jail, community service sentences, and fines as alternatives to prison. But other newspapers have continued in the same old inflammatory, fear-engendering vein. A small-town editor quoted with approval a reader's suggestion for helping the new governor overcome the problem he had inherited, the court order "to reduce [the] prison population so as not to inconvenience the prisoners too much." The proposal was to parole enough inmates by lottery to satisfy the court, and then to try a federal judge or ACLU attorney as codefendant of every parolee committing rape, murder, or other capital crimes.

The consistent failure of the press to report either the judge's reasons for his rulings or his reassurances that the population reduction could be delayed if any threat to the public safety could be demonstrated has contributed to misunderstanding, fear, and a hostile reaction to federal intervention. Not even the concluding statement of the May 1979 order appeared in press reports. The judge commented that the conditions of confinement have reinforced antisocial attitudes, promoted more criminal behavior, and "imperiled us all." Constitutionally adequate conditions, he said, "serve both our humaneness and our self-interest."

Three months into the 1979 legislative session, it became apparent that there was still no unity of purpose among the state leaders. Some alternative measures were passed. One was a bill allowing municipalities to set up alternative programs to deal with drunks. A resolution authorizing weekend jail terms in the community passed, was vetoed, and the veto was overridden. But bills to increase the felony limit from $20 to $50 or $100 were defeated; so was a measure calling for a fulltime parole board.

A routine house-cleaning measure to eliminate an obsolete statute providing for castration of mental patients and certain prisoners was amended to require castration of convicted rapists — and the measure failed by only two votes. A bill expanding eligibility for the restitution program and directing courts to give first consideration to restitution in preference to fines or imprisonment passed; but a resolution urging the state supreme court to recommend to trial courts that they use probation and restitution as alternatives to imprisonment was defeated. At present, a number of courts make minimal or no use of suspended judgment, probation, or restitution options and need encouragement to do so.

Another indication of the lack of unity of purpose came in an attack on the director of corrections that took on the proportions of a personal vendetta. Leading legislators, charging that the director had padded the budget to include items not required by the court order, demanded his ouster. The governor and Board of Corrections supported the director. The court said Oklahoma owed him a debt of gratitude "for the skillful, persistent fashion in which he has pursued his difficult responsibilities," and said his skills would be greatly needed for the implementation of the rulings. A legislative leader replied that if the judge liked the director so well, perhaps he would hire him as a court clerk.

A joint legislative committee appointed to investigate the director challenged the propriety of commissioning a firm headed by the former director of the National Clearinghouse to make the architectural study because the director had been working for the Clearinghouse when he developed the Master Plan. The correction budget specified that none of the firms that prepared the architectural studies were to be hired for new construction.

The committee demonstrated considerable flexibility in finding reasons for getting rid of the director. One of the original charges was that he had fired a deputy director for blowing the whistle on the budget padding. In the final report, the committee concluded that this same deputy director deserved to be fired but the director was at fault for not firing him sooner. When an attempt to cut the director's salary to force him to resign was unsuccessful, the director was specifically excluded from a cost-of-living increase given to all the other state employees.

In the closing moments of the session, the legislature slashed an additional $4 million from a compliance budget that had already undergone major surgery. One of the earlier cuts had eliminated authorization for additional probation and parole officers. The additional officers were not required by the court order, although they will be needed if effective use is to be made of the sentencing alternatives. The ability to make the cuts was cited as proof of how the director had padded the budget. This was a thoroughly misleading statement, since the court had already authorized spreading the appropriations for compliance over a two-year period instead of making the entire appropriation in one year. The budget, as finally passed, raises serious questions about whether compliance can be achieved.

The governor continued to support the director. The Corrections Board reaffirmed its support, terming the investigation a "witch hunt." A metropolitan paper editorialized that the ouster move "all falls into a familiar and troublesome pattern....It is time to ask whether any qualified administrator can make a real effort to improve the prison system without automatically antagonizing a Governor or powerful members of the Legislature or both." The director resigned, saying that the victims of the move to oust him were "[department] employees and prisoners."

The cost of prison building has been getting much attention in Oklahoma. But many of Oklahoma's leaders have avoided discussing two elements of the cost factor that should be brought to the attention of the public: the question of how many people it is really necessary to imprison and the question of how much maximum-security space is required.

Although the cost of keeping people behind bars is an appropriate consideration in determining how many and what kind of people the taxpayers want or can afford to imprison, the minimum figure of $10,000 per year to maintain each inmate is seldom mentioned. Supporting the present prison population of 4,200 costs the taxpayers $42 million a year.

It will take a more concerted effort than has yet been evidenced by legislators, the executive branch, and the judiciary to reduce the prison population from the present 4,200 to the 3,600 to 3,800 that can be housed constitutionally by January 1982, the final deadline for complete compliance. Supporting a prison population of 3,800 will still cost $38 million a year, as compared with $22 million for the smaller, 2,200 inmate population anticipated by the Master Plan. The public is not being advised of the relative costs, let alone the cost effectiveness of the options available to the prison system.

The second question, of how much maximum security is really necessary, is also seldom addressed. After the riot, the task force reported that Oklahoma had far too many offenders in maximum-security prisons and said space for 400 would be enough. The Master Plan called for only 300 maximum-security spaces. The three new prisons have been described by the Corrections Department as providing *maximum* security for *medium*-security inmates. When the third new prison is completed, over 1,000 of these maximum-security spaces for medium-security inmates will be available—more than three times as many as called for by the Master Plan. Renovation/rebuilding at the penitentiary will provide yet another 450 spaces, at a cost of $30,000 to $40,000 per cell.

If Oklahoma develops more alternatives to prison, some of the unconstitutional cellblocks could be closed instead of being replaced. The cost to the taxpayers would be reduced. The public would still be adequately protected.

But public discussion has not focused on these cost factors, nor on the relatively greater effectiveness of nonincarcerative alternatives. The citizens of Oklahoma are not being told what they need to know. Six years after the riot, in spite of some improvements, solutions to Oklahoma's overcrowding and overincarceration are still not in sight, though the longer these problems are neglected the bigger they become. The abdication of responsibility by public figures has kept the prison system malfunctioning still, and the public is paying a punishing cost for that malfunction.

26

Crime Policy in Denmark
How We Managed to Reduce the Prison Population

H. H. Brydensholt

The Goals of the Criminal Justice System

The Norwegian government's white paper on crime policy, which was published in 1978, stated that the goals of the criminal justice system could be defined as (1) to combat crime, while (2) complying with fundamental principles of justice and humanity and (3) maintaining a balance between the cost of criminal justice policy and the benefits to society of that policy.

Although they do not all provide the same definitive statement of their goals, the Scandinavian countries, it is fair to say, do have the same objectives in criminal justice. And I would guess, these objectives are shared by other countries as well.

With regard to the first goal, we have not been very successful so far: As in other Western industrialized nations, our level of crime has

Source: *Crime and Delinquency*, Vol. 26, No. 1 (January 1980), 35-41. Reprinted with the permission of the publisher.

increased. In the last part of this article, I will return to the issue of what should be done about criminality. It is important, however, to stress immediately that while Denmark's depenalization policy, which has been developed over the last decade, has had goals in addition to that of reducing crime, a more lenient crime policy does not necessarily run counter to this fundamental objective. If anything, it seems that a more lenient—and more flexible—penal policy affords more genuine possibilities for avoiding an outbreak of serious crimes than does a stricter system.[1]

Criminality in Denmark

After a peak in criminality during the Second World War, we experienced a relatively stable period in the 1950s. The number of offenses against the penal code reported each year (excluding such minor offenses as traffic violations) was approximately 125,000. However, in the late 1950s and 1960s, Denmark, like other Western nations, saw a tremendous increase in crime rates. This growth in crime was especially rapid during the last part of the 1960s, with the rate of reported crimes rising by 1970 to 300,000. From 1970 to 1974, crime continued to increase, but at a slower rate, reaching 325,000 reported offenses in 1974. During 1975 and 1976 we saw an unexpected but not unwelcome drop in crimes reported per year, to less than 280,000. In 1977 and 1978, crime again increased—to 310,000 reported offenses in 1977 and 340,000 in 1978.

The type of crime accounting for the greatest proportion of these figures is, as in the other Scandinavian countries, offenses against property. Sexual offenses comprise only about 1 percent of the total number, and violence is a part of less than 2 percent of the reported crimes. Each year, there occur between 30 and 40 murders among Denmark's over 5 million inhabitants, the majority involving people who know one another. This compares favorably with the number of deaths by traffic accident, which has reached a yearly figure of 800. If the murder rate in the United States were the same as that in Denmark, the number of homicide victims would be about 1,600, instead of 20,000.

What accounts for the changes in criminal activity in Denmark? One thing seems obvious: Crime has something to do with the conditions in which people live. It is impossible to believe that entire generations are biologically different from one another. Rather, the dramatic changes in the level of criminality must be related to citizens' (particularly young males') position in our society. While no one has isolated the causes of the fluctuations in crime levels, and no one believes that simple explanations will cover the entire question, noticeable changes in crime trends can be seen to correspond with major changes in Danish society that occurred around 1958, 1966, 1974, and 1977.

In 1958, with the election of a new government in Denmark, began the period of what is called the second industrialization. During the late 1950s and early 1960s a majority of the farm workers went from the rural areas to the towns, leaving less than 10 percent of the working population occupied in farming. Drug use among youngsters began in Denmark around 1966. The pressing need of drug users for immediate cash could explain to some extent the rapid increase in theft and burglaries in the mid-1960s. Moreover, drug use was only one side of the new youth culture, which accepted none of the social norms without question. It is not surprising that respect for other people's property would decrease.

The energy crisis in 1974 meant that for the first time in many years there was a high rate of unemployment, especially among youngsters. One reading the the textbooks on crime would expect widespread unemployment to result in an increasing number of criminals. Yet we saw a noticeable fall in criminality. It has been suggested that this decline can be attributed more to a slowdown in crime by recidivists than to a decreased number of new offenders.

Several explanations for this curtailment of crime among exoffenders have been offered. First, the decrease in crime may be a result of Denmark's policy of providing unemployment insurance. Danish citizens who are forced into unemployment receive about 90 percent of a "normal" income as unemployment compensation. Exoffenders, who often have difficulty holding jobs, will not be offered jobs for a longer period and thus be able to continue to collect their high unemployment payments. If jobs were available, they would be transferred quickly by the employment authorities to the general social welfare system, where they would receive only about half what is considered a normal wage. According to this explanation, society paid criminals so well that they stopped their criminality. A second explanation attributes the fall in crime to a process of destigmatization. While the person who is out of work in a society with full employment may be severely stigmatized, if many ordinary citizens are forced to be unemployed, the exoffender's status automatically rises.

But what is the explanation, then, for the upturn in crime two years later? Many youngsters in Denmark remain unemployed, so why has the crime situation changed?

Perhaps this is a result of the large number of youngsters entering into criminality for the first time. It may well be that many youths are bored with forced inactivity and thus are easily attracted to any offer of excitement. If this is true, it indicates a very dangerous situation. There will be no more important crime prevention measure in the next years than to secure work for these youngsters.

The Decrease in the Prison Population

The prison population remained amazingly stable through the 1960s, even while criminality was growing rapidly.[2] Although crime figures more than doubled during the 1960s, the daily prison population remained at about 3,500. However, the early 1970s brought an increasing number of inmates. We were in the situation of either having to secure more prison space or to change our criminal law so that imprisonment was used less frequently.

When the prison population was at about 3,500, this figure could be divided as follows: 800 persons were being held in custody before trial, 500 were serving a short, fixed term of imprisonment (called "haefte") often used for minor offenders (especially drunk drivers), 300 were serving indeterminate or "semideterminate" sentences (most of these inmates were youths serving a specific semideterminate sentence called "youth prison," lasting between one and four years), and about 1,900 were serving fixed prison sentences.

About 30,000 people pass through the prison system each year, a large proportion of them persons held for short periods in the local jails who later receive a sanction which does not involve deprivation of liberty. In addition, there is a high turnover of drunk drivers, who normally receive ten to thirty days of haefte.

In 1973, when the prison population was rising, Danish penal law was changed in several fundamental respects. We eliminated the indeterminate and semideterminate sanctions. Today a judgment involving deprivation of freedom is nearly always a fixed sentence. Use of indeterminate sanctions had been shown to result in prolonged periods of incarceration—periods disproportionate to the offense committed. Moreover, neither indeterminate nor semideterminate sanctions resulted in significantly lower rates of recidivism than did fixed periods of incarceration.[3]

This was an important change. But the "depenalization" law passed simultaneously was even more significant. Under this reform, the relatively minor property crimes were handled more leniently. More people were placed on probation. Shorter sentences were given to property offenders: The maximum sentence for first-time property offenders, including burglars, was lowered from two years to one and one-half years, and repeat offenders now face two and one-half instead of three years of incarceration.

Part of this law reform was a major administrative change. Until 1973, the probation administration was a publicly funded, separate organization in the criminal justice system. With fewer people being incarcerated and more placed on probation in the community, it was necessary to transfer some of the resources from the penal institutions to probation. Such a transfer could only be accomplished if the responsibility were placed in one administration; therefore, probation was placed under the same management as the prison system.

The penal policy in Denmark has been a success in decreasing the prison population. The daily average number of persons incarcerated has dropped from 3,500 to 3,000. We now have 700 persons in custody before trial, 500 serving brief, fixed sentences, and 1,800 serving prison sentences.

Why Do We Wish Fewer People in Prison?

In a report on alternatives to imprisonment which was published in 1977, we find in the introductory remarks a summary of some of the viewpoints which have governed the diminishing role of incarceration in the Danish penal system.[4]

First there are general humanitarian concerns. Incarceration is difficult to tolerate. The harm caused by confinement often extends beyond the deprivation of liberty itself to broken family life, loss of work, stigmatization. While presumably the deprivation of freedom has always been a harsh punishment, the ill effects of incarceration appear more pronounced today. Perhaps this is because there is a more common understanding of the criminal's situation. In addition, compared with previous conditions, the society from which the inmate is excluded has more to offer — in terms of more spare time, better working conditions, and more material welfare. It can be argued that exclusion from society today is a greater punishment than was true in the past.

Another part of the debate has focused on the effectiveness of incarceration as a penal measure. Deterrence has long been regarded as an important goal of punishment. But opposed to the belief that offenders are deterred from future criminal activity by temporary incapacitation is recent research focusing on inmates' personalities. The findings here do not support deprivation of freedom as a suitable means of resocialization; on the contrary, it seems that deprivation of freedom more often strengthens feelings of insecurity, apathy, and aggressiveness toward the community, damages further the inmate's self-respect, and promotes identification with those who display patterns of criminal behavior.[5] Studies of recidivism also indicate that deprivation of freedom is less effective than other forms of punishment in preventing repeated offending.[6] Even if the methodological problems apparent in the research to date force us to view the results with certain reservations, it is important to note that no research has yet been able to show that deprivation of freedom is more effective in preventing recidivism than are other penal measures.

A third reason for reassessment of the role of incarceration is that offenses against property, which dominate the Danish crime statistics, are looked upon today differently than was the case in the past. The general growth in wealth and the prevalence of theft insurance mean that this offense is not as burdensome for the victim as in previous years. Consequently, offenses against property are seen as not necessarily requiring such serious sanctions. Incarceration can be resorted to less often.

Finally, it has been argued that incarceration is a costly measure. In Denmark, it costs about $90 million per year to run the prisons.

These arguments are not in themselves decisive. Deprivation of freedom normally prevents the offender from committing new offenses during the period of incarceration. This effect should not be ignored. Even if it is difficult to prove that deprivation of liberty does have a general deterrent effect, this severe sanction may be decisive in establishing the authority of the criminal justice system — an important condition for maintaining a general law-abiding attitude among members of society. Incarceration is sometimes a necessary means for society to express its sincere disapproval of a criminal act. This is particularly true in a country that does not have — and does not wish to have — capital punishment.

Thus, Denmark's depenalization policy is not a matter of not using incarceration any longer. It is a matter of using incarceration more carefully, for shorter periods. Probably the best argument for our depenalization policy is to envision the situation we would have had if we had not set about reforming the penal system.

In the beginning of the 1970s, the number of prisoners in England and that in Denmark were comparable. England, with its 50 million inhabitants, had about 35,000 persons incarcerated, whereas Denmark, with about 5 million inhabitants had approximately 3,500 inmates. England did not depenalize; if anything, the sentences became longer. The result is that they now have more than 42,000 prisoners and severe problems in the prison system. The policy in Denmark has made it possible during the same period to regulate the prison population and conditions and to transfer resources from the institutions to the probation service. This has enabled us to intensify our work with offenders at an earlier stage.

The End of the Depenalization Period — And Then What?

Denmark, like the other Scandinavian countries, is still in the process of depenalization. Committees reviewing policies in all these countries recommend further depenalization—a criminal justice system with fewer incarcerated.

In order to comply with these recommendations, sentences could be shortened still more. This could be done either by more lenient judgments by the courts or by earlier release of inmates. In Denmark, we are presently discussing whether inmates might be released after having served one-half of their sentences rather than waiting until they have served two-thirds of their terms, as is now the case. New alternatives to incarceration are also being discussed, such as community service, which is not yet used in any of the Scandinavian countries.

The consequence of the suggestions under debate in Denmark would be a further reduction in the daily prison population, from approximately 3,000 to about 2,500 inmates.

As was mentioned at the beginning of this paper, we have not been successful in achieving the main goal of criminal justice, namely, to reduce crime. One can foresee that a crime policy which is able to meet only part of the goals of criminal justice cannot continue. It may be that we will achieve our goals only by looking outside the criminal justice system for the answers.

The declining birth rate today indicates that the number of youngsters in the most crime-prone years will drop by the 1980s. We may expect that the decreased birth rate will mean more employment opportunities, although this is difficult to predict with certainty. In the meantime, it is crucial that our school systems, our social welfare system, and our communities work to involve youngsters in our society. The criminal justice system must be able to participate in that effort.

In Denmark we created some ten years ago a central crime prevention board, where public officials joined with representatives from the private sector to create crime prevention programs. Initially, this board was most concerned with what is called target hardening, to stem the rising number of property crimes. Now, however, the interest has broadened, and the board is working to stimulate planning in the local communities. The board follows with great interest town planning and its impact on criminal activity. The idea of considering crime prevention when we develop our towns is relatively new.

There is also recent development of what are called "anti-institutions," a type of living collective housing both staff and their "clients." These seem to be particularly successful with comparatively difficult clients.

Finally, it should be mentioned that we are trying to link the criminal justice system and labor organizations. In some ways this is probably more difficult in a country like Denmark, which depends on a national social welfare system, than it would be in a country like the United States, where private enterprise is still very important in maintaining the standard of living. We believed too long that our criminal justice and other social problems would be solved by hiring expertise. We ought to have learned sooner that it would not be possible to solve those serious problems without involving the public. A country like the United States has an advantage in this respect that we lack—namely, the survival of the citizens' willingness to volunteer. We still have much to learn about that.

Footnotes

[1]Ulla Bondeson, Kriminalvard i Frihed [Criminal Care in Liberty] (Stockholm, Sweden, 1977); Norman Bishop, "Beware of Treatment," in Some Developments in Nordic Criminal Policy and Criminology, Scandinavian Research Council on Criminology (Norrkoping, Sweden: Kriminalvardsstryrelsen, 1975); and Britta Kyvsgaard, Straffesystemets Virkning [The Effect of Punishment], mimeo. (Copenhagen, Denmark, 1978).
[2]Nils Christie, Hvor Tett et Samfunn? [How Close a Society?] (Cophenhagen, Denmark; Oslo, Norway, 1975).
[3]Karl O. Christiansen et al., Effektiviteten af Forvaring og Soefoengsel [The Effectiveness of Indeterminate Compared with Determinate Punishment] (Copenhagen, Denmark, 1972).
[4]Alternativer til Frihedsstraf—et Debatoplaeg [Alternatives to Deprivation of Liberty—Information for the Debate] (Copenhagen, Denmark, 1977).
[5]Ulla Bondeson, Fangen i Fangsamhallet [The Prisoner in the Prison Community] (Stockholm, Sweden, 1974).
[6]Bishop, "Beware of Treatment."

27

Save Parole Supervision

Robert Martinson
Judith Wilks

The increasing attacks on the institution of parole in the United States today fail to distinguish between parole as a method for releasing offenders from (or returning offenders to) imprisonment and parole as a method for supervising offenders in the community. These two distinct functions need to be separately evaluated for an overall assessment of the usefulness of parole and its fairness in our system of criminal justice.

The parole release (and revocation) decision is inseparable from the indeterminate sentence. Decisionmaking is a quasi-judicial process carried on by small groups of appointed officials organized into Parole Boards. Parole supervision, on the other hand, is not dependent on the indeterminate sentence. It is a method for controlling, helping, or keeping track of offenders in the community. For hundreds of thousands of convicted offenders, it is a major institutional alternative to extended periods of imprisonment. The supervision functions of parole are carried on by an extended network of thousands of agents

Source: *Federal Probation*, Vol. 41, No. 3 (September 1977), 23-27.

organized into parole district offices and divisions.

The essential criterion of parole as a quasi-judicial process is simple fairness .and equity. Such issues are especially critical when unreviewed discretion involves deprivation of liberty. Many critics have rightly argued that the parole decisionmaking process is lamentably brief for such an important decision, lacking in essential elements of due process, frequently arbitrary and subject to political interference, and based in part on a myth that parole boards have the ability to accurately predict when a particular offender is "ready" for parole.

The usual criterion for assessing parole supervision has been how *effective* it is in reducing the criminal behavior of those under supervision. Such effectiveness need not be gained at the price of unfairness. On the contrary, since the consequence of engaging in criminal behavior is to be reimprisoned, supervision which is effective directly contributes to fairness in the sense that fewer offenders are deprived of their liberty. By preventing or inhibiting criminal behavior, effective parole supervision insures that fewer offenders will be rearrested, convicted, and returned to prison.

Unfortunately, in their haste to restrict or eliminate the Parole Board decision-making function (and the indeterminate sentence on which it rests), some critics propose to throw the baby out with the bath water. Yet there is no reason why a mandatory and definite parole sentence could not be substituted for the present system of parole board discretion and conditional release under threat of revocation for rule-breaking.[1] And those who propose such radical surgery would do well not to speak in the name of the offender for there is grave danger that the overall consequence of abolishment of parole supervision would be to consign larger numbers of offenders to prison.

One critical empirical question that must be answered is: Would the abolition of the present system of parole supervision increase or decrease the rates at which persons released from incarceration would be reprocessed into the criminal justice system? Previous research has not addressed this question. Such research deals primarily with variants of parole supervision within the existing system.[2] Inferences from such research are speculative and do not permit a "...direct comparison of offenders under parole supervision with offenders set entirely free."[3]

Parole has never been a universal method for releasing offenders from incarceration, and therefore in most jurisdictions in the United States some persons are released on parole supervision while others are released at the expiration of their terms, i.e., "set entirely free." Clearly, the most obvious research method, available to researchers since parole was established in the United States, would be controlled comparisons òf persons released under parole supervision with comparable persons released directly from imprisonment without parole supervision. This is the method to be used in the present analysis.

The Survey

The data presented in table 1 are taken from a larger survey of criminal justice research. The survey was designed to provide a standard procedure for maximizing the accumulation of existing information so that substantive questions can be answered and decisions taken on matters of public policy. For a description of the research procedure, the classification of documents received, and the variables coded, it is necessary to read the preliminary report.[4] The present substudy illustrates the utility of the procedure adopted.

Two key concepts were employed in collecting, coding, and organizing the data taken from more than 600 recent documents: the "batch" and the "computable recidivism rate."

Batch. —A "batch" is any number of persons at some specifiable location in the criminal justice system for whom a "proper" recidivism rate is computable. A proper recidivism rate must specify what *proportion* of a batch are recidivists. The term "parent batch" refers to a universal set which contains two or more batches. For example, a universal set of, say 1,000 male and female parolees may be broken into one batch of 800 *male* parolees and one batch of 200 *female* parolees. Each of these batches is coded as "exclusive" since together they exhaust the parent batch and have no members in common. All batches in table 1 are exclusive batches with an N of 10 or more.

Recidivism Rate. —The primary unit of analysis in the survey is the computable recidivism rate. Each such rate specifies what proportion of any batch shall be identified as "recidivists" according to whatever operational definition of recidivism is utilized by the researcher. Such an operational definition will normally specify the length of time which the batch was followed up in addition to the criminal justice action (arrest, suspension, conviction, return to prison, and so forth) which led to the decision to classify a particular person as a "recidivist." All such definitions were coded into seven categories. Three of these categories—arrest, conviction, and return to prison with a new conviction —were judged to be appropriate for a comparison of parolees and persons released from incarceration with no supervision ("max out").[5]

The term "system re-processing rate" specifies precisely what is being measured in table 1. An "arrest," for example, is an event that can occur to a person under the jurisdiction of criminal justice, and an arrest *rate* simply reports what proportion of any batch included in table 1 were reported as being reprocessed in this way in the documents coded in the survey.

Each recidivism rate in the survey has been coded with additional items of information. The coding system developed was guided by the primary aim of the accumulation of knowledge based on the existing state of the art in criminal justice research. Codes were designed to maximize the information produced by the standard procedures now used in the body of documents encountered. Many of the items specify critical methodological features of the study, such as whether the batch is a population or a sample, the type of research design utilized, months in followup, months in treatment, the type of population or sample (e.g., "termination" sample), and so forth. Since studies report information on the characteristics of batches in a bewildering variety of ways, a standard attribute code was developed so as to maximize the reporting of such information as educational attainment, current offense, race, class position, family status, and so forth.[6] In addition, it was possible to code a considerable number of batches (and therefore rates) with such information as mean age, months in incarceration, sex, whether the batch consisted primarily of narcotics cases or persons with alcohol problems, and so forth.

Procedure

The procedure adopted was to exhaust the survey data base of all meaningful comparisons between adult offenders released from incarceration to parole supervision and comparable groups of adult offenders not released to parole supervision ("max out"). This was a simle sorting operation with an IBM counter-sorter. From a total pool of 5,804 recidivism rates for batches of adult persons in the United States and Canada released under parole supervision, those rates which fell in the category of "arrest" (N = 235), "conviction" (N = 135), and return to prison with a new conviction" (N = 738) were sorted out. A similar sort for adult max out rates resulted in 44 arrest rates, 26 conviction rates, and 73 return-to-prison-with-new-conviction rates. The total number of rates produced by these initial sorts are found at the bottom of table 1.

The cards were then sorted on the variables which had been coded in the survey making no distinction between items which were primarily methodological (e.g., time in followup) and those which were primarily descriptive of a batch (e.g., mean age, sex, percent property offenders). All code categories for which at least two rates were reported for both parole and max out were located. Mean rates for these code categories were computed, and are presented in table 1.[7]

TABLE 1.—*Mean recidivism rates*

Batch Characteristic	Definition: Arrest Parole X	N*	Max Out X	N	D°*	Conviction Parole X	N	Max Out X	N	D	New Prison Sentence Parole X	N	Max Out X	N	D
1. Batch N=100-499	26.9	84	32.8	12	5.9	20.5	68	25.9	22	5.4	11.0	227	14.7	44	3.7
2. Male	25.2	174	39.5	32	14.3	19.1	85	29.6	21	10.5	11.3	393	14.3	58	3.0
3. % White=0 to 24.9	20.8	38	31.0	17	10.2	12.8	18	22.8	6	10.0	13.3	24	22.8	6	9.5
4. Total Population	20.8	62	37.7	22	16.9	13.9	31	28.1	25	14.2	9.7	593	14.5	67	4.8
5. Termination Sets	24.4	206	42.1	25	17.7	21.3	79	35.7	17	15.4	10.9	603	14.9	71	4.0
6. After-Only Research Design	25.2	96	42.3	27	17.1	21.8	60	28.9	25	7.1	10.9	581	14.8	73	3.9
7. Research done in 1970's	24.0	178	43.6	42	19.6	18.1	66	28.9	25	10.8	9.8	543	14.8	73	5.0
8. Standard Treatment	27.4	129	43.0	39	15.6	19.3	96	29.9	26	10.6	10.3	584	14.9	72	4.6
9. 7-12 Months Follow-up	24.6	85	43.7	12	19.1	15.6	66	22.8	6	7.2	8.7	250	5.2	15	-3.5
10. 19-24 Months Follow-up	28.4	41	57.5	10	29.1	20.9	11	32.5	5	11.6	11.0	170	11.2	15	.2
11. 25-36 Months Follow-up	28.9	25	49.5	4	20.6	17.8	15	27.5	10	9.7	15.5	79	18.9	16	3.4
12. Measured Only After Treatment	28.3	8	43.4	36	15.1	46.3	11	33.2	15	-13.1	14.9	48	13.9	62	-1.0
13. % Property Offenders 50-74.9	16.6	39	34.5	6	17.9	13.0	70	22.8	6	9.8					
14. % First Offenders 0-24.9	29.5	32	37.5	10	8.0	13.8	14	22.8	6	9.0					
15. Not Primarily Narcotic Users	32.5	5	32.5	5	0	5.9	7	22.8	6	16.9					
16. Not Primarily Alcohol Problems	43.4	9	36.2	6	-7.2	13.7	12	22.8	6	9.1					
17. % White 25-49.9	27.8	39	51.2	9	23.4	44.5	7	30.7	13	-13.8					
18. Mean Age 25-34.9	22.2	51	40.5	25	18.3	20.9	28	23.1	7	2.2					
19. % High School Graduates 0-24.9	25.5	67	41.2	9	15.7	19.8	17	22.8	6	3.0					
20. Measured over Same Time at Risk	22.6	26	44.0	19	21.4	18.7	55	18.9	9	.2					
21. Months Incarcerated= 12-17	17.3	36	40.8	8	23.5	17.5	10	28.2	19	10.7					
22. % From Broken Families 50-74.9	32.3	9	32.5	5	.2	19.3	23	22.8	6	3.5					
23. Comparison Group	28.3	79	42.5	15	14.2						9.9	126	14.5	9	4.6
24. Batch N=50-99	20.9	53	64.5	4	43.6						12.6	62	15.5	10	2.9
25. Sample	25.9	62	48.1	22	22.2						14.0	145	16.3	11	2.3
26. "E" Group	23.7	84	42.5	5	18.8										
27. % Property Offenders 25-49.9	21.1	29	48.5	10	27.4										
28. Batch N=10-49	22.8	72	44.1	28	21.3										
29. Primarily Narcotics Users	29.0	20	29.5	6	.5										
30. Mixed Sex Batch	28.6	39	51.7	9	23.1										
31. % From Broken Families 0-24.9	29.3	31	51.2	3	21.9										
32. % High School Graduates 25-49.9	33.5	10	37.0	4	3.5										
33. Lowest Class	34.1	22	45.8	8	11.7										
34. Non-Random Research Design	24.4	93	43.9	17	19.5										
35. 1-6 Months Follow-up	15.5	61	29.5	12	14.0										
36. 13-18 Months Follow-up	30.1	16	32.5	5	2.4										
37. Months Incarcerated= 24-29	29.5	32	31.2	3	1.7										
38. Months Incarcerated= 30-36	36.2	6	59.5	6	23.3										
39. % Property Offenders 0-24.9						20.5	15	30.5	10	10.0					
40. Highest Class						20.8	19	22.8	6	2.0					
41. Batch N=500+											9.3	378	13.9	18	4.6
42. 37-60 Months Follow-up											13.5	87	18.4	18	4.9
43. 60+ Months Follow-up											14.1	22	25.4	7	11.3
TOTAL	24.5	235	42.9	44	18.4	19.7	135	29.9	26	10.2	10.5	738	14.8	73	4.3

*N = Number of rates   **D = Max Out Mean minus Parole Mean

Discussion

Item 1 can be used to illustrate how the table should be read. For parole, there were 84 recidivism rates where "arrest" was the measurement of recidivism and for which the batch size fell between 100 and 499. The mean of these 84 rates was 26.9. For this same batch size (100-499), there were 12 max out rates, and the mean of these rates was 32.8. The difference between these two means is 5.9.

Reading across the table, for the "conviction" definition the mean rates for parole and max out were 20.5 and 25.9, respectively. For the "return to prison with new conviction" definition these means were 11.0 and 14.7. Turning to a different batch size of 50-99 (item 24), one notes that comparisons could only be made for two of the three definitions. For some variables comparisons were possible for only one definition.

This table presents data in a manner which is similar to the procedure of simultaneously controlling for adulthood, definition of recidivism, place in the criminal justice system (i.e., parole vs. max out), and at least one additional variable. Given the number of rates available, it would have been possible to have controlled for one (or even more) variables in addition to the four specified above. For reasons of time, these additional controls were not attempted.

It is interesting to note that in *74 of the 80 comparisons contained in table 1, the mean of the recidivism rates for parole is lower than for max out.* This is the case whether the final variable controlled is methodological or sociodemographic. For the arrest definition, the differences *in favor of* parole range from a low of 0.2 (item 22) to a high of 43.6 (item 24). For conviction, the differences in favor of parole range from 0.2 (item 20) to 16.9 (item 15). For new prison sentence, the differences in favor of parole range from 0.2 (item 10) to 11.3 (item 43).

In 6 of the 80 comparisons, the mean of the rates for max out is equal to or lower than the mean for parole. These six cases are unsystematically distributed throughout the table. In three instances the final control variable is methodlogical; in three it is sociodemographic. Two cases fall under the arrest definition; two under conviction; and two under return to prison. These six exceptions do not suggest to us any particular set of conditions which might be further explored to discover subgroups of offenders, or contexts, for which max out would be a superior policy for criminal justice.

Data contained in our Preliminary Report provided a starting point for this analysis. This initial data (based on 3,005 rates coded at that time) indicated that the mean of the rates for parole (25.4) was somewhat lower than the mean of the rates for max out (31.6). This six percentage point difference resulted from a comparison which did not further control for the definition of recidivisim, for adult vs. juvenile, or for any of the other variables utilized in table 1. Increasing the total number of rates, and simultaneously controlling for four additional variables has led to the discovery of larger mean differences between parole and max out.[8]

Summary

Those who propose the abolition of parole supervision in this country often speak of "fairness to the offender." It is difficult to detect in table 1 evidence of such fairness. On the contrary. The evidence seems to indicate that the abolition of parole supervision would result in substantial increases in arrest, conviction, and return to prison. Those who wish to eliminate the unfairness of parole board decisionmaking might well concentrate on finding a specific remedy for this problem, a remedy which would not increase the very "unfairness" they deplore. At the very least, the data in table 1 should give pause to those policymakers and legislators who have been operating on the unexamined assumption that parole supervision *makes no difference*. In face of the evidence in table 1 such an assumption is unlikely.

Footnotes

[1] See J. Wilks and R. Martinson, "Is the Treatment of Criminal Offenders Really Necessary?," *Federal Probation*, March 1976, pp. 3-9.

[2] See, for example, D. Lipton, R. Martinson, and J. Wilks, *The Effectiveness of Correctional Treatment*. New York: Praeger Publishers, 1975, sections on Probation and Parole.

[3] D.T. Stanley, *Prisoners Among Us: The Problem of Parole*, The Brookings Institution, Washington, D.C., 1976, pp. 181-2.

[4] See, R. Martinson and J. Wilks, *Knowledge in Criminal Justice Planning, A Preliminary Report*, October 15, 1976, pp. 58 (processed).

[5] The other four categories were: 100% minus "success" rate; short of arrest (i.e., AWOL, absconding, suspension, and similar); return to prison for technical violation; and return to prison for technical plus new conviction. Three of these categories were eliminated because they cannot happen to max out groups. The fourth — 100% minus "success" rate — was eliminated because of possible problems in interpreting the meaning of the measure.

[6] The proportion in which any attribute was present in a batch was coded as follows: 1 — 0-24.9%; 2 — 25-49%; 3 — 50-74.9%; and 4 — 75-100%.

[7]Multiplying the total number of coding categories (97) by the three definitions gives a total of 291 possible comparisons if sufficient data had been present. Eliminating 39 cases where data were reported as "unknown," 38 cases in which there were less than two rates in a category of either parole or max out, and 134 cases in which no data were reported leaves the 80 comparisons reported in table 1.

[8]This method is an application of standard research procedures. See, for example, P.F. Lazersfeld, "Interpretation of Statistical Relations as a Research Operation," in: *The Language of Social Research* (P.F. Lazersfeld and M. Rosenberg, eds.), Glencoe, Ill.: The Free Press, 1955.

28

Alternatives to Incarceration
A Conservative Perspective

Charles Colson and
Daniel W. Van Ness

In Michigan, conservative Republican legislators Jack Welborn and William Van Regenmorter worked with liberal Democrat Carolyn Cheeks Kilpatrick to pass a Community Corrections Act (CCA). The result: Non-violent offenders will be punished in their communities instead of prison, which will save money and ease the state's prison overcrowding crisis.

In Indiana, Republican State Sen. Ed Pease led a successful legislative effort to establish home detention as a means of easing the pressure of the state's expanding prison population. Russ Pulliam, editorial writer of the conservative Pulliam newspaper chain, voiced support for the legislation as "one step in the right direction for the future of the criminal justice system in Indiana" (*Indianapolis News* Jan. 20,1988). (The bill was included in The Council of State Governments' *Suggested State Legislation*, 1989).

Source: *The Journal of State Government*, Vol. 62 (March/April 1989), 59-64, published by the Council of State Governments. Reprinted by permission of the publisher and the authors.

In Florida, conservative businessman Jack Eckerd and former Federal Bureau of Prisons Director Norm Carlson are leading a campaign for expanded use of house arrest, drug treatment and restitution centers as alternatives to imprisonment for non-violent offenders.

In Alabama, conservative Democratic Rep. Claud Walker is sponsoring a Community Corrections Act aimed at reducing the large percentage of non-violent inmates in state prisons. Alabama Commissioner of Corrections Morris Thigpen and the Alabama Sheriffs Association are backing the bill.

In Arizona, Republican State Sen. Tony West sponsored the Community Punishment Act. The legislation, which recently passed with the support of Arizona Chief Justice Frank Cordon and Maricopa County Chief Presiding Judge B. Michael Dann, will provide communities with state money to establish restitution, community service, victim-offender reconciliation and other non-prison programs for non-dangerous offenders.

Conservatives are often typecast as champions of the "lock 'em up and throw away the key" battle cry of this "get tough on crime" era. Yet, increasingly, all around the country, conservatives of both parties are advocating alternatives to incarceration for non-violent offenders. They may well be the single most potent force for practical, prudent criminal justice reform today.

What's Going On?

No one can deny the crying need for reform in our nation's criminal justice system. In December 1988 there were 627,402 state and federal prisoners in American institutions—twice as many as in 1978 (Department of Justice press release April 23, 1989). The prison population explosion has filled prisons to overflowing. Federal prisons are 73 percent over capacity, while state prisons are on average 20 percent over capacity, according to the Bureau of Justice Statistics (BJS 1988a).

Prison systems in 45 states have been sued because of overcrowding. In 37 states, at least one major institution is under court order or consent decree. In nine of those 37 states, the entire prison system is under court order. Litigation is pending in eight states (National Prison Project 1988).

The future looks no brighter. The National Council of Crime and Delinquency (NCCD 1988a) estimates that U.S. prison populations will increase by an additional 50 percent in the next 10 years.

Although our country is incarcerating more people than ever, violent and property crimes continue to escalate (BJS 1988b). The indiscriminate "get tough" approach is a grand success in filling prisons. But it fails miserably at reducing crime.

Thankfully, many conservatives actively are pushing saner, wiser solutions to crime's stranglehold on our nation and the prison population explosion.

Why conservatives? Based on Justice Fellowship's work with politicians across the United States, it's clear that many see alternatives to incarceration for non-violent offenders as a natural extension of conservative political philosophy. Legislators cite the following principles: Punishment is appropriate; it should serve victims' needs; public safety is essential; local is better, and wise use of limited government resources is needed.

Let's look at each.

Punishment is appropriate. Since the first "penitentiary" was established in 1789, American criminal justice has been predicated on the belief that crime is the result of environmental or psychiatric factors. Criminals were seen as victims and were sent to prison to be rehabilitated.

This human engineering approach has proven a dismal failure. Studies over the last two decades consistently have concluded that three out of four ex-offenders are rearrested within four years of their release from prison (Federal Bureau of Investigation 1975; Petersilia, Turner and Peterson 1986). Far from rehabilitating offenders, prisons seem better suited to train them in the finer arts of crime.

Pursuing false dreams of rehabilitation undermines the principle of personal accountability. No matter how many environmental factors weigh upon the individual, committing a criminal act is a personal choice. By treating victimizers as victims, society robs them of the dignity belonging to moral agents. They are denied the opportunity to "pay the price" and move on with life. C.S. Lewis ([1949] 1983) put it this way, "To be punished, however severely, because we have deserved it, because we 'ought to have known better' is to be treated as a human person made in God's image."

Treatment programs should be available to offenders who would be helped by them—but justice requires that offenders also must be held accountable for their behavior.

The issue should not be *whether* to punish but *how*. The problem is that our society has increasingly equated "punishment" with "prison" and seems unable to conceive of the notion of punishments aside from prison. Prisons are, of course, necessary for violent offenders. But nearly 50 percent of the American prison population is behind bars for non-violent offenses. Many of them would pose little danger to their communities; they are imprisoned solely for punishment.

For the reasons that follow, many conservatives are concluding that society is not well served by punishing non-violent offenders behind bars. Sound alternatives to prison are available. Restitution, community service and intensive supervision probation are tough and effective punishments that limit freedom and place demands for compensation upon offenders.

Punishment should serve victims' needs. While victims suffer most from crime—physically, emotionally and financially (to the tune of $13 billion per year) (BJS 1988c)—victims' interests are represented least. From the moment a crime is committed, through the time the offender is convicted and sent to prison, the victim is virtually ignored by the criminal justice system. As Roberta Roper whose daughter was murdered seven years ago, said, "Crime doesn't pay—but victims do."

This injustice has sparked the growth of victims' rights groups across the United States. In addition to supporting an increased role for victims in the system, many have promoted restitution and other alternatives to incarceration—not to make life easier for offenders but to benefit victims.

For example, the Alabama Victims Compensation Group and Victims of Crime Against Leniency are supporting the Alabama Community Corrections Act because it holds offenders accountable for their crimes and provides for victim assistance officers to help victims secure restitution and compensation. In Maryland, Justice Fellowship worked with the effective and well-respected Stephanie Roper Committee to promote recently passed mandatory restitution legislation.

Victim restitution must become an essential part of criminal punishments. This a matter of simple justice. In an article describing the Sentencing Improvement Act of 1983, U.S. Sens. William Armstrong, R-Colorado, and Sam Nunn, D-Georgia, (1986) recognized the importance of alternative punishments based on restitution: "Because of growing public concern for crime victims, the restitution concept holds great promise of gaining broad public support. . . . Recent surveys indicate that a great percentage of Americans would prefer to have the non-violent offender repay his victim rather than serve time at public expense."

Public safety is essential. Non-violent offenders who might be sentenced to alternative punishments are taking up precious prison space that should be reserved for violent criminals. (As noted, nearly half of all state prisoners were convicted of non-violent crimes. And 34 percent have never committed a violent crime (BJS 1988d).)

But, prisons are so overcrowded that many states rely on early release to reduce prison populations. This means that some dangerous offenders are let out well before they have served their full sentence. This is the irony of the "get tough" response to crime: By indiscriminately sending more people to prison, communities are less safe.

The case of Charlie Street is illustrative. Street was released from Florida's Martin Correctional Institution in the fall of 1988 after serving only half of his sentence for attempted murder. Ten days later, he gunned down two Dade County police officers — a tragedy that could have been avoided if Street had been kept off the streets and in prison where he belonged. As Jack Eckerd wrote in the *Orlando Sentinel* (Dec. 4,1988), "We must restore sanity to the system, slamming the door and keeping it shut on violent and career criminals like Charlie Street, while expanding alternate punishments for non-violent offenders."

Any discussion of public safety eventually includes the issue of deterrence. The argument that prisons alone deter is defeated by the facts. Swift and certain punishment deters, not harsh punishment that is neither swift nor certain.

Consider the odds. The federal government reports that, out of 100 crimes, 33 will be reported to the police and seven will result in an arrest. Four will end with a conviction, with one offender going to jail, one to prison and two to probation. In other words, for every 100 crimes committed in the United States, one person goes to prison (Colson and Van Ness 1989).

Can we reasonably believe that doubling or tripling the number of people in prison would significantly deter crime? Would a 2 or 3 percent chance of imprisonment actually deter more crime than a 1 percent chance of imprisonment?

Fortunately, experienced criminal justice practitioners know that tough alternative punishments are feared more by convicted offenders than prison. Trial judges in Florida, for example, say that defendants request prison sentences to avoid the state's tough Community Control Program.

Alternatives promote public safety in other ways as well. For example, they keep the non-violent offender out of prison, the ideal training ground for becoming a more accomplished and dangerous criminal. The Rand Corporation found in a 1986 study (Petersilia, Turner and Peterson) that a group of probationers committed fewer new crimes than an identical group of ex-prisoners. The researchers concluded that "imprisonment was associated with a higher probability of recidivism."

A federal study of Georgia's Intensive Probation Supervision program (National Institute of Justice 1987) found that probationers committed fewer new crimes than comparable prisoners and no violent new crimes.

Community safety depends on increased use of community sanctions.

Local is better. Many alternatives to incarceration significantly benefit local communities. Community Corrections Acts, for example, allow communities to tailor programs to meet their own needs, by dealing with non-violent offenders in their own ways. This also means that communities are involved with their own offenders, who will most likely continue to live in the community after serving their sentences.

Local punishments benefit the state as well. Every offender who stays in a local program is one less person taking up scarce prison space at state expense.

Community service performed by offenders can be another important local benefit. Instead of sending offenders to state prisons, some communities reap the benefits of free or low-pay labor for charitable or governmental agencies. Genesee County, New York, has honed this practice into an art form. Since the establishment of the county's widely acclaimed Genesee Justice program in 1981,offenders performed more than 97,000 hours of community service for 118 community agencies, a total value of $389,000 (Genesee County Sheriff's Department 1988).

Wise use of limited government resources. There is no question that states will have to increase their prison capacities. But state governments cannot afford to rely on prison construction as the sole means to solve the overcrowding crisis. It costs an average of $15,900 to keep an inmate in prison for one year (Camp and Camp 1988). In fiscal 1987 alone state and federal governments spent almost $5 billion in new prison construction (American Correctional Association 1988).

This is placing an extraordinary strain on state budgets. Norman Carlson (1988), writing of the situation in Florida, summarizes the dilemma facing many states, "Constructing sufficient prison space is not a viable solution. The tremendous costs involved in building and operating the required number of new prisons would overwhelm the limited resources available in the state treasury and would compete with other high priority needs, such as education, medical care and transportation."

Explaining why he worked so hard for passage of the Michigan Community Corrections Act, Michigan State Rep. William Van Regenmorter (1988) said, "Michigan's prison system has been overcrowded since 1975. (In). . . 1984, the system held about 300 prisoners more than its intended capacity. To combat this problem, the Department of Corrections constructed many new prisons, almost doubling the system's capacity in just three years. The result of this expensive building program? The system was still overcrowded, this time by some 3,000 prisoners!"

And because of the extraordinary increase (141 percent over the last five years) in the corrections budget—due to the massive prison construction program (*Grand Rapids Press* Jan. 2, 1989)—Michigan now faces cuts in social service programs.

New prison construction costs an average of $80,000 per maximum security cell. The total cost of all current or planned prison construction will be $25 billion (NCCD 1988b). States cannot afford to make such budget-busting investments in concrete and steel condominiums with bars.

To reduce overcrowding and avoid bankrupting other key state programs, conservatives argue in favor of investing in alternatives to prison, so that prisons can be reserved for the dangerous offenders who must be locked away from society. Some states are taking initiatives to do so.

Program Profiles

Community Corrections Acts (CCAs). These acts provide a statewide mechanism allowing local governments to design, develop and deliver—and state governments to fund—local correctional tools such as intensive supervision, restitution, community service, and drug and alcohol treatment. Thirteen states now have CCAs.

Tennessee diverted 504 offenders from prison in fiscal 1987-88 at a cost of $7,599 per offender, compared to the state average of $19,710 for incarceration. In addition, offenders sentenced to community corrections paid $59,145 in restitution to victims and performed 76,294 hours of community service. The estimated total savings to the state was $6.1 million (Mike Jones, Tennessee Department of Corrections, telephone interview September 1988).

Virginia diverted 699 felons from its prisons and jails in fiscal 1987-88. As a result, it saved more than $8 million, which does not include savings realized by diverting more than 6,500 local felons and misdemeanants from jails. Diverted offenders performed 229,812 hours of community service and paid $76,870 in restitution (Gwen Cunningham, Virginia Department of Corrections, telephone interview, September 1988).

House arrest confines offenders to their own homes. They are not allowed out except for approved activities such as health care, special religious services, community service or employment, which in turn most often leads to restitution payments to victims (Petersilia 1987). Many jurisdictions are using electronic surveillance measures to ensure compliance.

Florida's Community Control Program is a nationally recognized house arrest program. Established in 1983, Community Control uses community service and restitution sanctions for some 8,000 offenders statewide. The cost to the state is $2,650 per year per offender, which is 80 percent less than the $13,140 cost for imprisonment (Carlson 1989). By reducing prison commitments by 180 people a month, Community Control has proven a valuable weapon in Florida's fight against overcrowding. Because only 9 percent of its offenders commit new crimes, it is also an effective weapon against crime.

Intensive Probation Supervision (IPS). The key to this program's success is low caseloads. Ideally, officers maintain caseloads of 15-25 people—as opposed to the supervision possible when harried officers in "normal" probation programs carry caseloads of between 120 and 300 offenders. In many IPS programs, offenders must make daily contact with their officers. Most intensive supervision programs require offenders to maintain employment or go to school and to abide by a strict curfew. Many also include restitution and community service as sanctions.

Illinois regularly supervises 570 offenders in its IPS program—a ratio of 25 offenders for every two officers. The annual cost per offender is $2,367. Since the program was established in 1984, Illinois has collected approximately $1 million in restitution, taxes, fines and court costs. Its Intensive Probation Supervision participants performed 145,349 hours of public service valued at $489,921. All told, the state saved $7.7 million in the last five years through IPS (Anderson 1988). And prospects look good for expanding the program to more offenders.

Restitution centers are residential facilities designed to house offenders requiring more supervision than regular or intensive supervision probation but less than total confinement in prison. These centers, which are a tightened-up version of "work release" with a focus on restitution, are used in six states as an alternative to imprisonment.

Georgia's restitution centers can house 2,600 offenders yearly. During fiscal 1987, the state collected from offenders $256,817 in restitution, $626,516 in family support, $1.4 million in room and board, $940,274 in fines and court fees and $1.4 million in taxes. The offenders also performed community service worth $266,516. The annual cost per offender was $8,249. Seventy-five percent of the residents successfully complete the program (Larry Anderson, Georgia Department of Corrections, telephone interview, 1988).

Florida's Probation and Restitution Centers can hold 382 offenders, far below the 900 offenders who would have qualified for the program in 1987, according to a 1988 report by the state Office of the Auditor

General. The annual cost per offender is $10,909, which the state partially defrays by collecting average annual fees of $1,900 per offender. Jack Eckerd and Norm Carlson are among those calling for expanded use of these centers in Florida.

Conclusion

No one could deny the severity of America's criminal justice crisis. The time has come for real solutions rather than overheated rhetoric that fuels public passions, reinforces stereotypes about prisons and prisoners and, in the end, results in taxpayers being punished far more than offenders.

Historically, conservatives have been at the forefront of many great movements in the West: the battle for abolition of the slave trade and of slavery, the fight to end industrial abuses in the late 19th century and in efforts to establish public education. We believe the criminal justice arena is one in which conservatives are beginning to lead the way toward measures that will benefit offenders, victims, correctional officials and taxpayers.

Crime is not a partisan issue. Pursuing alternatives to prison for non-violent offenders will take the endurance, creativity and cooperation of men and women from every political perspective. And conservatives, working with moderates and liberals, can play a key role in forging that public consensus for effective criminal justice policy.

References

Administrative Office of the Illinois Courts. 1988. *Illinois Intensive Probation Supervision: Statewide Summary, Quarterly Statistical Report.* Prepared by Gregg Anderson. Springfield: Administrative Office of the Illinois Courts, July.

American Correctional Association. 1988. *1988 Directory: Juvenile and Adult Correctional Departments, Institutions, Agencies — Paroling Authorities*, ed. Anthony P. Travisono. College Park, MD: American Correctional Association.

Armstrong, William L., and Sam Nunn. 1986. "Alternatives to Incarceration: The Sentencing Improvement Act." *Crime and Punishment in Modern America*, ed. Patrick B. McGuigan and Jon S. Pascale, 337-348. Washington DC: Free Congress Research and Education Foundation.

Bureau of Justice Statistics (BJS), Department of Justice. 1988a. *Prisoners in 1987.* Washington DC: GPO, April.

_____. 1988b. *Criminal Victimization 1987.* Washington DC: GPO, October.

_____. 1988c. *Report to the Nation on Crime and Justice*. 2d. ed. Washington, DC: GPO.

_____. 1988d. *Profile of State Prison Inmates 1986*. Prepared by Christopher A. Innes. Washington, DC: GPO, January.

Camp, George M., and Camille Graham Camp. 1988. *The Corrections Yearbook 1988*. New York: Criminal Justice Institute.

Carlson, Norman A. 1988. *Findings and Recommendations on Florida's Prison Crisis*. Tallahassee: Florida Prison Crisis Project, March-April.

_____. 1989. *Florida's Prison Crisis*. Tallahassee: Justice Task Force, January.

Colson, Charles, and Daniel W. Van Ness. 1989. *Convicted: New Hope for Ending America's Crime Crisis*. Westchester, IL: Crossway.

Council of State Governments. 1989. *Suggested State Legislation*, Vol. 48. Lexington: Council of State Governments.

Federal Bureau of Investigation. 1975. Crime in the United States 1975. *Crime in the United States 1975: Uniform Crime Reports for the United States*. Washington, DC: GPO.

Genesee County (NY) Sheriff's Department. 1988. *Genesee Justice 1987-88 Annual Report: Community Service/Victim Assistance Program*. Batavia, NY: Genesee County Sheriff's Department.

Lewis, C.S. [1949] 1983. The Humanitarian Theory of Punishment. Reprint, in *God in the Dock: Essays on Theology and Ethics*, ed. Walter Hooper, 287-294. Grand Rapids: William B. Eerdmans.

National Council on Crime and Delinquency (NCCD). 1988a. *Crime and Punishment in the Year 2000: What Kind of Future?* San Francisco: NCCD.

_____. 1988b. *Illusory Savings in the War Against Crime*. San Francisco: NCCD, July.

National Institute of Justice. 1987. *New Dimensions in Probation: Georgia's Experience with Intensive Probation Supervision*. Prepared by Billie S. Erwin and Lawrence A. Bennett. Washington, DC: GPO, January.

National Prison Project. 1988. *Status Report: The Courts and Prisons*. Washington, DC: National Prison Project.

Petersilia, Joan, Susan Turner and Joyce Peterson. 1986. *Prison versus Probation in California: Implications for Crime and Offender Recidivism*. Santa Monica: Rand.

Petersilia, Joan. 1987. *Expanding Options for Criminal Sentencing*. Santa Monica: Rand.

State of Florida Office of the Auditor General. 1988. *Performance Audit of the Department of Corrections Community-Based Facilities Program*. Tallahassee: Office of the Auditor General, March.

Van Regenmorter, William. 1988. "Helping Young Offenders in Michigan." *The Banner*, Nov. 14.

29

New Dimensions in Probation

Georgia's Experience With Intensive Probation Supervision

Billie S. Erwin and Lawrence A. Bennett

Georgia's Intensive Probation Supervision (IPS) program, implemented in 1982, has stirred nationwide interest among criminal justice professionals because it seems to satisfy two goals that have long appeared mutually contradictory: (1) restraining the growth of prison populations and associated costs by controlling selected offenders in the community and (2) at the same time, satisfying to some extent the demand that criminals be punished for their crimes. The pivotal question is whether or not prison-bound offenders can be shifted into Intensive Probation Supervision without threatening the public safety.

A new research study, partially funded by the National Institute of Justice, suggests that intensive supervision provides greater controls than regular probation and costs far less than incarceration. The study was conducted by the Georgia Department of Corrections, Office of Evaluation

Source: *National Institute of Justice Research in Brief*, January 1987. U.S. Department of Justice, January 1987, 1-7.

and Statistics, and was assisted by an Advisory Board funded by the National Institute of Justice. This *Research in Brief* summarizes the findings.

The Georgia Program

The IPS program began in 1982 as a pilot in 13 of Georgia's 45 judicial sentencing circuits. By the end of 1985, it had expanded to 33 circuits and had supervised 2,322 probationers.

While probation programs with varying degrees of supervision have been implemented throughout the country, Georgia's IPS is widely regarded as one of the most stringent in the Nation. Standards include:

- Five face-to-face contacts per week;
- 132 hours of mandatory community service;
- Mandatory curfew;
- Mandatory employment;
- Weekly check of local arrest records;
- Automatic notification of arrest elsewhere via the State Crime Information Network listing;
- Routine and unannounced alcohol and drug testing.

The supervision standards are enforced by a team consisting of a Probation Officer and a Surveillance Officer. The team supervises 25 probationers. In some jurisdictions, a team of one Probation Officer and two Surveillance Officers supervises 40 probationers.

The standards are designed to provide sufficient surveillance to control risk to the community and give a framework to treatment-oriented counseling. The counseling is designed to help the offender direct his energies toward productive activities, to assume responsibilities, and to become a law-abiding citizen.

Most offenders chosen for the IPS pilot program were already sentenced to prison, presented an acceptable risk to the community, and had not committed a violent offense. A risk assessment instrument was used to screen offenders. While the majority of those selected fell into the category of nonviolent property offenders, a large number of individuals convicted of drug- and alcohol-related offenses also were included as the program developed. Some of these offenses also involved personal violence.

Of the 2,322 people in the program between 1982 and 1985, 370 (or 16 percent) absconded or had their probation revoked. The remaining

1,952 were successfully diverted from prison; many are still under some form of probationary supervision. Some have successfully completed their sentence.

The Evaluation Findings

The evaluation evidence strongly suggests that the IPS program has played a significant role in reducing the flow of offenders to prison. The percentage of offenders sentenced to prison decreased and the number of probationers increased. The kinds of offenders diverted were more similar to prison inmates than to regular probationers, suggesting that the program selected the most suitable offenders. IPS probationers committed less serious crimes during their probation than comparable groups of regular probationers or probationers released from prison. The extensive supervision required seems to exert significant control and thus gives better results.

The cost of IPS, while much greater than regular probation, is considerably less than the cost of a prison stay, even when construction costs are not considered. In addition, society receives thousands of hours of community service from IPS offenders. Criminal justice practitioners seem to accept the program as suitable intermediate punishment. Judges particularly like it because it increases local control.

The evaluation addressed seven major issues:

1. *Did the program divert offenders from prison to an alternative operation?* The evidence indicates that intensive probation supervision diverted a substantial number of offenders from prison.

Georgia sentencing statistics from 1982 through 1985 show a 10 percent reduction in the percentage of felons sentenced to incarceration. At the same time, the percentage of offenders placed on probation increased 10 percent (from 63 percent in 1982 to 73 percent in 1985). Jurisdictions with intensive supervision teams showed an increase of 15 to 27 percent in the percentage of offenders on probation, markedly higher than the statewide average increase of 10 percent.

A 10 percent reduction in the percent of felons who were incarcerated represents major progress in easing prison crowding. The precise extent of the impact of intensive probation supervision cannot be determined, however, because many factors influenced judges' decisions to consider alternative sentences. Nevertheless, in view of the shift toward increased use of probation, the influence of intensive supervision must be considered substantial.

2. *Would the felons who were placed in the IPS program have gone to prison if the program had not existed?* Because Georgia does not have determinate or presumptive sentencing guidelines, the judicial circuits historically have exhibited a great deal of sentencing disparity. In general, sentences in the rural circuits are more severe than in urban circuits. For this reason, selecting offenders for the program according to crime type or risk measure may not have achieved equal impact among the various circuits in diverting offenders from prison.

Hence, IPS administrators targeted a particular type of offender— specifically serious but nonviolent offenders who, without the intensive supervision option, would have gone to prison in the jurisdiction where they were sentenced. This carefully reasoned decision reflected the administrators' desire to achieve maximum support from the judiciary.

The evaluation results indicate that 59.4 percent of the IPS cases were more similar to those incarcerated than to those placed on probation. The results also suggest that 24.6 percent of those actually incarcerated were very similar to those probated. The evidence seems clear: the offenders actually sentenced to IPS resembled those incarcerated more than those who received probation.

3. *Was risk to the community reduced?* The experience suggests that IPS sufficiently controls offenders so that risk to the community is markedly limited. The recidivism rates are considerably better for IPS offenders than for groups under regular probation and for those released from prison. IPS offenders commit fewer and less serious crimes.

Of the 2,322 offenders sentenced to the IPS program:

- 68 percent are still on probation under IPS or regular probation caseloads;
- 15 percent have successfully completed their sentences;
- 1 percent were transferred to other jurisdictions;
- 16 percent have been terminated from the program and returned to prison for technical violations or new crimes.

Only 0.8 percent of the IPS probationers have been convicted of any violent personal crimes (including simple battery, terroristic threat, etc.). Most new crimes have been drug- and alcohol-related offenses. To date, no IPS probationer has committed a subsequent crime that resulted in serious bodily injury to a victim. Of the 2,322 cases admitted to the program, the following serious crime convictions have resulted: 1 armed robbery, 6 simple assaults, 4 simple battery offenses, 1 terrorist threat, 18 burglaries, 19 thefts, and 3 motor vehicle thefts.

Table 1 shows the number and percent of rearrests, reconvictions, and reincarcerations for selected samples of offenders sentenced during 1983. Prison releasees had the highest rate of rearrest in all risk categories. IPS probationers had a higher rate of rearrest than regular probationers, which is not surprising considering the higher level of surveillance.

The recidivism pattern that begins to emerge from Table 1 involves greater intervention (e. g., more incarceration, tighter supervision) paired with more negative outcomes. This pattern tends to hold for most risk groups except offenders with high risk classifications. Offenders with high risk classifications who had been incarcerated showed the lowest percentage of reincarcerations in State prison; however, this same subgroup had the highest rate of rearrest, reconviction, and reincarceration in jail.

The apparent variation in the go-to-prison rate may be attributed to some unknown factor rather than differences in offenders' behavior. For example, it is not unusual for a Georgia judge to decide that an offender may have been released from prison too soon. When that individual appears before the judge on a subsequent offense, the judge will often use jail, county work camps, or some other method of detention and supervision to ensure more direct control over the offender and the period of incarceration.

Recidivism patterns also may be affected by the selection process for the incarcerated sample. This group included only those who had been released for 18 months at the time of the study. Because screening for this group was done in December 1983, only those offenders who were released before July 1984 could be tracked. Thus, those tracked had experienced a short period of incarceration—2 to 6 months. The early release means they were apparently deemed less serious offenders. This suggests that comparisons with more serious offenders released from prison would reflect an even more favorable view of the IPS group.

Table 2 shows the number of convictions for various crimes for the three groups of offenders. The IPS group was convicted of fewer serious new crimes against persons than either of the other two groups. Although not shown in Table 2, minor repeat offenses, primarily marijuana possession, were numerous. Judges reacted strongly in such cases since they felt the offender had already been given his last chance. Serious offenses were, however, remarkably infrequent.

While many IPS probationers were convicted for possession of marijuana and habitual alcohol-related offenses, the most serious new offenses were 4 burglaries and 1 armed robbery in which no one was injured. The regular probationers had more serious offenses; they committed 8 burglaries, 1 rape, and 2 aggravated assaults in addition

Table 1

Outcomes for offender groups after 18-month tracking by risk classification[a]

Offender classification	No. of Cases	Rearrested		Reconvicted		Sentenced to jail or prison		Incarcerated in State prison	
Low risk		No.	%	No.	%	No.	%	No.	%
IPS probationers	12	5	41.6%	3	25.0%	3	25.0%	2	16.7%
Regular probationers	11	3	27.0%	0	0.0%	1	9.1%	1	9.1%
Prison releasees	13	6	46.2%	5	38.5%	4	30.8%	3	23.1%
Medium risk									
IPS probationers	62	21	33.9%	10	16.1%	10	16.1%	9	14.5%
Regular probationers	58	20	34.5%	14	24.1%	9	15.5%	6	10.3%
Prison releasees	12	7	58.3%	6	50.0%	4	33.3%	2	16.7%
High risk									
IPS probationers	69	24	34.5%	19	27.5%	14	20.3%	11	15.9%
Regular probationers	73	22	30.1%	18	24.7%	13	17.8%	10	13.7%
Prison releasees	47	27	57.4%	21	44.7%	10	21.3%	6	12.8%
Maximum risk									
IPS probationers	57	25	43.6%	15	26.3%	12	21.1%	11	19.3%
Regular probationers	58	26	44.8%	16	27.6%	11	19.0%	8	13.8%
Prison releasees	25	16	64.0%	9	36.0%	7	28.0%	6	24.0%
Total for all risk groups									
IPS probationers	200	80	40.0%	37	18.5%	39	19.5%	33	16.5%
Regular probationers	200	71	35.5%	48	24.0%	34	17.0%	25	12.5%
Prison releasees	97	56	57.8%	41	42.3%	25	25.8%	17	17.5%

[a] Numbers and percentages do not add across the columns because the categories are separate but not mutually exclusive. A percentage of those offenders arrested are convicted. Some of those convicted are placed in jail while others are returned to prison.

Risk scores are based on a Wisconsin instrument; scores are (0-7) Low Risk, (8-14) Medium Risk, (15-24) High Risk, and (25 and over) Maximum Risk.

Table 2

New serious crimes committed during 18-month followup period

Type of Crime	IPS probationers (No. = 200)		Regular probationers (No. = 200)		Prison releasees (No. = 97)	
	No.	%	No.	%	No.	%
Sale of Marijuana	0	0.0%	1	0.5%	0	0.0%
Sale of Cocaine	0	0.0%	1	0.5%	0	0.0%
Theft by Taking	4	2.0%	4	2.0%	3	3.2%
Auto Theft	0	0.0%	1	0.5%	0	0.0%
Burglary	4	2.0%	8	4.0%	13	14.0%
Aggravated Assault	0	0.0%	2	1.0%	3	3.2%
Robbery	0	0.0%	2	1.0%	0	0.0%
Armed Robbery	1	0.5%	0	0.0%	2	2.2%
Rape	0	0.0%	1	0.5%	2	2.2%

to other less serious new crimes. The prison releasees were convicted of the most new crimes: 13 burglaries, 3 aggravated assaults, 2 rapes, and 2 armed robberies. This comparison suggests that IPS surveillance provided early detection of uncooperative behavior or substance abuse and effectively reduced danger before citizens were harmed.

Although more IPS probationers violated the conditions of probation than regular probationers (7 percent compared to 4.5 percent), this might be anticipated because IPS probationers were so closely supervised. What might not be expected is the very low number who absconded. Only one of the sample of 200 IPS probationers absconded compared to four of the 200 regular probationers.

4. *How much did the program cost?* Preliminary estimates suggest a savings of $6,775 for each case diverted from prison (see Table 3). If all 2,322 offenders placed in IPS through the end of 1985 were diverted, considerable savings were realized—more than $13 million.

It should be noted that these estimates are based on incarceration costs ($30.43 per day) and supervision costs only. The estimates do not include any capital outlay, which could quite legitimately be included because the prisons in Georgia are full. If the 1,000 offenders under the IPS program at any given time had been incarcerated, they would have filled two moderate-sized prisons which, if constructed, would have cost many millions of dollars.

Table 3

Comparison of costs per offender
(average days incarcerated or under supervision)

Incarcerated Offenders	Cost
255 days @ $30.43 = $7,759.65	$7,759.65
(Excludes capital outlay)	
IPS Probationers	$984.66
196 days @ $4.37 under IPS = $856.22	
169 days @ $.76 under regular probation = $128.44	

Cost avoidance per IPS probationer = $6,774.69

Another benefit of IPS is the thousands of hours of public service IPS offenders provide. If these hours are valued at even minimum wage, the contribution to society would be considerable.

Probation supervision fees were critical to financing IPS. In 1982, the Georgia Department of Corrections instituted a policy that allowed judges to order probationers to pay supervision fees. The fees currently range from $10 to $50 per month. The policy followed an Attorney General's ruling that existing statutes permitted court-ordered fee collection if the fees were used to improve probation supervision. IPS was implemented at the same time the probation fee collection system was initiated. No funds were requested from the legislature.

Judges, who had been vocal in requesting stricter supervision standards, were advised that intensive supervision would be phased in using resources made available through fee collection. The amount of money collected from fees exceeded expectations. Over the 4 years of operation, the money collected for probation fees exceeded IPS costs and was used for numerous additional special probation needs. This does not mean that IPS probation fees alone have supported the program — regular probation fees also were included. Georgia judges impose probation fees on a case-by-case basis. (The issue of probation supervision fees is of considerable interest — what level of fees should be levied on which offenders; what is the most effective collection process; and what kinds of penalties are imposed for nonpayment — but represents an entire study outside the scope of this *Brief*.)

5. *What kinds of cases have been assigned to the IPS program?* Looking at the 2,322 offenders sentenced to the program through 1985, the following profile emerges: 68 percent were white, 89 percent were male, 46 percent were 25 years old or younger, and another 24 percent were between 26 and 30 years old. Forty-three percent were convicted of property offenses, 41 percent of drug- and alcohol-related offenses, and 9 percent were convicted of violent personal crimes.

6. *What kinds of cases were most successful in the IPS program?* Drug offenders responded better to the IPS program than they did to regular probation (90 percent success rate during the 18-month followup study). Frequent contact during the evening and on weekends and the urinalysis monitoring may be particularly effective in supervising drug offenders.

The finding that offenders convicted of drug- and alcohol-related offenses had the highest success rates raises interesting questions because the program initially considered discouraging substance abuse offenders from being accepted in the program. But judges were obviously looking for constructive alternatives for substance abuse cases; hence staff training and urinalysis capabilities were increased.

Females succeeded at a slightly higher rate than males, as they did under regular supervision. There was no significant difference in outcome by race.

The evaluators used discriminant analysis techniques to predict which offenders might be most effectively supervised under an intensive program. These techniques enabled the evaluators to predict 64 to 68 percent of the variation in outcome. The analysis identified risk score as the most important variable in predicting that a probationer is likely to fail in the IPS program. Being a property offender was the next most important predictor. Sex of the offender, need score (a scale depicting the social service needs of the probationer), race, and drug possession each made small additional contributions to the predictions.

7. *How well has the program been accepted?* Judges are now among the strongest supporters of the program in part because the program has a high degree of accountability. A judge can contact an IPS officer about a case knowing that the officer has had direct, recent contact with the offender. The officer knows what the offender is doing and how he is adjusting.

IPS staff have maintained high morale throughout the life of the program despite long, irregular work hours and heavy paperwork. Few have abandoned the program; most who leave the program have been promoted to other jobs. Probation Officers who are interested in joining the program must add their names to a waiting list.

The Staff

Conflicts between the treatment and enforcement functions of a Probation Officer are well documented. One of the most interesting findings of the IPS evaluation is the near impossibility of separating treatment from enforcement. The Georgia design places the Probation Officer in charge of case management, treatment and counseling services, and court-related activities. Surveillance Officers, who usually have law enforcement or correctional backgrounds, have primary responsibility for frequently visiting the home unannounced, checking curfews, performing drug and alcohol screening tests using portable equipment, and checking arrest records weekly. The Surveillance Officer becomes well acquainted with the family and the home situation and is often present in critical situations. Both the Probation and Surveillance Officers report a great deal of overlap of functions and even a reversal of their roles.

Because the Surveillance Officer is in frequent contact with the probationer, a close supportive relationship often develops. The Probation Officer spends a great deal of time with court matters and screening potential cases and is thus sometimes viewed as the representative of the repressive aspects of probation. Such divergent roles could lead to conflict and general dysfunction. However, the small caseloads contribute to close, often daily communication among the staff. Thus the probationer's needs — whether for control or support — are clearly identified and the team develops a coordinated plan and follows it closely.

The evaluators report that one major benefit of the team approach may be the support that officers give one another. This enables them to maintain high morale in very demanding jobs. During the evaluation period, each officer became absorbed in attaining the goals of the cases rather than simply performing according to the job description. Roles overlapped and officers exhibited an impressive, cooperative team spirit. Some officers interchanged roles whenever circumstances required scheduling adjustments. Staff seemed to function with mutual respect and concern for each other and for the continuity of supervision.

Smooth staff functioning, however, was not achieved by accident. The program's Probation Officers were selected from among the most experienced and best available. The Surveillance Officers were hired by the Probation Division specifically for the new program. In addition, true teams might not have emerged without careful attention to training. A National Institute of Corrections grant supported concentrated staff training coordinated through the Criminal Justice Department of Georgia

State University. The freshly trained and invigorated staff were seen as emissaries of the new intensive supervision, and their energetic and dedicated response to the program may well have contributed significantly to the program's success.

IPS is a Successful Option in Georgia

IPS has proven itself to Georgia officials and has become an integral part of the corrections system. Intensive Probation Supervision is a highly visible probation option that satisfies public demand for a tough response to crime while avoiding the costs of prison construction.

The cost of IPS, while much greater than regular probation, is considerably less than the cost of a prison stay, even when construction costs are not considered. In addition, society receives thousands of hours of community service from those in the IPS program. Criminal justice practitioners seem to accept the program as a suitable intermediate punishment. Judges particularly like it because it increases local control.

In Georgia, IPS is seen as one option on a continuum of increasing levels of control. Probation administrators, mindful of the public's increasing demand that probation clearly demonstrate appropriate punishment, have responded with a creative range of options. The options have varying degrees of severity and intrusiveness.

One rapidly growing alternative is the Community Service Program in which probationers perform court-ordered community service under the conditions of regular probation. The Community Service Program is far less intensive and less costly than most and is therefore able to manage a large volume of cases. Other alternative sanctions include placement in a community diversion center and Special Alternative Incarceration, which is a 90-day "shock" incarceration program.

By providing a series of graduated options, Georgia's Department of Corrections has responded seriously to repeat violators but also has shown a commitment to try alternatives to prison whenever possible. Instead of a stark prison-versus-probation decision, judges have a wider choice of sanctions. A highly innovative staff has taken the initiative to use the full range of options.

The attention focused on approaches developed in Georgia for identifying and diverting offenders from prison is well deserved. Georgia has exhibited ingenuity and commitment to try new ways to address a nationwide problem. The lessons gained through Georgia's experience are applicable in other locations that are experiencing similar problems with prison costs and crowding, although the population of offenders who could be diverted may vary a great deal. Jurisdictions that are considering implementing programs such as IPS should not only study Georgia's program; they should also define the target group in terms of their own needs. There is no magic formula, but Georgia's experience demonstrates that enough people can be diverted to achieve significant cost savings without serious threat to the community.

30

Experimenting With Community Service
A Punitive Alernative to Imprisonment

Richard J. Maher and Henry E. Dufour

Introduction

Many veterans of World War II recount the wisdom of judges who punished their youthful infractions by offering them a choice between jail or induction into the Army. Those who have had this experience often attribute their term of "community service" as a turning point, a time when they prioritized their values and began a productive life. No doubt the first court that ordered community service was inspired to do so long before World War II's manpower need.

The notion that work, community service or otherwise, is good for the spirit is well-founded in Judeo-Christian teaching. Considering society's well-established belief in the therapeutic value of hard work

Source: *Federal Probation*, Vol. 51, No. 3 (September 1987), 22-27.

and the giving of self to others, it is no wonder that the concept of community service as an alternative to imprisonment has gained broad acceptance. It is routinely used throughout the United States, England, and other English-speaking countries.

For the past two decades, criminal justice professionals have experimented with community service orders. They have been used in lieu of fines or cash restitution to punish the offender by restricting his leisure, and sometimes as alternatives to imprisonment. Using community service orders as an alternative to imprisonment will be our concern.

Background

During the past quarter century, major changes have occurred in the American correctional system. In spite of the dollars that have been spent and the programs that have been conceptualized and put into place, there is still a great deal of skepticism about the system and its ability to deal with criminals. As a matter of fact, some writers claim that the system might best be described as a nonsystem because of the widespread feeling that nothing seems to work. Crime is a real threat to many, and they are frightened by the thefts and acts of violence that touch their lives and those of their loved ones. Rates of recidivism appear to be as high as ever, and the public seems disenchanted, frustrated, and frightened.

These attitudes about the system are longstanding and were clearly identified and addressed in 1967 by the President's Commission on Law Enforcement and the Administration of Justice. The commission noted that "a major goal of corrections is to make the community safer by preventing the offender's return to crime upon his release."[1] There are probably very few individuals who would disagree with that statement, but the question has always been how can this aim be best accomplished?

The concept of institutional treatment was once seen as the answer to this question, but it now seems apparent that other avenues must be explored because of public and professional questions about the pragmatism of such an approach.

Some of these questions were brought into sharp focus by Robert Martinson in the spring of 1974. At that time, he published an article in *The Public Interest* titled "What Works? Questions and Answers About Prison Reform." His conclusions had a sobering impact on the advocates of treatment, for he found very few programs that were successful in the rehabilitation of offenders.

> . . .It is just possible that some of our treatment programs are working to some extent, but that our research is so bad that it is incapable

of telling. Having entered this very serious caveat, I am bound to
say that these data, involving over two hundred studies and hundreds
of thousands of individuals as they do, are the best available and
give us little reason to hope that we have in fact found a sure way
of reducing recidivism through rehabilitation.[2]

The general public is usually not aware of academic publications of
this type so their concerns about crime and the prison system must arise
from other sources such as TV, newspapers, and personal experiences.
It appears to these writers that these sources have disseminated sufficient
information throughout our society to bring about a recognition of the
failure of corrections and to produce a sense of frustration in the man
in the street. Warren Young attributes this "widespread disillusion with
imprisonment as a penal sanction to four main themes in penal policy:
the influence of humanitarianism; skepticism about the effectiveness of
imprisonment as an instrument of treatment or a means of deterrence;
prison overcrowding; and economic stringencies."[3]

These statements represent a set of social, cultural, and economic
realities of the 1980s that must be dealt with by the correctional manager.
None of these themes can be dealt with by the quick-fix route, and all
of them seem likely to be with us for some time. With these thoughts
in mind, it seems that currently the best alternative is the strengthening
of current community-based programs and the development of additional
options to prison, such as community service orders.

A publication of the National Institute of Mental Health summarizes
the arguments made in 1971 in favor of community-based programs.

> Until alternatives to institutionalization are demonstrated to be more
> effective than imprisonment in preventing further crime, a major
> rationale for the use of community programs will be that correctional
> costs can be considerably reduced by handling in the community
> setting a large number of those offenders normally institutionalized.
> Experimental/demonstration projects in intensive intervention have
> shown that for a large number of institution candidates incarceration
> is clearly unnecessary. Thus, if society is still determined, in the
> light of this evidence, to keep those offenders in prisons and training
> schools, it must be willing to pay the price. The central question
> becomes: Are the goals of punishment and custodial control worth
> the high costs of constructing institutions, and maintaining the
> inmate in the institution, as well as the observed and the still
> unknown personal and social costs incurred through exposing
> individuals to the institutional experience?[4]

Since we cannot afford to pay the price, it seems that community
service orders must be explored for a limited number of carefully selected
individuals. Such a program satisfies those of a liberal political

persuasion by keeping the offender out of prison and providing the best opportunity for treatment and/or positive change to take place. On the other hand, the conservative who believes in punishment should be somewhat mollified by the fact that the client must provide the required service and earn a living afterward. In some regards, this may be more demanding than the typical prison experience.

Discussion

The merits of community service as a sentencing alternative have been demonstrated throughout the United States and elsewhere. Approximately one-third of the states have passed legislation giving sanction to community service as an alternative to imprisonment. The United States Congress has been slow to sanction and define appropriate community service, but by terms of the *Comprehensive Crime Control Act and Criminal Fine Enforcement Act* of 1984, it is mandated that any convicted felon who receives a sentence (not a Class A or B felony) must be ordered to pay a fine, make restitution, and/or work in community service.[5] Since the early 1960s, U.S. Federal Courts have often chosen to suspend sentences and impose a special condition of probation directing offenders to perform community service work for public or charitable organizations.

The British Parliament granted the first legislative authority for community service orders. Under the Criminal Act of 1972 (Sections 14-18), such orders were sanctioned as an experiment. In 1973, legislative authority was consolidated under the Powers of the Criminal Courts Act. British law defined the Community Service Order as a distinct alternative to imprisonment. However, these orders are limited in their application by virtue of the statutory guidelines imposed by Parliament. The law set a minimum of 40 and a maximum of 240 hours of work to which an offender may be sentenced. These limits are believed to be motivated by genuine social and economic concerns. With the high unemployment rate in Britain over the past years, there was a need to assure protection of free labor. With this in mind, probation departments have been selective in choosing work projects for offenders.

It is also generally recognized that there are practical parameters to what may be expected from offenders assigned to community service. The order should not be so stringent that it might be regarded as unfair or as forced servitude; however, if community service is to be accepted as a credible alternative to imprisonment in the United States, its parameters must not be set too narrowly.

Experience in the United States has clearly demonstrated the benefits of community service orders. When properly administered, community service has enhanced respect for the probation service and the court in the community with nonoffenders and offenders alike. These orders alone, or combined with other special probation conditions, offer the court a broad range of sanctions, sanctions which can be tailored to the seriousness of the offense and to the individual offender's needs.

Community service, when used as an alternative to imprisonment, is also a deterrent. It punishes, provides for reparation, and assists in resocializing the offender. United States District Judge Joseph L. Tauro expounded the benefits of such orders in 1983 when he said:

> In the appropriate case, a public service order can be a progressive, productive alternative to jail. It provides the chronically wounded tax payer with a rare double barrelled break. Hard earned tax dollars are not wasted on housing and feeding the offender, and the offender's public service assignment is something of a dividend to the taxpayer in terms of expanded manpower service. Moreover, a meaningful, closely supervised public service sentence can provide a daily reminder to the offender that he has in fact committed serious anti-social behavior.[6]

Community service orders should focus on the offender's need for resocialization and on the protection of the community. United States Federal Courts have recognized that conditions of probation must be reasonably related to the treatment of the offender and the protection of the public from future crime.[7] This recognition carries with it the presumption that offenders with a history of violence or those who otherwise represent a serious risk to the community will be precluded from consideration. Determining who is an appropriate candidate is best addressed at the presentence report stage of the sentencing process.

At sentencing, an offender must be made to understand that serious antisocial behavior has resulted in his conviction and that the consequence may be imprisonment. Therefore, the community service alternative, possibly accompanied by other special conditions, may be severe. Such an order is more than a stringent form of probation. It must be harsh enough to be viewed by the public and the offender as a serious alternative, a sentence as credible as incarceration.

The probation office, offender, and recipient of community service must work together closely to attain maximum benefits. An offender's success on community service depends on the tailoring of the court order to his circumstances and on his ability to accept his obligation. He must be disciplined and punctual. In addition to his work assignment, he must abide by all other conditions of probation. It is essential that communication be good between the probation officer, offender, and work project supervisor. Even when good communication exists, myriad problems may arise which often involve the probation officer. Unlike an offender in custody, the community service offender is not removed absolutely from family, social relationships, and other commitments. The imposition of a stringent public service order may create a set of stresses and problems to which the probation officer must be sensitive and able to assist in resolving.

If the court determines an individual is to be given a community service order, the probation department should have a suitable work program in place and a specific task tentatively arranged. The intricacies of developing programs, screening candidates, and supervising community service orders offer a challenge to probation services. To meet this challenge, probation departments should allocate adequate personnel and material resources. The Administrative Office of the United States Courts has created specialist positions for probation officers charged with developing and administering community service programs. As the use of such orders grows, the need may develop for a community service division of probation. As noted, Britain developed such a division because of the preponderance of such orders and in recognition of the unique skills required to address public service needs.

As the experiment continues, so do the experiences. In the summer of 1985, the United States Probation Office, Northern District of Georgia, was alerted that an unusually large number of nonviolent first offenders would be entering guilty pleas. Most were involved in major frauds and other serious offenses. Others were involved peripherally in cocaine sales. Many of these individuals were local residents. It was certain that some would receive community service orders. In anticipation, the Probation Department made arrangements for offenders to participate in two group work programs. These programs could offer a wide range of work experiences to suit the court's purpose and also match the abilities of various individuals who would be sentenced. But the probation staff did not anticipate that the court would order such extensive community service work in lieu of incarceration. The lengthy hours demanded, coupled with other special conditions of probation, would test the known practical limits of community service orders.

As indicated, participation in two group programs was set up by the probation staff. Each agency offered the advantage of experience working with community volunteers. The agencies were familiar with liability issues and were willing to meet their obligation as it related to the court order. One agency offered an added advantage in that it had previously engaged in a Federal public service project with the court. That experience had been very successful. Also, both agencies had extensive enough labor needs to absorb the hours demanded of the probationers.

The first program agency served was a non-profit historical association. The association was founded to raise funds and to restore the Wren's Nest, the Atlanta home of Joel Chandler Harris. Harris, a renowned southern author, is best known for the creation of the Uncle Remus tales. Since 1913, his house has been a museum. In spite of its deteriorating condition and location in a blighted neighborhood, approximately 10,000 visitors were drawn to it last year. If the Wren's Nest was accepted as a suitable site, the work provided by assigned offenders would accelerate the restoration efforts, thus bringing improvement to a depressed area. Tourist visitation is expected to increase substantially and to produce needed revenue for the community.

The Wren's Nest director learned of the offender community service program and made an inquiry to the probation office. While Wren's Nest officials entertained the idea of using community service offenders, they expressed reluctance over the employment of criminals. A meeting was scheduled at the Wren's Nest between agency staff and a probation officer to address the many points of mutual concern.

During the meeting, the probation officer found the Wren's Nest staff very professional. The agency and its work need appeared suitable for community service assignments. This meeting and subsequent ones proved to be productive, and groups of offenders were assigned. The offenders worked on Saturdays, and because of reservations on the part of the Wren's Nest staff, a probation officer came on site and worked with and supervised the crew.

After a few weeks, the supervision of the offenders was left to a Wren's Nest staff member. The probation officer came by at the end of the day to inquire about and to observe the quality of work done. The Wren's Nest staff members grew comfortable dealing with offenders and demonstrated they could meet their obligation to the court order. As an example, on one occasion an offender attempted to claim one and one-half hours he did not earn. He was called to task by the agency supervisor, the probation officer was notified, and the problem was resolved.

With the weekend crew producing tangible results and the magnitude of the project's labor need becoming apparent, the probation department assigned a weekday work crew. Three offenders were selected to work sixteen hours each week. These three would be joined by a fourth on one of the weekdays. The task was physically strenuous and none of the four was accustomed to hard labor. Nonetheless, their efforts soon impressed the staff and the project architect. Accordingly, a staff member commented with pleasure that in a short time the offenders "did a mountain of work.'' Often the offenders rented tools at their own expense, donating the expenditures to the effort.

However, from these positive efforts and attitudes, an unanticipated problem resulted. The offenders heard the director discuss the price estimate for taking down a diseased oak tree. In spite of liability issues previously discussed and without the director's knowledge, the offenders purchased a chain saw and removed the diseased tree. Afterward, they split the wood and rented a machine to grind the stump below ground level. An excellent job was done. However, because of the liability concerns, the incident brought the staff, offenders, and the probation officer together, effecting closer communication.

This strengthened communication also sensitized the Wren's Nest staff to the offenders' circumstances. In addition to their community service, two of the offenders were under house arrest, and three were confronted with revocation of professional and business licenses. Although there was little hope of these licenses being retained, the Wren's Nest director got involved by offering to be a character witness at state hearings and by drafting a supportive letter. The offenders who previously felt some distance from the staff began to feel they were an integral part of the Wren's Nest effort. Their self-esteem was bolstered. Thus, the improved relationship enhanced the probation department's objectives.

The second group project was also a bonus to probation department efforts. This project was established at the Atlanta Cerebral Palsy Center. The center is a school and day center which primarily provides services for children but also has a number of adult clients.

The Cerebral Palsy Center is funded by United Way and relies on community volunteers to supplement the paid staff. Further, they are experienced with using well-screened offenders. A few years ago, the center employed 19 offenders on community service orders. All but one of these offenders performed extremely well, and a few stayed and continued working even after completion of their obligation.

Unlike the first group assigned to the center, this immediate group of offenders, it was decided, would be under a very restrictive order. Three of the offenders were assigned 40 public service hours per week for 6 months, 12 months, and 18 months respectively. These same three were also placed in a halfway house for 6 months and received the maximum fine relative to their offense.

The court left no doubt that it viewed the offenses as serious and intended a punishment as severe as imprisonment. These orders were experimental and tested the practical limits of community service orders.

The Cerebral Palsy Center's structure and experience offered an ideal testing ground for the intense orders. The center could use assistance in a wide variety of tasks. Each offender at the center was targeted during the sentencing process, and the center was consulted on each prospective assignment prior to sentencing. Thus, the probation orders were tailored to both the center's requirements and the offender's needs and talents.

In each instance, the community service order and other special conditions took into account the individual's ability to comply with the order. The financial resources of each were carefully reviewed. Four of the five assigned offenders would continue full- or part-time paid employment.

The offender who received the most severe community service order nearly managed to maintain his personal standard of living. His wife went to work, and he took 30-hour per week employment. Through this joint effort and the sale of his business, the offender preserved his home and other assets. His child enjoyed some continued stability, and Sunday was reserved for leisure and family outings. The offender highly valued these Sundays, reporting them to be the major benefit of community service in lieu of imprisonment.

Few problems occurred at the Cerebral Palsy Center which required the probation officer's attention. As at the Wren's Nest, the Cerebral Palsy Center staff took an active interest in the offenders and the resocialization effort. One offender was offered a part-time position at the center which could be done continuous to his 8-hour public service. On another occasion, the center director approached a probation officer with a complimentary "problem." An offender was sent on an errand usually done by the paid maintenance crew, and he returned in 30 minutes with the job done. In good humor, it was pointed out that the same job had never been done in less than one and one-half hours by the paid staff.

In each of the Cerebral Palsy Center placements, the work was done with enthusiasm, and the center staff members demonstrated their appreciation. The probation officers involved stayed in close communication with the center staff and the offenders. All had a favorable experience.

It appears the merits of public service orders as tested proved practical. The purposes of punishment were met, and sufficient measures were taken to assure public safety. The work programs were structured and supervised, thus providing compensation to the community. The severity of the orders was a sufficient deterrent, and at the same time, provided positive experiences for the offenders.

Conclusion

The community service experiment will continue. Faced with crowded prisons and limited tax dollars, the government must find practical and cost-effective means of punishing crime. It is not necessary to imprison many nonviolent offenders. Many such offenders have traditionally been imprisoned because the courts and the public have not recognized that there are credible and effective alternatives. Motivated by apparent benefits, many jurisdictions have successfully achieved legislation giving sanction to community service orders. Needed direction and support have been gained. However, in many cases, legislation has inappropriately limited the hours which may be ordered. Such legislation has served to restrict the use of community service as a credible alternative to imprisonment.

The community service alternative is in its infancy. Programs, guidelines, and the practical limits of its use demand more experimentation and refinement. The courts and their probation departments are in a unique position to experiment with and to give direction to community service. A concerted effort is owed our society.

Footnotes

[1] The President's Commission on Law Enforcement and the Administration of Justice, *The Challenge of Crime in a Free Society*. Washington, DC: U.S. Government Printing Office, 1967, p. 165.

[2] Robert Martinson. "What Works? — Questions and Answers About Prison Reform." *The Public Interest*, Spring 1974, p. 49.

[3] Warren Young. *Community Service Orders*. London: Heinemann, 1979, p. 4.

[4] National Institute of Mental Health. *Community Based Correctional Programs*. Washington, DC: U.S. Government Printing Office, 1971, p. 34.

[5] Rozina Wilks. "Legal and Liability Issues in Court Ordered Community Service Programs," a paper presented to the Midwest Criminal Justice Association, October 1985.

[6] J.L. Tauro. "Sentencing: A View From the Bench." *New England Journal on Criminal and Civil Confinement*. Summer 1983, p. 323.

[7] *United States* v. *Atlantic Richfield*, 465 F.2d 58, 61 (7th Cir., 1972); *Porth* v. *Tamplar*, 453 F.2d 330, 331 (10th Cir., 1971).

Bibliography

Wilks, Rozina. "Legal and Liability Issues in Court Ordered Community Service Programs." A paper presented to the Midwest Criminal Justice Association, October 1985.

Tauro, J.L. "Sentencing: A View From The Bench." *New England Journal on Criminal and Civil Confinement*. Summer, 1983, 9 (2) 323-330.

United States v. *Atlantic Richfield*, 465 F.2d 58, 61 (7th Cir., 1972); *Porth* v. *Templar*, 453 F.2d 330, 331 (10th Cir., 1971).

Corbett, Ronald P., Jr. and Fersh. "Home as Prison: The Use of House Arrest."
   Federal Probation, March 1985, pp. 13-77.
Perrier, C. David and Pink. "Community Service: All Things to All People."
   Federal Probation, June 1985, pp. 32-38.
"36,000 Hours of Useful, Constructive Work—Instead of Prison." *Ulster
   Commentary*, October 1980, p. 1.
"Alternatives to the Use of Custody," *Ulster Commentary*, October 1980, p. 1.
North Wales Combined Probation and After Care Service. "Community Service
   Scheme," 1 April 1975 — 31 December 1980, pp. 1-18.
Merseyside Probation and After Care Committee. "Annual Report for Year Ending
   31 December, 1979."
American Bar Association Project on Standards for Criminal Justice, "Standards
   Relating to Probation." Approved draft, 1970.
The Federal Judicial Center, "As a Matter of Fact. An Introduction to Federal
   Probation," January 1973.
Dershowitz, Alan M. "Criminal Sentencing in the United States: An Overview,"
   Crime and Justice. Del Mar, CA: Publishers, Inc. 1977, pp. 269-78.
Sellin, Thorsten. "A Look at Prison History," *Crime and Justice*. Del Mar, CA:
   Publishers, Inc. 1977, pp. 279-84.
Young, Warren. "Community Service Order," London, Neinemann Educational
   Book Ltd. 1970.
The President's Commission on Law Enforcement and the Administration of
   Justice. *The Challenge of Crime in a Free Society*, Washington, DC: U. S.
   Government Printing Office, 1967, p. 165.
Martinson, Robert. "What Works?—Questions and Answers About Prison
   Reform." *The Public Interest*, Spring 1974, p. 49.

31

Electronic Monitoring of Offenders Increases

Annesley K. Schmidt

Officials in 33 States were using electronic monitoring devices to supervise nearly 2,300 offenders in 1988—about three times the number using this new approach a year earlier, according to a National Institute of Justice survey.

In 1988, most of those monitored were sentenced offenders on probation or parole, participating in a program of intensive supervision in the community. A small portion of those being monitored had been released either pretrial or while their cases were on appeal.

The first electronic monitoring program was in Palm Beach, Florida, in December 1984. Since then an increasing number of jurisdictions have adopted electronic monitoring to better control probationers, parolees, and others under the supervision of the criminal justice system.

To inform agencies considering monitoring programs, and to track the growing use of electronic monitoring, the National Institute has surveyed monitoring programs for the last 2 years. This article reports on the 1988 survey, compares the responses with those of the previous year, and sketches a contemporary picture of the use of electronic monitoring.

Source: *National Institute of Justice Reports*, No. 212, U.S. Department of Justice, January/February 1989, 1-4.

Where Are the Programs?

As shown in exhibit 1, 33 States in all regions had monitoring programs, a substantial increase over the 11 States with programs in 1987.

The level of monitoring activities varies widely. Florida and Michigan, with 667 and 461 electronically monitored offenders, respectively, account for a large proportion of the offenders—49.5 percent.

Many monitoring programs involve limited numbers of offenders. Responses were received from more than one locality in almost every State with such programs. Yet as exhibit 1 shows, 7 States were monitoring between 25 and 49 offenders, and 12 were monitoring fewer than 25. Two States had established programs but were not monitoring any offenders on the date information was gathered. One State's program had not quite begun by February 14, 1988.

Monitoring programs have been developed by a broad range of State and local criminal justice agencies, from departments of corrections, probation, and parole, to court systems, sheriff's offices, and police departments. Some began a few days or weeks before the survey response date. About a quarter of the programs had been operating 4 months or less. Others, like the one in Palm Beach County, were more than 3 years old. Regardless of the length of time in operation, most programs were monitoring fewer than 30 offenders.

The two States with the largest number of electronically monitored offenders structure their programs differently. In Michigan, the State Department of Corrections monitors most offenders, and local courts, sheriffs, or private agencies monitor the rest.

In contrast, the Florida Department of Corrections monitors only a little over half the participating offenders. Another quarter are monitored by city or county agencies, including sheriff's offices, local departments of corrections, and police departments. Most of the rest are monitored by one of several private agencies that offer monitoring services, and a very small number are monitored by a Federal demonstration project.

Florida is a microcosm of the country as a whole in that monitoring activities take place in all areas—large metropolitan areas, medium-sized cities, small towns, and rural areas—by all levels of government. The government may provide the service with its own staff or contract for it. These public agencies represent all elements of the criminal justice system, including police departments, sheriffs, courts, correctional systems, and probation and parole agencies.

Exhibit 1.

Number of offenders being electronically monitored on February 14, 1988

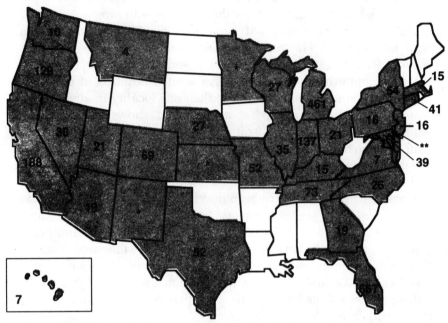

* Programs exist, but no offenders were being monitored on this date.
** No response.
Note: There are no programs in Alaska.

Who is Being Monitored and
What Kinds of Offenses Did They Commit?

The characteristics of the 2,277 offenders monitored in 1988 do not differ much from those of the 826 who were monitored in 1987. Both years, the programs monitored mostly men, with women constituting 12.7 percent of monitored offenders in 1988 and only 10.2 percent in 1987.

Survey results show that offenders monitored in 1988 were convicted of a wide range of criminal violations (see exhibit 2).

A quarter (25.6 percent) of offenders were charged with major traffic offenses. Most of the offenders in this group (71 percent) were charged with driving under the influence or while intoxicated. The other offenses in this category reflect primarily current or previous drunk driving convictions such as driving on a revoked or suspended permit.

Exhibit 2.

Electronically monitored offenders categorized by offense

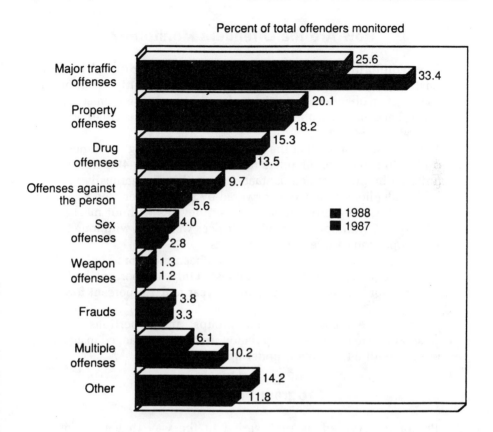

Percent of total offenders monitored

Major traffic offenses	25.6 / 33.4
Property offenses	20.1 / 18.2
Drug offenses	15.3 / 13.5
Offenses against the person	9.7 / 5.6
Sex offenses	4.0 / 2.8
Weapon offenses	1.3 / 1.2
Frauds	3.8 / 3.3
Multiple offenses	6.1 / 10.2
Other	14.2 / 11.8

■ 1988
■ 1987

In 1988, however, a smaller proportion of major traffic offenders were monitored than in 1987. This change reflects the expanding number of programs run by State departments of corrections, such as Michigan and Florida. Offenders monitored by these two States generally had committed more serious offenses. These State programs included prison-bound offenders or parolees and releasees from State institutions.

Property offenders were strongly represented. They committed a few closely related offenses—burglary (28 percent), thefts or larcenies (39.6 percent), and breaking and entering (16.6 percent).

Drug law violators constituted 15.3 percent of monitored offenders, with slightly over half of these charged with possession of drugs and the rest charged with distribution.

How Are the Offenders Monitored?

The monitoring equipment used can be roughly divided into two kinds: continuously signaling devices that constantly monitor the presence of an offender at a particular location, and programmed contact devices that contact the offender periodically to verify his or her presence (see box).

Survey results show that the continuously signaling equipment was used for 56 percent of offenders nationwide. Another 42 percent were monitored by programmed contact devices that mechanically verified that the telephone was being answered by the offender, and 2 percent were monitored by programmed contact devices without mechanical verification. Continuously signaling devices were used with roughly the same proportion of offenders in 1988 as 1987.

In 1988, however, many offenders had been monitored only a short time—54.1 percent for 6 weeks or less. Only 4.1 percent had been monitored for between 6 months and a year and 1.4 percent for more than a year.

Offenders belonged to all age groups, in proportions roughly corresponding to the general population. In 1988 they ranged in age from 10 to 79, with 54.9 percent under age 30.

Program Features. . .

Programs surveyed in 1988 varied in the way they paid for the sanction, the intensity of supervision, and failure rates.

Who pays? The survey answers show that in most programs the offenders do, with the exception of the Florida Department of Corrections. Charges are based on a sliding scale, with a maximum fee of $15 a day.

How often is the computer output reviewed? Some programs review it only during normal business hours (e.g., 9 to 5, Monday through Friday). Others provide continuous computer coverage and respond to the report of a violation at any time of the day or night, weekday or weekend.

How do offenders fare in these programs? Some programs reported that few participants had failed to complete the program successfully

How Electronic Monitoring Equipment Works

Electronic monitoring equipment receives information about monitored offenders and transmits the information over the telephone lines to a computer at the monitoring agency. There are two basic types: **continuously signaling devices** that constantly monitor the presence of an offender at a particular location, and **programmed contact devices** that contact the offender periodically to verify his or her presence.

Continuously signaling devices

A continuously signaling device has three major parts: a transmitter, a receiver-dialer, and a central computer.

The transmitter, which is attached to the offender, sends out a continuous signal. The receiver-dialer, which is located in the offender's home and is attached to the telephone, detects the signals sent by the transmitter. It reports to the central computer when it stops receiving the signal and again when the signal begins.

A central computer at the monitoring agency accepts reports from the receiver-dialer over the telephone lines, compares them with the offender's curfew schedule, and alerts correctional officials about any unauthorized absences. The computer also stores information about each offender's routine entries and exits so that a report can be prepared.

Programmed contact devices

These devices use a computer programmed to telephone the offender during the monitored hours, either randomly or at specified times. The computer prepares a report on the results of the call.

Most but not all programs attempt to verify that the offender is indeed the person responding to the computer's call. Programmed contact devices can do this in several ways. One is to use voice verification technology. Another is to require the offender to wear a wristwatch device programmed to provide a unique number that appears when a special button on the watch device is pressed into a touchtone telephone in response to the computer's call.

A third system requires a black plastic module to be strapped to the offender's arm. When the computer calls, the module is inserted into a verifier box connected to the telephone. A fourth system uses visual verification at the telephone site.

while others reported that almost half had not completed the program. Most of the failures resulted from infractions of program rules such as not abiding by curfew hours or using alcohol or drugs.

The precise reasons for the variations in program completion rates are unclear, but one factor seems to be the control of intake. Some programs can refuse to accept offenders that they deem inappropriate for the program but others cannot.

. . . And Some Problems

Survey respondents noted a variety of problems that they had for the most part resolved. Some programs, for instance, initially had difficulty gaining acceptance within their agencies for either the program or the equipment that would be used. After proper training and successful tests of the program, however, confidence grew.

Offenders had to learn to handle the equipment properly and understand what was expected of them. Their families also had to adapt to limiting their use of the telephone so the computer calls could be received.

Other problems were related to the equipment itself. In several jurisdictions, there was a "shakedown" period when operators learned to use the equipment correctly, interpret the printout, and deal with power surges and computer downtimes.

Poor telephone lines, poor wiring, and "call-waiting" features on the telephones caused other technical problems. Occasionally, an offender's home was located too close to an FM radio station or other strong radio wave broadcaster. Some difficulties were overcome by repairing lines or wires or by using radio-frequency filters.

A few program managers said they had encountered unanticipated costs—for extra telephone lines, special interconnections, underestimated long-distance charges, and supplies. Most of those surveyed, however, thought equipment manufacturers were responsive to their concerns.

The Future of Electronic Monitoring

Electronic monitors have been available commercially for only a short time, but their use has grown rapidly. Recent discussions with manufacturers suggest the growth continues. Some existing monitoring programs have expanded, and more programs have been launched since the 1988 survey was completed.

The National Institute of Justice is following use of the sanction and supporting ongoing research that will help policymakers decide if, when, and for whom the sanction is appropriate in their own jurisdictions. Institute research is assessing how well electronic monitoring of offenders protects the community.

Part VI

Critical Problems and Issues in Corrections

Introduction

Correctional officials seem perpetually to be plagued by problems and embroiled in controversy. Each day brings a new set of emergencies, ranging from escape plots and suicide attempts to plumbing problems and work stoppages. Correctional administrators and staff have little choice but to respond to the seemingly unending barrage of crises on a day-to-day basis. Consequently, they rarely have the time to reflect soberly on possible solutions to emerging problems or to develop long-term plans to cope with these problems.

Readers of the first five sections of this book certainly are well aware that the problems of contemporary corrections are numerous and intractable. No single volume can possibly do justice to all of the issues that need to be addressed as corrections moves into the twenty-first century. Nevertheless, the editors of this volume have selected six readings that examine correctional problems and issues that clearly have emerged as particularly troublesome in recent years.

First, Hans Toch, the nation's leading authority on the psychological consequences of imprisonment, explores the extreme difficulties prison officials encounter when dealing with inmates who are severely mentally ill. Professor Toch's "The Disturbed Disruptive Inmate: Where Does the

Bus Stop?'' reviews the prison careers of several ''disturbed disruptive'' inmates. These prisoners pose unusually severe disciplinary and mental health problems for staff, and they are extremely dangerous to themselves as well as to others. Typically, correctional and mental hospital officials resort to ''bus therapy''—a procedure in which troublesome inmates are shuttled back and forth from prison to mental hospital. The result is that they rarely, if ever, receive the kind of intense, specialized, long-term treatment they need.

A relatively new problem faced by prison administrators—and one that will become steadily worse in the 1990s—is how to meet the special needs of elderly prisoners. As a result of the increase in crime by older Americans and the long-term effects of the many state mandatory sentencing laws passed in recent years, American prisons will house a growing number of inmates who are well past the age of 50. In ''Growing Old Behind Bars,'' Professor Sol Chaneles of Rutgers University examines the various kinds of convicts who will make up the geriatric prison population of the future. As Chaneles points out, few of our prisons are prepared to handle the health care of this rapidly increasing segment of the prison population.

Another type of offender with special needs is the juvenile female offender. Frequently overlooked by criminal justice researchers and misunderstood by the general public, incarcerated adolescent females are more likely than their male counterparts to be locked up for mere status offenses (running away from home, curfew violations, and other offenses that would not be considered crimes if committed by an adult). Yet they are less likely than incarcerated adolescent males to receive the kind of vocational and educational programming needed for personal growth and economic independence. In ''The Forgotten Few: Juvenile Female Offenders,'' Ilene R. Bergsmann explains how gender bias and stereotyping have led to the inequitable treatment of juvenile offenders. She concludes by calling for correctional educators and administrators to implement gender-neutral policies that will ensure equitable and effective programs for all juvenile offenders.

One of the many controversial issues in corrections is the use of drug testing. A consensus has emerged among the courts that pretrial detainees and convicted prisoners can be subjected to random, unannounced drug testing. Similarly, an overwhelming majority of courts have upheld drug testing as a condition of probation or parole. However, the constitutionality of subjecting prison guards and other correctional employees to urine testing or other types of drug testing remains unsettled. In our next selection, ''Employee Drug-Testing Policies in Prison Systems,'' Randall Guynes and Osa Coffey report the results of a recent survey of the prison-employee drug-testing policies of 48 states and the Federal Bureau of Prisons. The survey, published in August 1988 by the National Institute of Justice, showed that 19 state correctional departments and the Federal Bureau of Prisons conducted drug testing of either staff or applicants. The authors also discuss such matters as testing procedures and technology, the costs of testing, and agency handling of employees who test positive.

The number of state correctional agencies that require employees to submit to drug testing is likely to increase throughout the 1990s as a result of two 1989 U.S. Supreme Court decisions. First, in *Skinner v. Railway Labor Executives' Association*, the Court upheld the mandatory breath, blood and urine testing of railroad employees after major train accidents. Second, in *National Treasury Employees v. Von Raab*, a five-to-four majority upheld a U.S. Customs Service program requiring all employees seeking promotion or transfer to drug-enforcement jobs to undergo urinalysis. Although neither decision authorizes mandatory, *unannounced* testing of public employees, most federal courts can be expected to follow the lead of the U.S. Court of Appeals for the Seventh Circuit, which relied heavily upon the *Von Raab* precedent when it recently permitted the mandatory, unannounced testing of prison employees who come into regular contact with inmates, who have opportunities to smuggle drugs to inmates, or who carry firearms (*Taylor v. O'Grady*, 888 F.2d 1189 (7th Cir. 1989)).

Without doubt, one of the most difficult and ominous problems facing prison officials in the 1990s will be the threat posed by acquired immune deficiency syndrome (AIDS). AIDS most frequently results from the sharing of infected needles by intravenous drug users and from homosexual contact. The use of illicit drugs is a common aspect of the pre-imprisonment lifestyles of many prisoners. Moreover, homosexual activities and the use of illegal drugs are prevalent in all too many jails and prisons. In "AIDS: The Impact on Corrections," Mark Blumberg discusses some of the most difficult questions that prison officials must confront in order to prevent the spread of AIDS in their facilities. Professor Blumberg carefully analyzes the arguments for and against such policies as mass screening, condom distribution, and segregation of AIDS-infected inmates, and he makes it clear that this is still another correctional problem with no easy solution.

Even if there are no easy solutions, is it possible that private corporations could do a better — and less costly — job of running prisons and jails than the state and federal governments have done? This is the intuitively appealing idea behind one of the most important recent developments in American corrections — the privatization of corrections, often known as "prisons for profit." As of February 1990, officials in seven states—Arizona, California, Florida, Kentucky, New Mexico, Tennessee, and Texas—had awarded contracts to operate certain jails or prisons to private prison businesses, and many other states contract with private agencies to provide such services as medical and dental care (*National Law Journal*, February 19, 1990, pp. 32-34). The movement toward privatization, however, has been met with both high praise and sharp criticism. In "Privatization of Corrections: Defining the Issues," Ira P. Robbins, professor of law at American University, considers the possible advantages and disadvantages of privatization. Professor Robbins also explores some of the most important policy issues and legal questions concerning "for profit" prisons. He concludes that it would be foolish to rush toward the privatization of prisons without a thoughtful and thorough review of the many complex issues that are involved.

32

The Disturbed Disruptive Inmate
Where Does the Bus Stop?

Hans Toch

If prisons had yearbooks, there are inmates who would unquestionably be voted "least likely to succeed." Among convicts who would qualify for this honor is a long-term New York prisoner who has served 13 peripatetic years of a 20-year sentence. By "peripatetic" I mean that the inmate has been frequently transferred or "shuttled." Ed (as we shall call the prisoner) has experienced 30 institutional moves, a career which, in a prison system, is an index of continued unpopularity.

One reason for Ed's singular status becomes clear when one reviews his folder. Ed's disciplinary dossier is horrendously long and variegated. Some of the recorded infractions suggest that Ed may occasionally be disoriented ("out of place," "loitering"), and that he has difficulties adjusting to prison routine. Some of the difficulties may

Source: *Journal of Psychiatry and Law* (Fall 1982), 327-349. Reprinted with the permission of the publisher.

appear simple (Ed is "repeatedly late for mess—[he] has been warned but insists on being late"), but others are more obviously complex ("had dirty cell and had burned his blanket and pillow cases"). Ed is responsible for strings of personal attacks against fellow-inmates and sometimes against guards. Some of these incidents are serious (e.g., "attempted to strangle inmate X"). Similarly serious is a series of suicide attempts and self-mutilation efforts, including an episode in which Ed cut his own throat.

Twelve of Ed's transfers—approximately one each year—placed him in a residential mental health setting. The first such transfer occurred straight out of prison reception. At the time, Ed was experiencing what was diagnosed as an "acute depressive reaction." In Ed's case, difficulties arose from the bizarre form his so-called "depressive reactions" tended to take. As an example, Ed's disappointment with a Christmas turkey shipment not only included manifestations of despondency, but (according to an officer's report) "he [Ed] put an edible portion of turkey in the garbage can, poured water over his head at 12:00 midnight and swallowed a cigarette butt instead of a pill." Private rituals such as these create disciplinary incidents; tardiness occurs, for example, because "I have to wash up and kiss [his family's photograph]...because I respect God and my family." Violence has mystifying origins. An officer is assaulted "because he called me wise guy and cocky"; a fight breaks out when Ed insults a group of black inmates whom he has never met, the day after arriving at a new institution for a predictably short stay.

Other incidents are clear psychotic episodes. A report describes Ed "eating feces from the mess hall toilet"; it notes that he has "burned his hands under boiling water from the faucet" the previous day. Another report describes Ed

> screaming without any reason, laughing inappropriately looking at his family pictures and stating that he will kill them, pouring hot water over his body, talking to himself and picking up and moving things back and forth constantly.

Extreme problems arise where such incidents take (as they do) blatantly destructive or self-destructive turns. The same report continues:

> His condition has become quite critical today, when he started putting his hand in an electric fan, putting his hand in the cigarette lighter socket, burning his hands and arms with cigarettes... threatened to stick his finger in an electric socket while having his foot in a pail of water in his cell.

Outbursts oscillate between attacks on others, such as sleeping fellow-inmates, and attacks on self. The rationale is invariably delusional—for instance, "a voice told me"; "I had the urge to get rid of myself because I had the devil in me"; "the officer [whom Ed assaulted] tried to kill my son—tried to nail me to a cross"; or "hear voices that my wife and children are dead."

Ed's dilemma, and that of the system, are eloquently described (under the evaluation heading "adjustment in prison,") by a prison-employed psychiatrist. The psychiatrist writes:

> Instead of discussing this as Ed's adjustment to prison, one might more appropriately consider this as the Department of Correction's (and Mental Health's) adjustment to Ed. The psychotic episodes were successfully handled by providing hospitalization and/or medication and counseling. Long-term rehabilitation has taken a second place with day-to-day handling being the main consideration. Ed has neither the ability nor the inclination to analyze his own problems and has requested transfers when he could not cope with the pressures of prison life. The transfers were effected without any fuss because Ed's desire to move was equalled, if not exceeded by, the institution's desire to get rid of the problem.

No one, however—least of all, Ed—has "gotten rid" of the problem, which we sense may climax in a completed suicide attempt. Ed is not served because he falls between the cracks of management options and because he is a notorious hot potato. More seriously, Ed defies our capacity to understand who and what he is. He is a conceptual Humpty Dumpty separated into two watertight and irreconcilable components, Ed the "mad" component and Ed the "bad" component.

It is paradigmatic that there is increased concern in the prison field about the prevalence of inmate mental health problems. One hears the topic broached in prison staff interactions ranging from superintendents' meetings to conversations with guards. A federal agency (the National Institute of Corrections) reports that "during recent... Advisory Board hearings, the increase in the number of mentally ill and retarded inmates was identified as a major concern of practitioners."[1] Similar alarm today revolves around perceived dramatic increments in prison violence. The impression is that many more inmates have serious adjustment difficulties, and that a "new violence-prone breed" of offender is abroad in the land.

Such staff impressions matter because they coincide with the advent of prison overcrowding, which poses unscheduled stressors for inmates and also decreases services available to them.

But such difficulties are at least familiar, and in theory at least can be responded to by improving and expanding on what we now do. Such is not the case with composite syndromes such as Ed's—syndromes that *combine* mental health and adjustment difficulties. Such syndromes *of necessity* are inappropriately and ineffectively responded to through existing modalities. The composite (disturbed *and* disruptive) inmate falls between available chairs. He does so because standard responses separately address (mental health or management) problems that are obviously linked. Unsurprisingly, inmates who have disciplinary and mental health problems are notoriously refractory to treatment and their careers through the system are biographies of escalating conflict and suffering. Inmates such as Ed are also at present uncharted and not understood. They mystify peers and staff, inspire fear and aversion, and spawn impotence based on a sense of our ignorance. Presumptively, the impotence extends to community settings faced with such persons, not only to criminal justice and mental health settings, but also to neighborhood groups, schools, and families.

As a category, disturbed disruptive inmates (DDIs) have no theoretical standing, and one reason why the combination "disturbed-disruptive" (DD) is a non-concept is because we are often placed in a "forced choice" situation where what someone does must be interpreted as symptomatic of an underlying disturbance or where we must react to it as a responsible exercise of unfettered malevolence. This occurs because symptomatic behavior and premeditated recalcitrance have mutually exclusive implications as to consequence and culpability. Even where the presence of both manifestations is obvious in the same individual, at any given point we may have to categorize one manifestation as relevant and the other as not.

In practice, the disturbed disruptive person tends to be conceptually segmented over time into a "disruptive" person and a "disturbed" person. At one juncture (for instance, when prison staff review the inmate's latest assault on an officer) they must unambiguously class him as disruptive; at a subsequent juncture (such as after the inmate's "voices" have instructed him to hang himself in the disciplinary segregation cell to which his disruptiveness has taken him) they must adjudge him psychotic. To be sure, the segmentation becomes increasingly unstable with chronicity of disturbance and disruptiveness patterns. Such chronicity makes the DD combination obvious, but invites a second "forced choice" involving selection of the pattern to be regarded as primary in classifying the person. With regard to this choice, the uninviting nature of the person's disruptive behavior reliably overwhelms decisions, and inspires caretakers to classify the person so as to make him primarily the client of other caretakers. This tendency is reinforced by the fact that symptoms of disturbance tend to wax and wane over time.

The competition of rival diagnostic efforts (sometimes referred to as "ping ponging") results in a tendency to shuttle the disruptive disturbed person to mental health settings (invoked by caretakers of disruptive inmates) from which he is returned to mainline disciplinary or custodial settings (by caretakers of the disturbed). This procedure is called "bus therapy," and it reveals pressure to make the "bus stops" as brief as decency permits. In *Corrections Magazine,* reporter Wilson notes that

> administrators from mental health and corrections agencies will each maintain in theory that they are best qualified to handle the "mad and bad." But in practice, neither wants to deal with him. The frequent result is a brutalizing series of transfers....There are, says Rowen [of the AMA] "problems in both camps. Correctional administrators, wanting to get rid of their bad apples, will ship them off to mental health. And the mental health administrators don't want to monkey around with acting-out clients, so they send them back."[2]

Three prison experts, Freeman, Dinitz, and Conrad, conclude that

> neither mental hospitals nor prisons welcome the disturbed and dangerous inmate....The resulting "bus therapy" expresses the reluctance which both kinds of institutions feel in contemplation of the burden of this kind of inmate. Until courts and administrators can establish rules to govern the disposition of such inmates their programming will be punctuated by bus movements which are clearly not intended for their benefit.[3]

Bus therapy obfuscates the disruptive-disturbed syndrome because the inmate who gets on the bus is labeled disturbed and the one who exits (presumptively after "therapy") is adjudicated disruptive. Such judgments are even made before the person gets on the bus. Recently, an *APA Monitor* reporter claimed that he had been told by a forensic mental health administrator that "corrections officials have sought to use psychologists to control—not necessarily help—prisoners. Prison staff have been known to ask mental health care personnel to get troublemakers committed or given medication....And psychologists have been 'obliged' to honor such requests...in order to keep their jobs."[4] The administrator later pointed out that he had been misquoted, but *Corrections Magazine* also tells us that "a common criticism by psychiatrists of prison administrators is that they want the doctors to handle the problem cases, which are not always psychiatric problems."[5] A prominent clinician (Vicky Agee), by contrast, recalls that

> We discovered that Mental Health institutions are for Mentally healthy patients—not rotten patients, who obviously were not psychotic—but had behavior problems. We drove our disturbed delinquents there—they beat us back—with the diagnosis of "manipulation"....[We] tried to outplay Mental Health at the "Name Game." They won, of course—you can't help but win when you hold

all the cards....Most of the game revolves around the Psychotic
versus Character Disorder names....Character disorders (which I
think means anybody who intimidates, messes over, or hurts people)
particularly do not belong in hospitals, because they are untreatable.[6]

Such charges are not made out of whole cloth, because "games"
such as those referred to by Agee are played on the record. Illustrative
is a case I have reviewed of a disruptive and disturbed prisoner who
was finally committed after having (1) attempted to hang himself twice
in one week, and (2) set fire to his mattress and pajamas (while occu-
pying them). This inmate was returned with the diagnosis "Explosive
personality disorders—antisocial personality disorders." Later the
same inmate was again committed. The report noted that "he hanged
himself last night and was unconscious when he was found." The
resulting "trip" was short and unproductive. However, the prison
superintendent almost immediately returned the inmate, certifying
that "it has been reported to me that this...resident's emotional condition is deteriorating. He has remained depressed, despondent and
has smeared feces on his body and all over the room. He is reportedly
reacting to auditory hallucinations and has had a serious attempt at
suicide, by hanging, one hour after his return to prison." Only one
week later, the same inmate reappeared with the discharge diagnosis
"Antisocial personality disorder 301.70." The following year, he was
again institutionalized. This time, the referring staff noted that the
inmate was "hearing voices telling him to kill himself—got 'rope' last
night but didn't use it. Harassed by other inmates to 'bug out.'" They
also reported that

> in the last two days he has made two suicidal attempts by hanging
> and set his mattress on fire. He says he is responding to voices
> telling him to kill himself....On examination this morning he was
> smeared with feces, says that he did this to baptize himself since
> the water in his toilet was turned off....He has been having
> difficulty adjusting to the open prison population and has mani-
> fested paranoid ideation.

The prison psychiatrist diagnosed the case as one of "paranoid
schizophrenia." The hospital psychiatrist (six weeks later) entered
"No diagnosis or condition on Axis I; Antisocial personality disorder."

For most inmates the game is played more honestly and with more
integrity, without callousness and risk as embodied in the example.
The issue often revolves around remission, or the onset and termination of acute psychotic episodes. Discharges certifying "full remission"
are often followed within weeks, days, or hours by renewed manifestations of symptoms. The fact is demonstrable, but need not reflect on

the validity of diagnoses. Among other things, as was pointed out somewhat bluntly to Wilson by an informant, "the mental health system drugs them up...gets them sufficiently passive, and sends them back to prison, where they don't give them their medication. Then they decide they have 'regressed,' and they send them back to mental health."[7]

The precise proportion of inmates who experience "bus therapy " is unknown. Equally to-be-established is the assumption that disturbed disruptive inmates are disproportionately subject to expeditious shuttling. A disproportion of expedited transfer would be predicted based on (1) the availability to mental health staff of their patient's disciplinary record, which is calculated to inspire caution in any reasonable man; and (2) the tendency, of some DDIs at least, to resist therapeutic ministrations. Less sanguine predictions could be based on the assumption that psychotropic medication levels can be more or less adjusted to neutralize disruptive tendencies. Of course, if medication regimens are deployed as "therapy," it is improbable that lasting change will occur, and shuttling is therefore likely to continue.

Failure to recognize the integrity of the DD cluster not only contaminates the understanding and treatment of DDIs, but also affects our view of disruptive nondisturbed and disturbed nondisruptive inmates. Where such inmates are conceptually merged with DDIs the result contains heterogeneous melanges whose attributes are understandably mystifying. For instance the Mecklenburg Correctional Center, the maxi-maxi-institution of the Virginia Department of Corrections which contains inmates deemed seriously disruptive, records that "twenty-seven percent of disruptive inmates have been previously committed to a mental health facility for treatment. Of these with prior psychiatric commitments, the average inmate has been committed on 2.12 occasions." Another case in point is provided in an Ohio study of intractable inmates by Myers and Levy, in which intractability is defined as "a chronic disciplinary and adjustment problem within the prison."[9] Myers and Levy discovered, among other things, that "the intractable group had a higher frequency of sick calls (about twice as high), with tension as the primary complaint (22%), and tranquilizers as the primary prescribed medication (44%)."[10] They also noted that "the Psychometric Test results shows that the intractable group scored lower on all IQ, grade level, and psychometric aptitude tests," and that "the intractable group had higher scores on the MMPI (Depression) Scale."[11] The psychometric data are particularly revealing. In the distribution of composite IQ scores (Optic and WAIS) the range of scores for the intractable group extended to a bottom score of 52 (compared to low scores of 72 and 77 for the "tractable" group), and the range for revised Beta scores was 47 to 112 for "intractable" inmates and 79 to 121 for the "tractable" group. Such statistics matter a great deal because prison syndromes in which extremely limited intelligence is a prominent feature seem to be disproportionately represented among DDIs.

The admixture of DDIs and disturbed nondisruptive inmates produces problems of similar complexity. One such problem is that diagnoses that (illegitimately) consider disruptiveness as a criterion highlight antisocial (psychopathic, sociopathic) features, which can be discounted as untreatable, and hence as nonpathological. The noninclusion of antisocial personality disturbances helps students such as Monahan and Steadman to arrive at the "cautious conclusion" that "there is no consistent evidence that the true prevalence rate of nonpsychotic mental disorder is higher among inmate populations than among class-matched community populations."[12] Presumptively different exclusion and inclusion criteria permit authorities such as the President's Commission on Mental Health to contrarily infer that "a high percentage of jail and prison inmates (markedly higher than in the nonprison population) are mentally handicapped."[13] This question is among issues that are unlikely to be resolved unless defensible lines are drawn between DDIs and disturbed nondisruptive inmates.

If DDIs are reliably differentiated from other inmates, some but not all of whose attributes they share, patterned differences *within* behavior dimensions—differences in disciplinary careers and mental health histories—not only can emerge, but are likely to do so. We expect different DD cross-fertilizations such that a given act (like sleeping under the bed) can be disruptive (it interferes with the mandatory custodial body count) but can be pathologically tinged (it can be designed to ward off delusional danger), nonpathologically motivated (designed to resist custody), or ambiguously framed (aimed at ameliorating a psychosomatic backache). The disruptive act that is pathologically motivated (for instance, tearing a bedsheet to produce a rope with which to commit suicide) is as unambiguously disruptive (by destroying "state property") as the same act designed for gain (for pulling contraband from a neighbor's cell), but the quality of the disturbed disruptive act held up to scrutiny will meaningfully differ from that of its nondisturbed counterpart.

Some disruptive behavior patterns, such as cycles of extrapunitive and intrapunitive behavior, are probably most unique to DDI syndromes. Burtch and Ericson note that "a classic statement of the commingling of homicidal and suicidal impulses was propounded by Sigmund Freud in *Mourning and Melancholia*."[14] The "commingling" may be less than universal, but may aptly characterize a subgroup of syndromes in the DDI population, such as the inmate Ed.

Studies of disruptiveness in mental hospitals consistently show that chronic patterns are sharply targeted in a minority of patients. One study cited by Smith found that "2 percent of patients accounted for 55 percent of all violent incidents."[15] A Canadian team surveyed 198 patient assaults, and discovered that "13% (N = 18) of the patients committed 61% of the assaults."[16] Clearly, disturbed disruptive patients exist as do DDIs. They exist, however, in small proportions that can be further reduced by chemical straightjacketing to the negligible levels reported in some studies.[17]

The most critical questions obviously revolve around the psychological link between disturbed and disruptive behavior. Where patterns of disturbance and recalcitrance coexist in the same person, the interconnection is an empirically to-be-investigated issue. Continuity of personality *presupposes* a connection. Common sense warns against *assuming* a connection. I have noted elsewhere that

> A schizophrenic who assaults people is a psychotic and is violence-prone. Both facts may diminish the person's popularity, but the combination does not make him a violent psychotic. If the patient obeys voices that tell him to kill, our understanding increases by considering this fact, but in most cases, the link between behavior and emotional and cognitive problems is more remote.[18]

The point of the comment is not that psychopathology and disruptiveness are unrelated, but that we cannot explain one by referring to the other. A diagnosis is a shorthand label for the person's disturbed behavior; it is not a summary of his disruptive behavior; this makes it unsurprising, for example, that, as Kozol, Boucher, and Garofalo note, "the terms used in standard psychiatric diagnosis are almost totally irrelevant to the determination of dangerousness."[19] The same caution applies in reverse. Disruptiveness—which invites disapproval and provokes anxiety—can impair diagnosis of pathology rather than illuminating it.

In exploring DD syndromes, the validity of findings is enhanced by approaching pathology and disruptiveness separately, and then determining what links (if any) can be surfaced where (if) patterns intersect. This calls for reliable criteria for independently diagnosing pathology and disruptiveness, inquiry into differences between DD patterns and non-DD patterns of pathology and disruptiveness, subcategorization of disruptiveness patterns in the DD group, and a search for DD patterns linking disturbance patterns to patterns of disruptiveness.

These links matter. If we are to address the problems and behavior of a disturbed disruptive inmate, it matters whether the inmate's disruptiveness is behavior premised on a delusional view of social reality; is a reaction to pressures that are routine for the average inmate but become overwhelming for the handicapped inmate; results from aversive peer reactions to the person's obnoxious symptoms;

represents a last-ditch gesture deployed to secure needed support; is a pathetic form of protest against intolerable dependence or represents a failure of precarious self-controls. Surfacing and categorizing such links—and drawing out possible implications they may have for action—should be a high-priority enterprise. And it is not as difficult a challenge as the resistance to it may imply. A few summary examples follow to show that the task of surfacing pathology—disruptiveness links can often be met simply by carefully reviewing the folder.

Take the case of George (again, not his real name). George is a large inmate (he weighs over 200 pounds) who is serving the 11th year of a 25-year term. His disciplinary record features a profusion of minor violations (mostly refusals to participate in activities or to obey orders). There are also more serious incidents. Many of these involve assorted acts of ponderous destructiveness: there is a profusion of notations such as "put his hand through window," "threw a pail of hot water at reporting officer," "threw a lightbulb and books on gallery, banged on the wall with his fists," "cut a square piece of material out of his state blanket," "destroying state sink," "flooded his section with water... tore a bible into pieces," "damaged cell door," "broke a glass against wall." There are also recorded fights and attacks on fellow-inmates, some pretty ineffectual. (Once, for example, George approached an officer "demanding to have another inmate's cell open so he could get him because he was a rat.") There are also a number of suicide attempts, and several self-protective requests.

Relatively early in his sentence, George drank a large quantity of acid; in explaining his motives, George reported that he was being harassed by fellow-inmates, who made reference to "his crime and time to serve." The incident was classed as a psychotic depressive reaction. In another incident George cut his wrist and requested transfer because "he claims some inmates called him a 'rat.'" He later attempted suicide after he was (completely predictably) passed over by the parole board. There is general agreement in prison about George being "a person of marginal intelligence who has emotional problems," and staff have also discovered that many of George's emotional problems have to do with his inability to digest or handle stress experiences or routine demands. George always withdraws—if he can—from situations that tax him because of their challenge or complexity. If he cannot withdraw, he explodes. He manages simple demands. For example, he likes a "dining hall assignment with strict supervision."

George has been assigned to a special program—a decent therapeutic community—where he remains after two years, generally under medication. Program staff have observed that George is "unable to learn anything except the most concrete concepts, is further unable to synthesize and learn from his experiences and further is generally unable to process logical thinking and subsequently reach productive conclusions." Among other things, George "doesn't really understand how to get along with other people on any more than a basic concrete level, involving exchange of goods and services." As a result, George

> has been observed on numerous occasions to involve himself in the trade or transfer of material goods with other inmates...with the same predictable results. Usually, he very quickly over-extends himself financially, and when he is unable to withstand the pressure of repaying his financial debt or when he is unable to withstand the pressure of the person to whom he is indebted, he ordinarily acts out in some way,

Once George is bailed out (or once he has survived the consequences of ill-advised chronic trading and gambling), he invariably renews his self-defeating financial career, alternating between contriteness, emotional breakdowns, and dramatic explosions of impotent rage. Given no evidence of change, therapeutic staff understandably feel that their program, which is designed to achieve personal impact, is wasted on George. They consequently demand his transfer as often as they can. Unfortunately, no alternative plausible placement comes to anyone's mind.

Ben has recently left our state prison system after serving four years of a seven-year prison sentence. His disciplinary record is studded with preemptive fights and threats against staff. Three months into Ben's sentence, for example, an entry charges him as follows:

> you were seen with a "large push broom" and you were holding it over your head. You were expounding loud sounds and directed your anger to the employees. You were attempting to incite other inmates to riot and hurt the officers. But before you were able to assault employees, another inmate disarmed you of the broom.

> You were ordered to return to your room but refused. Only after additional officers arrived on the scene did you return to your room. ...You resisted being pat frisked and handcuffed....

Between such emotionally charged prison disturbances, other incidents are recorded that have a different quality. Some are self-destructive incidents (entries such as "threatened to cut up — counseled and released," "fire in cell"), but most are self-insulating incidents — they reflect Ben's reluctance to leave his cell for program involvement (notations such as "did not go to gym," "refused to work," "skipped school").

A few weeks prior to the push-broom incident — two months after Ben's entry into the system — he was seen by a psychiatrist, who observed that Ben was "mildly depressed with vague reference to auditory hallucinations." In the interview transcript, Ben is reported as saying that "he could not take the pressure of population in the block." He expressed fear of the inmates and correction officers around him. But also (insightfully, as it happens) Ben "expressed the desire to be in a set up where there are not too many people around him." Within days, Ben was again observed "depressed, nervous and crying," and *on the day prior to the pushbroom incident* he was referred

> because of an episode of depression during which time he made threats to "kill himself before others do it." *Inquiry...revealed that he was approached by other inmates in homosexual relationships and felt depressed and anxious about this.* (The finding proves crucial.) [Emphasis added.]

One week later, Ben's disciplinary record was reviewed with him, and he observed (again, insightfully) "that he [always] felt depressed prior to getting into trouble." The sequence (feeling of pressure and depression leading to ideas of reference and explosions) was to repeat itself time after time during Ben's prison stay, including in several self-destructive episodes: the first of these occurred after all of Ben's belongings were stolen by fellow-inmates; in the second, officers "confirmed the staff's opinion that Ben was being pressured by Smith and that as a result of this pressure he decompensated to the point where he became extremely paranoid and eventually suicidal."

Like George, Ben is kept afloat in prison through placement in a special ameliorative program, with the evidence suggesting (as staff put it) "that if Ben were to be transferred to general population at this time, he would be unable to cope with the pressures of prison life and as a result he would decompensate to the point where he could no longer function." Unfortunately, even special programs have their pressures. Ben therefore indulges in numerous "sudden violent attacks against individuals who he 'thought' were going to hurt him...though investigation of the incidents failed to reveal any basis in fact to Ben's assumptions that he was being threatened by the man he attacked." Only in complete isolation (keeplock) did Ben's behavior prove exemplary.

In Ben's case, the relationship between his disturbance and disruptiveness is direct; under stress, Ben's tenuous controls give way. As observed by an interviewing psychiatrist, "when Ben is sick, he becomes paranoid and does not get along with people and causes fights."

Dave has served eight years of a life sentence, and he has accumulated a long, variegated, and serious disciplinary record. Dave has on numerous occasions been seen by prison psychiatrists, who have maintained him—very much at his own request—on psychotropic medication, tranquilizers, and sleeping pills. Dave's psychiatric stock in trade are fear, (demonstrable) anxiety, depression, and (alleged) insomnia. These commodities are systematically used to secure medication, favorable program recommendations, and ameliorations of custody. Dave's level of disturbance is real; in the words of a classification analyst, "he obviously has deep psychological, emotional problems;" a psychiatrist notes, "this man is in a constant anxiety state since his admission to the penal system." But equally real is the flagrant manipulation pattern based on Dave's disturbance—particularly, the threatened risk of completing suicide.

Dave's folder is studded with injunctions to custody by mental health staff, such as "I have notified the security person to keep a close watch on Dave because he may try to hurt himself again;" "this man should be considered a definite suicidal risk....I would suggest to treat him gently and avoid punishment at this stage"; "in view of the inmate's past history of [suicidal behavior] and mental disorder, it seems advisable to the writer not to place this man under undue pressure. Otherwise, it is difficult to predict what this man will do. Moreover, I believe he should be given back his kitchen job...one of his major grievances;" and "I feel if at all possible, he should be out of the metal shop, but of course this is up to the assignment board."

There are also notations such as "patient manipulates environment in order to get habit forming drugs"; and "he has been on Dalmane for over 7 years in other institutions and certainly is addicted to it. I feel this man is manipulating to get Dalmane"; and "diagnostic impression: addiction to Valium and Dalmane"; these notations appear in the folder in the later stages of Dave's career.

Because of Dave's combination of pathology and manipulativeness, he is viewed as a test of prison and mental health staff forbearance. His advent at one assignment (the mess hall) is greeted with the entry "the word has spread far and wide that this man is a creep." The document concludes "as long as inmate behaves himself in the mess hall, I have no objection to his being there, of course; but once he starts to act up, I probably will recommend that he see the psychiatrist." This sequence (like others) ends with Dave "acting up," seeing the psychiatrist, and making the best of his chronically bad situation.

My last example, Frank, recently completed a checkered nine-year prison term, including 18 institutional transfers (five to mental health settings) and 80-plus disciplinary infractions. Upon entry into the system a decade ago, Frank initiated an impressive sequence of disruptiveness—incidents such as "throwing food at an officer"; "broke bed—used pieces for weapons—smashed light fixture in cell," alternating with incidents of self-insulation. With respect to the latter, there are report entries such as "he refused to come out of his cell today," and "the Sgt. informed me that Frank was just standing in the center of his cell"; and "he came up to the desk and mumbled something inaudibly...he refused to speak...and he left."

Frank's paradoxic flight-fight pattern has been in evidence, in unabated cycles, for nine years. Frank's explosions are so frequent that they include his diagnostic interviews. During one interview Frank was offered an apple (a generous gesture or a projective test borrowed from Genesis?) and "after receiving the apple from the psychiatrist, he washed it in the sink and then quickly turned around and threw it at the facility psychiatrist. Frank then proceeded promptly to slap the facility psychiatrist about his face." Other interviews move from unresponsiveness and incoherence into towering rages.

Frank's explosions have been punctuated with after-hours yelling, throwing and smashing of objects, and persecutory beliefs freely (and loudly) expressed. Such behavior has contributed to Frank's growing unpopularity among peers, as well as among staff. One forgets that most of Frank's time is occupied with episodes of quiet restlessness, muteness, unresponsiveness, and inactivity (including refusals to eat), and reports of quiet hallucinations (such as Frank "hears voices which tell him, 'Brush your hair.'").

Now Frank is back in the community, and we do not know what he is up to. We do know that only three months prior to Frank's release, he "punched another inmate without provocation;" he also "bangs on the walls while taking a shower and shows sudden mood swings from laughter to hostility and agitation...standing for long periods of time in one place...sloppy, untidy and unkempt in his appearance...was delusional." At the expiration of his sentence (three months later), Frank had to be released. A final entry in Frank's folder reads:

> Frank was discharged (maximum) from prison and did not want to leave the institution. Dr. W., the institutional psychiatrist, tried to talk to the inmate and the inmate struck him in the side of the face, knocking his glasses off. Inmate was requested by Department of Corrections personnel to leave the premises on several occasions. He would leave temporarily and kept returning. Eventually...the inmate was arrested for harassment and given 15 days in [the local] County Jail.

The irony of this scene has to do with Frank's inability to manage not only the prison situation, but its absence.

Frank is admittedly an uninviting client, and so are Ed, George, Ben, and thousands of others who are similarly situated. Such persons are as uninviting when they terrorize school yards and prison yards as when they contaminate neighborhoods or vegetate under medication in hospitals.

The uninvitingness of setting and person, of course, are mutual. We cannot cope with Frank who cannot cope with his world—or at least,

with the settings that he disrupts and disturbs. Frank's settings can—
within limits—help themselves. They can expel their Franks and Eds
and Georges (always with cause and to other settings) or secrete them
to neutralize them in inhouse places of exile, for statutory terms. These
are holding patterns and they are unstably, warily, and uncomfortably
sustained.

The Franks and Georges who find their world inhospitable have no
recourse. To Ed, Frank, and their peers, social settings are dumping
grounds, variations on inhospitality, always painful, uncongenial, mystifying, irritating, and harsh. The options Frank and his peers have are
non-options—to alternately lash out and retreat, to fight without hope
of winning, and to flee without hope of surviving.

To escape the dilemma we must face Frank's despair, which
requires suspending our concern with Frank's obnoxiousness, with the
"management problem" Frank presents. Frank's bus must somehow be
made to stop. It must stop long enough so that we can resonate to the
bankruptcy that underlies Frank's disruptiveness. This means that we
must understand Frank's cornered explosions as well as the self-
insulating efforts we conventionally associate with psychological
extremity.

Eventually, we must generate new ameliorative settings and restora-
tive settings for Frank and Ed and Ben. We must care for these walking
wounded, for men driven to extremes by a despair that transcends and
surpasses the range of the familiar—of mental illness in its more
passive and congenial manifestations.

Footnotes

[1]National Institute of Corrections, *NIC Program Plan for the Fiscal Year 1983*
(Washington, D.C., July 1982).
[2]R. Wilson, "Who Will Care for the 'Mad and Bad'?" 6 *Corrections Magazine*
5-17, at 8 (1980).
[3]R.A. Freeman, S. Dinitz, and J.P. Conrad, "A Look at the Dangerous Offender
and Society's Efforts to Control Him," *American Journal of Correction*, January-
February 1977, pp. 25-31, at 30.
[4]D. Reveron, "Mentally Ill—and Behind Bars," *APA Monitor*, March 1982,
pp. 10-11.
[5]Wilson, *supra* note 2, at 14.
[6]V.L. Agee, "The Closed Adolescent Treatment Center," *Utah Correctional
Association Annual Conference*, September 10, 1981.
[7]Wilson, *supra* note 2, at 8.
[8]Mecklenberg Correctional Center, "Mecklenberg Treatment Program," mimeo-
graphed (Boydton, Virginia, December 1, 1981).

[9]L.B. Myers and G.W. Levy, "The Description and Prediction of the Intractable Inmate" (Columbus, Ohio: Battelle, 1973), p. *ii*; see also, 15 *Journal of Research in Crime and Delinquency* 214-28 (1978).

[10]Myers and Levy, *supra* note 9, at 15 (1973).

[11]*Id.* at 16.

[12]J. Monahan and H.J. Steadman, "Crime and Mental Disorder: an Epidemiological Approach," in *Crime and Justice: An Annual Review of Research*, ed. N. Morris and M.H. Tonry (Chicago: University of Chicago Press, in press).

[13]Wilson, *supra* note 2, at 6.

[14]B.E. Burtch and R.V. Ericson, *The Silent System: An Inquiry into Prisoners Who Commit Suicide* (Toronto, Canada: University of Toronto, 1977), p. 45.

[15]A.C. Smith, "Violence," 134 *British Journal of Psychiatry* 528-29 (1979).

[16]V.L. Quinsey, "Studies in the Reduction of Assaults in a Maximum Security Psychiatric Institution," 25 *Canada's Mental Health* 21-23 (1977).

[17]M.G. Kalogerakis, "The Assaultive Psychiatric Patient," 45 *Psychiatric Quarterly* 372-81 (1971).

[18]H. Toch, "Toward an Interdisciplinary Approach to Criminal Violence," 71 *Journal of Criminal Law and Criminology* 646-53, at 649 (1980).

[19]H.L. Kozol, R.J. Boucher, and F.R. Garofalo, "The Diagnosis and Treatment of Dangerousness," 18 *Crime and Delinquency* 371-92, at 383 (1973).

33

Growing Old Behind Bars

Sol Chaneles

  William David Smith is one of the oldest of some 43,000 inmates currently serving time in the federal prison system. He claims to be 84, although prison records say he was born in 1916. On his birthday in April, he received no greeting cards, no telephone calls, no birthday cake. I was his first visitor in a year and we celebrated with cold cheeseburgers and soft drinks from vending machines in the visitors' lounge of the United States Penitentiary in Terre Haute, Indiana.

  Smith, who was transferred in June to the Federal Medical Center in Rochester, Minnesota, has spent 22 years in state and federal prisons, in stretches of 8 months to 6 years, for robbery, grand larceny and kidnapping, among other crimes. Like many chronic offenders, he has a positive self-image to go with his long record. The image shows in the stories he tells about himself. "There was this bank job in I-o-way. I spent six months casing it before I made the hit. I knew where city and county cops would be. For the next few months I lived real good and partied every night." He can poke fun at himself, too. "I hit a supermarket for $11,000 and hid the money bag in a wooded area a few miles away. When I went back a few weeks later to pick up the loot, a groundhog had dug a hole and hauled the bag away . . . like a common thief." He takes his greatest pride in what he sees as his ability to outwit

Source: *Psychology Today*, Vol. 21, No. 10 (October 1987), pp. 47, 49, 51.
Reprinted with the permission of the publisher.

the law. He laughed when he told me: "If I got caught for everything I did, they'd hang me."

There was even a touch of professional and paternal pride when he described another crime. "My son, my grandson and me robbed a bank near where my son lived just out of Tul-see, Oklahoma. The job went off all right, but there was so many people in the bank who recognized my son. I told him it was dumb to rob a bank in your own hometown. They're both doing time in the federal prison at El Reno."

Despite thinning hair and a quiet, reflective manner of speaking, Smith looks much younger than his age as he stoically lists his infirmities: coronary problems, arthritis in both legs, failing eyesight, most teeth missing and "a touch of diabetes." Inmate number 024-45030 is one of an increasing number of prisoners growing old behind bars.

Several broad social and psychological trends have combined to produce this graying of our prisons. They include: the overall aging of our population, combined with an even faster-rising level of expectations among older people; a "get-tough" policy that has resulted in longer mandatory sentences; and increased normalization of life inside prisons.

Elderly people, in general, are living longer and living better as their income increases faster than that of any other age group. The image of a "tattered coat upon a stick," as Yeats put it, has been replaced by one of vigorous men and women in jogging suits. Detachment, serenity and wisdom are no longer the ultimate virtues for elderly Americans.

Tax reductions, rent control, subsidized senior citizen housing and recreational centers, increased public advocacy, Medicare, pension guarantees and increasing Social Security benefits—all have helped bring the elderly back into the mainstream with a vengeance. They are more physically able to get what they believe they deserve, and more seem willing to use force to get it. Figures on admissions to state prisons, for example, show that, compared to younger people, a much higher percentage of older people are being incarcerated for murder and manslaughter (see table).

Other statistics confirm that older people are committing more serious crimes than in the past. From 1976 to 1985, the arrest rate for rape committed by men over 65 increased 155 percent. For men 60 to 64, the increase was 112 percent. During the same 10 years, the rate of arrests among the same two groups increased 39 percent and 60 percent for all sex offenses, and 30 percent and 33 percent for larceny-theft.

There were nearly 600,000 inmates 18 and over in our federal, state, county and municipal prisons on January 1, 1987. According to my estimates, about 10 percent of these were over 50 and facing the prospect of release only when they are well past 60. By the year 2000, if present

Admissions to State Prisons, 1982

AGE AT ADMISSION

Offense	Total	Less than 18 years	18-24 years	25-34 years	35-44 years	45-54 years	55-64 years	65 years and over
All Offenses	100.0%	100.0%	100.0%	100.0%	100.0%	100.0%	100.0%	100.0%
Murder	4.3	4.5	3.1	4.2	6.3	8.8	11.0	18.4
Manslaughter	2.6	1.7	1.6	2.6	4.3	5.1	9.8	16.8
Rape	2.6	3.8	2.4	2.6	2.9	2.9	2.5	1.0
Robbery	17.6	28.4	20.1	17.1	10.9	7.6	4.6	2.6
Assault	6.6	4.8	5.7	6.9	8.1	9.1	9.1	8.7
Burglary	27.2	36.2	34.9	23.2	15.6	11.3	7.3	4.1
Larceny	10.4	8.6	10.5	10.2	11.1	10.7	7.8	3.6
Auto Theft	1.8	2.3	2.1	1.4	1.3	1.5	0.9	2.0
Forgery, Fraud, Embezzlement	6.2	1.4	4.3	7.5	8.6	9.4	7.5	4.1
Drugs	8.0	0.8	5.1	10.5	12.0	9.8	8.0	9.7
Public Order	5.3	2.3	3.1	5.6	8.9	13.7	19.8	17.3
Other Offenses	7.4	4.6	6.4	7.7	9.4	9.4	11.0	11.7
Number of Admissions*	100,814	2,674	44,423	37,209	11,507	3,696	1,109	196

*Includes other sexual assault, other violent offenses, other property offenses, and miscellaneous offenses.

Source: United States Department of Justice, Bureau of Justice Statistics, Special Report: "Prison Admissions and Releases, 1982."

trends continue, the number of long-term prisoners over 50 should be around 125,000, with 40,000 to 50,000 over 65.

Even these figures only hint at the real increase in crime by the elderly. I believe the facts are obscured by a double standard of law enforcement toward older men and women. Except for the most serious crimes, such as murder, police and prosecutors are inclined to overlook offenses by the elderly, especially women. They often don't make arrests, or if they do, the charges are dismissed. There are probably no more than a thousand women over 65 in U.S. prisons.

Even so, more old people are being sent to prison today and more young people under 30 are getting long mandatory sentences that will keep them imprisoned until they are old. This does not mean that we face a tidal wave of crime. Rather, these facts reflect the "get-tough" policy that emerged following the Vietnam years. Public acceptance of the policy has helped overcome resistance to committing large sums for new prisons. At the current rate of construction, about a thousand state and county prisons will be built by the year 2000, at a cost that has been estimated as high as $200,000 a cell. These figures do not include the cost of new federal prison facilities.

The increased number of prisoners of all ages is less a result of more arrests and more convictions than it is of longer sentences and vastly increased use of mandatory minimum sentences. The increased number of older first-time offenders is less a result of any policy to get tough on the elderly than it is of the fact that older people are more active, more prone to taking what they want. Their greater visibility also makes them more prone to arrest and conviction.

A third reason more old people will grow very old in prison and more young people will grow old there is that conditions on the inside have become, over the last decade or so, closer to those on the outside. Although there are a few prisons in which rich, older mobsters and former government officials live a reasonably pleasant life at minimum-security facilities, most prisons are still harsh and often unthinkingly cruel environments. But the horrors of the past have been reduced to some extent by prison reforms and court decisions upholding the rights of prisoners to decent living conditions.

As a result, many social patterns of the free community now continue behind prison walls. The intense stimulus deprivation of the past has often been replaced by informational abundance, especially for older offenders. In many cases, there are uncensored television sets in each cell and current motion pictures available on video.

New Jersey is a proving ground for what is taking place nationally concerning crime by the elderly and the aging of the prison population. The state has responded to the increase in violent crime with a stern get-tough policy: mandatory minimum sentences of 30 to 50 years for some crimes and authorization of hundreds of millions of dollars for new prisons. New Jersey has also developed long-range plans for a sizable geriatric prisoner population, one unlike any seen in the past.

Four kinds of convicts make up this population. The first, such as Smith, is the chronic offender who has grown old during one major sentence or in a steady series of shorter stretches. The second group consists of those under 30 who have been sentenced to long mandatory terms. The characteristics of these prisoners are clear. My research suggests that among those who will be at least 60 to 70 before they are released, 80 percent have led an actively abusive life involving drugs, alcohol and hallucinogens. Many have been intensely promiscuous bisexuals. Most place high value on physical strength, aggressiveness, violence and predatory behavior expressed through gang membership.

One prison official referred to these young inmates, who face a virtual lifetime in prison, as "jiveass, drug-oriented prisoners." Another described them as "jitterbug celebrities proud of their 50-year mandatory minimum." But without the support of drugs, the drug economy and gang crime, their bravado soon turns to depression and anger. They realize that they may never again walk on a city street and that they face abandonment by family and friends. Their rage often turns into exploitative behavior towards elderly prisoners.

Allen Benowitz, age 40, is serving a 30-year sentence for homicide, with, he says, "only 25 more to go, unless I work harder on myself." Benowitz is the third type of geriatric prisoner, the middle-aged man, often a repeater, who probably won't be released until he is very old. By working hard, he means attending group therapy sessions regularly. Through them and countless hours of introspection, he has "finally come to understand who I am and what my potential is. I have mellowed. When I get out I'll know how to use my creative energies."

Benowitz's chief motivation for making himself into a different person is to win favorable parole consideration after his mandatory minimum of 15 years. "That's only 10 more years," he exclaims, with optimism sparkling in his blue eyes. He will not admit to himself that people convicted of homicide are often not paroled after serving the mandatory minimum. But he does all he can by keeping to himself, avoiding trouble with guards and inmates, keeping fit by running and lifting weights and admitting responsibility for his crimes.

Benowitz, at 40, looks considerably older. The only son of Polish-Jewish immigrants, he has been in trouble most of his life. After he was sent to Trenton State Prison five years ago, his wife divorced him. "She just disappeared with our two sons, aged 14 and 12. She must have gone to Texas or someplace like that and changed her name." He assures me that he will soon make an effort to locate his sons and work out a relationship with them.

Sam Malone represents the fourth type of elderly prisoner, the convict who is serving time for his first serious offense, often murder. A youthful 72-year-old black man who was born in Georgia and raised in Newark, New Jersey, Malone has a quick, philosophical turn of mind. He is proud of his accomplishments and ability, eager to describe how much money he saved and invested wisely during a 40-year career in construction. He repeats, obsessively, that he will win his release because he can prove that the prosecutor made a number of serious, reversible errors during his trial. Malone was convicted of shooting and killing a handicapped 84-year-old neighbor in a senior citizens' residence and received a mandatory sentence of 30 years.

The way he describes his life inside echoes what many prison personnel say about old-timers. "Most never get mail or visits," they say. "They are loners who go their own way." "They are usually comfortable in a secure environment, although they are constantly hustled and cheated by younger inmates.''

Malone, a widower for the past eight years, receives only a few letters from his 24 children and grandchildren, most of whom live less than an hour from the prison. He speaks to them occasionally on the telephone. With no real work assignments, he and other elderly inmates are allowed to feel retired, to go about the prison without the restrictions placed on young inmates. Malone keeps up with the news by watching television in his cell and looks forward to better times. ''I've lived a good life,'' he says. ''I'm relaxed. I'm happy.'' On the wall of his cell he has taped a number of sayings, including his favorite: ''I'm doin' bad and don't need help.''

One thing that makes life inside prison go smoothly for older prisoners is having money to spend on themselves and others. Benowitz's mother helps him out. Smith and Malone have savings and Social Security payments to draw on. Benowitz told me that when young prisoners gamble with older ones and lose, they refuse to pay their debts. When the older men lose, the younger ones not only insist on prompt payment but extort much more for late payments. To give themselves better control over their money, Smith and Malone have both arranged to have their benefits sent to friends they can count on outside.

For prisoners over 62 who are receiving Social Security payments, the checks provide a standard of living higher than that enjoyed by nearly all other inmates and bring privileges traditionally enjoyed behind bars only by convicted public officials, business people and mobsters. ''With the Social Security,'' Smith says, ''I don't have to touch my savings. I usually buy $60 worth of stuff at a time in the commissary. Except for the few cigars I need for myself, I give the rest away in exchange for favors.''

For Malone, the checks are a way to get things that are officially prohibited in prison. ''There's a place in one of the blocks we call 'Times Square.' It's run by the young fellows who use most of their time building up their physique. You can buy nearly anything you want there — sex, drugs, booze.''

Although a federal law that took effect in 1984 requires suspension of payments to all new prisoners convicted of a felony, the Social Security Administration doesn't know how many payments have been stopped. While the law is probably being well enforced in federal prisons, it is unlikely that the states are complying fully; they are traditionally reluctant to return money to the federal treasury.

Elderly inmates, such as Smith and Malone, who aren't confined to a wheelchair or bed are expected to participate in such routine activities as going to meals, outdoor recreation, tidying the cell and clean-up tasks.

"Even if," as Texas prison statistician Larry Farnsworth put it, "all it means is sweeping a two-foot square of corridor." But the growing number of elderly inmates who require more-than-average care is causing administrators to consider the need for special facilities.

By the year 2000, the number of people over 65 is expected to increase 21 percent in the general population. In prisons, I estimate the increase will be 50 percent. Many of these 85 and over, the fastest-growing segment of the elderly population, will require complex, round-the clock health care, creating new cost burdens.

According to William Kelsey, health care administrator for Pennsylvania's Department of Corrections, the money spent for prison health services in that state soared from $1.23 million in 1973 to $16.7 million in 1986. Eyeglasses and dentures are provided and even open-heart surgery is performed when needed. Large prisons with infirmaries have set aside a section to care for elderly inmates dying of cancer and inoperable heart conditions. Some of the wards house elderly inmates suffering from Alzheimer's disease and organic brain disorders.

While the federal prison system maintains hospital at Springfield, Missouri, that cares for some elderly inmates, it is not really equipped for gerontological care. No research has been done within the federal prison system to gauge the future requirements of its aging population.

New York State's Commissioner of Correctional Services, Thomas A. Coughlin III, states a position shared by many prison officials: "The elderly prisoners are in fact a minority. In general, healthy inmates over the age of 60 get only what other inmates get—work, visits, recreation—nothing special because of their age."

34

The Forgotten Few
Juvenile Female Offenders

Ilene R. Bergsmann*

Adolescent female offenders have been described as a "specialty item in a mass market" (Grimes, 1983). Generally overlooked and frequently ignored, relegated to a footnote, and perceived as sexually deviant and in need of protection, these young women have received scant attention from members of the juvenile and criminal justice communities.

What about the juvenile female offender? Who pays attention to her special needs? Unfortunately, the courts and law enforcement pay too much attention for the wrong reasons, while litigators, legislators, and juvenile correctional administrators pay too little attention, also for the wrong reasons. During the past 25 years, few research studies, congressional inquiries, or lawsuits have focused on juvenile female offenders. Even when research is conducted on juvenile offenders, the data are not disaggregated by sex. When the Bureau of Justice Statistics provides valuable and much-needed data on juveniles in the justice

*This article was written as part of a U.S. Department of Education, Women's Educational Equity Act Program grant to the Council of Chief State School Officers. The author wishes to thank Glenda Partee of the council and Denis Shumate, superintendent of the Youth Center at Beloit, Kansas, for their helpful comments and suggestions on the article.

Source: *Federal Probation*, Vol. 53, No. 1 (March 1989), 73-78

system, one or two tables at most provide information by gender. *Uniform Crime Reports* data published by the Federal Bureau of Investigation also provide little information by gender.

Class action suits based on parity of programs proven effective for adult women to increase their educational and vocational training opportunities while in prison have not been filed on behalf of young women. Questionable correctional policies and practices are all too frequently the subject of policy debates within departments of youth services while in adult departments of corrections these same procedures have become the subject for litigation (Collins, 1987).

This article addresses the problems of young women in the juvenile justice system, including a description of who the female adolescent offender is, gender bias and stereotyping by correctional educators and administrators, and much-needed policy changes to ensure equitable programs.

Profile of a Juvenile Female Offender

Young women in trouble with the law are typically 16 years old, live in urban ghettos, are high school dropouts, and are victims of sexual and/or physical abuse or exploitation. Most come from single parent families, have experienced foster care placement, lack adequate work and social skills, and are substance abusers. Over half of these adolescent females are black or Hispanic (Bergsmann, 1988; Crawford, 1988; Sarri, 1988).

For youths in secure confinement, property crimes account for nearly 41 percent of all offenses, possession of drugs accounts for nearly 7 percent, status offenses 9 percent, and violent crime 32 percent (Beck, Kline and Greenfield, 1988). Although the number of females in correctional facilities has remained about the same between 1975 and 1985 (17,192 and 17,009, respectively), a shift has occurred between placement in public and private facilities. In 1975, 53 percent of the female youthful offenders were in public institutions; in 1985, only 40 percent were in such institutions (Kline, anticipated 1989).

In a self-report study conducted by the American Correctional Association Task Force on the Female Offender (Crawford, 1988), 62 percent of the juveniles indicated that they were physically abused, 47 percent with 11 or more incidences of abuse. Thirty percent said the abuse began between ages five and nine, another 45 percent said onset occurred between 10 and 14 years of age. In most instances, parents were the primary abusers.

Sexual abuses follow similar but slightly less harsh patterns. Fifty-four percent of the juvenile females were victims of sexual abuse, 40 percent with abuse occurring once or twice, 33 percent with 3 to 10 occurrences. The age of onset of abuse occurred before age 5 in about 16 percent of the youths, from ages 5 to 9 for nearly 33 percent, and from ages 10 to 14 for nearly 40 percent. Fathers, stepfathers, and uncles accounted for nearly 40 percent of the attackers. Other research conducted on the national, state, and local levels show both higher and lower figures than those cited by Crawford. All, however, document the close connection between physical/sexual abuse and running away from home (Geller and Ford-Somma, 1979; Chesney-Lind, 1987).

Although most of the females were not convicted of drug abuse, self-report data indicate that they are frequent users of controlled substances, with alcohol, marijuana, speed, and cocaine the most frequent drugs used (Crawford, 1988).

Sarri predicts that 90 percent of all youthful female offenders will be single heads of households who will spend 80 percent of their income on housing and child care (1988). Yet, a majority of these youths, who have failed to obtain a high school diploma or a GED and are educationally disadvantaged, also suffer from societal biases against women and minorities.

A majority (64 percent) of female juvenile offenders in secure facilities indicate that a member(s) of their family has been incarcerated. Most (80 percent) also report being runaways. Contrary to staff perceptions, over half report growing up with love and acceptance. Typical of most teenagers, over 80 percent say that peers and friends influence them (Crawford, 1988).

Many teen-age female offenders suffer from low self-esteem. Self-report data show that over half have attempted suicide, 64 percent of whom have tried more than once. They express reasons such as being depressed, life is too painful to continue, and no one cares (Crawford, 1988). While offenders are not a precise mirror of young women in society in the depths of their feelings of poor self-worth, studies demonstrate that lack of self-esteem is generally a common problem among young women. In a study begun in 1981 to measure the self-confidence of high school valedictorians, salutatorians, and honor students, males and females in roughly the same percentages believed that they had "far above average" intelligence at graduation. Four years later as college seniors, 25 percent of the males continued to share this opinion while none of the females did (Epperson, 1988). If women with above average intelligence, leadership ability, and the opportunity to achieve higher education experienced feelings of low self-esteem, it is not too difficult to understand how young women from broken homes, urban ghettos, poor schools, and abusive families develop feelings of despair and hopelessness about themselves and their chances for success.

Gender Bias and Stereotyping in the Juvenile Justice System

Differential treatment of females and males prevails in the juvenile justice system. Sexual promiscuity, including immoral conduct, has prevailed for much of the last 100 years as one basis for locking up juvenile females. Girls are expected to conform to traditional roles within the family and society. They should be inconspicuous; passive in their dealings with others and take few, if any, risks; and obedient to their parents, teachers, and elders. Boys, on the other hand, are expected to be rowdy, boisterous, and get into trouble now and then. They should be aggressive, independent, and strive for great achievements. As Chesney-Lind explains. "From sons, defiance of authority is almost normative whereas from daughters it may be seen as an extremely serious offense. And because so much of the adolescent female sex role evolved to control female sexual experimentation so as to guarantee virginity upon marriage, such defiance is virtually always cast in sexual terms" (Chesney-Lind, 1978).

The courts view female adolescents as "more vulnerable and in need of protection than boys" (Grimes, 1983) and thus have used their "discretionary powers in the service of traditional sex roles . . . (while they) appear to be less concerned with the protection of female offenders than the protection of the sexual status quo" (Datesman, Scarpitti and Stephenson in Sarri, 1983). Of all the juveniles who appeared in court in 1984, females represented 45 percent of all status offender cases compared with only 19 percent of all delinquency cases. Of this 45 percent, 62 percent were runaways (Snyder et al., 1987).

While young women comprised 14 percent of all juveniles in custody in 1985, they represented 52 percent of all status offenders (Bureau of Justice Statistics, 1986). *Uniform Crime Reports* data show that 18 percent of all female juvenile arrests are for curfew and loitering violations and running away, yet only 6.4 percent of male juvenile arrests are for these offenses (Federal Bureau of Investigation, 1987). The 1987 Children in Custody survey indicates that the number of female status offenders has increased since 1985 while the number of male status offenders has declined (Allen-Hagen, 1988). Today, less than 2 percent (1.6 percent) of males are held in training schools for the commission of status offenses compared to 9.3 percent of all females (Beck, Kline and Greenfield, 1988).

Parents, law enforcement officers, and school administrators are inextricably linked to young women's contacts with the law. Often parents use the courts as a route to mending family feuds or as a last resort for addressing problems with promiscuous and sexually active daughters. Because judges have similar parental concerns, they tend to react sympathetically. Rarely are the courts employed as a quick fix for sons who exhibit similar sexual behaviors.

Female sexual activity also frequently becomes part of the record that judges and other court officers review, including levels and types of sexual activity and numbers of children, regardless of the offense for which they are being tried. According to several judges in Missouri, such information is almost never found in delinquent male records (Grimes, 1983).

Police contribute to the differential treatment of these adolescent females as well. Not only do they tend to arrest more females for sexual and relational activities than for criminal conduct, they also promote a different set of sanctions for them. Dating back to the 1950s, research has shown that girls were more likely than boys to be: 1) referred to social or welfare agencies rather than being released from custody; 2) placed on informal probation supervision; and 3) placed in secure treatment facilities for the commission of status offenses (Chesney-Lind, 1982). Females arrested for status offenses often remain in detention longer than males, according to a Minnesota study in which 82.9 percent of all status offenders held beyond the statutory limit were females (Osbun and Rode, 1982). And, 12 percent of all status offenders placed in secure detention are females contrasted with 9 percent for males (Snyder et al., 1987).

Self-report data, on the other hand, indicate that males engage in at least the same amount of sexual activity as females but rarely are arrested for such behavior. Adolescent females in self-report studies indicate that their engagement in criminal activity is greater than what court intake records show. If these studies are accurate, the number of females involved in criminal activity would remain below that of males, but the types of offenses for which they would be arrested would be much the same (Geller and Ford-Somma, 1979; Sarri, 1983; Chesney-Lind, 1987). As Chesney-Lind maintains, ". . . it is reasonable to assume that some bias (either unofficial or official) is present within the juvenile justice system and functions to filter out those young women guilty of criminal offenses while retaining those women suspected of sexual misconduct" (1982).

A third source of referral to juvenile courts is through the school system. In a study conducted in nine public and parochial high schools in the Midwest, 11 percent of all court referrals come from the schools (Sarri, 1983). These youths have become so disruptive that the teaching and administrative staff are no longer able to contain them.

Administrative Disinterest

Like their adult counterparts, adjudicated juvenile females find themselves with few programs and services to meet their needs for developing socialization and life skills and an awareness of the world of work and their role in it. In the community, services are geared to preventing further physical or sexual harm but not to developing vocational and life skills (National Council of Jewish Women, 1984).

In secure confinement, the amount of staff time to work with these adolescents is limited to the average length of stay of 8 months (Bergsmann, 1988). Yet, it is during incarceration that these young women should be acquiring some of the tools they will need for economic independence and personal growth. The barriers to providing equitable treatment of these females come from several sources: 1) the traditional view of young women held by many female and male correctional administrators and staff; 2) the small number of females who, because of their limited population, are housed in co-correctional (co-educational) facilities; 3) limited resources that are mostly channeled to the males who constitute 93 percent of the incarcerated juvenile population; and 4) lack of program and service integration among state and local education, health, labor, and youth services agencies.

When educationally disadvantaged delinquent females enter the juvenile justice system, they also encounter administrative resistance in the provision of appropriate resources and programs to meet their unique needs. Departments of corrections and youth services rarely, if ever, designate a central office position to coordinate female programs and services (Ryan, 1984). Co-educational institutions are often the result of financial/administrative decisions based on the small number of females and the large number of male offenders. Often, the young women are imposed on all-male facilities in which policy and procedure frequently are not written from an equity perspective and where programs and services are more appropriate for males than females.

Workforce Changes in the 1990s

The traditional or stereotypical orientation of many youth services managers towards delinquent women is a great disservice not only to these young women but also to society. Major economic and workforce changes are anticipated during the 1990s, changes that will most certainly impact women and minorities. Consider the major trends for our economic future that the Hudson Institute forecasts for the year 2000: a growing economy, fueled by an increase in service-related jobs over manufacturing; a workforce that is "growing slowly, becoming older, more female and more disadvantaged," as well as minority; and jobs that require higher skill levels than those of today (Johnston, 1987). In other words, highly skilled employees will have greater employment options while the least skilled will face greater joblessness.

The 1990s will see more women and minorities entering the labor pool. Nearly 66 percent of all new workers will be women, many of whom will be poor single heads of households; non-whites will constitute 29 percent of the new workforce. Although women will continue to work in jobs that pay less than those for men, they also will have greater opportunities for high-paying professional and technical positions. And, even with entry-level positions, employers who are facing a shrinking labor pool are beginning to invest time and money in finding and training new workers. Unless women offenders, who are disproportionately minority, receive sufficient education and training to perform the more complex jobs projected for the coming years, our economy will suffer and their poverty, dependence, and criminal activity will escalate (Johnston, 1987; Packer, 1988).

As jobs become more sophisticated, young women offenders, who have minimal occupational skills, will find it increasingly difficult, if not impossible, to become employed in an occupation with more than poverty-level wages. Many are high school dropouts, and nearly 26 percent suffer educational disadvantages, including learning disabilities and emotional problems (Bergsmann, 1988). Their exposure to vocational education is often limited to traditional programs of cosmetology, office skills, and food services. The Department of Labor's statistics on women, especially women and girls who are minorities, are not encouraging. In 1984, the unemployment rate for black female teenagers was almost three times as great as for white female teens, and for Hispanic women unemployment rates were almost 4 percent above the rates of all women (Council of Chief State School Officers, 1986).

Policy Considerations

The inequitable treatment of juvenile female offenders is often exacerbated by the lack of adequate social and life skills programs and pre-vocational and vocational training programs that are critical for these youths in order to achieve economic and emotional self-sufficiency. Recognizing this problem, the American Correctional Association (ACA) has called for both juvenile and adult women offenders to receive programs comparable with those provided to males, as well as services that meet the unique needs of females. Integral to its policy on "Female Offender Services" is the provision for "access to a full range of work and programs designed to expand economic and social roles of women, with emphasis on education; career counseling and exploration of non-traditional as well as traditional vocational training; relevant life skills, including parenting and social and economic assertiveness; and pre-release and work/education release programs" (1986).

The Correctional Education Association (CEA) concurs with the need for appropriate education for women offenders. Its standards, promulgated in 1988, include a mandatory standard on educational equity which states that, "Institutions housing females provide educational programs, services and access to community programs and resources equitable with those provided for males within the system." This means that small numbers and thus high per capita costs of program delivery cannot be used to justify a lack of equitable programs that are defined "in terms of range and relevance of options, quality of offerings, staff qualifications, instructional materials and equipment, and curriculum design." Pennsylvania is the first state to use the standards to assess the status of its educational programs. A program to enforce the standards is being developed to ensure that all participating jurisdictions would be required to provide equitable educational programs for juvenile female offenders.

Troubled and delinquent offenders have often been the stepchildren of the educational system. Today, these offenders fall within the "at-risk" category of youths whose multiple problems have made their odds of educational success difficult at best. Many of these teenagers have failed academically, been chronic truants, and when they do go to school, frequently act out. Unfortunately, when they enter the juvenile justice system, education, one of their greatest needs and surest routes for entering the economic and social mainstream becomes second to security, which takes preference above all else.

A Bill of Educational Rights for incarcerated youth has been called for (Price and Vitolo, 1988) which seeks "to establish minimum standards for protecting their rights and assuring them of an education program designed to meet their needs." Included in this Bill of Educational Rights are the rights to: 1) ". . . a public education fostering (youth) development as productive members of society" guaranteed by Federal policy that mandates education for all juvenile offenders; 2) a curriculum that "emphasize(s) the core subjects and skills" including basic academics and independent living skills that use a competency-based system for awarding credits; 3) "a thorough educational assessment" that appropriately identifies and addresses different learning styles and needs; 4) education on "affective development" to focus on positive self-esteem and interpersonal relationships; 5) special education services; 6) state-certified instructors to design a curriculum consistent with the community's educational standards; 7) an educational program that meets "recognized community standards leading to a diploma" in order that youths can continue their education on release; and 8) transition services on release to assist with reintegration back to school, entry into a vocational education program, or job placement.

Inherent in this Bill of Educational Rights are many important elements for delinquent female offenders. These youths need academic encouragement, counseling to improve their self-esteem, introduction to the world of work to encourage them to consider high paying careers, vocational education courses, independent living skills, and transition planning and assistance.

Institutions interested in implementing the provisions of the ACA's policy on female offenders, the CEA standards, including the standard on equity, and the provisions of the Bill of Educational Rights could do so by: 1) developing equitable educational opportunities for adolescent females delivered through a continuum of interrelated programs and 2) establishing a collaborative educational program that links youth service staff with employees in the state departments of education, labor, and employment and training both inside and outside the training school.

To achieve pre-vocational, vocational, health, and life skills, a comprehensive, coordinated service delivery system must be in place within the institution and continue through transition back into the community. Such services include testing and evaluation; pre-vocational and vocational training; independent living and social skills; health education, including human sexuality; individual and group counseling; substance abuse programs and pre-release planning, including a network of support in the community.

Underlying any fundamental change in the way these youths perceive themselves is the need to raise their self-esteem. Contributing to many of these girls' involvement in the juvenile justice system is their poor self-esteem, brought on by abuse and/or exploitation at home, poor academic achievement, little assistance from teachers and administrators and minimal school involvement (Finn, Stott and Zarichny, 1988) and the myriad of social and economic problems in which they have grown up. They tend to underestimate their abilities; fail to consider a full range of career opportunities; become pregnant and then a single parent; perform poorly in school; be overly dependent on young men; fear success and assertiveness; and have an excessive need for external approval (Agonito and Moon, no date). Training school staff, not just educators, must work with these young women to enhance self-esteem through academic and vocational education programs that instill self-confidence and staff-offender interactions based on acceptance and approval.

More subtle, but equally compelling, is the need for staff members to be gender neutral in their interactions with all youthful offenders. For example, teachers need to design curricular materials that incorporate women and minorities. They should employ classroom strategies that encourage female participation, e.g., females, especially minority females, need more "wait time" than other students during classroom interaction. In co-correctional facilities, females should be included fairly in all classroom interactions. Finally, testing and counseling programs should avoid career segregation and stereotyping (Sadker and Sadker, 1988).

Conclusion

Little time, and even less effort, has been devoted to the juvenile female offender in the last century. Criminal and juvenile justice administrators pursue problems that are seemingly more pressing, such as crowding, or those that are more vocal, such as litigation. Researchers study juvenile offenders, generalizing their theories of male juveniles to females. Unfortunately, the adolescent female offender has been silent for so long that the few administrators and researchers who do champion her special needs are often unheard and even when heard go unheeded.

The differential treatment of females and males in the juvenile justice system begins with the schools, continues with law enforcement and the courts, and is perpetuated by the correctional system. Many delinquent females are locked up for running away from home as a result of physical and/or sexual abuse or exploitation. Many others suffer from low self-esteem, inequitable treatment in school from teachers and administrators, and inequitable programs during incarceration.

The need for educational equity for these offenders is paramount. Teachers must begin to design curricula with females in mind and interact in a gender-free environment. Law enforcement officers must stop arresting females for running away and for other status offenses. Judges and magistrates must stop treating girls differently from boys in the length of confinement in detention and the length and types of sentences imposed. Correctional educators and other staff must begin to provide equitable programs and services for this adolescent female population. Only then will female juvenile offenders have the opportunity to develop the social and educational/vocational skills to compete in the ever-changing technological world in which we live.

References

Agonito, R. and Moon, M. *Promoting Self-Esteem in Young Women.* Albany, NY: The State Department of Education, Division of Community Relations and Intercultural Relations, no date.

Allen-Hagen, B. *Children in Custody, Public Juvenile Facilities, 1987.* Washington, DC: Department of Justice, Office of Juvenile Justice and Delinquency Prevention, 1988.

American Correctional Association. *Public Policy for Corrections: A Handbook for Decision-Makers.* Laurel, MD: American Correctional Association, 1986, pp. 28-31.

Beck, A., Kline, S., and Greenfield, L. *Survey of Youth in Custody, 1987.* Washington, DC: Department of Justice, Bureau of Justice Statistics, 1988.

Bergsmann, I.R. *State Juvenile Justice Education Survey.* Washington, DC: Council of Chief State School Officers, 1988.

Chesney-Lind, M. "Young Women in the Arms of the Law." In L.H. Bowker (ed.), *Women, Crime and the Criminal Justice System.* Lexington, MA: Lexington Books, 1978, pp. 171-96.

_____. "Guilt by Reason of Sex: Young Women and the Juvenile Justice System." In B.P. Price and N.J. Sokoloff (eds.), *Criminal Justice System and the Law.* New York: Clark Boardman Co., Ltd., 1982, pp. 77-103.

_____. "Girls' Crime and Women's Place: Toward a Feminist Model of Female Delinquency." Paper presented at the American Society of Criminology, Montreal, Canada, 1987.

Collins, W. *Collins: Correctional Law, 1987.* Olympia, Washington, 1987, pp. 125-133.

Correctional Education Association. *Standards for Adult and Juvenile Correctional Education Programs.* College Park, Maryland, 1988.

Council of Chief State School Officers. *Equity Training for State Education Agency Staff.* Washington, DC: Resource Center on Educational Equity, 1986.

Crawford, J. *Tabulation of a Nationwide Survey of Female Inmates.* Phoenix, AZ: Research Advisory Services, 1988.

Epperson, S.E. "Studies Link Subtle Sex Bias in Schools with Women's Behavior in the Workplace." *Wall Street Journal.* September 16, 1988, p. 27.

Finn, J.D., Stott, M.W.R., Zarichny, K.T. "School Performance of Adolescents in Juvenile Court." *Urban Education,* 23, 1988, pp. 150-161.

Geller, M. and Ford-Somma, L. *Caring for Delinquent Girls: An Examination of New Jersey's Correctional System.* Trenton: New Jersey Law Enforcement Planning Agency, 1979.

Grimes, C. *Girls and the Law.* Washington, DC: Institute for Educational Leadership, 1983.

Johnston, W.B. *Workforce 2000.* Indianapolis, IN: Hudson Institute, 1987, pp. 75-104.

Kline, S. *Children in Custody 1975-1985: Census of Public and Private Juvenile Detention, Correctional, and Shelter Facilities, 1975, 1977, 1979, 1983, 1985.* Washington, DC: Department of Justice, Bureau of Justice Statistics, anticipated 1989.

National Council of Jewish Women. *Adolescent Girls in the Juvenile Justice System.* New York: National Council of Jewish Women, 1984.

Osbun, L.A. and Rode, P.A. *Changing Boundaries of the Juvenile Court: Practice and Policy in Minnesota.* Minneapolis, MN: University of Minnesota, 1982, pp. 33-49.

Packer, A. "Retooling the American Worker." *The Washington Post,* July 10, 1988, p. C3.

Price, T. and Vitolo, R. "The Schooling of Incarcerated Young People." *Education Week,* 27, June 15, 1988, pp. 27, 36.

Ryan, T.A. *State of the Art Analysis of Adult Female Offenders and Institutional Programs.* Columbia, SC: University of South Carolina, 1984, p. 22.

Sadker, M. and Sadker, D. *Equity and Excellence in Educational Reform.* Washington, DC: The American University, 1988, pp. 25-26.

Sarri, R.C. Keynote remarks. Conference on Increasing Educational Equity for Juvenile Female Offenders. Washington, DC: Council of Chief State School Officers, 1988.

———. "Gender Issues in Juvenile Justice." *Crime and Delinquency,* 29, 1983, pp. 38-97.

Snyder, H.N., Finnegan, T.A., Nimick, E.H., Sickmund, M.H., Sullivan, D.P., and Tierney, N.J. *Juvenile Court Statistics 1984.* Pittsburgh, PA: National Center for Juvenile Justice, 1987.

United States Department of Justice, Federal Bureau of Investigation. *Crime in the United States 1987.* Washington, DC: U.S. Government Printing Office, 1987.

———. *Children in Custody 1985.* Washington, DC: Bureau of Justice Statistics, 1986.

35

Employee Drug-Testing Policies in Prison Systems

Randall Guynes and Osa Coffey

Drug use in the workplace increasingly demands attention by employers, particularly in potentially dangerous work environments such as law enforcement and corrections that require full mental and physical alertness. These positions not only involve public trust but are inherently stressful and thus at high risk for substance abuse.

Earlier National Institute of Justice reports reviewed the response of police departments to employee drug use.[1] This report deals with actions taken by prison systems to deal with drug use by correctional staff, job applicants, or both. Inquiries to all 50 State correctional systems and the Federal Bureau of Prisons brought replies from 48 States and the Bureau. Among the findings were these:

- The Bureau of Prisons and less than half the States now test employees or job applicants for drugs.
- Most of the systems that test began their programs within the last 4 years.
- Most respondents do not consider drug abuse among staff members a major problem.

Source: National Institute of Justice, *Research in Action*, U.S. Department of Justice, August 1988, 1-6.

- Most agencies began drug testing because of problems with contraband, work performance, or both, and in response to public concerns about drug abuse in general.
- Of the systems with testing programs, most test only employees suspected of drug use. Only two systems reported random testing of staff, and that was limited; eight systems test job applicants.
- Special staff training on drug abuse remains limited and is more likely to be available in agencies that test employees or applicants.
- Few agencies have written policies and procedures for drug testing programs.
- Few grievances or lawsuits have resulted from drug testing to date.
- False positives were a common result on first tests; therefore many systems require a second test whenever the first proves positive.
- Most agencies with testing programs contract with laboratories or hospitals to conduct the tests at an average cost of $20 to $30 each.
- In the 15 States with unions, 7 unions have taken no stand, 1 union supported drug testing, and the remaining 7 opposed it.

Who to test

As shown in Exhibit 1, only 19 State correctional agencies and the Bureau of Prisons (41 percent of respondents) currently conduct drug testing of either staff or applicants. (By comparison, earlier studies showed testing by 73 percent of a sample of police departments.)

Four additional States indicate they plan to start a testing program. Twelve test only employees suspected of drug use; six test all applicants and those employees suspected of use; two States test only employees.

Only two States conduct random testing of staff, and one of those limits staff testing to preservice training. Georgia is the only State with random weekly testing of staff, and that program is limited to the Reidsville maximum security institution.

Reasons for testing

Asked why drug testing was initiated, 44 percent of respondents cited problems with contraband, 29 percent cited problems in work

---

Exhibit 1
Employee drug testing in State prison systems

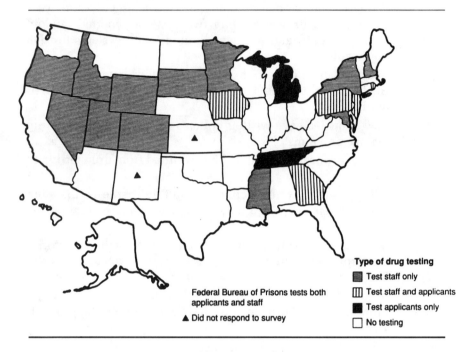

performance, and 27 percent mentioned public concerns about drug use.

Respondents from systems that do test employees for drugs indicated they perceive a relationship between drug tests and contraband more frequently than those from systems that do not test. No empirical evidence, however, either corroborates or refutes the perception that correctional employees who use drugs are more likely to be involved in drug contraband.

In virtually all States, an employee caught with drug contraband is turned over to the local or State police and charged with possession. Testing for drugs may or may not be part of the police arrest procedure.

Agencies that limit their testing of employees to those suspected of drug abuse did not indicate whether their limitation was established because it would raise fewer legal questions, whether it was due strictly to a sense of necessity, or whether cost was a consideration.

Legal questions about testing arise most frequently with regard to the fourth amendment, which prohibits *unreasonable* searches and seizures.

When testing is limited to those suspected of drug abuse, departments have to make determinations as to what constitutes reasonable grounds. Suspicion is usually based on an employee's appearance, manner, or actions that raise questions about the employee's ability to perform assigned duties.

Testing procedures

Another sensitive area is testing procedure. Care must be taken that urine samples reach the laboratory unadulterated while the individual's rights to privacy and due process are respected. Without proper procedures and reliable tests, grievances and legal actions are likely.

Of 20 correctional systems that test, only 13 indicated they have written policies and procedures. (Virtually all the 33 police departments in earlier surveys had written procedures.) Two jurisdictions reported that State law provided the necessary policy.

Policies ranged in length from a few lines in the general personnel policies to separate, detailed policy and procedural orders.

Many of the policies provide a detailed description of the "chain of custody"; i.e., records of everyone who physically handles the container from the moment the sample is provided to the time it enters the laboratory process.

Most of the policies also cover other requirements: a second test when the first has proven positive; issues of confidentiality; actions to be taken if the person refuses the test or if the test is positive. The majority of agencies (16) require that the sample be provided under the direct observation of a same-sex supervisor.

Testing technology

Agencies use several different types of drug tests (Exhibit 2), the most popular being EMIT (enzyme multiplied immunoassay technique) for the first test and gas chromatography for the second. Agencies received test results in from 1 to 6 days; on average, within 3 days.

The EMIT test is inexpensive and is utilized as a basic screen for opiates, barbiturates, cocaine, and marijuana. The National Institute on Drug Abuse has reported that the immunoassay method has the advantage of short analysis time and "moderate to good sensitivity and specificity."[2] Seven correctional agencies reported using their own equipment and conducting their first tests in the facility at a very low cost.

Exhibit 2
Testing technology used

	1st test	2nd test*
EMIT	12	1
Gas chromatography	2	6
Thin-layer chromatography	1	0
Radioimmunoassay	1	0
Respondent unsure	4	10

* The three States that use gas and thin-layer chromatography do not have second tests routinely performed. In these cases a repeat test may be made if necessary.

Gas chromatography is a more sensitive technique that can detect small amounts of drugs; however, it is a slower process requiring more expertise.[3] Correctional agencies that use this technique usually do so as a second test to confirm previous findings or to screen out false positives.

Cost of testing

Cost is of concern to correctional agencies, and reported drug-test costs range from $2 to $100. The $100 figure, however, included personnel, transportation, and related expenditures as well as the laboratory work.

Most agencies provided only the cost of the test procedure. Agencies that used outside laboratories cited prices in the $20-$30 range. The lowest figure, $2, was from an agency that uses an in-house "desktop" tester for first tests only.

The low cost of desktop testing, however, must be balanced against the fact that it is generally less accurate than results from full-scale carousel equipment. Considering this and the high incidence of desktop false positives (44 percent of a limited sample of 98 cases discussed later), agencies utilizing desktop testing need to consider more sophisticated equipment — either in-house or outside — for confirmatory second tests.

How agencies face dispositions, training

Testing is not the only approach correctional agencies have taken regarding drug abuse. Some agencies are providing drug abuse training for staff, either in-service or at the training academy. As Exhibit 3 indicates, most agencies that test also provide staff training. Only 35 percent of agencies without drug testing provide drug abuse training (including one agency whose training program was in development at the time of this study).

Exhibit 3
Systems providing training on drug abuse

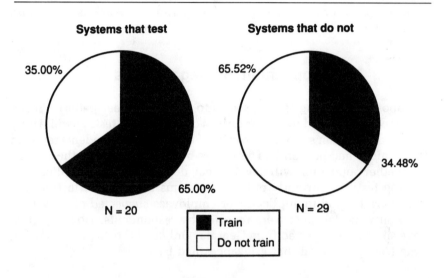

Agencies were also asked about their disposition of subjects testing positive. Those that test applicants require testing as a condition of employment and reject anyone who refuses to take the test or who tests positive. Six of the eight agencies that test applicants provided estimates of test results. Rejection rates due to positive tests ranged from 0.7 to 11 percent.

While most systems were candid about the failure rate among applicants, the number and disposition of staff members testing positive for drugs were impossible to obtain. The systems did not have figures on the number of employees tested nor on employees refusing tests or testing positive.

Respondents from 10 agencies provided data on the disposition of cases in which results were positive, but warned the figures were only approximations. Cumulatively, they provided disposition information for 98 cases. Of these, 43 were cleared through a second test, 38 were fired, 3 resigned, and 2 were referred to a treatment program. In 12 cases, the disposition was unknown.

Although only a few cases were identified as having been referred in the limited data obtained, correctional agencies claim to use a variety of drug treatment referral sources, shown in Exhibit 4.

A small number of agencies that conduct drug testing of employees indicated they base referrals on work performance rather than on test results alone. In these instances failure to attend the employee assistance program (EAP) or continued poor work performance are used as cause for termination.

Opposition and legal issues

Opposition to drug testing seems to fall in no clear pattern. Seven respondents reported that their unions opposed drug testing while only one reported union support for testing. Seven other respondents reported their unions had no stand. (There were no unions in five of the States.)

Whether opposition will develop may depend on future applications of drug testing. Currently only two systems use *random* testing. All others are limited to applicants or employees *suspected* of drug use.

Initially, no lawsuits were reported by respondents. However, two have since been reported from Georgia. Only 6 of the 20 systems using drug testing reported that grievances had been filed.

Exhibit 4
Drug treatment referral resources

Referred to	Testing States	Nontesting States
Employee assistance programs (EAP)	8	19
Community programs	1	16
Mental health division	0	2
No referrals	0	2
Unknown	1	0

The relative lack of opposition may simply reflect the limited application of drug testing. Thirteen of the testing programs were less than 2 years old, and most cases other than applicant testing originate based on observation of work performance.

Conclusion

Most respondents did not consider employee drug abuse a major problem. One respondent called particular attention to the fact that virtually all of the facilities in the State were in rural areas where drugs were less prevalent. Others said they were more concerned about contraband and inmate drug use.

Though most respondents saw no significant employee drug problem, Warden Lanson Newsome of Georgia State Prison was among a few who believe they face very serious problems. He initiated random testing in 1984, and according to the warden, 40 percent of the tests then were positive. By 1985, the positives had dropped to 10 percent.

Responses from 4 States indicated plans to initiate testing the following year, and another 13 States were discussing such plans.

Perhaps the biggest surprise of the survey was that only seven States and the Federal Bureau of Prisons test applicants. (In an earlier study of police departments, 73 percent tested applicants.) New programs being considered may well begin at the applicant stage; at present, agencies seem more likely to identify drug problems *after* hiring than to screen applicants.

The survey reflects a surprising dearth of written policies and procedures. The small number of formal grievances shows the low visibility of testing problems to date. However, operating a testing program without carefully prescribed policies and procedures can leave an agency exposed to constitutional challenge.

The future of employee drug testing in corrections is difficult to forecast. The problem is highly significant in a few systems and not considered much of a problem in others. However, the fact that 4 States are planning to implement drug testing for correctional employees and 13 others are considering it indicates an awareness of the drug problems being generally recognized across the country.

Correctional officials may do well to concentrate their antidrug efforts on policy development and on the effectiveness of applicant screening until results of police departments' drug policies become better known.

Random drug testing at Georgia State Prison

Random testing for drugs began at Georgia State Prison in 1984 in response to staff and administration concerns over contraband.

All 742 employees, including the warden, are included in the program. Every Monday morning the names of all employees are placed in a box. Twenty names are pulled; urine samples are collected that morning and transported to the prison's lab, where the first test is performed.

If the result is positive, the sample is sent to Atlanta for two additional tests. Anyone who tests positive on all three tests is terminated.

Employees who acknowledge a drug problem and seek assistance through the EAP before being tested positive are kept in service, and nothing is entered in their personnel file. They must, however, remain drug free and not test positive at any time. During their involvement with the EAP, they are tested as frequently as the EAP coordinator finds necessary, either through the Department of Corrections, the EAP, or the employee's private physician.

Warden Lanson Newsome indicated the program has met its goals. At first, approximately 40 percent of all tests were positive; the figure today is about 10 percent.

The warden said there has been a tremendous reduction in drug contraband within the prison, reporting that they are not collecting nearly the amount of drugs and drug contraband during shakedowns now as they did before the testing program and drug dealings between staff and inmates are notably lower.

To date there have been no grievances filed by current employees. There are, however, two lawsuits in the court system, filed by terminated employees.

Footnotes

[1]Barbara A. Manili et al., *Police Drug Testing*, Washington, D.C., National Institute of Justice, October 1987; J. Thomas McEwen, Barbara Manili, and Edward Connors, "Employee Drug Testing Policies in Police Departments, *Research in Brief*, Washington, D.C., National Institute of Justice, October 1986.

[2]National Institute on Drug Abuse, *Urine Testing for Drugs and Abuse*, n.d.: 31.

[3]*Urine Testing*, n. 2 above: 33.

36

AIDS
The Impact on Corrections
Mark Blumberg*

Introduction

Correctional institutions in the United States are faced with problems related to overcrowding, violence, lack of sufficient resources, inadequate rehabilitation programs, and a shortage of trained personnel. The threat posed by acquired immune deficiency syndrome (AIDS) adds a new and potentially frightening dimension to these difficulties. This disease is transmitted in the United States primarily through homosexual activity and the sharing of infected needles by intravenous (IV) drug users. Consequently, fear has been expressed that prisons and jails, because they house a large number of IV drug addicts and provide an environment that presents many opportunities for homosexual activity, may become breeding grounds for the spread of AIDS.

Correctional administrators must confront a variety of new and complex issues as they struggle to develop policies that are designed to prevent transmission of this ailment within the institutional setting.

Source: Prepared especially for *The Dilemmas of Corrections, Second Edition* by Mark Blumberg.

*The author would like to express his gratitude for Ken Haas, Allen Sapp, and Scott Christianson for providing helpful comments and ideas.

Many of these are issues that the outside society has already faced: mandatory testing, the question of whether to segregate infected persons, the appropriate content of educational programs designed to slow the spread of AIDS (i.e., whether to teach abstinence or "safer sex"), and the question of condom distribution. At the heart of the debate is the following question: should prisons and jails adhere to the practices of the larger society or is the institutional environment so unique that deviations from these established policies are acceptable?

This article explores the issues that AIDS poses for the corrections system. After a brief discussion of the medical and social aspects of this disease, epidemiological data are presented that address the following questions:

1) How many inmates have been diagnosed with AIDS?
2) What are the social characteristics of these inmates?
3) How do they differ from the characteristics of persons with AIDS in the community?
4) Is the AIDS virus being transmitted with great frequency in the nation's prisons and jails?

The data pertaining to these questions are followed by an examination of the pros and cons with respect to the various policy options that are designed to prevent the transmission of this disease within the correctional system. The discussion includes a synopsis of the findings from several surveys that have examined the direction that correctional policies are taking in this area. Finally, some of the legal issues that have arisen as correctional administrators formulate policies to control the spread of AIDS within jails and prisons are explored.

The AIDS Epidemic

Definition of AIDS, ARC and HIV

The very first case of AIDS in the United States was diagnosed in June 1981 (Morgan and Curran, 1986: 459). Yet during the next seven years, more than 64,000 additional cases were reported to the U.S. Public Health Service (CDC, 6/20/88). By the year 1991, it is projected that approximately 270,000 Americans will develop "full-blown" AIDS and 179,000 people will die from this ailment (Morgan and Curran, 1986: 461). However, to understand the full scope of this epidemic, two other and larger categories of infected individuals must also be considered:

those infected with the Human Immunodeficiencies Virus (HIV) and those suffering from AIDS-related complex (ARC).

It is estimated that between 1 and 1.5 million Americans have become infected with HIV, the viral agent that causes AIDS (CDC, 12/18/87: 804). The great majority of these seropositives[1] appear healthy but they are able to infect others. Because the incubation period is so lengthy (mean = 7 years), it is not known what proportion of seropositive persons will eventually develop "full-blown" AIDS. A recent study suggests the percentage may be as high as 99 percent (Lui, Darrow and Rutherford, 1988: 1334). At this point in time, the available data indicate that 20 to 30 percent will progress to this stage within 5 years (Koop, 1986: 12).

The second largest group of infected persons has AIDS-related complex (ARC). This term is applied to those individuals who display a wide variety of symptoms related to HIV infection, but who do not meet the strict clinical definition of AIDS as established by the Centers for Disease Control (CDC). Because there is not a firm definition of what constitutes ARC, data with respect to the prevalence of this condition are rather sketchy. However, it has been estimated that between 50,000 and 125,000 Americans suffer from ARC (Institute of Medicine, 1986: 7).

A smaller number of people actually meet the clinical definition of AIDS. To be classified as a person with AIDS, an infected individual must be diagnosed as having one of the opportunistic infections[2] or cancers that plague victims of full-blown AIDS. Such persons are generally quite ill and survive an average of one year after being diagnosed with this condition (Rothenberg et al., 1987: 1298).

Mode of Transmission

HIV is transmitted only through sexual contact, through contact with infected blood, or from an infected mother to a newborn infant (Friedland and Klein, 1987). There is overwhelming evidence that casual contact with infected persons does not transmit AIDS. Studies of individuals who resided in the same household as AIDS patients and who shared plates, cooking utensils, toilets, and other objects with these infected persons over an extended period of time have concluded that not a single individual has become infected except through sexual contact or by sharing needles (Friedland et al., 1986).

In the United States, approximately 90 percent of AIDS cases have been reported among two risk groups: homosexual/bisexual males and IV drug users (Centers for Disease Control, 6/20/88: 1). Despite exaggerated claims to the contrary (Masters and Johnson with Kolodny, 1988), there is little evidence to suggest that the disease is "breaking-out" of the "high-risk" groups into the general population. Only four percent of the cases have been linked to heterosexual transmission (Centers for Disease Control, 6/20/88: 1) and the great majority of these have occurred among the female sex partners of IV drug users (Friedland and Klein, 1987: 1129).

Social Stigma

Because AIDS is a recent phenomenon evoking fears of the unknown, because it is associated in the public mind with practices that are viewed as immoral by many people (i.e., homosexuality and drug addiction), and because it is a horrible disease, a great social stigma has attached to this ailment. Infected persons have often been treated as outcasts and subjected to various forms of discrimination. Many cases have been reported in which persons with AIDS or individuals merely carrying HIV have been denied housing, terminated from employment, forced to leave school, or subjected to other forms of harassment. In Arcadia, Florida, the home of three infected hemophiliac brothers who had attempted to enroll in public school was set on fire (Rosellini and Goode, 1987).

Treatment

At present, there is no cure for AIDS and no vaccine to protect against the virus. In fact, most public health experts do not believe that a general vaccine to prevent AIDS will be available until the mid-1990s, at the earliest (Weisburd, 1987: 329). Physicians are able to treat some of the opportunistic infections that plague AIDS patients. However, the only drug approved to treat AIDS itself is azidothymidine (AZT). Both AZT and the costs of medical treatment for AIDS patients are very high. A recent study estimated that the lifetime medical costs (including AZT) for each person with AIDS will rise to approximately $61,800 by 1991 (Hellinger, 1988: 309).

Persons with AIDS in Prisons and Jails

In each of the last three years, the National Institute of Justice (NIJ) in conjunction with the American Correctional Association (ACA) has surveyed all 50 state prison systems, the Federal Bureau of Prisons (FBOP), and over 30 large county/city jail systems in order to determine the number of inmates who have been diagnosed with full-blown AIDS in America's prisons and jails (Hammett, 1986; 1987; and 1988). These data indicate that the number of cases in correctional facilities is increasing, but at a slightly slower pace than in the general population. By October 1, 1987, a cumulative total of 1,964 confirmed cases had been reported. This was an increase of 59 percent over the previous year when 1,232 cases had been reported and this compares with an increase of 61 percent for the U.S. as a whole (Hammett, 1988: 23).

The incidence of AIDS among inmates is not distributed evenly among correctional systems. The majority of cases are concentrated in three states: New York, New Jersey and Florida (Greenspan, 1988: 7). Because New York has the largest number of inmates with AIDS and because AIDS is now New York's leading cause of death among prisoners (Wormser, 1987), the most comprehensive demographic data have been compiled by the New York State Commission of Correction (Gido and Gaunay, 1987). This research concluded that almost all inmate deaths attributable to AIDS were among males (96 percent), that a disproportionate number were black or Hispanic (88 percent) and that 95 percent had a history of intravenous drug use (p. 2).

Impact of IV Drug Use

Outside the institution, male homosexual behavior is the most common risk factor among persons with AIDS. Approximately 70 percent of all reported cases have occurred among members of this risk group (Centers for Disease Control, 6/20/88: 1). Among inmates, however, IV drug use is the key risk factor for developing AIDS. As previously noted, almost all cases have occurred in prisoners with a history of IV drug use. With the exception of California, IV drug users constitute the majority of inmates with AIDS in all states (Greenspan, 1988: 7). In addition, the largest concentration of confirmed cases has been reported in those states (i.e., New York and New Jersey) where the rate of seroprevalence[3] among addicts tends to be quite high. Epidemiological data indicate that between 50 and 60 percent of IV drug users in New York City and northern New Jersey are seropositive as compared with a rate of less than 5 percent in most other sections of the nation away from the East Coast (CDC, 12/18/87: 2). Because "shooting galleries"[4] are typically found in the northeast, a substantial proportion of addicts in this region have become infected with HIV.

IV drug use also explains the disproportionate number of minority group members who have been victimized by this disease. The National Institute on Drug Abuse (NIDA) estimates that 70 percent of the nation's 1.28 million IV drug addicts are black or Hispanic (Stengel, 8/17/87: 13).

For this reason, HIV infection is much more common in poor inner-city neighborhoods. Thirty-nine percent of AIDS patients are members of these racial-ethnic groups. This proportion is approximately double their representation in the general population. One-third of the AIDS cases among minorities are attributed to IV drug use as compared with just five percent among whites (Stengel, 8/17/87: 13). Excluding homosexual and bisexual men with AIDS, the ratio of persons with AIDS is 12.0 to 1 for blacks and 9.3 to 1 for Hispanics as compared with whites (CDC, 12/18/87: 10).

Minorities constitute an even greater proportion of those diagnosed with AIDS in the correctional setting. One reason is the greater prevalence of IV drug use in poor, disadvantaged neighborhoods. Another is that prison and jail populations contain both a disproportionate number of minorities as well as IV drug users. Nonetheless, the fact remains that this epidemic has placed a tragic burden on some of the most powerless individuals in our society.

Prevalence and Transmission of HIV Within Institutions

Most epidemiological studies have concluded that the rate of seroprevalence within the general inmate population is quite low (3 percent). Among prisoners who are at "high risk"[5] for AIDS, the proportion of seropositives is somewhat higher (Hammett, 1987: xxi). An exception to this pattern was observed in New York State. The New York Department of Health tested 500 new inmates from New York City who had recently been admitted to the prison system and found that 15 percent were seropositive (Criminal Justice Newsletter, 4/15/88: 1). Because both New York State and the New York corrections system have a substantially greater number of AIDS cases than any other state, this finding is not unexpected.

Although the rate of infection among prisoners is generally quite low, many correctional administrators remain concerned that seropositive inmates will transmit HIV to others within the institution through homosexual activity or by sharing contaminated needles or tattoo equipment. Although no cases have been documented in which an inmate seroconverted[6] during incarceration, "logic and common sense both suggest that even in the best managed correctional institutions, there may be at least some transmission of the AIDS virus occurring among inmates" (Hammett, 1987: 15). However, there is little doubt that incarcerated IV drug users face far less risk of becoming infected with HIV than is the case for addicts who remain on the street.

Several states have attempted to determine whether HIV is being transmitted within the institution. These studies indicate that very few prisoners who have been continuously incarcerated over a substantial period of time are infected. Maryland authorities observed that only two out of 137 such inmates were seropositive (Vaid, 1987: 238). Similar findings have been reported in New York and Florida (Hammett, 1988: 31). However, because the upper limit of the incubation period for AIDS has not been established, it is uncertain whether these inmates actually seroconverted during incarceration.

Mass HIV screening of all inmates *both* upon entry and at release has been instituted in four states—Alabama, Idaho, New Hampshire and West Virginia (Greenspan, 1988: 6). These data should eventually provide some indication of how frequently the AIDS virus is being transmitted within the prison. However, because Alabama is the only state among these systems with a substantial number of AIDS cases, it is questionable whether these findings will be generalizable to systems that contain a large number of inmates with AIDS (i.e., New York, New Jersey, and Florida).

Measures to Control HIV Infection

Mass Screening

In the U.S., public health authorities have attempted to control the spread of HIV through education, voluntary testing, and by counseling persons at high-risk. With the exception of immigrants and military personnel, most testing has been conducted on a voluntary basis. From the beginning of the epidemic, correctional administrators have debated whether this approach is appropriate in prisons and jails. Before discussing the controversy regarding mandatory testing, it is necessary to touch upon the available technology for diagnosing HIV.

The current blood test is not able to predict which seropositive individuals are likely to develop full-blown AIDS nor at what point symptoms may appear. The test cannot detect the AIDS virus; it merely detects the presence of antibodies to HIV. Because the human immune system will generally not develop antibodies until 6 to 12 weeks[7] after exposure (Petricciani and Epstein, 1988: 236), persons tested during this period will be seronegative[8] despite the fact that they are able to infect others. These results are commonly referred to as "false negatives." They pose a real concern for any program of mass screening.

Advantages

Mandatory mass screening involves testing all inmates or all incoming inmates for HIV infection. A more limited version involves testing only members of high-risk groups (i.e., homosexuals, IV drug users or prostitutes). Proponents argue that mass screening is the best way to identify seropositive inmates. Such a policy provides correctional administrators with an opportunity to target education and prevention programs. In addition, infected individuals can be placed under special supervision to insure that they do not transmit the virus to others. Supporters of this policy argue that institutions must take action to identify infected inmates and to prevent the spread of this virus or they will be held civilly liable. Finally, it is suggested that mass screening could provide a more accurate projection of how many cases of full-blown AIDS will eventually develop. This will enable correctional officials to plan more effectively and to seek an appropriate level of funding to meet future needs.

Disadvantages

Critics of mass screening do not accept these rationales. They respond to the claim that education and prevention efforts can be targeted by asserting that these programs must be directed toward all inmates. It is asserted that all prisoners should be encouraged to refrain from high-risk behavior, not just those identified as seropositive. Furthermore, opponents of mass screening are opposed to the practice of segregating infected individuals from the inmate population. Because any system of mass screening would produce some false negatives, it is not possible to identify all infectious inmates. The problems that this raises with respect to any segregation policy are discussed in the next section.

Opponents of mass screening are also skeptical about the civil liability concern. They note that institutions already have rules that prohibit those types of conduct which can transmit HIV (i.e., sexual contact and IV drug use). As a consequence, inmates who engage in these practices do so at their own risk. Most correctional lawyers argue that the institution would not be held liable unless an inmate became infected through a sexual assault (Hammett, 1987: 35).

The claim that correctional institutions must be able to project accurately the number of future AIDS cases is not disputed. However, critics of mass screening note that anonymous testing procedures can satisfactorily achieve this goal. In fact, the CDC is using anonymous testing to determine the prevalence of HIV in ten geographically diverse correctional institutions across the nation (Corrections Digest, 6/1/88: 1). Blood samples are coded in such a manner as to insure that prison officials do not learn the names of infected inmates.

Opponents of mass screening also argue that such a policy is not a wise expenditure of resources and that it will create a class of outcasts within the institution. Fear is expressed that seropositive inmates will be subjected to harassment, discrimination, and violence within the prison, and that they will also encounter difficulties in obtaining employment and housing upon release.

Finally, there is the question of how prisoners will respond to the knowledge that they are seropositive. Because institutions contain a substantial number of individuals with sociopathic personalities, it can be argued that inmates who learn they are carrying a deadly virus will be more likely to engage in predatory behavior.

Current Policy

Despite the objections raised by civil libertarians, the trend is toward greater use of mass screening. Thirteen states[9] now require that all incoming inmates be tested for HIV (Greenspan, 1988: 7). A survey taken just a year earlier indicated that only three jurisdictions followed this policy (Hammett, 1987: xx). In addition, the Federal Bureau of Prisons and five states[10] are now testing all inmates prior to release (Greenspan, 1988: 7). It is noteworthy, however, that none of the correctional systems with the largest number of AIDS cases have chosen to follow this policy. In fact, one state actually decided not to conduct mass screening because correctional officials did not wish to deal with the administrative consequences of a large number of seropositive inmates in the population (Hammett, 1987: 34).

The pressure to conduct widespread testing of inmates has come from politicians, not state correctional officials (Greenspan, 1988: 8). Both the National Association of State Corrections Administrators (Vaid, 1986: 3) and the National Commission on Correctional Health Care (Criminal Justice Newsletter, 5/2/88: 3) are opposed to this policy. Nevertheless, state legislators have continued to propose statutes which require mandatory testing.

Segregation

In addition to contending with the controversy concerning testing, correctional administrators must also decide whether to separate infected prisoners from the inmate population. Segregation can be undertaken for medical reasons,[11] to protect an infected individual from violence, or as a general policy to prevent the transmission of HIV within the institution. It is the latter rationale which raises a great deal of controversy and is thus the focus of our attention.

Advantages

Proponents of segregation assert that this is necessary to prevent the transmission of HIV within the institution. In making the case for this policy, advocates make the following arguments: 1) Previous research indicates that homosexual activity is a fact of life in prison. Nacci and Kane (1983: 35) report that 30 percent of male inmates have had a homosexual experience as an adult in prison. However, data from another institution (Wooden and Parker, 1982: 50-51) indicated that 65 percent of the male prisoners have had sex with another male during their current period of incarceration; 2) Other sexually transmitted diseases (e.g., rectal gonorrhea) are sometimes transmitted in the correctional setting; 3) Tattooing (although prohibited in most institutions) is a very common practice[12] and illicit drug use probably takes place as well to some extent; and 4) Studies conducted within various institutions conclude that a small proportion of inmates are sexually assaulted during incarceration (see Bowker, 1980: 2-3).

Disadvantages

Civil libertarians are opposed to the practice of segregation except for valid medical reasons or in cases involving protective custody. They argue that because HIV is not spread through casual contact, separate facilities are not necessary. In fact, the CDC opposes special housing for AIDS patients except when medically necessary. Critics contend that institutional segregation undermines the basic public health message that AIDS is not transmitted except through intimate contact.

Opponents of this practice also express concern because infected inmates are often placed in substandard living quarters and denied an opportunity to participate in certain work assignments, rehabilitation, and recreation programs or to be eligible for work release. Furthermore, because these prisoners are excluded from many institutional programs, they frequently also lose the opportunity to earn "good time" credit toward eventual release.

The problem of false-negative HIV test results has already been noted. Vaid (1987) has suggested that a policy of mandatory testing and segregation could actually be counter-productive for this reason. Because individuals who remained in the general prison population would be perceived as HIV-free, inmates might be encouraged to continue engaging in high-risk behavior due to the mistaken notion that all infectious persons had been placed in isolation. Furthermore, such a policy could conceivably place seropositive inmates in greater jeopardy as well. Believing that they have little to lose, these individuals might continue to engage in risky activities. However, it is possible that repeated exposure to the virus may increase the likelihood that a seropositive individual will eventually develop full-blown AIDS (Gostin, 1986: 11).

Segregation raises other problems as well. Critics note that it can become very expensive. In those jurisdictions that have a large number of infected inmates, this policy may require the development of what is, in fact, a second corrections system. Officials may be required to duplicate many existing institutional programs. As the number of cases continues to grow over the next few years, this could become an administrative nightmare.

Clearly, correctional administrators have a legal as well as an ethical responsibility to pursue policies that minimize the transmission of HIV within the institution. However, it is questionable whether a blanket policy of segregation is the best way to accomplish this objective. As an alternative, prisons and jail administrators could reduce the incidence of high-risk behavior through such steps as increased supervision, hiring more correctional officers, intensive educational programs, and harsh penalties for sexual assault (Vaid, 1987: 238). In addition, the classification process can be used to identify inmates who are likely to engage in predatory behavior as well as those who are likely to be victimized. Bowker (1980: 11) notes that the latter are "more likely to be middle class, young, inexperienced, convicted of minor property offenses, and slight of build." This is an important piece of information for correctional officials who wish to place potentially vulnerable prisoners under special supervision.

Current Policy

Policies regarding segregation vary greatly among state correctional systems. Inmates with full-blown AIDS are more likely to be segregated than either ARC cases or seropositive individuals. Only 10 percent of state/federal prison systems and 18 percent of city/county jail systems continue to isolate[13] all three categories (Hammett, 1988: 86). In fact, there is a clear trend away from blanket segregation. The number of jurisdictions that are making decisions on a case-by-case basis has increased sharply over previous years. More correctional facilities are now making housing determinations based on medical, behavioral, and security considerations.

Distribution of Condoms

Another important decision that correctional administrators must confront is the issue of condom distribution.[14] Because condoms can reduce the risk of HIV infection, many educational campaigns outside the prison have emphasized the use of condoms as a means of avoiding exposure to the virus. Such campaigns have often been controversial with critics charging that they encourage people to engage in casual sexual activity. The debate over "safer sex" vs. abstinence is even more intense in the area of corrections. Although most correctional systems allow inmates to be provided with "safer sex" information (generally through outside speakers), only New York City, Mississippi, and Vermont actually make condoms available for use by inmates within the institution[15] (Hammett, 1988: 92). Jail officials in Philadelphia and San Francisco are currently considering this step (Criminal Justice Newsletter, 7/1/88: 5).

Advantages

Advocates of condom distribution assert that homosexual behavior is a fact of life in many institutions and that officials should give inmates access to these devices as a means of protecting them from disease. It is asserted that such conduct will occur despite the best efforts of policy makers and administrators to eliminate sexual activity within the institution. Furthermore, they point to desperate attempts by inmates who "are fashioning makeshift condoms out of trash can liners, bread wrappers and other plastic bags" in an attempt to protect their health (Criminal Justice Newsletter, 7/1/88: 5).

Disadvantages

Critics of condom distribution note that sexual activity is prohibited within institutions and that many states have statutes which criminalize homosexual behavior. They argue that this step would imply tacit approval of such conduct by correctional administrators. There is also concern about how the public might react as well as fear that inmates might use condoms to make weapons or hide contraband (Hammett, 1988: 92). Finally, there is the question of whether condoms actually offer significant protection against HIV infection during anal intercourse (CDC, 3/11/88: 136).

Those jurisdictions that have chosen to distribute condoms report few problems. New York City has not experienced any cases in which inmates used condoms to make weapons or conceal contraband (Hammett, 1988: 92). Inmates receive condoms from medical personnel who must dispense AIDS information and counseling with regard to "safer sex" along with these prophylactic devices (Criminal Justice Newsletter, 7/1/88: 6). The same policy is followed by Vermont officials. Mississippi, on the other hand, allows these items to be sold in the prison commissary (Greenspan, 1988: 9).

Release of Persons with AIDS

Denial of Parole

How should persons with AIDS be treated with respect to parole? Sometimes, correctional officials hear arguments that infected inmates should be denied release on parole (Vaid, 1987: 250). It is asserted that such persons present a serious danger to the health of others and that the state has an obligation to protect its citizens from infection. However, others assert that to deny parole solely on medical grounds would constitute punishment based on illness and therefore violate the Constitution (Robinson v. California, 1962).[16] Because HIV is not transmitted through casual contact, persons in the community could protect themselves by not engaging in the types of high-risk behavior that spread this disease. Following this line of reasoning, it would be inappropriate to deny release to a convicted sex offender who was infected with the virus. These parolees would pose no greater risk to the public than the one million other seropositives already in the population.

Early Release

Others have advanced another argument—that inmates with AIDS who present no danger to the community should be eligible for early release from prison. Recently, the New York State Division of Parole announced that 50 prisoners who were seriously ill with this disease had been released as soon as they had become eligible for parole (Sullivan, 3/7/87: 1). Under this policy, release is not automatic; inmates must demonstrate evidence of good conduct and not present a danger to the community. The state argues that this policy demonstrates compassion toward those who are terminally ill.

Although most jurisdictions with a large number of institutional AIDS cases have not followed the lead of New York, there are several reasons why correctional administrators may wish to consider this approach. For example, the cost of treatment for prisoners with AIDS is quite high and inmates are not eligible for medicaid reimbursement or social security disability. As a consequence, correctional systems which must care for many individuals with AIDS will face enormous budgetary pressures. Second, there is the issue of whether prisons and jails can provide satisfactory medical care. Gido and Gaunay (1987) have concluded that inmates with AIDS in New York survive, on the average, less than half as long as such patients on the outside (p. 28). This raises the question of whether institutions are able to provide the kinds of treatment that these patients require. Third, there is also a humanitarian consideration. Should gravely ill individuals who pose no risk to the community be forced to spend their final days in prison, isolated from family and friends?

Conditions of Parole

The HIV epidemic poses other parole-related issues as well. Specifically, may a parolee who continues to engage in high-risk behavior be subject to revocation for this reason? On the one hand, it can be asserted that the purpose of parole is to prevent the commission of additional crimes and that revocation under these circumstances is therefore inappropriate. However, others argue that the purpose of parole is to protect the community, regardless of the nature of the threat. This debate is complicated by the fact that twelve states have enacted statutes which make it a crime to expose another person to HIV (Weisenhaus, 8/1/88: 1). Is it therefore appropriate to revoke parole for this behavior only in those jurisdictions?

Disclosure

Finally, there is the question of disclosure. What obligation does a parole officer have to notify a spouse or sex partner that a releasee is infected with HIV? This is similar to the dilemma that currently confronts physicians. Does the well-being of others outweigh the need to protect patient confidentiality? Clearly, there is no simple answer. In some states, there are statutes that prevent disclosure of HIV test results to third parties. Parole officials in these jurisdictions can protect the health of persons who may be at risk by counseling inmates that they have an ethical obligation to notify all potential sex or needle partners of their HIV status.

HIV and the Corrections Officer

Three consecutive surveys of correctional institutions reveal that not a single staff member has become infected through his or her work (Hammett, 1988: 15). Nonetheless, correctional officers have often expressed a great deal of fear that their employment places them at increased risk of contracting this life-threatening ailment. Incidents have been reported in which staff members refused to perform assigned tasks (e.g. transport a seropositive inmate) because they feared infection. Some officers working in AIDS units have demanded hazardous duty pay and/or reduced working hours (Hammett, 1988: 106). In Maryland, an association representing correctional officers has filed a lawsuit seeking to compel the mandatory testing of all inmates and the disclosure of all seropositive results to staff working in the institution (Criminal Justice Newsletter, 7/15/88: 4).

It has been alleged that the following types of situations could place correctional officers in jeopardy: 1) contact with infected blood as a result of actions taken to terminate a fight among inmates; 2) being bitten or spat upon by an infected prisoner; or 3) a puncture wound from a sharp object in the course of a search. Examination of the facts regarding HIV transmission suggests that it is highly unlikely that any staff member will become infected under any of these circumstances.

Because AIDS is a blood-borne disease, some correctional officers argue that they may be at risk as a result of actions taken to break up fights. If one of the participants who is bleeding is seropositive and if the staff member has an open sore, there is a theoretical possibility that transmission could occur in this manner. However, the fact remains that we are one decade into the AIDS epidemic and there are no documented cases in which this has happened. Clearly, the risk posed by such incidents is more theoretical than real. Correctional officers who follow recommended CDC procedures (e.g., bandaging open sores, wearing latex gloves when contact with blood is expected, etc.) have little reason to be concerned.

HIV has been isolated not only in blood, but in saliva as well. For this reason, it might appear that spitting or biting incidents pose a real danger of infection. However, this is not the case. For one thing, the virus cannot pass through intact skin. Second, because the level of HIV present in saliva is minuscule, it has been estimated that one quart would have to enter the bloodstream for infection to occur (Hammett, 1988: 16). Not surprisingly, there are no reported cases in which transmission has occurred through either biting[17] or spitting (Hammett, 1988b: 2).

Needlesticks and puncture wounds are another source of anxiety for correctional officers. Because staff members often conduct searches of areas hidden from public view, there is concern regarding cuts or punctures that result from needles or other sharp objects that are contaminated with blood. Correctional officers must be trained to conduct such searches with great care. Whenever possible, flashlights should be utilized to eliminate the necessity of placing hands or fingers in darkened areas. Inmates should be required to empty their own pockets during body searches. In addition, officers should always wear gloves during cell or body searches. Although gloves do not offer complete protection from cuts, correctional personnel can take comfort from the fact that the risk of transmission associated with needlesticks is extremely low. Studies of health care workers indicate that less than one percent of those persons who prick themselves with HIV contaminated needles actually become infected (Friedland and Klein, 1987: 1127).

Correctional officers face far less danger from AIDS than from stab wounds or other risky aspects of their job. Thus, it is incumbent upon administrators to provide all staff (and inmates) with accurate information regarding the nature of this virus. Educational material must not only explain how AIDS is transmitted, but how it is not transmitted as well. In addition, correctional officers should be trained to follow the recommended CDC guidelines for avoiding infection. These precautions include keeping all wounds properly bandaged, the use of gloves when contact with blood or other body fluids is expected and careful cleaning up of spills of blood or body fluids (CDC, 11/15/85).

Certain jurisdictions have gone well beyond these recommended procedures. Some institutions have placed restrictions on work assignments that are available to infected inmates. Others require these individuals to use separate shower or toilet facilities (Hammett, 1987: 55). Alabama insists that seropositive prisoners wear surgical masks whenever they leave their cells and that they use alcohol or ammonia to clean the telephone receiver after each use (Criminal Justice Newsletter, 5/16/88: 1). Not only are such restrictions unnecessary, they may also increase the level of anxiety by undermining the basic educational message that HIV is not transmitted through casual contact.

Legal Issues

Numerous lawsuits have been filed that raise issues related to the correctional management of AIDS. Most have been initiated by inmates, a smaller number by correctional officers, and in a few instances, by unions who represent staff members. In some suits, inmates have demanded that all fellow prisoners be tested for AIDS or that seropositive individuals be segregated from the general population. Others have been filed by infected inmates challenging either differential treatment within the institution or denial of certain privileges. Numerous other issues have been litigated as well. Unfortunately, a discussion of the entire range of cases is beyond the scope of this article.

Almost all suits have been decided in favor of correctional authorities. Infected inmates have lost cases that sought to overturn the following institutional practices: segregation (*Cordero v. Coughlin*, 1985); disqualification from work release programs (*Marsh v. Alabama Department of Corrections*, 1987); denial of conjugal visits (*Doe v. Coughlin*, 1986); denial of outside exercise (*Macke v. Cowles*, 1987); and exclusion from a community work program (*Williams v. Sumner*, 1986). Correctional officials have also prevailed in cases in which inmates seeking protection from HIV sought to impose mandatory screening (*Jarret v. Faulkner*), separation of infected prisoners (*LaRocca v. Dalsheim*, 1983), and an end to the sharing of kitchen utensils, toilet facilities, clothing and bed linen with infected inmates (*Wiedman v. Rogers* and *Mayberry v. Martin*). Clearly, the latter case demonstrates ignorance with respect to how AIDS is transmitted.

An issue that has concerned administrators since the beginning of the AIDS crisis is the question of civil liability for transmission within the institution. To date, few cases have addressed this issue and no court has awarded damages for this reason. Because the virus is transmitted almost exclusively through sexual activity or needle-sharing, it is highly unlikely that inmates would prevail under these circumstances. As previously noted, judges and juries are likely to take the view that inmates engage in such activities at their own risk. Indeed, this outcome is most probable if administrators have undertaken extensive educational programs to insure that inmates are knowledgeable with respect to the dangers posed by unsafe sex or needle-sharing. For this reason, AIDS education is necessary not only to reduce needless anxiety on the part of inmates and staff, but to minimize the risk of civil liability as well.

In previous cases, correctional employees have been forced to pay damages arising from homosexual rapes which occurred as a result of reckless or callous disregard for inmate safety by a member of the staff

(*Smith v. Wade*, 1983). Because administrators are required to adhere to a standard of reasonable care in protecting inmates, it is imperative that officials take steps to minimize the likelihood that such incidents will occur. Although it may be difficult to prove that HIV infection resulted from a particular sexual assault, inmates making this claim would have a much stronger case than would inmates who engaged in consensual sexual activity.

The Future

The years to come will bring with them many more cases of full-blown AIDS within the nation's prisons and jails. If the epidemic continues on its present path, jurisdictions that currently have relatively few inmates with AIDS will be confronted with a large increase in the number of reported cases. Indeed, the geographic distribution of AIDS patients in correctional institutions is less uneven than it was several years ago. This trend will continue, although those correctional systems in the mid-Atlantic region will probably still account for a disproportionate share of institutional cases.

The future impact of this epidemic on corrections, in all probability, will be shaped by events that take place outside the institution. For example, policy makers may decide to distribute clean needles to IV drug addicts. This step could contribute to a significantly lower rate of new HIV infection among intravenous drug users. Because almost all inmates with AIDS have been infected through IV drug use, the number of future AIDS cases in the nation's prisons and jails could be greatly reduced as a result of this step.

Advances in medical science also have the potential to change the picture. It is conceivable that researchers will discover a drug that prevents asymptomatic seropositives from developing ARC or full-blown AIDS. This would greatly lessen the severity of the epidemic and its impact on the correctional system. Another hope is that additional treatments will become available. Although this would prolong life expectancy for AIDS patients, correctional systems might be confronted with even higher medical costs and, as survival rates improved, more current cases of full-blown AIDS to manage.

Finally, there is a feature of the AIDS epidemic that is not likely to change. In the early 1980s, medical researchers learned how HIV is transmitted (i.e., sexual contact, needle-sharing, contaminated blood and perinatally). No evidence of additional modes of transmission have been discovered since that time. Because scientists do not expect to learn anything new in this regard, it is clear that we currently possess the technical know-how to prevent additional cases of this disease. Regardless of what decisions are reached with respect to mandatory testing and segregation, administrators must give the highest priority to educational campaigns that teach inmates and staff about behaviors that transmit HIV and those that do not. Not only will such information serve to protect these individuals from infection, it will also eliminate much needless anxiety and concern.

Footnotes

[1] The term "seropositive" refers to individuals whose blood test indicates that they have been exposed to Human Immune-Deficiency Virus (HIV), regardless of whether or not they manifest symptoms of illness.

[2] Opportunistic infections are ailments that affect persons with a damaged immune system.

[3] The term "seroprevalence" refers to the proportion of individuals in a specific group who are seropositive.

[4] "Shooting galleries" are locations where drug users gather to "rent" needles and syringes. It is not uncommon for the same equipment to be shared by numerous addicts in a short period of time.

[5] High-risk groups include homosexual/bisexual males, IV drug users and prostitutes (who frequently are IV drug users).

[6] The term "seroconvert" refers to a positive HIV blood status by an individual who formerly was not infected.

[7] Some persons do not develop antibodies until several months after exposure to the virus.

[8] The term "seronegative" refers to those individuals whose HIV blood test indicates that they have *not* been exposed to the virus.

[9] These states include Alabama, Colorado, Georgia, Idaho, Iowa, Missouri, Nebraska, Nevada, New Hampshire, New Mexico, Oklahoma, South Dakota, and West Virginia.

[10] These jurisdictions include Alabama, Idaho, Mississippi, New Hampshire, and West Virginia.

[11] Because AIDS patients have an impaired immune system they sometimes must be isolated to protect them from catching infectious conditions that do not threaten healthy persons.

[12] Although there are no documented cases of HIV transmission as a result of sharing tattoo needles (Vaid, 1987: 239), there is concern that this common practice among inmates may be quite risky.

[13] Segregation does not include those jurisdictions that single-cell infected inmates.

[14] A policy that would generate far more controversy is the distribution of clean needles to inmates. Not only would this create a security problem, it would be a tacit admission that authorities are unable to stop the smuggling of illicit drugs into the institution.

[15] The state of Washington dispenses condoms, but only for conjugal visits. In addition, some jurisdictions provide inmates with condoms upon release (Hammett, 1988: 92).

[16] In *Robinson*, the U.S. Supreme Court invalidated a California statute making narcotics addiction a crime punishable by imprisonment and noted that even one day in jail for the "crime" of having a common cold would constitute cruel and unusual punishment.

[17] In a biting incident, there may be contact with blood. However, it is the assailant who comes in contact with the blood of the victim. Unless the former was bleeding from the mouth, it is highly unlikely that the latter would become infected with HIV.

References

Bowker, Lee H. (1980). *Prison Victimization*. New York: Elsevier.

CDC (Centers for Disease Control—1988). *AIDS Weekly Surveillance Report.* U.S. Public Health Service (June 20).

_____ (1988). "Condoms for Prevention of Sexually Transmitted Disease," *Morbidity and Mortality Weekly Report*. Vol. 37, No. 9 (March 11).

_____ (1987). "Human Immunodeficiency Virus Infection in the United States," *Morbidity and Mortality Weekly Report*. Vol. 36, No. 49 (December 18).

_____ (1985). "Recommendations for Preventing Transmission of Infection with Human T-Lymphotropic Virus Type III/Lymphadenopathy—Associated Virus in the Workplace," *Morbidity and Mortality Weekly Report*. Vol. 34, pp. 681-86.

Corrections Digest (1988). "CDC Funding Study to Measure the Spread of AIDS in U.S. Prison Population" (June 1).

Criminal Justice Newsletter (1988). "Of Inmates from New York City, 15% Show Exposure to AIDS Virus" (April 15).

_____ (1988). "Correctional Health Group Urges No Mass Screening for AIDS" (May 2).

_____ (1988). "ACLU Challenges AIDS Tests and Segregation of Alabama Inmates" (May 16).

_____ (1988). "Condoms for Inmates at Issue in Philadelphia, San Francisco" (July 1).

_____ (1988). "Maryland Correctional Officers Sue for AIDS Testing of Inmates" (July 15).

Friedland, Gerald H., Brian R. Saltzman, Martha F. Rogers et al. (1986). "Lack of Transmission of HTLV-III/LAV Infection to Household Contacts of Patients with AIDS or AIDS-Related Complex with Oral Candidiasis," *The New England Journal of Medicine*. Vol. 314 (February 6).

Friedland, Gerald H. and Robert S. Klein (1987). "Transmission of the Human Immunodeficiency Virus," *The New England Journal of Medicine*. Vol. 317 (October 29).

Gido, Rosemary and William Gaunay (1987). *Acquired Immune Deficiency Syndrome: A Demographic Profile of New York State Inmate Mortalities, 1981-1986*. New York State Commission of Correction (September).

Gostin, Larry (1986). "AIDS Policies Raise Civil Liberties Concerns," *National Prison Project Journal* (Winter), pp. 10-11.

Greenspan, Judy (1988). "NPP Gathers Statistics on AIDS in Prison," *National Prison Project Journal* (Summer), pp. 5-8.

Hammett, Theodore M. (1986). *AIDS in Correctional Facilities: Issues and Options*. National Institute of Justice, Washington, D.C. (April).

_____ (1987) *AIDS in Correctional Facilities: Issues and Options*, 2nd edition. National Institute of Justice, Washington, D.C. (May).

_____ (1988). *AIDS in Correctional Facilities: Issues and Options*, 3rd edition. National Institute of Justice, Washington, D.C. (April).

_____ (1988b). *Precautionary measures and protective equipment: Developing a reasonable response*. National Institute of Justice, Washington, D.C. (January).

Hellinger, Fred J. (1988). "Forecasting the Personal Medical Care Costs of AIDS from 1988 through 1991," *Public Health Reports*. Vol. 103: 3 (May-June).

Institute of Medicine (1986). *Confronting AIDS: Directions for Public Health, Health Care, and Research*. Washington, D.C.: National Academy Press.

Koop, C. Everett (1986). *Surgeon General's Report on Acquired Immune Deficiency Syndrome*. Washington, D.C.: U.S. Public Health Service.

Lui, Kung-Jong, William W. Darrow and George W. Rutherford, III (1988). "A Model-Based Estimate of the Mean Incubation Period for AIDS in Homosexual Men," *Science*. Vol. 240 (June 3).

Masters, William and Virginia Johnson with Robert Kolodny (1988). *Crisis: Hetero-Sexual Behavior in the Age of AIDS*. New York: Grove Press.

Morgan, W. Meade and James W. Curran (1986). "Acquired Immunodeficiency Syndrome: Current and Future Trends," *Public Health Reports*. Vol. 101, No. 5 (September-October).

Nacci, Peter L. and Thomas R. Kane (1983). "The Incidence of Sex and Sexual Aggression in Federal Prisons," *Federal Probation*. Vol. 47, No. 4 (December), pp. 31-36.

Petricciani, John C. and Jay S. Epstein (1988). "The Effects of the AIDS Epidemic on the Safety of the Nation's Blood Supply," *Public Health Reports*. Vol. 103, No. 3 (May-June).

Rosellini, Lynn and Erica E. Goode (1987). "AIDS: When Fear Takes Charge," *U.S. News and World Report*. (October 12), pp. 62-70.

Rothenberg, Richard, Mary Woelfel, Rand Stoneburner, et al. (1987). "Survival with the Acquired Immunodeficiency Syndrome," *The New England Journal of Medicine*. Vol. 317, No. 21 (November 19).

Stengel, Richard (1987). "The Changing Face of AIDS: More and More Victims are Black or Hispanic," *Time*. (August 17), pp. 12-14.

Sullivan, Ronald (1987). "New York State Paroles 50 Men Sick With AIDS," *New York Times*. (March 7), section I, p. 1.

Vaid, Urvashi (1986). "Balanced Response Needed to AIDS in Prison," *National Prison Project Journal*. No. 7 (Spring), pp. 1-5.

_____ (1987). "Prisons." In Burris Dalton and the Yale AIDS Law Project (eds.) *AIDS and the Law: A Guide for the Public*. New Haven, CT: Yale University Press, pp. 235-50.

Weisburd, Stefi (1987). "AIDS Vaccine: The Problems of Human Testing," *Science News*. Vol. 131 No. 21 (May 23).

Weisenhaus, Doreen (1988). "The Shaping of AIDS Law," *The National Law Journal*. Vol. No. 47 (August 1).

Wooden, Wayne S. and Jay Parker (1982). *Men Behind Bars: Sexual Exploitation in Prison*. New York: Plenum Press.

Wormser, Gary P. (1987). "AIDS in Prisons." In Wormser, Stahl and Bottone (eds.) *AIDS and Other Manifestations of HIV Infection*. Park Ridge, NJ: Noyes Publications, pp. 48-66.

Cases

Cordero v. Coughlin, 607 F Supp. 9 (S.D. N.Y. 1985).

Doe v. Coughlin, 509 NYS 2d 209 (N.Y. App. 1986).

Jarret v. Faulkner (S.D. Indiana), No. IP85-1569-C.

LaRocca v. Dalsheim, 120 Misc. 2d 697 (N.Y. 1983).

Macke v. Cowles (W.D. Missouri). Consolidated Cases No. 86-4447-CV-c-5, Magistrate's Report (October 1, 1987).

Marsh v. Alabama Department of Corrections (N.D. Alabama), No. CV-86-HM-5592-NE. (April 10, 1987).

Mayberry v. Martin (E.D., North Carolina), No. 86-341-CRT).

Robinson v. California, 370 U.S. 660 (1962).

Smith v. Wade, 461 U.S. 30 (1983).

Wiedman v. Rogers (E.D., North Carolina), No. C-85-116-G).

Williams v. Sumner (C.D. Nevada, 1986).

37

Privatization of Corrections
Defining the Issues
Ira P. Robbins

Although something must be done about the sordid state of our nation's prisons and jails, we should not permit the purported benefits of privatization to thwart consideration of the broad, difficult policy questions that are involved.

Even as the public is demanding that more criminals be incarcerated and that their sentences be lengthened, the problems of America's prisons and jails continue to plague, if not overwhelm, us. More than two-thirds of the states are currently under court order to correct conditions that violate the United States Constitution's prohibition against cruel and unusual punishment. There many important questions, but there are still no clear, satisfactory answers.

The last few years have thus witnessed diverse, controversial developments. Some, like the voluntary accreditation of correctional facilities by the Commission on Accreditation for Corrections, have begun to take root. Others, like a 1982 proposal in Congress to build an Arctic penitentiary for serious offenders,[1] have been inconsequential. Yet the number of prisons and the cost of housing them still mount. Prison and

Source: Reprinted with permission of the author from *Judicature*, Vol. 69, No. 6 (April-May 1986), 324-331.

jail populations have doubled in a decade, and—with preventive detention, mandatory-minimum sentences, habitual-offender statutes, and the abolition of parole in some jurisdictions—there is no relief in sight. Some states are even leasing or purchasing space in other states. And it is costing the taxpayers approximately $17 million a day to operate the facilities, with estimates ranging up to $60 a day per inmate. Several commentators have not so facetiously noted that we could finance college educations at less cost for all of the inmates in the country.

To reduce some of this stress on the system, a new concept has emerged: the privatization of corrections, occasionally known as "prisons for profit." The idea is to remove the operation (and sometimes the ownership) of an institution from the local, state, or federal government and turn it over to a private corporation.

At the outset, it should be emphasized that private prisons are different from the notion of private *industries* in prison—Chief Justice Burger's "factories with fences" proposal[2]—which seeks to turn prisoners into productive members of society by having them work at a decent wage and produce products or perform services that can be sold in the marketplace. (In the process, the prisoners can also pay some of the costs of their incarceration, and, we would hope, gain some self-esteem.)

Privatization is also different from the situation in which *some* of the services of a facility—such as medical, food, educational, or vocational services—are operated by private industry. Rather, the developing idea, which may turn out to be a lasting force or just a passing fad, is to have the government contract with a private company to run the *total* institution.

Advantages and Criticisms

Privatization has sparked a major debate. Its proponents—including not only some corrections professionals, but also major financial brokers who are advising investors to consider putting their money into private prisons—argue that the government has been doing a dismal job in its administration of correctional institutions. Costs have soared, prisoners are coming out worse off than when they went in, and while they are in they are kept in conditions that shock the conscience, if not the stomach.

The private sector, advocates claim, can save the taxpayers money. It can build facilities faster and cheaper, and it can operate them more economically and more efficiently. With maximum flexibility and little or no bureaucracy, both new ideas (like testing new philosophies) and routine matters (like hiring new staff) can be implemented quickly. Overcrowding — perhaps the major problem of corrections today — can be reduced.

A final — and significant — anticipated benefit of privatization is decreased liability of the government in lawsuits that are brought by inmates and prison employees.

The critics respond on many fronts, beginning with two major constitutional objections: the mere fact that the government would no longer directly be operating the institutions cannot shift liability under the Federal Civil Rights Act, 42 U.S.C. § 1983, pursuant to which most prison-condition litigation is brought; and, in any event, the government does not have the power to delegate to private entities the authority for such a traditional and important governmental function. In brief, critics argue that, to be properly accountable, the government must operate its prisons and jails and be subject to liability.

As a policy matter, moreover, they claim that it is inappropriate to operate prisons with a profit motive, which provides no incentive to reduce overcrowding (especially if the company is paid on a per-prisoner basis), nor to consider alternatives to incarceration, nor to deal with the broader problems of criminal justice. On the contrary, the critics assert that the incentive would be to build more prisons and jails. And if they are built, we will fill them. This is a fact of correctional life: The number of jailed criminals has always risen to fill whatever space is available.

Cost-cutting measures will run rampant. Conditions of confinement will be kept to the minimum that the law requires. As a reporter for *Barron's* has written: "[T]he brokers, architects, builders and banks . . . will make out like bandits."[3] But questions concerning people's freedom should not be contracted out to the lowest bidder. In short, the private sector is more interested in doing well than in doing good. This idea was succinctly expressed recently by the director of program development of Triad America Corporation, a multimillion-dollar Utah-based company that has been considering proposing a privately run county jail in Missoula, Montana: "We'll hopefully make a buck at it. I'm not going to kid any of you and say we are in this for humanitarian reasons."[4]

Privatization also raises concerns about the routine, quasi-judicial decisions that affect the legal status and well-being of the inmates. To what extent, for example, should a private-corporation employee be allowed to use force — perhaps serious or deadly force — against a prisoner? It is difficult enough to control violence in the present public-correctional system. It will be much more difficult to assure that violence is administered only to the extent required by circumstances when the state relinquishes direct responsibility. Another important concern is whether a private employee should be entitled to make recommendations to parole boards, or to bring charges against a prisoner for an institutional violation, possibly resulting in the forfeiture of good-time credits toward release. With dispersion of accountability, the possibility for vindictiveness increases. As an employee who is now in charge of reviewing disciplinary cases at a privately run Immigration and Naturalization Service facility in Houston told a *New York Times* reporter last year: "I'm the Supreme Court."[5]

Finally, the critics claim, the financing arrangements for constructing private facilities improperly eliminate the public from the decision-making process. Traditionally, correctional facilities have been financed through tax-exempt general-obligation bonds that are backed by the tax revenues of the issuing governmental body. This debt requires voter approval. Privatization abrogates this power of the people. In Jefferson County, Colorado, for example, the voters twice rejected a jail-bond issue before E.F. Hutton underwrote a $30 million issue for private-jail construction.[6] The corporation can build the institution and the government can lease it. The cost of the facility then comes out of the government's appropriation, avoiding the politically difficult step of raising debt ceilings. Once the lease payments have fulfilled the debt, ownership of the facility shifts to the governmental body.[7] This position was acknowledged by Senator Alfonse D'Amato (R-N.Y.),[8] who proposed a bill in 1984 to provide federal investment and rehabilitation tax credits and accelerated-depreciation deductions for private-prison construction.[9]

One example of the potentially egregious effects of reducing accountability and regulation concerns a proposal by a private firm in Pennsylvania to build a 720-bed medium- and maximum-security interstate protective-custody facility on a toxic-waste site, which it had purchased for $1. The spokesperson for the Pennsylvania Department of Corrections is reported to have said: "If it were a state facility, we certainly would be concerned about the grounds where the facility is located. [As for a private prison, there] is nothing in our legislation which gives anyone authority on what to do."[10] In the face of proposed legislation in Pennsylvania to place a one-year moratorium on the construction or operation of private prisons, the company has since abandoned its plan. It reportedly is now attempting to sell the toxic-waste site for $790,000, and is seeking to open the protective-custody facility in Idaho.[11]

Constitutional Issues

The relative advantages and disadvantages of privatization are not merely academic, for more than 30 institutions—immigration, juvenile, work-release, and halfway-house facilities—are now owned and operated by private groups. Further, a few of the above issues have preliminarily been litigated.

There are two major constitutional questions regarding the privatization of corrections: whether the acts of a private entity operating a correctional institution constitute "state action," thus allowing for liability under 42 U.S.C. § 1983; and whether, in any event, delegation of the corrections function to a private entity is itself constitutional. In this section, I shall address the caselaw pertaining to these questions.

State Action

When a private party, as compared with a government employee, is charged with abridging rights guaranteed by the Constitution or laws of the United States, the plaintiff, in order to prevail under 42 U.S.C. § 1983, must show that the private party was acting "under color of state law." The reason for this is fundamental. The Fifth and Fourteenth Amendments, which prohibit the government from denying federal constitutional rights and which guarantee due process of law, apply to the acts of the state and the federal governments, and not to the acts of private parties or entities.[12]

The ultimate issue in determining whether a person is subject to suit for violation of an individual's constitutional rights is whether "the alleged infringement of federal rights [is] 'fairly attributable to the State.'"[13] A person acts under color of state law "only when exercising 'power possessed by virtue of state law and made possible only because the wrongdoer is clothed with the authority of state law.'"[14]

Three basic tests have been used to determine "state action":[15] the public-function test; the close-nexus test; and the state-compulsion test. State action will be held to exist if any one of these tests is satisfied. I believe that, in the private-prison context, *each* of these tests for state action is satisfied.

Public-Function test. The case that is perhaps most directly relevant to state action in the private-prison context is *Medina v. O'Neill.*[16] Sixteen inmates of the privately run Houston Immigration and Naturalization Service facility who had been confined in a single, windowless, 12-by-20-foot cell that was designed to hold six persons sued the private corporation and the INS. Another issue in the case was that one private security guard, who had not been trained in the use of firearms, had been using a shotgun as a cattle prod when the gun went off, killing one inmate and seriously wounding another.

The plaintiffs claimed that they had been unconstitutionally deprived of life and liberty, arguing, *inter alia*, that the INS had a duty to oversee their detention and that the defendant's failure to do so constituted state action. In opposition, the federal defendants contended that at all times the plaintiffs were in the custody of the private company, and, therefore, that the problems stemming from the plaintiffs' detention arose from purely private acts. Thus, the defendants averred that there was no state action.

The federal district court, in 1984, rejected the defendants' argument, finding "obvious state action" on the part of both the federal defendants and the private company.[17] The court noted that, although there was no precise formula for defining state action,[18] the Supreme Court has recognized a "public function" concept, which provides that state action exists when the state delegates to private parties a power "traditionally exclusively reserved to the State."[19] As the Supreme Court stated in 1982 in *Rendell-Baker v. Kohn*,[20] "the relevant question is not simply whether a private group is serving a 'public function'. . ., [but] whether the function performed has been 'traditionally the *exclusive* prerogative of the State.'"[21] The *Medina* court found that detention came squarely within this test.

More recently, in August 1985, the United States Court of Appeals for the Eleventh Circuit, in *Ancata v. Prison Health Services, Inc.*,[22] addressed the question whether a private entity that was responsible for providing medical care to county jail inmates was liable, under section 1983, to the estate of a deceased county-jail prisoner who, following recalcitrance and improper diagnosis and treatment by doctors of the private health service, was diagnosed as having leukemia. Finding the state action issue so well settled as not to require extended discussion, the unanimous court of appeals panel stated:

> Although Prison Health Services and its employees are not strictly speaking public employees, state action is clearly present. Where a function which is traditionally the exclusive prerogative of the state (or here, county) is performed by a private entity, state action is present.[23]

Close-nexus test. Another standard that enlightens state-action jurisprudence is the "close-nexus" test. The inquiry here is "whether there is a sufficiently close nexus between the State and the challenged action . . . so that the action of the latter may be fairly treated as that of the State itself."[24]

A good example of the application of this test is *Milonas v. Williams*.[25] The plaintiffs, former students of a school for youths with behavior problems, brought an action against the school on the ground that it had used a "behavior modification" program that allegedly violated their constitutional rights. Specifically, the plaintiffs claimed that the school administrators, acting under color of state law, had caused them to be subjected to antitherapeutic and inhumane treatment, resulting in violations of the cruel and unusual punishment clause of the Eighth Amendment and the due process clause of the Fourteenth Amendment.

The unanimous panel of the court of appeals found state action, because "the state ha[d] so insinuated itself with the [school] as to be considered a joint participant in the offending actions."[26] The court made this determination after considering the following factors: many of the plaintiffs had been placed at the school involuntarily by juvenile courts and other state agencies acting alone or with the consent of the parents; detailed contracts were drawn up by the school administrators and agreed to by many local school districts that placed boys at the school; there was significant state funding of tuition; and there was extensive state regulation of the educational program at the school. These facts "demonstrate[d] that there was a sufficiently close nexus between the state sending boys to the school and the conduct of the school authorities so as to support a claim under Section 1983."[27]

Application of the close-nexus test to the private-prison context should yield the same result, especially considering, among other factors, the involuntary nature of the confinement, the detailed nature of the contracts between the government and the private entities, the level of government funding,[28] and the extent of state regulation of policies and programs.[29]

State-compulsion test. Like the public-function test and the close-nexus test, the state-compulsion test can also result in improper state action, in violation of 42 U.S.C. § 1983. The inquiry is whether the state had a clear duty to provide the services in question.

In *Lombard v. Eunice Kennedy Shriver Center*,[30] for example, the plaintiff—a mentally retarded person who was a resident of a state institution that had contracted with a private organization for medical services—sued under 42 U.S.C. § 1983, alleging that he had been denied adequate medical care, that he had been subjected to inappropriate medical treatment, and that his property had been improperly managed. The defendants contended that, because the private organization that provided all of the medical care about which the plaintiff complained was a private entity, the state could not be held accountable for the acts of the private corporation and, further, that the corporation could not be held responsible for not conforming with constitutional and statutory requirements that are applicable only to governmental entities. In short, the issue was "whether the acts and omissions of the [private entity] constitute[d] state action for purposes of the Fourteenth Amendment, and whether [it] acted 'under color of law' for the purposes of 42 U.S.C. § 1983."[31]

The court responded to these questions in the affirmative, stating that "[t]he critical factor in our decision is the duty of the state to provide adequate medical services to those whose personal freedom is restricted because they reside in state institutions."[32] The court added:

> [I]t would be an empty formalism to treat the [private entity] as anything but the equivalent of a governmental agency for the purposes of 42 U.S.C. § 1983. Whether the physician is directly on the state payroll. . . or paid indirectly by contract, the dispositive issue concerns the trilateral relationship among the state, the private defendant, and the plaintiff. Because the state bore an affirmative obligation to provide adequate medical care to plaintiff, because the state delegated that function to the [private corporation], and because [that corporation] voluntarily assumed that obligation by contract, [the private entity] must be considered to have acted under color of law, and its acts and omissions must be considered actions of the state. For if [the private entity] were not held so responsible, the state could avoid its constitutional obligations simply by delegating governmental functions to private entities.[33]

The foregoing statement virtually summarizes the experiences of the courts on the question of whether the acts of private entities performing functions that are delegated by the state constitute state action. In the context of detention—whether in a prison, a jail, an immigration facility, a juvenile facility, or a mental-health center—the answer is clearly affirmative.

Delegation

In *Ancata v. Prison Health Services*[34]—which involved the contracting out by the county of the provision of medical care to incarcerated individuals—the United States Court of Appeals for the Eleventh Circuit recently stated:

> Although [the private entity] has contracted to perform an obligation owed by the county, the county itself remains liable for any constitutional deprivations caused by the policies or customs of the [private entity]. In that sense, the county's duty is non-delegable.[35]

In other words, there is an area of overlap between state action and the propriety of a delegation of governmental powers: Government liability cannot be reduced or eliminated by delegating the governmental function to a private entity. But the non-delegation doctrine goes further than that, holding that some governmental functions may not be delegated *at all*. Whether the privatization of corrections would be held invalid under that doctrine is debatable; certainly the answer to that question is less clear than is the answer to the question whether such a delegation constitutes state action.

The Constitution provides that "[a]ll legislative Powers herein granted shall be vested in a Congress of the United States. . . ."[36] Strictly interpreted, this clause prohibits Congress from delegating its legislative powers to any other institution.[37] Due to societal changes, advances, and complexities, however, a strict adherence to the doctrine of non-delegation is not possible.[38] Practicality necessitates that many of the comprehensive regulations that are required by modern life be delegated, for they are often too intricate and detailed for the direct legislative process. Thus, Congress—under the "necessary and proper" clause of the Constitution[39]—can "delegate authority . . . sufficient to effect its purposes."[40] But *which* purposes? Can the governmental functions of incarcerating, punishing, deterring, and rehabilitating criminals constitutionally be delegated to private entities?

Historically, the Supreme Court expressed an antipathy to the delegation of policymaking responsibility to private organizations.[41] Although it has been suggested that the continued vitality of this position is suspect,[42] as the doctrine has not been employed to invalidate a delegation in more than 50 years (with similar experience in many states),[43] the doctrine at the least retains important influence by requiring that Congress provide an articulation of policy along with any delegation of authority. This requirement not only limits agency excesses, but it also facilitates the practicality of judicial review of agency action.[44] Nevertheless, it may be that, with a sufficiently broad delegation of a traditionally exclusive governmental function, the doctrine might be used once again.

In many areas, the courts have regularly allowed private entities to exercise authority that could be characterized as amounting to a deprivation of a property or liberty interest.[45] The area of family law provides a familiar example.[46] And it is also true that, even in areas that are traditionally thought of as belonging in the realm of public rather than private decisionmaking, courts have tolerated broad delegation of lawmaking power to private bodies.[47]

There comes a point, however, where concerns about the fairness of decisionmaking that affects the interests of individuals in what is so clearly a governmental function must outweigh the need for unchanneled exercises of expertise and claims of efficiency and reduced cost.[48] Whether that point is reached with privatization of corrections is a very difficult question, without any good, clear, recent help from the caselaw. Even if such a delegation is constitutional, however, that does not necessarily mean that it is wise to transfer this most basic function of government—the doing of justice—to private hands.[49]

Other Important Questions

Although there has been litigation on some of the issues that are likely to be raised concerning the privatization of corrections, the concept has yet to be fully tested, for there are presently no primary medium- or maximum-security adult facilities in the country that are owned or operated by private bodies.

Such adult correctional facilities are different from juvenile, immigration, work-release, and halfway-house facilities. Juvenile facilities, for example, typically require only minimum security, while adult institutions can range from minimum to maximum security. As a result, higher costs for security may be incurred by the private contractor. As the security level increases, so too will concern for escapes, assaults, and prison discipline. Moreover, the special problems of long-term confinement must be considered, for the length of imprisonment in an adult facility is certain to be much longer than the length of stay in a juvenile, detention, or INS facility. Further, the political climate surrounding an adult facility will usually involve stronger public opposition, since the inmates will pose more of a threat to the immediate community. This opposition could delay, as well as increase the cost of, plans to contract with the private sector. For these reasons and others, notwithstanding the claims of proponents of privatization, it may be that lower cost is not an advantage of privatization for adult primary institutions.[50]

If the concept of privatization of corrections does take hold, however, we should move slowly and cautiously, for statutes may have to be amended or repealed, and comprehensive contracts will have to be drafted narrowly and unambiguously. Among the many questions, both general and specific, that will have to be confronted are the following:

What standards will govern the operation of the institution?

Who will monitor the implementation of the standards?

Will the public still have access to the facility?

What recourse will members of the public have if they do not approve of how the institution is operated?

Who will be responsible for maintaining security and using force at the institution?

Who will be responsible for maintaining security if the private personnel go on strike?

Where will the responsibility for prison disciplinary procedures lie? For example, will private personnel be permitted involvement in quasi-judicial decisions, including not only questions concerning good-time credit, but also recommendations to parole boards?

Will the company be able to refuse to accept certain inmates—such as those who have contracted AIDS?

What options will be available to the government if the corporation substantially raises its fees?

What safeguards will prevent a private contractor from making a low initial bid to obtain a contract, then raising the price after the government is no longer immediately able to reassume the task of operating the prisons (for example, due to a lack of adequately trained personnel)?

What will happen if the company declares bankruptcy (for example, because of liability arising from a prison riot), or simply goes out of business because there is not enough profit?

What safeguards will prevent private vendors, after gaining a foothold in the corrections field, from lobbying for philosophical changes for their greater profit?

Questions like these present some hard choices—but ones that will have to be addressed if we should seriously move toward the private ownership and operation of correctional institutions.

Symbolism: The Hidden Issue

In its 1985 policy statement on privatization, the American Correctional Association began: "Government has the ultimate authority and responsibility for corrections."[51] This should be undeniable. When it enters a judgment of conviction and imposes a sentence, a court exercises its authority, both actually and symbolically. Does it weaken that authority, however—as well as the integrity of a system of *justice*—when an inmate looks at his keeper's uniform and, instead of encountering an emblem that reads "Federal Bureau of Prisons" or "State Department of Corrections," he faces one that says "Acme Corrections Company"?

This symbolic question may be the most difficult policy issue of all for privatization: Who *should* operate our prisons and jails—apart from questions of cost, apart from questions of efficiency, apart from questions of liability, and assuming that prisoners and detainees will retain no fewer rights and privileges than they had before the transfer to private management? In an important sense, this is really part of the constitutional-delegation issue, in that it could be argued that virtually anything that is done in a total, secure institution by the government or its designee is an expression of government policy, and therefore should not be delegated.[52] I cannot help but wonder what Dostoevsky — who wrote that "[t]he degree of civilization in a society can be judged by entering its prisons"[53] — would have thought about privatization of corrections.

Further, just as the prisoner should perhaps be obliged to know — day by day, minute by minute — that he is in the custody of the state, perhaps too the state should be obliged to know — also day by day, minute by minute — that it alone is its brother's keeper, even with all of its flaws. To expect any less of the criminal-justice system may simply be misguided.

Conclusion

We should not be swayed by brash claims, such as the one by a private-facility owner who told a *New York Times* reporter: "I offer to forfeit my contracts if the recidivism rate is more than 40 percent."[54] Nor should we be fooled by the "halo effect" — that is, that the first few major experiments will be temporarily attractive because the private administrators, being observed very closely, will be under great pressure to perform. Prison operation is not a short-term business. We should further be wary that private-corrections corporations may initiate advertising campaigns to make the public feel more fearful of crime than it already is, in order to fill the prisons and jails. Finally, and most importantly, we should not permit the purported benefits of prison privatization to thwart, in the name of convenience, consideration of the broader, and more difficult, problems of criminal justice.

To be sure, something *must* be done about the sordid state of our nation's prisons and jails. The urgency of the need, however, should not interfere with the caution that must accompany a decision to delegate to private companies one of government's most basic responsibilities — controlling the lives and living conditions of those whose freedom has been taken in the name of the government and the people. At the least, the debate over privatization of corrections may provide an incentive for government to perform its incarceration function better.

Referring to privatization, the Director of the National Institute of

Justice recently stated: "[W]hen we have opportunities to do things more efficiently and more flexibly without in any way harming the public interest, we would be foolish not to explore them to the fullest." [55] What the public interest is, however, and where day-to-day government power should reside, are questions that are too important to leave only to criminal-justice professionals and academics. Whatever direction we may take on privatization, we must generate a thoughtful and deliberate review of the complex issues that are involved, for resolution of these issues will say a great deal about how we, as a society, wish to be perceived. To rush toward privatization, therefore, is clearly inappropriate.

Footnotes

[1] See H.R. 7112, 97th Cong., 2d Sess. (1982) ("Arctic penitentiary Act of 1982") (introduced by Rep. Leboutillier).

[2] Keynote Address by Warren E. Burger, National Conference on "Factories with Fences": The Prison Industries Approach to Correctional Dilemmas (June 18, 1984), reprinted in Robbins, ed., Prisoners and the Law ch. 21 (New York, NY: Clark Boardman, 1985).

[3] Duffy, Breaking Into Jail, Barron's, May 14, 1984, at 20, 22.

[4] Deseret News, June 20-21, 1985, at B7 (statement of Jack Lyman); see also infra n. 50.

[5] New York Times, Feb. 19, 1985, at A15 (statement of Corrections Corporation of America employee John Robinson).

[6] Rosenberg, Who Says Crime Doesn't Pay?, Jericho, Spring 1984, at 1, 4; see also National Institute of Justice, The Privatization of Corrections 45 (Washington, DC: U. S. Government Printing Office, 1985).

[7] See National Institute of Justice, supra n. 6, at 40-50.

[8] See New York Times, Feb. 17, 1985, at A29.

[9] See S. 2933, 98th Cong., 2d Sess. (1984) ("Prison Construction Privatization Act of 1984"). Senator D'Amato has stated that, although he supports the private ownership of prisons, he does not support their private operation. See New York Times, Feb. 17, 1985, at A29.

[10] Levine, "Private Prison Planned on Toxic Waste Site," National Prison Project Journal, Fall 1985, at 10, 11.

[11] See Elvin, "Private Prison Plans Dropped by Buckingham," National Prison Project Journal, Winter 1985, at 11. On March 21, 1986, Pennsylvania Governor Dick Thornburgh signed a bill imposing a 15-month moratorium on private prisons, to allow a panel to study the issues. See New York Times, Mar. 23, 1986, at 16; New York Times, Mar. 20, 1986, at A22.

[12] See Shelley v. Kraemer, 334 U.S. 1, 13 (1948); Civil Rights Cases, 109 U.S. 3, 11 (1883).

[13] Rendell-Baker v. Kohn, 457 U.S. 830, 838 (1982) (quoting Lugar v. Edmondson Oil Co., 457 U.S. 922, 937 (1982)). The Supreme Court in Lugar found state action when state officers had acted jointly with a private creditor to secure the plaintiff's property by garnishment and prejudgment attachment.

14 *Polk County v. Dodson*, 454 U.S. 312, 317-18 (1981) (quoting *United States v. Classic*, 313 U.S. 299, 326 (1941)); *see also Evans v. Newton*, 382 U.S. 296. 299 (1966).
15 The constitutional standard for finding state action is identical to the statutory standard for determining "color of state law." *See Lugar v. Edmondson Oil Co.*, 457 U.S. 922, 929 (1982).
16 589 F. Supp. 1028 (S.D. Tex. 1984).
17 *Id.* at 1038.
18 *See Burton v. Wilmington Park Auth.*, 365 U.S. 715, 722 (1961).
19 *Flagg Bros., Inc. v. Brooks*, 436 U.S. 149, 157 (1978); *see also Jackson v. Metropolitan Edison Co.*, 419 U.S. 345, 352 (1974).
20 457 U.S. 830 (1982).
21 *Id.* at 842 (quoting *Jackson v. Metropolitan Edison Co.*, 419 U.S. 345, 353 (1974)).
22 769 F.2d 700 (11th Cir. 1985).
23 *Id.* at 703; *see also Lawyer v. Kernodle*, 721 F.2d 632 (8th Cir. 1983) (private physician hired by county to perform autopsies was acting under color of state law); *Morrison v. Washington County*, 700 F.2d 678 (11th Cir.) (refusing to dismiss physician employed by county from section 1983 action), *cert. denied*, 464 U.S. 864 (1983); *Perez v. Sugarman*, 499 F.2d 761 (2d Cir. 1974) (finding state action for private institution's acts where the City of New York had removed a child from the mother's custody and placed the child in a private child-care institution); *compare Calvert v. Sharp*, 748 F.2d 861 (4th Cir. 1984) (no state action found where private doctor had no supervisory or custodial functions, whose function and obligation was solely to cure orthopedic problems, and who was not dependent on the state for funds), *cert. denied*, 105 S. Ct. 2667 (1985).
24 *Jackson v. Metropolitan Edison Co.*, 419 U.S. 345, 351 (1974).
25 691 F.2d 931 (10th Cir. 1982), *cert. denied*, 460 U.S. 1069 (1983).
26 *Id.* at 940.
27 *Id.*; *see also Woodall v. Partilla*, 581 F. Supp. 1066, 1076 (N.D. Ill. 1984) (finding sufficient nexus between private food corporation and state to constitute state action); *Kentucky Ass'n for Retarded Citizens v. Conn*, 510 F. Supp. 1233, 1250 (W.D. Ky. 1980) (finding sufficient nexus between private residential-treatment center and state), *aff'd*, 674 F.2d 582 (6th Cir.), *cert. denied*, 459 U.S. 1041 (1982); *compare Calvert v. Sharp*, 748 F.2d 861, 863-64 (4th Cir. 1984) (finding insufficient nexus between private doctor and state on the particular facts), *cert. denied*, 105 S. Ct. 2667 (1985).
28 On the question of the private entity's dependence on the state for funds, *see Blum v. Yaretsky*, 457 U.S. 991, 1011 (1982); *Rendell-Baker v. Kohn*, 457 U.S. 830, 841 (1982).
29 On the question of whether the particular function is subject to extensive state regulation, *see Blum v. Yaretsky*, 457 U.S. 991, 1007-08, 1009-10 (1982); *Rendell-Baker v. Kohn*, 547 U.S. 830, 841 (1982).
30 556 F. Supp. 677 (D. Mass. 1983).
31 *Id.* at 678.
32 *Id.*
33 *Id.* at 680.
34 769 F.2d 700 (11th Cir. 1985).
35 *Id.* at 705.
36 U.S. Const. art. I, § 1.
37 *See* Davis, *Administrative Law* § 3.4 (3d ed. 1972).
38 *See* Schwartz, *Administrative Law* § 2.1 (2d ed. 1984).
39 U.S. Const. art. I, § 8, cl. 18.

40 *E.g.. Lichter v. United States*, 334 U.S. 742, 748 (1948).

41 *See A.L.A. Schecter Poultry Corp. v. United States*, 295 U.S. 495, 537 (1935); *see also* Washington *ex rel. Seattle Title Trust Co. v. Roberge*, 278 U.S. 116 (1928).

42 *See, e.g., FPC v. New England Power Co.*, 415 U.S. 345, 353 (1974) (Marshall, J., concurring and dissenting); *see also* Tribe, American Constitutiona Law § 5-18, at 291 (1978).

43 *See A.L.A. Schecter Poultry Corp. v. United States*, 295 U.S. 495 (1935); *Panama Refining Co. v. Ryan*, 293 U.S. 388 (1935).

44 *See American Power and Light Co. v. SEC*, 329 U.S. 90, 106 (1946). "The delegation doctrine is alive, but not well articulated or coherently applied by the Supreme Court." Schoenbrod, *The Delegation Doctrine: Could the Court Give It Some Substance?*, 83 Mich. L. Rev. 1223, 1289 (1985). *See generally* Comment, *The Fourth Branch: Reviving the Nondelegation Doctrine*, 1984 B.Y.U. L. Rev. 619; Note, *Rethinking the Nondelegation Doctrine*, 62 B.U.L. Rev. 257 (1982).

45 *See generally* Note, *The State Courts and the Delegation of Public Authority to Private Groups*, 67 Harv. L. Rev. 1398, 1399 (1954).

46 *See, e.g., Parham v. J.R.*, 442 U.S. 584, 602-03 (1979); *Wisconsin v. Yoder*, 406 U.S. 205 (1972).

47 *See. e.g., Todd & Co., Inc. v. SEC*, 557 F.2d 1008 (3d Cir. 1977).

48 *See* Jaffe, *Law Making by Private Groups*, 51 Harv. L. Rev. 201 (1937).

49 *See infra* nn. 51-53 and accompanying text.

50 *See, e.g., New York Times*, May 21,1985, at A14 (reporting $200,000 in cost overruns for privately operated prison in Tennessee); *see also* American Federation of State, County, and Municipal Employees, Position on Contracting Out Correctional Facilities (July 1985). Kenneth F. Schoen, former Commissioner of Corrections in Minnesota, has stated: "Private operators claim they can build prisons more cheaply. While more efficient administration of construction may reduce costs, the savings are lost to the higher cost of private borrowing, against public bonds. And, since prison construction is financed through tax shelters, the effect is to narrow the national tax base, shifting the burden of financing jails to our lower-income taxpayers." Schoen, *Private Prison Operators, New York Times*, Mar. 28, 1985, at A31.

Further, privatization of prisons and jails may cost the government more than public ownership and operation of the facilites would cost because, by delegating the incarceration function, the state may waive the defense of sovereign immunity in ordinary negligence actions. *See* Opinion Letter from W.J. Michael Cody, Tennessee Attorney General, to Shelby A. Rhinehart, Tennessee State Representative, at 2, 10-11 (Nov. 27, 1985).

51 American Correctional Association, National Correctional on Private Sector Involvement in Corrections (Jan. 1985).

52 *Cf. Carter v. Carter Coal Co.*, 298 U.S. 238 (1936): "The power conferred upon the majority is, in effect, the power to regulate the affairs of an unwilling minority. This is legislative delegation in its most obnoxious form; for it is not even delegation to an official or an official body, presumptively disinterested, but to private persons whose interests may be and often are adverse to the interests of others in the same business." *Id.* at 311.

As the executive director of the Vera Institute recently stated: "Justice is not a service, it's a condition, an idea." *New York Times*, Sept. 17, 1985, at A17 (statement of Michael E. Smith). This theme is echoed by the president of the Police Foundation: "Being efficient does not mean that justice will be served." *Id.* (statement of Hubert Williams).

[53] Dostoevsky, *The House of the Dead* 76 (C. Garnett trans. 1957).

[54] *New York Times*, Feb. 11, 1985, at B6 (statement of Ted Nissen, president of Behavior Systems Southwest).

[55] 16 Corrections Dig. 2 (1985) (statement of James K. Stewart).

This article is adapted from testimony that I presented before the Subcommittee on Courts, Civil Liberties and the Administration of Justice of the House Committee on the Judiciary, 99th Congress, 1st Session, Nov. 13, 1985.

The reader should be aware that I served as the Reporter on Legal Issues for the National Institute of Justice's National Forum on "Corrections and the Private Sector" (Feb. 1985) and am currently serving as Reporter for the American Bar Association Criminal Justice Section's study on the privatization of corrections. Although the analyses, conclusions, and points of view expressed herein are my own, and do not reflect the positions of the Federal Judicial Center or the National Institute of Justice, a slightly modified version of this paper served as the Report that accompanied a Resolution presented by the ABA Criminal Justice Section to the ABA House of Delegates, recommending that "jurisdictions that are considering the privatization of prisons and jails not proceed . . . until the complex constitutional, statutory, and contractual issues are satisfactorily developed and resolved." The Resolution was passed by the House of Delegates at its February 1986 meeting.